Belize

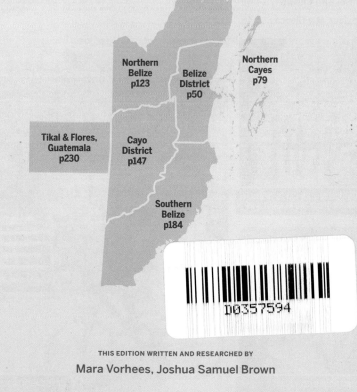

Northern
Belize
p123

Belize
District
p50

Northern
Cayes
p79

Tikal & Flores,
Guatemala
p230

Cayo
District
p147

Southern
Belize
p184

D0357594

THIS EDITION WRITTEN AND RESEARCHED BY
Mara Vorhees, Joshua Samuel Brown

Contents

PLAN YOUR TRIP

ON THE ROAD

NOHOCH CHE'EN CAVES BRANCH ARCHAEOLOGICAL RESERVE P89

RON WATTS / GETTY IMAGES ©

LIGHTHOUSE REEF P121

JEFF HUNTER / GETTY IMAGES ©

JOHN SONES SINGING BOWL MEDIA / GETTY IMAGES

CAYE CAULKER P104

Contents

Welcome to Belize

With one foot planted in the Central American jungles and the other dipped in the Caribbean Sea, Belize combines the best of both worlds.

Under the Sea

You've heard that the Belize Barrier Reef is the second longest in the world. But have you heard that this reef is home to more than 100 different kinds of coral and some 500 species of fish? This alluring underwater world is undoubtedly the top attraction in Belize. Snorkelers swim through translucent seas, gazing at a kaleidoscope of coral, fish and turtles; divers go deeper, investigating underwater caves and walls and the world-renowned Blue Hole.

The turquoise waters are inviting even for those who choose to remain above the surface. Kayakers glide from one sandy, palm-dotted islet to another; windsurfers and sailors skim across the surf by the power of the breeze; sunbathers lounge on the dock, lulled into relaxation by the gentle lapping; and foodies feast on delectable fresh fish, spiny-tailed lobster and other creatures of the sea.

In the Jungle

Inland, a vast network of national parks and wildlife sanctuaries offers a safe haven for wildlife, which ranges from the industrious cutter ants to the national animal of Belize, Baird's tapir. Bird-watchers aim their binoculars at some 570 species, which roost along the rivers and lagoons and in the broadleaf forest. Of course, many of these birds and animals are elusive, but keen-eyed visitors can easily spot spider monkeys and howler monkeys, peccaries, coatimundis, *gibnuts*, American and Morelot's crocodiles, green iguanas and countless species of birds. Even the showy keel-billed toucan – the national bird of Belize – occasionally makes an appearance in public.

In the Land of the Maya

If that's not enough adventure for you, Belize is also home to one of the world's most mysterious civilizations – the ancient Maya. The country is sprinkled with archaeological sites that date to the Maya heyday, known as the Classic Period (AD 250–1000). Enormous steps lead to the tops of tall stone temples, often yielding 360-degree jungle views. Curious climbers can explore excavated tombs and examine intricate hieroglyphs, while adventurers can descend deep into natural caves to see where the Maya kings performed rituals and made sacrifices to the gods of their underworld.

Why I Love Belize

By Joshua Samuel Brown, Author

With its Spanish-speaking neighbors to the south and west and the laid-back Caribbean to the east, Central America's youngest nation offers a cultural mélange – including Maya, *mestizo*, Garifuna, Creole, Mennonite and more – unrivaled in Central America. Belize is home to verdant jungles, from the Maya Mountains in the southwest to the Shipstern Nature Reserve in the northeast, not to mention ancient ruins, remnants of bygone days as part of the greater Maya kingdom. Then there are the beaches, miles of white sand and blue sea dotted with a nigh-uncountable number of islands big and small. So what's not to love?

For more about our authors, see page 320

Belize

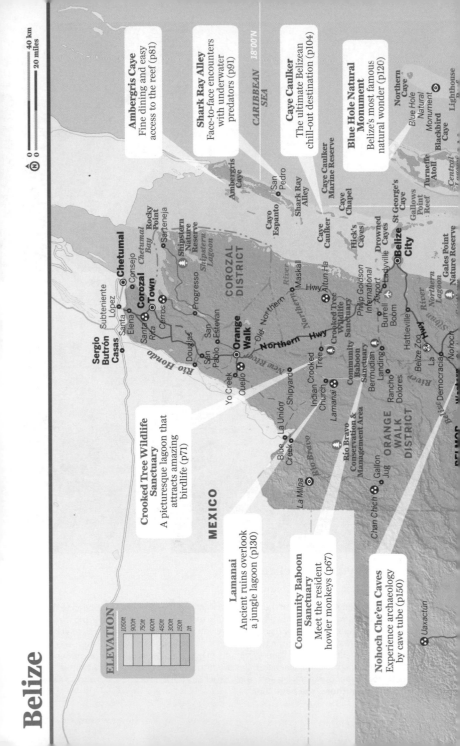

ELEVATION

1050ft
900ft
750ft
600ft
450ft
300ft
150ft
1ft

0   40 km
0   20 miles

Ambergris Caye
Fine dining and easy access to the reef (p81)

Shark Ray Alley
Face-to-face encounters with underwater predators (p91)

CARIBBEAN SEA

18°00'N

Caye Caulker
The ultimate Belizean chill-out destination (p104)

Blue Hole Natural Monument
Belize's most famous natural wonder (p120)

Crooked Tree Wildlife Sanctuary
A picturesque lagoon that attracts amazing birdlife (p71)

MEXICO

Lamanai
Ancient ruins overlook a jungle lagoon (p130)

Community Baboon Sanctuary
Meet the resident howler monkeys (p67)

Nohoch Che'en Caves
Experience archaeology by cave tube (p150)

Sergio Bután Casas

Subteniente López

Santa Elena · Santa Rita · Corozal · Corozal Town

Consejo · Chetumal

Chetumal Bay · Rocky Point · Sarteneja

Shipstern Nature Reserve · Shipstern Lagoon

Cerros · San Estevan

Progresso

COROZAL DISTRICT

San Pablo

Douglas

Río Hondo

Yo Creek · Orange Walk · Orange Walk

Quello · New River · Maskall · Altun Ha · Old Northern Hwy

Northern Hwy

Shipyard

Indian Church

Lamanai

La Unión

Blue Creek

Río Bravo

La Milpa

Río Bravo Conservation & Management Area

Gallon Jug

Chan Chich

Crooked Tree Wildlife Sanctuary · Crooked Tree

Northern River

Community Baboon Sanctuary · Bermudian Landing · Rancho Dolores

Burrell Boom · Philip Goldson International Airport

ORANGE WALK DISTRICT

Belize Zoo · Hattieville

La Democracia

Belize City

Ladyville

Northern River

Sibun River

Gales Point Nature Reserve

Northern Lagoon

BELIZE

Bóise Democracia

Western

Nohoch

Uaxactún

Cayo Espanto · San Pedro

Ambergris Caye

Shark Ray Alley

Caye Caulker Marine Reserve · Caye Caulker

Caye Chapel

Hick's Caye

Drowned Cayes

St George's Caye

Gallows Point Reef

Belize City

Turneffe Atoll

Central

Northern Caye

Blue Hole Natural Monument

Blackbird Caye

Lighthouse Reef

N

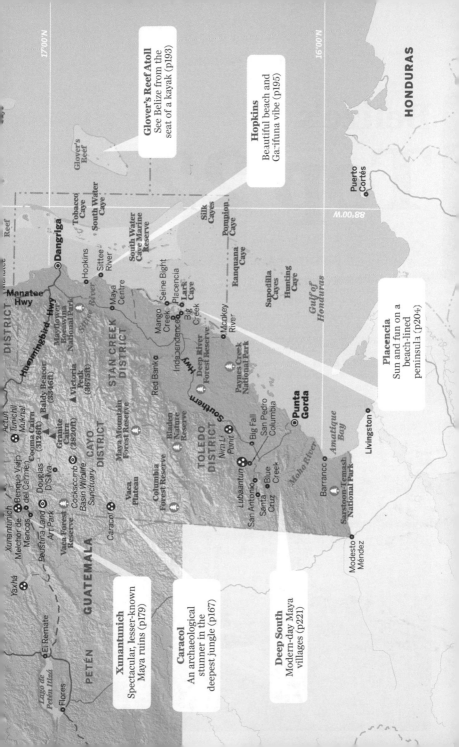

Glover's Reef Atoll
See Belize from the seat of a kayak (p193)

Hopkins
Beautiful beach and Ga'ifuna vibe (p195)

Placencia
Sun and fun on a beach-lined peninsula (p204)

Xunantunich
Spectacular, lesser-known Maya ruins (p179)

Caracol
An archaeological stunner in the deepest jungle (p167)

Deep South
Modern-day Maya villages (p221)

HONDURAS

GUATEMALA

PETÉN

Lago de Petén Itzá

Flores

El Remate

Yaxhá

Melchor de Mencos

Benque Viejo del Carmen

Xunantunich

Deustria Land Art Park

Vaca Forest Reserve

Actun Tunichil Muknal

Cooma Cairn

Granite Cairn (2920ft)

Baldy Beacon (3346ft)

Douglas D'Silva

Cockscomb Basin Wildlife Sanctuary

Vaca Plateau

Caracol

Maya Mountain Forest Reserve

Columbia Forest Reserve

Bladen Nature Reserve

CAYO DISTRICT

Mountain Pine Ridge

▲ Victoria Peak (3675ft)

Sibun River

Manatee Hwy

Hummingbird Hwy

DISTRICT

Dangriga

Hopkins

Sittee River

Maya Centre

Sittee River

STAN CREEK DISTRICT

Mango Creek

Seine Bight

Placencia

Big Creek

Independence

Red Bank

Deep River Forest Reserve

Monkey River

Southern Hwy

Paynes Creek National Park

TOLEDO DISTRICT

Big Fall

San Pedro Columbia

Nim Li Punit

Lubaantun

San Antonio

Santa Cruz

Blue Creek

Punta Gorda

Barranco

Moho River

Sarstoon-Temash National Park

Amatique Bay

Livingston

Modesto Méndez

Reef

Tobacco Caye

South Water Caye

Glover's Reef

South Water Caye Marine Reserve

Silk Cayes

Pompion Caye

Ranquana Caye

Lark Caye

Sapodilla Cayes

Hunting Caye

Gulf of Honduras

Puerto Cortés

17°00'N

16°00'N

88°00'W

Belize's
Top 22

Kayaking Glover's Reef Atoll

1 Lying like a string of white-sand pearls, Glover's Reef Atoll (p193) consists of half a dozen small islands surrounded by blue sea as far as the eye can see. Its unique position, atop a submerged mountain ridge on the edge of the continental shelf, makes it an ideal place for sea kayaking, both between the islands and around the shallow central lagoon. Get a kayak with a clear bottom and you're likely to see spotted eagle rays, southern stingrays, turtles and countless tropical fish swimming beneath as you paddle.

Diving the Blue Hole

2 The sheer walls of the Blue Hole Natural Monument (p120) drop more than 400ft into the blue ocean. Although it is half filled with silt and natural debris, the depth still creates a perfect circle of startling azure that is visible from above. The wall of the Blue Hole is decorated with a dense forest of stalactites and stalagmites from times past. A school of reef sharks – as well as plenty of invertebrates and sponges – keeps divers company as they descend into the mysterious ocean depths.

GREG JOHNSTON / GETTY IMAGES ©

Snorkeling Shark Ray Alley

3 Local fisherfolk used to come to Shark Ray Alley (p90) to clean their catch, and their discards would attract hungry nurse sharks and southern stingrays. As a result these predators have long become accustomed to boats, which nowadays bring snorkelers instead of fishers. Shark Ray Alley is the top snorkeling destination in Hol Chan Marine Reserve, a protected part of the Belize Barrier Reef that harbors an amazing diversity of colorful coral and other marine life.

Ambergris Caye

4 Also known as La Isla Bonita, Ambergris Caye (p81) is the ultimate tropical paradise vacation destination (and that's what Madonna thought, too). Spend your days snorkeling the reef, kayaking the lagoon or windsurfing the straits; pamper yourself at a day spa or challenge yourself at a yoga class; ride a bike up the beach or take a nap at the end of your dock. After the sun sets, spend your evenings enjoying the country's most delectable dining and most happening nightlife.

Garifuna Drumming

5 Dangriga and Punta Gorda both provide opportunities to study drumming and drum-making with Garifuna drum masters, but for something really special head to the Garifuna village of Hopkins to take part in a drumming ceremony at Lebeha education and cultural center (p200). The ceremony is led by local drummer Jabbar Lambey, whose drum jams draw drummers and other musicians from around the village, the country, and even the world. For a really swinging time, come on down when the moon is full.

Caye Caulker

6 A brisk breeze is almost always blowing (especially between January and June), creating optimal conditions to cruise across the water on sailboat, windsurfer or kiteboard. The world's second-largest barrier reef is just a few miles offshore, beckoning snorkelers and divers to frolic with the fish. The mangroves teem with life, inviting exploration by kayak. All these adventures await, yet the number-one activity on Caye Caulker (p104) is still swinging in a hammock, reading a book and sipping a fresh-squeezed fruit juice. Paradise.

Altun Ha

7 You've drunk the beer, now visit the ruins that inspired the Belikin beer bottle label. The most accessible of Belize's ancient ruins, Altun Ha (p69) displays 10 different structures dating from the 6th and 7th centuries, and it was also the site of some of the richest archaeological excavations in Belize, although the artifacts have long since been removed. You'll get your exercise climbing to the tops of the temples to take in the panorama of the surrounding jungle.

Crooked Tree Wildlife Sanctuary

8 Belize is for the birds. Nowhere is that statement truer than at Crooked Tree (p71), a fishing and farming village centered on a picturesque lagoon. The wetlands attract hundreds of bird species (276 to be exact), including dozens of migrants who stop on their way north or south. Bird-watching is best during the drier months (February to May), when the lagoon dries up and the birds congregate around the remaining puddles. Expert guides will lead you by boat or on foot to spot and identify your feathered friends.

Lamanai

9 Spanning all phases of ancient Maya civilization, the ruins at Lamanai (p130) are known for their stone reliefs, impressive architecture, and their marvelous setting that overlooks the New River Lagoon and is surrounded by some of Northern Belize's densest jungle. Arrive at this outpost by boat, allowing up-close observation of birds and wildlife along the New River. While on site, hear the roar of the howler monkeys while climbing the steep facade of the High Temple and admiring the deformed face on the Mask Temple.

HENRY GEORGI / GETTY IMAGES ©

DAMIAN TURSKI / GETTY IMAGES ©

Belize Carnival

10 This is not the usual pre-Lenten extravaganza that takes place in other parts of the Caribbean in anticipation of the fasting season. In the 1970s, Belizeans started celebrating their own Carnival (p55) in September, as a spicy addition to the national holidays. Revelers don outrageous costumes and take to the streets in Orange Walk, Corozal Town and especially Belize City. In a flurry of movement, music and color, neighborhood camps design floats and wear costumes that depict local cultures and customs.

Xunantunich

11 Amazing things come in small packages. Though Xunantunich (p179) isn't Belize's biggest archaeological site, it's still one of the most impressive. After taking a hand-cranked ferry across the Mopan River, you'll walk through bird- and butterfly-filled jungle, until you reach a complex of temples and plazas that dates back to the early Classic Maya period. Once there, you can explore a number of structures and plazas, and even climb to the top of 130ft-high El Castillo for a spectacular 360-degree view.

Jungle Hiking

12 If it's off the beaten path you're after, take a hike in one of Belize's many protected areas, such as Mayflower Bocawina National Park (p198) or Cockscomb Basin Wildlife Sanctuary (p202). With jungle, mountains, waterfalls, swimming holes and even some small Maya ruins, you'll feel like you've left civilization and the 21st century behind entirely. Off the tourist trail, you'll be sharing the park with countless birds, mammals, reptiles and, no doubt, a resident squad of black howler monkeys. Cockscomb Basin Wildlife Sanctuary (p202)

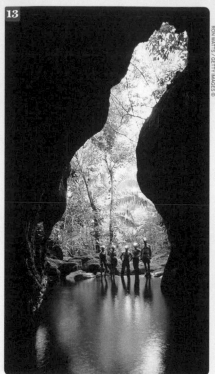

RON WATTS / GETTY IMAGES ©

Nohoch Che'en Caves Branch

13 Picture yourself on a tube on a river under blue skies... Ahhh... Hold on tight, though, as within a few minutes of your trip's launch the sky will be replaced by total darkness as you're pulled down into the very bowels of the earth. After entering the Nohoch Che'en Caves Branch (p89) you'll float through an underground network, experiencing wonders unseen in the world above, from schools of eyeless cave fish, to stalactites and strange Maya paintings high on the cave ceilings. For an even cooler time, try a sunset trip.

Maya Villages

14 To experience Maya life firsthand, take a trek through the villages of Belize's Deep South, where ancient and contemporary Maya culture exist side by side, and rituals and folklore continue to play an important role in everyday life. From the ancient ruins of Lubaantun (p223) to even more remote spots like Jalacte (p226) and San Benito Poite (p226), your trek will take you through some of Belize's most beautiful jungle villages and allow you to interact with a people whose civilization once surpassed Rome in political influence and grandeur.

Deep-Sea Fishing

15 The Northern Cayes are the base for anglers who are drawn to the flats offshore – a prime spot to pull off a 'Grand Slam' (reeling in a permit, tarpon and bonefish in one outing). The remote Turneffe Atoll (p119) is home to a handful of all-inclusive resorts that cater to folks who are focused on the fish and only the fish. Alternatively, Ambergris Caye (p81) and Caye Caulker (p104) are both perfectly situated for fishing-orientated day trips.

Ambergris Caye

Caracol

16 Step out of the modern world and into the ancient world at Belize's largest Maya site (p167), where you'll spend the day wandering through a city that once rivaled Tikal in political influence. Standing in the central area of temples, palaces, craft workshops and markets, you'll feel the power and glory of ancient Caracol. At 141ft, Caana (which means Sky Place) is still the tallest building in Belize. In addition to being the country's preeminent archaeological site, Caracol also teems with jungle wildlife.

The Hummingbird Highway

17 Arguably Belize's most beautiful stretch of road, the Hummingbird Hwy (p155) offers unparalleled views of the Maya Mountains as it winds through jungles, orchards and tiny villages. The highway also offers plenty of reasons to stop for a few hours (besides a near constant procession of postcard-perfect vistas). Explore St Herman's Cave, hike the jungle loop trail, or have a dip in the crystal-clear Blue Hole. If you prefer showering with a view, the Barquedier Waterfall is down the road. Scenery along Hummingbird Hwy (p155)

DANITA DELIMONT / ALAMY ©

Hopkins

18 Halfway between the hustle of Dangriga and the tourist vibe of Placencia lies slacked-out Hopkins (p195), a low key Garifuna town where life hasn't changed much in decades. Children walk the town's one street selling their mothers' freshly baked coconut pies and chocolate brownies; local men catch fish by day and play drums at night; and the pace of life is pleasantly slow. Best of all is the beach, which is as pretty as any in Southern Belize, but it is never crowded.

Belize Zoo

19 Humane, earthy and educational, even people philosophically opposed to the very concept of caged creatures will approve of this zoo (p75). As a halfway house and rehabilitation center for injured, orphaned and rescued Belizean jungle animals, the Belize Zoo is a fabulous and friendly place to get a good look at 125 species of indigenous animals and birds that are difficult to spot in the wild. The zoo hosts myriad educational programs for kids and adults, including a festive birthday party for April the tapir, the national animal of Belize.

Placencia

20 It isn't off the beaten path, true, but there's a reason so many feet beat the path to Southern Belize's most popular spot (p204). This small village is just too chilled out to not spend some time kayaking, sailing, or just walking barefoot on the beach by day, and drinking rum drinks by night. As for dining, it has two of the area's best restaurants (Rumfish and Omar's Creole Grub), so your culinary cravings will be well catered for.

Community Baboon Sanctuary

21 The 'baboons' at this sanctuary (p67) are not really baboons, but rather black howler monkeys, an endangered species in Central America. The 'sanctuary' is not exactly a protected area, but rather a network of private properties where the howlers live. Thanks to this community-based, grassroots effort, property owners have agreed to preserve their land for the benefit of the resident monkeys. Although the sanctuary encompasses about 20 sq miles, guides take tourists to a small area where the welcoming troop allows for up-close observation of the funny monkeys.

Half Moon Caye Natural Monument

22 Part of the Lighthouse Reef Atoll, Half Moon Caye (p121) provides a nesting ground for the rare red-footed booby bird. Thousands of these rare water fowl make their homes in the treetops, alongside the magnificent frigate bird and 98 other species. Dive the Half Moon Caye Wall (or snorkel the surrounding shallows); enjoy a picnic on the beach; then hike across the island and climb the observation platform to get a good look at the boobies.

Need to Know

For more information, see Survival Guide p293

Currency
Belize Dollars (BZ$)

Languages
English, Kriol, Garifuna, Spanish

Visas
For most nationalities, visas are issued upon entry for up to 30 days.

Money
ATMs are widely available; credit cards are accepted at most hotels, restaurants and shops.

Cell Phones
Local SIM cards can be used in European and Australian phones. Other phones must be set to roaming.

Time
Belize is in the Central Time Zone (GMT/UTC minus six hours)

When to Go

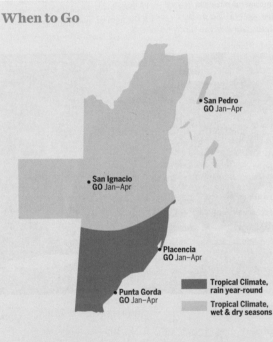

- San Pedro
  GO Jan–Apr

- San Ignacio
  GO Jan–Apr

- Placencia
  GO Jan–Apr

- Punta Gorda
  GO Jan–Apr

Tropical Climate, rain year-round

Tropical Climate, wet & dry seasons

High Season (Dec–Apr)
➡ Expect sunny skies from February to April

➡ Prices for accommodations increase by 30–50%

➡ Extra-high 'peak' prices from mid-December to mid-January; reservations are essential during this period

Low Season (May–Nov)
➡ Heavy rainfall from June to November, especially at night

➡ Hurricanes possible between August and October

➡ Few tourists; prices for accommodations drop significantly

Useful Websites

Belizean Journeys (www.belizeanjourneys.com) Online magazine covering life and nature in Belize.

Belize Forums (www.belizeforum.com/belize) User forum discussing all topics Belizean.

BelizeNews.com (www.belizenews.com) News and views from around the country.

Government of Belize (www.belize.gov.bz) Official GOB website.

Lonely Planet (www.lonelyplanet.com/belize) Destination information, hotel bookings, traveller forum and more.

Important Numbers

Belize has no regional, area or city codes. Dial a seven-digit local number from wherever you are in the country

Country code	☎501
Directory assistance	☎113
Emergency	☎911
International access code	☎00
Operator assistance	☎115

Exchange Rates

Australia	A$1	BZ$2.08
Canada	C$1	BZ$1.97
Europe	€1	BZ$2.64
Guatemala	Q1	BZ$0.26
Japan	¥100	BZ$2.06
Mexico	1 peso	BZ$0.17
New Zealand	NZ$1	BZ$1.71
UK	UK£1	BZ$3.08
USA	US$1	BZ$2.02

For current exchange rates see www.xe.com.

Daily Costs

Budget: less than BZ$150

➡ Dorm bed BZ$25–40

➡ Excellent, filling, cheap street food

➡ Take the bus; snorkel under the dock

Midrange: BZ$150–300

➡ Double room with private bathroom BZ$100–200

➡ Dine at local restaurants

➡ Take a snorkeling tour or a river cruise

Top End: more than BZ$300

➡ Luxury accommodations from BZ$240

➡ Fancy restaurants in resort areas

➡ Transportation by rental car or organized tours

Opening Hours

Outside of banks, phone companies and government offices you'll generally find most opening hours to be flexible. Restaurants and bars tend to keep longer hours during high season, but will also close early if they wish (if business is slow etc).

Banks 8am-2pm or 3pm Mon-Thu & 8am-4pm or 4:30pm Fri

Pubs & Bars noon-midnight (or later)

Restaurants & Cafes 7-9:30am (breakfast), 11:30am-2pm (lunch) & 6-8pm (dinner)

Shops 9am-5pm Mon-Sat, some open Sunday

Arriving in Belize

Philip Goldson International Airport Many hotels and resorts offer airport shuttles. Taxis into town cost around BZ$50. No public buses run (p303).

International Bus Services Frequent buses from Guatemala and Mexico travel to border towns; daily express buses go all the way to Belize City. One nightly bus runs from Belize City to Cancun Airport.

International Boat Services

Chetumal, Mexico, to San Pedro

Livingstone and Puerto Barrios, Guatemala, to Punta Gorda

Puerto Cortés, Honduras, to Belize City, Placencia and Dangriga

Getting Around

Transport in Belize is cheap and occasionally efficient. A website offering updated schedules and other transport-related info is http://belizebus.wordpress.com.

Car Belize drives on the right side of the road. All major highways are paved, but none have shoulders or dividing lines. Speed bumps are common but not all are marked.

Bus Most travel in Belize is done by bus. All towns from Corozal to Punta Gorda are serviced by one or more of a variety of private bus services, and you can usually flag down a bus on the highway.

Boat Caye Caulker and Ambergris are serviced by ferries from Belize City; there is also a boat from Corozal to Ambergris with a Sarteneja stop. No regular boats to the smaller islands and cayes, but passage can be arranged with a private boatman from Dangriga, Hopkins or Placencia, or through resorts and hotels.

Air Two companies (Maya Island and Tropic Air) fly between all major towns in Belize. Planes are small, flights are short and generally affordable, and both companies enjoy good safety records.

For much more on **getting around**, see p305

If You Like…

Sun & Fun

Who doesn't love some sun and fun? Not to state the obvious, but this is the Caribbean, so you're probably hoping to spend at least a few days soaking up some rays and dipping your toes in the turquoise blue.

Hopkins Some of the best beaches in Southern Belize, with only about 20% of the tourist traffic of nearby Placencia. (p195)

Caye Caulker The ultimate chill-out destination, with a laid-back village vibe and easy access to the sea. (p104)

Ambergris Caye If the hustle and bustle of San Pedro are too much for you, head to one of the luxurious resorts on the North Island, where there are no interruptions to the sun, sea and sand. (p81)

Placencia A beach-lined peninsula offering ample opportunities for swimming, sunning, snorkeling and scuba diving. (p204)

Diving & Snorkeling

Life under the sea is dramatic and diverse, from the fantastical coral formations and the kaleidoscopic fish that feed there to the massive and sometimes menacing creatures that lurk in deeper waters.

Glover's Reef Right on the reef, Glover's Reef offers some of the most pristine diving and snorkeling opportunities you'll find in the country. (p193)

Blue Hole Natural Monument Seen from the sky, this national landmark is a perfectly round, perfectly blue bull's eye. Seen from underwater, it's a sheer wall, adorned with stalactites and stalagmites, descending into the darkness. (p120)

Turneffe Elbow The convergence of currents at the Elbow attracts huge congregations of cubera snappers, horse eye jacks, Atlantic spadefish, reef sharks and king mackerel. (p119)

Hol Chan Marine Reserve Shallow waters offer excellent conditions for snorkeling, especially at Shark Ray Alley, but divers will be thrilled by the shipwreck at Amigos Wreck. (p82)

Caves

The erosive action of water on the relatively soft limestone of the Maya Mountains has produced numerous underground rivers and caves. Many of the caves were ritual sites for the ancient Maya, as they were considered to be close to the underworld.

Actun Tunichil Muknal This unforgettable all-day experience takes you deep into the eponymous cave, where you will see first-hand the evidence of the Maya rituals of food offerings, blood-letting and human sacrifice. For nights after you'll dream of shimmering flowstone rock formations, giant stalactites and phallic stalagmites. (p157)

Nohoch Che'en Caves Branch Archaeological Reserve A unique and distinctly Belizean activity, cave-tubing combines the mystery of spelunking with the cool (in temperature and fun) adventure of river-rafting. Float through this underground network of caves, where, through the light of your headlamp, you'll see wonders unseen in the world above, all the while being carried gently on the river's back. (p150)

Animals

The animal life is the star of the show in Belize, thanks to conservation of the forests and reefs. From monkeys to manatees, you can see these creatures in their natural habitat.

Green Hills Butterfly Ranch An unforgettable experience for animal lovers is meditating amongst fluttering butterflies and hummingbirds at the Green

Above) Diving with turtles, Lighthouse Reef (p121)
Below) Kayaking on the Caves Branch River (p151)

Hills Butterfly Ranch in Cayo District. (p160)

Community Baboon Sanctuary Get up close and personal with a troop of black howlers at this community-based, grassroots monkey refuge. (p67)

Swallow Caye Wildlife Sanctuary As many as 30 West Indian manatees inhabit the waters around Swallow Caye. Observers watching from the boat will see these gentle giants surfacing for air, then diving back down to their sea-grass feast. (p108)

Belize Zoo Perhaps the happiest zoo in the world, this amazing (and privately funded) zoo houses wildlife that have been injured or otherwise rescued throughout the country. (p75)

Birds

If you're into birds, you probably already know that Belize boasts 570 resident and migratory species. On the shores of the rivers and lagoons or deep in the forest, keep your binoculars on hand, for your feathered friends are here.

Crooked Tree Wildlife Sanctuary Giant jabiru storks congregate here in April and May, but the lagoon is home to hundreds of bird species year round. Look for boat-billed herons, snail kites and black-headed hawks, among many others. (p71)

Red Bank This tiny village near Placencia is home to the spectacular scarlet macaw, which feasts on the forest fruits from January to March. (p214)

Río Bravo Conservation & Management Area Use La Milpa Field Station as your base and start ticking off your list of bird species. Without even trying, you're likely to spot birds as varied as the collared aricari, oscillated turkey, pygmy kingfisher, ruffous hummingbird, black-headed trogon and plenty of turkey vultures. (p133)

Outdoor Adventure

Come to Belize for action and adventure, to mount seemingly insurmountable temples, to dive to the ocean's darkest depths, and to feel the heat of the jungle and the salty air of the sea.

Deep South Travel through Toledo's Deep South, visiting lush jungles, swimming holes, waterfalls, jungles and Maya ruins, which exist between the area's small but vibrant Maya villages. (p221)

Glover's Reef These islands are ideal for hopping. Kayak the limpid waters, admiring the prolific marine life from above. (p193)

Placencia A plethora of sailing activities awaits the adventurous. Many operators offer combination snorkeling/sailing trips, a great way to experience the waves over and under. (p204)

Mountain Pine Ridge In the remote west, the highlands of the Maya Mountains are covered with pine forest, an unexpected aberration on the landscape. Big Rock Falls are the impressive waterfalls at Privassion Creek. (p164)

Ecochic Resorts

Ecotourism was practically invented here. Thanks to a progressive populace, Belize offers myriad ways for travelers to tread lightly, from beach resorts powered by solar energy to jungle lodges built from reclaimed hardwoods.

Black Rock River Lodge The perfect base for a jungle adventure, where slate-and-wood cabins sit on the banks of a rushing river, surrounded by towering cliffs and 13,000 acres of national park. (p181)

Chan Chich Lodge One of the original ecolodges, Chan Chich sits on 200 sq miles of private wildlife preserve on the Guatemalan border. (p135)

Turneffe Atoll All of the beach resorts on Blackbird Caye are taking steps to preserve the spectacular environment of the surrounding atoll. (p119)

Thatch Caye Resort An island paradise, Thatch Caye is eco-friendly, rustic-chic, luxurious without being ostentatious, and offers great beaches, snorkeling, fishing and an amazing over-the-water bar. (p195)

Maya Ruins

For almost 3000 years, the ancient Maya civilization flourished in Belize, building towering temples as tribute to their god-like rulers. The remains of these once-mighty city-states are scattered throughout the country and are prime for exploration.

Xunantunich It isn't Belize's biggest Maya ruin, but Xunantunich may be one of the prettiest, and definitely among the easiest to get to. The view from El Castillo is worth the climb. (p179)

Caracol Once the most powerful kingdom of the Maya world, Caracol covers a vast, jungle-clad area atop the Vaca Plateau. The centerpiece is the 141ft Caana (Sky Palace), which is still the tallest structure in Belize. (p167)

Lamanai Spanning all phases of ancient Maya civilization, the ruins at Lamanai are among the oldest and the largest Maya sites in the country. (p130)

Music

A rich diversity is evident in the music of Belize, where you'll hear rhythms and instruments representing Creole and calypso, Maya and Garifuna.

Maroon Creole Drum School Head to Emmeth Young's Maroon Creole Drum School on the outskirts of Punta Gorda and learn traditional drum crafting and playing with a genuine Creole master. (p215)

Watina Andy Palacio's last album is the ultimate Garifuna showcase, with each song riffing on a different Garifuna rhythm, and all of the lyrics in Garifuna language. (p276)

Placencia Live music is definitely on the menu in the bars of Placencia on Friday and Saturday nights, when the town rocks past midnight to the sounds of punta, reggae, Garifuna drumming and more. (p204)

Legends Burger House Come for the burgers but stay for the live music, which rocks the house two nights a week. (p100)

Month by Month

January

The dry season has not officially started, but don't tell the tourists. The holidays bring a huge influx of people and an increase in prices. Visitors might see some rain, but (hopefully) not enough to spoil their good time.

New Year

Many Belizeans kick off the New Year in very active ways. Burrell Boom hosts a long-standing New Year's Day horse race. Hundreds of spectators cheer on the cyclists who ride from Corozal to Belize City as part of the Krem Annual New Year's Day Classic.

February

The dry season is upon us, so visitors will enjoy sunny skies and warm temperatures day after day. Prices for accommodations remain relatively high.

Birding

Lagoons and rivers begin to dry up and birds become easier to spot, as they congregate around the limited remaining water sources. Migration also significantly increases the number of species you might tick off your list. Prime birding conditions continue through to May.

Fiesta de Carnaval

The exact dates vary with the church calendar, but this pre-Lenten festival always includes music, dancing, costumes and parades. The festivities take place throughout northern Belize, but mostly in San Pedro.

Closing of the Lobster Season

The lobster's mating and spawning season is from mid-February to mid-June. Belize respectfully gives the crustaceans some privacy, closing the season for trapping lobsters on February 15.

March

The dry season persists. Plus: tourists and residents keep enjoying blue skies and warm temperatures. Minus: everyone should be careful to minimize water consumption.

Baron Bliss Day

On March 9 (or the closest Monday), Belize pays tribute to its greatest benefactor. Part of Bliss' legacy is a trust that funds an annual boat race in Belize City, and other towns follow suit by hosting smaller races and regattas.

La Ruta Maya Belize River Challenge

Participants from all walks of life join teams to compete in this grueling, four-day canoe race. Following the original trade and transport route, the race runs along the Macal and Belize Rivers from San Ignacio to Belize City. See also www.larutamayabelize.com.

April

The weather is still dry and it's beginning to get hot, especially in the southern parts of the country.

Expect extra crowds during the weeks before and after Easter.

✨ Holy Week

Various services and processions are held in the week leading up to Easter Sunday. Good Friday and Easter Monday are official state holidays, so most places of business are closed all weekend.

June

Dry season gradually turns to rainy season in May and June. Rivers start to swell and dirt roads get muddy. Visitors who can tolerate a few raindrops will enjoy the peaceful atmosphere and lower prices.

✨ Lobster Season Reopens

Lobster season reopens on June 15 and the coastal towns and fishing villages celebrate! Fun food festivals take place in Caye Caulker, San Pedro and Placencia, with music, drinking and plenty of seafood. See also www.sanpedrolobsterfest.com and www.placencia.com.

August

Weather is hot, humid and wet, wet, wet. Belizeans are on the lookout for hurricanes and tourists make themselves scarce.

✨ Costa Maya Festival

People with Maya in their blood or in their souls come from all parts of Central America and Mexico to celebrate Maya coastal culture in San Pedro. See also www.internationalcostamayafestival.com.

September

It's the height of hurricane season, but it's also the most festive month in Belize, which celebrates its national holidays with gusto.

✨ September Celebrations

The holidays commence on the Battle of St George's Caye Day, with ceremonies and celebrations around the country. For the next 10 days, Belize hosts carnival parades and fun competitions. The celebrations culminate with outdoor concerts on September 21, Independence Day.

November

The rain starts to let up. As temperatures drop in the northern hemisphere around Thanksgiving, the trickle of tourists turns into a steady stream.

✨ Garifuna Settlement Day

A celebration of one of the country's richest minority cultures, this national holiday on November 19 commemorates the Garifuna arrival on Belizean soil in 1832. The country gets down with lots of drumming, dancing and drinking, especially in Dangriga, Hopkins and Punta Gorda, where celebrations may last several days.

December

December still brings some rain, but not enough to deter the many travelers who want to spend their holidays in the tropics. Most lodgings are extra expensive in the last two weeks of the month.

✨ Christmas Day

Belizeans celebrate Christmas much like North Americans, decorating their houses with colorful lights weeks ahead. Most people spend Christmas Day sharing meals with family and friends. In some places, festivities continue until January 6, when Garifuna *jonkonu* dancers go from house to house.

Itineraries

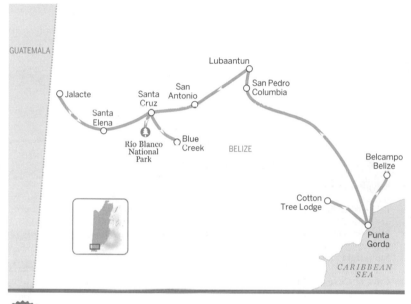

 **Deep South**

Exploring Belize's Deep South takes time, so give yourself at least five days. **Punta Gor-da** is a chilled-out town and natural spot to begin your trek. If you'd like to experience some luxury, book yourself in at **Cotton Tree Lodge** or **Belcampo Belize**, among the finest ecolodges in Belize. Punta Gorda is blessed with one of the country's best informa-tion centers, so stop by the Belize Tourism Board and get the latest info on Maya village homestays and guesthouses. If drumming interests you, visit Emmeth Young's Maroon Creole Drum School. Next, head to **San Pedro Columbia** and use it as a base to explore nearby **Lubaantun**. Later, head further still to the small Maya villages of **San Antonio**, **Santa Cruz** and **Santa Elena**, stopping for a hike and a swim at beautiful **Río Blanco National Park**, or caving at **Blue Creek**. If you want to go into the deepest south, visit **Jalacte** – the end of the road, for now!

The Whole Enchilada: From Corozal to Punta Gorda

1 MONTH

Belize is small enough that you might see the whole country in a month. This itinerary leads the way, starting in the quaint Mestizo town of **Corozal**, just south of the Mexican border. Spend one day in **Orange Walk**, where you can cruise the New River and explore the Maya ruins at **Lamanai**. Then head east to the small fishing village of **Sarteneja** for some amazing wildlife-watching at **Shipstern Nature Reserve**.

From Sarteneja, catch the fast ferry to San Pedro. Whether you stay on **Ambergris Caye** or **Caye Caulker** it doesn't matter, but allow yourself at least four days to chill out in a hammock, kayak out to the reef, frolic with the fish and feast on fresh seafood.

When you head back to the mainland, don't bypass the animal-lovers' sights in the Belize District, including the **Community Baboon Sanctuary** and the **Belize Zoo**. If you're into birds, spend a night or two around the **Crooked Tree Wildlife Sanctuary**. Further west in Cayo, take four or five days and choose your own adventure, whether it be delving deep into the caves at **Actun Tunichil Muknal** or **Barton Creek**, horseback riding at **Mountain Equestrian Trails**, climbing the tall temples at **Caracol** or **Xunantunich**, or all of the above.

Backtrack east to the beautiful Hummingbird Hwy, which carries you south across the thickly forested northern foothills of the Maya Mountains. Stop at **Ian Anderson's Caves Branch Jungle Lodge** for some cave exploration, jungle expeditions and abseiling down bottomless sinkholes.

By now you have been away from the water for way too long, so spend a few days in the coastal village of **Hopkins** to absorb some Garifuna rhythms. From here, you can hike the beautiful jungle trails at **Mayflower Bocawina National Park** or **Cockscomb Basin Wildlife Sanctuary**.

If you're still thirsting for sun and fun, you have a choice. If you're looking for something civilized, head south to **Placencia** to enjoy lovely sandy beaches, lively bars and lots of water sports. If you're looking for something uncivilized, indulge your tropical-island fantasies at **Glover's Reef**, which has an irresistible low-key vibe and brilliant diving and snorkeling. Finish up in **Punta Gorda**, the southernmost town in Belize.

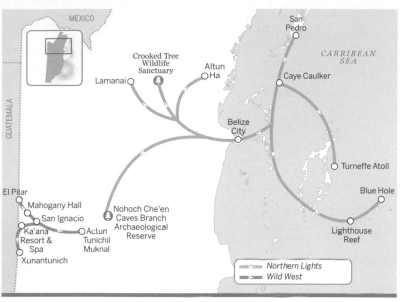

Legend:
Northern Lights
Wild West

1 WEEK Northern Lights

If you only have a week to spare, there is no sense moving around too much. However from your base on one of the Northern Cayes, you have access to an impressive array of activities on land and sea.

Choose **Caye Caulker** or **San Pedro**, as they are closest to the mainland. (We prefer Caye Caulker – not only for its easygoing vibe, but also for its easy access to **Belize City**, which is only 45 minutes away by water taxi.) From here, you can take snorkel or dive trips to **Turneffe Atoll** and **Lighthouse Reef**, the latter home to the amazing **Blue Hole**.

You can also use either of these islands as a base for day trips to the mainland. Spend a day in the Belize District to spy on birds at **Crooked Tree Wildlife Sanctuary** or to see the Maya ruins at **Altun Ha**.

It's also an easy trip to eastern Cayo District, where you can go cave-tubing in the **Nohoch Che'en Caves Branch Archaeological Reserve** or zip-lining through the forest canopy. You can also head north to the Maya ruins at **Lamanai**, enjoying a peaceful boat ride on the New River along the way.

3 DAYS Wild West

On day one head to **San Ignacio** to get a feel for the town, perhaps visiting nearby Maya site Cahal Pech and having a great meal at Ko-Ox Han-nah. San Ignacio has plenty of good midrange hotels, so save your money for a night at a really good ecolodge later. Make sure you arrange a tour to explore the amazing ritual cave of **Actun Tunichil Muknal**, which, travel time included, will take up all of your second day. Don't check out of your hotel though, as you'll no doubt be exhausted when you get back to San Ignacio.

On your third day, wake up early and do a half-day trip to either **Xunantunich** or **El Pilar** before checking into one of the better hotels or ecolodges in western Cayo: Mahogany Hall is closest to **El Pilar**, and has an amazing pool, patio and rushing river, while the fabulous **Ka'ana Resort & Spa** is closer to Xunantunich. Ka'ana has a full spa where the knots in your back, arms and legs from all that hiking, exploring, temple-climbing and caving will be kneaded until all that is left are fond memories of three days well spent.

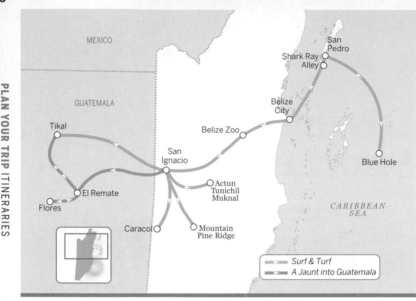

MEXICO

GUATEMALA

San Pedro

Shark Ray Alley

Belize City

Tikal

Belize Zoo

San Ignacio

Blue Hole

El Remate

Actun Tunichil Muknal

Flores

CARIBBEAN SEA

Caracol

Mountain Pine Ridge

Surf & Turf
A Jaunt into Guatemala

2 WEEKS Surf & Turf

This traditional Belize sampler gives you the best of both worlds – a taste of the jungle and a glimpse of the sea – all within your two weeks of vacation time.

Start your trip at holiday central: **San Pedro** on Ambergris Caye. Snorkel or dive among coral gardens and observe the inhabitants of **Shark Ray Alley**. Use San Pedro as your launching pad for dives at **Blue Hole** and other atoll sites.

After a week of sun and fun, make your way to dry land and head out along the Western Hwy. Stop on the way to visit the recovering and rescued animals at the **Belize Zoo**.

In Cayo, base yourself at a luxurious jungle lodge or a more affordable hotel in **San Ignacio**. From here, you can explore caves loaded with ancient remains, such as **Actun Tunichil Muknal**; travel by canoe or inner-tube along jungle rivers; dip beneath the waterfalls of the **Mountain Pine Ridge**; or explore Belize's greatest Maya site, **Caracol**.

If you have the time and inclination, venture over the border into Guatemala, where you can visit the region's most significant Maya archaeological site at **Tikal**.

5 DAYS A Jaunt Into Guatemala

Across the border and within easy reach lie the glory and splendors of the ancient Maya world: scores of ancient ruins surrounded by lush rainforests, and a few really lovely towns thrown in for good measure. Taking it all in would take months, so allow us to suggest a five-day compromise.

Leaving San Ignacio on the morning of the first day, head directly to **El Remate**. The lakefront town makes a lovely base and has accommodations in all budget ranges. Head to **Tikal** early the next morning and spend the day exploring this fascinating ancient Maya city. Having made arrangements to spend the night at one of Tikal's three hotels, you can enjoy the sunset from the top of Temple IV at your leisure. Spend the first half of the third day exploring Tikal further (it's worth it) before heading back to El Remate to relax.

On your remaining days, hang out in **Flores** and soak up the town's island ambiance, perhaps taking a half-day trip to one of the parks, villages or smaller ruins that are in the area.

Plan Your Trip
Diving & Snorkeling

Belize is a world-class destination for diving and snorkeling – after all, the world's second-longest barrier reef parallels the country's entire coastline. From Cayes North, Central and South to stunning offshore atolls, whatever your level of underwater experience you'll find a place to explore and indulge in Belize.

Northern Cayes

The two main centers in this northern sector of the barrier reef are Ambergris Caye (p83) and Caye Caulker (p108), both of which are a short flight or boat ride from Belize City.

Ambergris Caye is the largest offshore island and the most developed, so it attracts most of the visiting divers. Many choose Ambergris for the variety and quality of its accommodations and nightlife, though it is pretty laid-back compared with other Caribbean destinations. Many of the accommodations along the shoreline have their own dive shops on site. Ambergris also has the only hyperbaric chamber in Belize.

Caye Caulker, a few miles to the south of Ambergris Caye, is smaller and more laid-back, but also a popular choice. Although prices are generally lower on Caye Caulker than Ambergris, this does not apply to snorkeling and diving, perhaps due to the more limited choices. (There are only three dive shops on Caulker.)

It is also possible to dive the northern reefs and the atolls on a daily basis from a base in Belize City (p54), where there are currently two major dive operators.

The barrier reef is only a few minutes by boat from either island. Diving here is quick and easy, though visibility is not

Plunging In

When to Go
December to July

What to Read
Lonely Planet Diving & Snorkeling: Belize by Mark Webster

Reef Creature Identification and Reef Fish: Florida, Caribbean & Bahamas by Paul Humann & Ned Deloach

Three Adventures: Galapagos, Titicaca, the Blue Holes by Jacques Yves Cousteau

www.scubadivingbelize.com
www.ambergriscaye.com/diving

Where to Stay
Glover's Reef Atoll, Stann Creek
Caye Caulker, Northern Cayes
Ambergris Caye, Northern Cayes
Salt Water Caye, Stann Creek

Best for Snorkeling
Hol Chan Marine Reserve, **Caye Caulker Marine Reserve**, Northern Cayes
Long Caye, Glover's Reef Atoll

Best for Diving
Blue Hole Natural Monument, **Half Moon Caye Natural Monument**, Lighthouse Reef
Turneffe Elbow, Turneffe Atoll
Long Caye, Glover's Reef Atoll

always prime and the water can be somewhat surging. Some divers will put up with a longer boat ride to get better visibility and drop-off clarity. Most of the dive shops offer similar deals in terms of the sites they visit and the prices of their packages. All of the dive shops take boats out to Turneffe and Lighthouse Reef Atolls.

Hol Chan Marine Reserve

At the southern end of Ambergris Caye is Hol Chan Marine Reserve (p82), which was established more than two decades ago. The profusion of marine life is a testament to the reserve's success. A lot of Hol Chan Marine Reserve is shallow and in many cases the sites are better for snorkeling, but divers have the opportunity to explore a sunken ship at Amigos Wreck. Although the reef is fishier in the south of this section, the north holds more formations, with deep spur-and-groove cuts and interesting terrain.

Central Cayes

Close to the big city but far enough away to be another world apart, the small isles and resorts on the Central Cayes are idyllic and convenient for barrier reef divers. They're normally not as busy as the reefs further north; it is quite possible to go the whole day and not see another dive boat.

If you're staying on the mainland, Hopkins (p195) is the main base from which to explore the Central Cayes. A boat ride to the dive sites is about 30 minutes on good days. Beautiful on sunny, calm days with sandy flats, reefs and old staghorns peeking above the surface, the dives are done

in the deep passes in the middle of the reef. Near are nine passes or cuts; the dive involves a descent to between 35ft and 55ft and then a swim along the deep drop-off looking for denizens.

Alternatively, depart from Dangriga for the offshore resorts on the Central Cayes. Tobacco Caye (p192) is a tiny 5-acre island only 10 miles from Dangriga. Dotted with rustic hotels and guesthouses, it offers a low-key atmosphere. This caye sits right on the edge of the barrier reef, provides excellent snorkeling, and is one of the few beach-diving locations in Belize. South Water Caye (p192) is a little larger and offers more expensive accommodations, but also sits on the crest of the barrier reef, offering beach diving and spectacular snorkeling.

South Water Caye Marine Reserve

Encompassing both Tobacco Caye and South Water Caye, this 62-square-mile marine reserve protects a unique reef system; indeed, Tobacco Caye has been the base for an Earthwatch (p301) reef-study project for several years.

There is a variety of reef topographies to be explored, ranging from shallow-water coral gardens to spur-and-groove formations, and, of course, the drop-offs from the reef edge. A little further south, the spurs and grooves change to what is known locally as a double-wall reef system. Here there are two separate systems, the first of which slopes sharply seaward from depths of 40ft down to 120ft. This is followed by a wide sand channel with isolated coral outcrops and pillars, and then a second coral reef rising to 60ft before it plunges over the wall beyond scuba-diving depths.

LIVE-ABOARD BOATS

If you are a truly dedicated diver wanting to maximize the number of dives during your trip, then choosing a live-aboard boat is the only way to go. Your 'hotel' moves with you to the dive site, which gives you the opportunity to dive four or five times a day, including night dives. The boats that operate in Belizean waters are comfortable and well equipped, and will even pamper you with hot showers on the dive deck and warm towels to wrap up in. If you do not need dry land and nightlife, then this is definitely the way to see the best that the barrier reef has to offer. All boats depart from Belize City and operators organize all ground transfers for you. Live-aboard boats in Belize include the Belize Aggressor III (www.aggressor.com) and Sun Dancer II (www.dancerfleet.com).

LEARNING TO DIVE

Have you ever wondered what it would be like to swim along a spur-and-groove reef system, to tunnel through underwater caves or to peer over a drop-off into the blue and watch schools of fish cruise by? Your trip to Belize is a great opportunity to find out. Learning to dive is not as difficult as you might think, and most of the larger dive centers offer 'try dives' to see if the sport appeals to you.

The PADI system is now the most popular certification program worldwide. The first step is the basic Open Water Diver qualification, which usually requires three days of instruction. It is possible to complete the full three-day program while you are in Belize, or you might undertake your basic theory training close to home and complete your dives in Belize under the PADI referral system. You can hire everything from fins and mask to a full scuba kit, which saves on baggage weight and provides the opportunity to test different equipment before investing in your own.

Belize's best spots for novice divers include:

➡ **Mexico Rocks**, off Ambergris Caye (p90)

➡ **Hol Chan Cut**, south of Ambergris Caye (p90)

➡ **Half Moon Caye Wall**, in Lighthouse Reef (p121)

➡ **Faegon's Point** and **Tobacco Cut**, near Tobacco Caye (p192)

➡ **Long Caye Lagoon** and **Long Caye Cut**, Glover's Reef (p193)

➡ Any site near **Placencia** (p204)

➡ **Silk Cayes** or **Mosquito Caye South**, near Placencia (p204)

Southern Cayes

The Southern Cayes have developed into a diving hot spot, with excellent sites around the Silk Cayes and Laughing Bird Caye. The base for these dives is the popular resort town of Placencia (p204). The sandy peninsula has some of the best beaches in Belize, while laid-back restaurants, colorful beach huts and even some five-star Hollywood-name hideaways have been erected among the tiny Garifuna villages. Dive shops are scattered around town, as well as being connected with specific resorts.

Gladden Spit & Silk Cayes Marine Reserve

The northernmost point of the southern reef area constitutes the Silk Cayes Marine Reserve. Blue-water action takes the form of whale sharks, bull sharks, hammerheads, dolphins and shoaling fish, all due to the seasonal spawning of cubera snapper. Looking for whale sharks in blue water is hard work, however, and not always fruitful (especially since they are night feeders). But from April to June, the spawning snappers attract the whale sharks and other predators into Gladden Spit, which is only about 12 miles off the barrier reef.

All year round, dives in the Silk Cayes can produce sightings of spotted eagle rays, turtles, moray eels, southern stingrays, large grouper, barracuda, king mackerel, dolphins and several shark species, as well as many smaller tropical reef fish and invertebrates. Manta rays appear with more frequency during winter months when the water temperatures drop, starting in December and January.

The reef table here is much wider and so it takes a little longer to reach the barrier reef by boat; however, the numerous islands with large expanses of coral reef and connecting channels between them are a bonus, providing a host of alternative dive and snorkeling sites on the way to and from the reef.

Laughing Bird Caye Faro Reef System

Laughing Bird Caye appears to be all that is left of another submerged atoll, its approximately 2.5 acres of land seemingly diminishing with passing storms and wave action. The caye got its name from the many laughing gulls that once nested here, but most of their nesting areas have since been swallowed by the rising sea. Pelicans and osprey still use the island as nesting grounds, as do sea turtles. Laughing Bird Caye is one of Belize's national parks and a part of the Belize Barrier Reef Reserve System World Heritage site (p285), which includes the island and surrounding reefs.

Within the faro is a system of patch reefs and coral ridges boasting luxuriant hard-coral growth and a variety of sponges and soft coral. The tremendous diversity of fish and invertebrate life in the inshore waters around the island make them ideal for both snorkeling and diving. There are several dive sites at the north and south of the island, all with basically the same marine life and terrain, although in the north it is possible to go a bit deeper.

Offshore Atolls

There are only four atolls in the Caribbean and three of them are right here off the coast of Belize. All three – Turneffe Atoll, Lighthouse Reef and Glover's Reef – lie offshore from the barrier reef, rising from great depths to just a few feet above sea level. You can dive them on day trips from the main islands, choose one of the atoll-based resorts or take a live-aboard boat that concentrates on diving the atolls.

Turneffe Atoll

Turneffe Atoll (p119) is the largest of the offshore trio and comprises a series of islands that runs north–south. Here you will find an area dominated purely by mangrove islands, where juveniles of every marine species are protected until they make their way into the wider waters. Sand flats, shallow gardens and life-filled walls are all highlights of Turneffe dives.

The Elbow is the most beloved Turneffe dive site, with its enormous schools of pelagic fish and pods of dolphins. Visibility varies widely depending mostly on the wind direction. A lot of wave action can stir things up in the mangroves, carrying nutrients into the water and reducing visibility. But more often, the deep water around the atolls guarantees excellent visibility and some of the most thrilling wall-diving you'll find anywhere.

The northwest site moorings such as Sandy Slope and Amber Head normally sit in 35ft to 40ft of water and the reef becomes a spur-and-groove system that leads to a vertical wall. This drops to a sandy shelf around 100ft to 120ft at most sites, then falls off again past sport-diving limits. The northwest side is protected from the occasional strong eastern and southeastern winds that sometimes blow in.

When the wind shifts to the north-northwest, blowing down from the US Gulf, conditions are better to dive on the

---

SAFETY GUIDELINES FOR DIVING

Before embarking on a scuba diving, skin diving or snorkeling trip, carefully consider the following points to ensure a safe and enjoyable experience:

➡ Possess a current diving certification card from a recognized scuba diving instructional agency (if scuba diving).

➡ Be sure you are healthy and feel comfortable diving.

➡ Obtain reliable information about physical and environmental conditions at the dive site (eg from a reputable local dive operation).

➡ Be aware of local laws, regulations and etiquette about marine life and the environment.

➡ Dive only at sites within your realm of experience; if available, engage the services of a competent, professionally trained dive instructor or dive master.

➡ Be aware that underwater conditions vary significantly from one region, or even site, to another. Seasonal changes can significantly alter any site and dive conditions. These differences influence the way divers dress for a dive and what diving techniques they use.

➡ Ask about the environmental characteristics that can affect your diving and how local, trained divers deal with these considerations.

SURF SAFARI BIG FIVE

African adventurers have long had their famed 'Big Five' list of must-see big game animals, and the Caribbean now boasts its own version for those who prefer a surf safari. For the wet set, the Big Five includes a selection of the coral reef's most notorious predators. With a couple of trips out to the reef and a little luck, you should be able to complete this checklist. In fact, one visit to Shark Ray Alley will get you nearly halfway home.

➡ **Shark** Even the nurse shark that you are most likely to encounter will on first sight cause a Spielbergian shiver, but that should soon pass after you watch your guide tickle its belly.

➡ **Stingray** These demons of the deep come armed with venomous, spike-tipped tails. The spotted eagle ray is the bigger and badder ray; it cruises the coral in Belize and is rarer to see.

➡ **Barracuda** Reaching 6ft in length and possessing powerful jaws with multiple rows of razor-sharp teeth, meet the pit bull of the reef, capable of a thrusting propulsion when it makes a deadly strike.

➡ **Moray eel** Easily concealing their 5ft-long bodies in a dark pocket of the reef or a crevice in the sea floor, these elongated serpents lie in wait for a quick-strike ambush on passing prey.

➡ **Octopus** With eight arms to hold you, the most cunning of the reef's predators is armed with a sharp beak for biting into fish, and suction cups to pry open shellfish. It is also prey for barracudas, sharks and eels, but can make itself elusive in a cloud of ink.

east side, at sites such as Grand Bogue II and Front Porch. This reeftop and wall starts a bit deeper, in the 40ft to 60ft range, and is known for being less of a slope and quite sheer in some spots. The reeftop also has interesting swim-throughs and some tight spurs and grooves.

Being the closest atoll to the coast, Turneffe is a quick trip from Ambergris Caye and Caye Caulker, although there are also resorts on Blackbird Caye (part of Turneffe Atoll).

Lighthouse Reef

At about 50 miles offshore, Lighthouse Reef (p121) is the atoll that lies furthest to the east. Lighthouse Reef is probably the best-known atoll in Belize and it is certainly the most popular, due to the Blue Hole. While this icon of Belize diving makes the atoll a major attraction, it is really the stunning walls, many swim-throughs and superb blue water that make it a favorite with both longtime, experienced Belize divers and complete novices.

Lighthouse Reef is home to Half Moon Caye Natural Monument (p121), a national park managed by the Belize Audubon Society, where a colony of rare red-footed boobies can be observed up close. There are a few fantastic dive sites nearby, such as Aquarium and Painted Wall. Other sites in the vicinity include the coral-covered Long Caye Wall.

Dive boats go out to Lighthouse Reef from both Ambergris and Caye Caulker, but the easiest way to see these sites is via a live-aboard boat. The commute from site to site is minimal, and divers can take advantage of early-morning dives and fascinating night dives. Alternatively, there are a few small lodges on Long Caye, while camping is allowed on Half Moon Caye.

Glover's Reef

In southern Belize, divers will find the third of the Belizean atolls. Of the three, Glover's Reef (p193) sees the least amount of human contact and remains largely unexplored. Glover's Reef Atoll was named after the 17th-century pirate John Glover, who used the remote islands as a base for raids against treasure-laden Spanish galleons heading to and from the Bay Islands of Honduras.

First recognized as a bird sanctuary in 1954, it has long been atop the conservation list, getting various conservation

RESPONSIBLE DIVING

Please consider the following tips when diving and help to preserve the ecology and beauty of reefs:

➡ Never use anchors on the reef, and take care not to ground boats on coral.

➡ Avoid touching or standing on living marine organisms or dragging equipment across the reef. Polyps can be damaged by even the gentlest contact. If you must hold on to the reef, only touch exposed rock or dead coral.

➡ Be conscious of your fins. Even without contact, the surge from fin strokes near the reef can damage delicate organisms. Take care not to kick up clouds of sand, which can smother organisms.

➡ Practise and maintain proper buoyancy control. Major damage can be done by divers descending too fast and colliding with the reef.

➡ Take great care in underwater caves. Spend as little time within them as possible as your air bubbles may be caught within the roof and thereby leave organisms high and dry. Take turns to inspect the interior of a small cave.

➡ Resist the temptation to collect or buy coral or shells, or to loot marine archaeological sites (mainly shipwrecks).

➡ Ensure that you take home all your rubbish and any litter you may find as well. Plastics in particular are a serious threat to marine life.

➡ Do not feed fish.

➡ Minimize your disturbance of marine animals. *Never* ride on the backs of turtles.

designations in 1978 before finally being declared a complete marine reserve in 1993, then a Unesco World Heritage site in 1996. There is a marine research station on Middle Caye and the remains of an ancient Maya settlement are being studied on Long Caye.

Located about an hour's boat ride from the mainland, Glover's Reef rises from abyssal depths of well over 2000ft; indeed, a dive site located midway between Long Caye and Middle Caye is known as The Abyss. Oval in shape, the reef is comprised of more than 700 patch reefs within a 100-sq-mile lagoon. Just to the south is one of the Caribbean's deepest valleys, where depths reach 10,000ft.

There are several rustic outpost resorts here for divers and fishers, each occupying its own island and offering an ecofriendly existence. Otherwise, there is day-boat diving from Hopkins and Placencia, and live-aboard boats occasionally cruise this far south.

The chance of seeing dolphins, mantas and whale sharks keep adventurous divers coming back for more. The spectacular walls and hard-coral formations are just a few minutes from the islands that fringe the eastern side of the atoll. If you get the chance, dive the west side of the atoll as well to explore some wonderful swim-throughs and caves.

Plan Your Trip
Belize Outdoors

Belize's extraordinary array of national parks and wildlife and marine reserves provides an incredible stage for the adventure traveler. Saltwater activities abound along the nation's 240 miles of coastline, while inland the cool waters of Belize's network of rivers provide routes for canoeing and river-tubing. Lush mountains and dense forests provide an exotic setting for jungle treks and wildlife-viewing excursions.

Fishing

This angler's paradise is home to 160 miles of barrier reef, hundreds of square miles of flats, and dozens of jungle-lined rivers and lagoons – all of which teem with a great variety of fish. The best months are May through July, with their hot sunny weather, though every species has its ideal time and place. Spin fishing, fly-fishing and trolling can all be enjoyed year-round.

Tarpon, snook and jacks inhabit the estuaries, inlets and river mouths, while bonefish, permit and barracuda are found out in the lagoons and flats. The coral reefs support grouper, snapper and jacks, and the deeper waters beyond are home to sailfish, marlin, pompano, tuna and bonito. The flats off the cayes and mainland raise realistic hopes of the angler's 'Grand Slam': permit, tarpon and bonefish all in one day. Catch-and-release is the norm for these fish and for most snook. Check with your guide or hotel about the regulations for your area and season.

The most popular fishing bases are in the Northern Cayes, especially San Pedro (p85) and Caye Caulker (p110), but there are also fishing outfits in Sarteneja (p144) and Belize City (p54).

For tarpon and bonefish, Belize's southern waters, from Placencia to Punta Gorda, are gaining in popularity. It's easy to charter a boat in places such as Glover's Reef

Essentials

When to Go

Fishing May to July
Kayaking December to May
Sailing & Windsurfing February to April
Caving January to April
Hiking & Horseback Riding January to May

Resources

Destinations Belize (www.destinationsbelize.com) is full of useful information on fishing in Belize, including fish guides, tide charts and fishing location descriptions.

Belize by Kayak: A Guide to Sea Kayaking in Belize, by Kirk Barrett, is out of print but still useful for planning routes.

Cruising Guide to Belize and Mexico's Caribbean Coast, by Freya Rauscher, provides comprehensive information for anyone navigating these complicated waters.

Best for...

Fishing Ambergris Caye
Kayaking Glover's Reef Atoll
Sailing Placencia
Windsurfing Caye Caulker
Caving Actun Tunichil Muknal
Hiking Hidden Valley Inn, Mountain Pine Ridge
Horseback Riding Mountain Equestrian Trails, Cayo

(p193), Hopkins (p195), Placencia (p204) and Punta Gorda (p215).

River fishing for big tarpon, snook, cubera snapper and 35lb to 100lb jewfish is also practicable year-round. The Sibun and Belize Rivers and Black Creek are the most frequently fished rivers, but the Deep, Monkey, Temash and Sarstoon Rivers in the south are good, too.

Lodges and guides may have equipment to rent but it's best to bring your own tackle.

Kayaking

The translucent waters of the Caribbean are as inviting for kayakers as they are for divers and snorkelers. It's amazing how much underwater life is visible from above the surface, and you can enjoy snorkeling and bird-watching as you go.

If you fancy some kayaking, consider staying at one of the resorts or hotels on the Placencia peninsula or Ambergris Caye, many of which provide free kayaks for guests. At San Pedro, Caye Caulker, Hopkins, Placencia village and Punta Gorda, you can rent a kayak for anywhere between BZ$30 and BZ$60 per day. Glover's Atoll Resort (p194) rents out single/double touring kayaks by the week for BZ$290/450.

If you want to see Belize with a paddle in your hands, a number of Belize- and North America–based firms offer recommended kayaking holidays:

Belize Kayak Rentals (522-3328, in USA 800-667-1630; www.belizekayaking.com; s/d per day BZ$70/110, per week BZ$420/700) If you prefer to go it alone on your kayaking expedition, this branch of Island Expeditions rents out kayaks from its base camp in Dangriga. Consultants are on hand to help you plan your route. Also offers weekly packages, which include a boat charter out to the cayes.

GAP Adventures (in USA 416-260-0999; www.gapadventures.com; 8-day trip BZ$2800) Using Placencia as a base, GAP's trip gives you eight nights of island-hopping on the cayes.

Island Expeditions (in USA 800-667-1630; www.islandexpeditions.com; 5-/10-day package BZ$3280/4600) This ecologically minded company takes tours departing from Dangriga and spends the night at rustic lodges on Tobacco Caye, Southwater Caye and Coco Plum Caye. Island Expeditions also does tasty combo trips, which include hiking in the jungle or visiting Maya ruins.

SeaKunga (523-3644, in USA 800-781-2269; www.seakunga.com; 8-day trip BZ$2160-2900;) SeaKunga offers a variety of excellent kayaking tours, including both sea kayaking and river kayaking. It is based in Placencia, but some of the tours are based on Glover's Reef or Sapodilla Cayes.

LA RUTA MAYA

One morning in March the waters of the Macal River beneath San Ignacio's Hawkesworth Bridge are the gathering place for a colorful flotilla of three-person canoes. They are assembled for the start of **La Ruta Maya Belize River Challenge** (www.larutamayabelize.com), a grueling four-day race down the Belize River to Belize City, where they arrive on Baron Bliss Day, a national holiday in memory of a great Belizean benefactor (p56). From relatively humble beginnings in 1998, the race has grown rapidly into Central America's biggest canoe event, attracting international and Belizean canoeists.

Even though it's all downstream, this is no gentle paddle. The fastest teams cover the river's 170 or so winding and beautiful miles from San Ignacio to Belize City in around 19 hours, while the slowest take around 36 hours. The race is divided into four one-day stages: Hawkesworth Bridge to Banana Bank Lodge near Belmopan (around 50 miles); Banana Bank to Bermudian Landing (60 miles including Big Falls Rapids); Bermudian Landing to Burrell Boom (35 miles); and Burrell Boom to Belcan Bridge, Belize City (25 miles).

In addition to being Belize's largest competitive sporting event, La Ruta Maya is an impressive conservation effort, as all proceeds are donated to local environmental efforts to revitalize and sustain Belizean waterways.

Slickrock Adventures (✉in USA 800-390-5715; www.slickrock.com; 5-/9-night package BZ$2590/3950) These top-class water-sports holidays are based on Long Caye, Glover's Reef, and combine sea kayaking, surf kayaking, windsurfing, snorkeling and diving. Accommodations are in stilt cabanas, and the meals are notable.

Canoeing

Canoes are more common than kayaks on inland rivers, especially the Mopan and Macal Rivers near San Ignacio. Both have some rapids, so be sure to choose a stretch of river that's right for your level. Many lodge accommodations in the area rent out canoes, and tour outfits in San Ignacio (p172) will also take you out on guided trips.

One of the most unusual canoe trips is the underground river through Barton Creek Cave (p161). Another nice place to use a canoe is the bird paradise of Crooked Tree Lagoon (p71).

Sailing

A day's sailing on crystal-clear Caribbean waters, with a spot of snorkeling or wildlife watching topped with an island beach BBQ, is a near-perfect way to spend a day. These tours depart from San Pedro (p89), Caye Caulker (p109) or Placencia (p204).

Some of these companies offer multiday sailing and camping trips, as well as popular boozy sunset and moonlight cruises. Raggamuffin Tours and Seahawk Sailing (p109) both do relatively economical island-hopping sails to Turneffe Atoll, Lighthouse Reef and Placencia. At San Pedro (p87) you can rent small craft by the hour or longer for light sailing on your own.

On longer sailing trips you can reach not only Belize's hundreds of islands but also the attractive Guatemalan ports of Lívingston and Río Dulce, the Honduras' Bay Islands and much of the rest of the eastern Caribbean. Several companies offer charters out of Hopkins, Placencia and San Pedro:

Belize Sailing Charters (✆523-3138; www.belizesailingcharters.com; Placencia) The sailboat *Seaker* specializes in customized trips for couples and small groups. The live-aboard boat comes with its own two-person crew, which will run the ship and prepare meals. Bareboat charters can also be arranged.

Under the Sun (✉in USA 800-285-6967; www.underthesunbelize.com; Hopkins; 8-day trip BZ$4400) The Lodge Hopper's Special is an outstanding eight days of Caribbean cruising on an 18ft Hobie Cat, with plenty of stops for snorkeling, fishing, kayaking and hammocking. Instruction is provided for novice sailors. Accommodations in lodges on the cayes, food, guide and support boat are all included in the price.

TMM Yacht Charters (✆226-3026, in USA 800-633-0155; http://sailtmm.com; San Pedro; per week BZ$7800-18,000) Based in San Pedro, TMM offers five different catamarans; custom itineraries include all of the islands and atolls.

Moorings (✉in USA 888-952-8420; www.moorings.com; Placencia) Odd that a luxury catamaran like the ones offered by Moorings should be called a 'bareboat.' Based in Placencia, Moorings offers a seven-day itinerary around the Central Cayes, but it's all subject to customization.

River-Tubing

River-tubing is the latest rage in Belize, blessed as the country is with many gentle and temperate watercourses that work their way through gorgeous scenery. You may wonder what exactly is involved, but it's not too complicated: it requires sitting in an inflated inner-tube and floating or paddling along a river. You go downstream most of the time and the only technique you need to know is how to avoid getting beached, eddied or snagged on rocks while continuing to face the right direction.

The Mopan River near San Ignacio is a popular spot for river-tubing, and you can leave from Bullet Tree Falls (p176) or San José Succotz (p179). Most lodges offer tubes and transportation for their guests, or you can rent tubes at the river's edge and go it alone.

The best of all Belizean tubing adventures is the float in and out of a sequence of caves on the Caves Branch River inside the Nohoch Che'en Caves Branch Archaeological Reserve (p150). People come on day trips from all over Belize for this. Book a tour or just show up and hire a guide at the entrance.

PLAN YOUR TRIP BELIZE OUTDOORS

Windsurfing & Kitesurfing

With a light-to-medium warm easterly breeze blowing much of the time and the barrier reef offshore to calm the waters, conditions on Caye Caulker (p110) and Ambergris Caye (p86)are ideal for wind-surfing. Regulars here boast occasional runs of 10 miles. You do have to take care with the boat traffic though, especially at San Pedro. Mellower beaches can be found in Hopkins (p195), home to a small but dedicated group of windsurfers. Winds are biggest (typically 10 to 17 knots) from February through April.

Kitesurfers also use sailboards but they catch the wind with a kitelike sail high in the air, to which they're attached by a harness and long cords. You can do introductory courses on Ambergris Caye or Caye Caulker. If you are a dedicated kitesurfer, sign up for a Kitecruise (www.kitexplorer.com), which is like a live-aboard ship for kitesurfing.

Caving

The karstic geology of parts of western Belize has produced many extensive and intricate cave systems, which are fascinating, challenging and awesome to investigate. To the ancient Maya, caves were entrances to Xibalba, the underworld and residence of important gods. Many Belizean caves today still contain relics of Maya ceremonies, offerings or sacrifices, and this archaeological element makes cave exploration doubly intriguing. One of the few caves in the country that you can enter without a guide is St Herman's Cave (p155), but even there you are required to take a guide if you want to go more than 300yd into the cave.

The most thrilling caves in the west of the country include Actun Tunichil Muknal (p157), with its evidence of human sacrifice; Barton Creek Cave (p161), which you explore by canoe; Che Chem Ha (p183), with its vast array of ancient pottery; and the caves in the Nohoch Che'en Caves Branch Archaeological Reserve (p150).

Hiking

In Belize, hiking usually means guided walks in search of birdlife, as well as other flora and fauna. Many lodges have access to trails on their own or nearby properties that you can walk by yourself, but more often lodge walks are with a guide who'll show you the animals and plants along the way. Several places offer night walks, which can be real eye-openers. Lodges with access to hiking trails include the following:

➡ Chan Chich Lodge (p135) Chan Chich is set on 130,000 acres of protected land, so you can imagine there might be some good hiking. In fact, the lodge maintains 9 miles of trails for birding and wildlife watching, with or without a guide.

➡ Macaw Bank Jungle Lodge (p163) Located on 50 beautiful acres in the foothills of the Maya Mountains, Macaw Bank is ripe for exploration, and includes a trail along the eponymous river.

➡ Black Rock River Lodge (p181) Trails departing from the lodge have enticing names like Mountain Summit, Vaca Falls and Vista Loop, promising challenging climbs, waterfalls and wonderful views.

➡ Blancaneaux Lodge (p166) Guided hikes include an early-morning bird walk and a late-night 'jaguar quest,' as well as an all-day jungle trek and a special orchid-hunting walk.

CAREFUL CAVING

➡ Remember that caves and their contents are extremely fragile. Don't disturb artifacts or cave formations, and try to avoid tours with large groups of people.

➡ For your own well-being, check the physical demands of a cave trip beforehand.

➡ Remember that some caves are subject to flash floods during rainy periods.

➡ An extra flashlight and a spare set of batteries is never a bad idea.

➡ If you have claustrophobic tendencies or are terrified of the dark (or bats), it's no shame to admit that caves are not for everyone!

Whether you're planning to hike or horseback ride for an hour or for a day, it's best to be prepared. Be ready for the hot sun, the hungry mosquitoes, the bird sightings and the ever-present possibility of finding a swimming hole.

➡ Water

➡ Hat & sunscreen

➡ Insect repellent

➡ Binoculars

➡ Swim gear

➡ Hidden Valley Inn (p167) Some 90 miles of signposted trails lead to numerous waterfalls (amongst other destinations) in the private Hidden Valley reserve.

Many of the nature preserves and national parks also have well-developed and well-maintained jungle trail networks that you can walk with or without guides:

➡ Cockscomb Basin Wildlife Sanctuary (p202) The well-marked hiking trails are excellent for birding and wildlife-watching, though you're unlikely to spot a jaguar.

➡ Mayflower Bocawina National Park (p198) It's only 11 square miles, but it contains about 7 miles of hiking trails (including the access road) to jungle, mountains, waterfalls and Maya ruins.

➡ Shipstern Nature Reserve (p144) There is a short nature trail that circles the visitors center, but a real appreciation of Shipstern requires taking a longer guided hike to Xo-Pol or along Thompson Trail.

➡ Río Bravo Conservation & Management Area (p133) The country's largest protected area has a network of hiking trails and ranger roads; walks depart from both of the field stations.

Horseback Riding

Belize has an active equestrian community. A growing number of lodges offers rides to their guests and – in some cases – nonguests.

➡ Backpackers' Paradise (p145) At BZ$30 per hour, Backpackers probably has the cheapest horseback riding in the country; it's also one of the few places that will let you ride without a guide (as long as you know how!).

➡ Banana Bank Lodge (p151) Near Belmopan, Banana Bank is a highly recommended lodge with a well tended stable of 150 horses, where you can enjoy anything from a two-hour ride to a multiday riding package.

➡ Black Rock River Lodge (p181) Black Rock keeps about a dozen horses at its small stable. Go on horseback to explore an unexcavated Maya site or the Flour Camp Cave system.

➡ Crystal Paradise Resort (p162) Guided horseback rides go to Cristo Rey Falls or Cahal Pech. Bring a bathing suit so you can take a dip in the local swimming hole.

➡ duPlooy's Jungle Lodge (p181) Offers all levels of horseback riding, ranging from a short one-hour excursion to the Belize Botanic Gardens, to a longer journey to Cristo Rey Falls (with river crossings).

➡ Mountain Equestrian Trails (p161) This rustic resort offers individual rides and riding-based holidays that combine lowland jungles and Mountain Pine Ridge.

Plan Your Trip

Weddings & Honeymoons

Getting married in Belize is surprisingly easy and affordable. Most upscale resorts and hotels offer wedding packages and services, which simplifies the planning process enormously. For a more customized approach, there are a few wedding planners working in the most popular destinations – Caye Caulker, San Pedro and Placencia.

A Wedding in Paradise

When to Say I Do
January to May

Best Book
Destination Wedding... The Fine Print by Rahmieneh Ortiz

Websites
Belize Tourism Board (www.travelbelize.org)

Wedding Planners
Barefoot Perfect Weddings (www.barefoot perfectweddings.com)

I Do (www.idobelizeweddings.com)

Mayan Ruins Weddings (www.mayanruins weddings.com)

Romantic Travel Belize (www.romantictravel belize.com)

Sally Gilham (www.weddingscayecaulker.com)

Secret Garden (www.secretgardenplacencia.com)

Tropical Weddings (www.weddingbelize.com)

Photographers
Conch Creative (www.conchcreative.com)

Jose Luis Zapata (www.joseluiszapata.com)

Demian Solano (www.demiansolano.com)

Olivera Rusu (www.oliverarusuphoto.com)

The Big Event

Do you dream of a beach wedding, exchanging vows with your beloved as the sun drops into the sea? How about an exotic jungle ceremony, serenaded by the roar of a waterfall? It's all possible in Belize, and the ranks of wedding planners and event coordinators are eager to make the dream come true for you and your mate. Here are a few questions to consider when starting to plan your special day:

Formal vs Informal

If you are hoping for a formal affair with fine china and a stretch limo, Belize is probably not the place for your destination wedding. In Belize the wedding party is more likely to arrive by golf cart rather than limousine. If you prefer going barefoot to wearing heels, you've come to the right place.

Intimate vs Inclusive

Is it going to be just you and your lover saying 'I do'? There is no more romantic place to elope. Will you be accompanied by a few family and friends? Perfect, they will have a ball in Belize. Do you have a host of of relatives that *must* be there? Now things are getting complicated. Keep in mind that Belize is a small country, and there are not many resorts that can handle very large parties. You will have many more choices if you limit your guest list to a few dozen instead of a few hundred.

Traditional vs Not

Most Belize weddings take place on the beach, in the jungle, or even atop Maya ruins, but there are plenty of options for the traditionalist, too. You'll have no problem finding a quaint seaside chapel for your church wedding or a beautiful blooming patch of tropical loveliness for your garden wedding.

Resort vs Not

Whether you're thinking beach or jungle, colonial or native, there are countless resorts and hotels that can provide a perfect locale for your event. Think about it, many of these places already have gorgeously manicured grounds, a restaurant for your reception, accommodations for your guests and (probably) a professional event planner to ensure all the arrangements are exactly what you have in mind. Of course, perhaps what you have in mind does not happen at a resort.

Legal Requirements

Three days, two passports and one justice of the peace. That's about all it takes to get married in Belize, which is one reason that destination weddings are becoming so popular here. Of course, the jaw-droppingly gorgeous setting doesn't hurt, but everyone appreciates the easy logistics too.

The government bureaucracy that oversees such things is the **Belize Registry Department** (☎227-7377; Treasury Lane, Belize City; ⏰8am-noon, 1-5pm Mon-Fri). Here's what it takes to make your marriage legal:

HOW TO HAVE A PERFECT HONEYMOON

Just married? Now it's time for you to relax, to share some adventures and to get to know each other even better. Here's how you can make your honeymoon in Belize extra romantic:

➡ **Accept Compliments** Many resorts and lodges offer complimentary champagne, room upgrades and other perks to newlyweds. Be sure to look into special packages and inform the staff that you are honeymooning when you make your reservation.

➡ **Have Breakfast in Bed** The last thing you want to worry about is waking in time for breakfast or going out to scrounge something to eat. Reserve a room with a kitchenette so your hot coffee and fresh juice are on hand when you awaken. A nice alternative is a place that serves breakfast in your room.

➡ **Go Easy on the Adventure** Honeymoons are for enjoying each other's company, not for over-exerting and exhausting yourselves. Don't try to pack in too much – remember that swinging in a hammock with your sweetheart is a very important part of your trip.

➡ **Avoid Tour Groups** Picture it: you can't hear the sweet-nothings being whispered into your ear, because a complete stranger is yammering away about her hip surgery. The easiest way to avoid this scenario is to avoid tour groups. Splurge on a private tour. Or – better yet – figure out how to get there on your own.

➡ **Make a Spa Date** A couple's massage is a wonderful sensual experience you can enjoy together. Many spas offer this service by candlelight, by the sea or even under the stars. For extra indulgence, go for a honeymoon package that includes pedicures and facials.

➡ **Dine on the Dock** Look out for resorts and restaurants that offer private dining, sometimes on the beach or at the end of the dock. Sure, you'll be sharing meals in private for the rest of your life, but here's your chance to have someone cook for you and wait on you.

TIE THE KNOT THE BELIZEAN WAY

So you've decided to go the nontraditional route; now the fun begins! Here are a few ideas for a truly memorable and uniquely Belizean wedding:

➡ **Sunset Sail** Come with me to the Sea of Love. Charter a catamaran and exchange your vows as you sail off into the sunset together (literally and figuratively).

➡ **Private Island** Belize has hundreds of them; take over your very own island on your special day.

➡ **Maya Temple** Exchange your vows atop the High Temple (no bloodletting or human sacrifice required).

➡ **Bubbly Wedding** Let the fish be your witness at an underwater affair. Glug glug glug.

➡ Obtain the application for a marriage license from the Register General (available by fax or in person).

➡ Complete the application and have it notarized by a justice of the peace (the Register General can provide contacts for JPs in your area).

➡ Both parties must be in Belize for three days before submitting your application to the Register General. Submit your application, along with photocopies of your passports showing your photograph and your arrival date. If either party has been married before, proof of divorce or widowhood is also required.

➡ For overnight service, the application costs BZ$500, plus a BZ$10 administrative fee. If you don't need expedited service, the fee is only BZ$200 plus administrative fee.

➡ When it's ready, pick up your marriage license and go get married!

➡ The marriage ceremony must be performed by a justice of the peace, a minister of a registered church or a boat captain. Two witnesses (one male and one female) must be present.

➡ After the ceremony, the marriage must be registered in the Belize Department of Registry.

➡ Your marriage is legal and valid anywhere in the world. Congratulations!

Plan Your Trip
Travel with Children

Belize has some special ingredients for a family holiday. It's affordable, especially compared to other Caribbean destinations; it's safe, especially compared to other Central American destinations; and it's small and easy to navigate. Belizeans are famously friendly, and families are no exception to this rule. Indeed, kids often break down barriers between tourists and residents, sometimes opening doors to local hospitality.

Belize for Kids

Fun & Games

Attractions in Belize – sea life, exploring caves, climbing ruins, watching for birds, wildlife and bugs – will delight kids as much as grown-ups. Most tours and activities can easily accommodate children and teenagers, although they are generally not appropriate for toddlers and babies. With these wee ones, activities might be limited to playing on the beach, swimming in the sea and swinging in the hammock. That's not the worst vacation either.

Most towns and tourist destinations have parks and public beaches where your little ones can frolic with the locals. If your child speaks English, there'll be no language barrier to mixing with local kids.

Be aware that your children may experience a touch of culture shock, especially at the visible poverty.

Food

Your kids will probably be happy to eat most typical Belizean foods such as sandwiches, rice and beans, fried chicken and hamburgers. Bakery goods, pasta and

Best Regions for Kids

Belize District
Many of the Belize District activities and attractions are designed with the cruise-ship passenger in mind. Turns out that cruisers and kids have some of the same criteria: fun stuff that's easy to reach and easy to enjoy in a limited time frame.

Northern Cayes
The boat ride itself is a sort of adventure. Once you reach these paradisiacal islands, the adventure continues with swimming, snorkeling, sailing, kayaking and more traditional beach fare.

Cayo District
Older kids especially will enjoy the wild west and all of its jungle activities.

pizzas are additional favorites. Tropical fruit smoothies are delicious and healthy.

Health

For the most part, Belize is safe and healthy for you and your family. Be cautious concerning insect bites, sunburn and, of course, water and sanitation.

Transportation

If you do not intend to do much traveling around the interior, consider going local. Public intercity transport is usually on old American school buses that have retired to Belize, so your kids will probably be familiar and comfortable (as long as the journey is not too long). Most car-rental companies can provide child seats – usually free of charge – but it's advisable to inquire when you make your reservation. Around the cayes, most transportation is by boat, which is a fun activity in itself.

Children's Highlights

Belize has begun to attract plenty of families for an exciting and exotic adventure vacation. Here's why:

Action & Adventure

➡ As long as your kids are not afraid of the dark, they'll be thrilled by cave-tubing at **Nohoch Che'en Caves Branch Archaelogical Reserve** or canoeing into **Barton Creek Cave**, both in Cayo.

➡ All of the **Maya ruins** offer a chance for kids to run, climb and explore.

➡ Many lodges offer **jungle horseback riding**, but the best are Banana Bank and Mountain Equestrian Lodge, both in Cayo.

➡ Ride the **zip line** across the jungle canopy at **Mama Noots** in Stann Creek.

➡ Besides hiking, biking, kayaking and horseback riding, **Bacab Eco Park** in Belize District also has an amazing swimming pool.

Animal Encounters

➡ Kids get a kick out of fish. Take them **snorkeling** in Glover's Reef or at Hol Chan Marine Reserve near Ambergris Caye.

➡ Sightings (and hearings) of the black howler monkey are practically guaranteed at the **Community Baboon Sanctuary** in Belize District.

➡ Children love to get up-close-and-personal with the animals at the **Belize Zoo**. Even teens are keen on the night safari.

➡ Kids come face to face with some scaly monsters at the **Green Iguana Exhibit** at the San Ignacio Resort Hotel.

➡ Everyone is delighted by the flutter magic at **Green Hills Butterfly Ranch**.

Beach Retreats

➡ For traditional sun-and-sand activities like sandcastle-building, kite-flying and wave-wading, beaches are the best at **Hopkins** or **Placencia**.

➡ Snorkeling and kayaking are on your doorstep at family-friendly **Thatch Caye**.

FOR YOUR BUDDING BIOLOGIST

Several organizations offer excellent programs that combine adventure and education, designed specifically for the younger set.

➡ **Belize Zoo** (www.belizezoo.org) Kids between 12 and 17 years old can attend Conservation Camp, a five-day program exploring the waterways and wildlife of the Sibun River.

➡ **Oceanic Society** (www.oceanic-society.org) Your family (kids must be over 10 years) can join Oceanic Society biologists for a family field study, which combines science and snorkeling, to learn about dolphins, manatees and sea turtles at Turneffe Atoll.

➡ **International Zoological Expeditions** (www.ize2belize.com) The IZE family adventure explores the rainforest around Blue Creek in Toledo and the sea and reef around South Water Caye.

➡ Kiddie pool, playground and children's yoga classes are just the beginning of the fun at **Ak'bol Yoga Retreat** on Ambergris Caye.

➡ Sports facilities, game rooms and loads of activities are designed specially for kids at **Costa Maya Reef Resort** on Ambergris Caye.

Jungle Lodges

➡ On the Hummingbird Hwy, **Ian Anderson's Caves Branch Jungle Lodge** delivers many exciting land adventures in one handy place.

➡ Your family can sleep in a tree house at **Parrot Nest Jungle Lodge** in Bullet Tree Falls.

➡ **Trek Stop** is an affordable ecolodge in Cayo with loads of kid-friendly fun.

➡ Explorers will get lost and found again in the jungle maze at **Hickatee Cottages** in Punta Gorda.

➡ The cool cabins at **Cotton Tree Lodge** in Toledo are connected by a jungle boardwalk. Just down the road is **Cyrila's Maya Belizean Chocolate**, where the kids can learn to make delicious Maya chocolate.

Rainy-Day Destinations

➡ Life-size replicas of Garifuna homesteads and logging camp scenes bring history to life at **Old Belize** outside of Belize City.

➡ Learn about the life cycle of the butterfly and play disc golf at **Tropical Wings Nature Center** in Cayo.

Planning

Successful travel with children requires some forethought.

When to Go

Kids are less likely to tolerate the tropical showers that occur often during the rainy season. Considering that Belize is an outdoor-activity sort of place, you're better off taking your children during the drier months (December to May).

Before You Go

Make sure your children are up to date on all their routine vaccinations like chicken pox and measles, in addition to the special vaccinations recommended for Belize.

What to Pack

In the towns and tourist destinations grocery stores are stocked with basic necessities, but you are not guaranteed to find the exact brand your child is accustomed to, so make sure you bring enough supplies. Other more specialized children's items might be difficult to find.

Where to Stay

➡ Most hotels, lodges and resorts welcome children – some with special activities and even child-care. Many places allow children (usually under the age of 12) to stay for free or at a reduced rate. The icon 🖪 indicates accommodations that are family friendly.

➡ Look for suites, cabins and condos that have the possibility of self-catering (eg in-room kitchenette). Eating at 'home' is an easy way to save money on meals, to make sure everybody gets to eat what they want and to avoid waiting for tables and the other hassles of dining out with children.

➡ Inquire in advance about the availability of high chairs and cribs at your accommodations. Some resorts and restaurants may be able to provide these upon request but it's worth finding out for certain so you can make alternative arrangements if necessary.

Regions at a Glance

This little country's 9000 sq miles are crammed with diversity, most evident in the geographical contrast between the sea and jungle regions. The Northern Cayes and the coastal destinations in Southern Belize are prime destinations for diving, snorkeling and other water sports (not to mention hammock-swinging and drinking rum cocktails); the dense forests of Cayo and Belize Districts and inland parts of Northern and Southern Belize are better for birding, wildlife-watching and other jungle adventures.

Ethno-cultural differences are also apparent between regions. The Mestizo influence is greatest in Northern Belize, while the Maya and Garifuna cultures thrive in Southern Belize. Creole culture is most vibrant in Belize District.

Belize District

Birding
Wildlife
Maya Ruins

Feathered Friends

Crooked Tree Wildlife Sanctuary is undoubtedly the country's top destination for birds and for people who like to watch birds. The lagoon and its environs are home to some 276 species; don't forget your binoculars.

Furry Friends

'Friends' is the operative word here, since the wildlife is not quite as 'wild' as in other parts of the country. Nonetheless, refuges such as the Community Baboon Sanctuary and the Belize Zoo are fabulous places to meet and greet the native species. Sightings are guaranteed!

Tall Temples

Altun Ha is significantly smaller than some of the country's other Maya sites, but it's still an impressive exhibit of ancient craftsmanship and labor. It's also well maintained and easy to access as a day trip from Belize City or the Northern Cayes.

p50

Northern Cayes

Activities
Food
Beaches

Under the Sea

Whether you're a certified diver or a novice snorkeler, the number-one reason to come to the Northern Cayes is to frolic with the fish and admire the colorful coral. This is world-class diving and snorkeling, accessible from any of the northern cayes or outer atolls.

Fruits of the Sea

The proliferation of fancy resorts and hotels has at least one positive consequence: amazing food. Thanks to fresh seafood and talented chefs, Ambergris boasts the country's best (and most expensive) eating.

Lounging by the Sea

OK, we admit it: the cayes do not have super fine beaches. The coastline is dominated by mangroves and sea grass, instead of vast stretches of sand. But that doesn't mean that it's not spectacularly beautiful, with picturesque docks providing plenty of places for swimming, sunbathing and hammock swinging.

p79

Northern Belize

Maya Ruins
Wildlife
Food

New River & Old Ruins

The beauty of Lamanai is not only that it's a vast, exquisite archaeological site (the country's second largest), but also that it's surrounded by lush rainforest and accessible primarily by boat. The jungle river cruise combined with the exploration of the ruins makes this one of the most popular and rewarding ways to spend a day in Belize.

Where the Wild Things Are

It's a little-known fact that the wild things are actually in Northern Belize. The remote corners of Corozal and Orange Walk are home to two of the country's most pristine and best-protected nature preserves: Rio Bravo Conservation & Management Area and Shipstern Nature Reserve.

Hot & Spicy

We can thank the Mestizo and Mexican population for spicing up the cuisine in Northern Belize.

p123

Cayo District

Ecolodges
Maya Ruins
Activities

Ecochic

When it comes to natural attractions, Cayo has everything (except the beaches!). The district's ecolodges are among the best in the country, taking full advantage of the region's natural splendors. From remote Black Rock River Lodge to the exquisite Hidden Valley Inn, you'll surely find a perfect setting for your jungle adventure.

Ancient Cities

For almost 3000 years, the ancient Maya civilization flourished in Belize, building towering temples as tributes to their god-like rulers. The remains of these once-mighty city-states are scattered throughout the country, with the most magnificent ones in Cayo.

Nonstop Adventure

Spelunking, cave-tubing, zip lining, horseback riding, hiking, bird-watching and more make Cayo an adventurer's paradise. You'll get tired, wet and dirty, but you won't get bored.

p147

Southern Belize

Beaches
Wildlife
Food

Sun & Sand

Hopkins and Placencia both have excellent, barefoot-perfect beaches. If you really want to go all-out, head to any of Southern Belize's Cayes for beachcombing, snorkeling, and of course, beachside hammocking (which in Belize is considered a sport).

Wild & Wonderful

Southern Belize is home to some of the country's finest nature reserves, including Cockscomb Basin Wildlife Sanctuary and Mayflower Bocawina National Park. Your chances of spotting stunning birds, reptiles and small mammals are very high, and you're almost guaranteed to hear the distant roar of howler monkeys.

Sweet & Spicy

Southern Belize is a great place to eat traditional Garifuna dishes, not to mention amazing seafood. Whatever you do, don't miss the chance to take a sampling tour of Marie Sharp's (hot sauce) Factory.

p184

Tikal & Flores, Guatemala

Maya Ruins
Jungles
Activities

Archaeological Bliss

The spectacular ruins of ancient Tikal and Yaxhá are the reason most visitors come to the Peten region, but those with a serious interest in the Maya will want to explore further, visiting the many smaller (and not so small) sites that dot the landscape.

Into the Wild

The parts of this region that feature towns and paved roads are small by comparison with the vast majority of the area, which is covered in jungle and accessible only to those willing to trek by foot, horseback or helicopter; Peten is firmly on any off-the-beaten path traveler's list.

Fun for All

There's more to this region than just the Maya ruins; activities include water sports on beautiful Lake Peten, hiking through nature reserves, zip lining across jungle canopies and exploring the beautiful island town of Flores.

p230

On the Road

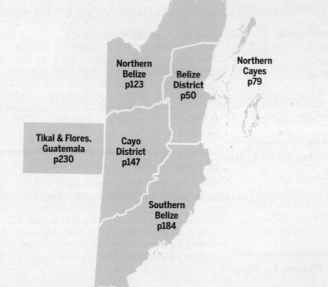

Belize District

Best Places to Eat

➡ Celebrity Restaurant,
Belize City (p60)

➡ Dit's Restaurant, Belize
City (p60)

➡ Amigos, Monkey Bay (p77)

Best Places to Stay

➡ Crooked Tree Lodge,
Crooked Tree (p71)

➡ Maruba Resort Jungle Spa,
Maskall Village (p70)

➡ Black Orchid Resort,
Burrell Boom (p66)

➡ Belize Zoo Jungle Lodge,
Belize Zoo (p75)

Why Go?

What a contrast is the district that shares its country's name! Belize District comprises 1600 sq miles at the heart of the country, and includes its largest population center and some of its most pristine tropical bush.

Belize City gets a bad rap for its impoverished areas, some of which are plagued by crime and violence. But the seaside city also embodies the country's amazing cultural diversity, its neighborhoods packed with people, restaurants and shops that represent every ethnicity.

A few miles out of the city center, the gritty Caribbean urbanism crumbles, revealing a landscape of vast savanna that stretches to the north, dense tropical forest to the west, and lush marshland to the south. There is plenty to see and do in Belize District – so much that a week-long visitor could spend their entire vacation here, sampling the country's Maya heritage, Creole culture and luxuriant wildlife, all within an hour's drive of the city.

When to Go

Belize District offers a few notable cultural events that might lure visitors outside of the normal tourist season, between January and April. In May the village of Crooked Tree goes nuts for a weekend during the annual Cashew Festival. In September Belize City engages in two weeks of festivities starting on National Day (September 10), including a huge carnival parade, bands, parties, music and dancing.

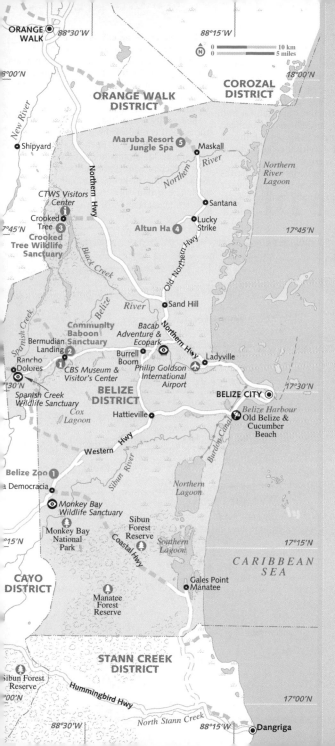

Belize District Highlights

① Getting a first-hand introduction to all of the native species at the **Belize Zoo** (p74)

② Spending a night surrounded by the roar of howler monkeys at the **Community Baboon Sanctuary** (p67)

③ Cruising the lagoon and marveling at the birdlife at **Crooked Tree Wildlife Sanctuary** (p71)

④ Admiring the jungle view from atop the Temple of the Masonry Altars at **Altun Ha** (p69)

⑤ Indulging in an afternoon of luxurious pampering in the jungle at the **Maruba Resort Jungle Spa** (p70)

BELIZE CITY

POP 63,700

Belize City does not exactly top the list of tourist destinations in Belize. In fact, many visitors choose to bypass the country's only major urban area. This may be because the country's main attractions are natural and nautical, rendering superfluous a prolonged visit to its only metropolis. An additional explanation is that the city has a bad reputation for poverty and crime.

Even those who admire its raffish charms and cultural vibrancy (and, to be fair, there's plenty of this) admit that – unlike the rest of the country – the city is not particularly relaxed. This said, the government has gone to greater lengths in recent years to make visitors feel safer in the city, including increasing the number of armed police and specially uniformed tourist police in areas frequented by travelers.

Belize City is the historical (if no longer the actual) capital of the nation, making it an interesting place to spend a day or two. Its ramshackle streets are alive with colorful characters who represent every facet of Belize's ethnic makeup, especially the Creoles. The urban scenery encompasses not just fetid canals and grungy slums, but also

Belize City

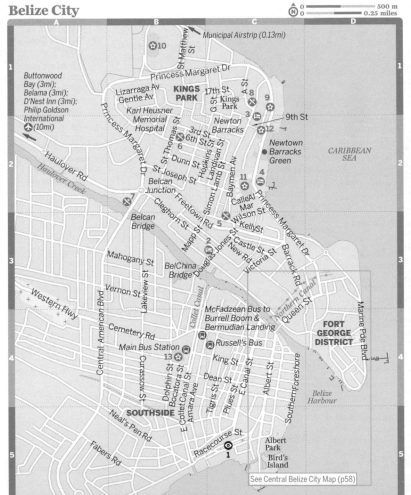

0 — 500 m
0 — 0.25 miles

Municipal Airstrip (0.13mi)

Buttonwood
Bay (3mi);
Belama (3mi);
D'Nest Inn (3mi);
Philip Goldson
International (10mi)

Matthew St
Princess Margaret Dr
Lizarraga Av
Gentle Av
KINGS PARK
17th St
A St
Karl Heusner
Memorial
Hospital
3rd St
6th St
Kings Park
Newton
Barracks
9th St
St Thomas St
Hopkins St
Landivar St
Lamb Av
Baymen Av
Newtown
Barracks
Green
CARIBBEAN SEA
Dunn St
St Joseph St
Belcan
Junction
Freetown Rd
Simon Lamb Av
Calle Al Mar
Wilson St
Princess Margaret Dr
Haulover Rd
Haulover Creek
Princess Margaret Dr
Cleghorn St
Mapp St
Kelly St
Belcan
Bridge
Mahogany St
BelChina
Bridge
Douglas Jones St
Castle St
New Rd
Victoria St
Barrack Rd
Vernon St
Western Hwy
Lakeview St
Collet Canal
Northern Canal
Queen St
Marine Pde Blvd
Cemetery Rd
Central American Blvd
McFadzean Bus to
Burrell Boom &
Bermudian Landing
Russell's Bus
FORT
GEORGE
DISTRICT
Main Bus Station
Curassow St
Dolphin St
Bocatora St
Collet Canal St
Amara Ave
King St
Dean St
Tigris St
Plues St
E Canal St
Albert St
Southern Foreshore
Belize
Harbour
SOUTHSIDE
Neal's Pen Rd
Fabers Rd
E Collet Canal St
Racecourse St
Albert
Park
Bird's
Island

See Central Belize City Map (p58)

handsome colonial houses, seaside parks, bustling shopping areas and sailboats that bob at the mouth of Haulover Creek. You might find Belize City menacing, but you certainly won't find it dull.

Haulover Creek separates the downtown commercial area (focused on Albert St) from the more genteel Fort George district to the northeast. Hotels, guesthouses and places to eat are found on both sides of the creek, with the majority of the city's high-end hotels being in Fort George. The northern end of the city has been undergoing much needed road construction so, as the saying goes, 'expect delays'. The Swing Bridge, which crosses Haulover Creek to link Albert St with Queen St, is the hub of the city, and – some say – the heart of Belize itself.

History

Belize City owes its existence to the harbor at the mouth of Haulover Creek, a branch of the Belize River, down which the Baymen (early British woodcutters) floated lumber from their inland camps. After the rainy season the Baymen would come to the coast to dispatch their lumber overseas and spend most of the proceeds on rum. Popular lore has it that the settlement – at first just a few huts surrounded by mosquito-ridden swamps –

grew on a landfill of mahogany chips and rum bottles, deposited by the Baymen.

The settlement had little significance until 1779, when the Spanish briefly captured St George's Caye. 'Belize Town' then became and remained the British headquarters in Belize.

During the 19th century the town grew on both sides of Haulover Creek, with the British merchants' homes and buildings of the ruling elite clustered along and near the southern seafront. African slaves and their descendants lived in cabins further inland. By the 1880s the town had a population of around 5000; the great majority were Creoles descended from the British and their slaves, though whites still held all the power and wealth. Belize City witnessed most of the significant events on the long road to Belizean independence, including riots in 1894, 1919 and 1950.

The city was devastated by hurricanes in 1931 and 1961. It was 1961's Hurricane Hattie that spurred the government to build a new capital at Belmopan, 52 miles inland. This left Belize City, and particularly the Creole population, feeling neglected, which led to an increase in emigration by those seeking to escape the overcrowding, unemployment and poor sanitation.

Since the 1980s and 1990s the city has been plagued by drug use and gang violence, which have contributed to tough conditions for the city's underemployed working class. Middle-class residential areas have developed on the northern and northwestern fringes of the city, while the central areas either side of Haulover Creek remain the country's cultural and commercial hub.

The 21st century has brought about a dramatic transformation in the city – albeit in a tiny corner. Cruise liners anchor off the coast of Belize City and with them come the day tourists, who head for the 'Tourist Village' – a large purpose-built facility at the mouth of Haulover Creek. Since 2004 the city has welcomed about 850,000 cruise-ship passengers every year (up from around zero at the turn of the millennium).

○ Sights

Museum of Belize   MUSEUM
(Map p58; www.nichbelize.org; Gabourel Lane; admission BZ$10; ☉8:30am-5pm Mon-Fri) This modern museum in the Fort George district provides an excellent overview of the story of Belize. Housed in the country's former main jail (built of brick in 1857),

the museum preserves one cell in its original state, complete with inmates' graffiti; if you thought your hotel room was cramped, think again! Fascinating historical photos and documents bear testimony to the colonial and independence eras, and the destruction wrought by hurricanes.

The Maya Treasures section, upstairs, is rather light on artifacts (most of Belize's finest Maya finds were spirited away to other countries) but there are some impressive examples of Maya jade, as well as some ceramics and sculpture. You'll also find plenty of informative models and explanations of the major Maya sites around the country. Other sections of the museum are devoted to Belize's highly colorful postage stamps, and its insect life, with full detail on the disgusting manner in which the human botfly uses living human flesh to nourish its larvae. The museum also has a good little gift shop.

Government House   HISTORIC SITE

(House of Culture; Map p58; Regent St; admission BZ$10; ⊙9am-4pm Mon-Fri) Fronting the sea down at the end of Regent St, this handsome two-story wooden colonial mansion served as the residence of Britain's superintendents and governors of Belize from the building's construction in 1814 until 1996. The house, one of the oldest in Belize, is now a cultural center and museum – worth a visit for its historic exhibits, colorful displays of modern Belizean art, spacious colonial ambience and grassy gardens. It was here, at midnight on September 21, 1981, that the Union Jack was ceremonially replaced with the Belizean flag to mark the birth of independent Belize. Displayed in the gardens is the tender from Baron Bliss' yacht.

St John's Cathedral   CHURCH

(Map p58; Albert St; ⊙6am-6pm) Immediately inland of Government House stands St John's Cathedral, the oldest Anglican church in Central America. It was built by slave labor between 1812 and 1820 using bricks brought from Britain as ballast. Notable things to see inside are the ancient pipe organ and the Baymen-era tombstones that tell their own history of Belize's early days and the toll taken on the city's early settlers.

A block southwest is **Yarborough Cemetery**, where you'll see the graves of less prominent early citizens – an even more turbulent narrative of Belize, which dates back to 1787.

Swing Bridge   LANDMARK

(Map p58) This heart and soul of Belize City life, crossed by just about everyone here just about every day, is the only remaining manually operated bridge of its type in the world. Its operators rotate the bridge open, usually at about 6am and 5:30pm, Monday to Saturday, just long enough to let tall boats pass, bringing vehicles and pedestrians in the city center to a halt. It's quite a procedure, and if you're in the right place at the right time, you might even get to help out. The bridge, a product of Liverpool's ironworks, was installed in 1923, replacing an earlier bridge that had opened in 1897.

The Swing Bridge is ground zero for hustlers looking to part tourists from their valuables. You are likely to be approached by seemingly friendly sorts with outstretched hands asking, 'Where you from?' Be advised that the chances of said encounter resulting in a mutually beneficial cultural exchange are slim to none.

Downstream from the bridge, Haulover Creek is usually a pretty sight, with small yachts and fishing boats riding at anchor.

Image Factory   GALLERY

(Map p58; www.imagefactorybelize.com; 91 N Front St; ⊙9am-5pm Mon-Fri) FREE The country's most innovative and exciting art gallery, near the Caye Caulker Water Taxi Terminal, stages new exhibitions most months, usually of work by Belizean artists. Opening receptions are usually held early in the month; cocktails are served on the Image Factory's deck, which looks out on Haulover Creek. The adjoining shop sells art, gifts and the country's best range of books.

Baron Bliss Tomb   MONUMENT

(Map p58) At the tip of the Fort George peninsula lies the granite Baron Bliss Tomb, the final resting place of Belize's most famous benefactor, who never set foot on Belizean soil while alive. Next to the tomb stands the **Fort George Lighthouse**, one of the many benefits the baron's munificence has yielded the country.

🏊 Activities

Although most divers and snorkelers base themselves out on the cayes, it is actually quicker to access some of the best sites directly from Belize City. Some hotels in the city offer their guests diving and snorkeling outings. Other reputable operators include Sea Sports Belize and Hugh Parkey's Belize Dive Connection.

The usual destinations are the barrier reef, Turneffe Atoll and Lighthouse Reef. Prices (including equipment) range from around BZ$240 for a two-tank dive at the barrier reef, to BZ$400 or so for a three-tank dive at Lighthouse Reef (usually including the Blue Hole). A day's snorkeling runs from around BZ$150 to BZ$300. Sea Sports Belize can also take you sea or river fishing.

☞ Tours

Popular day-trip activities and destinations from Belize City include: cave-tubing at Nohoch Che'en Caves in Cayo; visits to the Maya ruins at Lamanai in Orange Walk, Altun Ha, Xunantunich in Cayo and even Tikal in Guatemala; birding at Crooked Tree Wildlife Sanctuary; and viewing the animals at the Community Baboon Sanctuary or the Belize Zoo. Several hotels offer tours to their guests.

Many taxi drivers in town are part-time tour guides; they might give you a sales pitch as they drive you around the city. These cabbies/guides can be quite knowledgeable and personable and may suit you if you want a customized tour; in general, you can negotiate such tours for around BZ$200 per day. Hotel staff can often make personal recommendations of cabbies known to them. Make sure your guide has a Belize Tourism Board (BTB) license.

Discovery Expeditions ADVENTURE TOUR
(☑ 223-0748; .www.discoverybelize.com; 5916 Manatee Dr, Buttonwood Bay) Specializes in mainland tours to Maya sites, national parks, caves, zip-lines, horseback riding and river kayaking.

Hugh Parkey's
Belize Dive Connection ADVENTURE TOUR
(Map p58; ☑ 220-4024; www.belizediving.com; Marine Pde Blvd, Radisson Hotel) Offers diving and snorkeling tours to most nearby cayes and reefs, as well as kayaking and wildlife tours. Hugh Parkey also operates the highly rated **Belize Adventure Lodge** (www.belizeadventurelodge.com) on nearby Spanish Lookout Caye.

S&L Travel TOUR
(Map p58; ☑ 227-7593, 227-5145; www.sltravelbelize.com; 91 N Front St) A very reputable agency that offers half-day and full-day trips inland as well as customized trip packages throughout the country.

Sea Sports Belize ADVENTURE TOUR
(Map p58; ☑ 223-5505; www.seasportsbelize.com; 83 N Front St) A PADI dive shop that also specializes in wildlife-encounter tours, river cruises, barrier-reef snorkeling and manatee- and dolphin-spotting.

★ Festivals & Events

Belize International
Film Festival FILM FESTIVAL
(www.belizefilmfestival.com) Showcases films produced in Belize and in other Central American and Caribbean countries. Takes place at the Bliss Centre for the Performing Arts.

Baron Bliss Day REGATTA, CANOE RACE
(⊙ March 9) Belize City is the end-point for La Ruta Maya canoe race. Other Baron Bliss festivities include a regatta in front of Fort George Lighthouse.

September Celebrations PATRIOTIC
(www.septembercelebrations.com; ⊙ September 10-21) Starting on National Day and culminating on Independence Day, two weeks of citywide patriotic celebrations keep the locals dancing in the streets. The **Belize Carnival** (www.belizecarnival.com), a street festival held during this time, sees Belizeans don colorful costumes and dance to Carribean beats.

🛏 Sleeping

Accommodations are found both north and south of Haulover Creek. The top-end places are to the north, and most of the midrange and budget places are to the south.

Bayview Guest House GUESTHOUSE $
(Map p52; ☑ 223-4179; www.belize-guesthouse-hotel.com; 58 Baymen Ave; s/d without bathroom BZ$35/50, s/d BZ$50/65; ❈ 🛜) Located in the quiet northern end of town in Newtown Barracks, this guesthouse is part of a family home run by a Taiwanese family. Its eight rooms are very clean and simply furnished with tile floors and white-washed walls. The large, gated yard, filled with fruit trees, is a great place to decompress after a day hanging out in the city.

Ma Ma Chen Guesthouse GUESTHOUSE $
(Map p58; ☑ 223-4568; 7 Eve St; r BZ$60; ❈) Rooms are small and cell-like at this Taiwanese-owned budget guesthouse north of the Swing Bridge. On the bright side, the Chen family runs a great vegetarian cafe in the same building.

Belcove Hotel HOTEL $
(Map p58; ☑ 227-3054; www.belcove.com; 9 Regent St W; s/d with shared bathroom BZ$55/65, s/d with private bathroom BZ$69/80, deluxe rooms d/tr

BZ$104/115; ✻ 🛜) Freshly painted and impeccably clean, the family-owned Belcove occupies a bright-yellow-and-burgundy building overlooking Haulover Creek. Staff is courteous and accommodating, and manager Myrna is deeply knowledgeable about the area. The creekside setting is atmospheric, and Marlin's restaurant (right next door) serves excellent seafood.

Sea Breeze Guesthouse   GUESTHOUSE $

(Map p58; 🖉 203-0043; info@seabreeze-belize. com; 18 Gabourel Lane; s/d with shared bathroom BZ$45/50, r with private bathroom BZ$55-80; ✻ 🛜) This little family-run guesthouse is a budget traveler's dream, though the razor wire surrounding the place makes it look like the owners are planning to withstand more than just the usual crime of Belize City – a zombie apocalypse, perhaps? The location in Fort George is safe, convenient and quiet – an easy walk from the water taxi or from the facilities at the Tourist Village; the nine rooms are super clean and comfortable for the price; and the Kalam family offers low-key but accommodating service. The place lacks the hang-out and hook-up atmosphere of more popular backpacker places, but for functionality and value it's unbeatable.

Caribbean Palms Inn   GUESTHOUSE $

(Map p58; 🖉 227-0472; 26 Regent St; dm BZ$36, r with shared/private bathroom BZ$72/140; ✻ 🛜) A rambling two-story house showing some wear and tear. Furnished with wrought iron and wood, the rooms are fairly basic, but all have private bathrooms, hot-water showers and air conditioning. The owners are very friendly and there's a nice rear terrace and comfy indoor sitting area.

Seaside Guest House   HOSTEL $

(Map p58; 🖉 632-7660; www.seasideguesthouse. org; 3 Prince St; dm BZ$40, d with private bathroom BZ$90; @) This longtime budget favorite, located in a central but rough-and-tumble neighborhood, is a classic two-story wooden house with a mellow, sociable vibe. The rooms are small, and the per-bed price is a bit high for what you get. On the plus side, there are chill-out spots on the 1st and 2nd floors. On the minus side, the place is noisy, locks don't work well, and both internet and hot water are intermittent. If you want to experience the real Belize City, this as good a place as any in which to do it.

Bakadeer Inn   GUESTHOUSE $$

(Map p52; 🖉 223-0659; bakadeerinn@gmail.com; 74 Cleghorn St; s/d BZ$92/106; ✻ @ 🛜) This little guesthouse receives rave reviews for clean, comfortable rooms and professional service,

---

BLISS OF BELIZE

Only Belize could have an annual holiday in honor of a national benefactor with a name like Baron Bliss. Born Henry Edward Ernest Victor Bliss in Buckinghamshire, England, in 1869 (the title 'Baron' was hereditary), Bliss was a man with a powerful love of the sea and of sailing. So much so, in fact, that he left his wife and his native land for the Caribbean in 1920, spending the next six years living aboard his yacht *Sea King II* off the Bahamas and Trinidad. After a bad bout of food poisoning in Trinidad, the baron took up an invitation from Belize's attorney general, Willoughby Bullock, to drop his anchor off the country on January 14, 1926.

Sadly, Baron Bliss' health took a decisive turn for the worse before he could leave his yacht; his doctors pronounced that the end was nigh. On February 17, 1926, the baron signed a will aboard the *Sea King II*, leaving most of his £1 million fortune to Belize. On March 9 he died. He had, apparently, fallen in love with Belize without ever setting foot on its soil.

The testament decreed that a Baron Bliss Trust be set up to invest his bequest, and that all income from it be used for the permanent benefit of Belize and its citizens, while the capital sum was to remain intact. No churches, dance halls or schools (except agricultural or vocational schools) were to be built with Bliss Trust moneys, nor was the money to be used for any repairs to or maintenance of the Trust's own projects.

Over the decades the Baron Bliss Trust has spent more than US$1 million on projects such as the Bliss Centre for the Performing Arts, the Fort George Lighthouse (beside which lies the baron's tomb) and the Bliss School of Nursing, which are all in Belize City; and several health centers and libraries around the country. An annual national holiday, Baron Bliss Day, is celebrated on or close to March 9, the anniversary of the good man's death.

and guests love the onsite restaurant. Unfortunately the neighborhood feels dodgy, so avoid walking around here at night.

Chateau Caribbean Hotel · HOTEL $$
(Map p58; ☑ 223-0800; www.chateaucaribbean.com; 6 Marine Pde Blvd; s/d/tr/ste BZ$158/178/198/218; P❋⊛) This converted colonial mansion in the Fort George district offers a spacious lobby, bar and dining room overlooking the Caribbean. Rooms are breezy and gracefully appointed with big beds, large windows with white curtains, and wicker furniture on which to sit with a suitably colonial beverage (gin and tonic, anyone?). The whole place has an appealing air of faded grandeur.

Coningsby Inn · GUESTHOUSE $$
(Map p58; ☑ 227-1566; coningsby_inn@btl.net; 76 Regent St; d/tr BZ$119/131; ❋@⊛) A friendly and comfortable small hotel in an attractive colonial-style house, the Coningsby is recommended for attentive service and tight security. Rooms are fairly Spartan and show some wear, but there is plenty of inviting common space, including a breezy balcony and a lovely dining room. Also on offer: excellent breakfasts (BZ$10), laundry service and tours. The location offers easy access to downtown Belize City, but it can be noisy.

D'Nest Inn · B&B $$
(☑ 223-5416; www.dnestinn.com; 475 Cedar St, Belama; s BZ$136-152, d BZ$164-184; ❋⊛) Your hosts Gaby and Oty have evidently put a lot of care into this retreat on the northern edge of town. The individually decorated rooms have four-poster beds and other Victorian-era antiques, handmade quilts and floral wallpaper. Even more enticing, a lush garden beckons with blooming orchids and allamandas, singing birds and quiet corners. It's easy enough to travel the 3 miles into town by taxi or by bus, but in all honesty you probably won't want to leave this tropical paradise.

Villa Boscardi · B&B $$
(☑ 223-1691; www.villaboscardi.com; 6043 Manatee Dr, Buttonwood Bay; s/d BZ$150/178; ❋@⊛) Set in a secure middle-class suburb, this guesthouse and its charming hosts will smooth away any stresses that Belize City's rougher edges might induce. The seven rooms are large and elegant, built with Belizean materials and decorated with fresh, bold colors and prints. Breakfasts of eggs and pastries are served in the cozy sitting area, and all guests have access to shared kitchen facilities. The guesthouse is about 4 miles northwest of the city center; there are at least five restaurants within walking distance and it's even safe to walk there.

Princess Hotel & Casino · HOTEL $$
(Map p52; ☑ 223-0638; www.princessbelize.com; Barrack Rd; s/d BZ$230/250, ste BZ$280; P❋@⊛❋) This six-story seafront hotel in the north of the city is also an entertainment and social center, with bustling public areas – in fact, a better place to visit for a bit of diversion than a place to stay. Clocks at reception show the time in Las Vegas, Miami and Cancún. The rooms are ample, pretty much what you'd expect for the price at a seaside casino. Prices for all rooms include breakfast, and there's an excellent little coffee shop (and even a movie theater) downstairs.

Great House · GUESTHOUSE $$$
(Map p58; ☑ 223-3400; www.greathousebelize.com; 13 Cork St; s/d BZ$280/300; P❋@⊛) This historic colonial-style mansion was built as a private home in 1927 on a piece of prime Fort George real estate. Nowadays the Great House features 12 graceful rooms that are individually decorated, all with hardwood floors and furniture, ceiling fans and floral prints. Many perks assure your warm welcome, including fresh fruit and hot coffee upon arrival. The Great House is across the street from the Radisson, so it offers easy access to the big hotel's restaurants and services.

Radisson Fort George Hotel · HOTEL $$$
(Map p58; ☑ 223-3333; www.radisson.com/belizecitybz; 2 Marine Pde Blvd; d BZ$340-400; P❋@⊛❋) Available at the city's top hotel are 102 conservatively decorated rooms with all the comforts. While offering top international-class service, the Radisson avoids the cultural detachment that often comes with such packages, with local woods, furnishings and decorations conferring genuine Belizean character. There are three classes of room: Club Tower (the fanciest option, in a glass tower where the marble-floored rooms all enjoy a full sea view); Colonial (in the original hotel structure, with fine wooden furnishings and partial sea views); and Villa (the least expensive, across the street from the main hotel). Besides two swimming pools, two restaurants and bars, the hotel has its own dock, home to Hugh Parkey's Belize Dive Connection.

Central Belize City

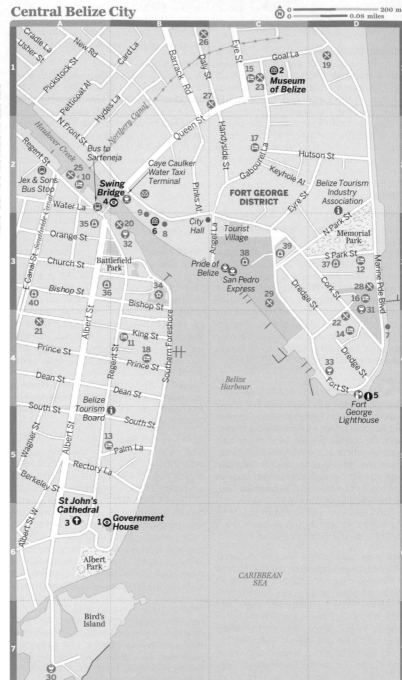

N

0 —————— 200 m
0 —————— 0.08 miles

Cradle La
Usher St
New Rd
Card La
Pickstock St
Petticoat Al
Hydes La
N Front St
Northern Canal
Haulover Creek
Regent St
Jex & Sons
Bus Stop
Water La
Bus to
Sarteneja
Swing
Bridge
Caye Caulker
Water Taxi
Terminal
Barrack Rd
Daly St
Eye St
Goal La
Queen St
Handyside St
Gabourel La
Keyhole Al
Hutson St
Museum
of Belize
FORT GEORGE
DISTRICT
Belize Tourism
Industry
Association
Memorial
Park
N Park St
S Park St
Eye St
Cork St
Marine Pde Blvd
Pinks Al
Angel La
City
Hall
Tourist
Village
Pride of
Belize
San Pedro
Express
Dredge St
Fort St
Southern Foreshore
Belize
Harbour
Fort
George
Lighthouse
E Canal St
Southside Canal
Orange St
Church St
Battlefield
Park
Bishop St
Bishop St
Prince St
Prince St
King St
Regent St
Albert St
Dean St
Dean St
South St
South St
Belize
Tourism
Board
Palm La
Rectory La
Wagner St
Albert St
Berkeley St
Albert St W
St John's
Cathedral
Government
House
Albert
Park
Bird's
Island
CARIBBEAN
SEA

Central Belize City

✗ Eating

Most of the fancier restaurants are in the hotels in the Fort George and Newtown Barracks districts, north of the Swing Bridge; you'll find some reliable local restaurants in the commercial area south of the Swing Bridge. In addition to the restaurants listed here, you can also chow down very happily at some of the bars and restaurants listed under Drinking.

Moon Clusters Coffee House   CAFE $
(Map p58; ☎ 203-0139; 25 Daly St; ☺ breakfast & lunch Mon-Sat) The coolest cafe in town, serving up six types of espresso as well as pastries such as donuts and muffins.

Marlin's Seafood   SEAFOOD $
(Map p58; Regent St; mains BZ$7-10; ☺ breakfast, lunch & dinner Mon-Sat) On a busy stretch of Regent St, this casual family-run seafood place overlooks Haulover Creek. Choose one of the seafood specials listed on the chalkboard – such as chimole fish or conch soup – then take a seat at a picnic table, which comes complete with river views.

Cenie's Deli   CAFETERIA $
(Map p58; Regent St, Commercial Center; pastries BZ$3, lunch BZ$8-10; ☺ breakfast & lunch) You'll get hearty, low-priced meals and friendly service here. At breakfast, fry-jacks (lightly fried pancake slices), eggs, bacon, sausage and a fresh juice are yours for under BZ$8. Lunch is served cafeteria-style from 11am until the food is gone. Rice-and-beans dishes are the stock in trade.

Pepper's Pizza   PIZZERIA $
(Map p52; 4 St Thomas St; pizza BZ$5-15; ☺ lunch & dinner; 🖉) One outlet in a chain of pizzerias that you will find throughout the country. It's a simple place with counter service and a long list of crispy-crust pizzas. It's worth stopping if you have a hankering for a slice.

Ma Ma Chen
Restaurant   TAIWANESE VEGETARIAN $
(Map p58; 7 Eve St; mains from BZ$5; ☺ breakfast, lunch & dinner; 🖉) Looking for an antidote to meat-heavy Belizean cuisine? Look no further: Ma Ma Chen's is a genuine Taiwan-style vegetarian restaurant, serving tofu,

brown rice and vegetable dishes. The seating area is cozy and bright, and the meals are fresh, filling and healthy.

Save U
SUPERMARKET $

(Map p52; Sancas Plaza, Belcan Junction; ☺8am-9pm Mon-Sat, 8am-2pm Sun) This modern supermarket is convenient for loading up on supplies before heading out into the wilds of Belize.

Brodie's
DEPARTMENT STORE $

(Map p58; 2 Albert St; ☺8:30am-7pm Mon-Thu, 8:30am-8pm Fri, 8:30am-5pm Sat, 8:30am-1pm Sun) This department store has the best downtown groceries.

Nerie's II Restaurant
BELIZEAN $

(Map p58; cnr Queen & Daly Sts; mains BZ$8-15; ☺breakfast, lunch & dinner) Nerie's offers most accompaniments imaginable to rice and beans, including curried lamb, stewed cow foot, lobster, *gibnut* and deer. You can start things off with a choice of soups, including chicken, *escabeche* (with chicken, lime and onions), *chirmole* (with chicken and a chili-chocolate sauce) or cow foot, and round it off with cassava pudding. Nerie's has another outlet – **Nerie's I Restaurant** (Map p52; Douglas Jones St; ☺Mon-Sat) – on the north side.

Le Petit Café
BAKERY $

(Map p58; Cork St; pastries BZ$1-5, sandwiches BZ$11-14; ☺breakfast, lunch & dinner; 🖉🖶) For muffins, croissants, cookies and a wide variety of coffee drinks, stop in at this excellent little cafe and bakery run by the Radisson. There is another outlet in the Caye Caulker water taxi terminal.

Dit's Restaurant
DINER, BAKERY $

(Map p58; 50 King St; snacks BZ$3, mains BZ$6-12; ☺breakfast & lunch) Dit's is a local favorite, a fine place to get rice-and-beans Belizean standards, sandwiches and Mexican dishes such as *panades* and *salbutes* (variations on the tortilla). Especially good are the desserts, coconut and lemon pies, milk shakes and juices.

★Celebrity Restaurant
INTERNATIONAL $$

(Map p58; 📞223-7272; www.celebritybelize.com; cnr Marine Pde Blvd & Goal Lane; mains BZ$20-30; ☺11am-11pm; 🖶) We love Celebrity because it is a semi-swanky place that is not inside a

hotel. It has an extensive menu that includes American favorites such as steaks and sandwiches, Mexican fare including fajitas and quesadillas, plenty of pasta dishes and a few Mediterranean surprises such as hummus, kofta and kebabs. That said, the chef's specialty is seafood – and you are in Belize, after all – so why not sample the grilled snapper or lobster Hollandaise? The ambience is casual, with a happening bar and sea views.

Wet Lizard
MEXICAN $$

(Map p58; Fort St; dishes BZ$12-18; ☺breakfast & lunch cruise-ship days only) Inside the Belize Tourist Village but also accessible from the street, the Wet Lizard provides solid servings of mainly Belizean and Tex-Mex food amid bright tropical colors, Jimmy Buffet songs and plenty of cruise-ship passengers.

Chon Saan Palace
CHINESE $$

(Map p52; cnr Kelly & Nurse Seay Sts; dishes BZ$12-30; ☺lunch & dinner; 🖉) The Chon Saan has been beloved in Belize City since it opened in the 1970s. The extensive menu has more than 200 items, including plenty of fresh seafood (which you can see swimming around in the tanks). Favorite dishes include chicken with cashew nuts, lobster in black bean sauce and Singapore-style chow mein.

Sumathi Indian Restaurant
INDIAN $$

(Map p52; 📞223-1172; 19 Baymen Ave; dishes BZ$18-38; ☺11am-11pm Tue-Sun; 🖉) New location, same owners, same great food. Belize City's best Indian restaurant provides a huge range of flavorsome curries, tandooris and *biryanis* (spicy rice with meat or vegetables), with plenty of vegetarian options, all in generous quantities. Bollywood films on the TV intensify the mood. It does meals to go if you prefer.

Stonegrill Restaurant
GRILL $$

(Map p58; www.radisson.com/belizecitybz; 2 Marine Pde Blvd, Radisson Fort George Hotel; mains BZ$20-35; ☺11am-10pm) At this thatched poolside restaurant at the Radisson you get to grill your own meal – steak, fajitas, shrimp, chicken satay and the like – on super-hot volcanic stones. It's fun, tasty and free of added fat.

Smoky Mermaid
CARIBBEAN $$

(Map p58; 13 Cork St; mains from BZ$20; ☺breakfast, lunch & dinner) Attached to the Great

House guesthouse, the Smoky Mermaid serves tasty Caribbean and international food on a lovely patio, which features tinkling fountains and towering tropical trees. The meals are dependably good and the servings satisfying.

🍷 Drinking & Nightlife

Top-end hotel bars are a focus of Belize City social life, especially on Friday evenings. It's more fun than it might sound, pulling in a range of locals, expats and tourists. Outside the hotels there are only a few dependably respectable places to drink.

The hub of Belize City nightlife is, fortuitously enough, located in the relatively safe Newtown Barracks area in the north of town. It's here you'll find the Princess Hotel & Casino entertainment complex and the best nightclubs. The local press publicizes upcoming events.

Bird's Isle Restaurant BAR
(Map p58; Bird's Isle; ⊙10:30am-2:30pm, 5:30pm-late Mon-Fri, 10:30am-10pm Sat) Bird's Isle may be the best that Belize City has to offer. An island oasis at the southern tip of town, it manages to defy the urban grit that lies just a few blocks away. Locals and tourists alike flock to the open-air *palapa* to partake of sea breezes, fresh-squeezed juice and cold beers, as well as delicious burgers and tasty snacks such as conch fritters. Thursday from 8:30pm to 1am is karaoke night; the bar also has live music occasionally.

Caesar's Palace CLUB
(Map p52; ☑223-7624; 190 Barrack Rd; cover men BZ$5, women free; ⊙10pm-4am Fri & Sat) The music and crowd here have a strong Latino element. People start turning up at about 10:30pm, and the action on and around the small dance floor can get pretty lively as the night wears on.

MJ's Grand BAR
(Map p52; 170 Barrack Rd; ⊙4pm-1am Mon-Fri, 4pm-3am Sat & Sun) You may get to enjoy some funky Belizean rhythms here, but karaoke starts up at 10pm most nights. MJ's is popular with locals both for its indoor pool tables and outdoor terrace tables overlooking Newtown Barracks Green.

Tropicana Lounge LOUNGE
(Map p58; ☑601-9001; 5 Fort Street; ⊙1pm-midnight Tue-Sat) Located right on the waterfront, The Tropicana is a cool place to relax,

have a drink, party with friends and enjoy enjoy occasional live music.

Riverside Cafe BAR
(Map p58; Regent St; ⊙10am-11pm) This funky urban cafe is hidden behind the Commercial Center on busy Regent St. The bamboo building is furnished with a tin roof and picnic tables – a decidedly pedestrian setting in which to quaff a beer and watch the activity on Haulover Creek. If you are hungry, there is always some spicy curry or stewed chicken on the stove in the back. Loud music and lots of local character.

Vogue Bar & Lounge BAR
(Map p52; www.princessbelize.com; Barrack Rd, Princess Hotel & Casino; ⊙noon-midnight Sun-Wed, noon-2am Thu-Sat) The lounge at the Princess gets lively on Friday nights when a mixed young crowd launches a new weekend. A DJ helps get things moving from 9pm Thursday to Saturday.

Radisson Poolside Bar BAR
(Map p58; www.radisson.com/belizecitybz; 2 Marine Pde Blvd, Radisson Fort George Hotel; ⊙11am-10pm) The Friday happy hour (5pm to 9pm) is very popular; often there is live music and sometimes there's a DJ.

Baymen's Tavern BAR
(Map p58; www.radisson.com/belizecitybz; 2 Marine Pde Blvd, Radisson Fort George Hotel; ⊙10am-10pm) The main bar at the Radisson is friendly and sociable, with a pleasant outdoor deck.

⭐ Entertainment

Bliss Centre for the Performing Arts MUSIC, THEATER
(Map p58; ☑227-2458, 227-2110; www.nichbelize.org; Southern Foreshore) Operated by the Institute for Creative Arts, the revamped Bliss Centre has a fine 600-seat theater that stages a variety of events throughout the year. Look for concerts of traditional Belizean music and shows celebrating Belize and its culture. Annual events include the Belize Film Festival and the Children's Art Festival in May.

Princess Hotel & Casino CASINO, BOWLING ALLEY, CINEMA
(Map p52; Newtown Barracks; ⊙noon-4am) The casino at the Princess Hotel is an informal and fun place to try to boost your budget, with roulette, poker and blackjack tables, plus hundreds of slot machines and a floor show with dancing girls kicking up their heels at 10pm.

You need to show ID such as your passport or driver's license to enter (minimum age is 18).

The complex is also where you will find Belize's only eight-lane (or any-lane, for that matter) **bowling alley** (⊘ 11am-11pm). The two-screen **movie theater** (⌨ 223-7162; admission BZ$10) shows first-run Hollywood films, though usually a bit later than their US release dates.

For spectator sports, the main venues are the **MCC Grounds** (Map p52; cnr Barrack Rd & Calle al Mar), for football and cricket; **Rogers Stadium** (Map p52; Dolphin St) for softball; and the **Marion Jones Sporting Complex** (Map p52; Princess Margaret Dr), which is used for various events.

🛍 Shopping

Albert St and its side streets are the main shopping thoroughfares, with stores dealing in everything from clothes and domestic appliances to spices and music.

You'll find decent gift shops at the Museum of Belize, the Radisson, the Princess Hotel and Old Belize. For a unique handicraft shopping experience, check out Belize Central Prison (p73) in Hattieville.

National Handicraft Center SOUVENIRS
(Map p58; 2 S Park St; ⊘ 8am-5pm Mon-Fri, 8am-4pm Sat) This store carries the best stock of high-quality Belizean arts and crafts at fair prices. Attractive buys include shade-grown coffee and local chocolate, carvings in zericote and other native hardwoods, slate relief carvings of wildlife and Maya deities, and CDs of Belizean music.

Tourist Village Flea Market SOUVENIRS
(Map p58; Fort St; ⊘ 8am-4pm, cruise-ship days only) On the street outside the Tourist Village, local vendors set up tents and tables to sell their wares, which include T-shirts with snappy slogans, original jewelry, woven bags and blankets, and plenty of carved wooden items. Quality varies widely and prices are negotiable. This is one of the few places in Belize where vendors are not afraid to engage the hard sell. On noncruise days, the selection is limited, but you might find a few scattered tables.

**Tourist Village
& Brown Sugar Mall** SOUVENIRS
(Map p58; Fort St; ⊘ 8am-4pm, cruise-ship days only) This waterfront complex exists for the convenience of cruise-ship passengers, who disembark here on their land trips. Noncruise tourists may enter from the street

with a temporary pass, obtainable on presentation of an identity document such as a passport. Most of the shops are liquor stores and international jewelers, but there is at least one excellent art gallery, and the shop Maya Jade, which features beautiful jewelry.

Image Factory ART, BOOKSTORE
(Map p58; 91 N Front St; ⊘ 9am-5pm Mon-Fri) This art gallery has the country's best range of books, including international literature, and titles on Belizean and Caribbean society and history. There is also one room that is packed with paintings and other local art.

Brodie's DEPARTMENT STORE
(Map p58; 2 Albert St; ⊘ 8:30am-7pm Mon-Thu, 8:30am-8pm Fri, 8:30am-5pm Sat, 8:30am-1pm Sun) Brodie's is the biggest department store in the country. Some of the 'departments' are pretty small, but it's still a good place to look for clothing and incidentals.

Augusto Quan Ltd OUTDOOR EQUIPMENT
(Map p58; 13 Market Sq) An excellent hardware store stocking tools, camping gear, sports gear and even the kitchen sink (really...it sells plumbing supplies). A good place to hit before heading into the bush.

Venus Photo Lab PHOTOGRAPHY
(Map p58; cnr Bishop & E Canal Sts) The best place in town for photographic supplies.

ℹ Information

DANGERS & ANNOYANCES

Not to put too fine a point on it, but Belize City isn't exactly the relaxed place the rest of the country is. Hotel windows are barred and front doors are often kept locked even during the day. Street crime is common. You are likely to spend most of your time in the commercial district (east of Southside Canal around Albert and Regent Sts) and in the Fort George district, both of which are safe during daylight hours.

Most violent crime occurs in the Southside district, south of Haulover Creek and west of Southside Canal. While much of it is violent crime between gang members, non-intergang crime (both petty and violent) is an increasing concern in Belize City. Stay on the main roads or take a taxi when you're going to or from the main bus station or other bus stops in this area. Even in the middle of the day these streets can have a threatening atmosphere.

After dark, it's best to take a taxi anywhere you go in the city. If you must walk, stay on better-lit major streets and don't go alone if you can help it. Get advice from your hotel about safety in specific neighborhoods.

Police maintain a fairly visible presence in the main areas frequented by tourists in Belize City, and will intervene to deter hustlers and other shady characters, but you can't rely on them to always be where you need them. Take the common-sense precautions that you would in any major city: be wary of overly friendly strangers; don't flash wads of cash, cameras, jewelry or other signs of wealth; don't leave valuables lying around your hotel room; don't use illicit drugs; and avoid deserted streets, even in daylight.

EMERGENCY

Ambulance (☑90, private ambulance 223-3292)

Crime Stoppers (☑224-4646, 922) To report crimes.

Fire Service (☑227-2579, 90)

Police (☑911, 90) Tourist police wear a special badge on the left shoulder and patrol central areas of the city. There are police stations located on Queen St and Racoon St.

INTERNET ACCESS

Angelus Press (10 Queen St; per hr BZ$3.50; ☺7:30am-5:30pm Mon-Fri, 8am-noon Sat) Office-supply store and internet cafe with a reasonable supply of books with Belizean themes.

KGS Internet (60 King St; per hr BZ$3; ☺8am-7pm Mon-Fri, 8am-6pm Sat) Will also burn CDs for BZ$3.50.

Maya Coffee (158 N Front St; per hr BZ$5; ☺8am-5pm Mon-Fri) Kevin Chen's coffee shop, just across from S&L Travel, sells souvenirs and books, as well as peddling internet access.

LAUNDRY

G's Laundromat (22 Dean St; wash per load BZ$10; ☺7:30am-5:30pm) Wash and dry in about 1½ hours. Most hotels can arrange laundry service at similar prices.

MEDICAL SERVICES

Belize Medical Associates (☑223-0304, 223-0303, 223-0302; www.belizemedical.com; 5791 St Thomas St; ☺24hr emergency services) Private hospital in Kings Park district with a good reputation among expats.

Brodie's (☑227-7070; 2 Albert St; ☺8:30am-6pm Mon-Thu, 8:30am-8pm Fri, 8:30am-5pm Sat, 8:30am-1pm Sun) This department store has a very well-stocked pharmacy.

Karl Heusner Memorial Hospital (☑223-1564, 223-1548; Princess Margaret Dr; ☺24hr emergency services) A public hospital in the north of town.

MONEY

The following banks exchange US or Canadian dollars, British pounds and, usually, euros. The ATM at First Caribbean International Bank ac-cepts foreign Visa cards while the Belize Bank ATM also accepts MasterCard, Cirrus and Plus cards. Most ATMs are open 24 hours, though it's highly recommended that you visit them during daylight hours.

Belize Bank (60 Market Sq) The ATM is on the east side of the building.

First Caribbean International Bank (21 Albert St)

Scotiabank (cnr Albert & Bishop Sts)

POST

Main post office (N Front St; ☺8am-5pm Mon-Thu, 8am-4:30pm Fri)

TELEPHONE

Public card-operated phones can be found around the city. You can also rent a cell phone from the Radisson Hotel for BZ$22 per day plus usage charge. **BTL** (☑227-7085; 1 Church St; ☺8am-6pm Mon-Fri) has indoor booths for phone-card calls, country-direct calls to Canada and the UK, and collect calls.

TOURIST INFORMATION

Belize Tourism Board (BTB; ☑227-2420, 227-2417; www.travelbelize.org; 64 Regent St; ☺8am-5pm Mon-Thu; 8am-4pm Fri) Pick up maps, magazines, and all sorts of information relating to travel around Belize. This is also where you will find the cruise-ship schedule, which is published and distributed on a bi-annual basis.

Belize Tourism Industry Association (BTIA; ☑227-1144; www.btia.org; 10 N Park St, Belize City; ☺8am-noon & 1-5pm Mon-Fri) The BTIA is an independent association of tourism businesses, actively defending 'sustainable ecocultural tourism.' The office provides leaflets about the country's regions, copies of its *Destination Belize* annual magazine (free), and information on its members, which include many of Belize's best hotels, restaurants and other tourism businesses. The website has a plethora of information.

ⓘ Getting There & Away

AIR

Belize City has two airports: Philip Goldson International Airport (BZE), which is 11 miles northwest of the city center off the Northern Hwy; and the Municipal Airstrip (TZA), around 2 miles north of the center. All international flights use the international airport. Domestic flights are divided between the two airports, but those using the Municipal Airstrip are cheaper (often significantly). The following airlines fly from Belize City:

American Airlines (☑223-2522; www.aa.com) Direct flights to/from Miami and Dallas/Fort Worth.

❶ AVOIDING THE CRUISE CROWD

If you intend to explore the sights in Belize District and eastern Cayo District, it's worth planning your itinerary around the cruise-ship schedule. Stop by or call the BTB office to find out on which dates cruise ships will be in port. On these days you'll want to avoid destinations and tours that are within striking distance of Belize City, as they will be overrun with cruise-ship passengers. The most popular day trips for cruisers are the Maya ruins at Altun Ha and cave-tubing at Nohoch Che'en Caves Branch Archaeological Reserve.

Continental Airlines (☎ 822-1062; www.continental.com) Direct flights to/from Houston.

Delta Air Lines (☎ 225-2010; www.delta.com) Direct flights to/from Atlanta.

Grupo TACA (☎ 227-7363; www.taca.com) Direct flights to/from Houston and San Salvador (El Salvador).

Maya Island Air (☎ 223-1362, 223-1140; www.mayaairways.com) Located at the Municipal Airstrip. Direct flights to Caye Caulker, Dangriga, Placencia, Punta Gorda and San Pedro (Ambergris Caye).

Tropic Air (☎ 226-2012; www.tropicair.com) Direct flights to Caye Caulker, Dangriga, Placencia, Punta Gorda, San Pedro and Flores.

US Airways (☎ 225-3589; www.usairways.com) Direct flights to Charlotte, North Carolina.

BOAT

Caye Caulker Water Taxi (CCWT; ☎ 203-1969, 226-0992; http://cayecaulkerwatertaxi.com; 10 N Front St, Caye Caulker Water Taxi Terminal) Provides the main boat service that connects Belize City with Caye Caulker and San Pedro (Ambergris Caye). Departures to Caye Caulker (one way/return BZ$15/30, 50 minutes) and San Pedro (one way/return BZ$20/40, 1½ hours) are at 8am, 9am, 10:30am, noon, 1:30pm, 3pm and 4:30pm.

If there are more than enough passengers for one boat, one will go directly to San Pedro. An extra boat, to Caye Caulker only, goes at 5:30pm. On request from passengers the boats will stop at Long Caye or Caye Chapel (one way BZ$20).

There are always a few companies offering some competition to Caye Caulker Water Taxi. Names and locations change from year to year, but prices tend to mirror those of CCWT.

San Pedro Belize Express Water Taxi (☎ 223-2225; www.belizewatertaxi.com; Front St, Brown Sugar Mall) Eight departures a day (approximately every 75 minutes from 7:45am to 5:45pm) from the dock near the Tourist Village to Caye Caulker and San Pedro. Also operates one daily boat to and from Caye Caulker to Chetumal, Mexico (via San Pedro).

Pride of Belize (☎ 607-9837; http://www.prideofbelize.com/; Caye Caulker Water Taxi Terminal) Operates a weekly ferry service between Belize City and Puerto Cortés (Honduras), stopping in Dangriga to clear customs and pick up passengers. The boat departs Belize City from the Caye Caulker Water Taxi Terminal at 9am each Saturday, reaching Dangriga at 10:30am and Puerto Cortés at 2:30pm. The return boat leaves Puerto Cortés at 10:30am each Monday, arriving in Dangriga at 3pm and Belize City at 4:30pm. One-way tickets are adult/child BZ$145/70.

BUS

Belize City's **main bus station** (Cemetery Rd) is the old Novelo's terminal next to the canal, now painted Rastafarian red, gold and green. Most buses leave from here or from the next-door **Pound Yard bus stop** (Cemetery Rd).

To judge from the barely legible handwritten schedules that adorn the walls, the country's intercity bus system is utter chaos. Indeed, there are dozens of companies that ply the main routes out of Belize City – south to Punta Gorda, west to Benque Viejo del Carmen and north to Corozal. It's actually simpler than it seems, since plenty of buses ply the main routes and prices and service do not vary much between companies.

Belmopan (BZ$5 to BZ$10, 1¼ hours, 52 miles) Nearly all southbound buses and all westbound buses pass through Belmopan. Any bus heading to Belmopan can drop you anywhere along Western Hwy.

Benque Viejo del Carmen (BZ$8 to BZ$12, 2½ to three hours, 80 miles) Buses depart every half hour from 5am to 9:30pm.

Bermudian Landing (BZ$5, one hour, 27 miles) Russell's buses go from the corner of Euphrates Ave and Cairo St at noon and 4pm from Monday to Saturday. McFadzean buses depart from the corner of Cemetery Rd and Amara Ave three or four times a day from Monday to Saturday, with the earliest bus at noon.

Burrell Boom (BZ$4, 45 minutes, 20 miles) All buses to Bermudian Landing pass through Burrell Boom. You can also catch any bus traveling along the Northern Highway, get out at the Burrell Boom turnoff and hitch 3 miles to the village.

Chetumal, Mexico (BZ$16, three hours, 102 miles) The Belize Bus Owners Cooperative operates an express bus departing daily at 6am, 9am and 11am. Alternatively, take one of the frequent northbound buses to Corozal, from where there are additional buses going over the border every half hour or so.

Corozal (BZ$10 to BZ$15, 2½ to 3¼ hours, 86 miles) Buses run north to Corozal every hour from 6am until 6pm.

Crooked Tree (BZ$5, one hour, 36 miles) Jex & Sons runs buses from the corner of Regent St W and W Canal St at 10:45am from Monday to Saturday, with additional buses departing in the late afternoon from Magazine St. You can also take any northern bus and hitch from the turnoff.

Dangriga (BZ$10 to BZ$14, 2½ to three hours, 107 miles) All southbound buses to Punta Gorda stop in Dangriga.

Flores, Guatemala Línea Dorada/Mundo Maya runs two daily buses to Flores (BZ$50, five hours, 145 miles) or Tikal (BZ$60) departing at 9:30am and 1pm. San Juan operates a bigger, more comfortable bus that plies this same route, departing at 9:30am and 2:30pm. All of these buses depart from the Caye Caulker Water Taxi terminal.

Guatemala City (BZ$110, 250 miles) The Línea Dorada/Mundo Maya buses to Flores continue on to Guatemala City.

Orange Walk (BZ$5 to BZ$7, 1½ to two hours, 57 miles) Hourly; all buses to Corozal and Sarteneja stop in Orange Walk.

Punta Gorda (BZ$24 to BZ$28, six to seven hours, 212 miles) The terminus for the southern lines — the main one operated by James. Buses depart hourly from 5:15am to 6:15pm.

San Ignacio (BZ$14 to BZ$22, two to 2½ hours, 72 miles) All westbound buses to Benque stop in San Ignacio.

Sarteneja (BZ$10, 3½ hours, 96 miles) Light blue buses depart twice a day from Regent St just northwest of the Swing Bridge; you can also catch this bus in Orange Walk.

CAR & MOTORCYCLE

The main roads in and out of town are the Northern Hwy (to the international airport, Orange Walk and Corozal), which heads northwest from the Belcan Junction, and the Western Hwy (to Belmopan and San Ignacio), which is the westward continuation of Cemetery Rd. Cemetery Rd gets its name from the ramshackle Lord's Ridge Cemetery, which it bisects west of Central American Blvd.

Auto rental firms in Belize City include the following:

Budget (223-2435, 223-3986; www.budget-belize.com; Mile 4 Northern Hwy) There is also an office at Philip Goldson International Airport and another in Placencia.

Crystal Auto Rental (223-1600; www.crystal-belize.com; Mile 5 Northern Hwy) One of the best local firms; allows vehicles to be taken into Guatemala. Check its website for medium- and long-term rental specials. There's another branch at Philip Goldson International Airport.

Euphrates Auto Rental (227-5752, 610-5752; www.ears.bz; 143 Euphrates Ave, Southside) Local firm that offers some of the best deals in town.

Hertz (223-5395, 223-0886; www.hertz.com; 11A Cork St, Fort George District) Hertz also has a branch at Philip Goldson International Airport.

Thrifty (207-1271; www.thrifty.com; 715 Gibnut St) Additional outlet at Philip Goldson International Airport.

Getting Around

Though many of the spots where travelers go are within walking distance of each other, it's always safest to take a taxi after dark.

TO & FROM THE AIRPORTS

There is no public transportation to or from either airport. The taxi fare to or from the international airport is BZ$50. An alternative is to walk the 1.6 miles from the airport to the Northern Hwy, where fairly frequent buses pass heading to Belize City. Taxis from the Municipal Airstrip to the center of town cost around BZ$10.

CAR & MOTORCYCLE

Belize City has the heaviest traffic in the country and, owing to ongoing construction (especially north of the Swing Bridge), traffic can sometimes be messy to say the least. There's a limited one-way system, which is easy to work with. If you need to park on the street, try to do so right outside the place you're staying. Never leave anything valuable on view inside a parked car.

TAXI

Cabs cost around BZ$7 for rides within the city, give or take; if it's a long trip from one side of town to the other, expect to be charged a bit more. Confirm the price in advance with your driver. Most restaurants and hotels will call a cab for you.

ALONG THE NORTHERN HIGHWAY

The Northern Hwy stretches from Belize City and into Orange Walk District, passing by the communities of Ladyville and Burrell Boom (west of which you'll find the Community Baboon Sanctuary and Spanish Creek Wildlife Sanctuary). At Sand Hill the road forks. To the west, the Northern Hwy continues to Orange Walk, passing the turnoff for the Crooked Tree Wildlife Sanctuary. To the east, the Old Northern Hwy leads to the Maya ruins of Altun Ha.

Burrell Boom

POP 1500

A tranquil and charming village, Burrell Boom occupies a quiet bank of the Belize River, just 19 miles north of Belize City and 3 miles west of the Northern Hwy. Founded in the 18th century, the village takes its name from the iron chains, or 'booms', that loggers extended across the river to trap the mahogany logs that were sent from further upriver. You can still see the boom and anchors on display in Burrell Boom Park in the village center.

Burrell Boom is only a few miles from the Community Baboon Sanctuary, but otherwise there are no big tourist draws in the immediate vicinity. Rather, the village's attraction is the exquisite natural setting, ideal for canoeing, birding and croc-spotting. Locals take advantage of the lush fruit trees and distill a huge variety of fruit wines, especially sweet berry and cashew wines.

This sleepy village comes to life every year in March when the annual canoe race known as La Ruta Maya passes through. Contestants spend their third night at the town's Old River Tavern, making that an ideal location for observers to hunker down with a cocktail and watch the fun.

The village's proximity to the international airport and the Northern Hwy make it a convenient and comfortable base from which to explore the rest of the country. That's the beauty of this place: it may be off the beaten track, but the track is only a few miles away so it's always easy to get back on.

◉ Sights

★ **Bacab Adventure & Eco Park**   PARK
(☑ 225-2587, 225-3537; www.bacabecopark.com; BZ$10; tour prices vary) ✿ Part nature preserve, part theme park, Bacab claims to offer 'Something for Everyone' – which is no idle boast. The place is set on more than 500 acres of delicious jungle, through which wind hiking trails and waterways. A nature hike will likely reward observers with a glimpse of resident howler monkeys or multiple bird sightings. But adventurers might wish to explore the reserve on horseback (best scheduled a day in advance), by kayak or even by mountain bike.

The place is perfect for families as it offers a plethora of 'safer' activities, including a huge swimming pool with a waterfall. More than 25 native butterfly species inhabit the Wild Wings Butterfly House, while a congregation of rescued crocodiles has laid claim to its own private watering hole. While this place was established with the cruise-ship tourist in mind, days when the ships aren't in (schedules change all the time; call the front desk to find out) are absolutely serene. The staff is warm and friendly and service absolutely top notch.

While Bacab is loads of fun, its goal is more complex, as management has undertaken an intensive reforestation effort, planting more than 25 species of native trees.

Bacab has a gift shop and a beautiful palapa-roofed restaurant that serves American, Caribbean and Belizean cuisine; so again, there is something for everyone. While plans are underway to build overnight accommodations, as of the time of writing overnight visitors can camp out for BZ$10 per person – tents can be provided. To get to Bacab, turn off the Burrell Boom road into Ridge Lagoon Estates and follow the signs.

🛌 Sleeping & Eating

Black Orchid Resort   RESORT $$$
(☑ 225-9158; www.blackorchidresort.com; d riverview/courtyard BZ$330/280, ste BZ$450; ⓟ❄️🛜🏊🛗) ✿ Guests rave about the attentive service and comfortable accommodations at this classy riverside resort. There are 16 spacious rooms with big beds made of mahogany; bedspreads are sprinkled lightly with hibiscus flowers. Mexican-tiled bathrooms and private balconies provide the perfect place to sip your morning coffee and listen to the birds awaken. Rooms are enhanced by funky wall murals, painted by a local Maya artist. All rates are for double rooms, but small discounts are available for solo travelers. The verdant flower-filled grounds stretch down to the river, where complimentary canoes, kayaks and paddle boats are available for guests' use. Other amenities include a nice restaurant, a small gift shop and plenty of adventure tours. Bonus: free airport transfers.

ℹ Getting There & Away

Both Bacab Eco Park and Black Orchid Lodge will arrange transfers from Belize City or from the international airport, so it's unlikely you will be dependent on public transportation. That said, five buses a day pass through Burrell Boom to/from Belize City (although three of them are very early in the morning). There are no buses on Sunday. Alternatively, buses ply the Northern Hwy every hour, so if you can get a lift from the village to the highway turnoff, you won't have to wait long.

Community Baboon Sanctuary

No real baboons inhabit Belize; but Belizeans use that name for black howler monkeys, an endangered species that exists only in Belize, northern Guatemala and southern Mexico. The Community Baboon Sanctuary (CBS; www.howlermonkeys.org) is an amazing community-run, grassroots conservation operation (run by local women's organizations) that has engineered an impressive increase in the primate's local population.

CBS occupies about 20 sq miles, spread over several Creole villages in the Belize River valley. More than 200 landowners in seven villages have signed pledges to preserve the monkey's habitat, by protecting forested areas along the river and in corridors that run along the borders of their property. The black howlers have made an amazing comeback in the area, and the monkeys now roam freely all around the surrounding area.

The CBS Museum & Visitor's Center (245-2009, 245-2007; cbsbelize@gmail.com; Bermudian Landing; admission BZ$14; 8am-5pm) has a number of good exhibits and displays on the black howler, the history of the sanctuary, and other Belizean wildlife. Included with the admission fee is a one-hour guided nature walk on which you're likely to get an up-close introduction to a resident troop of black howlers. Along the way the trained local guides also impart their knowledge of the many medicinal plants. Alternatively, the Visitor's Center also offers night hikes, canoe trips and croc-spotting tours.

There are also nearly 200 bird species here to keep wildlife-watchers busy. The center can also connect you with local homestays providing both food and lodging.

Sleeping & Eating

Bring your own lunch when you visit the Baboon Sanctuary, as there are no restaurants in the village. Bed & Breakfast (d incl 2 meals BZ$84) is available in local homes around the village. Conditions are rustic (not all places have showers or flush toilets), but there's no better way to experience Creole village life and support the community. Book at the Visitor's Center.

There are also a few private lodges in the village:

★ Howler Monkey Resort   LODGE $$
(607-1571; www.howlermonkeyresort.bz; cabins from BZ$120-170; P❄🛜🐾👪) ✎ Ed and Melissa Turton's beautiful, rustic jungle lodge consists of seven cabins of varying size and proximity to the river, set on 20 jungle-filled acres above a bend in the Belize River. This is the place to come to hear the howler monkeys roar at night and watch birds, agoutis, iguanas and even the occasional crocodile roam during the day. Ed and Mel are excellent wildlife guides (and chefs), and their resort has trails to explore, canoes to rent (BZ$80 per day) and even a swimming pool. One feature of the resort that should appeal to budget travelers is that prices are for the cabins themselves, so splitting between four or six people becomes quite cheap indeed. All cabin rentals include

---

THE MONKEY THAT ROARED

Listen! Up in the sky! It's a jet plane! It's a Harley Davidson! It's a Led Zeppelin! No, it's a howler monkey.

Just how loud is the vociferous simian? The howl of the howler monkey routinely reaches 88 decibels, which is on average louder than a lion's roar, an elephant's trumpet or a Maria Sharapova serve. This makes the howler the loudest of all land animals. A hollowed-out bone in the throat gives the 20lb primate the anatomical ability to crank up the volume.

The male monkeys make all the noise. Howler troops, which number about a dozen members, are matriarchal. The females only need one or two mature males around to defend their preferred patch of rainforest from hungry rivals. So early in the morning and late in the afternoon, when the dominant male traipses up to his treetop trapeze to make his booming broadcast, *stay away!*

There are officially nine species of howler, but only one in Belize – the Yucatan black howler, which happens to be the largest of the kind. Belizeans refer to it as a baboon, but that is a misnomer. The baboon is an Old World monkey; the howler is strictly New World. Even if you do not see a howler monkey on your trip to Belize, you will likely hear one. Its haunting cry carries as far as 5 miles.

breakfast and dinner for two at the couple's onsite dining room, with additional meals available for around BZ$16.

Another surprisingly excellent feature of the Howler Monkey Resort is its newly built bat house; that is, an old cabin that's been converted to a bat sanctuary. The benefit of this to visitors isn't obvious at first, but becomes so once you realize that the bats pay their rent by keeping the area nearly mosquito free.

Nature Resort   CABAÑAS **$$**
(☑ 223-3668; naturer@btl.net; cabañas BZ$110-120; P ✿) Right next to the Visitor's Center, this little resort was closed during the time of our last visit, but may be opened again by the time you read this. Contact the Visitor's Center for information.

❶ Getting There & Away

Bermudian Landing is 28 miles northwest of Belize City and 9 miles west of Burrell Boom. Buses depart from the CBS Museum & Visitor's Center to Belize City (BZ$5, one hour) very early in the morning, with a few departures at 3:30pm and 4pm from Monday to Saturday. Buses leave Belize City from the corner of Amara Ave and Cemetery Rd and depart at noon, 12:20pm, 3:30pm, 4pm, 4:30pm, 5pm and 5:30pm. There's also one bus a day leaving from the main terminal at 6pm. The bus costs BZ$3 and takes one hour.

Rancho Dolores

POP 200

This pristine 5900-acre **Spanish Creek Wildlife Sanctuary** runs 5 miles along the length of the Spanish Creek, beginning by the small Creole/Maya community of Rancho Dolores. Here you will find the wildlife sanctuary **visitors center** (☑ 630-3312, 602-2740), the green building between the bridge and the cemetery.

Like the Community Baboon Sanctuary, the Spanish Creek Wildlife Sanctuary is run by a grassroots, community-based group; unlike CBS, it is not well organized. In theory, local guides take tourists horseback riding, canoeing and hiking along the **Spider Monkey Trail**, which starts about 2 miles downstream from the village; in reality, the visitors center is staffed only sporadically and the wildlife sanctuary does not see enough visitors to keep guides on call – so it might be difficult to make such arrangements.

Though there are no hotels in Rancho Dolores, there is a **homestay program** (per person BZ$30) with families throughout the village. In addition to providing rooms and meals, host families can act as guides and liaise between guests and the general community.

Rancho Dolores is located 17 miles west of the junction at Burrell Boom. You will pass through several villages along the way (as well as the Community Baboon Sanctuary) and Rancho Dolores is at the end of the road. Be warned: the last few miles are on a very shoddy dirt track; 4WD vehicle is recommended. One bus per day leaves Belize City, at 5pm Monday to Friday and 1pm Saturday, from the corner of Amara Ave and Orange St. It arrives at Rancho Dolores about an hour later. The same bus departs Rancho Dolores at 5am Monday to Saturday.

Old Northern Highway

If you wish to get a sense of what Belize was like before the tourist boom, take a drive along the Old Northern Hwy, which forks off from the 'new' Northern Hwy about 20 miles north of Belize City. The road was apparently completely paved during colonial rule, but it's not clear whether the government of Belize has done much maintenance since independence. Just joking (sort of).

For the first stretch, the 'highway' is mostly paved but very narrow. It traverses about 10 miles of dense jungle and tiny villages before reaching the turnoff for the Maya ruins at Altun Ha.

⊙ Sights

Altun Ha   RUIN
(http://nichbelize.org; adult/child under 5 BZ\$10/ free; ⊙7am-5pm) Altun Ha, the ruins that have inspired Belikin beer labels and Belizean banknotes, stands 34 miles north of central Belize City, off the Old Northern Hwy.

During its peak in the Classic Period (AD 250–1000), Altun Ha was a rich and important Maya trading and agricultural town with a population of 8000 to 10,000. The entire site covered some 1500 acres, but what visitors today see is the central ceremonial precinct of two plazas surrounded by temples, excavated in the 1960s and now looking squeaky clean following a stabilization and conservation program from 2000 to 2004.

Altun Ha existed by at least 200 BC, perhaps even several centuries earlier, and flourished until the mysterious collapse of Classic Maya civilization around AD 900. Most of the temples date from around AD 550 to 650, though, like many Maya temples, most of them are composed of several layers, having been built over periodically in a series of renewals.

In Plaza A, structure A-1 is sometimes called the **Temple of the Green Tomb**. Deep within it was discovered the tomb of a priest-king dating from around AD 600. Tropical humidity had destroyed the garments of the king and the paper of the Maya 'painted book' buried with him, but many riches were intact: shell necklaces, pottery, pearls, stingray spines used in bloodletting rites, ceremonial flints and the nearly 300 jade objects (mostly small beads and pendants) that gave rise to the name Green Tomb.

The largest and most important temple is the **Temple of the Masonry Altars** (B-4). The restored structure you see dates from the first half of the 7th century AD and takes its name from altars on which copal was burned and beautifully carved jade pieces were smashed in sacrifice. This is the Maya temple that's likely to become most familiar during your Belizean travels, since it's the one depicted (in somewhat stylized form) on Belikin beer labels.

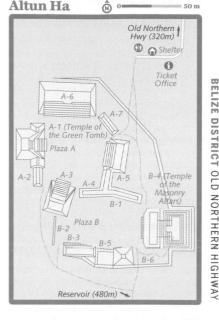

Excavation of the structure in 1968 revealed several priestly tombs. Most had been destroyed or desecrated, but one, tomb B-4/7 (inside the stone structure protruding from the upper steps of the broad central staircase), contained the remains of an elderly personage accompanied by numerous jade objects, including a unique 6in-tall carved head of Kinich Ahau, the Maya sun god – the largest well-carved jade object ever recovered from a Maya archaeological site. (Look for the jade head illustration in the top left corner of Belizean banknotes.)

A path heading south from structure B-6 leads 600yd through jungle to a broad pond – the main **reservoir** of the ancient town.

Modern toilets, and drinks and souvenir stands are near the ticket office, and the site has good wheelchair access.

🛏 Sleeping & Eating

Mayan Wells Restaurant   BELIZEAN **\$\$**
(☑225-5505; www.mayanwells.com; Altun Ha Rd; camping per person BZ\$10, r BZ\$80, lunch BZ\$12-20; ⊙lunch Mon-Fri; @) Mayan Wells is 1.4 miles from the ruins, on the road in from the Old Northern Hwy, and makes a fine stop for lunch or refreshments. Traditional Belizean lunches of rice, beans, stewed chicken and a drink are served under a *palapa* (thatched-roof shelter), beside a cenote

WORTH A TRIP

MARUBA RESORT JUNGLE SPA

An oasis of luxury in the middle of dense broadleaf forest, **Maruba Resort Jungle Spa** (☑ 225-5555; www.maruba-belize.com; Mile 40½ Old Northern Hwy; s/d BZ$350/400, junior ste BZ$540, ste from BZ$670; P ❀ 🛜 🏊 🍴) takes the jungle-lodge-and-spa concept to extremes of expensive pampering. Lush tropical grounds harbor individually designed rooms in a variety of African, Creole, Maya and even Gaudíesque styles – including honeymoon and 'fertility' suites, and a jungle tree house. All are spacious, stylish and even a bit glamorous. There are two pools with hot tubs, waterfalls and romantic daybeds with privacy curtains. The tree-house restaurant serves good seafood and game, healthy salads and fresh-squeezed juices to nonguests as well as guests.

For the active, there is a range of adventures and tours, including horseback riding and jungle excursions. For the self-indulgent, there is a full range of decadent spa treatments, including body scrubs (BZ$150 to BZ$230), mud wraps (BZ$140 to BZ$170) and aromatherapy (BZ$180). The specialty is the Mood Mud Massage (BZ$180), which uses scented or unscented 'mud' lotions to revitalize the skin, relax the muscles and enhance the mood. The romantic Couples Mood Massage is popular with honeymooners. There are a variety of half-day packages available to visitors who can't spend the night.

Maruba is about 2 miles north of Maskall village (13 miles north of Altun Ha).

amid lovely tropical gardens. If you fancy staying here, there's a cozy mosquito-netted *cabaña* with private bathroom and hammock-slung veranda that accommodates up to four adults. Otherwise you can camp. Birders and other nature lovers will particularly enjoy this hospitable place.

ⓘ Information

DANGERS & ANNOYANCES

North of Altun Ha, the quality of the road declines drastically, and north of Maskall it's all gravel all the time. Indeed, Maskall is the only civilization of any note along the Old Northern Hwy, so there's nobody to ask for help when you get a flat tire. Locals advise avoiding the northern part of this highway and approaching Altun Ha and Maruba from the south (even if you are coming from northerly points such as Orange Walk or Corozal).

ⓘ Getting There & Away

Many tours run to Altun Ha from Belize City/Caye Caulker, or from San Pedro on Ambergris Caye.

To get here with your own vehicle, turn off the Northern Hwy 20 miles from Belize City at a junction signed 'Altun Ha,' then drive 11.5 miles along the paved but narrow and often potholed Old Northern Hwy to Lucky Strike village, where a better paved road heads off west to Altun Ha (2.4 miles).

Buses to Maskall, four times daily from the main bus station in Belize City, will drop you at Lucky Strike. Heading back to the city, buses leave only in the early morning, so the trip is feasible only if you spend the night at one of the local lodges. Traffic along the jungle-lined Old Northern Hwy tends to be light, so if you're hitchhiking prepare to wait.

Crooked Tree

POP 900

Founded in the early 18th century, Crooked Tree – 33 miles from Belize City – may be the oldest village in Belize. The story goes that the village got its name from early logwood cutters who boated up Belize River and Black Creek to a giant lagoon marked by a tree that seemingly grew in every direction. These 'crooked trees' (logwood trees, in fact) still grow in abundance around the lagoon. Until the 3.5-mile causeway from the Northern Hwy was built in 1984, the only way to get here was by boat, so it's no wonder life still maintains the slow rhythm of bygone centuries.

Crooked Tree village is the gateway to the eponymous wildlife sanctuary, quite possibly one of the best birding areas in Belize. It is well worth a visit for anyone who loves nature or anyone who enjoys a peaceful rural community with an interesting history and a beautiful setting. It's best to stay the night so you can be here at dawn, when the birds are most active. Don't forget your binoculars!

The obvious reference point in the village is the 'Welcome to Crooked Tree' sign, at a junction 300yd past the visitors center as you enter the village from the causeway.

◉ Sights & Activities

Crooked Tree
Wildlife Sanctuary   WILDLIFE RESERVE
(CTWS; admission BZ$8) ✍ Between December and May migrating birds flock to the lagoons, rivers and swamps of the massive Crooked Tree Wildlife Sanctuary, which is managed by Belize Audubon. The best birdwatching is in April and May, when the low level of the lagoon draws thousands of birds into the open to seek food in the shallows.

That said, at any time between December and May bird-watchers are in for hours of ornithological bliss. Boat-billed, chestnut-bellied and bare-throated tiger herons, Muscovy and black-bellied whistling ducks, snail kites, ospreys, black-collared hawks and all of Belize's five species of kingfisher are among the 276 species recorded here. Jabiru storks, the largest flying bird in the Americas, with wingspans of up to 12ft, congregate here in April and May, and a few pairs nest in the sanctuary in the preceding months.

At the entrance to the village, just off the causeway, stop by the CTWS visitors center (⊘ 8am-4.30pm) to browse the interesting displays, books and information materials for sale. It's here that you'll be asked to pay your admission fee. The helpful, knowledgeable staff will provide a village and trail map, as well as information on expert local bird guides.

Walking Trails   WALKING
A series of reasonably well-signposted walking trails weave along the lakeshores and through and beyond the village. About 3 miles north of the village center is an excellent 700yd boardwalk and an observation tower, which allows access to swampy areas of thick, low vegetation around the lagoon's edge. From January to May you can reach the boardwalk by driving and walking; the rest of the year you'll need a boat to reach it.

Boat Tours   BOAT TOUR
(up to 4 people BZ$180) Any of the local hotels can arrange a boat tour of the lagoon. This activity is particularly worthwhile from December to February, before the level of the lagoon has dropped off dramatically. Expert guides know which birds live in every nook and cranny of the swampland.

South of the lagoon, Spanish Creek and Black Creek harbor plenty of birds all year in their thick tree cover. Black Creek is also home to black howler monkeys, Morelet's crocodiles, coatimundi and several species of turtle and iguana; Spanish Creek gives access to Chau Hix, an ancient Maya site with a pyramid 80ft high.

✷ Festivals & Events

Crooked Tree is home to a great number of cashew trees and the village's annual Cashew Festival during the first weekend in May. The festival celebrates the cashew harvest in a big way, with music, dancing and lots of cracking, shelling, roasting and stewing of cashews, as well as the making of cashew cake, cashew jelly, cashew ice cream, cashew wine (not unlike sweet sherry) and cashew you-name-it. The harvest season continues into July.

🛏 Sleeping & Eating

Tillett's Village Lodge   GUESTHOUSE $
(☏ 607-3871, 245-7016; www.tillettvillage.com; r from BZ$70; tr cabaña BZ$120; lakeside cabin BZ$200; P ❋) The Tilletts are a local Crooked Creek clan who have reared some of the most celebrated bird guides in the country. Their guesthouse has five simple rooms (two with air-con, the rest fan-cooled) with linoleum floors, comfortable beds, hot showers and an assortment of original artwork featuring the local birdlife. The Tilletts also have three *cabañas* (including one on the lagoon) that are fan-cooled and fully furnished. The little restaurant serves excellent Creole cooking (meals BZ$8 to BZ$16). Tillett's is on the main street, 500yd north of the 'Welcome to Crooked Tree' sign.

A pioneering family in Belize's ecotourism field, the Tilletts naturally offer excellent tours around the area, including trips to Altun Ha, Lamani, Belize Zoo and elsewhere. They also lead horseback tours, nature walks and, of course, birding trips on the lagoon.

★ Crooked Tree Lodge   CABINS $$
(☏ 636-3396, 626-3820; www.crookedtreelodge-belize.com; camping per person BZ$20, cabañas BZ$120-176; P 🛜 🐕) ✍ Mick is a British pilot who served for years in Belize; Angie was born and bred in Crooked Tree. This delightful couple has found their little plot of paradise and – lucky for us – they welcome visitors! The cozy wood *cabañas* all have private porches that overlook the lagoon, providing perfect sunrise views. The self-service waterfront bar and open-plan dining room are wonderful and welcoming. Homemade meals – served family-style –

are moderately priced and delicious (breakfast or lunch BZ$20, dinner BZ$30). Angie will also help you arrange any sort of tour or activity that you wish. Mick and Angie provide reusable water bottles, campers are welcome to use the fridge, and they'll provide lifts to the highway. The lodge is located at the north end of the village; cross the causeway and turn right at the 'Welcome to Crooked Tree' sign.

Jacana Inn   HOTEL $$
(☑604-8025, 620-9472; www.jacanainn.com; r from BZ$100; 🖥🐶) Run by the Nicholson family, this newly opened hotel sits on a gorgeous spot on the banks of the northern lagoon and offers 12 basic but comfortable rooms perfect for birders visiting Crooked Tree. Mrs Nicholson will provide breakfast and lunch with advance notice for a small fee, and locally made wines are available for sale.

Bird's Eye View Lodge   HOTEL $$
(☑225-7027, 203-2040, in USA 570-588-0844; www.birdseyeviewbelize.com; camping per person BZ$20, s BZ$120-180, d BZ$160-240; P❄@) Aptly named, this lodge has an excellent spot for viewing the waterfowl that inhabit the sanctuary's main lagoon. Catering to bird-watchers for almost 15 years, the Lodge's 20 rooms are of ample size, with many recently renovated to include new beds, ceiling fans, Mexican-tile floors and stained wood wainscoting. The more expensive rooms upstairs have private balconies that yield lovely vistas over the lagoon. Meals (BZ$24 to BZ$30) are served in a bright dining room. The lodge offers lagoon boat tours (BZ$200), nature walks with experienced bird guides (per person per hour BZ$20), horseback riding (per hour BZ$30) and canoe rental (per person per hour BZ$10). The Bird's Eye View Lodge is about 1 mile south of the 'Welcome to Crooked Tree' sign.

❶ Getting There & Away

To reach Crooked Tree village, turn off the Northern Hwy 33 miles north of Belize City and drive across the causeway into the village. The wildlife sanctuary visitors center is immediately on the right. From the 'Welcome to Crooked Tree' sign, other posts will direct you to the various lodges.

Jex & Sons runs buses to Belize City (BZ$5, one hour) that leave the village early in the morning.

Most hotels will arrange transfers from Belize City or from the international airport for BZ$100

to BZ$150 for up to four people. Alternatively, your host will probably be willing to fetch you from the Northern Hwy turnoff, which means you can take any northbound bus from Belize City.

ALONG THE WESTERN HIGHWAY

The Western Hwy stretches from Belize City through the village of Hattieville, and on to Belmopan and Cayo District. This part of Belize District is mostly agricultural, offering wide vistas of farmland with glimpses of the Mountain Pine Ridge in the distance. At Hattieville a good paved road heads north to hook up with the Northern Hwy, which is an excellent way to avoid the city when driving around Belize District.

Old Belize

Located just 5 miles outside of Belize City, this strange museum and adventure park was apparently designed to provide hurried cruise-ship tourists with a neatly encapsulated version of Belizean history and culture. Somebody soon realized that most cruisers are looking for sun and fun more than history and culture, so they built a beach (with requisite beach bar). As demand grew for more action and adventure, Old Belize added a giant water slide and a zip line.

If you are in Belize for one day (as cruise-ship passengers are) Old Belize is a place where you can sample a little bit of everything. If you happen to be here for longer than one day there are plenty of other places where the history and culture, sun and fun, and action and adventure are more authentic and more rewarding. You will, however, have to venture further than 5 miles outside of Belize City.

⊙ Sights

Old Belize Exhibit   MUSEUM
(☑222-4129, 222-4286; www.oldbelize.com; adult/child BZ$10/6, child under 6 free; ⊙8am-4pm Tue-Sat, 10am-4pm Sun & Mon; P) This is the original Old Belize, which manages to pack the country's entire ecological, archaeological, industrial and political history into a 45-minute tour. It starts in the rainforest, with reproductions of the tropical trees and limestone caves that you'll find (for real) just a few miles west. A Maya exhibit has reproductions of some temples and tombs, which you also might see (for real) just a few miles north of here.

The most interesting parts of the museum are the industry exhibits, which display some genuine artifacts, such as a sugarcane press and a steam-powered sawmill. There is also a reproduction of the interior of a Garifuna home, as well as a life-size model of a Belize Town street from the early 20th century.

Your trip through the plastic bowels of Old Belize ends at the gift shop, which is actually pretty well stocked with interesting knickknacks, including T-shirts, rum, chicle gum and Cuban cigars.

Cucumber Beach   BEACH
(www.oldbelize.com; admission BZ$30, zip line BZ$40) If you are desperate for some beach time but you can't leave the mainland, this artificial beach is not a terrible option. It's a 350ft stretch of sand facing the sea, with plenty of thatched-roof huts surrounding a tranquil lagoon. A massive water slide – also known as Slippery Conch – drops from a 50ft platform into the lagoon. There is also a 650ft zip line that runs across the lagoon

and beach. The friendly beach bar serves all your favorite fruity cocktails, plus there are showers and changing facilities.

Apparently, back in the 1950s this plot of land was owned by an American grower and trader who exported all kinds of vegetables (including cucumbers) to the US. This port was used to package and load the produce-laden boats, and thus earned the name Cucumber Beach.

❶ Getting There & Away

Any westbound bus will drop you at the Old Belize entrance (BZ$2, 10 minutes from Belize City).

Hattieville

POP 1300

The village of Hattieville – 15 miles southwest of Belize City – takes its name from the infamous Hurricane Hattie that wreaked havoc around the country in 1961. A refugee camp was set up to shelter the many residents of

---

DON'T MISS

BELIZE CENTRAL PRISON

Only in a country as laid-back as Belize could a fully functioning prison also be considered a tourist attraction. It's the only prison in Belize (the name 'Hattieville' is to Belizeans what 'San Quentin' is to Americans) and, as such, it houses criminals of all stripes, from pickpockets to murderers. But don't come looking for some sort of American-style corporate-owned Supermax with imposing concrete walls topped with electrified razor ribbon. The 'Hattieville Ramada' (as it's called on the streets) looks more like a summer camp, its main prison buildings are set back from the road and surrounded by farmland, where the prisoners work. So what makes the prison worth a visit?

Two words: gift shop.

Belize Central Prison (Mile 2 Burrell Boom Rd, Hattieville) has a **gift shop** (⊙9am-3pm) that sells items from the reformatory's renowned woodshop. Inside the small shop (located on the road and outside of the actual prison itself) you'll find hand-carved walking sticks, traditional masks, religious icons such as crucifixes, statues depicting saints, a host of carved Jesus figures, and even beautifully crafted wooden doors. All items in the shop are meticulously crafted by the prisoners themselves from locally grown wood including mahogany, teak and sandalwood. There's also a variety of smaller items, including jewelry, cards, calendars, hammocks, clothing and other assorted knickknacks, all of which have been made by the prisoners themselves.

This most unusual penal facility is part of the larger vision of an organization called the **Kolbe Foundation** (📞225-6190; www.kolbe.bz), which took over the management of the once-notorious government prison and restructured it in a way that was more in line with the foundation's Christian philosophy. Rather than merely punishing criminals by sequestering them from society, the Kolbe approach focuses more on rehabilitation through education and skills development. In addition to the various craft-making shops inside the prison, there are also small-scale animal farms and gardening operations that supply some of the prison's food. One of the long-term goals of the foundation is for the prison to be self-sustainable; as such, all funds earned by gift-shop sales go back to the maintenance of the prison, meaning that your purchases directly assist in the rehabilitation of Belize's criminal element (who might otherwise wind up robbing you on your next visit to Belize).

Belize City who were left homeless after the devastating storm. Many residents ended up staying permanently, and so was born the village of Hattieville.

🛏 Sleeping

Orchid Garden Eco-Village RESORT $$$
(☎ 225-6991; www.trybelize.com; Mile 14.5 Western Hwy; d incl breakfast & dinner for 2 BZ$280; P 🛜 🏊 🐾) ✐ Built in a natural setting encompassing 43 acres of jungle savanna (half of which is designated as a protected sanctuary), Orchid Garden is a super convenient and rather exotic place to base yourself during your time on the mainland. The onsite hotel is comfortable but understated; the rooms are large and sparsely decorated, giving the place a 'meditation center' feel. In addition to the lodging, the ecovillage has nature trails, beautifully cultivated gardens, a swimming hole, a butterfly corridor, an iguana reserve and a small museum with archaeological and geological exhibits.

The location, 15 miles outside of Belize City, makes the Orchid Garden an excellent choice for those looking to avoid staying in Belize City itself. The proprietors offer a wide variety of nature- and culture-oriented day trips all over central Belize, including meals and transportation. The Orchid Garden Restaurant is also excellent, serving dishes prepared using vegetables and herbs from the family's own organic garden. Vegetarian dishes are especially excellent (in fact, the website offers a seven-day 'vegetarian tour' of Belize).

The main focus of Orchid Garden is multi-day packages that include meals and tours; check the website for full rates and details.

Belize Zoo

You probably won't see a jaguar in the wild, but you will see one at this charming little zoo, which specializes in protecting native species and educating the population about them.

HURRICANE WATCH

Hurricanes have long bedeviled the Belizean coast, leaving their marks in very visible ways. For example, the Split on Caye Caulker was created when Hurricane Hattie whipped through here in 1961. This is the same storm that motivated the Belizean government to build a new inland capital at Belmopan.

The effects of these tropical storms are not only physical: hurricane season is engrained in the brains of the residents, who long remember the last evacuation and always anticipate the next one. Any visitor to Belize is likely to engage in at least one conversation about the most recent tempest (more, if it was a bad one). Here are a few of the lowlights from Belizean hurricane history:

➡ **Hurricane Five (1931)** One of the deadliest seasons in Atlantic-coast hurricane history. Hurricane Five hit the coast of Belize on a national holiday, meaning that emergency services were slow to respond. The entire northern coast of the country was devastated, and around 2500 people were killed.

➡ **Hurricane Hattie (1961)** This history-making hurricane killed 275 people and destroyed much of Belize City. Afterward, survivors apparently roamed the rubble-strewn streets in search of food and shelter. Many moved to refugee camps, which later morphed into permanent settlements – the origins of Hattieville. Hurricane Hattie provides the backdrop for Carlos Ledson Miller's novel *Belize* and Zee Edgell's *Beka Lamb*.

➡ **Hurricane Iris (2001)** This devastating Category-4 storm made landfall in southern Belize, destroying many rural Maya villages and leaving upward of 10,000 people homeless. Off the coast south of Belize City, a live-aboard dive ship capsized, killing 20 people. Joe Burnworth recounts the tragic tale in his book *No Safe Harbor*.

➡ **Hurricane Richard (2010)** The ravages of this Category-1 hurricane were still evident around the Belize District at the time of research. The only loss of life was a US filmmaker who was mauled by a jaguar; the jaguar escaped when a tree fell on its cage.

Recent scientific evidence suggests that the strength of hurricanes increases with the rise of ocean temperatures. So as our climate continues to change, countries such as Belize are likely to experience more frequent and more intense hurricane hits.

◉ Sights

★ **Belize Zoo**   ZOO
(☑822-8000; www.belizezoo.org; Mile 29 Western Hwy; adult/child BZ$30/10; ⊙8am-5pm) The story of the Belize Zoo began with filmmaker Richard Foster, who shot a wildlife documentary entitled *Path of the Raingods* in Belize in the early 1980s. Sharon Matola – a Baltimore-born biologist, former circus performer and former US Air Force survival instructor – was hired to take care of the animals. By the time filming was complete, the animals had become partly tame and Matola was left wondering what to do with her 17 charges. So she founded the Belize Zoo, which displays native Belizean wildlife in natural surroundings on 29-acre grounds. From these beginnings the zoo has grown to provide homes for animals endemic to the region that have been injured, orphaned at a young age or bred in captivity and donated from other zoos.

Many of the animals in Belize Zoo are rescue cases, that is, wild animals that were kept as pets by individual collectors. The zoo makes every attempt to recondition such animals for a return to the wild, but only when such a return is feasible. In cases where return is impossible (as is the case with most of the zoo's jungle cats, who have long since forgotten how to hunt, or never learned in the first place), they remain in the zoo: perhaps not the best life for a wildcat, but better than winding up in Zsa Zsa Gabor's closet.

The zoo has many animals you're unlikely to see elsewhere – there are two fat tapirs (a Belizean relative of the rhino), *gibnuts*, a number of coatimundi (they look like a cross between a raccoon and a monkey), scarlet macaws, white-lipped peccaries, pumas and many others. But what really sets Belize Zoo apart is that the perimeters – and in some cases, even the enclosures of individual animals – are relatively porous. This means that the wildlife you'll see inside enclosures are outnumbered by creatures who have come in from the surrounding jungle to hang out, eat, or – just maybe – swap tales with incarcerated brethren. Among the animals you'll see wandering the grounds are Central American agouti (also called bush rabbits), huge iguanas, snakes, raccoons, squirrels and jungle birds of all sorts.

Take a night tour (one of the best ways to experience Belize Zoo, as many of the animals are nocturnal) and you'll be just as likely to see a *gibnut* outside enclosures as in. You'll also be able to hear ongoing long-distance conversations between the zoo's resident black howler monkeys and their wild relatives just a few miles away.

If most zoos are maximum security wildlife prisons, then the Belize Zoo is more like a 'country-club jail.' Some would even call it a halfway house for wild animals that can't make it on the outside. We call it a must-visit.

🛏 Sleeping & Eating

Belize Zoo Jungle Lodge   LODGE $
(☑822-8000; tec@belizezoo.org; Mile 29 Western Hwy; camping per person BZ$15, dm/cabaña/guesthouse BZ$60/120/130; [P]) 🍴 Formerly known as the Tropical Education Center (TEC), the zoo's lodgings are set on 84 acres of tropical savanna with lush gardens and plenty of wildlife. A treetop viewing platform and savanna nature trails give plenty of opportunities to spot the animals and birds in their natural habitat. Located about a mile from the zoo, this is an excellent accommodation option, especially for those who want to do night tours at the zoo (BZ$30 with a minimum of five people).

Sleeping options run from dorm beds in the 'Savannah Castle' (set up mainly for student groups), to neat wooden Forest Cabañas on stilts. Two 'VIP guesthouses' overlook the center's own small lake (home to Morelet's crocodiles). All options have good mosquito screens. If you want meals here, you need to request them in advance.

The Jungle Lodge is 0.9 miles off the Western Hwy, from a signposted turning 50yd east of the zoo; staff can pick you up from the zoo.

Juice, snacks, and other assorted items are available in the zoo's **gift shop** (⊙8am-5pm). It's an easy drive a couple of miles along the highway to one of the good restaurants near Monkey Bay Wildlife Sanctuary.

Savanna Guesthouse   GUESTHOUSE $$
(☑822-8005; www.belizesavannaguesthouse.com; Mile 28½ Western Hwy; r incl light breakfast BZ$120; 🛜) 🍴 Opened by Richard and Carol Foster, the naturalist and filmmaker couple who began the Belize Zoo in 1987, Savanna Guesthouse sits on the site of the original Belize Zoo, where it all began. The hotel is off the grid and solar powered.

ℹ Getting There & Away

Any nonexpress bus from Belize City heading along the Western Hwy will drop you at the zoo entrance (BZ$4, 45 minutes).

Monkey Bay

The Monkey Bay Wildlife Sanctuary stretches from the Western Hwy to the Sibun River, encompassing areas of tropical forest and savanna, and providing an important link in the biological corridor between coastal and inland Belize. Across the river is the remote Monkey Bay National Park, which together with the sanctuary creates a sizable forest corridor in the Sibun River Valley. The park and the sanctuary get their name from a bend in the river – called a 'bay' in Belize – once noted for its resident black howler monkeys. Though the species had all but disappeared in the area, it has returned in significant numbers, thanks in no small part to the work done at the sanctuary.

Monkey Bay
Wildlife Sanctuary   WILDLIFE RESERVE
(☑822-8032; www.belizestudyabroad.net; Mile 31½ Western Hwy; canoeing per person BZ$70) ✦ Established in the 1980s by Matthew and Marga Miller, this 1.7-sq-mile wildlife sanctuary and environmental education center offers lodging and activities for casual travelers, as well as internship activities for those with a more long-term interest in Belize. A well-stocked library provides plenty of reference and reading matter on natural history and the country.

Activities center around the Sibun River, which attracts sweaty travelers (and other kinds of wildlife) to its inviting **swimming hole**. Around 230 bird species have been identified at the sanctuary. Larger wildlife such as pumas and coatimundi have been spotted on the 2-mile track running down beside the sanctuary to the river.

Other activities include **canoeing** and trips to nearby **Tiger Cave** (per person BZ$100). In the dry season, guides take adventurers about 12 miles north to Cox Lagoon, which is home to jabiru storks, deer, tapirs, black howlers and lots of crocodiles.

🛏 Sleeping & Eating

Within a few hundred yards along the Western Hwy on either side of Monkey Bay Wildlife Sanctuary are two fun eateries that are often filled with just-off-the-plane travelers happily adjusting to the fact that they're on holiday. The restaurants are also worth noting if you're spending the afternoon at the Belize Zoo (which is just a few miles northeast).

Monkey Bay
Wildlife Sanctuary   CAMPGROUND, CABINS $
(☑822-8032; www.belizestudyabroad.net; camping per person BZ$15, bunkhouse per person BZ$35, d BZ$50, cabin BZ$90; [P][@][🛜][🗲][♦]) ✦ Accommodations at the sanctuary range from camping out on raised platform decks to mosquito-screened bunkhouses, to private rooms in the field house. All of these options have shared bathroom facilities with rainwater showers. It may be rustic, but it's a comfortable and affordable way to spend the night out in the wild. The amenities demonstrate ecological principles in action, with biogas latrines (though there are also four new flush toilets) producing methane for cooking, rainwater catchment and partial

---

MONKEY BAY WILDLIFE SANCTUARY

If you are yearning to get your hands dirty and do some good in the world, plan to spend some time at Monkey Bay Wildlife Sanctuary as a **volunteer** (☑822-8032; www.belizestudyabroad.net; per week BZ$300). The price includes meals and accommodations, as well as internet access and access to the library and other facilities (including the swimming hole!). In exchange, volunteers are expected to work at least 30 hours a week. Most work is outdoors, including maintenance jobs like composting, landscaping and other physical fun. Volunteers must give one month's advance notice before arrival and commit to a minimum of one week of work. Fortunately, the work schedule is flexible enough to allow for additional exploration around Belize.

Students are also invited to come to Monkey Bay as interns. The terms are similar, except the interns must give two months' notice and commit to working for at least one month. Their tasks are also more varied, including kitchen and hospitality work, as well as more substantive projects like researching local planting techniques, working with local conservation groups, assisting with wildlife care (especially for the iguanas), and developing materials and planning events for environmental education. Most importantly, interns have the support of the very knowledgeable staff, as well as access to contacts throughout the community, so they will certainly gain an in-depth understanding of the country.

solar energy. Meals are available within the sanctuary but should be arranged at least a day in advance (BZ$14 to BZ$22).

Cheers   AMERICAN, BELIZEAN **$$**
(✆ 822-8014; www.cheersrestaurant.bz; Mile 31¼ Western Hwy; cabañas BZ$130-140, meals BZ$15-30; ☺ breakfast, lunch & dinner) This large, airy and friendly restaurant serves hearty meals, from all-day breakfasts to French-dip roast beef sandwiches to excellent Cuban tilapia. Naturally, rice, beans and stewed chicken are served as well. If you fancy spending the night, there are three *cabañas* that are simple, spacious and slightly elegant. The location – about 500yd east of the Monkey Bay turnoff – is convenient for an overnight if you are heading further west.

Amigos   AMERICAN **$$**
(Mile 31¾ Western Hwy; mains BZ$12-22; ☺ 8am-10pm) Amigos serves both American and Belizean cuisine in a distinctly Belizean setting (a mosquito-screened *palapa* house) drenched in pure American whimsy (walls covered in kitschy signs and bumper stickers). Carnivores should order the BBQ pork ribs (BZ$22); those with a serious sweet tooth won't want to miss Amigos' desserts. It's 200yd west of the sanctuary turnoff.

ℹ Getting There & Away

Any nonexpress bus doing the Belize City–Belmopan run will drop you at the sanctuary turnoff (220yd from the main entrance) or at Cheers or Amigos (BZ$4, 50 minutes from Belize City).

ALONG THE COASTAL ROAD

The Coastal Rd – also known as the Manatee Hwy – heads south from the Western Hwy, and runs parallel to the coast (appropriately enough) for 36 miles to the town of Dangriga. The Coastal Rd is gravel, which means it is slow going at the best of times, and often impassable during the rainy season. Some rental car companies advise against driving on the Coastal Rd, which is not really 'a shortcut to Placencia' as it is sometimes called.

Gales Point Manatee

POP 345
The Creole village of Gales Point Manatee sits on a narrow peninsula that juts out about 2 miles into the Southern Lagoon, one of a series of interconnected lakes and waterways between Belize City and Dangriga. The village was initially founded around 1800 by runaway slaves from Belize City escaping south into jungle and lagoon country. A more beautiful spot you'd be hard pressed to find; to the west, jungle-clad limestone hills rise above the plains that end on the shores of the Southern Lagoon; to the east, also across the lagoon, sits the narrow stretch of forest and mangrove swamp that separates the lagoon from the Caribbean Sea.

Since 2008, however, Gales Point has been hit by a series of hardships: hurricanes, an economic downturn, and a complete loss of regular bus services have turned this once-vibrant village into something of a ghost town.

So why come? For the spectacular beauty and superlative wildlife attractions. Gales Point is home to the highest concentration of West Indian manatees in the Caribbean, and the nearby beaches are the primary breeding ground for hawksbill turtles in Belize. The 14-sq-mile Gales Point Wildlife Sanctuary (which covers the Southern and adjoining lagoons) offers some of the most amazing bird-watching opportunities in the country.

Getting lost in Gales Point Manatee would be difficult – the town's only street runs about 2.5 miles north from the Coastal Rd to the tip of the peninsula, and if you walk too far either east or west you'll be wading in the lagoon. Once you hit town from the south (the only way you can hit town, barring an amphibious landing), you'll pass by the police station, Ionie's B&B and Gentle's Cool Spot. Saunter further up the road and you'll wind up at Manatee Lodge at the end of the peninsula.

◉ Sights & Activities

Nature tours bring most visitors to Gales Point Manatee, and for the majority of these you'll need to hire a guide with a boat; all accommodations can set you up with one (your hosts will certainly be able to connect you with a guide, if they aren't guides themselves). In addition to fishing, the lagoons surrounding Gales Point Manatee are specifically noted for birding, turtling and, of course, manateeing.

Manatee-Watching   BOAT TOUR
Manatees graze on sea grass in the shallow, brackish Southern Lagoon, hanging out around the Manatee Hole, a depression in the lagoon floor near its east side that is fed

DRUMMER DONE GONE

For years one of the major draws of Gales Point Manatee was **Emmeth Young**, one of Belize's pre-eminent Creole drummers. In 2010 the musician, teacher and drum maker moved his Maroon Creole Drum School (p215) to the outskirts of Punta Gorda. So if you're looking to study drum-and-beat-making with the master, you'll want to head south. It's a bit further to go, but at least the roads are paved.

by a warm freshwater spring. The manatees rise about every 20 minutes for air, allowing spectators views of their heads and sometimes their backs and tails. A 1½-hour manatee-watching boat trip costs BZ$100 for up to four people. Manatee-watching can also be combined with other activities.

Turtle-Watching   BOAT TRIPS

Around 100 hawksbill turtles, which are protected in Belize, as well as loggerheads, which aren't, lay their eggs on the 21-mile beach that straddles the mouth of the Bar River, which connects the Southern Lagoon to the sea. For both species, this is the main nesting site in the country. Turtle-watch outings from Manatee Lodge during the nesting season involve a boat trip down the river, then a 4-mile nocturnal beach walk to look for nesting turtles (BZ$350 for up to four people).

Bird-Watching   BOAT TRIPS

In the **Northern Lagoon**, about 45 minutes from Gales Point Manatee by boat, is **Bird Caye**, a small island that is home to many waterfowl, including frigate birds, great egrets and toucans. Gentle's Cool Spot combines trips here with a stop at the Manatee Hole for BZ$190.

Fishing   FISHING

Large tarpon quite often break the surface of the Southern Lagoon. You can also fish for snook, snapper, jack and barracuda in the lagoon and rivers. A half-/full-day trip for up to three people costs around BZ$350 from Manatee Lodge.

☞ Tours

Manatee Lodge offers a wide range of trips at fixed prices; rates elsewhere can be lower. Raymond Gentle of Gentle's Cool Spot charges BZ$125 for a tour of up to four

people to 'see' the manatees. (Swimming with the manatees is no longer permitted).

🛏 Sleeping & Eating

Ionie's B&B   CABINS **$**

(☑220-8066; s/d without bathroom BZ$33/38) This B&B is run by friendly Ionie Samuels (also a justice of the peace, if you've matrimony in mind). This house on stilts has dingy, simple rooms, fans and shared bathrooms with cold showers. Good-sized Belizean meals for under BZ$10 include a drink.

Gentle's Cool Spot   CABINS **$**

(☑668-0102; d/tr BZ$35/55, mains BZ$6; **P**) Three small rooms with cold-water showers, double bed, a tiny window and little else go for BZ$30. A room with three double beds in a higher house on stilts goes for BZ$55. Ms Gentle also does hair braiding for BZ$40. Anyone with hair long enough to braid and an hour to kill is welcome.

Manatee Lodge   HOTEL **$$**

(☑662-2154; www.manateelodge.com; r BZ$170, breakfast/lunch/dinner BZ$22/18/32; **P @ 🛜**) The only midpriced lodge in the area, Clifton and Nancy Bailey's Manatee Lodge takes up the tip of the Gales Point peninsula and is situated in a beautiful garden surrounded on three sides by the Southern Lagoon. The eight rooms, spread over two floors, are spacious and comfortable, with bathtubs and lots of varnished wood. There is a large sitting/reading room with a lovely, breezy veranda that overlooks the lagoon. There is also a dining room for guests of the lodge. The lodge is most popular with groups, individual travelers, nature lovers and fishermen. A wide range of activities is on offer, and canoes and a sailboat are provided free for guests.

❶ Getting There & Away

Gales Point Manatee is located about 1 mile off the Coastal Rd; the turnoff is 22 miles off the Western Hwy and 14 miles from the Hummingbird Hwy. The Coastal Rd and the road into the village are mostly unpaved, but quite drivable in a normal car during the dry season. In the rainy season, those without a 4WD risk getting stuck in the mud.

There are no longer regularly scheduled buses to Gales Point Manatee.

The best way to travel to or from Gales Point Manatee for those who can afford it is by boat via a network of rivers, canals and lagoons stretching from Belize City. The trip takes about two hours, and costs around BZ$400 for up to four people. Arrangements can be made through the Manatee Lodge.

Northern Cayes

Best Places to Eat

➡ Sandro, Caye Caulker (p117)

➡ Lazy Croc BBQ, Ambergris Caye (p99)

➡ Hidden Treasure, San Pedro (p99)

➡ Habaneros, Caye Caulker (p117)

Best Places to Stay

➡ Caribbean Villas Hotel & Bird Sanctuary, San Pedro (p93)

➡ Ak'bol Yoga Retreat, Ambergris Caye (p95)

➡ Barefoot Beach Belize, Caye Caulker (p114)

➡ Sea Dreams Hotel, Caye Caulker (p112)

Why Go?

Daydream a little. Conjure up your ultimate tropical island fantasy. With over 100 enticing isles and two amazing atolls, chances are that one of the northern cayes can make this dream a reality.

If you imagined stringing up a hammock on a deserted beach, there is an outer atoll with your name on it. Pining to be pampered? You can choose from an ever-growing glut of ritzy resorts on Ambergris Caye. San Pedro is prime for dancing the night away to a reggae beat, while Caye Caulker moves at a slower pace.

But the islands are only the beginning: the Northern Cayes' richest resource lies below the surface of the sea. Only a few miles offshore, the barrier reef runs for 80 miles, offering unparalleled opportunities to explore canyons and coral, to face off with nurse sharks and stingrays, and to swim with schools of fish painted every color of the palette.

When to Go

During the peak tourist season – from December to April – prices for accommodations are significantly higher – sometimes by as much as 50%. The trade-off is that the weather is predictably warm and wonderful. If you happen to find yourself on the cayes during the hot summer months you can enjoy the opening of lobster season, which is celebrated with much fanfare on Ambergris and Caye Caulker. In August San Pedro is the site of Belize's biggest street festival, the International Costa Maya Festival.

Northern Cayes Highlights

1 Availing yourself of the amazing array of aquatic activities – from kitesurfing and paddle-boarding to snorkeling and diving – in laid-back **Caye Caulker** (p104)

2 Being surrounded by nurse sharks and stingrays at **Shark Ray Alley** (see boxed text, p90)

3 Watching the sun set and feeding the tarpons at San Pedro's **Sunset Restaurant** (p98)

4 Kayaking to investigate the birdlife at the **Caye Caulker Forest Reserve** (p105)

5 Catching sight of a West Indian manatee frolicking in the shallow waters off **Swallow Caye Wildlife Sanctuary** (p108)

6 Cruising out to Lighthouse Reef to descend into the darkness of the **Blue Hole Natural Monument** (p120) and spying on the rare red-footed booby at **Half Moon Caye** (p121)

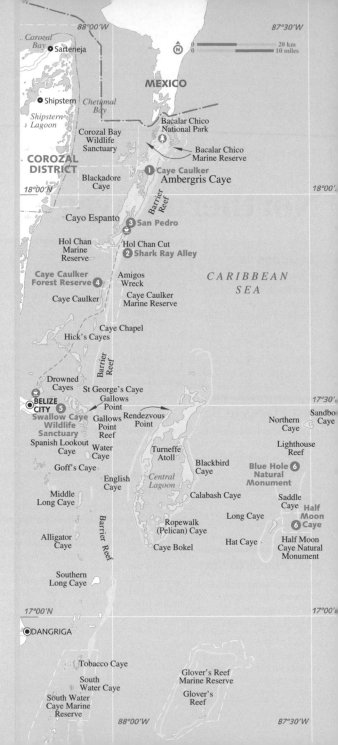

ℹ Getting There & Around

Scheduled flights and regular passenger boats go from Belize City to San Pedro (on Ambergris Caye) and Caye Caulker, and from Corozal to San Pedro. Northern Caye (Lighthouse Reef) also has an airstrip. No scheduled boats run to/from the outer islands, but most of the lodges located there provide transportation for their guests.

AMBERGRIS CAYE

POP 11,300

When Madonna sang about her dreams of San Pedro, she was referring to the captivating capital of Ambergris Caye, which has since adopted the inevitable nickname La Isla Bonita. Of course, it was more than 20 years ago when Madonna crooned about all the nature being wild and free. She might not recognize the place today, with condos being constructed on every corner and golf carts whizzing through the streets.

Nonetheless, Ambergris (am-*ber*-griss) Caye exudes the atmosphere of a tropical island paradise, where sun-drenched days are filled with fruity drinks and water sports. The island is long and thin, measuring 25 miles long and 5 miles across at its widest point, though much of it is less than half a mile across. Although resorts are being erected up and down the coast, its outer reaches are still practically uninhabited. The remote northern extremity abuts Mexican territory, and the Hispanic influence is evident in language, customs, food and fiestas.

Though the entire island is often called San Pedro, technically that is the name of the town that dominates the southern half. Once a laid-back little village dotted with colorful Caribbean houses, San Pedro is starting to resemble a typical tourist town, lined with souvenir shops and beach bars. The sandy streets were recently replaced with concrete, rapidly increasing the number of cars and golf carts on the roads (not to mention the speeds at which they drive). The beach is built up, though thankfully no buildings are higher than three stories.

Despite the overdevelopment complaints, San Pedro has protected its most valuable asset, the barrier reef, which is only a half-mile offshore. If you are passionate about water sports, San Pedro will seduce you: dive operators lead tours to more than 35 sites, both local and beyond. And if you don't want to look at the fish, surely you'll want to eat them, as San Pedro is home to the country's most imaginative and appetizing dining scene.

History

Once the southern tip of the Yucatán Peninsula, Ambergris Caye was an important Maya trading post. Around 1500 years ago, in order to open up a better trade route between the Yucatán coast and mainland Belize, the Maya dug the narrow channel at Bacalar Chico that now separates Ambergris from Mexico.

As with their counterparts on the mainland, the local Maya inhabitants gradually retreated to the bush as contact with the Europeans became more frequent. Whalers in the 17th century probably gave the island its current name, which derives from the waxy gray substance used in perfume production that comes from the intestines of sperm whales. According to folklore, British, French and Dutch pirates used the island's many coves as hideouts when ambushing Spanish ships, so they may also be responsible for the title. Small treasure troves have been discovered on the island, and gold coins and old bottles have been washed ashore, all evidence of pirates using the island for its freshwater, abundant resources and hidden coves. These swashbucklers turned into mainland loggers who partly depended on manatees and turtles from the Northern Cayes for their survival.

Ambergris Caye was not significantly populated until the War of the Castes, when the war in the Yucatán first forced Mestizos, and then Maya, across Bacalar Chico and onto the island. The town of San Pedro (named for Peter, the patron saint of fishermen) was founded in 1848.

Ownership of the island was bandied about between a group of wealthy British mainlanders. Finally, in 1869, James Hume Blake purchased the land for US$625 with the gold of his wife, Antonia Andrade, a rich Spanish refugee widow from the Yucatán. The Blake family converted much of the island to a coconut plantation, conscripting many of the islanders to work the land.

The coconut business thrived for less than a century. By the 1950s it had been all but destroyed by a series of hurricanes. In the 1960s the Belize government forced a purchase of Ambergris Caye and redistributed the land to the islanders.

While the coconut industry declined, the island's lobster industry began to develop. The market for these crustaceans skyrocketed once refrigerated ships came to the island. San Pedro lobster catchers formed cooperatives and built a freezer plant on their island.

Perhaps inevitably, the waters close to Ambergris Caye were overfished. Fisherfolk looked to supplement their income by acting as tour, fishing and dive guides for the smattering of travelers who visited the island. Today lobster stocks have partly recovered with the aid of size limits and an annual closed season, but tourism and real estate are the booming businesses on Ambergris.

◉ Sights

A narrow channel splits Ambergris Caye in two segments, known as South Island and North Island. Most services and many hotels, as well as the airstrip, are within walking distance of each other in San Pedro's town center, on the South Island. Some of the water taxis from Belize City and Caye Caulker dock on the reef side of the island right in San Pedro's center. Both the Thunderbolt boat service from Corozal and the Water Jets service from Belize City dock on the lagoon side.

North of town a toll bridge crosses the channel (vehicles BZ$10, bikes BZ$2). From here, a dirt road, suitable for 4WDs, golf carts and bicycles, runs north for several miles. Rumor has it that it won't be long before this road is paved and runs all the way to the southern edge of Bacalar Chico National Park (13 miles).

The northernmost section of the North Island constitutes Bacalar Chico National Park, and the surrounding waters form Bacalar Chico Marine Reserve. The western shore has mangroves and wildlife along much of its length.

Many hotels and resorts are strung out along the coast both north and south of town. Cycling is a very convenient way to get around. Otherwise, a water shuttle runs between Fido's Dock and the North Island resorts.

Hol Chan Marine Reserve MARINE RESERVE
(www.holchanbelize.org; admission BZ$20) 🖉 At the southern tip of Ambergris, the 6.5-sq-mile Hol Chan Marine Reserve is probably Belize's most oft-visited site. Its spectacular coral formations and abundance and diversity of marine life, not to mention its proximity to the cayes, make it the country's number one spot for diving and snorkeling.

Hol Chan is Mayan for 'Little Channel,' which refers to a natural break in the reef, also known as **Hol Chan Cut**. The channel walls are covered with colorful corals, which in turn harbor an amazing variety of fish life, including moray eels and black groupers.

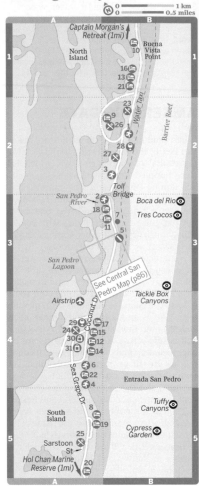

Ambergris Caye

Although the reef is the primary attraction of Hol Chan, the marine reserve also includes sea-grass beds and mangroves. The sea grass provides a habitat for nurse sharks and southern stingrays, which lend their name to **Shark Ray Alley**. Snorkelers are guaranteed the chance to get up close and personal with both species, due mainly to the fact that the animals are used to getting fed by tour boats.

All dive operators and nautical tours offer trips to Hol Chan. For information and displays on marine life, visit the **Hol Chan Visitors Center** (Caribeña St; ☺9am-5pm).

Ambergris Caye

Bacalar Chico National Park & Marine Reserve   MARINE RESERVE
(admission BZ$10, tour BZ$180) ✦ At the northern tip of Ambergris Caye, Bacalar Chico is part of the Belize Barrier Reef Reserve System World Heritage Site, declared in 1996. At the time of research, the park was only accessible by a 90-minute tour-boat ride from San Pedro or Sarteneja in Northern Belize.

On the way up from San Pedro, boats might stop at **Cayo Iguanu**, better known as 'bird island,' as it is the nesting ground for the roseate spoonbill and the reddish-brown egret. The next stop is the **San Juan ranger station**, at the northern tip of the island, where there is a nature trail and some small Maya ruins to explore. From here, the boat motors through the **ancient channel** that was dug by seafaring Maya about 1500 years ago. Now the narrow channel separates Ambergris Caye from the Mexican mainland.

Boat trips to Bacalar Chico usually make several snorkel stops along the way. The coral is extra colorful around here, as there is significantly less damage from boats and tourists. Besides the bountiful fish and birdlife, you have the chance of seeing crocodiles and manatees, as well as green and loggerhead turtles.

If the waters are calm, boats go to **Rocky Point**, notable as one of the few places in the world where land meets reef.

In theory the return trip is on the east side of the island, but this requires a quick detour outside the reef, so in rough seas the boats travel up and down the western side of the island.

Not all tour operators run trips to Bacalar Chico, due to the long travel distance, so plan ahead and inquire in advance about trips.

🏃 Activities

If you're into water sports, you'll be in ecstasy on Ambergris. The town is awash with tour companies and individuals organizing scuba diving, snorkeling, windsurfing, sailing, swimming and fishing trips.

Diving

Many hotels have their own dive shops that rent equipment, provide instruction and organize diving excursions. Numerous dive sites are within a 10- to 15-minute boat trip from town. Most popular (and affordable) is undoubtedly Hol Chan Marine Reserve, south of the island.

Prices do not usually include admission to the marine reserves, which is BZ$20 for Hol Chan and BZ$80 for the Blue Hole.

A one-tank local dive, without equipment, costs BZ$80 to BZ$100; with two tanks it's BZ$140 to BZ$150. Night dives are BZ$100 to BZ$120, including a headlamp. Three-day open-water dive courses cost about BZ$950, including equipment. A one-day Discover Scuba Diving course (offered by most of the dive shops) costs BZ$300 to BZ$320.

Day trips further afield to the Blue Hole and Lighthouse Reef (three dives) or Turneffe Elbow (three dives) cost BZ$370 to BZ$500.

The following is a list of some reputable independent dive operators; a few also run a full range of nondiving tours.

Ambergris Divers   DIVING
(Map p86; ☑ 226-2634; www.ambergrisdivers.com) Located next to Tackle Box. Offers half-day trips (BZ$120) including one tank at Hol Chan and a snorkeling stop at Shark Ray Alley. Also offers night dives (BZ$100) and full-day trips to north Ambergris (BZ$240) and the offshore atolls (from BZ$370).

Amigos del Mar Dive Shop   DIVING
(Map p86; ☑ 226-2706; www.amigosdive.com) Runs two local trips each day, one departing at 9am and another at 2pm. Also specializes in day trips to Turneffe and Blue Hole. Shares a dock with the Coastal Xpress Island Ferry.

Aqua Scuba Center   DIVING
(Map p86; ☑ 670-4775; www.aquascubacenter. com; Shark's Pier) Offers many different multi-day dive packages, as well as day tours and courses at competitive rates. It also goes fishing and snorkeling.

Belize Academy of Diving   DIVING
(☑ 600-4753; www.belize-academy-of-diving.com) Specializes in various courses and training, as well as dive trips to Hol Chan and Shark Ray Alley (BZ$110), the Turneffe Elbow (BZ$370) and the Blue Hole (BZ$500). Located 7 miles north of San Pedro at the Costa Maya Reef Resort.

Belize Diving Adventures   DIVING
(Map p86; ☑ 226-3082; www.belizedivingadven-tures.net) Highlights include the Blue Hole (BZ$500 including park fee) and the Turn-effe Elbow (BZ$370). Single-/double-/triple-tank dives run BZ$86/140/200, while the price of night dives varies. Fishing and land tours also available.

Bottom Time Dive Shop   DIVING
(Map p86; ☑ 893-3825; www.sanpedroholiday. com) Popular deep-water diving destinations include Cypress Canyons, Tres Cocos and M&M Caverns, while Hol Chan and Mexico Rocks are the preferred shallow-water sites. Located on the dock in front of San Pedro Holiday Hotel.

Ecologic Divers & Training Center   DIVING
(Map p86; ☑ 226-4118; www.ecologicdivers.com) Specializes in early-morning dives (BZ$120), which depart every day at 7am, and night dives (BZ$120), which depart at 5:30pm. Otherwise, single-/double-/triple-tank dives are BZ$90/150/200. Divers receive a free CD with photos from their dive.

Patojo's Scuba Center   DIVING
(Map p82; ☑ 226-2283; www.ambergriscaye. com/tides) Connected with Tide's Beach Re-sort, this small, family-run operation offers knowledgeable and personal service. There are local dives (BZ$90 to BZ$200) and off-shore trips (BZ$330 to BZ$500), as well as fishing and snorkeling. Multiday dive pack-ages available.

Snorkeling

The most popular destinations for snor-keling excursions include Hol Chan Marine Reserve and Shark Ray Alley (BZ$90 includ-ing park fee) or Mexico Rocks and Tres Co-cos (BZ$50 to BZ$80). Snorkeling operators usually offer two daily half-day trips (three hours, two snorkel stops), departing at 9am and 2pm.

Full-day trips go to the northern tip of Ambergris (six hours, three stops) for around BZ$170. Trips to Bacalar Chico also make several snorkel stops. Most of the dive operators and all of the tour companies of-fer various versions of these snorkeling trips.

Most dive boats take snorkelers along if they have room, but snorkelers sometimes get lost in the shuffle on dive boats, so you are better off joining a dedicated snorkel tour whenever possible. Unfortunately, snorkel tours do not often run to Blue Hole, so if you have your heart set on snorkeling around the edge of this World Heritage Site you'll have to tag along with the divers.

If you don't want to opt for a tour you can paddle out to the reef from some of the North Island resorts. You can snorkel under the dock at Ramon's Village. It does not support the extensive life that the reef does, but it is free.

Grumpy and Happy   SNORKELING
(☑ 226-3420, USA 1-888-273-9226; www.grumpy-andhappy.com) If you want to enjoy your time with the fish – without having to make conversation with other people – sign up

with this husband-and-wife team who offer private custom snorkel trips. They cater to special-needs snorkelers with prescription masks and a specially designed, easy-to-climb ladder. There is no storefront, so make arrangements by phone or online.

Searious Adventures   SNORKELING, SAILING
(Map p86; ☑ 226-4202, 662-8818; www.searious-adventuresbelize.com) Combine snorkeling and sailing with the catamaran snorkel tour (BZ$100). This long-running, respected outfit offers all the standard snorkel trips, as well as special snorkel trips to Bacalar Chico (BZ$180) and Blue Hole (BZ$260). Located on the beach in front of Ruby's Hotel.

Manatee-Watching

The best offshore manatee-watching is off Swallow Caye near Belize City. Tours usually include a lunch and snorkel stop, in addition to a cruise through the manatee habitat. This trip is slightly cheaper (and travel times are shorter) from Caye Caulker, where folk are also working on manatee conservation.

Tanisha Tours   BOAT TOUR
(Map p82; ☑ 226-2314; www.tanishatours.com; Boca del Rio; ♿) Guide Daniel Nuñez takes his guests to the mouth of the Belize River to see the manatees, then continues up the river for more sightings of birds, crocodiles and plenty of howler monkeys. Different packages include different activities, from cave tubing to zip lining to visits to the baboon sanctuary. Call for current prices.

Seaduced by Belize   BOAT TOUR
(☑ 226-2254; www.seaducedbybelize.com; Tarpon St, Vilma Linda Plaza; ♿) See the manatees at Swallow Caye, have lunch at Goff's Caye, feast at a beach BBQ and snorkel at Coral Gardens; all for BZ$205.

The all-day tour with Searious Adventures (p85) also includes lunch and two snorkel stops, as well as a viewing of the manatees at Swallow Caye. The BZ$180 fee does not include park fees.

Swimming

Although sandy beaches are plentiful, sea grass at the water line makes entry from the shore unpleasant, so you'll mostly be swimming from piers in waters protected by the reef. When you do this, watch carefully for boats: there's plenty to see down under if you snorkel, but you often can't see or hear if a boat is coming your way. Have someone look out for you. Ramon's Village Pier, dis-

tinguished by its four *palapas* (thatched-roof open-sided huts), is good for swimming and snorkeling.

All beaches are public and most waterside hotels are generous with their deck chairs, but a proprietorial air is developing about the piers, which are also supposed to be public. The beach in front of the Banana Beach Resort is clear of sea grass, and the nearby pier is good for swimming. Of course, the further north or south you go on the island, the fewer people there are on the piers.

Fishing

San Pedro draws fishing enthusiasts who are anxious to take a crack at Belize's classic tarpon flats, which cover over 200 sq miles. The ultimate angling accomplishment is the Grand Slam: catching bonefish, permit (best from March to May) and tarpon (best from May to September) all in one day. In the reef, fishers get bites from barracuda, snapper, jacks and grouper.

Deep-sea fishing is less of a drawcard; most people are here for the reef. There are, however, stories of giant marlin caught out in the deep beyond. In December there is a deep-sea fishing tournament hosted by the Belikin beer company.

Fishing is mostly on a catch-and-release basis, but your fishing guide might clean and cut your catch if you intend to eat it. In addition to the fishing specialists listed here, some of the dive shops also offer fishing trips, including Patojo's Scuba Center and the Aqua Scuba Center.

Go Fish Belize   FISHING
(Map p82; ☑ 226-3121; www.gofishbelize.com; 7 Boca del Rio) In addition to fly fishing, reef fishing and deep-sea fishing, this long-standing outfit also organizes backcountry outings (BZ$550 to BZ$700) for tarpon, bonefish and snapper, as well as night fishing (BZ$700) and combo fishing/BBQ/snorkeling outings (BZ$900). Prices are per boat, with each boat holding four guests, except for the backcountry trip which holds two.

Rock Fishing Team   FISHING
(☑ 601-3865; www.belizefishfinder.com) Specializing in deep-sea fishing. Half-/full-day outings start at BZ$1100/1700, with cheaper smaller-boat outings available when weather conditions allow. Fly-fishing and reef fishing are also on the menu (half-/full-day BZ$450/590). Make arrangements by phone or online.

Central San Pedro

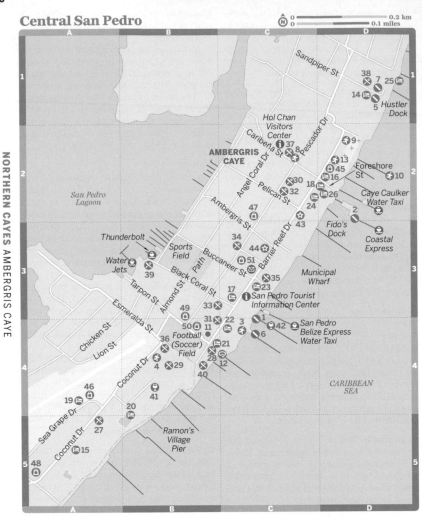

NORTHERN CAYES AMBERGRIS CAYE

Tres Pescados FISHING
(Map p86; ☑ 629-2599, 226-3474; www.belizefly.com; Barrier Reef Dr) All the gear you need to go fly-fishing at the Ambergris flats, as well as guide services (full/half-day BZ$700/350). The fly shop also offers a variety of courses ranging from courses for beginners to advanced fly-fishers.

Water Sports

Ambergris is ideal for wind-powered sports: the offshore reef means the waters are always flat, but there is no shortage of breeze to power your craft. The windiest time of year is between January and June, when the wind speed is usually between 12 and 20 knots.

Aquatic Sports Belize WATER SPORTS
(Map p86; ☑ 226-4601; www.aquaticsportsbelize.com) Located in front of the San Pedro Holiday Hotel, this place rents all forms of water transport, from Hobie Cats (BZ$70 per hour) and sailboards (BZ$60 per hour) to paddle boats (BZ$40 per hour) and kayaks (BZ$30 per hour). This is also the place to get snorkel gear (BZ$20) if you want to check out the fish around your dock.

Central San Pedro

Sailsports Belize WATER SPORTS
(Map p82; ☑ 226-4488; www.sailsportsbelize.com) Right in front of Caribbean Villas, this is the place that will put the breeze in your sail. You can sign up for sailing lessons for BZ$98 per hour or, if you're already your own captain, rent a Laser Pico (BZ$44 per hour) or a Hobie (BZ$76 to BZ$98 per hour) and set sail. Sailboards cost from BZ$44 to BZ$54 per hour, or you can get a lesson for BZ$98 per hour. More comprehensive instruction packages are also available.

You can also go kitesurfing, where the sail floats high up in the sky and pulls the surfer across the waves at alarming speeds. Two instructional courses are required before you can do it on your own: kite-control skills (BZ$330, 2½ hours) and board-control skills (BZ$330, 2½ hours). After that you can rent equipment (BZ$164 per half day) and fly with the wind.

San Pedro Watersports WATER SPORTS
(Map p86; ☑ 226-2888; sanpedrowsc@gmail.com) Stop by the kiosk in front of the Spindrift Hotel if you want a motor to power you along the water. This place rents Jet Skis (BZ$200 per hour) as well as paddle boats (BZ$20 for two hours).

Cycling
The North Island is a wonderful place for a cycle. With the breeze off the ocean and the palms shading your path, you can ride all the way up to Matachica Beach Resort and beyond. Just follow the sandy path that runs along the beach from Reef Village. There are a few places to stop for a fruit smoothie or an ice-cold Belikin beer along the way. Rent

bikes from **Joe's Bicycle Rentals.** (Map p86; 226-5371; cnr Pescador Dr & Caribeña St; per day/week BZ$15/80; ⊙8am-6pm)

Day Spas

If you have come to Ambergris Caye for a bit of rest and relaxation, you may want to schedule a day at the spa.

Art of Touch
DAY SPA

(Map p86; 226-3357; www.touchbelize.com; Coconut Dr, Sunbreeze Hotel) With the goal of healing body, mind and spirit, Art of Touch offers massage (BZ$140 to BZ$160), life transformation workshops (BZ$130) and group meditation (at 10am Sunday).

Black Orchid Spa
DAY SPA

(Map p86; 226-3939; Tarpon St, Vilma Linda Plaza) Massage, wrap, scrub and polish your body back into shape. Offers special massage and facial packages specifically aimed at gentlemen.

Just Relax Massage
DAY SPA

(666-3536; Boca Del Rio Beachfront) Certified massage therapist Shirlene Santino runs a small beachfront day spa out of a lovely white-cloth *palapa* tent on the beach. Shirlene specializes in Swedish, deep tissue and Belizean style massage (using coconut oil and incorporating a variety of deep tissue toxin-releasing techniques). Beachfront massages are BZ$80 per hour, and house calls are BZ$130. Just south of Hotel De Rio.

Mayan Secrets
DAY SPA

(Map p82; 226-3584; Tres Cocos, North Island) All treatments include a tropical drink and a soak in the garden mineral bath.

Ocean Essence
DAY SPA

(Map p82; 226-2310, 604-0766; ⊙10am-5pm) On a seaside dock a few minutes south of town, this tiny place wins the award for its location – literally *above* the water. In addition to ear candling (BZ$90), there are plenty more traditional treatments, as well as a romantic oceanside couples massage. Located just south of Xanadu Island Resort.

Sol Spa
DAY SPA

(Map p86; 226-2410; www.belizesolspa.com; Front St, Phoenix Resort; ⊙9am-6pm Mon-Sat) Sol Spa offers the whole range of body work and facial treatments, but the specialty is the Maya abdominal massage, a noninvasive technique inspired by Ix Chel, the goddess of medicine and fertility.

Xamen Ek Retreat & Spa
DAY SPA

(226-4455; www.xamanekbelize.com; North Island) Soothe your sunburn with a seaweed massage (BZ$170), stimulate your skin with a Bomba mud scrub (BZ$170) or indulge in a three-hour 'Head to Toe' overhaul (BZ$600).

Bliss Spa
DAY SPA

(665-1434; blissspabelize@yahoo.com; treatments from BZ$180) If you're truly looking to pamper yourself, check out this lovely spa on the grounds of the White Sands Cove Resort,

---

FEEDING THE FISH

To feed or not to feed? That seems as if it is always the question.

Feeding is common at Shark Ray Alley and other sites, as guides want to be able to guarantee a good time for their guests. Fish feeds usually mean close-up views, more interaction and – sometimes – incredible photographs.

Purists argue that feeding changes the fish's natural behavior; it may be harmful to their natural abilities to forage for food if they become dependent on humans. It certainly makes them more vulnerable to the hand that feeds them as, for example, the wrong kind of food can be harmful. For some people, fish feeds have a tinge of falseness, lessening the thrill of interacting with the creatures in their natural habitat.

This is a controversy that will undoubtedly continue as long as there are snorkel guides and dive masters who want to entertain their clients. One thing that is certain is that feeding should be left to the professionals: lurking barracuda can shred a hand in seconds; poor-sighted moray eels can leave an awful tear to the skin; aggressive stingrays can give you a mean hickey; and we all remember what happened to that Crocodile Hunter.

These (and other) fish are inherently dangerous and frequently present at fish-feeding sites. Professional guides know how to look out for fish that could pose a threat – and they know how to respond when something scary shows up. So, if there is going to be fish feeding taking place during your snorkel or dive outing, leave it to the guide so you can come home with all of your digits working!

where you can enjoy treatments ranging from massage and facials to various other forms of physical pampering.

Yoga
What better way to start a day in paradise than by saluting the sun?

Ak'bol Yoga Retreat   YOGA
(Map p82; ☑226-2073; www.akbol.com; North Island) With two open, thatch-roof yoga studios (one at the end of the dock), Ak'bol offers daily walk-in classes (BZ$30) in addition to the week-long yoga retreats that are scheduled throughout the year.

Phoenix Fitness Center   YOGA
(Map p86; ☑226-2410; www.belizesolspa.com; Front St, Phoenix Resort; BZ$30; ⊙9am Tue & Thu) The staff at Sol Spa also offer 75-minute yoga classes that are suitable for beginners or more advanced yogis.

☞ Tours

Nautical Tours
Most nautical tours include snorkeling, swimming and sunning; full-day trips also include lunch, and often a beach BBQ.

El Gato   BOAT TOUR
(☑226-2264, 602-8552; www.ambergriscaye.com/elgato; half-/full-day cruise BZ$100/130) Sail to Caye Caulker aboard the *El Gato,* stopping to snorkel if you like. Also offers sunset cruises (BZ$100).

Reef Runner Glass Bottom Boat   BOAT TOUR
(☑226-2172; www.ambergriscaye.com/reefrunner; half day tour BZ$90; ⊙9am & 2pm; ⊞) Here's a way to get a look at the reef without getting wet (if you don't want to). The standard half-day trip visits Hol Chan and Shark Ray Alley. Snorkeling is optional.

Seaduced by Belize   BOAT TOUR
(Map p86; ☑226-2254; www.seaducedbybelize.com; Tarpon St, Vilma Linda Plaza; ⊞) Offers family discounts and a range of sailing trips, including a sunset and full-moon cruise. Don't miss the full-day trip to Mexico Rocks and Robles Beach, complete with snorkel stops and beach BBQ.

Sea Symphony   BOAT TOUR
(Map p82; ☑226-2882; www.discoverybelize.com) This strange double-decker houseboat docks in front of the Exotic Caye Beach Resort. A two-hour evening cruise is BZ$20, or BZ$110 with appetizers and drinks. Available for private functions as well.

The all-day tour with Searious Adventures (p85) also includes lunch and two snorkel stops, as well as a viewing of the manatees at Swallow Caye. The BZ$180 fee does not include park fees.

Mainland Tours
Many visitors to Belize use San Pedro as their base and make excursions by plane or boat to other parts of the country. Mainland trips are operated by many of the dive and boat-tour firms.

Altun Ha (p69), the closest Maya ruin to the cayes, is one of the most popular day trips. If you have just one day and wish to see a sample of mainland attractions, you can pair Altun Ha with one or two other stops (BZ$150 to BZ$220). Trips go by boat across the San Pedro Lagoon, up the Northern River to Bomba village and then by bus to Altun Ha. One trip pairs Altun Ha with a stop at the exotic Maruba Resort Jungle Spa (p70). The time at Maruba can be filled with lunch, then swimming, horseback riding or spa treatments (at extra cost).

If you're interested in seeing more wildlife, you might combine Altun Ha with a trip to the Community Baboon Sanctuary (p67), Crooked Tree Wildlife Sanctuary (p71) or Belize Zoo (p75), all in Belize District.

Altun Ha is lovely, but it doesn't have the importance or architectural variety of Lamanai (p130). If you want a closer look at Maya history and ruins, consider the Lamanai River Trip (BZ$220 to BZ$300), which takes you up the New River (lots of bird and croc spotting) to the spectacular ruins in Orange Walk. This is a great tour, but it makes for a long day trip in a variety of vehicles – ocean boat, van, river boat and then back again.

Another option is a cave-tubing adventure (BZ$300 to BZ$380) at **Nohoch Che'en Caves Branch Archaeological Reserve** (admission BZ$10; 5-cave float BZ$70) in Cayo. Tours combine a river-tube float and a tour of a cave, where you'll see stalagmites and stalactites and possibly pottery shards and other evidence of the ancient Maya. At some point on the tour the group spends a few spooky moments in total darkness. This tour is often packaged with a trip to the Belize Zoo or the Zip-line Canopy Tour at Jaguar Paw Resort.

Tours going all the way west to San Ignacio, Xunantunich and Mountain Pine Ridge are available from San Pedro, but you'll spend most of the day getting to and from these sites. It's better to spend a few days in the west instead of trying to visit from the cayes.

NORTHERN CAYES AMBERGRIS CAYE

AROUND AMBERGRIS: WHERE TO DIVE & SNORKEL

You may not have too much choice about where to drop anchor, as dive masters usually choose the best sites based on weather conditions. Depending where you end up, here is what you'll find.

Mexico Rocks

This site, 4.5 miles north of San Pedro, is a unique patch reef at the northern end of the island. Snorkelers will find an incredible array of corals, including the *Montastrea annularis* corals, which are unique to the Northern Shelf Lagoon. Many small creatures inhabit the turtle grass and coral heads, including flounders, walking hermit crabs, conch, stingrays and hogfish. Schooling fish take refuge in the larger corals, while banded shrimp and Pederson shrimp have cleaning stations.

Boca del Rio (Statue)

The underwater terrain at Boca del Rio, 2 miles northeast of San Pedro, is a spur-and-groove system, featuring rolling coral hills and sandy channels. This is one of the few sites with healthy staghorn coral as well as plate corals. Around 90ft, there are big coral heads, barrels and tubes, and turtles are often spotted here. Near the mooring (in the shallows at 60ft) is a statue of Christ, which gives this site its alternative name of 'Statue.'

Tres Cocos

Tres Cocos is a bit deeper than most, with coral heads rising up to 50ft and a wall with spurs that spill out from 90ft to 120ft. The marine life here is wonderful, with thick growth of star corals, big plating corals, red rope sponges and soft sea whips, and gorgonians on the upper reaches of the spurs. The place is renowned for shoals of schooling fish, including snapper, horse-eye jack and spotted eagle rays.

Tackle Box Canyons

One mile offshore from the Tackle Box pier is this great site with big, steep coral grooves. There are swim-throughs in many places along the drop-off on the way to the outer reef. Gray angels, redband and stoplight parrotfish, and blue chromis hang out along the outer wall.

★ Festivals & Events

Fiesta de Carnaval   CULTURE
The weekend before Lent is a big party in San Pedro. The parades and costumes of more typical carnival celebrations are replaced with body-painting and flour-fighting – great fun to watch and even more fun to participate in.

San Pedro Lobster Festival   CULINARY
(www.sanpedrolobsterfest.com) As of 2007, the third week in June is dedicated to the spiny tail. San Pedro reopens lobster season with a block party, featuring live music, delicious seafood and the crowning of the Lobsterfest king and queen.

Costa Maya Festival   CULTURE
(www.internationalcostamayafestival.com) During the first weekend in August, participants from all over Central America celebrate their shared heritage. The streets of San Pedro are filled with music, parades, dancing and

drinking, culminating in a bodybuilding contest and the crowning of a festival queen.

🛏 Sleeping

Reservations are recommended for the winter season, between December and May. Almost all hotels accept major credit cards, though you may pay a steep surcharge. For more apartments, suites and condominiums, check www.ambergriscaye.com.

🛏 San Pedro

While it's fun to be in the middle of the action, some of the places right in the center can be noisy. If you are on a tight budget, you may have no other choice.

Pedro's Hotel   HOSTEL, HOTEL $
(Map p86; ☎226-3825, 206-2198, 610-5526; www.pedroshotel.com; Sea Grape Dr; r with bathroom & air-con BZ$120, s/d without bathroom BZ$30/50,

Tuffy Canyons

Tuffy Canyons, about 1.6 miles south of San Pedro, is marked by deep grooves and a long, narrow tunnel. This high-walled passage leads to an opening at 80ft to 90ft onto the reef drop-off. Look for some attractive sponges in the deeper reaches, and the occasional eagle ray passing by. Marauding nurse sharks hang around the entire dive. *Tuffy* was the name of a shrimp boat that met its demise here, and you may see some pieces of it at around 20ft.

Cypress Garden

Cypress Garden is home to resting nurse sharks, turtles, black grouper and tiger grouper. The pronounced undercuts provide habitat for arrow crabs and various shrimps, as well as drums of all sizes. The coral growth here includes flower coral, thin leaf lettuce coral and some nice stands of the rare pillar coral.

Hol Chan Cut

Four miles south of San Pedro, this site, part of the Hol Chan Marine Reserve, is famous for its ample sea life, including eagle rays, stingrays and shoaling schools of fish. The channel is lined with large coral, which hides black snapper, chubs, schoolmasters and mutton snappers, as well as moray eels and channel crabs. At the channel mouth, groupers, rays and sapper ride the current. Yellowtails are ubiquitous, but you might also spot tarpon.

Shark Ray Alley

Only snorkeling is allowed at this perennially popular spot, which is part of the Hol Chan Marine Reserve. Shark Ray Alley was traditionally a place for local fishers to clean fish, and the creatures attracted to the fish guts soon became a tourist attraction. As the name implies, the area is known for the big southern stingrays and mooching nurse sharks, which come right up to the boat when it first arrives.

Amigos Wreck

The one and only wreck on the reef is in Hol Chan Marine Reserve. Amigos Wreck is a 60ft barge, intentionally sunk to provide a marine habitat, now home to nurse sharks and large, green moray eels.

deluxe r BZ$130; ❄️📶♨️🏊) The cheapest budget option on the island, Pedro's is a longtime San Pedro party hotel favorite. The best deal at Pedro's is the brand-spanking new deluxe annex, which has 12 rooms featuring flat screen TVs with 110+ channels, air-con and en-suite bathrooms with hot showers. The slightly older hotel is a bargain, offering affordable wood-paneled rooms with air-con and hot water. The original 'hostel' has cell-like rooms with thin walls and shared (cold-water) bathrooms. Either way, you can lounge in hammocks, swim and sunbathe in the sweet pool, play poker and eat pizza at the sports bar on site, and sleep easy knowing you are saving your money for drinking and diving (and other important things). Pedro's also offers a money-back guarantee on tours booked through the hotel, to wit: 'if the tour isn't as good as we say it is, we will refund your money.'

Ruby's Beachfront HOTEL **$**
(Map p86; ☎226-2063; www.ambergriscaye.com/rubys; Barrier Reef Dr; d with/without bathroom BZ$80/50; 📶) This white-with-red-trim hotel near the water taxi dock is a local landmark and budget favorite. The most attractive feature of this long-standing backpacker fave is the downstairs cafe, which guarantees a delicious breakfast every morning. Guests enjoy their coffee on the large terraces that offer sweeping views of the active beachfront. Unfortunately the fan-cooled rooms themselves are pretty tired – but not bad value considering the price and location. Thin walls do little to block out the revelries of your neighbors, so you might as well join the party.

Hotel San Pedrano GUESTHOUSE **$**
(Map p86; ☎226-2054; sanpedrano@btl.net; Barrier Reef Dr; s/d/tr BZ$76/87/87, with air-con BZ$96/107/107; ❄️) There are no views from this 2nd-story streetside hostelry, but you might catch the breeze from the balcony. Relatively spacious rooms have two or three beds.

Thomas Hotel
GUESTHOUSE $

(Map p86; ☎ 226-2061; Barrier Reef Dr; s/d with fan BZ$65/85, d with air-con BZ$93; ❉ �fas) Rooms are equipped with TV and minifridge. The comfy little balcony out back sports a wonderful view of the building next door. Bit pricey for the ambiance.

★ Hotel del Rio
GUESTHOUSE, CABINS $$

(Map p82; ☎ 226-2286; www.ambergriscaye.com/hoteldelrio; Boca del Rio; d with/without air-con BZ$190/100, cabaña BZ$150-180; ❉ �fas ⩕) Just south of San Pedro River, this little lodge has a perfect spot on a quiet stretch of beach, and provides easy access into town. Three categories of room vary in size and layout. Most enticing are the thatched-roof *cabañas* (sleeping two to four people) that are clustered around the sandy grounds, with a central *palapa* that's ideal for socializing or swinging in a hammock. In the background, the two-story Casa Blanca houses the cheapest rooms, but even these have access to a shared balcony with cooling sea breezes and captivating sea views.

Coral Beach Hotel
HOTEL $$

(Map p86; ☎ 226-2013; www.coralbeachhotel.com; cnr Barrier Reef Dr & Black Coral St; d BZ$92; ❉) It doesn't get more central than this location, upstairs from the popular restaurant Crave and one block from the water-taxi dock. Adequate rooms are modern but dark, and hot showers deliver heat only intermittently.

Conch Shell Inn
HOTEL $$

(Map p86; ☎ 627-5202, 226-2062; www.ambergriscaye.com/conchshell; 11 Foreshore St; r downstairs-upstairs BZ$130/152; ❉ �fas) This pink-and-white beauty on the beach offers excellent value smack dab in the middle of town. Recently revamped, the 10 brightly tiled rooms are now equipped with tempurpedic beds, kitchenettes, and hammocks hanging on the shared balcony. The downstairs rooms do not have the kitchen area, but they do have direct access to the sweet sandy beach, lovingly furnished with lounge chairs and palm trees. Air-con is available for BZ$20 a night but the rooms are designed to take full advantage of ocean breezes, so you probably won't need it.

Tio Pil's Hotel
GUESTHOUSE $$

(Map p86; ☎ 226-2059; www.tiopilshotel.com; cnr Barrier Reef Dr & Caribeña St; s BZ$110-130, d BZ$130-150; ❉ �fas) When the slow-moving, sweet-talking Felipe Paz (aka 'Tio Pil') died in 2009, his family-run guesthouse was renamed in his honor. Formerly Lily's Caribbean Lodge, this longstanding favorite has a prime beach location and a long wooden balcony offering views of it all. Rooms are spacious and simple, with a modicum of style; if you get one facing the sea, the big, breeze-inducing windows are all you need. Downstairs, guests tend to congregate in the highly recommended beachfront restaurant.

Spindrift Hotel
HOTEL $$

(Map p86; ☎ 226-2018, 601-8977; www.ambergriscaye.com/spindrift; 45 Barrier Reef Dr; d BZ$107, d with patio/sea view BZ$170/220, beachfront apt BZ$300; ❉ �fas) This is a big concrete block in the middle of town – not the most attractive place, but the service is efficient and staff is warm and welcoming. Rooms are clustered around a central patio decked with potted plants; pay more for the ones with sea views. On the ground floor, the Mexican restaurant Caliente is a popular spot.

Changes in Latitude
B&B $$

(Map p86; ☎ 317-536-5160, 226-2986; www.ambergriscaye.com/latitudes; 36 Coconut Dr; d BZ$230; ❉ �fas ⩕) Unique in San Pedro for its intimate atmosphere, this B&B is a short block from the beach. The six rooms are small but stylish, with wood and bamboo adding Belizean flair. All rooms overlook a well-tended garden with an exotic flower-covered pagoda – a perfect place for guests to sip fruity cocktails and swap snorkeling tales. Other perks include a common kitchen and use of the pool and dock at the Belize Yacht Club next door.

San Pedro Holiday Hotel
HOTEL $$

(Map p86; ☎ 226-2014; www.sanpedroholiday.com; Barrier Reef Dr; r BZ$240-300, apt BZ$390; ❉ �fas ⩕) The central location is both a bonus and a shortcoming. Sure, there's great people-watching and easy access to everything, but this is a busy stretch of beachfront. So even though a painted picket fence surrounds a patch of sand that's only for guests, it doesn't get much privacy. Nonetheless, it's a pretty little place, with intricate wooden trim adorning the porches and decks. Light-filled rooms are simple but spacious, and there is an excellent on-site restaurant.

★ Caye Casa
BOUTIQUE HOTEL $$$

(Map p82; ☎ 226-2880; www.cayecasa.com; Boca del Rio; r BZ$250, ste BZ$300, villa from BZ$480; ❉ �fas ⩕ ⩕) At the quiet northern end of San Pedro town, Caye Casa stands out for its simplicity, sophistication and utter loveliness. The sweet colonial-style *casitas* and villas offer thatched-roof porches with wonderful sea views, fully stocked kitchens with stainless-steel appliances and limestone countertops, spacious tiled bathrooms and inviting king- and queen-sized beds. The hosts go above and beyond to ensure their guests' comfort and convenience (with plenty of help from resident pups, Reef and Caulker). Note the three-night minimum stay during peak periods.

Tide's Beach Resort HOTEL $$$
(Map p86; ☎ 226-2283; www.ambergriscaye.com/tides; Boca del Rio; s/d/tr BZ$220/250/280, ste from BZ$410; ❉❂❄) Set in a classic, colonial-style wooden building, Tides is an ultra-friendly place that primarily caters to divers, due to its affiliation with Patojo's Scuba Center (p84). But everyone will appreciate the classy rooms with high ceilings, polished wood floors and king-sized beds with funky, hand-painted headboards. A wooden balcony runs the width of the building, giving all rooms access to ocean views. Out front, a palm-shaded deck surrounds the swimming pool and the bartender serves up drinks to guests and locals alike.

Ramon's Village RESORT $$$
(Map p86; ☎ 226-2071; www.ramons.com; Coconut Dr; cabaña garden view/seaside/beachfront BZ$360/390/450, ste from BZ$450; ❉❄🛏) Guests love the exotic, faux-jungle setting at this luxurious beach resort with a giant Maya mask known as 'Rey Ramon' overlooking the grounds. Thatched-roof *cabañas* are surrounded by lush greenery and flowering hibiscus and bougainvillea, allowing for plenty of privacy. Beachfront *cabañas* are front and center with uninhibited Caribbean vistas; seaside *cabañas* are set back a bit, with a partially blocked view of the water. Ramon's boasts one of the best beachfronts on the island, with a dock for swimming and lounge chairs for sunning.

Blue Tang Inn GUESTHOUSE $$$
(Map p86; ☎ 226-2326, in USA 866-337-8203; www.bluetanginn.com; Sandpiper St; r BZ$248, ste with garden/ocean view BZ$348/398, deluxe ste BZ$438; ❉❂❄🛏) Named for one of the brightest and most beautiful fish on the reef, the Blue Tang lives up to this enticing image. Each of the suites at this beachside retreat includes kitchen facilities, dining furniture and living space. Big windows and vaulted ceilings make the rooms seem even bigger than they are. Many rooms have good sea

views, but for the best views of all, make your way upstairs to the rooftop – one of the highest vantage points on the island – for the true 360-degree panorama.

🛏 South of Town

If you need a vacation from your vacation, get out of San Pedro. South of town you can enjoy more peace and privacy, although you still have easy access to the restaurants and facilities in town. If you don't feel like making the trek (more than a mile in some cases), a few restaurants and bars cater to the southerners.

★Caribbean Villas Hotel & Bird Sanctuary RESORT $$
(Map p82; ☎ 226-2715; www.caribbeanvillashotel.com; Sea Grape Dr; studio BZ$178-210, ste from BZ$358; ❉❂❄🛏) These simple, sophisticated studios and suites are the best bargains on the island. Brightly painted walls, tile floors and wood trims adorn the oceanfront accommodations, all of which are equipped with kitchenettes. The suites range in size, so this is an ideal spot for families or groups. The jungly grounds of the Caribbean Villas are also home to a bevy of birds, which you can observe from the 'people perch' (also ideal for sunrises). Best of all, the pier protects some algae-covered equipment and local sedimentary rock, forming a sort of artificial reef that attracts a flurry of fish – a great snorkel spot just off your doorstep!

Banana Beach Resort RESORT $$
(Map p82; ☎ 226-3890; www.bananabeach.com; Sea Grape Dr; r BZ$230, ste poolside/oceanfront BZ$250/315; ❉❂❄🛏) This place may be too Daytona Beach for some tastes, but nobody can deny the excellent value it offers. It's a big, three-story concrete building with rooms set around two swimming pools or facing a clean stretch of beach. Attractive rooms have rattan furniture, ceramic artwork and woven tapestries; suites have fully equipped kitchens that are ideal for long-term stays. The place offers excellent week-long package deals.

Corona del Mar GUESTHOUSE $$
(Map p82; ☎ 226-2055; www.ambergriscaye.com/coronadelmar; Coconut Dr; d BZ$170-210, ste BZ$260; ❉❂) Friendly and efficient, this 12-room hotel is removed from San Pedro's hustle and bustle. Tile floors, wicker furniture and cool white hues give the rooms an

appealing tropical atmosphere (also aided – in some cases – by beautiful ocean views). Woody's Wharf stretches out from the white sandy beach into the sea, offering a perfect place to swim, sunbathe or swing in a hammock.

★Victoria House
RESORT **$$$**
(Map p82; ☎226-2067, in USA 800-247-5159; www.victoria-house.com; Sea Grape Dr; r from BZ$370, casitas BZ$596, villas BZ$1190-1810; ✷ 🛜 🏊 ➕) Two miles south of the airstrip, this elegant beach resort is one of the oldest on the island. A beautiful beach and grassy grounds are shaded by a healthy stand of palm trees; rooms are in thatched-roof *casitas* that feature colorful Caribbean themes, or colonial-style 'plantation' houses, with a sophisticated white-on-white scheme that oozes luxury. Villas are fully furnished with flat screen TVs, cable and a huge array of luxurious mod cons. It's a bit of a trek into town. Guests can rent golf carts for BZ$180, and complimetary bicycles and four daily shuttles will help get you into town. Considering the beautifully landscaped gardens, smooth sandy beaches, huge variety of activites on tap, personalized service and several highly touted restaurants, you might never leave the resort!

Mata Rocks Resort
BOUTIQUE HOTEL **$$$**
(Map p82; ☎226-2336; www.matarocks.com; Sea Grape Dr; r BZ$290-340, ste BZ$390-420; ✷ 🛜 🏊) Modern and minimalist, this intimate 17-room hotel is a little oasis on a pretty stretch of beach. The contemporary design, featuring hardwood or tile floors, stucco walls and high ceilings, gives every room a bit of an ocean view. Guests can enjoy the bikes, breakfast and rum punch, which are all complimentary.

Coral Bay Villas
HOTEL **$$$**
(Map p82; ☎226-3003; www.coralbaybelize.com; Coconut Dr; r BZ$300; ✷ 🛜 🏊 ➕) This attractive colonial-style hotel is set back from the ocean, which means that a wide, sandy swath is free for sunbathing, sand-castle building and hammock swinging. What's better, the beach gets very little foot traffic this far south, so it feels as if you have the whole place to yourself. Six deluxe condos are equipped with full kitchens, wireless internet access, cable TV and – lest you forget where you are – private verandas with sea views. Bikes and kayaks are available for guest use.

Coconuts Caribbean Hotel
HOTEL **$$$**
(Map p82; ☎226-2055; www.coconutsbelize.com; Coconut Dr; s/d/tr/q incl breakfast BZ$250/300/320/340, ste BZ$430-480; ✷ 🛜 🏊 ➕) Coconuts scores low on the subtlety scale (as you might expect, with a name like Coconuts), but it's not a bad place for a beach holiday. The true-blue concrete building forms a horseshoe around a central patio, giving all 30 rooms easy access to the pool (with swim-up bar) and the sea beyond. Rooms are rather nondescript, but are equipped with TVs, telephones, fridges and coffee makers.

Exotic Caye Beach Resort
RESORT **$$$**
(Map p82; ☎226-2870; www.belizeisfun.com; Coconut Dr; 1-bedroom condos BZ$300-350, 2-bedroom condos BZ$400-690; ✷ 🛜 🏊) By 'exotic,' they mean beachfront thatched-roof *cabañas*, a freshwater swimming pool and a friendly beach bar. The condos are nothing fancy (certainly not exotic), but the guaranteed views of the Caribbean's sparkling waters more than make up for this. There's an onsite yoga studio, fitness club with tennis courts and conference and meeting rooms. Divers, note that the on-site dive shop offers both recreational diving and adventure tours. The resort also rents kayaks (BZ$16 per hour).

Xanadu Island Resort
RESORT **$$$**
(Map p82; ☎226-2814; www.xanaduresort-belize.com; Sea Grape Dr; ste BZ$380-420, loft BZ$390-450, 2-bedroom apt BZ$450-700; ✷ 🛜 🏊 ➕) ✐ When the Travel Channel's Samantha Brown came to San Pedro, she stayed at Xanadu, so you know this place has something going for it. Ms Brown stayed in the oceanfront deluxe apartment, but you might opt for a slightly simpler studio or loft apartment. It doesn't really matter, as they are all fitted with every amenity and have an atmosphere of rustic luxury. The thatched-roof *cabañas* are clustered around an enticing beachfront freshwater swimming pool, shaded by palm trees. Bicycles, kayaks and snorkel gear are complimentary.

🛏 North Island

The North Island is where you should go if you really want to get away from it all. These resorts are all top end and mainly accessible by boat; you can travel in and out by golf cart or car to at least as far north as the Portofino Resort, but the island ferry is probably a more pleasant way to go.

Bella Vista Guest House GUESTHOUSE **$$**
(Map p82; ✆ 226-4047; http://bellavistabelize.
com; cabins BZ$160-190; ✸ 🛜) About 2.5 miles
north of town, four cozy *casitas* surround a
lagoon, which is home to fish, birds and the
occasional crocodile. The accommodations
are comfortable, with mahogany cabinets,
bamboo furniture and fully equipped kitchens. A long pier leads across the lagoon to
the beach. Facing the sea, you'll find two
large villas that are also available to rent.

Ak'bol Yoga Retreat RESORT **$$**
(Map p82; ✆ 226-2073; www.akbol.com; s/d
BZ$70/100, cabaña BZ$290-330; ✸ 🍴) Yogis,
rejoice! Ak'bol, or 'Heart of the Village,' is
a sweet retreat in a near-perfect location
about 1 mile north of town. The seven colorful *cabañas* have delightful details such as
handcrafted hardwood furniture and mosaic sinks with conch-shell faucets. Enjoy
plantation-style shutters that open to the
sea and mosaic-tiled showers that are open
to the sky. Alternatively, save your cash and
sleep in the rustic yoga barracks with shared
bathrooms. Either way, indulge in fabulous
food at the breezy beach bar and daily yoga
classes in the studio surrounded by sea.
Kids' camp available (which includes children's yoga).

★**Capricorn Resort** CABINS **$$$**
(Map p82; ✆ 226-2809; www.capricornresort.
net; d BZ$370; ✸) Unexpectedly luxurious,
Capricorn has three sweet and sumptuous *cabañas*, located about 3 miles north
of town. Decorated in rich jewel tones and
handmade artisan crafts, they feature romantic details such as private porches and
showers built for two. Capricorn heats up for
a few hours each evening, when people from
town boat in to dine at the outstanding restaurant. The grounds are a botanical wonderland, bursting with blooms of Belize's native plant species, while the small size means
that the local habitat was barely disturbed
by the construction of the *cabañas*, which
are made from hardwoods and thatch.

Costa Maya Reef Resort RESORT **$$$**
(✆ 226-4700; www.costamayareef.com; 1-/2-bedroom condos BZ$278/398; ✸ 🛜 ❄ 🍴) Big
rotunda-style buildings house 30 contemporary condos (which sleep four to six people).
The place is pretty innocuous, but all of the
activities and amenities are here, including

snorkeling and scuba, beachfront bar, free
bikes and kayaks, and loads of activities for
kids. Costa Maya is 6.5 miles north of San
Pedro, accessible only by the Coastal Express
ferry.

Xamen Ek Retreat & Spa RESORT **$$$**
(✆ 226-4455; www.xamanekbelize.com; cabaña
BZ$380, ste BZ$610-670, meal plan BZ$100;
✸ 🛜 ❄) Five miles north of town, Xamen Ek
is a delightfully secluded retreat with two
romantic *cabañas* and three vast suites facing the sea. The suites feature full kitchens
and spacious living areas that open onto the
beach, and 2 acres of tropical paradise are
home to birds galore. Yoga classes, spa treatments and dive packages available.

El Pescador Lodge & Villas RESORT **$$$**
(Map p82; ✆ 226-2398; www.elpescador.com;
standard r BZ$550, 1-/2-/3-bedroom villas
BZ$800/1250/1700; ✸ 🛜 ❄) 🌿 With the atmosphere of a charming old-time fishing
lodge and the amenities of a luxury hotel,
this 21-acre property is a sweet retreat for
anglers and adventurers, located 2.5 miles
north of the river. Set in an intimate colonial-style building, the sea-facing standard
rooms have polished hardwood floors and
colorful hand-woven tapestries. The villas
are nothing short of vast – perfect if you
have family or friends in tow. Fishing packages also available: see the website.

Captain Morgan's Retreat RESORT **$$$**
(✆ 677-9999; www.captainmorgans.com; casitas/
villas BZ$476/592; 🅿 ✸ 🛜 ❄) All you need to
know is that Captain Morgan's Retreat was
the filming location for the first season of
the reality TV show *Temptation Island* (if
you're not familiar with this show, be grateful). Enjoy thatched cabins with private
porches, three swimming pools and lots of
reggae music. Beware the timeshare sales
pitch! Located about 3 miles north of San
Pedro and accessible by Coastal Express island ferry. There's also an onsite casino featuring slot machines, blackjack, poker and
roulette. Open from 6pm to 2am.

White Sands Cove RESORT **$$$**
(Map p82; ✆ 602-773-1322, 226-3528; www.whitesandscove.com; 1-bedroom condos BZ$270-570,
2-bedroom condos BZ$470-770; ✸ 🛜 ❄) If you
want to get away from it all without giving up any of the comforts of home, White
Sands Cove – about 2.5 miles north of San
Pedro – is for you. Condos are furnished
with fully equipped kitchens, gas grills and

spacious living areas (where you can watch one of 60 channels on your big TV). The beach bar, freshwater pool and tropical spa ensure optimal relaxation, while active types can take advantage of the onsite dive shop or the complimentary bikes and kayaks. White Sands receives rave reviews for above-and-beyond service.

Portofino Resort
RESORT $$$

(📞678-5096; www.portofinobelize.com; beachfront cabañas BZ$500, ste from BZ$530, meal plan per person BZ$110; ❄️ 🛜 🏊) Who knew a thatched-roof cabin could be so chic? With high ceilings, huge picture windows, Mexican tiles and Guatemalan rugs, these lodgings are at once primitive and plush. The resort's total capacity is 32, making it wonderfully intimate. Access is by water only, but that doesn't stop gourmands from coming up by the boatload to dine at the world-class restaurant, Le Bistro (p100).

Matachica Beach Resort
RESORT $$$

(📞226-5010; www.matachica.com; bungalow BZ$500, ste BZ$650-700, beachfront casitas $830; ❄️ 🛜 🏊) Vying for the title of 'swankiest resort,' Matachica is extravagant, exotic and eclectic. This place is serious about the idea of tropical luxury, so down duvets and Frette linens cover the mosquito-netted beds, and each thatched-roof cottage has a private patio, hung with hammocks, of course. Other highlights include the award-winning Mambo Restaurant (p100) and the indulgent Jade Spa. It's 5 miles north of San Pedro.

Cocotal Inn & Cabanas
GUESTHOUSE $$$

(Map p82; 📞226-2097; www.cocotalbelize.com; d BZ$250-300, ste BZ$500; ❄️ 🛜 🏊 🍴) The Cocotal, located 2.5 miles north of town, has six rental units (with a sixth on the way as of this writing), each with a kitchenette. Look for a cool colonial atmosphere, with fans hanging from high mahogany ceilings, potted plants, tile floors and wicker furniture. The most charming unit is the cupola-topped *casita* with sunlight pouring through its skylights. It's all very secluded and sophisticated, and good value to boot. Complimentary bikes and kayaks available.

Journey's End
RESORT $$$

(📞in USA 800-460-5665; www.journeysendresort.com; r BZ$300, ste BZ$490, cabaña BZ$410-490, meal plan per person BZ$120; ❄️ 🛜 🏊 🍴) 🏊 Whether you want a view of the crystal-blue Caribbean or the emerald-green garden, your lodging at Journey's End will be spacious and sophisticated, with big windows, high ceilings and romantic four-poster mahogany beds. A dive shop, spa, restaurant and bar are at your doorstep. Besides pampering its guests, Journey's End makes a point of caring for its environs. Guests appreciate the biodegradable shampoos and soaps in the bathroom, and the homegrown, organic ingredients in the kitchen. Other efforts go unseen, such as the water conservation policy that includes collecting rainwater and reusing graywater. About 4.5 miles north of town, Journey's End is accessible by water taxi or Coastal Express island ferry.

🍴 Eating

Although there are plenty of options for cheap street food, pizza and sandwiches, it's hard to sit down at a San Pedro restaurant without paying as much as BZ$50 per person. Dining on Ambergris is startlingly expensive, especially by comparison with the rest of Belize. That said, diners usually get their money's worth, as Ambergris is home to the country's freshest seafood and most innovative chefs.

🍴 San Pedro

For the budget-conscious traveler, several small cafes in the town center serve cheap, simple meals. Try the food stands in front of the park, where a plate of chicken with rice and beans, BBQ meat or fish and other delicacies is under BZ$10.

Ruby's Café
BAKERY $

(Map p86; Barrier Reef Dr; pastries BZ$3-5; ⏰6am-6pm; 🍴) This tiny place is packed with locals during the morning hours. Nobody can resist the sweet and sticky cinnamon rolls, chicken-filled Johnny cakes, homemade banana cake, hot tortillas filled with ham, cheese and beans, and more. There is only one tiny table so grab your breakfast to go and find a shady spot on the beach.

Celi's Deli
FAST FOOD $

(Map p86; Barrier Reef Dr; deli items BZ$3-10, restaurant mains BZ$16-30; ⏰deli 6am-6pm, restaurant lunch & dinner) A fantastic find for breakfast or lunch, Celi's Deli serves food to go – sandwiches, meat pies, tacos, tamales and homemade cakes. You can take your snack across the street and eat on the deck in front of the San Pedro Holiday Hotel, where you'll also find Celi's Restaurant (Map p86), also recommended (especially for the Wednesday night beach BBQ).

My Secret Deli BELIZEAN **$**
(Map p86; Caribeña St; meals BZ$8-12; ☺breakfast & lunch) This is one secret too good to keep, especially for the budget-conscious traveler looking for good bargain eats. This family-run eatery serves filling Belize favorites such as stew chicken, steak and rice, and chunky chicken vegetable soups. Save room for the desserts!

Belize Chocolate Company SWEETS **$**
(Map p86; http://www.belizechocolatecompany. com; Barrier Reef Dr; ☺10am-7pm; 🛜) Run by Chris and Jo Beaumont, the same couple who manufacture the amazing (and Ambergis-produced) Kakaw brand chocolate, this newly opened cafe serves up the finest cacao products on the island. Come in for a taste of the couple's excellent chocolate, ranging from milk to dark (and everything in between). Especially refreshing in this hot clime is the Chococino, an iced chocolate drink made with French Press Coffee (BZ$8).

★**DandE's Frozen Custard** ICE CREAM **$**
(Map p86; www.dande.bz; Pescador Dr; ice cream from BZ$10; ☺2-9pm; 🛝) Don't be confused by 'frozen custard.' It's basically high-quality ice cream, made with eggs for extra richness, then churned as it freezes for extra dense creaminess. The flavors change frequently, often featuring local fruity flavors such as coconut, sour sop and mango. Alternatively you can't go wrong with 'not just' vanilla. DandE's also makes sorbet, but you're a fool if you forego the frozen custard.

NORTHERN CAYES AMBERGRIS CAYE

SAN PEDRO FOR CHILDREN

San Pedro is among the most 'developed' destinations in Belize, which means the island offers more facilities that cater to demanding tourists. (And let's face it, children are demanding.) There are very few sights, activities and amenities designed specifically for kids in San Pedro, but there are loads of ways to share the joys of surf, sand and sun with your little people.

Sights & Activities
Whether swimming, snorkeling or building sand castles, there's no end to the fun in the sun for your kids. A few pointers for making the most of it:

➡ Frequent the playground just south of the toll bridge.

➡ San Pedro beaches are not ideal for swimming so consider staying in a place with a swimming pool.

➡ Bring lots of books and teach your kids the joy of swinging in a hammock.

➡ Keep a running list of birds, bugs, lizards and other animals spotted (perhaps with illustrations provided by your child).

➡ Dig in the sand. (Pots and spoons work almost as well as shovels and pails.)

➡ Visit the fish! Kids as young as five or six years old enjoy snorkeling. Practice using a mask and snorkel in the bathtub before your trip.

➡ Let older kids paddle around in a kayak or a paddleboat.

➡ Ride bicycles. The main roads in town have a lot of traffic, but the North Island is quiet, beautiful and safe. Stick to the road if riding in the sand is too difficult.

➡ Take a family-friendly tour, such as the manatee tour offered by Seaduced by Belize (p85) or the Reef Runner Glass Bottom Boat (p89).

Sleeping & Eating
Look for the 🛝 icon in listings for restaurants and resorts that offer perks for little people.

Getting Around
The main forms of transportation around San Pedro are boat and golf cart, both of which can be dangerous for children if proper precautions are not taken. Keep small children in the arms of an adult. In town, the narrow roads get congested with traffic, but the beach is a pleasant place to push a stroller. The beach trail on the North Island is only suitable for a heavy-duty baby jogger. In both cases, the sandy trail might demand some extra exertion from the pusher.

Caramba! Restaurant BELIZEAN $$
(Map p86; ☎ 226-3850; www.ambergriscaye.com/caramba; Pescador Dr; burgers BZ$9-12, mains BZ$20-40; ⊙ lunch & dinner Thu-Tue; 🛜📶♿) Caramba is a busy place due to its excellent food, fun atmosphere and attentive service. Mexican and Creole dishes focus on fresh fish and seafood cooked in at least 10 tasty ways. The tropical decor (including the staff's festive attire) enhances your seafood feast.

Playa Chel INTERNATIONAL $$
(Map p86; Sandpiper St; sandwiches BZ$15-30, mains BZ$25-40; ⊙ breakfast, lunch & dinner) This lovely open-air *palapa* has hardwood tables, attractive decor and refreshing breezes. The menu is varied, offering American breakfast all day long, sandwiches, seafood and a large variety of Mexican specialties. The food is good and the beachside setting is unbeatable.

Crave CARIBBEAN $$
(Map p86; ☎ 226-3211; www.cravebelize.com; cnr Barrier Reef Dr & Black Coral St; mains BZ$22-36; ⊙ lunch & dinner Mon-Sat, dinner Sun) Travelers rave about Crave: top-notch service, fun-loving atmosphere and to-die-for cocktails. The menu is an eclectic blend of classic Caribbean and Mexican, including appetizers such as Caye lime shrimp or conch fritters, followed by Belizean BBQ or blackened fish.

El Patio Restaurant & Grill BELIZEAN $$
(Map p86; www.ambergriscaye.com/elpatio; Black Coral St; mains BZ$12-25; ⊙ lunch & dinner Wed-Mon) Potted plants, a flowing fountain and a candlelit interior make this sand-floored *palapa* an inviting setting for a romantic dinner. Grilled meats and seafood are the specialty, accompanied by fresh-squeezed, thirst-quenching fruit juices or ice-cold Belikin beers.

Jambel Jerk Pit CARIBBEAN $$
(Map p86; ☎ 226-3515; jambels@yahoo.com; Beachside, Sun Breeze Suites; mains BZ$16-30; ⊙ breakfast, lunch & dinner; ♿) New locations, same great Jamaican Jerk. Whether you want fish, chicken or pork – or the famous Jamaica Mi Crazy Shrimp – your order will be as spicy as you like it. Wednesday nights feature live reggae music and an all-you-can-eat buffet that will sate the hungriest Rasta Mon; Sunday is family fun day. Jambel also has a new location 5.5 miles north of the bridge at the Xamanek Resort.

Estel's Dine by the Sea BREAKFAST $$
(Map p86; www.ambergriscaye.com/estels; Buccaneer St; meals BZ$10-30; ⊙ 6am-5pm; 🖋) This long-standing breakfast favorite is basically an extension of the beach – complete with sandy floors and ocean breezes. Stop by for a breakfast burrito, fruit-filled jacks or an eye-opening coffee.

Blue Water Grill INTERNATIONAL $$$
(Map p86; www.bluewatergrillbelize.com; Sun Breeze Beach Hotel, Coconut Dr; starters & salads BZ$10-30, mains BZ$20-50; ⊙ breakfast, lunch & dinner; 🖋) It's hard to resist the huge open-air restaurant at this beachfront property, and almost everybody who comes to San Pedro ends up eating here at some point. Few are disappointed. The menu is wide-ranging and includes some safe options, such as pizza and pasta, as well as more adventurous Asian-influenced seafood dishes. The place is always busy, but it's big so you probably won't have to wait for a table.

Elvi's Kitchen BELIZEAN $$$
(Map p86; ☎ 226-2176; Pescador Dr; mains BZ$20-50; ⊙ lunch & dinner; ♿) This San Pedro institution has been around since the early days, serving up local specialties such as shrimp creole, fried chicken and conch *ceviche*. The funky tropical decor, loud marimba music and expensive T-shirts for sale (not to mention the overpriced main courses) give it a Disney-like atmosphere. But it's a good place to sample some authentic and filling local cuisine.

Wild Mango's INTERNATIONAL $$$
(Map p86; ☎ 226-2859; 42 Barrier Reef Dr; mains BZ$30-50; ⊙ lunch & dinner; 🖋) Exuding a carefree, casual ambience (as a beachfront restaurant should), this open-air restaurant manages to serve up some of the island's most consistent and creative cuisine. With a hint of the Caribbean and a hint of Mexico, the dishes showcase fresh seafood, Cajun spices and local fruits and vegetables. The place is usually packed – come early or make a reservation.

Sunset Restaurant INTERNATIONAL $$$
(Map p86; ☎ 226-2601; 10 Black Coral St; lunch BZ$20-25, dinner BZ$40-70; ⊙ lunch & dinner) With San Pedro town clustered on the east side of the island, the sunset on Ambergris often goes unnoticed. But not by the folks at Sunset Restaurant, which overlooks the lagoon at the back. The menu features lots of seafood, which is served steamed, sautéed,

grilled and in many other creative ways. But as gorgeous as the sunset is over the lagoon, it is not the main show at the Sunset Restaurant. That would be the monster tarpons who come flying out of the water to feast on the sardines offered by the staff (and guests).

🍴 South of Town

George's Kitchen   DINER **$**
(Map p82; Coconut Dr; meals BZ$6-12; ☺ breakfast, lunch & dinner Wed-Mon; 🖉) Opposite the entrance to Corona del Mar, this little seafood and sandwich shack is one of San Pedro's longstanding favorites. It's a homely little hole in the wall, but George and Maria make their guests feel like family. An excellent option for breakfast, with big omelets and other hearty egg dishes.

El Divino   INTERNATIONAL **$$**
(Map p82; www.bananabeach.com; Banana Beach Resort, Coconut Dr; breakfast BZ$10-16, mains BZ$20-40; ☺ breakfast, lunch & dinner; 🖉🖤) This streetside eatery gets heaps of praise, especially for its Caribbean rotisserie, grilled burgers and steaks. The beach-themed decor is not exactly subtle, as you will notice as soon as you catch a glimpse of the reef mural on the wall (or, even better, the sunset vista in the martini lounge). Staff members dressed in brightly colored tropical uniforms ensure a fun and friendly ambience.

Ali Baba   MIDDLE EASTERN **$$**
(Map p86; 🖉 226-4042; Coconut Dr; mains BZ$20-30; ☺ lunch & dinner) Ali Baba serves some good Middle Eastern and Mediterranean food, including Lebanese-style chicken dishes, rice and kebabs. It even has Egyptian-style *shisha* pipes (BZ$25).

★ **Hidden Treasure**   CARIBBEAN **$$$**
(Map p82; 🖉 226-4111; www.hiddentreasurebelize.com; 4088 Sarstoon St; lunch BZ$15-25, dinner BZ$40-70; ☺ lunch & dinner; 🖉) Living up to its name, Hidden Treasure is a gorgeous open-air restaurant set in an out-of-the-way residential neighborhood (follow the signs from Coconut Dr). Lit by candles, the beautiful bamboo and hardwood dining room is the perfect setting for a romantic dinner, which might feature almond-crusted grouper, Maya-spiced snapper wrapped in a banana leaf, or spare ribs marinated in a Garifuna spice rub. When you make your reservation, inquire about free transportation from your hotel.

Palmilla Restaurant   INTERNATIONAL **$$$**
(Map p82; 🖉 226-2067; www.victoria-house.com; Coconut Dr; mains BZ$30-60; ☺ breakfast, lunch & dinner; 🖉) The classy candlelit restaurant at Victoria House is overseen by New York–trained chef José Luis Ortega, who ensures high-quality cuisine for his discriminating guests. At lunchtime, you might prefer Admiral Nelson's Beach Bar, the hotel's casual, open-air cafe on the beachfront.

🍴 North Island

Some visitors take the dirt road only as far as Legends for lunch or the Palapa Bar for drinks, before heading back to San Pedro. Others travel up the coast by ferry for an exotic starlit evening at one of the North Island's excellent restaurants. You can expect unusual menus featuring excellent seafood dishes.

★ **Lazy Croc BBQ**   BBQ **$$**
(Map p82; 🖉 226-4015; meals BZ$12-20; ☺ 11am-3pm Thu-Sun) A sign points the way from the beach to this tiny shack with a back porch overlooking a lagoon that's also a croc breeding spot. This is Cheri and Ens' Lazy Crocc BBQ, easily the best BBQ place on Ambergris. Pull up a stool and watch for the resident crocs while you wait for the sweet and spicy BBQ. Chicken and ribs are fine but the pulled pork is divine; splurge on the sampler if you wish to try all three. The serving sizes are massive, but do your best to save some room for the decadent drunken rum cake. Cash only.

Legends Burger House   BURGERS **$$**
(Map p82; www.legendsburgerhouse.com; Tres Cocos; mains BZ$15-30; ☺ lunch & dinner Mon-Sat; 🖉🖤) A quarter of a mile north of the river, this cute red, white and blue clapboard house has 15 kinds of burgers named after local and international celebrities (as well as a few fictional characters). For a legendary experience, try the Sir Barry Bowen burger, which is topped with Belikin beer-battered shrimp. Got an appetite? Try the King Kong Burger – 8 5oz patties with cheese, bacon and a pound and a half of fries. It's BZ$50, but if you finish it in half an hour it's free. All burgers are available with animal-free black bean patties. Besides the burgers, this place has live music and a happening bar.

Cabana Coffee
CAFE

(Beachside, Captain Morgan's Retreat; Coffee drinks from BZ$4; ☉ 6:30am-1pm Sun-Fri) The only coffee shop on the north end of the island, this friendly little place sits on the beach in the grounds of Captain Morgan's Retreat and serves excellent espresso drinks as well as a small variety of pastries and baked goods, both sweet and savory.

Aji Tapas Bar & Restaurant
MEDITERRANEAN $$$

(Map p82; ☎ 226-4047; www.bellavistabelize.com; tapas BZ$20-26, mains BZ$30-48; ☉ lunch & dinner Wed-Mon; ✍) If you're in the mood for romance, book one of the six tables at this magical Mediterranean hideaway. Surrounded by blooming flowers and swaying palms, the dining area is only steps from the sea. The menu features a few classic tapas (such as garlic shrimp or bacon-wrapped dates), as well as some delectable seafood dishes (including highly recommended paella). Personalized service completes the delightful experience.

Mambo Restaurant
MEDITERRANEAN $$$

(☎ 220-5011; www.matachica.com; Matachica Beach Resort; mains BZ$40-80; ☉ breakfast, lunch & dinner) The Matachica Beach Resort's award-winning restaurant is as eclectic and exotic as the resort itself. Specializing in Mediterranean fare such as pasta and paella, the menu does not skimp on fresh seafood and local seasonal produce. While you are here, be sure to stroll around the grounds to thoroughly appreciate this tropical fantasy. Reservations required.

Rendezvous Restaurant & Winery
THAI, FRENCH $$$

(☎ 226-3426; www.ambergriscaye.com/rendezvous; mains BZ$40-60; ☉ lunch & dinner; ✍) Four miles north of town, Rendezvous is unique in San Pedro – if not Belize. Set in a ramshackle house on the beach, this colonial-style place artfully blends the flavors of French and Thai cuisine, with exquisite results. Try the Singapore-style chili crab, Thai pepper pork with roasted garlic chips, *pad thai* or fresh fish with coconut cream sauce and saffron and cilantro. House wines are made at the winery in the grounds. Rendezvous also offers wine tasting and has an excellent outdoor bar with a pier for swimming and sunbathing.

Capricorn Restaurant
INTERNATIONAL $$$

(Map p82; ☎ 226-2809; www.capricornresort.net; Capricorn Resort; mains BZ$50-70; ☉ lunch & dinner)

This restaurant's nouvelle cuisine has long been considered among the best in Belize. By day you can chill out under the *palapa* at the beach bar; at night the open-air restaurant is lit by festive twinkling lights. Dinner specials change daily, but they might include stone-crab claws with a garlic and herb dip, filet mignon with portobello mushroom sauce, or grilled lobster tail painted with garlic butter. Reservations are essential; book a table and it's yours for the night.

★ Le Bistro
EUROPEAN, CARIBBEAN $$$

(☎ 220-5096; www.portofinobelize.com; Portofino Resort; mains BZ$20-40; ☉ breakfast, lunch & dinner) With a chef trained in French and Italian cuisine, and a brilliant Belizean setting, the European-Caribbean fusion cuisine at Le Bistro makes perfect sense. The all-sauté menu features freshly caught snapper, lobster and other seafood prepared with diverse (and delectable) sauces. If you're feeling really romantic, inquire about private dining on the pier. A complimentary shuttle boat leaves Fido's Dock at 6:30pm; reservations recommended.

🍸 Drinking

Most hotels have comfortable bars, often with sand floors, thatched roofs and reggae music. The Lonely Planet–reviewed bars open from late morning till late at night (unless otherwise noted).

Palapa Bar
BAR

(Map p82; www.palapabarandgrill.com; North Island; ☉ 8am-10pm) This over-the-water *palapa* is about a mile north of the San Pedro bridge, and a popular place to hang out. Dishes are a mixed bag – Palapa serves good burgers and decent tacos, but the chicken wings are nothing to write home about. Still, it's a fantastic place for tropical drinks any time of day. There are no laws against drinking and floating, so when it's really hot you are invited to partake of a bucket of beers while relaxing in an inner tube. Happy hour is from 4pm to 6pm daily.

Legends Burger House
BAR

(Map p82; www.legendsburgerhouse.com; Tres Cocos; ☉ noon-midnight; ☎) There's a lot going on at Legends, even besides the burgers. There is live music two nights a week and there are ice-cold beers, wacky cocktails and sometimes even free jello shots. And there are walls crammed with memorabilia from all over the US of A. Bring something for the wall and get a free drink (license plate, poster, underwear...they don't care.)

Tackle Box
BAR

(Map p86; www.tackleboxbarandgrill.com; Shark's Pier) An island institution since 1981, the Tackle Box extends a warm welcome (usually with a reggae beat) to everyone arriving in San Pedro. No longer the dock for the water taxi, this is still an ideal first stop, where you can have a drink, unwind and get into the island frame of mind.

Wahoo's Lounge
BEACH BAR

(Map p86) Formerly the Pier Lounge, this otherwise innocuous sports bar has made a name for itself by hosting the weekly World Famous Chicken Drop (6pm Thursday). This form of entertainment – sort of like bingo with chickens – gives new insight to the origin of the term 'chicken shit.' The sand is divided by numbered squares and a chicken is put in the middle of it; participants place bets on where it will drop a turd. Give people enough alcohol and they are amused by anything. This place also has a giant plasma TV and plans to host other silly games.

BC's Beach Bar
BEACH BAR

(Map p86) This little shack on the beach is a hot spot for nachos and burritos and cold drinks. Local bands play on Thursday nights and Friday is trivia night. On the beach south of Blue Water Grill.

Crazy Canuck's
BEACH BAR

(Map p82; www.belizeisfun.com; Exotic Caye Beach Resort, Coconut Dr) Open to the cooling sea breezes; staff is friendly and regular patrons welcoming. Sunday is the big day, with horseshoe tournies in the afternoon and crowd-drawing live music in the evening. There's also live punta music on Monday nights, and pulled pork and live band karaoke on Tuesdays.

Pedro's Hotel
SPORTS BAR

(Map p86; 206-2198; www.pedroshotel.com; Sea Grape Dr) Come to eat pizza, play pool and watch sports on the big screen. With one hour's advance notice, Pedro can order any game for your viewing pleasure. Wednesday and Saturday are poker nights.

Roadkill Bar
BEACH BAR

(Map p82; Coconut Dr) Feels like a beach bar, but it's actually not on the beach. Burgers on Friday and karaoke on Wednesday night.

☆ Entertainment

Fido's
CLUB

(Map p86; www.fidosbelize.com; 18 Barrier Reef Dr; ⊙ 11am-midnight) This enormous *palapa* decorated with seafaring memorabilia attracts crowds for drinking, dancing and hooking up. There's plenty of seating, an extensive food menu and an ample-sized dance floor. Live music is on every night at 8pm – classic and acoustic rock, reggae and the occasional record spin.

Jaguar's Temple Club
NIGHTCLUB

(Map p86; www.jaguarstempleclub.com; Barrier Reef Dr; ⊙ 9pm-4am Thu-Sat) You can't miss this surreal Maya temple, complete with jaguar face, across from the central beachside park. The place does its very best to create a 'wild' atmosphere, with jungle dioramas setting the stage and lighting effects keeping it spooky. Hip-hop and breakbeat music keeps dancers on their feet. When you need to take a break, check out the streetside **Rehab Lounge** (⊙ 3pm-midnight Tue-Sun).

🛍 Shopping

Plenty of gift shops in the hotels and on and around Barrier Reef Dr sell T-shirts, beachwear, hammocks, jewelry and ceramics. But there are also interesting boutiques, fancy gift stores, art galleries and woodwork shops. Prices are high but you might find unique and artistic souvenirs. Sometimes artisans sell their woodwork and handicrafts from stalls on the street near the central park or on the beach, and you can often find Maya merchants selling locally made handcrafts close to the pier by Ak'Bol Yoga.

Orange Gifts
ART

(Map p82; www.orangegifts.com; Coconut Dr; ⊙ 10am-6pm) This is one of the biggest and best galleries in San Pedro (though it's a fraction of the size of the original location in Cayo). If you are into hand-carved wooden sculpture and furniture, paintings and ceramics by Belizean artists, and hand-woven textiles and handmade jewelry, you can do all of your shopping right here, in one place. There is another smaller location (Map p86; Pescador Dr; ⊙ closed Sun) near the airstrip.

Belizean Arts Gallery
ART

(Map p86; www.belizeanarts.com; Fido's, 18 Barrier Reef Dr; ⊙ 9am-10pm Mon-Sat) This is one of the country's best shops for local art and handicrafts, selling ceramics, wood carvings, Gari-

WORTH A TRIP

TACKLE BOX SEA BAR

Not to be confused with the same named bar at Shark's Pier, the **Tackle Box Sea Bar** (☎220-5880; www.tranquilitybayresort.com; meals BZ$40-80) is the restaurant at Tranquility Bay Resort, in the far north of the North Island. It is named after the original Tackle Box, which was destroyed by Hurricane Mitch in 1998. In fact, this place is a very close replica of the original Tackle Box, down to details like the sea green exterior and the interior bar constructed from a wooden speedboat.

The most awesome feature of the Tackle Box is the marine show that takes place here every night. Apparently, the original Tackle Box (which was located at Shark's Pier) kept a fish pen below the dock, where sharks and rays swam in circles for the viewing of the diners. The new Tackle Box does not need to keep anything in nets, because it is located right on Rocky Point, where the reef meets the shore. A huge variety of marine life swims freely around and under the restaurant dock, including tarpons, eagle rays and sharks. The fish are most active at night, when they put on an amazing show for the diners enjoying their meal on the dock.

Entertainment aside, the food at the Tackle Box is excellent. The menu features those creatures that are swimming below. Very fresh!

funa drums and antiques alongside affordable and tasteful knickknacks. You'll also find a decent selection of paintings by local and national artists. Rainforest-flora beauty products, including soaps, are on sale, too.

Caribe Creations CLOTHING
(Map p86; Barrier Reef Dr) Take a bit of Belizean style home with you: here you'll find custom-made clothes with Caribbean flair, ranging from beach cover-ups and do-rags to silky sarongs and wedding gowns, all in free-flowing fabrics with a distinctive island design. The motto is 'From cloth to clothes in 24 hours,' so if you don't see what you like, you can have it custom made.

Rum, Cigar & Coffee House FOOD
(Map p86; ☎226-2020; saul.rums@gmail.com; Pescador Dr; ⊗9am-9pm; 🛜) Catering to all of your vices with a good selection of fresh roasted coffee beans, local rums and cigars from all over the Caribbean. Stop by for a taste test, which will give you the chance to sample several coffee- and fruit-flavored liqueurs. The coffee can't be beat, and there's even free wireless so you can check your email.

Ambergris Jade ACCESSORIES
(Map p86; Spindrift Hotel, 45 Barrier Reef Dr) The Maya valued jadeite for its iridescent beauty and perceived powers. Different varieties were believed to enhance creativity, stimulate positive energy and offer protection from evil spirits. This so-called 'Jade & Maya History Museum' carries a wide variety of beautiful Guatemalan jade in the form of

jewelry and other carved objects. Also offers appraisal services.

Ambar ACCESSORIES
(Map p86; Fido's, 18 Barrier Reef Dr; ⊗9am-9pm Mon-Sat) Beautiful handmade jewelry in interesting and diverse styles, including plenty of options from the namesake stone. Custom designs made while you wait!

Pages BOOKS
(Map p86; www.pagesbookstorebelize.com; Vilma Linda Plaza, Tarpon St; ⊗9am-5pm Mon-Sat) The biggest and best bookstore in Belize, with an excellent selection of travel books and reference books about Belizean history and culture. This is also the place to trade in your used paperbacks and pick up a new novel to peruse on the beach.

C's Furniture World FURNITURE
(Map p86; Sea Grape Dr; ⊗10am-6pm Mon-Sat) If you are heading further into Belize, you are better off buying your wood products and furniture in Cayo, where prices are lower and the selection is more diverse. But otherwise, stop by C's to see the handiwork with mahogany, rosewood and teak.

Friki Tiki Toucan SOUVENIRS
(Map p86; ⊗8am-10pm) Sure, this place has loads of stuffed toucans and 'You better Belize it' T-shirts, but it also has a decent selection of music by Belizean artists, the full range of Marie Sharp's hot sauces, delicious locally grown coffee beans and decadent rum cake packed to travel. You

might even find a T-shirt or a baseball cap that you'd like to show off to your friends at home.

Gallery of San Pedro, Ltd ART
(Map p82; Coconut Dr) A wide variety of local arts and crafts, as well as lots of tapestries, hammocks and masks imported from Guatemala.

Little Old Craft Shop ARTS & CRAFTS
(Map p86; Coconut Dr) Ricardo Zetina crafts beautiful jewelry and figurines out of black coral, or 'King Coral,' which he harvests from deepest shelves of the reef.

Paradise Gallery & Frame ART
(Map p86; www.paradiseframe.com; Vilma Linda Plaza, Tarpon St; ⊙9am-5pm Mon-Sat) Although this place specializes in custom framing, it also showcases paintings and photography by local artists. It's a small but choice selection.

ⓘ Information

EMERGENCY
Medical, Fire & Police (☑911)
Police (☑206-2022; Pescador Dr)

INTERNET ACCESS
Caribbean Connection (cnr Barrier Reef Dr & Black Coral St; per hr BZ$10; ⊙7am-10pm) High-speed connections, CD burning, international phone calls, excellent coffee, unique jewelry.
Slurp & Surf Cyber Cafe (49 Lagoon St; per hr BZ$8)
Wayo's Beachside Beernet (Boca del Rio; per hr BZ$10; ⊙10am-midnight) International calls, fresh-squeezed juice.

INTERNET RESOURCES
Ambergris Caye (www.ambergriscaye.com) Excellent island information and a lively message board.
Goambergriscaye.com (www.goambergris-caye.com) Detailed information including comprehensive accommodations listings.

LAUNDRY
Candace's Laundromat (Slurp & Surf Cyber Cafe; ⊙8am-9pm Mon-Fri, 10am-6pm Sun) Offers full service and full-serve wash and dry.
Nellie's Laundromat (Pescador Dr; ⊙7am-9pm Mon-Sat)

MEDIA
Two rival weekly newspapers keep readers informed about news and events. Both are printed on Thursday.

Ambergris Today (www.ambergristoday.com)
San Pedro Sun (www.sanpedrosun.net) Includes a weekly column on the birds of Ambergris Caye.

MEDICAL SERVICES
Hyperbaric Chamber (☑226-2851, 684-8111; Lion St; ⊙24hr) Center for diving accidents, next door to the Lion's Club.
Lion's Club Medical Clinic (☑226-4052, 600-9071; Lion St) Across the street from the Maya Island Air terminal at the airport.
San Carlos Medical Clinic, Pharmacy & Pathology Lab (☑226-2918, emergencies 614-9251; 28 Pescador Dr) Treats ailments and does blood tests.

MONEY
You can exchange money easily in San Pedro, and US dollars cash and traveler's checks are widely accepted.
Atlantic Bank (Barrier Reef Dr; ⊙8am-2pm Mon-Fri, 8:30am-noon Sat) Near Buccaneer St; cash advances cost BZ$10 per transaction.
Belize Bank (Barrier Reef Dr; ⊙8am-3pm Mon-Thu, to 4:30pm Fri)

POST
Post office (Alijua Bldg, Barrier Reef Dr; ⊙8am-noon & 1-4pm Mon-Fri)

TOURIST INFORMATION
San Pedro Tourist Information Center (Barrier Reef Dr; ⊙10am-1pm Mon-Sat) Next to the town hall, this tourist information center has plentiful giveaway information.

ⓘ Getting There & Away

AIR
The San Pedro airstrip is just south of the town center on Coconut Dr. The Tropic Air terminal is at the north end of the strip, right on Coconut Dr, while the Maya Island Air terminal is on the west side of the strip.
Tropic Air (☑226-2338; www.tropicair.com) has hourly flights operating to/from Belize City's Philip Goldson International Airport (BZ$126, 20 minutes), as well as the Belize City Municipal Airstrip, 12 miles closer to town (BZ$70, 20 minutes). About half the flights stop at Caye Caulker (BZ$70, five minutes, six daily). Additional flights depart for Corozal (BZ$95, 20 minutes, five daily). All flights depart between 7am and 5pm daily.
Maya Island Air (☑226-2435; www.mayaair-ways.com) has prices and schedules similar to Tropic Air.

BOAT

Caye Caulker Water Taxi Association (☏ 226-0992; www.gocayecaulker.com/members/ccwta.html; Caribeña St) is the longest-standing and most reliable boat service to Caye Caulker (one way/round trip BZ$20/35, 45 minutes) and Belize City (one way/round trip BZ$30/55, 1½ hours). Boats leave San Pedro at 8am, 9:30am, 11:30am, 1pm, 2:30pm and 3:30pm (also 4:30pm weekends and holidays).

San Pedro Belize Express Water Taxi (☏ 223-2225; www.belizewatertaxi.com; Black Coral St, reef side) has services to Caye Caulker (one way/round trip BZ$20/35) and Belize City (one way/round trip BZ$30/55) at 7am, 11:30am, 2:30pm and 4:30pm, with a 6:30pm run that goes to Caye Caulker only.

Also operates one daily boat to Chetumal, Mexico (one way/round trip BZ$80/140) departing Caulker at 7:00am, San Pedro at 7:30 and reaching Chetumal around 11am. It returns at 3:30pm.

Thunderbolt (☏ 422-0026; www.ambergriscaye.com/thunderbolt; Buccaneer St, lagoon side) departs San Pedro's lagoon-side dock at 3pm for Corozal (one way/round trip BZ$45/85, two hours), stopping at Sarteneja upon request.

Water Jets (☏ 226-2194; www.sanpedrowatertaxi.com; Black Coral St, lagoon side) has four runs per day to Caye Caulker (one way/round trip BZ$24/40, 45 minutes) and Belize City (one way/round trip BZ$35/65, 90 minutes) at 6am, 10:30am, 3:30pm and 5pm. One daily boat to Chetumal (one way/round trip BZ$90/180, two hours) departs San Pedro at 8:30am and returns at 3pm.

① Getting Around

You can walk into town from the airport in 10 minutes or less, and the walk from the boat docks is even shorter. **San Pedro Taxi** (☏ 206-2076) drives minivans. From the airport, one or two people will pay BZ$10 to any place in town, or BZ$12 to BZ$20 to the hotels north or south of town.

BICYCLE

Many hotels and resorts provide bikes for their guests for a small fee or for free. Otherwise, you can rent a bike at Joe's Bicycle Rentals (p88).

BOAT

The **Coastal Express** (☏ 226-3231; www.coastalxpress.com; Caribeña St) operates an Ambergris-only water-taxi service north and south from Amigos del Mar. Boats run to the northern resorts from 5:30am to 11:30pm, with an additional 1am run on Wednesday, Friday and Saturday. Heading south, it runs

from 6am to 1am, with an additional 2am run on Wednesday, Friday and Saturday. The cost ranges from BZ$10 to BZ$40, depending on how far you are going; weekly passes for unlimited use are available. Many resorts and restaurants also offer a water-shuttle service into town.

GOLF CART

These days, traffic jams are not unusual in San Pedro, due to the glut of golf carts cruising the streets. Note that some golf carts are battery-powered and others run on gas; the former being more ecologically sound and the latter having greater endurance.

Carts Belize (☏ 226-4090; www.cartsbelize.com; Xanadu Island Resort, Sea Grape Dr) Rent a four-seater for a day/week for BZ$130/532, or a six-seater for BZ$294/844.

Island Adventures (☏ 226-4343; www.island-golfcarts.com; Coconut Dr) Rent a four-seater for BZ$120/500 per day/week.

Moncho's Cart Rentals (☏ 226-4490; www.sanpedrogolfcartrental.com; 11 Coconut Dr) Rents carts for a day/week for BZ$129/494. Moncho's will deliver your vehicle to your hotel for your convenience.

SEGWAY

A kind of a cross between a golf cart and a bicycle, a Segway is a motorized scooter that you can use for transportation or fun. Get one at **Segway of Belize** (☏ 226-3344; http://www.segwayofbelize.com; Fairdale Plaza, Coconut Dr) for BZ$56 for one hour. Guided Segway tours also available.

CAYE CAULKER

POP 1300

'No Shirt, No Shoes…No Problem.' You'll see this sign everywhere in Belize, but in no place is it more apt than Caye Caulker. Indeed, nothing seems to be a problem on this tiny island, where mangy dogs nap in the middle of the dirt road and suntanned cyclists pedal around them. The only traffic sign on the island instructs golf carts and bicycles to 'go slow,' a directive that is taken seriously.

The 1000 or so residents have traditionally made their living from the sea, specifically from the spiny lobsters and red snapper that inhabit the warm waters. The Caye has also long been a budget traveler's mecca, but in recent years tourists of all ages and incomes have begun to appreciate the island's unique atmosphere. On Caye Caulker there are no cars, no fumes and no hassles, instead just white sandy beaches, balmy breezes, fresh seafood, azure waters and a fantastic barrier reef right at its doorstep.

The easygoing attitude is due in part to the thriving Rastafarian culture on the Caye, which pulses to a reggae beat. If it's not Bob Marley blaring from a boom box on the beach, it's the latest in *punta* rock. Drumming groups gather on the beach and at local bars to get their Afro-Caribbean groove on. They play for themselves, but anybody is welcome to gather around and soak up the good vibes.

The island is an ideal base for snorkeling and diving adventures at the nearby reef. The northern part of the island – a tempting destination for kayakers is mostly mangroves, which are home to an amazing variety of birdlife. Other than that, all visitors should be sure to schedule in plenty of time for swinging in a hammock and enjoying the breeze (which is indeed a legitimate activity on Caye Caulker).

But Caye Caulker cannot remain so idyllic forever. The increase in visitors means more construction, more amenities and fewer fish. Some travelers even complain that the local Ra-sta guys are a 'bad element.' The northern part of the island – until now practically uninhabited – has been partitioned into lots that are on the market for sale and development. Come to Caye Caulker now, before paradise is lost.

History

Caye Caulker was originally a fishing settlement. It became popular with 17th-century British buccaneers as a place to stop for water and to work on their boats. Like Ambergris Caye, it grew in population with the War of the Castes, and is mainly a Mestizo island. It was purchased in 1870 by Luciano Reyes, whose descendants still live on the island. Reyes parceled the land out to a handful of families, and to this day descendants of those first landowners still live in the general vicinities of those original parcels. These islanders were self-sufficient and exported turtle meat until the turtle population was decimated.

During much of the 20th century coconut processing, fishing, lobster trapping and boat building formed the backbone of the island's economy. Caulker was one of the first islands to establish a fisherfolk cooperative in the 1960s, allowing members to receive fair prices for the lobster and other sea life pulled from their waters.

Caye Caulker remains a fishing village at heart, and fishing (as well as boat design and construction) continue. Tourism, which began as a small part of Caulker's economy in the late 1960s and 1970s (when small numbers of hippies found their way to the island), has become its prime economic mover, and the idea of Caulker without tourism would strike most Belizeans as ludicrous. Today, many islanders operate tourism-related businesses, but there are no plans for large-scale development. Caulker residents enjoy the slow rhythm of life as much as visitors do.

◉ Sights

Caulker village has three main north–south streets: Front, Middle and Back Sts. The streets are now officially called Avenidas Hicaco, Langosta and Mangle, though you're unlikely to hear the new names used.

In 1961 Hurricane Hattie carved 'the Split' through the island just north of the village. North of the Split is mostly undeveloped (although not for much longer, as the land has been subdivided for housing). A few folk live on the North Island just over the Split. The most northerly part of Caulker is the Caye Caulker Forest Reserve.

Caye Caulker Marine Reserve   MARINE RESERVE
🐟 Declared a marine reserve in 1998, the 61-sq-mile Caye Caulker Marine Reserve includes the portion of the barrier reef that runs parallel to the island, as well as the turtle-grass lagoon adjacent to the Caye Caulker Forest Reserve. Although the reef is regenerating after patchy hurricane damage, it is rich with sea life, including colorful sponges, blue-and-yellow queen angel fish, Christmas tree worms, star coral, redband parrotfish, yellow gorgonians and more. Between April and September snorkelers and divers might even spot a turtle or a manatee. All local snorkel and dive operators lead tours to the Caye Caulker Marine Reserve.

Caye Caulker
Forest Reserve   NATURE RESERVE
🐟 The northernmost 100 acres of the island constitute the Caye Caulker Forest Reserve, also declared in 1998. The littoral forest on Caye Caulker is mostly red, white and black mangrove, which grows in the shallow water. The mangroves' root systems support an intricate ecosystem, including sponges,

Caye Caulker

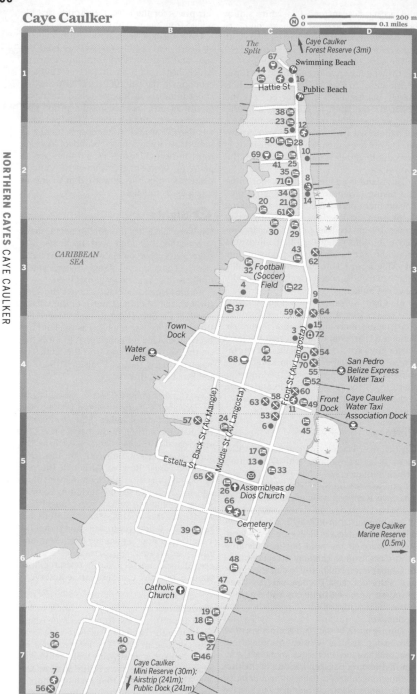

The Split

Caye Caulker
Forest Reserve (3mi)

Swimming Beach

Public Beach

Hattie St

CARIBBEAN
SEA

Football
(Soccer)
Field

Town
Dock

Water
Jets

Front St (Av Langosta)

San Pedro
Belize Express
Water Taxi

Front
Dock

Caye Caulker
Water Taxi
Association Dock

Back St (Av Mangle)

Middle St (Av Langosta)

Estella St

Assembleas de
Dios Church

Cemetery

Caye Caulker
Marine Reserve
(0.5mi)

Catholic
Church

Cave Caulker
Mini Reserve (30m);
Airstrip (241m);
Public Dock (241m)

Caye Caulker

gorgonians, anemones and a wide variety of fish. Besides the mangroves, the forest contains buttonwood, gumbo-limbo (the 'tourist tree'), poisonwood, madre de cacao, ficus and ziracote. Coconut palms and Australian pines are not native to this region, but there is no shortage of them.

Birdlife is prolific in the mangrove swamp, especially wading birds such as the tricolored heron and songbirds including the mangrove warbler. Somewhat rare species that can be spotted include the white-crowned pigeon, rufus-necked rail and black catbird. Inland lagoons provide habitat for crocodiles and turtles, all five species of crab, boa constrictors, scaly tailed iguanas (locally called 'wish willies'), geckos and lizards.

The forest reserve is an excellent (if ambitious) destination for a kayaker. Many places to stay have kayaks available for their guests; otherwise, you can rent one from Chocolate's Gift Shop (p118). You may prefer to paddle up the calmer west side of the island to avoid strong winds and rough seas. There is a visitors/research center and picnic area, and a platform trail through the mangrove forest.

Swallow Caye Wildlife Sanctuary
MARINE RESERVE

(☑ 226-0151; www.swallowcayemanatees.org; adult/child BZ$10/5) ✎ About 19 miles southwest of Caye Caulker, the vast Swallow Caye Wildlife Sanctuary spans nearly 9000 acres, including Swallow Caye and some parts of nearby Drowned Caye. Here the ocean floor is covered with turtle-grass beds, which support a small population of West Indian manatees.

For years guides have been bringing tourists to this spot in the hope of catching a glimpse of these gentle creatures as they chow down on the turtle grass. But the constant traffic put stress on the habitat, having the unintended effect of harming the manatees. After tireless efforts on the part of conservationists and guides, a wildlife sanctuary was finally established in 2002.

Now strict guidelines are in place to protect the manatees and to encourage them to stay in the area. Swimming with manatees is now forbidden by the Belizean authorities and signs have been posted to dissuade boat operators from using their motors near the manatees and from speeding through the area. (Propeller injuries are one of the chief causes of manatee deaths.) There is a permanent caretaker in these waters, although some complain that this is not enough to adequately enforce regulations.

Nonetheless, those who monitor the manatees are encouraged by the increase in numbers at Swallow Caye. Patient visitors are usually rewarded with several sightings of breeching and feeding manatees, often including a mother and calf swimming together.

🏃 Activities

Activity on the island focuses on water sports and sea life.

Diving

Common dives made from Caye Caulker include two-tank dives to the local reef (BZ$170 to BZ$200); two-tank dives in the Hol Chan Marine Reserve (p82) area (BZ$180, plus a BZ$20 marine-park fee); three dives off Turneffe Atoll (BZ$250 to BZ$330); and three-dive trips to the Blue Hole Natural Monument and Half Moon Caye (BZ$300, plus BZ$80 for park fees).

Belize Diving Services
DIVING

(☑ 226-0143; http://belizedivingservices.net) Professional and highly recommended dive shop that runs PADI-certification courses and Advanced Open Water courses. It specializes in excellent trips to Turneffe Elbow, but doesn't go to the Blue Hole. It is Belize's only technical training center.

Frenchie's Diving
DIVING

(☑ 226-0234; www.frenchiesdivingbelize.com) Offers full-day trips (three dives) to Blue Hole and Turneffe, and half-day trips (two dives) to Hol Chan, Caye Chapel or Spanish Bay. Night dives at Caye Caulker Marine Reserve cost BZ$120. It promises groups of 10 divers or fewer.

Snorkeling

It is possible to snorkel around the Split and off the pier near the airstrip, but to really experience life under the sea it's necessary to sign up with a tour operator and go out to the reef. Even though it is only a short boat ride offshore, only licensed guides are permitted to take snorkelers out to the reef, which aids in protecting this fragile ecosystem. Most guides are knowledgeable about the reef and adept at spotting and identifying many hidden creatures.

The most popular destination for snorkeling trips is Hol Chan Marine Reserve (p82) and Shark Ray Alley. Half-day trips (BZ$60) leave at 9:30am or 10:30am and 2pm. Full-day tours (BZ$100) include a stop in San Pedro for lunch (not included in the price).

Other half-day snorkeling trips visit the Caye Caulker Marine Reserve (BZ$60), departing at 10:30am and 2pm. Destinations include Coral Gardens, the Swoosh (a stand of coral near an opening in the reef where the current and swells attract a good variety of marine life) and Shark Ray Village, Caulker's own shark and ray habitat.

Some tour operators also take snorkel groups to Turneffe Atoll, a longer trip that promises a more pristine reef and an even greater variety of fish. Dedicated snorkel tours to Blue Hole and Lighthouse Reef are rare, although snorkelers are usually welcome to tag along with dive boats.

All of the tour operators in town take groups snorkeling, as do the sailing companies.

Carlos Tours
ADVENTURE

(☑ 226-0458, 600-1654; carlosayala10@hotmail.com; Front St; ♿) Carlos is an accomplished underwater photographer and offers all his guests a CD featuring photographs from their snorkel outing.

Anwar Snorkel & Tours TOUR COMPANY
(☑ 226-0327; www.anwartours.page.tl; Front St)
Well recommended.

Mario's Tours TOUR COMPANY
(☑ 226-0056, 602-1773; mariostours@yahoo.com;
Front St)

Manatee-Watching
Tours are available to monitor the manatees'
journey to Swallow Caye Wildlife Sanctuary,
and are followed by one or two snorkeling
stops and a lunch break at Sergeant's Caye
or Goff's Caye. If you don't have any luck
spotting manatees in the morning, the boat
might return to Swallow Caye in the afternoon to give it another go. The tour usually
lasts from 9am until 4pm and costs BZ$120
to BZ$150.

Chocolate Heredia was one of the first
Caulker fishermen to begin ferrying backpackers out to Swallow Caye on his fishing
boat. He has also played a crucial role in the
establishment of the wildlife sanctuary and
the continued protection of the sea mammals. **Chocolate** (☑ 226-0151; chocolate@btl.
net; Front St) still leads excellent and informative tours, however sporadically.

Red Mangrove Eco Adventures ECOTOUR
(☑ 226-0069; www.mangrovebelize.com) 🌿 Takes
groups to Swallow Caye.

E-Z Boy TOUR COMPANY
(☑ 226-0349; ezboytours_bze@yahoo.com) Takes
groups to Swallow Caye.

Sailing
Several companies organize sailing trips,
most of which are run in a similar fashion to
the snorkel tours, visiting two or three different sites – usually Caye Caulker Marine
Reserve and Hol Chan Marine Reserve – and
stopping somewhere for lunch. At BZ$90,
the price is similar to the regular snorkel
tours, but the difference is that your journey
will be wind powered. In general, the sailboats are large, meaning they can take larger groups than the little motorboats other
tour operators might use.

In addition to the snorkeling trips,
these companies might offer sunset cruises (BZ$40) and moonlight sailing trips
(BZ$60). Island-hopping trips include
overnight excursions to Lighthouse Reef
or Turneffe Atoll, as well as multiday
trips to the southern cayes and Placencia
(BZ$600). These tours usually involve one

LOBSTERFEST
Caulker hosts the original Northern
Cayes **Lobsterfest**, which kicks off
lobster-fishing season on June 15. The
streets are filled with *punta* drumming,
Belikin beer and grilled lobster. Other
activities include a fishing tournament,
canoe races, dance performances and –
of course – the Lobster Festival Pageant.

or two nights camping on the beach, as well
as plenty of snorkel stops.

Reef Watersports WATER SPORTS
(☑ 635-7219; www.reefwatersports.com; Avenida
Hicaco) This newly opened shop located right
at the split offers Jet Ski rentals (BZ$140
per ½ hour). It also does various packages
including wakeboarding and waterskiing.
Check the website for package details.

Raggamuffin Tours BOAT TOUR
(☑ 226-0348; www.raggamuffintours.com; Front St)
All-day trips to Turneffe Atoll cost BZ$150.
Three day sailing and camping trips to Placencia depart every Tuesday and Friday. Raggamuffin's has a reputation as a party boat.

Blackhawk Sailing Tours SAILING
(☑ 607-0323; blackhawksailingtours@hotmail.
com; Front St) Locally owned and operated
since 2000, Blackhawk does sailing/snor-
keling tours, overnight sailing trips and
sunset cruises.

Seahawk Sailing BOAT TOUR
(☑ 607-0323; www.nickmela.com/seahawk; Front
St) Fondly known as 'Aqua Man,' captain
Steve Wright is a Caye Caulker native who
invites tourists onto his 30ft sailboat.

Swimming
Hurricanes Mitch and Keith in 1998 and
2000, respectively, left strips of sand on
Caye Caulker where there once were sea
shrubs, and local authorities have also built
up sandy beaches. However, sea grass lies
under the water along much of the shore,
which doesn't make for pleasant wading or
swimming; you'll find the best swimming is
off the end of the docks that line the east
side of the island. The docks are supposed
to be public, but hotel owners have become
proprietorial, putting up gates to give privacy to their guests who use the sun lounges
and deck chairs provided.

Caye Caulker's **public beach** is at the northern end of the village at the Split. It's a popular spot for both tourists and locals, who drink at the Lazy Lizard and do cannonballs from the new diving board. The beach is small and scattered with debris – sunbathers lounge on a broken seawall that is crumbling into the ocean – but the water is cool and clean, thanks to the currents that pass through the Split. You can snorkel around here, but beware of boats cruising through deeper water on the north shore.

If you prefer to catch your rays without the clamor of crowds, there is a lesser-known **public dock** south of town, near the airstrip. The water is clear of sea grass, but fish hover in the shade underneath the dock, making for decent snorkeling. That said, getting out of the water is a bit precarious. There is no ladder, so you must wade in through the foliage or try to climb out onto the dock.

The surf breaking on the barrier reef is easily visible from the eastern shore of Caye Caulker. Don't attempt to swim out to it, as powerful boats speed through these waters. Crocodiles live in the waters on the west side of the island.

Windsurfing & Kitesurfing

With an easterly wind blowing much of the time, and its shallow waters protected by the barrier reef, Caulker has superb conditions for windsurfing and kitesurfing, especially between November and July. To rent equipment or sign up for lessons visit **Kitexplorer** ($226-4613; www.kitexplorer.com; Front St), which offers a three-hour introductory course (BZ$300) or a nine-hour basic course (BZ$740), as well as equipment rental for windsurfing (per hour BZ$34 to BZ$50). Experienced kiteboarders can sign up for a Kitesafari (half-/full-day BZ$160/300), which allows you to spend the whole time surfing downwind, stopping for a rest and lunch at remote islands along the way.

Fishing

Just about any skipper will take you fishing, and it's cheaper from here than from Ambergris Caye. Grand Slams are not unusual (catching permit, tarpon and bonefish all in one day); other fish often caught include snook, barracuda, snapper and shark, usually on a catch-and-release basis. If you venture out for deep-sea fishing, look for wahoo, sailfish, kingfish, snapper, grouper, jacks, shark and barracuda.

Half-/full-day fly-fishing or deep-sea fishing trips for two to three people run at BZ$400/600. Anglers Abroad and Tsunami Adventures will take anglers out for fishing in the deep water, flats or reef.

Anglers Abroad   FISHING
($226-0602; www.anglersabroad.com; Hattie St) Also offers adventurous overnight fishing and camping trips. If there's nobody in the office head to the Sea Dreams Hotel next door to arrange your tour.

Tsunami Adventures   ADVENTURE TOUR
($226-0462; www.tsunamiadventures.com; Front St) Bring home some barracuda, grouper or snapper; guided by retired fisherman Rolly Rosado. Tsunami also does a wide range of other tours.

Hiking, Cycling & Birding

Swim or paddle across the Split to reach the **north side**, as it is called, which is still untouched by the tourist boom. Only a handful of residents live along the main road, meaning there is plenty of opportunity for exploring the more remote parts, and spotting birds and even crocodiles. Alternatively, paddle all the way up to the northern end of the island to the Caye Caulker Forest Reserve (p105), which has a short trail that leads through the mangrove forest. It is an excellent place to spot water birds, including rails, stilts and herons, as well as ospreys and mangrove warblers.

The southern part of the island is also relatively undeveloped, especially in the interior, despite the fact that houses are being built along the coastline south of the airstrip. A rough trail suitable for hiking or biking follows the perimeter of the **southern tip**, beginning and ending at the airstrip. The airstrip itself is flanked on both sides by swampy marshland, making it a fantastic place to spot birds, including the killdeer, the black-necked stilt, the common black hawk and herons of all kinds. Be on the lookout for airplanes that fly in and out of here without paying much heed to who or what might be on the airstrip.

Just north of the airstrip, the **Caye Caulker Mini Reserve** is run by the Caye Caulker branch of the Belize Tourism Industry Association (BTIA). The small **visitors center** ($226-2251; ⊗9am-noon) has information on the island's flora and fauna, and a short interpretative trail (open 24 hours) runs through the littoral forest.

Spas

After swimming, snorkeling and sunning, you may be in need of a little hands-on healing.

Coco Plum Gardens   DAY SPA

(☑226-0226; www.cocoplum.typepad.com; Back St; ⊙8am-5pm) From chakra balancing and tarot readings to tropical-fruit facials and body massages. The octagon-shaped day spa was built from indigenous hardwoods and is set amid the lush garden of the Coco Plum.

Healing Touch Day Spa   DAY SPA

(☑206-0380; Front St; ⊙9am-5pm) Ms Eva Mc-Farlane can take care of all your beauty and body needs, including manicures and pedicures, Reiki, reflexology, body scrubs and aromatherapy.

🦾 Tours

Although most tour operators have their own specialties, many offer similar versions of the same trips. Prices are also similar. Most tour operators work closely together, consolidating tours on slow days and juggling overflow at busier times. Snorkel gear, water and fruit are included in the price of most boat trips.

Aside from boat tours, some companies also organize trips to the Belizean mainland, including those involving zip lining, cave-tubing and visiting Maya sites at Lamanai and Altun Ha.

The companies listed here are generalists, offering a wide variety of tours by land and sea.

Tsunami Adventures (p110) offers fishing and a wide range of other tours, including mainland trips, night tours of Caulker, scenic flights over the Blue Hole and various island-hopping trips.

E-Z Boy (p109) and **Red Mangrove Eco Adventures** (p109) take groups to Swallow Caye.

Contour   PADDLE BOARDING

(☑653-8515; www.contourbelize.com; Playa Ascencion/Front St) This newly opened shop brings something different to the world of Caulker Aquatic Recreation, taking visitors on sunset tours on a paddleboard. In addition to multi-hour tours, Contour also rents boards for BZ$36 per hour (with discounts for longer rentals), and provides free lessons.

Little Kitchen Adventure Tours   BOAT TOUR

(☑620-8086; littlekitchentours@gmail.com; Marvin Gainy St) Roy and Elisia's Little Kitchen

Adventure Tours does trips all around the area, including manatee tours, full-day sailing trips, sunset cruises and more. Call or email for prices.

Anda De Wata Tours   ADVENTURE TOUR

(☑666-7374; Luciano Reyes St) Does floating on an inner tube pulled behind a slow-moving boat sound like a dream come true? Anda De Wata's 90-minute boat-and-float tour (BZ$50) may be your own personal paradise! It also offers a variety of interesting snorkeling tours around local reefs.

Liberty Sailing Tours   SAILING TOUR

(☑206-0407; www.libertysailingtours.com) Does three-day sailing/camping trips to Placencia, camping out on cayes along the way. Outlay BZ$700 to cover everything from food to fishing/snorkeling gear and camping equipment.

🛏 Sleeping

Golf-cart taxis meet boats and flights upon arrival; they will take you around to look at a few places to stay. It's best to book in advance if you're coming at Christmas or Easter.

📍 Central Area

As you wander up Front St, you will see that there is an endless array of accommodation options (mostly budget), as local business owners rent out one or two rooms above or behind their shops.

Trends Beachfront Hotel   HOTEL $

(☑226-0094; www.trendsbze.com; r BZ$76-87) Trimmed in pink and blue, Trends is the first place you'll see when you step off the water taxi. With wide porches and vast shady grounds, it is a fantastic spot for watching the comings and goings on the island (and to and from the island). Rooms are simple and fresh, and come equipped with two double beds, ceiling fan and mini-fridge, but not much in the way of decoration. The idea – undoubtedly – is to get outside and enjoy the view.

Yuma's House Belize   HOSTEL $

(☑206-0019; www.yumashousebelize.com; Front St; dm/s/d BZ$27/55/62; 🛜) Formerly known as Tina's, this fun and funky hostel is just a few steps from the water-taxi dock, giving it a prime location in the center of town and at the water's edge. Yuma takes full advantage of the beachfront property, reserving a dock for guests and stringing up hammocks in the leafy garden. Crowded dorm rooms have fresh paint and new beds and mattresses. Shared facilities include two fully equipped kitchens, games and cold-water showers.

Dirty McNasty's Hostel
HOSTEL $

(☑636-7512; Crocodile St; dm BZ$28, d $66) What backpacker (or travel writer) could resist a place called Dirty McNasty's? Despite the name, this newly opened (indeed, only partially finished, with obvious expansion in the works) place is neither especially unhygienic nor foul, though there is a certain raffish pirate-ship quality about the place. Dorms and double rooms are clean enough, though obviously hostel-basic, and all rooms are equipped with hot showers for when things get too dirty and/or nasty.

Mara's Place
GUESTHOUSE $

(☑600-0080; 27 Front St; d BZ$93; @☏) The eight guest rooms in this two-story wooden structure are simple but spotless, cramped but comfortable. Not exactly luxurious, they nonetheless include a few perks you would not expect, such as a private verandah complete with hammock and reading material. There is a communal kitchen on the premises, and the sandy beach is right across the street, where Mara's has a private dock with lounge chairs and hammocks.

Bella's Hostel
HOSTEL $

(☑226-0360; bellas.hostel@yahoo.com; dm/d BZ$20/50, camping BZ$15; ☏) On the back side of the island, Bella's is a hideaway for the backpacker set, who can camp on the shady grounds or snag a bed in the lofty bunkhouse. You are likely to see travelers sharing a meal in the kitchen, playing cards on the balcony and taking advantage of free stuff such as canoes and bikes.

Ocean Pearl Royale Hotel
HOTEL $

(☑226-0074; oceanpearl@btl.net; Park St; r BZ$55-80, cabaña BZ$100; ❊☏) Located on a quiet side street, this small hotel is surrounded by sandy grounds strewn with palms and flowering trees that attract hummingbirds and other beauties. The 10 clean rooms are remarkably good value, with brightly painted walls and simple wood furnishings. A big airy lobby offers space for guests to congregate and swap island stories. The *cabaña* has a kitchenette. Free wi-fi and coffee in the morning makes this a great deal!

Jerimiah's Inn
HOTEL $

(☑630-3854; Front St; d with/without bathroom BZ$55/44; ☏) Another good budget choice, fan-cooled rooms at this small hotel right on the main drag are comfortable enough (though somewhat Spartan), surrounding a shared courtyard. Though across from the beach, a central location assures that you're never more than a stone's throw from Caulker's many aquatic attractions.

Tropical Oasis
HOSTEL $

(☑629-0511; karianne_mokkelbost@hotmail.com; La Posa St; dm BZ$25, cottage BZ$50) Perfect for backpackers, this ramshackle collection of huts and trailers offers dorms, cottages and even an outdoor kitchen centered around a communal outdoor chill-out spot.

Chinatown Hotel
HOTEL $

(☑226-0228; www.chinatownhotelbelize.com; Estella St; r BZ$55-100; ☏) This centrally located hotel has clean rooms with cable TV and aircon. Though nothing fancy, there's a decent Chinese restaurant and a cool bar with slot machines in the lobby.

★Sea Dreams Hotel
B&B $$

(☑226-0602; www.seadreamshotel.com; r BZ$210, apt BZ$310-410; ❊☏) A lovely guesthouse on the back side of the island, Sea Dreams offers a rare combination of easy access and sweet tranquility. Spend the day lounging around the Split, then retreat to the cozy accommodation just a few steps away. Original paintings by local artists adorn the colorful walls of the rooms and apartments, which are small but comfortable. Guests are invited to enjoy glorious sunset views from the private dock or over drinks at the rooftop lounge. Breakfast, bike and canoe use are included.

Amanda's Place
GUESTHOUSE $$

(☑226-0029; www.cayecaulkerrentals.com; Front St; apt from BZ$180; ❊☏☀) Amanda offers two art-filled apartments with kitchenettes and a cozy *casita*. Only a block back from the beach, the grounds are leafy and the attractive apartments each have a little porch from where you can watch street life and see the ocean.

Island Magic
HOTEL $$

(☑226-0505; www.islandmagicbelize.com; Front St; r BZ$220-260, penthouse 1-/2-bedroom BZ$370/570; ❊☏☀⛱) Offering excellent value for its accommodations and amenities, Island Magic has 10 spacious, earth-toned rooms with fully equipped kitchens and dining areas, with more expensive rooms offering glorious ocean views from their private balconies. Island Magic's two penthouse suites offer even more lovely views of the sea and surrounding island. The swanky swimming pool is one of the nicest on the island, though the fence blocks the view of the sea.

Seaside Cabanas
RESORT **$$**

(☑ 226-0498; www.seasidecabanas.com; r BZ$210, cabaña BZ$238-318; ✳ 🐾 ☀) Sun-yellow stucco buildings shaded by thatched-palm roofs exude a tropical atmosphere at this beachfront beauty. The interior decor features desert colors, rich fabrics and plenty of pillows. Most of the rooms occupy the main building facing the ocean; closer to the sea, concrete *cabañas* take advantage of the location with private rooftop decks; more expensive ones have terrace Jacuzzis.

Costa Maya Beach Cabanas
CABINS **$$**

(☑ 226-0432; www.tsunamiadventures.com; Front St; d BZ$110-130, apt BZ$150; ✳ 🐾 ⊞) Six two-story beachfront hexagon-shaped *cabañas* are clustered around a sandy courtyard. The wood-paneled interiors of the cheaper units are gloomy but each unit has a porch, perfect for catching sea breezes. The pricier beachfront units are fitted with kitchenettes, cable TV, air-con and private patios with wonderful views. Guests enjoy complimentary bicycles, beach chairs, swimming dock and canoes, as well as discounts on tours at Tsunami Adventures (p110).

De Real Macaw Guest House
GUESTHOUSE **$$**

(☑ 226-0459; www.derealmacaw.biz; Front St; r BZ$100-140, apt BZ$260; ✳ 🐾 ⊞) All the rustic lodgings dotting the leafy grounds here are inspired by the jungle, from *cabañas* built from pimenta sticks to the beachfront rooms with thatched-roof verandas. The decor continues with swinging hammocks and woven tapestries, but these rooms are also equipped with modern conveniences such as TVs, fridges and coffee makers. The main property is in a great central spot opposite the beach; additional apartments are in a less appealing location on Back St.

Casa Rosado
CABINS **$$**

(☑ 226-0029; www.cayecaulkerrentals.com; cabaña BZ$135-150, cabaña with kitchenette BZ$190; ✳ ⊞) Painted in pastels and trimmed with a seashell theme, these sweet cabins occupy a (usually) quiet spot overlooking the soccer field. Each is equipped with a shady porch and a comfy hammock, though lack ocean breezes.

Blue Wave
GUESTHOUSE **$$**

(☑ 206-0114; www.bluewaveguesthouse.com; Front St; d with/without bathroom BZ$150/140; ✳) Look for the attractive log-cabin-style house overlooking Front St, and you'll know you've arrived at the Blue Wave, an inviting guesthouse with several different accommodation options. 'Deluxe' rooms are spacious and stylish, with air-con, TV, private bathrooms and breezy balconies. Beneath the owners' clapboard house, there are three cheaper rooms with shared facilities.

Rainbow Hotel
HOTEL **$$**

(☑ 226-0123; www.rainbowhotel-cayecaulker.com; Front St; d BZ$200-230; ✳ 🐾) Bright blue paint, a couple of rainbows for decoration and upgraded rooms make this bunkerlike concrete building relatively appealing. Bottom-floor rooms open right onto the street, so you can sit out front and enjoy the street life. For privacy, choose a room on the top floor or rent one of the cottages (BZ$230 to BZ$280 for up to four people) at the back. All rooms have flat screen TVs, mini-fridges and coffee makers.

Pancho's Villas
HOTEL **$$**

(☑ 226-0304; www.panchosvillasbelize.com; Pasero St; d with/without kitchenette BZ$180/130; ✳ ✳ 🐾) Resembling a big square wedding cake with lemon-yellow frosting, Pancho's Villas is a little out of place on this quiet side street. The new building is decked out with all the modern amenities, such as kitchenettes, cable TV and the rest. Big on comfort and convenience, but small on style and sophistication.

Caye Caulker Plaza Hotel
HOTEL **$$**

(☑ 226-0780; cayecaulkerplazahotel.com; Av Langosta / Calle Al Sol; r BZ$120-200; ✳ 🐾 ⊞) This 32-room hotel offers good amenities including private bathrooms with hot showers, cable TV, in-room safes and mini refrigerators in every room. More expensive rooms have private balconies, while cheaper ones are on the ground floor. The beautiful rooftop terrace is open to all. Staff is friendly, and the location is central.

Leeside Rooms
GUESTHOUSE **$$**

(☑ 226-0020; www.cayecaulkerrentals.com; r BZ$150-170; ✳ 🐾) Boasting the island's most beautiful sunset view, these simple rooms have small verandas that overlook a small private beach and dock. Located on the back side of the island, there is less noise and less light than on Front St. The stylish interior design features high beds, tiled floors and walls hung with old maps. All rooms have cable TV, and management provides free bicycles and kayaks for guests.

★ **Caye Reef**   BOUTIQUE HOTEL **$$$**
(☑ 226-0381; www.cayereef.com; Front St; 1-bedroom apt BZ$330-400, 2-bedroom apt BZ$400-470; ❖ 🛜 ❄ ♿) The six apartments at Caye Reef have been designed with the utmost attention to detail – from the original artwork hanging on the walls to the swinging hammocks hanging on the private balconies. Room prices rise with the floor, with the most expensive rooms being on the 3rd floor. As comfortable and classy as they are, the apartments are not the main attraction of staying at Caye Reef. That would be the roof deck, complete with hammocks, hot tub and 360-degree sea views.

Iguana Reef Inn   RESORT **$$$**
(☑ 226-0213; www.iguanareefinn.com; standard r BZ$270-290, deluxe r BZ$310-330; ❖ 🛜 ❄) Set on sandy grounds fringed with palms, the Iguana Reef is both upscale and informal. It's the kind of place you can roam around barefoot by day but you might dress up for dinner. Bamboo furniture, Mexican tapestries and local artwork adorn the jewel-toned rooms. Outside, you can lounge poolside or swing in a hammock; at the end of the day, take your pick from the extensive menu of tropical cocktails in the *palapa* bar and watch the sunset. Breakfast included.

Jan's Place   GUESTHOUSE **$$$**
(☑ 226-0173; www.jansplace.net; Front St; apt BZ$250; ❖ 🛜 ♿) This charming yellow clapboard house has two self-contained apartments facing the sea; private porches with hammocks ensure maximum appreciation of this gorgeous view. Apartments contain kitchenettes, a dining area, two full-sized beds and mahogany furniture – not super fancy but very functional. In the grounds there is also a three-bedroom house available for rent (BZ$400 per night, three-night minimum) for families or groups.

Caye Caulker Condos   HOTEL **$$$**
(☑ 226-0072; www.cayecaulkercondos.com; Front St; ste BZ$240-270; ❖ 🛜 ❄ ♿) Inside this attractive salmon-colored concrete block on Front St sit eight sweet retreat suites. Each has a fully equipped kitchen, satellite TV and fancy bathrooms with romantic two-person showers made of stone. Suites each have a private balcony, and the rooftop terrace, with its 360-degree views, is an amazing feature (as is the property's lovely swimming pool).

🛏 South of Town

South of the cemetery, Caye Caulker is noticeably quieter and the beach sees much less foot traffic. Almost all of the accommodations south of town are in the midrange price bracket. The back streets at the south end of town are known as 'Gringo Heights,' for this is where many expats have bought property and built houses, and, with names such as 'Hummingbird Hideaway' and 'Canuck Cottage,' many of them are available for longer-term rentals (three days or more) via **Caye Caulker Rentals** (☑ 630-1008; www.cayecaulkerrentals.com).

Ignacio Beach Cabins   CABINS **$**
(☑ 226-0175; http://aguallos.com/ignaciobeach; d BZ$30-45, ste BZ$110; 🛜) In the far south of town, Ignacio offers simple waterfront lodging in weathered cabins on stilts. There is little foot traffic this far south, so it feels private and pristine. The cold-shower cabins all have easy access to the beach, but the pricier ones are at the water's edge, catching cool breezes and salty scents. Besides the great views from the verandas, the cabins, cheerfully painted though Spartan, are not without a certain rustic charm.

Tom's Hotel   HOTEL **$**
(☑ 226-0102; d without bathroom BZ$30, cabañas BZ$60; ❖) Owned by a local fishing family, this trim hotel south of the cemetery has long been a budget favorite, thanks to the private pier, rooftop deck and always affable management. The cheapest rooms are in the concrete building, with a wide shady veranda on which to meet your fellow travelers and enjoy the sea breeze. Otherwise, upgrade to the cozy *cabañas* with private facilities.

★ **Barefoot Beach Belize**   GUESTHOUSE **$$**
(☑ 226-0205; www.barefootbeachbelize.com; r BZ$138-158, ste BZ$258, cottages BZ$258; ❖ 🛜) Painted in candy colors, this perky place is on a quiet stretch of beach at the southern end of the village. Suites and cottages have kitchens and living space, with direct access to beach breezes; rooms are smaller but still spacious, with fridges, air-con and coffee makers. The whole place has a tropical theme, with plenty of floral prints and sea-themed artwork. Hammocks hang under a thatched-roof *palapa* at the end of a long deck, offering a perfect place to while away an afternoon. Your host, Susan Pelt, will make sure you have a great stay.

★**Maxhapan Cabanas** CABINS **$$**
(✆226-0118; maxhapan04@hotmail.com; 55 Av Pueblo Nuevo; s/d BZ$110/130; ✳🕙) In an unexpected location south of town, Maxhapan has sweet yellow *cabañas* clustered around a shady courtyard. At its center, a big *palapa* has hammocks and a bring-your-own bar, where guests can gather. Natural light floods the comfortable cabins, which are equipped with fridges, fans and televisions. Your host, Louise, guarantees your comfort and happiness throughout your stay. The only drawback is that it's not on the water, which explains why it's such a bargain. Free bikes are a bonus.

Tree Tops Guesthouse GUESTHOUSE **$$**
(✆226-0240; www.treetopsbelize.com; r with/ without bathroom from BZ$223/123, ste BZ$225; ✳@🕙) For years Doris and Terry have been winning accolades for their hospitality and helpfulness. The cool, clean rooms are decorated with international themes and original artistic touches. Set back from the beach, the three-story building is fronted by a pleasant palm-shaded garden, while a roof terrace with panoramic vistas towers over the treetops, giving the place its name.

Oasi GUESTHOUSE **$$**
(✆623-9401; www.oasi-holidaysbelize.com; Back St; apt BZ$150-190; ✳🕙) Oasi is surrounded by blooming tropical gardens, with a lovely wide veranda (hung with hammocks, of course). Woven tapestries and warm hues enrich the interior of the apartments, which are equipped with full kitchens. Hosts Luciana and Michael go above and beyond to ensure you enjoy your stay, offering expert opinions about local snorkel and dive trips. The guesthouse is away from town and away from the waterfront, but free bikes make for an easy trip.

Shirley's Guest House CABINS **$$**
(✆226-0145; www.shirleysguesthouse.com; r with/ without bathroom BZ$130/100, cabins with bathroom BZ$150; 🕙) At the far end of the island, just north of the airstrip, is this sweet and secluded spot, which caters for adults only. Lush and lovingly maintained, the grounds are fenced off from the beach, which might increase security but it does detract from the island's easygoing vibe. Five rooms are housed in the cottages, each with a sensational sunrise view. The wood-paneled interiors are simple, but fitted with fans, coffee makers and other necessities (as well as plenty of notices to keep guests in line).

Colinda Cabanas CABAÑA **$$**
(✆226-0383; www.colindacabanas.com; Playa Ascension; r BZ$98-278; ✳🕙) It's hard to miss Colin and Linda's brightly colored yellow and blue property, which sits south of the cemetery. The five *cabañas* and five suites are all nicely appointed with minifridges, coffee makers, hot showers and comfy double and single beds. The suite has a full kitchen and air-conditioning. All have balconies and hammocks.

Anchorage Resort HOTEL **$$**
(✆206-0304; www.anchorageresort.com; s/d/ tr/q BZ$134/158/182/206; ✳🕙🏊) This is not the place to come for style or swank, but if you're in search of a hammock strung from a coconut palm or a wooden pier stretching out to the sea to swim, snorkel or fish from, look no further. With floral bedspreads and dormitory furniture, the rooms are not going to win any design awards, but they are equipped with plenty of perks, such as king-sized beds, cable TV and private balconies with glorious sea views. The resort boasts one of the most beautiful stretches of beach on the island.

Tropical Paradise Hotel RESORT **$$**
(✆226-0124; www.tropicalparadise.bz; Front St; r BZ$86-100, cabins BZ$120-140, ste BZ$180-260; ✳🕙) With an ideal location just south of the cemetery, Tropical Paradise Hotel is Caulker's 'original beach resort.' It was one of the first places to clean out a stretch of sand, furnish it with painted lounge chairs and entice guests with fruity cocktails. These days there are plenty of more stylish places to stay, but these colorful clapboard cottages still offer decent value, especially when the various discounts for advanced booking are taken into account. The restaurant is a perennially popular place for guests to meet.

Lazy Iguana B&B **$$**
(✆226-0350; www.lazyiguana.net; d BZ$210; ✳🕙) Located on the island's southwest side, this place is off the beaten track and away from the beach. But you won't miss out on sea views: just head up to the rooftop patio for 360-degree panoramas. The four guest rooms – fitted with dark wood furniture and tiled floors – are prettily decorated in tones of gold, sage and cream. Common space includes two cool and comfy lounges, as well as a leafy garden overflowing with orchids.

✖ Eating

Indulge in the creatures of the sea, including spiny tail lobsters, shrimp, conch and all the fish of the reef. Seafood lovers take note: lobster season runs from mid-June to mid-February, and conch season runs from October to June only. There are plenty of street eats in Caulker, from ad-hoc beachside grills to the island's famous 'Cake Lady,' who shows up on Front St with a push cart filled with amazing homemade cakes right around dusk.

Pizza Caulker   PIZZERIA $
(☑206-0666; Front St; slice BZ$8; ☺lunch & dinner; ☑🍴) The sandy floor and reggae music lend a cool Rasta vibe to this friendly pizza place. Pizzas have crispy crust and light sauces, and takeout is available. If you choose to dine in, the bar serves potent rum drinks, with a two-for-one special every day until 7pm.

Glenda's Café   BELIZEAN $
(Back St; mains BZ$5-10; ☺breakfast & lunch Mon-Fri) Glenda's serves traditional Belizean food in a clapboard house on the island's west side. It has the best cheap breakfasts in town, from cinnamon rolls and orange juice to full breakfasts of bacon or ham, eggs, bread and coffee. Burritos, tacos, sandwiches and chicken with rice and beans are offered for lunch. Get there early for breakfast.

Barrier Reef
Sports Bar & Grill   INTERNATIONAL $$
(www.belizesportsbar.com; Front St; mains BZ$18-30; ☺9am-midnight; 🛜) This unlikely Canadian-run spot has surprisingly delicious food and good prices. On the other hand, service is nonchalant, at best. If you don't like the multiple TVs blaring sports interviews into the atmosphere, take a seat out front and enjoy the breeze off the ocean.

Syd's   BELIZEAN, MEXICAN $$
(Middle St; mains BZ$15-30; ☺lunch & dinner Mon-Sat) Syd's is a longstanding favorite for its good-value meals and convivial atmosphere. Out back there is a flower-filled patio, where you can dine to the soothing sounds of a gurgling fountain. Otherwise, the dining room is rather nondescript. No matter where you sit, you will be sated by the big plates of Belizean and Mexican food.

Bambooze   SEAFOOD $$
(Waterfront; mains BZ$15-25; ☺lunch & dinner; 🍴) Arguably the best location on the island, this casually cool bar and grill sits right on the beach, with swings hanging from the rafters and tables set up in the sand. Besides the Cajun specialties, you can feast on a huge seafood burrito or a delectable grilled-fish sandwich, washed down with a fruit smoothie.

Coco Plum Gardens   CAFE $$
(☑226-0226; www.cocoplum.typepad.com; Back St; mains BZ$20-30; ☺breakfast & lunch Mon-Sat; ☑) The highlight of the Coco Plum is the beautiful garden setting, overgrown with hibiscus, sea grape and coco plum (spot the ceiba tree at the entrance). Located off Back St near the airstrip, Coco Plum is off the beaten track but worth the walk for home-baked breads and wholesome breakfasts.

Happy Lobster   SEAFOOD $$
(Front St; mains BZ$18-30; ☺breakfast, lunch & dinner Wed-Mon; ☑) The lobster at this Caulker institution is actually not that happy, but you will be after eating big plates of fresh fish, spiced with Creole flavoring or sweetened with coconut. The place has plenty of vegetarian options, as well as a popular breakfast menu, and the front porch is a pleasant place to catch the breeze off the ocean and watch the activity on Front St.

Rainbow Grill & Bar   SEAFOOD $$
(Waterfront; mains BZ$10-25; ☺lunch & dinner Tue-Sun; ☑) Perched on a deck over the turquoise waters, this local favorite is evidence of Caulker's agreeable temperatures. By day, nibble on vegetarian plates, burgers, quesadillas, burritos and sandwiches. At night fancier fare includes fish, shrimp, conch and lobster cooked how you like it, from simple lemon with butter to Jamaican jerk or oriental style.

★ Rosa's Grill   SEAFOOD $$
('the Dock St'; mains BZ$8-16; ☺breakfast, lunch & dinner; ☑) Take your pick from the selection of amazing fresh fish and lobster on display at this friendly streetside cafe. Then head out back to the shade of the *palapa* while staff grill it up for you. Family-style seating at big picnic tables makes for a fun, lively atmosphere, and you'll likely make friends with the wait staff and the other guests sharing your table.

Little Kitchen Restaurant   BELIZEAN $$
(☑667-2178; Marvin Gainy St; meals BZ$6-20; ☺lunch & dinner) Elisia Flower's Little Kitchen is a 3rd-floor open-air restaurant on

Caulker's southwestern side serving traditional (yet artfully done) Belizean dishes including curry shrimp, coconut red snapper and excellent conch fritters (just to name a few). Little Kitchen's unique vantage point makes it a fine spot to watch the sun go down with a cocktail made with local rum, ginger wine or a fresh juice.

Amor Y Café BREAKFAST **$$**
(Front St; mains BZ$8-12; ⊘ breakfast & lunch; 🖋️)
There's no contest about the most popular breakfast spot on the island – this place is always busy, but you won't have to wait long for a table on the shaded porch overlooking Front St. Take your pick from fresh-squeezed juices, scrambled eggs or homemade yogurt topped with fruit, and don't miss out on the fresh-brewed coffee. If you have to pack a lunch, sandwiches are available to go.

La Cubana CUBAN **$$**
(Front St; mains from BZ$12; ⊘ breakfast, lunch & dinner) It'd be hard to miss this cheery (unless you're a pig) place, whose most prominent feature almost daily is a skewered piglet in various states of the roasting process by the front door. La Cubana serves seafood, chicken and (gasp) even a range of vegetarian dishes. But what brings people here nightly is the roast pork. Perhaps the best deal here is the all-you-can-eat buffet (BZ$28), an awesome spread with a variety of veggie dishes, meat dishes, desserts and, of course, the baby pig.

★**Sandro** ITALIAN **$$**
(Waterfront; mains BZ$25; ⊘ dinner) Stop in during the day to let Sandro know you will be coming for dinner, and ensure your place at one of four tables at this charming seaside shack. The open kitchen means you can watch the Italian chef work his magic with fresh pasta, grilled seafood and homemade garlic bread. *Delicioso!*

Magandon ITALIAN **$$$**
(📋 226-0025; Front St; mains BZ$30-50; ⊘ dinner; 🖋️) Formerly known as Don Corleone, Magandon still serves excellent Italian dishes, including gorgeous salads, pastas with aromatic sauces and substantial fish or meat main dishes. Pizza lovers take note: Magandon makes a pretty darn good pie as well!

★**Habaneros** INTERNATIONAL **$$$**
(📋 620-4911; habanerosdream@gmail.com; cnr Front & 'the Dock St'; mains BZ$25-50; ⊘ dinner Fri-Wed) Caulker's 'hottest' restaurant,
named for the habanero chili, is located in a brightly painted clapboard house in the center of town. Here chefs prepare gourmet international food, combining fresh seafood, meat and vegetables with insanely delicious sauces and flavors. Wash it down with a fine wine or a jug of sangria. Sit in the funky bar and sip a fruity cocktail or enjoy the buzz and eat by candlelight at the tables on the veranda. Reservations are recommended.

🍷 Drinking

I&I Reggae Bar BAR
(⊘ 6pm-midnight) I&I is the island's most hip, happening spot after dark, when its healthy sound system belts out a reggae beat. Its three levels each offer a different scene, with a dance floor on one and swings hanging from the rafters on another. The top floor is the 'chill-out zone,' complete with hammocks and panoramic views. Great place for a sunset drink.

Lazy Lizard BEACH BAR
(the Split; ⊘ 10am-Midnight) The Lazy Lizard is described as a 'sunny place for shady people' – and there is no shortage of the latter hanging about. It mainly serves beer to swimmers and sunbathers, but the seafood is also recommended.

Wish Willy's Bar & Grill BAR
(⊘ 5pm-late) This funky place is named for a scaly tailed iguana. Located on the back side of the island, it's a great place to watch the sunset, whether you're sipping a Belikin beer or feasting on the day's BBQ special.

Sand Box BAR
(Front St; ⊘ 8am-late) With outdoor seating facing the dock, and a happy hour from 3pm to 6pm, the Sand Box is an island institution. Locals and expats gather to socialize and catch up on gossip. If you can't check into your hotel straight away, make this your first stop coming off the water taxi.

Perla Del Mar COFFEE
(Calle Del Sol; internet per hr BZ$9; ⊘ 7am-9pm; 📶) This cool little coffee shop offers wi-fi, six internet kiosks and lovely coffee drinks (hot, iced and frozen).

🛍️ Shopping

Caulker has a few shops selling T-shirts, beach gear and souvenirs, but this is not the best place for shopping. Keep your eye out for colorful paintings and handmade jewelry by local artists.

Caribbean Colors
ART

(www.caribbean-colors.com; Front St; ⊘7am-9pm; 🔊) This shop stocks a collection of silk-screened fabrics, jewelry and paintings by the owner and artist Lee Vanderwalker, as well as pieces by about a dozen other Belizean artists. While you browse you can treat yourself to a hot coffee (the best on the island, some say), a cool smoothie, or even freshly caught sushi at the onsite **Caribbean Colors Art Cafe.**

Chocolate's Gift Shop
JEWELRY, CLOTHING

(Front St) Chocolate's wife Annie has souvenirs with international flair: gorgeous hand-woven textiles from Mexico and Guatemala; sarongs and clothing from Indonesia and Malaysia; and jewelry made from precious and semiprecious stones.

Coco Plum Giftshop
ARTS & CRAFTS

(🖉226-0226; www.cocoplum.typepad.com; Back St) Sometimes a spa and sometimes a restaurant, the Coco Plum is also – sometimes – a gift shop. There is an eclectic assortment of tropical-themed paintings, unique jewelry, carved wood pieces and reference books on natural healing. If you don't want to trek all the way down here, check out the smaller branch store on Front St.

Cooper's Art Gallery
ART

(Front St; ⊘noon-8pm Wed-Sun) Debbie Cooper's primitive painting style is a huge hit with tourists, who appreciate her colorful depictions of island life. The whimsical frames are designed and painted by her husband.

❶ Information

EMERGENCY
Police (🖉911, 226-0179; Front St)

INTERNET ACCESS
Caye Caulker Cyber Café (Front St; per hr BZ$8; ⊘7am-10pm) Air-conditioned; has a bar with happy hour from 3pm to 6pm.

Cayeboard Connection (Front St; per hr BZ$12; ⊘8am-9pm) Also does printing, sells water and coffee, sells books and has a book exchange.

Island Link (Front St; per hr BZ$9) This is not an internet cafe, but rather an internet ice-cream parlor, a concept that's long overdue.

INTERNET RESOURCES
CayeCaulker.org (www.cayecaulker.org) Includes links to an active message board, travel hints and loads of info.

GoCayeCaulker.com (www.gocayecaulker.com) The official site of the Caye Caulker branch of the Belize Tourism Industry Association (BTIA).

Offical Caye Caulker Website (www.cayecaulkerbelize.net) The village council's site, which has news of upcoming events.

LAUNDRY
Caye Caulker Coin Laundromat ('the Dock St'; wash, dry & soap per load BZ$20; ⊘7am-9pm)

Marie's Laundry (Middle St; per 8lb BZ$10)

MEDICAL SERVICES
Caye Caulker Health Center (🖉226-0166) Just off Front St, two blocks south of 'the Dock St.' Operates on a donation basis.

MONEY
Atlantic Bank (Middle St; ⊘8am-2pm Mon-Fri, 8:30am-noon Sat) Offer cash advances, as well as an ATM that functions on Cirrus and other international networks. It's the only cash machine on the island and is somewhat temperamental, so make sure you have some cash before you arrive.

POST
Post office (Caye Caulker Health Center Bldg; ⊘8:30am-4:30pm Mon-Fri)

❶ Getting There & Away

AIR
Both **Maya Island Air** (🖉226-0012; www.mayaairways.com) and **Tropic Air** (🖉226-0040; www.tropicair.com) stop at Caye Caulker en route from San Pedro (adult/child BZ$61/46) to Philip Goldson International Airport (one way BZ$109). Each company has flights four or five times a day. The airline offices are at Caye Caulker's newly renovated airstrip at the southern end of the island. **Tsunami Adventures** (🖉226-0462; www.tsunamiadventures.com; Front St) can also book tickets.

BOAT
Any of these services will stop at St George's Caye and Caye Chapel, but you must request these stops or arrange pick-up in advance.

Caye Caulker Water Taxi Association (🖉226-0992; www.cayecaulkerwatertaxi.com) runs boats from the main dock at the foot of 'the Dock St'. Departs to Belize City (one way/round trip BZ$20/35, one hour) at 8:30am, 10am, 1:30pm and 4pm (and 5pm Saturday, Sunday and holidays). Boats to San Pedro (one way/round trip BZ$20/35, 20 to 30 minutes) go at 8:45am, 11:20am, 2:20pm and 5:20pm.

San Pedro Belize Express Water Taxi (🖉223-2225; www.belizewatertaxi.com) departs from the pier in front of the basketball court. Service to San Pedro (one way/round trip BZ$20/35) at 7am, 9:45am, 12:45pm, 3:45pm and 6:15pm, and Belize City (one way/round trip BZ$20/35) at 7:30am, noon, 3pm and 5pm. You can also depart from Caye Caulker at 7am and make a connection in San Pedro to the boat to Chetumal, Mexico (one way/round trip BZ$80/150). **Water Jets** (226-2194; www.sanpedrowatertaxi.com; Lagoon dock) departs from the back dock on the lagoon side. Runs to San Pedro (one way/round trip BZ$24/40) at 7:45am, 10:45am, 3:15pm and 6:45pm, and Belize City (one way/round trip BZ$24/40) at 6:30am, 11am, 3:30pm and 6pm. The 7:45am boat to San Pedro connects with an 8:30am departure to Chetumal (one way BZ$80).

🅘 Getting Around

Golf cart taxis meet the arriving water taxis to escort passengers to their hotels. Otherwise, Caulker is so small that most people walk everywhere. If need be, you can rent a golf cart at **Caye Caulker Golf Cart Rentals** (226 0237; cnr Back St & Calle del Sol; per hr/day BZ$25/125). Bicycle rental is available all over the island.

OTHER NORTHERN CAYES

Most visits to the other northern cayes are made by day trip from Caye Caulker or San Pedro, usually as part of a trip to snorkel or dive the Turneffe Elbow or the world-famous Blue Hole. But you can stay on a number of the smaller and outlying cayes if you don't mind being stranded on an otherwise deserted island. Serious divers and fishers, nature lovers and honeymooners are the most common customers at the camps and resorts on these cayes, which are generally available as weekly (or partial-week) all-inclusive packages. Transportation by charter boat or flight is usually provided by the lodge; inquire about transportation when you book.

Cayo Espanto

Billed as 'a Private Island,' the ultra sumptuous **Cayo Espanto** (910-323-8355, in USA 888-666-4282; www.aprivateisland.com; villas incl all meals from BZ$2590; ❋ 🛜 ☒) resort has seven delightful villas (total capacity 18), each designed for maximum privacy and panoramic views. Each casa is luxuriously decked out, with king-sized beds dressed in high-thread-count designer sheets and draped in mosquito netting. Each one also has a private dock *and* a private plunge pool, and – in some cases – an alfresco shower. The most unusual option is Casa Ventanas, which is perched at the end of a long dock, surrounded by 360 degrees of crystal-blue loveliness.

One of the highlights of staying at Cayo Espanto is the exceedingly attentive service (all packages include the services of a personal house attendant). Prior to arrival, guests are invited to fill out a preferences survey, which is used to prepare for all aspects of the visit, including the menu. Chefs create artistic dishes according to your personal tastes and serve them in the privacy of your villa.

Cayo Espanto is 3 miles west of Ambergris Caye. It's not uncommon for celebrities to frequent the island, which has hosted the likes of Robert De Niro, Harrison Ford and Tiger Woods. Leonardo DiCaprio loved it so much that he bought neighboring **Blackadore Caye** to build his own environmentally friendly island resort. Stay tuned.

Turneffe Atoll

Of Belize's three coral atolls, the Turneffe Atoll is the largest and the closest to the mainland. At 30 miles long and 10 miles wide, Turneffe Atoll is alive with coral, fish and large rays, making it a prime destination for **diving, snorkeling** and **fishing**.

This atoll is dominated by mangrove islands. Mangroves are what make Belize diving special, as they are the nurseries on which almost all marine life depends to ensure juvenile protection and biological productivity. Although the atoll is best known for its walls, there are also many shallow sea gardens and bright sand flats inside the reef that are excellent sites for novice divers and snorkelers.

Undoubtedly, the highlight of Turneffe Islands diving is a spot called the **Turneffe Elbow**, where the current attracts big hungry fish in large numbers and affords one of the only drift dives in Belize. Other sites include **Front Porch**, in front of the Turneffe Island Lodge; **Myrtle's Turtle**, named for the resident green turtle that appears annually; and **Triple Anchor**, marked by three anchors remaining from a wreck. Fishing enthusiasts are attracted by the flats, which are ideal for saltwater fly fishing.

Turneffe Atoll is usually visited by day trip, as it's within easy reach of Caulker, Ambergris and Belize City to the north, and Glover's Reef and Hopkins village to the south. Even Placencia dive boats occasionally make the trip to Turneffe Elbow, at the southern tip of the islands. On rough days it's favored by San Pedro dive operators, because much of the trip can be made behind the barrier reef, protecting passengers from choppy open seas.

Incredibly, the Turneffe Islands have as yet no environmental protection. However, Belize University's Institute of Marine Studies monitors environmental impacts from a field station on Calabash Caye.

🛏 Sleeping & Eating

The lodging available on the Turneffe Islands is at all-inclusive resorts, which usually include diving, snorkeling and/or fishing tours for a minimum of one week.

Turneffe Flats Lodge   RESORT $$$
(📞232-9022, in USA 888-512-8812; www.tflats.com; Blackbird Caye; weekly diving/fishing packages BZ$4190/7200; ❄ 📶 📷) 🖊 Although its principal fame is as a fishing retreat with expert guides, this lodge on Blackbird Caye also offers dive trips that are often far less crowded than those from other resorts (because most of the other guests are out fishing). Accommodations are in spacious, terracotta-tiled duplex apartments, each with balcony and dramatic views of the waves crashing on the nearby reef. As a bonus, guests can feel assured that at least some of their money is going to a good cause, as Turneffe Flats Lodge donates 1% of its revenue to organizations that are working to promote conservation.

Oceanic Society   CABINS $$$
(📞in USA 800-326-7491; www.oceanic-society.org; Blackbird Caye; 5-day research programs from BZ$3750, family-education programs per week adult/child BZ$3900/3580; 📷) 🖊 The society has a field station about five minutes' walk from Blackbird Caye Resort. Accommodations here are in basic but comfortable white wooden beachfront *cabañas* with private porches. Participants spend eight days helping with natural history research, collecting

---

DON'T MISS

BLUE HOLE

At the center of Lighthouse Reef is the world-famous **Blue Hole Natural Monument** (marine fee BZ$80). The Blue Hole is an incomparable natural wonder and an unparalleled diving experience. It may not be the best dive in Belize, but it certainly ranks among the most popular. The image of the Blue Hole – a deep blue pupil with an aquamarine border surrounded by the lighter shades of the reef – has become a logo for tourist publicity and a symbol of Belize.

Inside, a sheer-sided wall drops about 100ft to an undercut filled with stalactites. Deep blue in the center, the hole forms a perfect 1000ft-diameter circle on the surface. It is said to be 430ft deep, but as much as 200ft of this may now be filled with silt and other natural debris.

Divers drop quickly to 130ft, from where they swim beneath an overhang, observing stalactites above and, sometimes, a school of reef sharks below. Although the water is clear, light levels are low, so a good dive light will enable divers to appreciate the sponge and invertebrate life. Because of the depth, ascent begins after eight minutes; the brevity of the dive does disappoint some divers.

This trip is usually combined with other dives at Lighthouse Reef. Experienced divers will tell you that those other dives are the real highlight of the trip. But judging from its popularity – most dive shops make twice-weekly runs to the Blue Hole – plenty want to make the deep descent.

On day trips the Blue Hole will be your first dive, which can be nerve-racking if you're unfamiliar with the dive master and the other divers, or if you haven't been underwater lately. It may be worth doing some local dives with your dive masters before setting out cold on a Blue Hole trip. An alternative is to take an overnight trip to Lighthouse Reef.

Snorkelers can enjoy a trip to the Blue Hole, too, as there's plenty to see around the shallow inner perimeter of the circular reef. But it's an expensive trip and you'll probably have to tag along on a dive boat.

Note: this trip involves two hours each way by boat in possibly rough; open waters. Also, there's a BZ$80 marine-park fee for diving or snorkeling at the Blue Hole; this is usually on top of the dive fees.

WORTH A TRIP

HALF MOON CAYE

The nesting ground of the rare red-footed booby bird, the **Half Moon Caye Natural Monument** (park fee BZ$20) is the most oft-visited of the Lighthouse Reef islands.

The caye has a **lighthouse**, excellent **beaches** and spectacular submerged walls that teem with marine flora and fauna. Underwater visibility can extend more than 200ft here.

Rising less than 10ft above sea level, the caye's 45 acres hold two distinct ecosystems. To the west is lush vegetation fertilized by the droppings of thousands of seabirds, including some 4000 red-footed boobies, the magnificent frigate bird and 98 other bird species. The east side has less vegetation but more palms. Loggerhead and hawksbill sea turtles, both endangered, lay their eggs on the southern beaches.

A **nature trail** weaves through the southern part of the island to an observation platform that brings viewers to eye level with nesting boobies and frigate birds. Along the path you'll see thousands of seashells, many inhabited by hermit crabs.

Organized boat trips, mainly from San Pedro and Caye Caulker, stop at Half Moon Caye on their way to/from the nearby Blue Hole. Camping is sometimes permitted and there is a picnic area and toilets, but you need to bring all your water. The Belize Audubon Society has a visitors center where you must register and pay a BZ$20 park fee on arrival. This part of the island is also used as a base camp for kayaking, snorkeling and diving holidays by adventure-tour company **Island Expeditions** (☑ in US 1-800-667-1630; http://www.islandexpeditions.com).

---

data and documenting the incredibly diverse wildlife (manatees, crocodiles, bottlenosed dolphins and hawksbill sea turtles, among others) that lives in the Turneffe Islands. Special **family-education programs** are worthwhile.

Blackbird Caye Resort RESORT $$$
(☑223-2767, 223-4449, in USA 888-909-7333; www.blackbirdresort.com; Blackbird Caye; weekly diving/snorkeling/kayaking packages from BZ$4540/3940/3940; 🏠✿🤙) 🍴 Blackbird offers snorkeling and diving as well, but is popular with kayakers as it has coral gardens, uninhabited islands and mangrove creeks all ripe for exploration. Kayakers can also paddle out to the reef for snorkeling. Accommodations are in separate roomy *cabañas* with private porches and hammocks, and meals are eaten in a huge *palapa* restaurant near the main dock.

Turneffe Island Resort RESORT $$$
(☑522-0382, in USA 800-874-0118; www.turnefferesort.com; weekly fishing/diving/resort packages BZ$5100/4400/3300; 🏠@) 🍴 At the southern tip of the atoll, the fanciest of the Turneffe resorts offers gorgeous *cabañas* with screened porches, wooden floorboards, and indoor and outdoor showers, all set amid coconut palms just yards from the beach. Proximity to the famous Elbow dive site means trips from the resort go there frequently; some of the best tarpon fishing is a three-minute boat ride away.

Lighthouse Reef

At 50 miles out, Lighthouse Reef is the furthest of the three atolls from the coastline. But it is probably the most visited, thanks to the allure of the mysterious **Blue Hole Natural Monument**. While this icon of Belize diving makes the atoll a major attraction, it is the stunning walls, heavily adorned with swim-throughs and clear blue water that make it a favorite of both longtime divers and complete novices.

Besides the Blue Hole, there is no shortage of fantastic dive sites, as well as a spectacular stop for bird enthusiasts. In addition to what follows, other sites in Lighthouse Reef include **Painted Wall**, named for the plethora of painted tunicates found here; the **Aquarium**, often visited as a second stop after the Blue Hole; and the **Cathedral**, known for its amazing variety of sponges. **Half Moon Caye Wall** is probably the best of the lot for its variety of coral formations along the wall and within canyons and swim-throughs. Of particular interest is a field of garden eels found on the sand flats near the wall. Snorkelers don't despair: the shallows around these sites are interesting as well.

In addition to Half Moon Caye and Long Caye, other islands in the atoll include Northern Caye, Sandbore Caye, Saddle Caye and Hat Caye. Northern Caye is a small but lovely island, home to **Lighthouse Reef Resort** – now closed – while the others are popular with mosquitoes and crocodiles.

GETTING TO CHETUMAL (MEXICO) BY BOAT

Many travelers chose to exit Belize by sea via either Water Jets (p104) or San Pedro Belize Express Water Taxi (p104), both of which offer fairly efficient ferry service on alternating days between Caye Caulker, San Pedro and Chetumal, Mexico. Daily boats leave Caye Caulker at 7am and stop in San Pedro to pick up passengers and clear immigration. Though theoretically the boat should leave San Pedro by 8:30am, the immigration line at San Pedro can move more slowly than at the land borders. In addition to the BZ$37.50 exit fee, passengers are also charged a BZ$10 'port fee.'

The trip between San Pedro and Chetumal takes around two hours. Once you've cleared immigration in San Pedro you'll be unable to leave the dock, but a small dockside snack kiosk will change the last of your Belize dollars for Mexican pesos or US dollars at reasonable rates. There's also usually a money-changer on the boat.

Upon entering the port of Chetumal, you'll be greeted by soldiers and your luggage will be gone over by drug-sniffing dogs before you're asked to pay the Mexican 'exit tax' of US$25 (MXN295) up front; save your receipt to avoid paying this tax again when exiting Mexico. Though it's more comfortable to get to Chetumal by boat than by land, the trip is only marginally faster, owing to bottlenecks in customs and immigration at both ends.

Long Caye

The contemporary version of a hippie commune, **Long Caye at Lighthouse Reef** (www.belizeisland.com) is an idyllic private island, 2.5 miles long and 3.25 miles wide, with white sandy beaches and plentiful coconut palms. It has been earmarked for development as an ecovillage, with strict ecoguidelines for anyone who wants to purchase property. The idea is to build using materials that are collected onsite; to utilize alternative sources of energy, such as solar and hydro; to minimize waste by recycling and composting; to minimize the impact of human presence on the local ecosystem; and to demonstrate that development can be managed in a sustainable way.

This is a project in progress, but there are already a couple of places to stay, a medical center with a decompression chamber, some houses and a couple of docks. Boardwalks, many already built, are to be used around the island to protect the wildlife underneath. Package prices include transfer from Belize City; otherwise, make arrangements for boat transport with your lodge (BZ$360).

Calypso Beach Retreat   B&B $$$
(☑in USA 303-264-8333; www.calypsobeachretreat.com; Long Caye; r incl breakfast BZ$250, beachcomber/snorkel packages per week BZ$1733/2690, diving/ fishing packages per week BZ$3590/3990; 🛜) ✎ Located on the northeast corner of the island, this B&B is built from tropical hardwoods, housing four charming guest rooms with priceless Caribbean sea views. Sleep in four-poster beds and feel the breeze off the ocean. The packages include all meals, or you can pay by the night and utilize the shared kitchen facilities. Diving and fishing packages are also available, as are other combinations.

Huracan B&B   B&B $$$
(☑in USA 518-253-7705; www.huracandiving.com; 4-night package s/d BZ$2200/3760; 🛜) ✎ The smallest dive lodge is also the sweetest, with only four rooms, each named for a Maya deity. King-sized beds are draped in mosquito nets and colorful throw pillows, giving the simple accommodations an air of tropical luxury. Delicious meals are served on the front deck. Packages include transportation by boat from Belize City, all meals and three days of glorious diving. Nightly rates are also available, as are seven day dive packages. Check the website for current deals.

Northern Belize

Best Places to Eat

➡ Cerros Beach Resort, Copper Bank (p143)

➡ Nahil Mayab, Orange Walk Town (p130)

➡ Patty's Bistro, Corozal Town (p139)

➡ Street food outside the Central Market, Orange Walk (p129)

Best Places to Stay

➡ Backpackers Paradise, Sarteneja (p145)

➡ Serenity Sands, Corozal Town (p138)

➡ Cerros Beach Resort, Copper Bank (p143)

➡ Almond Tree Resort, Corozal Town (p138)

➡ Chan Chich Lodge, Orange Walk District (p135)

Why Go?

Many travelers save a chunk of change by flying into Cancun and busing or driving down to their final destination. Passing through the flat farmland and provincial towns of Northern Belize, they may not be inspired to linger.

But what are they missing? This is a chilled-out stretch of Belize that is entirely void of crowds, with unbeaten paths, abundant wildlife and prices a fraction of those in the rest of Belize.

Northern Belize comprises two districts: Corozal and Orange Walk, both traversed by the straight, flat Northern Hwy. Off the main road, adventurous travelers will find pretty fishing villages, pristine jungles, ancient Maya cities and anachronistic Mennonite communities.

Then there's the food. Exhibiting influences from Mexico, Northern Belizean cuisine is more diverse and more daring than its southern counterpart. If you're ready to trade rice and beans for seafood *ceviche*, you've come to the right place.

When to Go

Weather conditions in the northern districts reflect those of the country overall. The best time to visit is during the dry season (January to April), or during the light months of the rainy season (November, December, May and June). But even the rainy season is not as rainy as it is down south. The local culture is on display during the Fiesta de Carnaval, the pre-Lenten throw-down that takes place in February or March.

Northern Belize Highlights

① Taking a riverboat tour along the New River to the magnificent Maya ruins of **Lamanai** (p130)

② Spotting crocs and other lagoon inhabitants at the **Shipstern Nature Reserve** (p144)

③ Getting a firsthand introduction to the traditional Mennonite community at **Little Belize** (p146)

④ Chilling in the laid-back fishing town of **Sarteneja** (p144)

⑤ Enjoying panoramic ocean views from the waterfront Maya temple at **Cerro Maya** (p143)

⑥ Discovering the unexcavated ruins and undisturbed wildlife at the **Río Bravo Conservation & Management Area** (p133)

⑦ Soaking up the saltwater breezes and Spanish colonial charm of **Corozal Town** (p136)

History

Located on the eastern fringe of the ancient Maya heartland, Northern Belize supported many settlements through history without producing any cities of the size or grandeur of Caracol, which lies further south in Belize, or Tikal in Guatemala. It was home to important river trade routes that linked the interior with the coast: the north's major Maya site, Lamanai, commanded one of these routes and grew to a city of up to 35,000 people during the Maya peak, known as the Classic Period. The city at Lamanai continued to serve as a Maya center until the Spanish arrived in the 16th century.

Meanwhile, another city grew up further west at La Milpa. During the late Classic Period La Milpa was home to 46,000 people, but archaeologists believe the city came to an abrupt end in the 9th century AD, possibly due to environmental and economic stresses brought on by drought.

A Spanish expedition into Northern Belize from the Yucatán in 1544 led to the conquering of many of the region's Maya settlements and, later, the creation of a series of Spanish missions distantly controlled by a priest at Bacalar in the southeastern Yucatán. Maya rebellion was fierce, and after a series of battles the Spanish were driven out of the area for good in 1640.

British loggers began moving into the region in search of mahogany in the 18th century. They encountered sporadic resistance from the now weakened and depleted Maya population, which had been ravaged by European-introduced diseases.

In 1847 the Maya in the Yucatán rose up against their Spanish-descended overlords in the War of the Castes ('Guerra de Castas' in Spanish), a vicious conflict that continued in diminishing form into the 20th century. Refugees from both sides of the conflict took shelter in northern British Honduras (as Belize was then called), with people of Spanish descent founding the towns of Orange Walk and Corozal, and the Maya moving into the forests and countryside. It wasn't surprising that intermittent hostilities took place in British Honduras. One group of Maya, the Icaiché, was repulsed from Orange Walk after fierce fighting in 1872. The border between Mexico and British Honduras was not agreed upon between the two states until 1893.

Caste War migrants from the Yucatán laid the foundations of modern Northern Belize by starting the area's first sugarcane plantations. Despite the sugar industry's many vicissitudes, it is now the backbone of the Northern Belize economy, with some 900 cane farms in the region.

Language

Due to Northern Belize's proximity to Mexico and Guatemala's Petén, and the Mexican or Guatemalan origins of many of the people living here, Spanish is the first language of many northerners, be they of Maya, Mestizo or Mexican origin or more-recent immigrant workers from El Salvador and Guatemala. However, nearly everybody speaks English as well.

ⓘ Getting There & Around

The Northern Hwy links Belize City with the Mexican border via the region's two main towns, Orange Walk and Corozal Town. Several bus companies service the route, with some going as far as Chetumal, 7 miles into Mexico. Approximately 30 daily buses run each way from Belize City to Corozal Town and beyond. There are also daily buses connecting Orange Walk Town with Sarteneja (though the nicest way to get to Sarteneja is by boat from Corozal Town). Both boats and flights connect Corozal Town with Sarteneja and San Pedro (Ambergris Caye) once a day.

ORANGE WALK DISTRICT

Orange Walk is one of the more spread-out and thinly populated districts in Belize. The Northern Hwy cuts through the district's population center in its far northeast, and most of the communities and attractions scattered west of this are connected by a network of (mostly) unpaved roads. A casual glance at the government-produced Belize travel map shows fairly extensive grid-roads west of the Northern Hwy that stretch out into towns with names like Yo Creek and August Pine Ridge. Though this gives the impression of larger communities in rural Orange Walk, these are actually farming communities; the neatly drawn lines represent farming roads and boundaries created by the farmers themselves, and not major towns bustling with activity.

Further west and to the south these grid roads disappear entirely, and you're in what Belizeans refer to as 'deep bush,' the backwoods jungle country that makes up most of Orange Walk District. It's here you'll find the vast Río Bravo Conservation & Management Area and, further out still, the village of Gallon Jug, and the ultra-exclusive Chan Chich Lodge.

Orange Walk Town

POP 16,000

Orange Walk Town is many things to many people: agricultural town, economic hub, Mennonite meeting place, street-food paradise...but it is not generally considered a tourist town. And the chances are pretty good that this won't change any time soon. This town of 16,000 souls – just 57 miles from Belize City – doesn't have much to keep travelers around for more than a day or two. Having said that, it is a useful base from which to make the superlative trip to the ruins of Lamanai and longer excursions into the wilds of Northern Belize. Orange Walk has a fine location beside the New River, which meanders lazily along the east side of town, and there are a few very nice (and reasonably priced) hotels and restaurants for visitors who choose to hang around for a bit.

History

Orange Walk Town was born as a logging camp in the 18th century, from where mahogany was floated down the New River to Corozal Bay. It began to develop as a town around 1850, when Mexican refugees from the War of the Castes arrived. These migrants, whose agricultural experience was welcomed by the British colonial authorities, started Northern Belize's first sugar boom (which lasted from the 1850s to the 1870s).

Meanwhile, tensions were on the rise between the settlers and the local Icaiché Maya. British loggers had been encroaching on lands that the Icaiché considered their own around the Rio Hondo (which today forms Belize's border with Mexico). Moreover, British Honduras had been supplying arms to the Cruzob Maya (bitter enemies of the Icaiché). In 1872 the War of the Castes came to Orange Walk when a force of some 150 Icaiché Maya attacked the town's Brit-

Orange Walk Town

ish garrison. After several hours of fierce fighting the Icaiché were repelled, and their leader Marcos Canul was fatally wounded. The attack went down in history as the last significant armed Maya resistance in Belize.

◎ Sights

Banquitas House of Culture   MUSEUM
(☑ 322-0517; Banquitas Plaza; ◎ 8:30am-5:30pm Mon-Fri) FREE The modern Banquitas House of Culture has an attractively displayed exhibit on Orange Walk's history. It's especially good on the local Maya sites, and has artifacts, maps and illustrations, as well as exhibits that change monthly. It's set in a pleasant, small, riverside park with an amphitheater.

Independence Plaza   HISTORIC SITE
The scant remains of two British forts in Orange Walk – Fort Cairnes and Fort Mundy – serve as reminders of the War of the Castes conflict. The flagpole behind Orange Walk's town hall is the only remnant of Fort Cairnes, while Independence Plaza marks the site of Fort Mundy.

Cuello   RUIN
FREE Close to Orange Walk Town, Cuello (*kway*-yo) is one of the earliest-known settled communities in the Maya world, probably dating back to around 2400 BC, although there's not much left to show for it. Archaeologists have found plenty here, but only Structure 350, a nine-tiered pyramid, is of much interest to the nonexpert. The pyramid was constructed around AD 200 to AD 300, but its lower levels date from before 2000 BC.

The site is on private property owned by Cuello Distillery (☑ 320-9085; Yo Creek Rd), 4 miles west of Orange Walk (take San Antonio Rd out of town). It is not really open to the public, although the distillery usually allows access if you call and make advance arrangements. A taxi to Cuello from Orange Walk costs about BZ$25, round trip.

Nohmul   RUIN
FREE Meaning 'Great Mound' in Mayan, Nohmul (noh-*mool*) was a town of 3000 people during the late Classic Period. The vast site covers more than 7 sq miles, though most of it is overgrown with grass and sugarcane. Sadly, Nohmul – and Belize – made international headlines as this guide went to print when much of the site's main structure was bulldozed by a construction company. In the aftermath Belizean police were conducting an investigation into the incident.

Though it is possible that the main pyramid is damaged beyond repair, as of this writing some of the structure remains standing. Should you wish to see what remains, a taxi to Nohmul from Orange Walk is about BZ$30, round trip.

◯⟩ Tours

Sugarcane and street tacos aside, the main reason travelers come to Orange Walk is to head out to the Maya ruins at Lamanai. Tour companies offer full-day trips (from 9am to 4pm) by riverboat that give visitors a chance to see the prolific birdlife along the New River and to learn about the history and archaeology at Lamanai. Any hotel can help make arrangements for this tour. The price includes a picnic lunch served in the shadow of the Maya temples. These companies usually require a minimum of four people to make the trip. You should probably reserve your place the day before, although you may be lucky on the morning you want to go.

NORTHERN BELIZE ORANGE WALK TOWN

Orange Walk Town

◎ Top Sights
1 Banquitas House of Culture C1
2 Flagpole B2
3 Independence Plaza C1

◯ Activities, Courses & Tours
4 Jungle River Tours C2
  Lamanai River Tours .... (see 8)

◯ Sleeping
5 Akihito Hotel B3
6 D'Victoria Hotel B4
7 Hotel de la Fuente C2
8 Lamanai Riverside Retreat D3
9 Orchid Palm Inn C2
10 St Christopher's Hotel C1

◯ Eating
11 Juanita's B3
12 La Hacienda A4
13 Lee's Chinese Restaurant B2
14 Nahil Mayab B3
15 Panificadora La Popular C2
  Paniscea Restaurant and Lounge . (see 1)
16 Torta Hut B2

◯ Drinking & Nightlife
  Lamanai Riverside Retreat .... (see 8)
17 Natural Balance B3

◯ Entertainment
18 La Tunnel Discothèque B2

PARTY TIME, SPANISH STYLE

One of the more colorful features of multi-ethnic Belize is the diversity of feasts and celebrations. Holidays in Northern Belize reflect the strong Mexican influence, with old-style Catholic Spanish roots.

A Northern Belizean Christmas is a distinctive festival. While Maya are gearing up for animistic deer dances and Brits are planning Boxing Day football parties, the north gets ready for **Las Posadas**. The tradition is more than 400 years old, and is practiced still in Mexico and Guatemala as well. It is based on Mary and Joseph's unsuccessful search for accommodations – Las Posadas means the 'the lodging.' For nine days, beginning on December 16, people participate in candlelit processions, singing hymns, stopping at designated homes, in a loose reenactment of the Bible story that culminates in a big Christmas Eve ceremony. In a secular spin-off from the tradition, Northern Belizeans still go around to each other's houses at Christmas time, being treated to holiday dishes, cakes and drinks.

The north is also the place to be in Belize at Carnaval time. Again, this festival is a product of the region's Catholic-influenced Mestizo culture. As a last hurrah before the Lenten fasting season, Northern Belize long celebrated **Fiesta de Carnaval**, with parades, costumes, cross-dressing and partying. Today, with the help of tourists and the expat community, San Pedro plays the role of little Rio. The festivities were so much fun that rest of the country decided to get in on it; so, since the 1970s, there is a second Carnaval held in connection with Belizean Independence Day in September.

Lamanai River Tours TOUR
(302-1600, 670-0700; per person BZ$100) Departing from the Lamanai Riverside Retreat, this company's tours include lunch and admission price. Travelers speak highly of Lamanai River Tours knowledgeable guides.

Reyes & Sons TOUR
(322-3327, 610-1548; per person BZ$80) Reyes & Sons keeps its boat docked by the Northern Hwy bridge over the New River, 5 miles south of town, but will pick you up at your hotel with advanced notice.

Dave's Eco Tours TOUR
(607-9929, 627-7955; www.davesecotours.com; 3 Pelican St, Maskall Village) Travelers speak well of David Chan's trips to Altun Ha, Lamanai, Cahal Pech and other Maya sights around Belize. David also does cave tubing, horseback riding and various nautical trips. Though based in Maskall (just outside of Altun Ha), Dave travels throughout the country.

Jungle River Tours TOUR
(302-2293; 20 Lovers' Lane; BZ$90) The Novelo brothers do a variety of other tours from Orange Walk.

🛏 Sleeping

Orchid Palm Inn INN $
(322-0719; www.orchidpalminn.com; 22 Queen Victoria Ave; basic s/d BZ$65/80, deluxe d BZ$110; P❄@📶) Set on a busy corner in the center of all the action, the little Orchid Palm Inn is a tiny island of tranquility. It has eight well-furnished and nicely decorated rooms that come in a variety of configurations, from singles to doubles with kitchenettes. Air-con is an additional BZ$10.

Lamanai Riverside Retreat GUESTHOUSE $
(302-3955; Lamanai Alley; r BZ$80; P❄@📶) Located right on the river, this place is about 24 miles from the namesake ruins, but boats headed to Lamanai do depart from here. It has only three rustic wooden rooms, with breezy balconies and mosquito-netted beds, and is far from the fanciest digs in town, but the jungly atmosphere and accommodating service are excellent. The owner is involved in the cataloging and protection of the area's crocodile population, and will be glad to tell you all about the crocs and other animals that call the river home. Adjoining the retreat is one of Orange Walk's more picturesque eating and drinking spots, so come for a beer even if the rooms are booked.

D'Victoria Hotel HOTEL $
(322-2518; 40 Queen Victoria Ave; basic r with fan/air-con BZ$50/75, deluxe r BZ$85; P❄📶❄) The fresh pink paint does not do much to brighten up this drab concrete hotel. Rooms are clean, boxy and basic, but some are rather musty.

St Christopher's Hotel HOTEL $
(302-1064; www.stchristophershotelbze.com; 10 Main St; r with fan/air-con BZ$66/98; P❄@📶) The flowering gardens and riverside setting

make this otherwise nondescript hotel an attractive place to stay. The rooms themselves are spacious but plain, although you might appreciate the colorful artwork and stenciled walls that adorn the pricier quarters. Your hosts – the Urbina family – are attentive and welcoming, in a low-key, unassuming sort of way.

Akihito Hotel
HOSTEL, HOTEL **$**

(⌂302-0185; cnr Queen Victoria Ave & Gravel Lane; dm BZ$15, d with shared/private bath BZ$30/45; ❋@🛜) The cheapest of the bunch, the Akihito has the goods for budget travelers. That means rooms are very plain but very clean. The family who runs the Akihito is a treasure trove of local information – the teenaged son's handmade map of Orange Walk will prove an invaluable tool for those who like to wander.

Hotel de la Fuente
HOTEL **$$**

(⌂322-2290; www.hoteldelafuente.com; 14 Main St; r BZ$70-110, ste BZ$150; P❋@🛜) This family-run hotel is smack dab in the center of Orange Walk, but most of the rooms are in a brand new building set back from the hustle and bustle (and noise) on the road. The clean, cozy rooms – all equipped with fridge and coffee maker – are probably the best in town, while the suite has a full kitchen. Foam mattresses ensure a good night's rest. By the time you read this, de la Fuente's owners will also be offering riverside cabins. Call them for more details.

🍴 Eating

Although there aren't many 'five-star eateries' in this working-class town, Orange Walk is known for its **street food**. Surrounding the town square are tiny cafes, snack stalls, fruit stands and pushcarts offering a veritable smorgasbord of Northern Belizean and Mexican foods, including rice and beans, tacos, tamales, stewed chicken, ice cream and more. Piped-in music and enticing aromas create an irresistible atmosphere, especially on Saturday afternoons. Everything is super cheap and hygiene standards are generally good. Some folks come from as far away as Corozal 'just to hang out and eat.'

Panificadora La Popular
BAKERY **$**

(Beytias La; pastries BZ$2-8; ⊙6:30am-8pm Mon-Sat, 7:30am-noon & 3-6pm Sun) Should you find yourself in Orange Walk during daylight hours, *do not pass go, do not collect $200;* go *directly* to this amazing bakery, grab a tray and a pair of tongs, and take your pick from the spread of sticky buns, cinnamon rolls, croissants and meat pies, which make for a perfect breakfast or lunch for the road. Good luck trying to decide.

Lee's Chinese Restaurant
CHINESE **$**

(11 San Antonio Rd; dishes BZ$12-20; ⊙11am-midnight; ☝) Orange Walk's most popular Chinese eatery, Lee's serves up a superior range of Hong Kong–style dishes. Aside from the blaring TV and the plastic table cloths, the atmosphere is festive and welcoming, with the stylish dragon-theme decor kept cool by whirring ceiling fans. The menu is extensive, including excellent seafood and vegetarian options.

La Hacienda
BURGERS **$**

(Northern Hwy; dishes BZ$10-15; ⊙11am-10pm Sun-Thu, 11am-midnight Fri & Sat) This spacious sports bar is a popular spot for locals and tourists alike to feast on tasty burgers and quaff Belikins. Food is reliably good and the TVs are also reliably on. Located about 1 mile south of town on the road to Belize City.

Torta Hut
FAST FOOD **$**

(Queen Victoria Ave; sandwiches BZ$3-6; ⊙4pm-midnight Thu-Tue) Not exactly street food, but certainly not a restaurant, the tiny Torta Hut is a food truck that parks at a busy intersection in the center of Orange Walk. The place keeps odd hours, easing the late-night munchies of passers-by with fat sandwiches stuffed with chicken, beef, pork, fish or shrimp.

Juanita's
BREAKFAST, BELIZEAN **$**

(8 Santa Ana St; dishes BZ$5-8; ⊙breakfast, lunch & dinner) You can tell from the number of dedicated locals who flock to this place that the food here is satisfying. Simple, clean and very well priced, Juanita's serves up eggs and bacon for breakfast, and rice and beans and other local favorites such as cow-foot soup during the rest of the day.

Come n' Dine Restaurant
BREAKFAST, BELIZEAN **$**

(Northern Hwy; BZ$7-12; ⊙breakfast, lunch & dinner) Unassuming and unexpected, this roadside restaurant serves some of the best Belizean food around. Located right next to the gas station on a crook on the Northern Hwy just a couple of miles south of town, it's well placed for road-trippers (but also worth the trip if you are staying in town). Look for excellent stews, steaks and stir-fries.

★ **Nahil Mayab** BELIZEAN, MEXICAN $$
(www.nahilmayab.com; cnr Santa Ana & Guadalupe
Sts; lunch BZ$8-20, dinner BZ$20-30; ⊙lunch only
Mon, lunch & dinner Tue-Sat; 🐶🖉📶) Decked in
exotic greenery and faux Maya carvings, the
dining room evokes the district's surround-
ing jungles, as does the pleasantly shaded
patio. It's a fun, kitschy atmosphere in which
to sample some Yucatecan-inspired food,
such as Ke'Ken (salt pork in tomato sauce)
or Cham Cham (empanadas). Less adventur-
ous eaters will appreciate the sandwiches,
burritos and good old-fashioned rice and
beans. The place looks like it might cater to
tourist groups, but the food is good enough
that it draws plenty of locals too.

**Paniscea Restaurant
and Lounge** CONTINENTAL $$
(meals BZ$12-40; ⊙11am-2pm & 5pm-2am Wed-
Mon) Located underneath the House of Culture on the banks of the New River, Lucy and
Doug's newly opened riverside restaurant
is quickly becoming Orange Walk's in spot
for food and drinks. Local faves like shrimp
ceviche (BZ$12) share a menu with grilled
imported steaks (prices vary; expect to pay
between BZ$24 and BZ$40). Other dishes
include smoked pork chop (BZ$24). There's
also a full bar with two flat-screen TVs.

🍸 Drinking & Nightlife

Orange Walk is a town where farmers from
all over northern Belize (including the area's
sizable Mennonite population) come to
swap tales, sell produce and feast on Chinese food.

Lamanai Riverside Retreat BAR
(Lamanai Alley; ⊙8am-10pm) With its breezy
deck and tables with lovely river views, this
restaurant bar gets crowded on weekends.
The menu is pretty extensive, but the place
is recommended mainly for drinking and
socializing.

Natural Balance CAFE
(San Antonio Rd; ⊙9am-5:30pm; 🐶) This Tai-
wanese-owned cafe serves fresh-brewed coffee drinks (iced and hot) as well as bubble
milk tea (popular in Asia but almost unknown in Belize). Light vegetarian snacks
are also available.

La Tunnel Discothèque DISCO
(South Park St) La Tunnel Discothèque is
lively at night but dead in the day. There are
other watering holes in this area as well.

❶ Information

Orange Walk lacks an official tourism information center, though hotels can provide local
information.

Belize Bank (34 Main St) Accepts all major
credit cards with BZ$4 fee and a limit of
BZ$500 per day.

Kai & A Internet Cafe (Queen Victoria Ave;
internet per hr BZ$4; ⊙7:30am-7:30pm)

Northern Regional Hospital (🖉322-2072;
Northern Hwy; ⊙24hr emergency services)
Located a half-mile north of the Pontoon Bridge
on the northern edge of town.

Police station (🖉322-2022; Hospital Cres)
Across from the library.

Post office (cnr Queen Victoria Ave & Arthur
St)

Scotia Bank (cnr Park & Main Sts) Accepts all
cards with BZ$4 fee; limit per day BZ$800.

❶ Getting There & Away

Orange Walk is the major Northern Belize hub
for buses plying the Corozal–Belize City route.
At last count there were six companies servicing
this route and between 25 and 30 buses a day
going in each direction. All buses pass through
the center of town before stopping on the west
side of Central Park or around the market to pick
up and drop off customers. Buses heading north
from Orange Walk begin at 7am and run until
9pm. Heading south to Belize City, buses begin
at 5am and run until 8:45pm. The trip to Belize
City takes between 1½ and two hours, and costs
between BZ$5 and BZ$7; the trip to Corozal is
slightly quicker and cheaper. Due to recent construction the Belize City–Corozal buses now stop
at a makeshift transit lot west of the cemetery,
but locals say this situation may (or may not)
change soon.

Buses to outlying regions depart from various
points around the market. Schedules are subject to change so you'll want to ask in advance
around the market or at your hotel.

The bus to Copper Bank (BZ$6, one hour)
leaves at 11:30am and 5pm, Monday to Saturday,
from a bus stop a half-block south of the market;
the one to Indian Church near Lamanai (BZ$8,
1½ hours) departs from the market at 3:30pm
on Monday, Wednesday and Friday; and the bus
to Sarteneja (BZ$8, 1½ hours) runs hourly from
the market between noon and 5pm Monday to
Saturday, and 3pm Sunday.

Lamanai

One of the biggest and best excavated Maya
sites in northern Belize, **Lamanai** (http://
nichbelize.org; BZ$20; ⊙8am-5pm) lies 24 miles
south of Orange Walk Town up the New

River (or 36 miles by unpaved road). The ruins are known both for their impressive architecture and marvelous setting, surrounded by dense rainforest overlooking the New River Lagoon. The translation of the word *lamanai* – which means 'submerged crocodile' in Mayan – gives a pretty good indication of the local residents of this jungly setting.

Most visitors approach Lamanai by guided river trip from Orange Walk, not just to avoid the long and bumpy road, but to take advantage of the river trip itself. The boat ride is an opportunity to observe the river's prolific and colorful birdlife, as well as crocs, iguanas, monkeys and other wildlife. Most guides who do the 1½-hour trip are experts in local archaeology and ecology, making this tour a two-for-the-price-of-one experience. Besides the beautiful jungle and lagoon, the river voyage passes the Mennonite community of **Shipyard** before reaching the ruin site. There are a number of excellent tour guides in Orange Walk who specialize in the journey.

History

Lamanai not only spans all phases of ancient Maya civilization but also tells a tale of ongoing Maya occupation and resistance for centuries after the Europeans arrived, equalling the longest known unbroken occupation in the Maya world. Lamanai was inhabited at least as early as 1500 BC, and was already a major ceremonial center, with large temples, in late Preclassic times.

It seems to have surged in importance (perhaps thanks to its location on trade routes between the Caribbean and the interior) around 200 or 100 BC, and its major buildings were mostly constructed between then and AD 700, although additions and changes went on up until at least the 15th century. At its peak it is estimated to have had a population of around 35,000.

When the Spanish invaded Northern Belize from the Yucatán in 1544, one of the most important missions they set up was Lamanai, where they had found a thriving Maya community. But the Maya never readily accepted Spanish overlordship, and a rebellion in 1640 left the Lamanai mission burned and deserted. Maya continued to live here until the late 17th or 18th century, when they were decimated by an epidemic, probably smallpox.

Archaeological excavations commenced as early as 1917, but large-scale digging, by David Pendergast of Canada's Royal Ontario Museum, only began in 1974. The painstaking work of uncovering the more than 700 structures found here will take several lifetimes, not to mention huge amounts of funding.

◉ Sights

Arriving at Lamanai by boat you'll probably first be brought to the small **museum**, which exhibits some beautiful examples of pottery, and obsidian and jade jewelry. Then you'll head into the jungle, passing gigantic guanacaste (tubroos), ceiba and ramón (breadnut) trees, strangler figs, allspice, epiphytes and examples of Belize's national flower, the black orchid. In the canopy overhead you might see (or hear) some of the resident howler monkeys. A tour of the **ruins** takes a minimum of 90 minutes, but can be done more comfortably in two or three hours.

Lamanai

Jaguar Temple   RUIN
This temple (Structure N10-9), fronting a 100yd-wide plaza, was built in the 6th century AD and modified several times up to at least the 15th century – a fine example of the longevity of the Lamanai settlement. The stone patterning on the lowest-level turns depicts two cleverly designed jaguar faces, dating from the initial 6th-century construction. On the opposite (north) side of the plaza is a set of buildings that were used as residences for Lamanai's royal elite.

Stela 9   RUIN
North of the elite residential complex, this intricately carved standing stone in front of Structure N10-27 was erected in AD 625 to commemorate the accession of Lord Smoking Shell in AD 608. He is shown in ceremonial regalia, wearing a rattlesnake headdress with quetzal feathers at the back, and holding a double-headed serpent bar diagonally across his body, with a deity emerging from the serpent's jaw at the top. The remains of five children – ranging in age from newborn to eight – were buried beneath the stela. Archaeologists believe the burial must have been highly significant, since offerings are not usually associated with the dedication of monuments.

Ball Court   RUIN
Not far west of Stela 9 is Lamanai's ball court, one of the smallest in the Maya world – but with the largest ball-court marker found yet! A ceremonial vessel containing liquid mercury, probably from Guatemala, was found beneath the marker.

High Temple   RUIN
North of the ball court, across a plaza shaded by trees, is Structure N10-43, the highest at Lamanai, which rises 125ft above the jungle canopy. Few large buildings in the Maya world were built as early as this one, which was initially constructed around 100 BC. This grand ceremonial temple was built from nothing on a site that had previously been residential, which indicated a dramatic surge in Lamanai's importance at the time. You can climb to its summit for fabulous panoramas over the rest of Lamanai, the New River Lagoon, and plains and forests stretching out on all sides.

Mask Temple   RUIN
To the northeast along a jungle path, the Mask Temple (Structure N9-56) was begun around 200 BC and was modified several times up to AD 1300. It has a 13ft stylized mask of a man in a crocodile headdress emblazoned on the southern part of its west face. Dating from about AD 400, this is one of the finest big masks in the Maya world, and unusual in that it is made of limestone blocks rather than plaster. A similar mask is hidden beneath the facade on the northern side. Deep within this building archaeologists found the tombs of a man adorned with shell and jade jewelry, and a woman from almost the same date. The pair are thought to be a succession of leaders – perhaps a husband and wife, or brother and sister.

Maya Structures   RUIN
At the far north end of the Lamanai site, and often missed by tour groups, this large platform, 120yd by 100yd in area, supports several large buildings up to 92ft high. Next to it is a river inlet that once formed an ancient harbor.

Colonial Structures   RUIN
Some 400yd south of Jaguar Temple are the remains of the thick stone walls of two Spanish churches, which were built by Maya forced labor from the remains of a temple. The southern church was built in 1544 and the northern one in the 1560s. Both were destroyed by the Maya, the second one in the 1640 rebellion. Unknown to the Spanish, the Maya placed sacred objects such as crocodile figurines inside the churches while building them. A 300yd path opposite the churches leads to the partly overgrown remains of a 19th-century sugar mill.

🛏 Sleeping & Eating

Lamanai Outpost Lodge   LODGE $$$
(☎ 670-3578, in USA 888-733-7864; www.lamanai. com; 2-night package per person BZ$1112-1310; 🅿 @ 🛜) For those who can afford it, the best option for fully exploring Lamanai is one of the package tours offered by this place. About 1 mile south of the ruins, this classy lodge is perched on a hillside just above the lagoon, and boasts panoramic views from its bar and gorgeous open-air dining room. The 20 thatched-roof bungalows, each with fan, private bathroom and veranda, are lovely and perfectly suited to the casual jungle atmosphere. Packages include meals, transfers to/from Belize City and two guided small-group activities per day. The list of activities ranges from visiting the ruins to observing howler monkeys, to starlight canoeing and nocturnal crocodile encounters. Birding is

big here: almost 400 species have been documented within 3 miles of the lodge.

ℹ Getting There & Away

If you decide to go without a guide, you can get to the village of Indian Church (next to Lamanai) from Orange Walk, but the bus goes only three times a week. You'll need to spend at least one night to catch the return bus early the next morning.

Río Bravo Conservation & Management Area

If you're looking for true, wild tropical rainforest, this is it. Encompassing 406 sq miles in northwest Belize, the Río Bravo Conservation & Management Area (RBCMA) takes up 4% of Belize's total land area and is managed by the Belizean nonprofit organization Programme for Belize (PFB; ☎227-5616, 227-1020; www.pfbelize.org; 1 Eyre St, Belize City; ☺8am-5pm Mon-Fri). The RBCMA harbors astonishing biological diversity – 392 bird species (more than two-thirds of Belize's total), 200 tree species, 70 mammal species, including all five of Belize's cats (jaguar, puma, ocelot, jaguarundi and margay). Río Bravo is said to have the largest concentration of jaguars in all of Central America.

Parts of the territory of the RBCMA were logged for mahogany and other woods from the 18th century until the 1980s, but distance and inaccessibility helped to ensure the survival of the forest as a whole. The area also contains at least 60 Maya sites, including La Milpa, the third-largest site in Belize.

At the RBCMA the PFB is seeking to link conservation with the development of

HOLLYWOOD VS HISTORY

The Maya is not one of the world's better-known ancient civilizations. Many of us learn about the Egyptians and the Romans at school, but when it comes to indigenous American history, common knowledge is more scant and sometimes inaccurate.

For example, some historians, archaeologists and anthropologists strongly debated *Apocalypto*, Mel Gibson's 2006 film about the ancient Maya civilization. They claim the epic was not only historically inaccurate, but also culturally insensitive.

Gibson did employ Amerindian actors who actually spoke the Yucatec Mayan language. And the film did capture many elements of the Maya culture, from the elaborate tattoos on their bodies to the jungle setting of their cities. But, according to some scholars, these details pale in comparison to the general misrepresentation of the civilization and the inherently colonialist message of the film.

Nobody denies that violence was an integral part of the ancient Maya culture. They were known to sacrifice humans to keep their gods happy. But there is no evidence that this took place to the extent depicted in the movie, and mass graves have not even been found at Maya sites. Rather, this is an aspect of the Aztec culture that was co-opted for the film. Most of the Maya's human sacrifices were rulers of rival kingdoms who were killed after their capture, or individuals who had been groomed for the honor.

Apocalypto also depicts crowds of slaves toiling under harsh conditions, but when you go to Tikal and Caracol you'll learn that these cities were likely built by ordinary citizens, who may have been conscripted or may have volunteered for the job.

Apocalypto does not convey that the Maya civilization endured for thousands of years and its accomplishments were many; art, architecture, astrology, spirituality, hieroglyphics, the calendar and more are not showcased in the movie.

Apocalypto ends with the arrival of the Spanish, which offers the first and only moment of peace in the entire film. They rescue our hero Jaguar Paw from his bloody fate, perhaps implying that the Spanish save the Maya from the violence they are perpetrating upon themselves.

In reality, the Maya cities (with the exception of Lamanai) had long since been abandoned by the time the Spanish arrived. The film does not touch on the violence the Spanish would inflict on the Maya in the coming years. Some experts estimate that the Maya population declined by as much as 90% within 100 years of the arrival of the Spanish.

So, viewer, beware: *Apocalypto* is a heart-racing, gut-wrenching, action-adventure film; a history lesson, it is not.

sustainable land uses. Programs include tree nurseries; extraction of nontimber products such as chicle, thatch and palm; experimental operations in sustainable timber extraction; and ecotourism.

History

Maya lived in this area as early as 800 BC. When Spanish expeditions first journeyed here the Maya were still using the same river trade routes, though by then their population was seriously depleted. Mahogany loggers moved into the area by the mid-18th century but were subject to intermittent attacks by the Maya for at least a century. By the late 19th century the Belize Estate and Produce Company (BEC) owned almost all of the land in northwestern Belize. The company carried out major timber extractions, floating mahogany and Mexican cedar out through the river system to the coast. With the advent of rail systems and logging trucks, operations flourished until overcutting and a moody market finally prompted the BEC to stop cutting trees in the early 1980s.

Intensive chicle tapping also took place throughout the 20th century, and you can still see slash scars on sapodilla trees throughout the RBCMA.

Belizean businessman Barry Bowen, owner of the Belikin brewery and the country's Coca-Cola distribution rights, bought the BEC and its nearly 1100 sq miles of land in 1982. He quickly sold off massive chunks to Yalbac Ranch (owned by a Texan cattle farmer) and Coca-Cola Foods. Meanwhile the Massachusetts Audubon Society was looking for a reserve for migrating birds. Coca-Cola donated 66 sq miles to support the initiative (a further 86 sq miles followed in 1992), and Programme for Belize was created to manage the land. Bowen also donated some land, and PFB, helped by more than US$2 million raised by the UK-based World Land Trust, bought the rest, bringing its total up to today's 406 sq miles.

◉ Sights & Activities

Bird-Watching TOUR
Considering the link to Mass Audubon, it's no surprise that Río Bravo is one of the country's prime birding areas. The conservation area may attract fewer birders than more accessible destinations like Crooked Tree, but it attracts more birds – more than 390 species to be exact. Due to its remote location and vigilant protection measures, Río Bravo is home to dozens of species that are rarely spotted in other parts of the country. Case in point: in 2005 the RBCMA was selected as the release site for the restoration of the amazingly majestic and globally threatened harpy eagle. Although you're unlikely to spot a harpy eagle, other large avian species are not uncommon, including the oscillated turkey, the crested guan and the ornate hawk eagle. The open area around La Milpa Field Station attracts fly-catchers, mannekins, redstarts, orioles, tanagers, trogons and hummingbirds, so you can lounge in your hammock with your binoculars and watch the show. Alternatively, guides take visitors on early-morning bird walks around the grounds for BZ$80 per person.

La Milpa RUIN
In the northwestern corner of the RBCMA, La Milpa is the third-largest Maya site in Belize, believed to have had a population of 46,000 at its peak between AD 750 and AD 850. Its 5-acre Great Plaza, one of the biggest of all Maya plazas, is surrounded by four pyramids up to 80ft high. Now the structures are all covered with jungle and inhabited by howler monkeys, evoking the mystery and history of the ancient ruins. Guides from the field station can accompany your hike to shed light on the function of the various structures, and to point out the stelae and other moss-covered artifacts that still remain in the area.

☞ Tours

From Hill Bank Field Station you can make arrangements to tour the lagoon by canoe or by boat, including nighttime croc-spotting. From La Milpa Field Station you can visit nearby Mennonite and Mestizo communities.

🛏 Sleeping & Eating

Visitors are invited to stay at one of two field stations (dm BZ$50-80, cabaña s/d/q BZ$130/200/220) that are managed by PFB. Hill Bank Field Station is in the southeastern part of the RBCMA beside the New River Lagoon (upstream from Lamanai), on the site of an abandoned logging station, where old wooden buildings and antique steam engines remain. La Milpa Field Station is in the northwest of the

CHAN CHICH LODGE

In the far western corner of Orange Walk District, in the midst of a 200-sq-mile private reserve, **Chan Chich Lodge** (☑ in USA 800-343-8009, tel/fax 223-4419; www.chanchich. com; standard s/d BZ$430/500, deluxe s/d BZ$530/600, meals per day BZ$140; ℗ @ 🛜) is one of the country's original ecolodges. The remote setting and pristine environs make this a picture-perfect location for a jungle lodge. It is also a destination in and of itself: many birders and wildlife enthusiasts arrive via charter flight from Belize City and spend the whole of their Belize visit right here.

Luxurious thatched *cabañas* surround the partly excavated ruins of an ancient Maya plaza. The *cabañas* are gorgeous – built from local hardwoods and furnished with ceiling fans, comfy king- or queen-sized beds and rustic yet modern decor. The lodge's distance from anywhere deters drop-ins, and the limited number of *cabañas* (not to mention the price) also keeps the crowds away.

Chan Chich lies within a private reserve known as the Gallon Jug Estate, which has been maintained by Belizean businessman Barry Bowen since his purchase of the BEC's lands in the 1980s. Intensive agriculture is practiced in a small part of the reserve, but the rest is subject to strict conservation. The lodge offers guided walks, vehicle tours and other activities throughout the day and night, and 9 miles of trails invite independent exploration. One tour goes to Gallon Jug, the center of the reserve's very orderly agricultural operations. Crops grown here include cacao and organic coffee beans, and another program aims to raise the quality of local beef using embryo transfer technology from English Herefords.

The lodge is about 25 miles south of La Milpa Field Station and 4 miles from the Guatemalan border. It's most easily reached by a 30-minute plane ride from Belize City (about BZ$500 per person round trip). Otherwise, you can drive from Belize City via Orange Walk Town (four hours, 130 miles), though the 73 miles from Orange Walk to the lodge are mostly unpaved. Be sure to obtain detailed driving instructions from lodge management before setting out. The lodge will also arrange a road transfer if you don't have your own vehicle.

RBCMA, 3 miles from La Milpa Maya site. Accommodations are similar at both sites. Lovely thatched *cabañas* come complete with private bathroom, hot water, fresh linens, veranda and mosquito nets. The six-person dorm rooms incorporate ecotechnology such as solar power and graywater recycling. There are plenty of hammocks in which to lie back and listen to birdsong. Delicious, filling **meals** (breakfast/lunch/dinner BZ$20/32/44) are prepared onsite and served family-style. Multiday packages are available.

❶ Getting There & Away

Most visitors rent a vehicle to get to either field station. La Milpa is about one hour from Orange Walk (via Yo Creek, San Felipe, Blue Creek and Tres Leguas); Hill Bank is about two hours from Belize City (via Burrell Boom, Bermudian Landing and Rancho Dolores). Call Programme for Belize or check the website for detailed directions and advice on road conditions (the later stages of both trips involve sections on unpaved roads, which can be impassable after heavy rains). PFB can also help arrange transfers from Orange Walk, Belize City or Lamanai.

COROZAL DISTRICT

The country's northernmost district, Corozal is wedged in between Orange Walk and the border. Its proximity to Mexico lends it a certain Spanish charm, and also offers easy access to travelers coming from Cancun or Chetumal. In recent years Corozal has been 'discovered' by outsiders, who are racing to buy up the affordable seaside property and build retirement homes on their little plots of paradise. However, this district is still relatively unknown to Belize-bound tourists, who don't often venture off the Northern Hwy.

The chunk of land that spreads south and eastward across the bay from Corozal Town is at once one of the least-visited and most visit-worthy spots in Belize. It's more compact than Orange Walk District, and most of the sights are well within striking distance – by boat or road – of Corozal Town itself. Though topographically not as dramatic as the west or the south (most of Northern Belize is fairly flat), this part of the country is sparsely populated and filled with pristine jungle, as well as the cool seaside town of Sarteneja and the amazing coastal Maya ruins at Cerros.

Corozal Town

POP 9100

Nine miles south of Mexico and 29 miles north of Orange Walk Town, Corozal has a vibe different from any other town in Belize. The Mexican influence is palpable on the streets of this provincial town, where you are likely to hear Spanish and eat tacos. Though it feels prosperous (especially by Belizean standards), most of the town's wealth comes from its position as a commercial and farming center – not from tourism. So while Corozal is a fine place to be a tourist, it escapes the holiday-ville atmosphere that haunts some other places in Belize.

With ocean breezes, affordable hotels, tantalizing food and easy access to the rest of the district, Corozal is worth a stop on the way to or from Mexico – if not a detour from your Belizean itinerary further south. The whole town is situated on Corozal Bay, and the waterfront is filled with parks, picnic tables and beachside *palapas* (thatched-roof open-air huts).

The town center is arranged around a town square, encompassing the plaza or 'Central Park,' post office and police station. The main highway passes through town as Santa Rita Rd and 7th Ave, briefly skirting the sea at the south end of town.

History

The ruins of the Postclassic Maya trading center, now called Santa Rita (probably the original Chetumal), lie beneath parts of modern Corozal. Across the bay, Cerros was a substantial coastal trade center in the Preclassic period.

Modern Corozal dates from 1849, when it was founded by Mexicans fleeing the War of the Castes. The refugees named their town Corozal after the Spanish word for cohune palm, a strong symbol of fertility.

For years Corozal had the look of a typical Mexican town, with thatched-roof homes. Then Hurricane Janet roared through in 1955 and blew away many of the buildings. Much of Corozal's wood-and-concrete architecture dates from the late 1950s. Like Orange Walk, the Corozal economy is based on sugarcane farming, although there's also quite a bit of trade with nearby Chetumal in Mexico as well.

◉ Sights

Santa Rita
RUIN

(⊙ dawn to dusk) **FREE** Santa Rita was an ancient Maya coastal town that once occupied the same strategic trading position as present-day Corozal Town, namely the spot between two rivers – the Rio Hondo (which now forms the Belize–Mexico border) and the New River (which enters Corozal Bay south of town). Much of Santa Rita remains unexcavated, but it's worth a short excursion out of town to explore the site. As of this writing plans were underway to begin conducting Maya-themed ceremonies (and even weddings!) at Santa Rita. Check with the folks at the Old Customs House to learn more.

To reach the Maya site, head out of town on Santa Rita Rd. Continuing north on the main highway toward Mexico, turn left at the Super Santa Rita store. Some 350yd past the store you'll find a wooded area on the right and in its midst a partially restored pyramid offering an amazing view of the surrounding town and bay.

Old Customs House
HISTORIC SITE

(cnr 2nd St South & 1st Ave; ⊙ 9am-5pm Mon-Fri) **FREE** Built in 1886, this fine old Spanish Colonial building once housed a bustling market and customs house. It was one of only 11 buildings spared by Hurricane Janet in 1955. Nowadays, the historic building houses a cultural center and museum, with exhibits of local artifacts and a reproduction of a Maya-Mestizo hut. It's a good place to catch up on what's going on in Corozal during your visit.

Town Hall
NOTABLE BUILDING

(✆ 422-2072; 1st St S; ⊙ 9am-noon & 1-5pm Mon-Fri) **FREE** A colorful and graphic **mural** by Belizean-Mexican artist Manual Villamor Reyes enlivens the lobby of the town hall. The mural depicts episodes from Corozal history including the War of the Castes, with the talking cross and the fall of Bacalar; the flight of refugees into British Honduras; the founding of Corozal; and Hurricane Janet. Across from the town hall, the landmark **clock tower** dominates the park.

Fort Barlee
HISTORIC SITE

At the center of town, this fort was built in 1849 by Caste War refugees for protection from attacks by hostile Maya. Remains of the brick corner turrets are still visible on the fort site.

Corozal Town

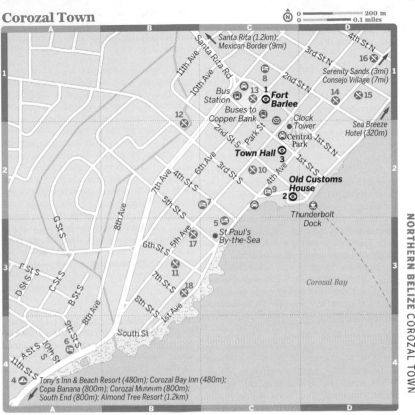

N 0 _____ 200 m
   0 _____ 0.1 miles

Corozal Town

⊙ Top Sights

⊟ Sleeping

⊗ Eating

✪ Entertainment

⊡ Shopping

Corozal Museum MUSEUM
(☏ 402-3314; 129 South End; ⊙ 9-11:30am & 2-4:30pm Mon-Fri) Called 'a Window to the Past', the exhibit at this little museum focuses on the experience of the East Indian population, who arrived around 1838 as indentured servants working on the sugar plantations. The museum is located about a half-mile south of town right on the Northern Hwy.

🛏 Sleeping

The nicest places to stay are in the south end, fronting the bay on Bayshore Dr and Almond Dr. The setting is sweet but it's a bit of a trek into town (20 to 30 minutes walking).

★ **Sea Breeze Hotel** GUESTHOUSE $
(☑front desk 422-3051, 661-9453; www.theseabreezehotel.com; 23 1st Ave; r BZ$40-70; P✳@🛜) Ah, Sea Breeze, a constant anchor of coolness in the sea of change that is the Corozal travel scene. Reminiscent of the kind of cheap and pleasant Key West hotel where Ernest Hemingway might have spent his last years, the hotel has plain but comfortable rooms, each with a queen-sized bed, desk and chair, and en suite with hot shower. The feature that would have appealed most to Papa Hemingway might well have been the usually lively and always fully stocked bar on the 2nd floor, complete with indoor and outdoor seating and a stunning view of Corozal Bay. Good food and strong coffee available on request, and the Sea Breeze's breakfasts are the stuff of legend.

Maya World Guest House GUESTHOUSE $
(☑666-3577; www.aguallos.com/mayaworld; 16 2nd St North; s/d BZ$45/55; @) 🖋 An offbeat and artistically done guesthouse, Maya World consists of two houses and an enclosed courtyard. The bright rooms in the front house have easy access to the wraparound veranda, and the house in back is the home of Byron Chu and his wife Jen. All rooms have shared bathrooms with solar-heated showers, as well as access to a shared kitchen. Gardeners and permaculture enthusiasts will especially want to spend hours hanging out in Byron's garden, at once fragrant and functional, containing herbs, vegetables, and a tall neem tree, reputed to have many healing qualities. Coffee, tea and filtered water are available throughout the day, and the Chu family will be happy to arrange tours in the area and make your stay memorable in general.

Caribbean Village CAMPGROUND $
(☑422-2725; www.belizetransfers.com; 7th Ave, South End; camping per person BZ$10, RVs BZ$40; @🛜🚼) You can't miss this place; it's the plot of land right off the main road on the south end of town with all the RVs parked on it. Lot spaces include all connections (water, electricity, sewage). There's also a campground with toilets and cold showers.

The owners, Henry and Joan Menzies, are licensed travel agents who rent vehicles (per day BZ$160) and book tickets throughout Central America.

★ **Almond Tree Resort** RESORT $$
(☑628-9224; www.almondtreeresort.com; 425 Bayshore Dr; d BZ$170, deluxe ste BZ$298; P✳🛜🐾🚼) Your warm and welcoming hosts are Lynn and Bob and their many pets (including the capricious coatimundi, Rocky). The town's most luxurious lodging, this gorgeous seaside inn offers spacious and stylish rooms with wonderful sea views, Caribbean-style furniture and temperpedic beds. Deluxe suites have full kitchenettes. The whole place is centered on lush grounds and a glorious swimming pool. Lynn's homemade meals are delectable but you will pay for them (home-cooked meals range from seafood dishes to pasta to steaks and go for between BZ$16 and BZ$32) From the Northern Hwy, turn onto Almond Dr a half-mile south of town, and follow the shoreline (and the signs) to Bayshore Dr.

★ **Serenity Sands** B&B $$
(☑669-2394; www.serenitysands.com; Consejo Rd; d BZ$170-180; P✳@🛜) 🖋 Located about 3 miles north of Corozal Town, this B&B is off the beaten track, off the grid and out of this world. The remote beachside setting offers the perfect combination of isolation and accessibility (though you'll need a vehicle to get here). Four gorgeous tiled rooms are decorated with locally crafted furniture and artwork, and each has a private balcony for watching the sunrise over the bay. Scrumptious breakfasts include homemade pastries, fresh fruit and organic eggs from the resident chickens. Aside from the delightfully serene setting and the top-notch service, the B&B has strived to reduce its environmental impact by preserving the local habitat, utilizing solar power and continuously improving waste management. To reach Serenity Sands, drive north out of town on 4th Ave, which turns into the Consejo Rd, and watch for the sign for the turnoff.

Mirador Hotel HOTEL $$
(☑422-0189; www.mirador.bz; cnr 4th Ave & 3rd St S; s/d/tr BZ$70/90/110, s/d/tr with air-con BZ$100/120/150; ✳@🛜) A stately hotel resembling a miniature Belizean version of New York City's famed Flatiron Building, the four-story Mirador's 20 rooms are all clean

and nicely arranged, with pastel-colored walls and tile floors, and most are enhanced by lovely ocean views. The rooftop patio is a welcoming respite; on good days it offers hammocks, lounge chairs and views clear out to Mexico.

Tony's Inn & Beach Resort　RESORT $$
(☑422-3555, 422-2055; www.tonysinn.com; Almond Dr; s/d/tr/q BZ$150/170/190/210; P ❄ @ 🛜 ⛱) This southside resort is the largest in town, with 24 uniform rooms on two floors surrounding a small garden. Spacious and comfortable rooms offer all necessities, such as hair dryers and cable TV, and there's free wi-fi throughout the property. There's a pool in the works, and Tony's Y-not ('Tony' backwards, get it?) Grill & Bar is a lovely seaside spot for food and drinks.

Las Palmas Hotel　HOTEL $$
(☑422-0196, 602-5186; www.laspalmashotelbelize.com; 123 5th Ave S; d/tw/tr from BZ$90/140/160; P ❄ 🛜) Thanks to the hard work of owner Charles Rublee, this renovated hotel has rooms with a crisp, minimalist feel, white stucco walls, wooden furniture and a southwestern motif. Two resident cats and a wrought-iron gate ensure good security. While a promised swimming pool has not materialized, Las Palmas offers plenty of gated parking for large groups.

Hotel Maya & Apartments　HOTEL $$
(☑422-2082; www.hotelmaya.net; 7th Ave, South End; s/d/tr/q BZ$68/75/89/89, s/d/tr/q with aircon BZ$89/100/100/126; ❄ 🛜) Run by the very friendly Rosita May, the Hotel Maya is a longtime favorite of budget-conscious travelers. Rooms are clean, and enlivened by colorful bedspreads and paintings done by local artists. Apartments are available for long-term rentals and, in addition to being a licensed travel agent, Rosita is a great source of local information.

Hok'ol K'in Guest House　GUESTHOUSE $$
(☑422-3329; www.corozal.net; 89 4th Ave; s/d with fan BZ$77/104, s/d with air-con BZ$92/120; ❄ @) With a Mayan name meaning 'rising sun,' this modern, well-run, small hotel overlooking the bay may well be the best value in town. The large, impeccably clean rooms are designed to catch sea breezes. Each has two double beds, a bathroom and a balcony with hammock. Hok'ol K'in also serves meals at reasonable prices (breakfasts are particularly good).

Copa Banana　GUESTHOUSE $$
(☑422-0284; www.copabanana.bz; 409 Bayshore Dr; r per day/week BZ$110/700; P ❄ 🛜 ⛱) Offering excellent value (especially appealing for longer-term visitors) this banana-yellow guesthouse has five beach-themed suites. The comfortable quarters all have access to a shared kitchen, laundry facilities and dining and sitting areas, not to mention the wonderful hammock-strung garden that blooms with tropical plants. The beach is just across the street. Bonus: free bicycles and free pickup from the bus station or the airstrip. Turn off the Northern Hwy onto Almond Dr (about a half-mile south of town) and follow the signs to Bayshore Dr.

Corozal Bay Inn　RESORT $$
(☑422-2691; www.corozalbayinn.biz; Almond Dr; cabañas BZ$110; P ❄ 🛜 ⛱) Ten cozy, colorful *cabañas* are set around a broad sandy area that faces the sea at the far southern end of town. Tucked in under thatched roofs, the *cabañas* are fully equipped (mosquito-netted beds, fridge, coffee maker) and nicely decorated (tile floors, bamboo furnishings). Corozal Bay Inn also has four budget *cabañas* for a mere BZ$50; these are similar to its regular *cabañas* but without the air conditioning. Alas, the resort's restaurant and bar has closed, but the outdoor pool is still a good place to chill out.

🍴 Eating

Travelers who pass through Corozal on their way to Southern Belize may want to spend an extra day in Corozal just to eat some great food before heading out into the land of stewed chicken and rice and beans. Check out the 2nd floor of the **Gabrielle Hoare Market** (6th Ave; ◷ 6:30am-5:30pm Mon-Sat, till 3pm Sun) for cheap eats in a lovely setting.

Corozal's seafront (or bayfront) seems to be enjoying something of a resurgence, with three new restaurants having opened up in the past few years.

Patty's Bistro　BELIZEAN $
(cnr 2nd St N & 4th Ave; meals from BZ$10; ◷breakfast, lunch & dinner) Though the location has shifted two blocks, management of this Corozal favorite has not changed, nor has its friendliness or overall decor. The yellow walls are hung with hokey beach art, and the tables are covered in plastic tablecloths, but the atmosphere is so welcoming that the informal decor only

ART IN THE PARK

The first Saturday of every month hosts an outdoor art exhibition and mini music festival in downtown Corozal, known as **Art in the Park** (http://corozal.com/culture/artinpark; ⊘5:30-10pm). Artists congregate in the Central Park to display their wares, with paintings, photography, woodwork and more. Music is performed live or piped in over the loud speakers and the whole town comes out to socialize.

adds to the charm. The place is best known for its conch soup (BZ$12), a thick potato-based chowder with vegetables, rice and chunks of conch meat, but more adventurous diners may want to go for the cow-foot soup (BZ$10). You'll also find more Mexican and Belizean fare on the menu, not to mention burgers, sandwiches and other standards.

Blue's Restaurant, Bar & Day Resort   PIZZERIA, BELIZEAN $

(Northern Hwy; meals BZ$12-24; ⊘Sun-Thu 10am-midnight, Fri & Sat 10am-2am; 🐾) Located on an inviting curve of beach just where the road turns south out of town, this semi-enclosed restaurant has indoor and beach-front seating with a spectacular view of the bay. (On a clear day – as most are around these parts – you can see the ruins at Cerros!) It has an outdoor stone oven, so pizza is a good dining choice at Blue's (they go for between BZ$18 and $BZ24), but Belize standards such as rice and beans, *ceviche*, salads and sandwiches are also available. There's also beer and fresh juices. Parents take note: Blue's also has a fine playground with swings, a jungle gym and even a reasonably well-cared-for trampoline.

RD's Diner   BELIZEAN $

(25 4th Ave; meals from BZ$10; ⊘breakfast, lunch & dinner) Rick and his staff go above and beyond to ensure a good time at this innocuous-looking eatery. The interior might be nondescript but it's an excellent place to sample some local specialties such as *gibnut* stew or rice and beans. Otherwise the menu offers a mix of Belizean, Mexican and straight-up continental fare such as burgers, salads and fried seafood. Service is a bit slow but exceedingly friendly.

Wood House Bistro   ASIAN $

(1st Ave; dishes BZ$8-22; ⊘lunch & dinner) A dime a dozen in Belize, cookie cutter Chinese restaurants are barely worth mentioning, which is why we're especially pleased that Corozal now has the quirky and pretty darn good Wood House Bistro at the southern end of town. Decor is charming, to say the least, with hand-painted scenes of animated splendor including a panda eating dumplings. Food is eclectic, offereing more than the usual fried chicken. Singapore-style noodles (BZ$12) are especially good, as are the Rangoon crab puffs (BZ$8). Egg rolls are best avoided by those with low grease tolerance.

Venky's Kabab Corner   INDIAN $

(☑402-0546; 5th St S; dishes BZ$8-15; ⊘10:30am-9:30pm) Chef Venky is the premier – and, as far as we know, only – Hindu chef in Corozal, cooking excellent Indian meals, both meat and vegetarian. The place is not much to look at on the inside, but the food is excellent and filling. Two main dishes and a few sides easily serve three people.

Cactus Plaza   MEXICAN $

(6 6th St S; snacks BZ$3-5, mains BZ$8-20; ⊘dinner Thu-Sun) You can't miss this building, which looks a bit like a cross between a Christmas tree and a Mexican fruitcake. On the menu you'll find tacos, *salbutes* and *panuchos* (fried corn tortillas with fillings), as well as shrimp, sea-snail or mixed-seafood *ceviches*. Beware the habaneros! There are also plenty of good drinks including *licuados con leche* (milkshakes) and fresh fruit juices.

Al's Cafe   DINER $

(5th Ave; snacks BZ$1-2, mains BZ$5-8; ⊘breakfast & lunch Mon-Sat, dinner Wed, Fri & Sat) This tiny local place is popular for tasty Mexican snacks and cheap daily lunch specials. Try the burritos with beans, chicken and cheese (and very hot habanero sauce)!

Chico's Tortilla Factory   BAKERY $

(25 7th Ave; tortillas per dozen BZ$1.25; ⊘6am-5pm) Not a sit-down restaurant, but a fun place to go to watch flour tortillas being made.

★Purple Toucan   MEXICAN, MAYAN $$

(☑622-9329; 52 4th Ave; meals BZ$15-30; ⊘11am-3:30pm & 6:30pm-11pm; 🧒) Joe and Yolanda's Purple Toucan serves some of the best food in Corozal. From Mayan *pork choc* (a grilled pork dish with onions, tomato and a delightfully savory sauce) to garlic shrimp to fish filet stuffed with shrimp, you're sure to find something you like at the Purple Toucan. Meals range from BZ$15 to BZ$30, but you can eat for under BZ$10 if you stick to the superb tacos. An excellent bar and friendly service have kept this place a Corozal mainstay for years.

Y-Not Grill & Bar INTERNATIONAL $$
(☑422-2055; www.tonysinn.com; Almond Dr; dishes BZ$15-32; ☺lunch & dinner) The waterfront restaurant at Tony's Inn offers a delightful setting and decent grub served under a breezy thatch-roofed *palapa* right on the waterfront, with dockside seating stretching out into the bay. The bar offers a fine selection of tropical fruity cocktails and other drinks.

☕ Drinking & Nightlife

To enjoy an aperitif in an atmospheric seaside setting, head to one of the southside hotel bars, such as the chilled-out **Corozal Bay Inn** (www.corozalbayinn.com; Almond Dr; ☺7am-late) or the upscale **Y-Not Grill & Bar** (www.tonysinn.com; Almond Dr; ☺11am-11pm or midnight).

Primo's Casita Bar BAR
(Front St; ☺noon-midnight Tue-Sun) Have a seat at this open-air bar and restaurant and enjoy the Corozal Bay breeze with a cold Belikin (BZ$3.50) or an even colder margarita or colada (BZ$10). If you're in the mood for something wilder, Primo's offers a host of special cocktails for between BZ$8 and BZ$15, half of which have names we can't print without blushing. Food is quite good as well, from filling homemade soups to burgers and excellent *ceviches*.

Cactus Plaza CLUB
(6 6th St S; ☺9pm-3am or 4am Fri-Sun) This colorful crazy Mexican restaurant heats up after dark with karaoke singing on Friday and Sunday and DJ-spinning on Saturday.

🛍 Shopping

If you're really desperate for retail therapy, your best bet might well be a quick trip up to the 'Free Zone' on the Belize–Mexico border.

Gabrielle Hoare Market SOUVENIRS
(6th Ave; ☺6:30am-5:30pm Mon-Sat, till 3pm Sun) Amid the fruit, vegetables and fish, you'll also find a few local craftspeople selling art, woodwork and tapestries. The 2nd floor has stores selling clothing and locally made clothing. You'll certainly find a greater selection further south (especially in the more tourism-focused towns).

ℹ Information

Agilarnet Café (60 4th Ave; internet per hr BZ$3; ☺7am-6pm Mon-Fri, 7am-3pm Sat) Internet access, printing services and computer repairs.

COROZAL FREE ZONE

Straddling the Belize–Mexico border at Santa Elena–Subteniente López, 9 miles north of Corozal Town, is a curious experiment in global capitalism going by the moniker 'Free Zone.' Though the name implies a kind of free-market free-for-all, with shops and stalls selling goods from both sides of the border at discounted rates to consumers from both sides of the border, the reality is, well...different.

In practice, the Free Zone resembles a shopping mall comprising loads of high-turnover small shops selling second-rate consumer goods from China, India and other export nations. Shops are staffed by both Belizean and Mexican workers, which apparently is where the notion of 'free' comes in, as both Belizeans and Mexicans are free to work there.

But not to shop. Unlike their Mexican counterparts, Belizeans can't just show up, shop and go home, due to restrictive import regulations and duties on the Belizean side of the border. In essence, the Free Zone is a bargain-basement shopping mall for consumers on the Mexican side of the border – one that Belizean customers can only utilize with some degree of bureaucratic wrangling.

So, the Free Zone is not open to Belizeans (or non-Belizean residents of Belize) but it is open to nonresident foreigners, eg tourists, who can shop duty-free. Shoppers can get excellent deals on alcohol, household appliances and brand-name shoes and clothing. It's cheap – *very* cheap – leading folks to speculate about the authenticity of those brand names. But they are good deals, nonetheless.

Here's the catch: the duty-free goods are for sale for use outside of Belize; if you bring your loot back into Belize, you are obliged to pay all applicable taxes.

Belize Bank (cnr 5th Ave & 1st St N) Situated on the plaza; ATM accepts all international credit cards, with BZ$500 limit and BZ$4 fee.

Corozal Hospital (☑ 422-2076) This hospital is located northwest of the center of town on the way to Chetumal (Mexico).

Immigration office (5th Ave; ☺ 8:30am-noon & 1-4pm Mon-Fri) Provides 30-day visa extensions for most nationalities.

Post office (5th Ave; ☺ 8:30am-noon & 1-4:30pm Mon-Thu, till 4pm Fri) On the site of Fort Barlee, facing the plaza.

Scotiabank (4th Ave) Currency exchange and cash advances; ATM accepts all international cards with BZ$800 daily limit and BZ$4 fee.

❶ Getting There & Around

AIR

Corozal's airstrip (CZH) is about 1 mile south of the town center. Taxis (BZ$10) meet incoming flights. Both **Tropic Air** (☑ 422-0356; www.tropicair.com) and **Maya Island Air** (☑ 422-2333; www.mayaairways.com) fly in and out of Corozal. Rosita at the Hotel Maya sells airline tickets to Belize City (via San Pedro; four or five daily, one way/return BZ$182/$314, one hour) and San Pedro (four or five daily, one way/return BZ$95/$190, 25 minutes). Prices may vary.

BOAT

Corozal is the natural jumping-off point for trips to Cerros, Sarteneja and San Pedro, and the town's only water-taxi service is **Thunderbolt.** (☑ 422-0026, 226-2904; 1st Ave) The advent of the Chetumal to San Pedro boat, combined with an overall tourism decrease in Corozal has made its service slightly less regular, but there are generally daily boats during high season. The boat leaves Corozal at 7am, returning from San Pedro at 3pm. It stops at Sarteneja and Cerros en route (upon request). The trip to Sarteneja takes 30 minutes and costs BZ$25/50 one way/return; San Pedro is two hours away and will cost you BZ$45/85 one way/return.

BUS

Corozal's main bus station is a key stop for nearly all of the myriad bus lines that ply the Northern Hwy down to Orange Walk and Belize City. At last count, 30 buses daily were doing the 2½-hour run from Corozal Town to Belize City, from 3:45am until 6:30pm; in the other direction, a similar number do the 15-minute run to the Mexican border.

In Chetumal, Mexico, buses from Corozal stop at the Nuevo Mercado (New Market), about 0.75 miles north of the town center. A few continue to Chetumal's intercity bus station, a further 0.6 miles north, from where buses leave for other destinations in Mexico. A taxi from the Nuevo Mercado to the bus station or town center is US$1. From Chetumal to Corozal, buses leave from the north side of the Nuevo Mercado from about 4:30am to 6pm.

Cerro Maya & Copper Bank

POP 500

The small fishing (and lobstering) village of Copper Bank (called San Fernando on some maps) is set on the shores of a brackish lagoon known as Laguna Seca (which is anything but dry). The village is a tiny place – consisting of just 500 souls – with a lazy hazy crazy tropical charm.

Although Copper Bank is only 9 miles from Corozal, it's isolated due to the poor condition of the roads and the necessity of crossing the New River by hand-crank ferry. Nonetheless, this tranquil little hamlet has just enough going on to make it an ideal place to hole up for a spell. The Maya ruins at Cerro Maya (also known as Cerros) are 2.5 miles north, overlooking Corozal Bay; and the New River and the surrounding jungles are ideal for fly-fishing, bird-watching and other outdoor adventures.

CRANK YANKING

If you're driving or riding through the back bush of Corozal District between Corozal Town and Sarteneja, you'll wind up fording two rivers in a distinctly Belizean way – via hand-cranked ferries that run along thick cables strung from riverbank to riverbank. This throwback to the early days of industrialization owes its existence to the low traffic density plying the roads. With too few vehicles to make building a bridge feasible, the low-tech (and low-impact) human-powered cable ferry was seen as a fine way to ensure that cars, bikes and motorcycles could get where they needed to go (even if only two at a time). The first is between Corozal and the town of Copper Bank, and the second on the way out of Copper Bank towards Sarteneja. They're slow and fun and, according to locals, they run 24 hours a day. Best of all, they're free.

CONSEJO VILLAGE

About 7 miles north of Corozal, Consejo Village is a sweet little fishing village set on Chetumal Bay, offering little more than a pristine stretch of beach and lovely sunrise views. Bring a book and your binoculars and you might be content to stay here for quite a while.

There aren't many amenities for tourists in Consejo Village. But there is a handful of folk who liked the place so much that they decided to stay, setting up a sort of outpost for expats at **Consejo Shores** (www.consejoshores.com) at the southern end of the village. Although there are no gates, it does have the exclusive atmosphere of a gated community.

The road between Corozal and Consejo is paved but pot-holed. A bus travels this route twice a day (departing from Corozal Central Sq at 8am and 3:40pm, and returning at 8:15am and 4pm). There is also a weekly boat service to Chetumal, which departs from the customs dock at 9am on Wednesday.

Casa Blanca by the Sea (☑423-1018; www.casablanca-bythesea.com; s/d BZ$130/150; P ❋ 🛜) is oddly out of place in modest Consejo. All the rooms at this upscale hotel have bay views and rattan furniture, and guests enjoy access to a private beach and day trips to Mexico. Even if you can't spend the night, the restaurant is a sweet spot for local seafood, cold drinks and fresh breezes.

⊙ Sights

Cerro Maya RUIN
(Cerros; admission BZ$20; ☺8am 5pm) The ruin at Cerro Maya is the only Maya site in Belize that occupies beachfront property. In late Preclassical times its proximity to the mouth of the New River gave it a key position on the trade route between the Yucatán coast and the Petén region.

Cerro Maya ('Maya Hill') is composed of a series of temples built from about 50 BC. The temples are larger and more ornate than any others found in the area, and archaeologists believe Cerro Maya may have been taken over by an outside power at this time, quite possibly Lamanai. Cerros flourished until about AD 150, after which it reverted rapidly to small, unimportant village status.

While the site is mostly a mass of grass-covered mounds, the center has been cleared and consolidated. Climbing **Structure 4** (a funerary temple more than 65ft high) offers stunning panoramic views of the ocean and Corozal Town just across the bay. Northwest of this, **Structure 5** stands with its back to the sea. This was the first temple to be built and may have been the most important. Large stucco masks flanking its central staircase have been covered over by stone walls for their protection.

Southwest of Structure 5, a third structure remains unexcavated, protected by an army of mosquitoes. Apparently **Structure 6** exhibits a 'triadic' arrangement (one main temple flanked by two lesser ones, all atop the same mound), which is also found in

Preclassical buildings at Lamanai and El Mirador in the Petén.

Be warned: Cerro Maya can get buggy, especially during the rainy season; cover up and don't skimp on the bug spray!

🛏 Sleeping & Eating

Copperbank Inn GUESTHOUSE $
(☑662 5281; www.copperbankinn.com; r inc breakfast BZ$70-90; P ❋ 🛜 ☀) This gracious plantation-style home stands out in the middle of modest little Copper Bank. With its wraparound veranda and exposed swimming pool, it is conspicuous, but nonetheless offers good value. Cool white-tiled rooms are decorated with gauzy curtains and stylish furniture, and meals are available at Maya Fusion, the excellent onsite restaurant. Management will assist with arrangements for boat trips and archaeological exploration, as well as trips to Chetumal.

★**Cerros Beach Resort** RESORT, CABINS $$
(☑623-9530, 623-9763; d/q cabaña BZ$80/120, mains BZ$12-15; P 🛜) About 3.5 miles north of Copper Bank, on the coast and surrounded by jungle, this rustic little beach resort is perhaps our favorite spot in northern Belize. What's so great about the Cerros Beach Resort? It isn't just its location, set as it is on the white-sand shore of the crystal blue side of Corozal Bay. Neither is it the facilities and amenities: four beautiful, hardwood, thatched-roof *cabañas* with hot solar showers and sea-facing porches, not to mention free use of kayaks and nature trails. Nor is it the highly recommended food prepared

by the owner, a former pastry chef from Miami who makes tangy, to-die-for *ceviche* and delicious, decadent chocolate cake. What makes us love this place is all these things and one other factor: Cerros Beach Resort is (almost) totally ecologically sustainable, operating on solar and wind power. Come for the kayaking, cake and *ceviche*; stay for the low-carbon footprint.

Maya Fusion   INTERNATIONAL **$**
(www.copperbankinn.com; meals BZ$12-25; ☺8am-8pm) Fomerly known as Donna's, the 1st floor of the Copperbank Inn is home to this great little restaurant. Maya Fusion serves freshly caught seafood, pastries, fresh juices and ice cream, all prepared in a Maya-style outdoor kitchen. The food is good and the vibe is super friendly.

🛈 Getting There & Away

All-weather roads run from Corozal to Copper Bank, punctuated by two rivers forded by hand-cranked cable ferry, and on to Cerros. For those without wheels of their own, getting to Copper Bank and Cerros is best done by boat.

Cerros is about 2.5 miles north of the village of Copper Bank. Bus schedules to Copper Bank don't permit day trips to Cerros; if you don't have your own vehicle you can visit on a guided tour from Corozal (typically costing BZ$80 per person) or get the Thunderbolt ferry to drop you.

🛈 GETTING TO MEXICO

The border crossing at Santa Elena (Belize) and Subteniente López (Mexico) is 9 miles north of Corozal and 7 miles west of Chetumal. If you are crossing from Mexico to Belize you will normally have to hand in your Mexican tourist card to Mexican immigration as you leave. If you plan to return to Mexico within the card's period of validity you are entitled to keep it and reuse it for your return visit. Officials at this border may charge US$10 to allow you to keep the card; this is still cheaper than the US$20 you would have to pay for a new card on your return.

Travelers departing from Belize by land have to pay BZ$37.50; this includes both the exit fee and a government-imposed conservation fee.

Bus travelers, heading in either direction, have to get off the bus and carry their luggage through customs.

Sarteneja

POP 2000

If you came to Belize in search of crystal-blue waters, delicious fresh seafood, fauna-rich forests and affordable prices, look no further than Sarteneja (sar-ten-*eh*-ha). The tiny fishing and shipbuilding village, located near the northeastern tip of the Belizean mainland, is a charming base from which to explore both the nautical and jungle treasures of the region. Stroll along the shoreline to admire the wooden sailboats that are still constructed in workshops around town.

The village spreads just a few blocks back from its long, grassy seafront. It's a delicious place to chill out for a few days. From this lovely seaside setting visitors can also head out to the Shipstern Nature Reserve and take birding, fishing and wildlife-watching trips all along the fabulous coast of northern Belize, including to Bacalar Chico National Park & Marine Reserve, on the northern tip of Ambergris Caye.

◉ Sights

Shipstern Nature Reserve   PARK
(www.shipstern.org; admission BZ$10; ☺8am-5pm) 🐾 This large nature reserve, which protects 43 sq miles of semideciduous hardwood forests, wetlands and lagoons and coastal mangrove belts, has its headquarters 3.5 miles southwest of Sarteneja on the road to Orange Walk. Lying in a transition zone between Central America's tropical forests and a drier Yucatán-type ecosystem, the reserve's mosaic of habitats is rare in Belize.

All five of Belize's wildcats and scores of other mammals can be found here, and its 250 bird species include ospreys, roseate spoonbills, white ibis and a colony of 300 pairs of American woodstorks, one of this bird's few breeding colonies in Belize. The Belizean nonprofit organization Shipstern Nature Reserve Belize is funded by the Swiss- and Dutch-based **International Tropical Conservation Foundation** (www.papiliorama.ch).

Admission allows access to both a small **museum** and **butterfly house** at the headquarters, as well as a short **botanical trail** that leads to an observation tower over the treetops. There are several other longer hiking trails, including **Thompson Trail**, which goes to the shore of the lagoon (accessible only in the dry season).

ZOE WALKER: CONSERVATION GURU

Wildtracks Conservation Programme is a nonprofit organization that is working towards a sustainable future for Belizean natural resources through conservation, research, education and development. The organization hosts both the Manatee Rehabilitation Centre and the Primate Rehabilitation Centre, neither of which is open to the public.

Where is the best place to see animals in the wild?
The Sarteneja Tour Guide Association (STGA) offers tours to Corozal Bay Wildlife Sanctuary, with the possibility of seeing manatees and dolphins (of course there are no guarantees), and to Bacalar Chico Marine Reserve, to snorkel the coral reef there. Shipstern Nature Reserve offers more land-based opportunities, particularly for bird-watching.

What's the best way to learn about local culture?
A new homestay program in Sarteneja allows travelers to experience the culture and way of life by staying with a family, with opportunities to learn Spanish and to make local tortillas. It is also a mechanism to reduce the dependency of these families on fishing. Contact the **Sarteneja Alliance for Conservation & Development** (SACD; www. sartenejaconservation.org) for details.

How can travelers promote wildlife conservation in Belize?
Voice concerns if a tour guide is not following best practices (eg chasing down manatees to get a better view, hitching a ride on sea turtles, teasing or feeding monkeys). The tour guides won't change unless the visitors express their dislike of these practices.

How can travelers get more involved?
Wildtracks doesn't take 'drop-in volunteers' but does recruit through **Global Nomadic** (www.globalnomadic.com). Generally, three-month placements are preferred.

SACD offers a number of opportunities to get involved in active management of Corozal Bay Wildlife Sanctuary, such as monitoring important target species that are vulnerable in the bay (West Indian manatees, bird-nesting cayes and native fin fish like cubera snapper, chiwa and mojarras).

Zoe and Paul Walker are the cofounders of Wildtracks Conservation Programme. Compiled with the assistance of the Sarteneja Alliance for Conservation & Development.

NORTHERN BELIZE SARTENEJA

Of course, the best way to see the lagoon and its birdlife is by taking a boat tour, which costs BZ$225 for up to four people (including lunch). As always, you'll see most in the early morning, so tours usually set out before sunrise.

About 40 minutes from the headquarters, **Xo-Pol** has a treetop hide overlooking a large forest-surrounded pond where you might see crocodiles, waterfowl, peccaries, deer and tapirs. Half-day birding tours are BZ$100 for up to four people. Rangers also take adventurers on overnight expeditions to Xo-Pol for BZ$250.

Any guesthouse in Sarteneja can help you arrange these longer tours. Don't forget your long sleeves, long pants and bug spray!

🛏 Sleeping & Eating

Sarteneja Village has a handful of small hotels, most of which double as restaurants. There are also a couple of bakeries, grocery stores and bars scattered around the village.

⭐**Backpackers
Paradise** CABINS, CAMPGROUND $
(☑423 2016; www.cabanasbelize.com; Bandera Rd, Sarteneja; camping BZ$7, cabañas with shared/private bathroom BZ$28/48, little/family house BZ$66/88; 🛜) Peaceful, sustainable and affordable, this is truly paradise. Backpackers is an idyllic 3-acre patch of unspoiled jungle and tropical farmland with camping, cabins and a great little restaurant (BZ$4 to BZ$8 for breakfast, BZ$10 to BZ$18 for lunch/dinner). It's no surprise that all sorts of travelers (not just backpackers) are making the trek into Northern Belize just to spend a few days here, walk jungle trails, eat tropical fruit from the trees, swim in the nearby ocean, or just lounge in hammocks in the comfy communal spaces. The *cabañas* are screened-in huts with thatched roofs and king-size beds, and two newly built houses sleep four to six. There's a communal kitchen, horses and bicycles for rent and plenty of other activities in the area. If you contact her in advance,

DON'T MISS

LITTLE BELIZE

Located on the eastern shore of Progresso Lagoon, Little Belize is an Old Order Mennonite community of approximately 2000 residents. Being among the more traditional Mennonite groups, these folks look as thought they've come straight from the prairie, driving around in horse-drawn carriages, men wearing broad-brimmed hats and overalls, women in long dresses and bonnets.

Like most Mennonite villages, Little Belize is an industrious place, with an economy thriving on farming. One of the largest employers in the village is Belize Exports Ltd, which grows papayas for export to North America.

Old Order Mennonites are typically an insular group, interacting with outsiders just enough to sell their wares. Tentatively opening itself up to rural tourism, Little Belize offers visitors a rare opportunity to get a closer look inside this enigmatic community. With advanced arrangements, visitors can tour the village in a horse-drawn buggy, visiting the papaya packing plant, a poultry farm, a wood workshop and other local industries. The half-day tour (BZ$100 per person) includes lunch in a private home. Some locals are also offering homestays in the village. Make arrangements in advance through the Shipstern Nature Reserve.

Little Belize is a 40-minute drive from Sarteneja, Corozal or Orange Walk. There is no public transportation available, but the Shipstern Nature Reserve can provide transportation.

the owner Nathalie will meet your bus or boat in her horse-drawn buggy.

Oasis Guesthouse   GUESTHOUSE $
(☑ 660-9621; Lagunita St; s/d BZ$50/60; P) Four clean and comfortable rooms, and a rooftop patio with a spectacular view of the bay and surrounding village. One block from the bay.

Candelie's Sunset Cabanas   CABINS $
(☑ 660-0561; candelies.cabanas@yahoo.com; N Front St; cabaña with fan/air-con BZ$80/120; P ✻ 🖱) At the west end of the waterfront street, Candelie's has two big, breezy *cabañas* and a dining room with an amazing mural that depicts Sarteneja's history.

**Fernando's Seaside
Guesthouse**   GUESTHOUSE $$
(☑ 423-2085; http://fernandosseaside.com; N Front St; d BZ$100; ✻) This small and colorful hotel has five rooms, each with two double beds, private bathrooms with hot showers, and ceiling fans. Fernando also arranges snorkeling, fishing and other trips around the area.

❶ Information

@Do's Cyber Cafe (internet per hr BZ$3; ◷ 9am-10pm; 🖱) While waiting for arrival and installation of computers, @Do's offered wi-fi access only at the time of research.

❶ Getting There & Around

You can rent good bicycles at Fernando's Seaside Guesthouse or Backpackers Paradise for BZ$4 per hour or BZ$20 per day.

With advance notice, the **Thunderbolt** (☑ 610-4475, 422-0026) ferry will stop in Sarteneja en route between Corozal and San Pedro. The ride to Corozal takes 30 minutes and sets you back BZ$30; to San Pedro you're looking at an hour and a half at sea and a cost of BZ$50.

Five buses do the Sarteneja–Orange Walk run (BZ$5, 1½ hours, hourly from noon to 5pm Monday to Saturday), returning the same day. On Sunday, there's only one bus from Sarteneja.

Sarteneja is 40 miles northeast of Orange Walk by a mostly unpaved all-weather road that passes through the village of San Estevan and the scattered Mennonite community of Little Belize. Drivers from Corozal Town can reach Sarteneja (43 miles) by taking the road toward Copper Bank. Turn right 6 miles from Corozal at a junction signposted to Progresso and Sarteneja. This road meets the road from Orange Walk Town shortly before Little Belize.

Cayo District

Best Places to Eat

➡ Ko-Ox Han-nah, San
Ignacio (p174)

➡ Benny's Kitchen, San José
Succotz (p180)

➡ Blancaneaux Lodge,
Mountain Pine Ridge (p166)

Best Places to Stay

➡ Black Rock River Lodge,
Chial Road (p181)

➡ Mahogany Hall, Bullet Tree
Falls (p178)

➡ Ian Anderson's Caves
Branch Jungle Lodge,
Hummingbird Highway
(p156)

➡ Trek Stop, San José
Succotz (p180)

Why Go?

Hiking, biking, birding, canoeing, kayaking, spelunking and all-around adventuring! The lush environs of the Wild West are covered with jungle, woven with rivers, waterfalls and azure pools, and dotted with Maya ruins ranging from small, tree-covered hills to massive, magnificent temples. Cahal Pech, Xunantunich, El Pilar and the mother of all Belizean Maya sites, Caracol, are all in Cayo.

Ancient history aside, Cayo teems with life in the here and now, from botanic gardens and butterfly houses to primeval jungles and rainforests, where the only thing that'll come between you and the wildlife is a pair of binoculars. Live it up in luxury in an exotic jungle lodge, or choose from dozens of lower-priced places in and around San Ignacio. If camping is your thing, just pitch your tent alongside the Macal River. No matter where you set up camp, you'll sleep well after a day of adventure in Cayo.

When to Go

Sun-drenched days and cooler nights make February and March a great time to explore Cayo. April and May are the height of the dry season: no need to worry about muddy shoes, but drink plenty of water. In July and August, summer showers bring an eruption of mangoes, avocados and breadfruit throughout the region.

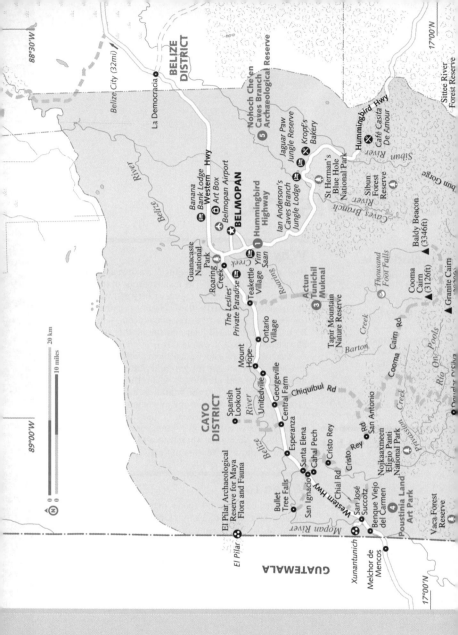

1 Driving along the **Hummingbird Highway** (p155)

2 Exploring the ancient ruins of **Caracol** (p167)

3 Serious spelunking at **Actun Tunichil Muknal** (p157)

4 Walking among the surreal art of **Poustinia Land Art Park** (p182)

5 Sunset cave-tubing at **Nohoch Che'en Caves Branch Archaeological Reserve** (p150)

88°30'W

89°00'W

17°00'N

BELIZE DISTRICT

Belize City (32mi)

La Democracia

CAYO DISTRICT

GUATEMALA

Belize River

Mopan River

El Pilar Archaeological Reserve for Maya Flora and Fauna

El Pilar

Bullet Tree Falls

San Ignacio
Santa Elena
Cahal Pech
Esperanza

Spanish Lookout
Unitedville
Georgeville
Central Farm

Mount Hope

Ontario Village

The Leslies' Private Paradise

Guanacaste National Park
Roaring Creek

Teakettle Village

Yim Saan

BELMOPAN

Belmopan Airport
Art Box
Banana Bank Lodge

Western Hwy

Hummingbird Highway

Ian Anderson's Caves Branch Jungle Lodge

St Herman's Blue Hole National Park

Jaguar Paw Jungle Reserve

Nohoch Che'en Caves Branch Archaeological Reserve

Kropf's Bakery

Hummingbird Hwy

Café Casita De Amour

Sibun River

Sibun Gorge

Sibun Forest Reserve

Caves Branch River

Roaring Creek

Actun Tunichil Muknal

Tapir Mountain Nature Reserve

Barton Creek

Chiquibul Rd

Cristo Rey
San Antonio
Cristo Rey Rd

Chial Rd

San José Succotz

Xunantunich

Melchor de Mencos

Benque Viejo del Carmen

Poustinia Land Art Park

Vaca Forest Reserve

Nojkaaxmeen Elijio Panti National Park

Privassion Creek

Cooma Cairn Rd

Thousand Foot Falls

Cooma Cairn

Baldy Beacon (3346ft)

Cooma Cairn (3126ft)

Granite Cairn

Rio On Pools

Sittee River Forest Reserve

N

0   20 km
0   10 miles

17°00'N

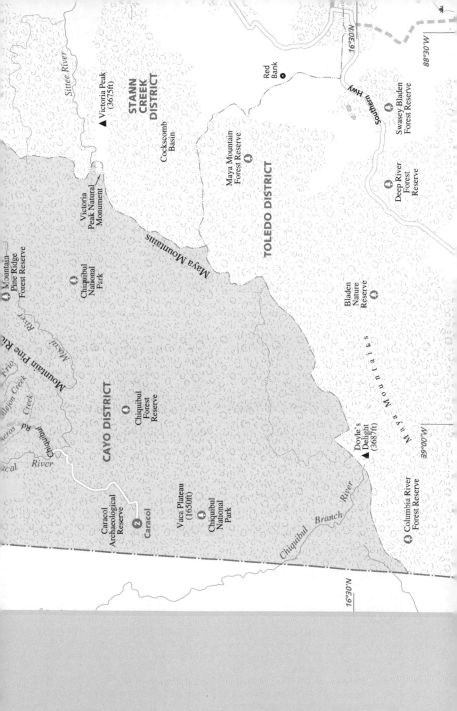

ℹ️ Getting There & Around

BUS

Buses run along the Western Hwy between Belize City and Benque Viejo del Carmen, stopping in Belmopan and San Ignacio. Passengers traveling between western and southern Belize need to change in Belmopan. Most destinations along the Western Hwy between Belize City, Belmopan and San Ignacio can be accessed by bus, as can some other spots in the region.

There are few bus services off the main highway. If you don't have your own vehicle, you'll need to take tours from San Ignacio (or from the lodges themselves) to access isolated lodges and attractions.

CAR

The Western Hwy is the region's artery, running across the country from Belize City through San Ignacio and Benque Viejo del Carmen and on to the Guatemalan border. The Hummingbird Hwy diverges south of Belmopan.

Unpaved or partially paved roads head off the main highway to villages, farms and remote lodges and attractions, the most important of these routes being Chiquibul Rd, which heads up and over the Mountain Pine Ridge, and Cristo Rey Rd, which links Chiquibul Rd with San Ignacio.

BETWEEN BELIZE DISTRICT & BELMOPAN

West of the Belize District, the Western Hwy speeds along for about 50 miles on smooth, unbroken pavement. This is probably the country's most heavily trafficked road. It leads to the capital, of course, but even more significantly it carries busloads of island-based tourists and cruise-ship passengers to inland adventures such as cave-tubing, zip lining and horseback riding.

About 11 miles east of Belmopan, a turn-off leads south to the Nohoch Che'en Caves Branch Archaeological Reserve and the Jaguar Paw Jungle Resort, two perennially popular attractions. In 2007 this road was paved, making it a quick and easy drive from the coast and bringing about an exponential increase in the number of visitors to the region.

◉ Sights & Activities

Guanacaste National Park PARK
(admission BZ$5; ☉ 8am-4:30pm) Belize's smallest national park is named for the giant guanacaste tree on its southwestern edge. Somehow, possibly thanks to the odd shape of its trunk, the tree survived the axes of canoe-makers and still rises majestically in its jungle habitat. Festooned with bromeliads, ferns and dozens of other varieties of plant, the great tree supports a whole ecosystem of its own.

Perched at the junction of the Western and Hummingbird Hwys, this 250,000-sq-yd park is an excellent place to break a drive. At the confluence of Roaring Creek and the Belize River, the park contains 2 miles of hiking trails that will introduce you to the abundant local trees and colorful birds. Birding is best here in winter, when migrants arrive from North America. After your hike, you can head down to the river for a dip in the park's deep swimming hole.

Nohoch Che'en Caves Branch Archaeological Reserve CAVING
(park admission BZ$10) Picture yourself on a tube on a river, with tamarind trees and Belizean blue skies... A few minutes after launch the sky will be replaced by total darkness as you and your comrades are pulled

---

DON'T MISS

SUNSET CAVE-TUBING

For a real adventure, book a sunset cave-tubing trip. Sunset trips differ from day trips in two key ways. First, while the park can get crowded during the day (especially on cruise-ship days), at 4pm it clears out, so there's unlikely to be anyone else on the river. And second, while you'll begin the hike before dusk and enter the cave at dusk, when you exit it will be beneath a canopy of stars, under which you'll float for the next 45 minutes with the sounds of the jungle's nocturnal wildlife coming at you from all sides. It's quite an unforgettable experience.

One of the pioneers of cave-tubing in Belize, **Vitalino Reyes** (☑832-2640, 602-8975; http://cavetubing.bz; per person depending on group size BZ$65-100) is also the only one currently offering sunset cave-tubing trips.

LOCAL KNOWLEDGE

MATTHEW KLINCK: CREATING HOLLYWOOD IN CAYO

In 2012 Canadian-born filmmaker Matthew Klinck started **Make-Belize Films** (www.make-belizefilms.com) to teach young Belizeans the skills to tell their stories using cinema. The project grew to create Belize's first homegrown full-length movie, *Curse of the Xtabai*.

Why did you choose Belize? While backpacking in San Ignacio I ran into some amazing young people building a film crane in a junkyard who dreamt of someday making movies. They couldn't afford a video camera and had no access to training, so I skipped the return flight and have been here ever since.

Why Cayo? The story called for pristine jungle, a river and a cave with road access and good places to camp. We found it all in Elijio Panti National Park behind San Antonio village. Mountain Equestrian Trails (p161) provided some tents, we shot the Xtabai flying scenes using Calico Jack's zip line (p162), and the underworld scenes we filmed in Actun Tunichil Muknal (p157).

The movie really makes Cayo look rugged, even foreboding. What difficulties did you encounter during the filming? A freak dry-season rainstorm soaked our gear and filled our tents with water. One of our actors was stung several times by a scorpion. Later the crew ate the scorpion. A swarm of killer bees attacked us in the middle of the jungle, and our leading lady was sure she was dying.

The story really resonated with Belizeans. Could you summarize it for non-Belizeans? Basically a group of students take on the Xtabai, an evil spirit of Mayan folklore, to save their village from its curse. A shaman leads them to a mysterious cave where they have to perform a ritual sacrifice.

Belize has been used as setting for only a handful of films – do you think this is likely to change? I see a bright future for production in Belize and the most exciting prospect is a new homegrown film industry for young Belizeans.

down into the very bowels of the earth, where you'll float through bracingly cold water in an underground network and witness – through the light of your headlamp – wonders unseen in the world above, from schools of eyeless cave fish and stalactites to strange Maya paintings high on the cave ceilings. Welcome to **cave-tubing**, possibly the coolest (and most family-friendly) thing you can do in the dark.

The country's most popular cave-tubing site is east of Belmopan. Here, the Caves Branch River flows through five caves, taking tubers between the open air and cool caverns, and giving them an up-close view of stalactites, stalagmites, crystalline formations and artifacts from ancient Maya rituals. The extensive network allows for exploration of side passages, which sometimes lead to other caves, such as the spectacular **Crystal Cave**.

Among the most highly recommended cave-tubing guides is Vitalino Reyes, a pioneer of the pursuit who begins his tubing trips with fascinating, information-filled jungle walks. During the walk he will show you which plants are good to eat, which will hurt you, and which ones will help you if you

confuse the first with the second. Vitalino is also an entomologist who delights in introducing his charges to tasty jungle bugs; and he has a penchant for handling tarantulas. Vitalino runs his trips both in the afternoon and at sunset.

To reach Nohoch Che'en Caves Branch Archaeological Reserve, turn south off the Western Hwy at Mile 37 (look for the 'cavetubing.bz' sign). Follow this road south for 6 miles until you come to the reserve's entrance.

Zip-Line Canopy Tour   TOUR
(tour BZ$110) On the grounds at Nohoch Che'en is the Zip-Line Canopy Tour, where you zoom through the treetops from platform to platform on six linked cable runs up to 200ft long. Trained guides give you a safety briefing and help you into your harness. The tour takes about two hours, but on busy cruise-ship days (best avoided) you'll be rushed through in less than an hour.

Banana Bank Lodge   HORSEBACK RIDING
(820-2020; www.bananabank.com; Mile 47 Western Hwy; 2-/4-hr jungle tour BZ$120/180) Set on a jungle- and pasture-covered property of more than 6 sq miles, Banana Bank has over 100 well-tended horses enjoying an

extensive grazing area and state-of-the-art stables. Besides miles of jungle and riverside trails, facilities include a round pen and a large arena for training and exercising the horses.

The turnoff to Banana Bank is 1 mile east along the Western Hwy from Guanacaste National Park. About 1 mile north of the highway, you reach a metal gong hanging beside a path leading down to the river. Bang the gong and someone will come from the lodge (on the opposite bank) to get you in a hand-operated ferry. It's also possible to drive to the lodge via a vehicle ferry over the Belize River just west of Roaring Creek village.

🛏 Sleeping & Eating

Belize Jungle Dome RESORT $$$
(☑822-2124; www.belizejungledome.com; Mile 47 Western Hwy; r standard/junior/ste/upper terrace BZ$231/297/352/396, breakfast/lunch/dinner BZ$18/22/44; P✳@🛜🏊) 🌊 This is, undoubtedly, an architectural oddity, but the signature dome deserves a mention, its skylights allowing sunlight to filter in, reflecting off the polished mahogany interior. Standard rooms, suites and terraces are fully equipped with modern conveniences, such as air-con, cable TV and internet, and have easy access to the central swimming pool. There's also an organic fruit orchard and an enticing treetop cafe from which to survey the domain. Drive to Belize Jungle Dome via the village of Roaring Creek.

Banana Bank Lodge RESORT $$$
(☑832-2020; www.bananabank.com; Mile 47 Western Hwy; chalets BZ$132-198, cabañas BZ$230-390, ste BZ$300-400, lunch/dinner BZ$20/30; P✳@🛜🏊) This lodge and equestrian center sits on the banks of the Belize River, 4 miles from Belmopan, and offers mahogany-and-thatch *cabañas* with a unique two-bedroom design with a sitting room, mosquito netting, ceiling fans and wrought-iron or carved-mahogany bedsteads. Budget 'chalet' rooms sleep five people. The lodge has a bird observation tower overlooking a lagoon, an orchid garden with over 50 species of orchid and some small Maya ruins onsite. While the horses at this equestrian center seem healthy and well tended, the presence of a caged jaguar might turn off people who feel that jungle animals are best left in the wild.

🛍 Shopping

Art Box ARTS & CRAFTS
(☑822-2233; www.artboxbz.com; Mile 46 Western Hwy; ⊙8am-5:30am Mon-Sat; 🛜) Right before the Belmopan airstrip sits this combination cafe-shop, a two-story purple building with climbing flowers and an outdoor deck. In addition to providing information on travel all around Cayo and Belize, Art Box sells locally made crafts and music. Stop in to use the wi-fi under the thatched-roof porch, linger to check out the local artwork in the 2nd-floor gallery, and stay for a cup of freshly brewed organic coffee.

BELMOPAN

POP 17,600

In 1961 Hurricane Hattie all but destroyed Belize City. Certain that a coastal capital would never be secure from further terrible hurricanes, the government decided to move. In 1971 it declared its intention to build a new capital in the center of the country, which would become Belmopan.

A grand new National Assembly was built to resemble a Maya temple and plaza, with government offices around it. Government needs have since outgrown these core buildings and an assortment of less-uniform government offices are spread out around the central green. While hardly geared toward recreation, Belmopan is a pleasant enough town. Many government ministries and other organizations are based here, as are a few embassies, giving the place an unexpected international atmosphere. Stick around long enough and it might just grow on you.

Belmopan is located 1 mile east of the Hummingbird Hwy, reached by either of two turnoffs, 1 and 2 miles south of the Hummingbird's junction with the Western Hwy, 50 miles from Belize City. Belmopan is a small place that is easily negotiated on foot. A ring road encircles the central area of town. The bus terminal and the main commercial area are within the west side of this ring.

⊙ Sights

Belize Archives Department MUSEUM
(☑822-2247; www.belizearchives.gov.bz; 26-28 Unity Blvd; ⊙8am-4:30pm Mon-Fri) Rotating displays on hurricanes, the Garifuna, Belmopan, Baron Bliss and other subjects. The extensive collections of photographs, newspapers,

Belmopan

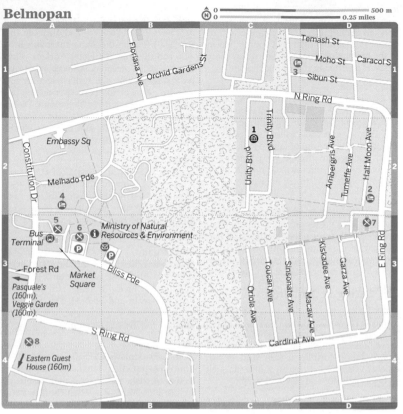

books, maps, documents, and sound and video archives are also open to the public.

🛏 Sleeping

El-Rey Inn HOTEL $
(📞 822-3438; www.belmopanhotels.com; 23 Moho St; r BZ$65-85; 🅿️ ❄️ 📶) An affordable option for budget travelers, this place is just outside the ring road, northeast of the green. Named after the affable owner, 'Elroy' Garbutt, the El-Rey has 12 plain, clean rooms equipped with private bathrooms and fans. More expensive rooms have air-con.

Eastern Guest House HOTEL $
(📞 625-9018; Constitution Dr; s/d BZ$38/49; 📶) A budget choice, in a very budget-unfriendly town. Rooms are very basic, fan-cooled and tolerable for a night.

Hibiscus Hotel HOTEL $$
(📞 610-0400, 822-0400; www.hibiscusbelize.com; Market Sq; s/d BZ$110/120; 🅿️ ❄️ 📶) 🦋 This Bel-

Belmopan

◎ Sights
1 Belize Archives Department C2

🛏 Sleeping
2 Bull Frog Inn.....................................D2
3 El-Rey Inn...C1
4 Hibiscus Hotel A2

🍴 Eating
Bull Frog Inn.................................(see 2)
5 Caladium Restaurant A3
Corkers...(see 4)
6 Food Stalls..A3
7 Moon Clusters Coffee Shop D3
8 Puccini's...A4

mopan favorite was bought by British couple Geoff and Samantha in 2011, and has since been renovated, making a good deal even better. Upgrades include new king and twin-sized beds, flat-screen cable-equipped TV and tea and coffee facilities in every room. Bird lovers take note: some of the profits from your stay go to support local avian conservation and rescue projects. The couple also runs Corker's restaurant, right next door. Adjacent to the bus station, Hibiscus isn't a bad place to spend an evening stuck in Belmopan.

Bull Frog Inn   HOTEL $$
(📞 822-2111; www.bullfroginn.com; 25 Half Moon Ave; s/d BZ$140/170; 🅿 ❄ @ 🛜) On the edge of the village green, just inside the ring road, the Bull Frog is a cheerful, civilized sort of place. The 25 rooms are void of any special atmosphere, but they are spacious and comfortable, complete with telephones and cable TV, while big bathrooms have strong, hot showers.

Yim Saan   HOTEL $$
(📞 822-1356; Hummingbird Hwy; s/d/tr BZ$94/94/120; 🅿 ❄ 🛜) This big hotel on the outskirts of Belmopan offers clean, crisp and sparsely decorated rooms with breezy balconies overlooking the parking lot. The downstairs restaurant serves decent Chinese food.

✖ Eating & Drinking

Food Stalls   STREET FOOD $
For a cheap meal, you can't go wrong at the food stalls just east of the bus station. They serve Mexican snacks such as burritos and *salbutes* (mini-tortillas, usually stuffed with chicken), as well as Belizean standards such as beans and rice and cow-foot soup.

Moon Clusters Coffee Shop   CAFE $
(E Ring Rd, 4 Shopping Center; coffee drinks BZ$3.30-11; ⊙ 11:30am-7pm Mon-Sat) The Aguilar family's excellent little coffee shop serves some of the best Java in Belize, from Cuban Dark Roast to the attitude adjustment, a five shot espresso drink that almost makes Belmopan seem exciting. There's also a variety of smoothies and ice cream drinks and a few snack items on the menu.

Veggie Garden   VEGETARIAN $
(43 Forest Dr; meals from BZ$7; ⊙ lunch & dinner Mon-Sat; 🍴) This Taiwanese vegetarian restaurant serves excellent meat-free dishes and fresh juices. The owners also run a small shop selling Chinese health and beauty products.

Caladium Restaurant   BELIZEAN $
(Market Sq; mains BZ$8-12; ⊙ 7:15am-8pm Mon-Fri, 8am-7pm Sat) Just across the street from the bus station, the Caladium is one of Belmopan's longest-standing family businesses. It offers a dependable menu of Belizean favorites, such as fried fish and coconut rice, conch soup and BBQ chicken.

Corkers   BRITISH $$
(📞 822-0400; Hibiscus Plaza, Melhado Pde; mains BZ$15-40; ⊙ 11am-8pm Mon-Wed, 11am-late Thu-Sat; 🛜🍴) Run by the same charming Brits who run the Hibiscus Hotel, Corkers offers a melange of excellent seafood, meat and pasta dishes – with plenty of choices for vegetarians – on a breezy patio overlooking (for what it's worth) exciting Belmopan. Dishes range from BZ$15 to BZ$40, with a few less expensive snack items and burgers. There's also a fully stocked bar.

Pasquale's   PIZZERIA $$
(cnr Forest Dr & Slim Lane; pizza BZ$22-60; ⊙ lunch & dinner; 🛜) Close to the bus station, this pizza joint has pizzas ranging in size from personal to 12 slice, and all the assorted toppings. Opened by Chicago natives, so you know it's gotta be good.

Bull Frog Inn   INTERNATIONAL $$
(www.bullfroginn.com; 25 Half Moon Ave; mains BZ$15-20; ⊙ breakfast, lunch & dinner; 🛜) This popular and breezy hotel-restaurant serves up good steaks and seafood. The adjoining bar is a popular watering hole, livened up by karaoke and live mariachi music.

Puccini's   PIZZERIA $$
(Constitution Dr; mains BZ$15-30; ⊙ lunch & dinner) This lively restaurant and bar has a great selection of pasta and other Italian dishes, as well as a few Mexican specialties. Take a seat at the open-air bar or sit inside and enjoy the air-con. Service is friendly but slow.

❶ Information

Belize Bank (Constitution Dr) and **Scotiabank** (Constitution Dr) keep regular banking hours and have 24/7 ATM access for all your money needs.

Check your email at **Pross Computers** (📞 601-3529; Constitution Dr; per hr BZ$6; ⊙ 9am-7pm Mon-Fri, to 6pm Sat; @). There's also an internet cafe next to the bus station.

Belmopan Hospital (📞 822-2264; off N Ring Rd) Just north of the center, this is the only emergency facility between Belize City and San Ignacio.

Immigration office (📞 822-3860; Dry Creek St; ⊙ 8am-noon & 1-5pm Mon-Thu, to 4:30pm Fri) Cayo's only immigration office offers 30-day visa extension stamps for BZ$50. It has moved since our last visit, so – hooray – you get to see more of lovely Belmopan!

Ministry of Natural Resources & Environment (📞 822-2226; www.mnrei.gov.bz; ⊙ 8am-noon & 1-4:30pm Mon-Fri) The Land Information

Center here sells the best topographic maps of Belize available, including 1:50,000 sheets.

Post office (⊙8am-noon & 1-5pm Mon-Thu, to 4:30pm Fri)

US Embassy (☎822-4011; http://belize.usembassy.gov; Floral Park Rd, Belmopan; ⊙8am-noon & 1-5pm Mon-Fri) From visa and passport information to marriage advice and hurricane preparedness tips, the US embassy can help. The website is comprehensive and easy to navigate – log on before you line up!

❶ Getting There & Away

AIR

Tropic Air (☎822-0920; www.tropicair.com) has one daily flight to Placencia (one way/return BZ$120/225, 30 minutes) and two to each of San Pedro (BZ$174/338, 55 minutes), Belize City Domestic (BZ$100/190, 25 minutes) and Belize City International (BZ$131/254, 25 minutes).

Belmopan's seldom-used airport is just a few miles east of the city.

BUS

Belmopan's **bus terminal** (☎802-2799; Market Sq) is Belize's main transit hub, and all buses (regardless of company) heading south or west from the Belize District, as well as north and west from Dangriga (and points south) stop in Belmopan. Along the Western Hwy, buses head east to Belize City (BZ$4, one hour) and west to San Ignacio (BZ$4, one hour) and Benque Viejo del Carmen (BZ$6, 1½ hours) every half-hour from 6am to 7pm. Along the Hummingbird Hwy, buses go south to Dangriga (BZ$6, two hours) once or twice an hour from 6:45am until 7:15pm.

From Dangriga, most buses continue on to Punta Gorda (BZ$18, 5½ hours).

Transfers to Hopkins and Placencia-bound buses can be made in Dangriga.

THE HUMMINGBIRD HIGHWAY

Passing through jungle and citrus orchards as it skirts the northern edges of the Maya Mountain range, the Hummingbird offers a near constant procession of postcard-perfect vistas. There are also plenty of reasons to stop and while away a few hours before hitting the Southern Hwy.

Chief among these may well be a visit to some of Belize's most amazing caves, many of which are located in this neck of the jungle. The 575-acre **St Herman's Blue Hole National Park** (admission BZ$8; ⊙8am-4:30pm) contains one of the few caves in Belize that you can visit independently. The visitors center (where flashlights can be rented for BZ$5) is 11 miles along the Hummingbird Hwy from Belmopan. From here a 500yd trail leads to **St Herman's Cave**. A path leads 300yd into the cave alongside an underground river. To explore deeper in the extensive cave system, with its huge caverns and classic Maya ceremonial chambers containing calcified skeletons and artifacts, you must have a guide.

Highly experienced Kekchi Maya guide **Marcos Cucul** (☎670-3116, 600-3116; www.mayaguide.bz) can sometimes be found at

---

WORTH A TRIP

THE LITTLE HOUSE OF LOVE

Just past the Bill Barquedier waterfall on one of the prettiest stretches of the Hummingbird Hwy sits a structure as adorable as it is out of step with the area's usual architecture. Its blue-and-peach-painted concrete 1st floor is oddly shaped, but in a way difficult to put your finger on. The wooden 2nd floor contains large windows and high peaked gables that would seem more in place on a Swiss ski chalet.

This is **Café Casita De Amour** (☎660-2879; Mile 16½, Hummingbird Hwy; meals from BZ$7.50; ⊙7:30am-5pm Tue-Sun), labor of love of a local couple. It's from the inside that the name 'little house of love' fully makes sense, for it's inside looking out that the structure's valentine shape (down to the shape of the door) becomes obvious. The love-themed cafe serves breakfast and lunch, *Eierkucken* (thick German crepes), milkshakes, coffee drinks, tropical fruit smoothies and the best hamburgers in Belize (made with local beef from Mennonite farms and homemade whole-wheat bread).

Surrounded by a jungle garden filled with orchids, hummingbirds and the occasional toucans, a more romantic day would be hard to find. Alas, the 2nd floor is the couple's private abode; however, they welcome campers to use the patch of flat grass in a quiet section of the back garden. There's a bathroom but no shower; however, the Billy Barquedier waterfall is just down the road.

WORTH A TRIP

KROPF'S BAKERY

This Mennonite **bakery** (✆632-2477; Mile 33 Hummingbird Hwy; ⊙7am-5pm) serves addictively good cinnamon rolls, banana bread and cookies, as well as other examples of Belize's finest baked goods. Kropf's also serves inexpensive breakfast all day using locally produced meat, cheese, eggs and preserves.
Look for the yellow house on the south side of the highway at Mile 33.

the visitors center (when he isn't leading jungle survival tours deep in the bush; check his website for more details). With over a decade's experience as an area guide, Cucul enjoys an excellent reputation. A three-hour spelunk costs BZ$100 per person. There's also a 1.5-mile aboveground **jungle loop trail** starting near the cave entrance, with a lookout tower at the area's highest point.

The **Blue Hole** for which the park is named is just off the highway, 1 mile east of the visitors center (an off-road trail connects the two). This is a 25ft-deep sapphire-blue swimming hole inside a 328ft-wide cenote that was formed when the roof caved in on one of the Sibun River's underground tributaries. An attendant at the Blue Hole parking area will collect your park fee if you don't have a ticket from the visitors center. Buses along the Hummingbird Hwy will drop you at the visitors center or Blue Hole entrance.

Further west down the road sits the small **Barquedier Waterfall** (admission BZ$8; ⊙9am-4pm), a magnificent waterfall sitting along a trail 15 minutes by foot from the Hummingbird Hwy. The falls cascade into a pool perfect for an afternoon swim or morning shower.

🛏 Sleeping & Eating

Ian Anderson's Caves
Branch Jungle Lodge   LODGE $$$
(✆in Belize 610-3452, toll free in USA & Canada 866-357-2698; www.cavesbranch.com; mile 41½ Hummingbird Hwy; d cabaña & bungalow BZ$338-$492, d ste & treehouse BZ$588-$1182, breakfast/lunch/dinner BZ$16/24/32; P🌐📶❄)
🍃 Ian Anderson's is a 90-sq-mile private jungle estate that acts as both starting point and nerve center for a variety of jungle activities, including horseback riding, cave-tubing, nocturnal jungle walks, day, night (and overnight) cave expeditions, as well as jungle and kayak expeditions. Check the website for a full description of what's on offer at the lodge. Accommodations are jungle-chic, and the restaurant serves excellent Belizean, Caribbean and international cuisine.

Visitors can indulge themselves in Anderson's beautiful riverside pool and hot tub, and enjoy meals and cocktails at the family-style restaurant overlooking the river. Most exclusive of the accommodations are the canopy tree houses overlooking the Caves Branch river. More like full Swiss chalets in a jungle setting, the treehouses feature beautifully carved four-poster beds, screened-in decks, beautiful outdoor tropical showers and a unique array of amenities, including in-room safes and high ventilation fans. Each carries an individual jungle-animal totem, with carvings and furnishings resembling the specific animal adorning each room.

More humble but no less lovely are the wooden *cabañas* closer to the river, which feature one double and one bunk bed, sleeping a family of four. These are lit by kerosene lamps, but have ceiling fans and bathroom lights. The lodge also has an onsite cheese factory and organic soap-making facilities, with sale proceeds benefiting the Belize National Youth Chess Foundation (one of Mr Anderson's many passions).

Most lodge guests book multiday packages including tours, accommodations, meals and more. Check the website for current deals.

BETWEEN BELMOPAN & SAN IGNACIO

The 22 miles of the Western Hwy between San Ignacio and the Belmopan turnoff wind through verdant, well-shaded countryside, with a number of villages strung along the road. The road to the Actun Tunichil Muknal cave heads off south at Teakettle Village, west of Belmopan. At Georgeville, Chiquibul Rd turns south off the highway, heading to Barton Creek and the Mountain Pine Ridge before joining with Cristo Rey Rd and circling back to the Western Hwy.

🛏 Sleeping & Eating

Lower Dover Field Station & Eco Lodge CABINS, CAMPGROUND **$$**
(Map p158; ☑834-4200; www.lowerdoverbelize.com; mile 59 Western Hwy; camping per tent BZ$20, bunk house per person BZ$30, d cabins with/without bathroom incl breakfast BZ$140/100, luxury a/c cabin BZ$200; P 🛜 🏠) 🏊 Located on 99 acres of prime jungle bush containing sparkling clear creeks with swimming holes, and extensive and largely unexcavated Maya ruins, Lower Dover is at once a place to hang out and a place for serious archaeological exploration. The bunkhouse sleeps six, and beautifully furnished cabins sleep three. Among the activities at Lower Dover are canoeing on the Belize River, swimming in one of the seven river-fed swimming holes, fishing and bird-watching. Lower Dover is also a fully functioning farm with chickens, ducks, sheep and well-labelled trees and plants. There's also a communal kitchen and a screened-in rec center with a pool table, dartboard and other amenities. Visit the station virtually at its photo-packed blog (ldfieldjournal.wordpress.com), which contains some of the last pictures of the ATM cave before the camera ban took effect. Note that the station is only open to archeologists for the months of June and July.

Leslies' Private Paradise RESORT **$$**
(☑822-2370; http://lesliesprivateparadise.com; Mile 51½ Western Hwy; cabins BZ$200-300, bush house BZ$500; P 🛜 🏠) Just a short drive from the nation's political center sits Bobby and Bernadette Leslies' Private Paradise. Four units, ranging from a raw-wood cabin (which accommodates three) to the Bush House, a two-story lodge sleeping seven, sit spread out among jungles and hills. All units are self-contained, with refrigerators, stoves and cutlery, and guests have access to amenities such as a patio BBQ grill, a beautiful swimming pool and a most serene hilltop meditation hut. The Leslies are a welcoming and charming family who'll do everything they can to make your stay in Belize memorable. Discounts are available for stays longer than a few days.

Orange Gallery HOTEL **$$**
(Map p158; ☑824-2341; www.belizegifts.com/guesthouse; Mile 60 Western Hwy; s/d/tr/q BZ$130/150/160/170; P ⚡ @ 🛜) Spread out over 7 acres, this friendly, family-run business is as excellent as it is multifaceted. The front-end **gift shop** is one of the best in the country, with a wide selection of Belizean souvenirs and handicrafts (including fine hardwood furniture, kitchenware and sculptures made right here in the family's own workshop). Behind the shop sits an open-air **restaurant** (breakfast & lunch BZ$14, dinner BZ$28) that serves delicious international cuisine incorporating ingredients from the family's own herb and vegetable garden. The final third is the hotel portion, which offers five clean rooms with hot showers, new air-con units and comfortable beds.

Wolf's Place CABINS **$$**
(Map p158; ☑605-4640; www.belize24.de; Mile 57 Western Hwy, Blackman Eddy; cabins BZ$70-130, breakfast BZ$15; 🛜) There are three huts on a hillside at this 1.5-acre German-run resort in the Western Hwy town Blackman Eddy. Cabins are well-furnished with queen-sized beds, a futon and en-suite cold-water shower. All are good deals for the price, with the best being the 'Eco-cabaña', an octagonal cabin with wraparound screened windows offering a good view of the surrounding countryside.

Amber Sunset Jungle Resort RESORT **$$$**
(Map p158; ☑824-3142, 824-3141; www.ambersunsetbelize.com; Mile 59, Western Hwy; d treehouse cabañas incl breakfast BZ$600-900; 🛜 ♿ 🏠) 🏊 Set atop a mountain with brilliant views of the surrounding Cayo District, this newly opened eco-resort is both high end and unique. Spread out over 28 hilly acres, Amber has five unique cabins, each named after one of the cultures that makes up the tapestry of Belizean life. Each cabin is built and furnished with locally sourced and crafted materials. Our favorite: the Garifuna, which features a king-sized bed suspended from ropes, indoor rock-tiled shower and an outdoor stone pool for bathing beneath the stars. Other rooms also have their own outdoor tubs. There's a beautiful onsite **restaurant** (meals from BZ$12) serving local and international cuisine and a hilltop pool with an attached bar, auspiciouslly named Wild Things. Guests at Amber Sunset can enjoy nature walks on the grounds and management will arrange tours to ruins, caves and other areas around Belize.

Actun Tunichil Muknal

One of the most unforgettable and adventurous tours you can make in Belize, the trip into **Actun Tunichil Muknal** (ATM) takes you deep into the underworld that the ancient Maya

Around San Ignacio

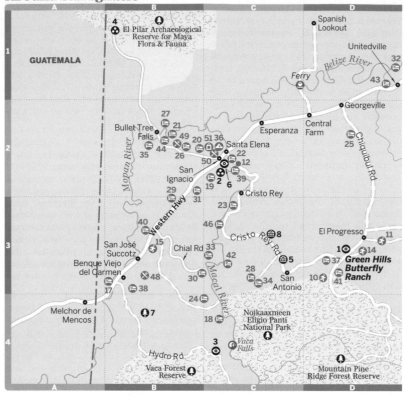

knew as Xibalba. The entrance to the **3-mile-long cave** lies in the northern foothills of the Maya Mountains, approximately 8 miles south of Teakettle Village on the Western Hwy. The trip is moderately strenuous, starting with an easy 45-minute hike through the lush jungle and across Roaring Creek (your feet will be wet all day). At the wide, hourglass-shaped entrance to the cave you'll don your helmet, complete with headlamp. To reach the cave entrance you'll start with a frosty swim across a deep pool (about 15ft across), so you must be a reasonably good swimmer. From here, you will follow your guide, walking, climbing, twisting and turning your way through the blackness of the cave for about an hour.

Giant shimmering flowstone rock formations compete for your attention with thick, calcium-carbonate stalactites dripping from the ceiling. Phallic stalagmites grow up from the cave floor. Eventually you'll follow your guide up into a massive opening, where

you'll see hundreds of pottery vessels and shards, along with human remains. One of the most shocking displays is the calcite-encrusted remains of the woman whom Actun Tunichil Muknal (Cave of the Stone Sepulchre) is named for.

In the cave's Main Chamber, you will be required to remove your shoes. Make sure you wear socks – not only to protect your feet from sharp rocks, but also to protect the artifacts from the oils on your skin.

The trip takes about 10 hours from San Ignacio, including a one-hour drive each way. A number of San Ignacio–based tour companies do the trip for around BZ$160 per person, including admission, lunch and equipment. You must be accompanied by a licensed guide.

As of 2012, cameras are no longer allowed inside the cave due to an incident involving a clumsy traveler, a dropped camera and the breaking of priceless artifacts.

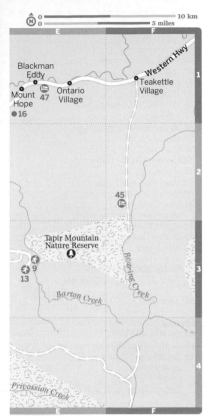

from a turnoff at Central Farm, from where a hand-crank ferry transports cars across the Belize River. About 5 miles down the Western Hwy (toward Belmopan), a newly paved road with bridge bypasses the old hand-crank ferry.

Spanish Lookout is an excellent place to see the Mennonites' industriousness in action. Surprisingly, this road is paved; unsurprisingly, it was the Mennonites – not the government – who paved it. They are the country's primary producers of dairy, meat, poultry and produce: here in Spanish Lookout you will find Quality Chicken, the biggest poultry producer, as well as Western Dairy, the only commercial dairy.

Since 2006 Spanish Lookout has been in the news thanks to the discovery of commercial quantities of oil in its environs. Understandably, drilling was highly controversial in this conservative community. A Mennonite spokesperson was quoted in the local press as saying: 'We would prefer not to have any production in our lands rather than money. Our way of life means more than money. Because of the laws of Belize we have to allow oil drilling' The Mennonites have since come to an agreement to share profits with the landowner and oil companies, but the developments are bringing big changes to this community.

Several buses a day go to Spanish Lookout (BZ$6, one hour) from San Ignacio, via Bullet Tree Falls.

If you want to get an earlier start, stay at **Pook's Hill Lodge** (Map p158; ☎ 832-2017; www.pookshilllodge.com; s/d/tr cabañas BZ$296/396/472, breakfast/lunch/dinner BZ$22/22/44; P @). Located off the dirt road that leads to ATM, this gorgeous lodge sits on the site of a small Classic Period Maya residential complex. Round thatch-and-stucco *cabañas* sport wraparound windows and immaculate natural-stone bathrooms. They are well spaced, allowing plenty of privacy. Set within a 300-acre private reserve, the grounds are lush with life, excellent for swimming, river-tubing and horseback riding. The birdwatching is also superb, from the lodge veranda or along the forest trails or river frontage on Roaring Creek.

Spanish Lookout

A thriving Mennonite community, Spanish Lookout (population 2000) is about 5 miles north of the Western Hwy, accessed

Chiquibul Road & Cristo Rey Road

Forming a loop encircling a large, beautiful swath of the Cayo District and leading into both the **Mountain Pine Ridge Forest Reserve** and **Caracol**, Chiquibul Rd (sometimes called Pine Ridge Rd) and Cristo Rey Rd both turn south off the Western Hwy. Heading west from Belmopan, you'll see the Chiquibul Rd turnoff at Georgeville. After 9 miles, Chiquibul Rd hooks up with Cristo Rey Rd, which then loops back north and connects with the Western Hwy in Santa Elena.

The only major population center on the loop is **San Antonio** (population 2000). Settled by Mayans from the Yucatán, the village gets its name from the statue of St Anthony in the town church. Though there are no hotels in town, **Sukunoob Maya Restaurant** (Cristo Rey Rd; meals from BZ$5; ☺ lunch & dinner) serves hamburgers and fries, fried rice dishes and excellent juices. There's a tiny grocery store

Around San Ignacio

just around the corner from Sukunoob with the only gas pump in town, in case you forgot to fill up for the long drive to Caracol.

◎ Sights

★ Green Hills
Butterfly Ranch   BUTTERFLY FARM
(Map p158; ☏834-4017; http://biological-diversity. info/greenhills.htm; Mile 8 Chiquibul Rd; adult/child BZ$20/10, group discounts available; ⏰8am-4pm, last tour 3:30pm) If butterflies make your heart flutter, don't miss the chance to see 20-plus exquisite native species at this amazing butterfly ranch, where biologists Jan Meerman and Tineke Boomsma breed butterflies for

research and educational purposes. Research activity includes tracking interaction between different species and compiling a field guide, as well as cultivating a botanical garden that supports the butterfly population. The ranch also boasts 13 species of hummingbird. For the protection of the butterflies, all tours are guided, and a minimum of two people are required for a tour. While the last scheduled tour leaves at 3:30pm, after-hour tours are available by appointment.

García Sisters' Place   MUSEUM
(Map p158; Cristo Rey Rd; ⏰7am-7pm) Half a mile before San Antonio (look for the color-fully painted facade), the García sisters

display and sell a wide assortment of black-slate carvings. These five sisters – born and raised right here in San Antonio – invented this craft, which is now widely imitated around Belize. Their carvings, selling for between BZ$10 and BZ$200, depict a variety of subjects, including local wildlife and Maya deities. You are likely to meet at least one of the sisters (or their wizened mother) working in the shop, doing their part to keep local arts and crafts alive.

Sa'c Tunich MUSEUM
(Map p158; ☎ 670-7806; Cristo Rey Rd; ⏱ 6am-6pm) Many refer to Sa'c Tunich as 'the living Maya site' because at first glance it looks like an excavated ruin. However, Sa'c Tunich is actually the museum-workshop of Maya artists Jose and Javier Magaña, who create contemporary Maya artworks from stone and clay, both for exhibition and for sale. A small gift shop sells artwork from both the brothers and other members of the family, and their sawmill employs local worker.

🏃 Activities

Mountain Equestrian Trails HORSEBACK RIDING
(Map p158; ☎ 669-1124, in USA 800-838-3918; www.metbelize.com; Mile 8 Chiquibul Rd; horseback tours BZ$122-180) For equestrians, nothing beats exploring the area from the back of a horse. The folks at MET arrange half- and full-day rides to the ancient city of **Pacbitun**, Barton Creek Cave and elsewhere. Horseback-riding trips include a picnic lunch and breaks for swimming and exploring, making for a glorious day away from civilization.

Barton Creek Cave CAVE
(Map p158; admission BZ$20) Barton Creek rises high in the Mountain Pine Ridge and flows north to join the Belize River near Georgeville. Along the way it dips underground for a spell, flowing through the Barton Creek Cave. During the Classic period the ancient

Maya interred at least 28 people and left thousands of pottery jars and fragments and other artifacts on 10 ledges. Today the cave is only accessible by canoe.

Peaceful canoe trips take you (in groups of six or fewer) about 750ft into the cave so you can get a look at the crystal cave formations, as well as the spooky skulls, bones and pottery shards that remain from the Maya. You must be accompanied by a guide to enter the cave. You can find one in San Ignacio, or check out **Mike's Place** (Map p158; ☎ 670-0451, 670-0441; adult/child BZ$130/65) just outside the cave entrance.

The drive here is precarious; the narrow and very rough 4-mile track to the cave heads east off Chiquibul Rd, about 5 miles south of the Western Hwy. Along the way you pass through the scattered traditional Mennonite farming community of Upper Barton Creek and ford both Barton Creek itself then one of its tributaries.

Chaya Garden Ashram YOGA
(Map p158; ☎ 666 7361, 652-9642; http://chayagardenashram.com/) Set on lush grounds next to a series of stunning natural waterfalls with an amazing swimming hole, Chaya Gardens offers yoga classes, massage treatments and excellent vegan and vegetarian meals. Drop-in yoga classes are BZ$20, massage is BZ$80 for an hour treatment, and the ashram also has a weekly program including meals and daily classes for BZ$420.

Bol's Cave CAVES
(Map p158; ☎ 664-3462; bjt_2005@hotmail.com; per person BZ$40) If you don't have the time to get to Barton Creek, you can still check out this smaller cave just before the entrance to Pine Ridge. Mr Fidencio Bol owns a 30-acre spot of hillside boasting an ancient Maya cave purportedly filled with over 1000 Maya artifacts dating from 950 BC to AD 450. A licensed guide, Mr Bol also

---

WORTH A TRIP

UNIVERSAL HEALING INSTITUTE & RETREAT

Difficult to categorize, the unique **Universal Healing Institute & Retreat** (Map p158; ☎ 677-7878; www.universalhealinginternational.com) 🏃 is spread out over a 150-acre organic jungle farm near the small village of **Unitedville**. Operators Yosiah and Linda offer medium and long-term retreats focusing on health and nutrition, yoga and spirituality, as well as courses in organic gardening and sustainability. Students and interns pay BZ$1200 per month to BZ$3000 per 90-day semester, depending on course selections. Private consulting, seminars and workshops are also available. Work exchange programs and long-term discounted internships are also available. Check the website for more details.

ⓘ VITAMINS

Looking to stock up on vitamins? Look in Spanish Lookout, which has Belize's only dedicated health-food store. **Reimers Health Food** (⌨823-0096; kbreimer@reimershealthfood.com; Bee Lane; ⊙8am-5pm Mon-Sat) stocks about the same selection of vitamins, supplements and other health products as you'd find at a good American supermarket.

gives tours of the area, including canoe tours down Barton Creek and through Barton Creek Cave, and overland tours around Caracol and Mountain Pine Ridge.

Calico Jack's   ZIP LINING
(Map p158; ⌨820-4078, from USA 301-792-2233; www.calicojacksvillage.com; El Progresso (7 Mile); per person BZ$80-124) Ever wanted to zip through a jungle canopy via a series of metal cables, harnesses and treetop platforms? This 365-acre property boasts a 9-run 16-platform zip line; various packages take you on different runs ranging from a 45-minute 'explorer' to a 90-minute 'ultimate adventure.' Adventurous visitors will want to ride the newly built jungle swing (BZ$50), which offers a trip across a canyon combined with a 55' free-fall.

🛏 Sleeping & Eating

Cool M Farm   HOMESTAY $$
(Map p158; ⌨824-2276; cool.m.farm@gmail.com; ¼ mile Cristo Rey Rd; cabañas d BZ$100, per extra person BZ$10; ⊕) ⌀ Spend a few days in a genuine Mennonite farm atomosphere at the Löhr family's 75-acre garden-filled dairy farm. Though on Cristo Rey Rd, Cool M is close enough to San Ignacio to be considered walkable. The farm has two lovely fan-cooled *cabañas* equipped with comfortable double beds, desks, modern bathrooms with hot showers and a sun porch overlooking the valley, meadows and (of course) the farm. Breakfast for two of organic eggs, yogurt, granola and bread (all from the farm) is included in the price; the family will also provide farm-fresh dinners, boxed lunches (including home-made bread and cheese) and even do laundry for an additional price. A unique and genuinely Belizean experience, a stay at Cool M may well be the highlight of your visit to Cayo.

Moonracer Farm   CABINS $$
(Map p158; ⌨667-5748, in USA 585-200-5748; www.moonracerfarm.com; Mile 9 Mount Pine Ridge Rd; cabañas d/q BZ$150/280, meals per day BZ$60; Ⓟ@🛜🛌) Just past the sign for Caracol, Moonracer occupies the former grounds of a wild feline rehabilitation center. The cats are gone, but the cages still stand. Moonracer Farm's one jungle cabin has two separate double rooms, each with two queen-sized beds handmade with local hardwood, full bathrooms with hot showers, and screened-in porches with hammocks. Kerosene lamps provide ambiance for the rooms, but the communal *palapa* kitchen and dining room has electricity and wi-fi. The location makes it perfect for bird-watchers and explorers looking to head out early to explore Caracol.

Maya Mountain Lodge   RESORT $$
(Map p158; ⌨824-2164; www.mayamountain.com; Mile ¾ Cristo Rey Rd; r small/standard/family BZ$194/243/341, cottages BZ$292, breakfast & dinner BZ$60; Ⓟⓧ❄🛜🛌) Lush gardens with a trail leading to a small, ancient Maya ceremonial site and the eight air-conditioned cottages with tile floors keep visitors coming back. Rooms all open onto a shared veranda and cottages have private porches with hammocks. Family units are more like efficiency apartments with complete kitchenettes, and all units have wi-fi. Owners Bart and Suzi Mickler pioneered many of the tours that are now widely offered throughout Cayo, and offer a variety of tours both on their verdant grounds and throughout the region.

Crystal Paradise Resort   RESORT $$
(Map p158; ⌨834-4016, 820-4014; www.crystalparadise.com; Cristo Rey Rd; garden r/garden loft/valley-view cabañas s/d/tr BZ$190/250/310, standard s/d/tr BZ$150/210/270; Ⓟ@) The Tut family's resort is spread out over well-tended gardens just above the Macal River, and offers utilitarian but comfortable *cabañas*. Most guests come here on packages that incorporate preplanned tours, including horseback riding, canoeing, Maya ruins and other activities. Breakfast and dinner are included.

Gumbolimbo Village Resort   RESORT $$
(Map p158; ⌨650-3112; www.gumbolimboresort.com; Mile 2 Chiquibul Rd; d incl continental breakfast BZ$224, breakfast/lunch/dinner BZ$18/12/45; Ⓟ@🛜🛌) ⌀ Perched high atop a hillside that is covered in gumbo-limbo trees (also known as the tourist tree due to its red, peeling bark), this resort offers four modern cab-

ins (tin and fiberglass roofed, not thatched) with cool white interiors and large glass doors surrounding a beautiful swimming pool. Rooms are sparse but spacious, with plenty of room for extra beds (sleeping up to four people). This place is surprisingly green (with the exception of the too-blue swimming pool), running completely on solar and wind power.

Macaw Bank Jungle Lodge LODGE $$$
(Map p158; ☑ 603-4825; www.macawbankjunglelodge.com; off Cristo Rey Rd; small/large cabañas BZ$220/290; P 🛜) 🏊 Getting to these gorgeous grounds – spread out along the Macal River – is an adventure in itself. Turn off Cristo Rey Rd about 3 miles south of Cristo Rey village, then drive another 3 miles on the narrow, overgrown dirt track. Once you're here, you won't want to leave, as this place is a wildlife wonderland, teeming with birds and other animals. Hike the network of trails, meditate beneath a 900-year-old bullet tree, explore an unexcavated Maya site or float down the river in a tube, then retire to your rustic, kerosene-lit cabin (though there is now basic solar-powered electricity) decorated with hand-hewn furniture, beautiful mosaic-tile floors and woven tapestries. A restaurant serving locally grown and sourced fruits, vegetables and meats is onsite, but meals must be ordered in advance.

Mountain Equestrian Trails RESORT $$$
(Map p158; ☑ 669-1124, in USA 800-838-3918; www.metbelize.com; s/d/tr/q BZ$220/264/308/352, breakfast/lunch/dinner BZ$16/22/40; P 🛜🍴) After a day of horseback riding, rest your weary body in one of 10 spacious thatched-roof *cabañas*, decorated with beautiful Maya tapestries and boasting lovely forest views. Kerosene lamps light the way (there is no electricity), making for a particularly romantic atmosphere. Good home-style meals are served in the *cantina* (canteen), while a wide deck offers wonderful views of the valley. Turn off Chiquibul Rd immediately opposite Green Hills Butterfly Ranch and drive about 0.75 miles on the unpaved road. Multiday packages including horseback riding, tours, accommodations and transfers are also available.

Table Rock Camp & Cabanas RESORT $$$
(Map p158; ☑ 834-4040; www.tablerockbelize.com; Cristo Rey Rd; camping with own/rented tent BZ$40/60, cabañas d BZ$250-370, per extra person BZ$40, breakfast/lunch/dinner BZ$20/24/50; P 🛜) 🏊 This exquisite little resort boasts five classy *cabañas*, each named for an exotic bird you might see on the grounds. The Kiskadee, Aracari and Motmot rooms are all furnished with custom-made four-poster beds, tile floors and thatched roofs. The newly built Oropendola and Laughing Falcon rooms are slightly larger, featuring king-sized beds, futons and thatched verandas. Delicious meals are served in the open-air *palapa* (thatched-roof shelter). The owners of Table Rock produce their own electricity, grow their own fruits and vegetables and use purified rainwater. Nonguest diners are welcome at the Table Rock restaurant with 24 hours' notice.

Mariposa Jungle Lodge LODGE $$$
(Map p158; ☑ 675-2113, 670-2113; www.mariposajunglelodge.com; Cristo Rey Rd; d BZ$330, per extra person BZ$50 ; P 🛜🌊) This luxurious

CAYO DISTRICT CHIQUIBUL ROAD & CRISTO REY ROAD

BELIZE WILDLIFE & REFERAL CLINIC

With a mission statement including the goals of establishing and managing a state-of-the-art veterinary clinic for wildlife and domestic animals in Belize, the **Belize Wildlife & Referal Clinic** provides educational opportunities and training for students, professionals and interested individuals. This nonprofit organization offers ongoing internships in wildlife medicine, rescue and rehabilitation. Internships focus on wildlife medicine, rescue and emergency medicine and conservation, and are designed to provide students with real-world experience while supporting wildlife rescue and conservation in the field. Some interns are pre-veterinary or animal science students, while others are veterinary students seeking clinical rotation credit in wildlife medicine.

Short-term internships ranging from two to six weeks for non-veterinary students are available for between BZ$1500 and BZ$2000 per week (including lodging, breakfasts and airport pick-up and drop-off). Various scholarships and work exchanges are available for students with genuine interest and skills, and the clinic is flexible and always interested in speaking with sincere potential interns and long-term volunteers.

Contact internship coordinator Justin Ford (jford@belizewildlifeclinic.org) or check out the website http://www.belizewildlifeclinic.org for more information.

jungle lodge offers six beautiful cabins, each named for a jungle creature or flower and featuring king-sized canopy beds dressed with Egyptian linens and mosquito nets, hardwood furniture and hand-thatched roofs. By the time you read this, the lodge will be offering a newly built suite (BZ$440), complete with wet bar, hot tub, flat-screen TV and recliner. With views of the rainforest or the mountain ridge, the screened porch is a perfect place to hang a hammock. There's a pool complete with barstools and a waterfall, and a full-service bar and restaurant. Ask about tours through the area, including the unique Village Culture Tour and trips to lesser-known caves and jungle areas.

Inn the Bush   CABINS $$$
(Map p158; ☑ 670-6364; www.innthebushbelize.com; Cristo Rey Rd; d cabins BZ$250, meals BZ$15-35; [P][✷]) Opened in 2009 by Robert and Roeni Wensenk, Inn the Bush sits atop a small hill. Two large cabins have massive four-poster mahogany beds, couches, full-sized bathrooms with hot showers and porches bigger than most hotel rooms, and a third family cabin has a second bed. A large *palapa* bar and dining area overlooks a most unusual above-ground swimming pool (shaped like two Belize dollar coins or a decapitated snowman). Meals featuring locally sourced meats and vegetables are served all day, but advance notice is requested. Robert and Roeni also offer camp spots (BZ$15 per person) for travelers wanting to pitch a tent in the bush.

Mystic River   CABINS $$$
(Map p158; ☑ 834-4101, 834-4100; www.mysticriverbelize.com; Cristo Rey Rd; cabañas d BZ$450, ste BZ$500; [P][📶]) This beautiful ecolodge on the bank of the Macal River (opened in 2009 by Nadege and Tom Thomas) features six beautifully furnished *cabañas* with Mexican tiled floors and high wooden ceilings, and three newly built one-bedroom suites. All feature spacious living areas and bathrooms, and river-facing verandas. Guests at Mystic River can hang out on the river with tubes, body boards and canoes, or take a hike (with or without horses) on the jungle trails that wind through Mystic River's 180 acres. The onsite restaurant serves breakfast, lunch and dinner. Meals vary from BZ$20 to BZ$45. Prices are per double occupancy; additional visitors are BZ$50. Low season discounts and packages are available. Check website for details.

❶ Getting There & Around

Buses from San Ignacio to San Antonio (BZ$4, one hour) run along Cristo Rey Rd, leaving San Ignacio at 11:30am and 4:30pm. Return buses leave San Antonio at 6am and 4:15pm.

MOUNTAIN PINE RIDGE AREA

South of San Ignacio and the Western Hwy the land begins to climb toward the heights of the Maya Mountains, whose arching ridge forms the border separating Cayo District from Stann Creek District to the east and Toledo District to the south.

In the heart of this highland area 200 sq miles of submontane (ie on the foothills or lower slopes of mountains) pine forest is the **Mountain Pine Ridge Forest Reserve**. The sudden switch from tropical rainforest to pine trees as you ascend to the Mountain Pine Ridge – a broad upland area of multiple ridges and valleys – is a little bizarre and somewhat startling. The reserve is full of **rivers**, **pools**, **waterfalls** and **caves**; the higher elevation means relief from both heat and mosquitoes.

◉ Sights & Activities

The pine forest is also a thriving ecosystem, covered with flora, traversed by river systems and replete with birds and other wildlife. The Macal River, Río Frio, Barton Creek and Roaring Creek all start up on Mountain Pine Ridge. From here they flow north to the Belize River and out to the sea, cascading across rocky cliffs and verdant hillsides along the way.

Thousand Foot Falls   WATERFALL
(lookout point admission BZ$4; ☉ lookout point 8am-5pm) Ten miles off Chiquibul Rd, the Thousand Foot Falls are reckoned to be the highest falls in Central America. Access them by turning onto Cooma Cairn Rd, then turn left after 7 miles at the '1000 Ft Falls' sign. You will reach a **lookout point** with a view of the falls plunging over the edge of the pine-covered plateau into the tropical broadleaf valley far below. The falls are in fact around 1600ft high, but the thin, long stream of falling water is unlikely to hold your interest for a long time. Birders should keep their eyes peeled for the rare orange-breasted falcon.

Mountain Pine Ridge Area

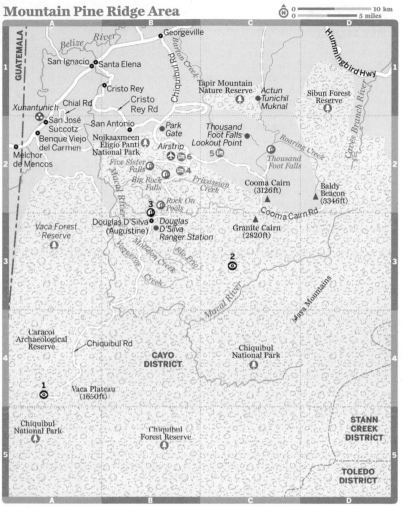

Ⓝ 0 ———————————— 10 km
0 ———————————— 5 miles

Mountain Pine Ridge Area

The highest point of the Mountain Pine Ridge is **Baldy Beacon** (3346ft), topped by a cluster of transmitter masts. Follow the signs a further 8 miles from the Thousand Foot Falls turnoff.

Privassion Creek   WATERFALL
(mini-tram lodge guests/nonguests free/BZ$5; ⏱ mini-tram 8am-5pm) The shorter (150ft) and wider **Big Rock Falls** on Privassion Creek are more powerful and, for many people, more beautiful and impressive than the

WORTH A TRIP

FIRE TEMPLE

Not far from the small Cayo village of Cristo Rey, **Ocean Spirit Fire Temple** (☑675-3721; winsomwinsom@yahoo.com) is home to spiritual healer and artist Winsom Omiala. Initiate of many rituals in Africa, Cuba, Central and North America, Winsom acts as a reader and spiritual healer, as well as offering workshops and classes, which incorporate yoga, dance and shiatsu massage. The temple also backs a yearly Festival of Lights, a gathering of artisans and craftspeople held on the third Saturday in March each year, which raises funds for the children of Cristo Rey.

Thousand Foot Falls. Take the road toward the former Five Sisters Lodge and, 1.5 miles past Blancaneaux Lodge, turn along a track to the left where a 'Five Sisters Lodge' sign points straight ahead. The track ends after about 175yd, and a foot trail continues 400yd down to the river. You can swim in the river and the falls are 100yd upstream. There's also a trail to the falls from Blancaneaux Lodge.

Five Sisters Falls, a set of smaller cascades with swimming pools and shelter pavilions at their base, are on the property of the former Five Sisters Lodge. From the lodge, walk along the trail for about 45 minutes, or take the hydro-powered **mini-tram**. Near the falls, Five Sisters maintains an impressive floral display of hundreds of species of orchids, bromeliads and palmettos.

Río Frio Cave & Río On Pools WATERFALL
Just off Chiquibul Rd, 2.5 miles north of Douglas D'Silva (Augustine), **Río On Pools** is a series of small waterfalls connecting pools that the river has carved out of granite boulders. It's a beautiful spot: the pools are refreshing for a dip and the smooth slabs of granite are perfect for stretching out on to dry off. A picnic area and outhouse are the only amenities here, but it's a popular spot for tour groups on their way back from Caracol.

In Douglas D'Silva itself, look for the signed turnoff to **Río Frio Cave**, less than 1 mile away. The river gurgles through the sizeable cave, keeping it cool while you go off and explore.

🍽 Sleeping & Eating

The Mountain Pine Ridge has a handful of places offering accommodations, meals, tours and activities – including some of the most luxurious lodges in the country. Although you might find a room if you show up unannounced, it's a long way to come for a 'No Vacancy' sign, so it's best to book in advance.

Pine Ridge Lodge CABINS $$
(☑606-4557, in USA 800-316-0706; www.pineridgelodge.com; d/tr/q incl breakfast BZ$180/233/286, lunch/dinner BZ$15/43; ℗) The most rustic of the Pine Ridge lodges has six little cabins decorated with Guatemalan handicrafts and original pieces created by local artists. Screened porches and hammocks are prime spots for relaxation. The Little Vaqueros Creek runs across the bottom of the grassy gardens, which are bursting with orchids. There's no electricity, but you'll come to love your kerosene lantern's soft glow, and the restaurant cooks up delicious meals using butane. The lodge is 4 miles along the Chiquibul Rd from the warden post.

★**Blancaneaux Lodge** RESORT $$$
(☑824-3878, 824-4912, in USA 800-746-3743; www.blancaneaux.com; cabañas BZ$640-1104, 2-bedroom villas BZ$1190-1300, lunch & dinner mains BZ$25-50; ℗ 🛜 ❄) Owned by movie director Francis Ford Coppola (who keeps a personal villa here, 'the Francis Ford Coppola Villa,' complete with attendant and private pool, yours for BZ$1734 per night), this indulgent 70-acre lodge offers 20 thatched cabins and luxury villas, spread around beautifully manicured gardens, with some looking right over the picturesque Privassion Creek. The lodgings feature beautiful tiled bathrooms, open-air living rooms in the villas, and handicrafts from Belize, Guatemala, Mexico and Thailand. Blancaneaux has its own stables, walking trails and riverside spa with a large hot pool. The newly built luxury *cabañas* feature their own plunge pools and outdoor showers, as well as indoor-style Japanese baths. There's also the Enchanted Cottage, a secluded one-bedroom stone cottage with fireplace, private pool, attendant and majestic view. This goes for BZ$2940

Two onsite restaurants serve Italian and Guatemalan cuisine; all room options include breakfast.

Hidden Valley Inn   RESORT $$$

(📞 866-443-3364, 822-3320; www.hiddenvalleyinn. com; d estate r/ste BZ$550/$750, breakfast/lunch/ dinner BZ$29/35/72; 🅿 @ 🆉) Hidden Valley Inn is set on 11 gorgeous sq miles of Mountain Pine Ridge, all for the exclusive use of its guests. The grounds straddle pine and tropical forest ecosystems, and have access to 90 miles of signposted trails, eight sets of waterfalls, some inviting swimming spots and spectacular lookouts. The 10 estate rooms and two estate suites feature earth-toned tapestries, brick fireplaces and mahogany furniture, creating a warm, intimate atmosphere that extends throughout. Suites are larger and feature granite tubs and screened-in porches. The lodge also offers a plethora of amenities, including free mountain bikes, yoga classes and more. It is situated 4 miles off the Chiquibul Rd, along Cooma Cairn Rd. Check the website for off-peak discount rates.

❶ Getting There & Away

There's no public transportation to this region, so you'll have to provide your own or arrange transit with one of the resorts. A taxi from San Ignacio should cost about BZ$100; lodge transfers are BZ$120 to BZ$150 for up to four people.

This area is among Belize's most sparsely populated. Outside of staff at area lodges, a few archaeologists, occasional troops on training exercises and a smattering of illegal squatters from Guatemala, you'll see few signs of (modern) human life in Mountain Pine Ridge.

CARACOL

Beyond the Pine Ridge, to the southwest, are the ruins of Belize's largest and most important Maya site, **Caracol** (admission BZ$30; ⊙ 8am-4pm). Once among the most powerful cities in the entire Maya world, this ancient city now lies enshrouded by thick jungle near the Guatemalan border, a 52-mile (much of this very rough) drive from San Ignacio that takes anywhere from three to four hours.

Sitting high on the Vaca Plateau, 1650ft above sea level, it's postulated that Caracol may have stretched over 70 sq miles at its peak (around AD 650). Nearly 40 miles of internal causeways radiate from the center to large outlying plazas and residential areas, connecting different parts of the city. At its height, the city's population may have approached 150,000, more than twice as many people as Belize City has today. Though they had no natural water source, the people of Caracol dug artificial reservoirs to catch rainwater and grew food on extensive agricultural terraces. Its central area was a bustling place of temples, palaces, busy thoroughfares, craft workshops and markets. Caracol is not only the pre-eminent archaeological site in Belize but also exciting for its jungle setting and prolific birdlife.

At the ticket office a small **visitors center** outlines Caracol's history and has a helpful scale model. A museum that's under construction will house much of the sculpture

---

LOCAL KNOWLEDGE

CAYO FOR FAMILIES

Jim and Jacquelyn Britt live in Barton Creek with their children, Kaitlyn, Logan and Cyan.

What's the best place for caving in Cayo? *Jim (dad):* The prevailing theory is ATM (p157), and it's hard to argue with that. But the Barton Creek Cave (p161) is magical and surreal. How many other caves can you glide through on a canoe?

What Cayo spots should be on any traveler's bucket list? *Jacquelyn (mom):* Apart from Barton Creek Cave, I would say Río on Pools (p166) and Big Rock Falls (p165). I would also include Xunantunich (p179).

How do you avoid poisonous snakes? *Kaitlyn (age 12):* Remember that the jungle is their territory, and they want to avoid you as much as you want to avoid them. If you're walking in the dark, carry a light.

Favorite jungle activities? *Logan (age 9):* There's a one-hour hike I sometimes take people on that goes up a windy trail up the mountain by our house and then comes back down through Barton Creek. I take a lot of people on that.

What games can kids play in Barton Creek? *Cyan (age 3):* I make sand castles on the beach on the creek. I paint using watercolors from the river rocks. I have tea parties with my dollies and animals. This morning I swung on the rope swing in my tutu!

found at Caracol. There are toilets, picnic tables and a small gift shop. Be sure to bring food, water and, if you're driving, a spare tire. Overnight stays are not permitted.

A system of trails meanders through Caracol, but Plazas A and B are the most excavated. The highlight is **Caana** (Sky-Place), which rises from Plaza B, and at 141ft is still the tallest building in Belize! Caana underwent many construction phases until its completion in about 800. It supports four palace compounds and three temples. High steps narrowing up to the top probably led to the royal family's compound, where **Structure B-19** housed Caracol's largest and most elaborate tomb. It contained the remains of a woman, possibly Lady Batz' Ek from Calakmul, who married into Caracol's ruling dynasty in 584. Climb to the top of Caana to feast upon one of the most magnificent views in all of Belize. On the way down, don't miss the hidden tombs around the back on the left side.

South of Plaza B, the **Central Acropolis** was an elite residential group with palaces and shrines. To its west, Plaza A contained many stelae, some of which are still in place. Atop **Structure A-2** is a replica of a stela found here in 2003 that is engraved with the longest Mayan inscription found in Belize. Structure A-6, the **Temple of the Wooden Lintel**, is one of the oldest buildings at Caracol. One of its lintels (the one to the left as you enter the top chamber) is original.

South of the Temple of the Wooden Lintel is the A Group Ballcourt, where the all-important **Altar 21**, telling us so much about Caracol's history, was found. A replica of the 'altar,' actually a ball-court marker, sits in the middle. Further south is one of Caracol's many **aguadas** (reservoirs), and beyond that the **South Acropolis**, a Classic period elite residential complex where you can enter two tombs.

Caracol

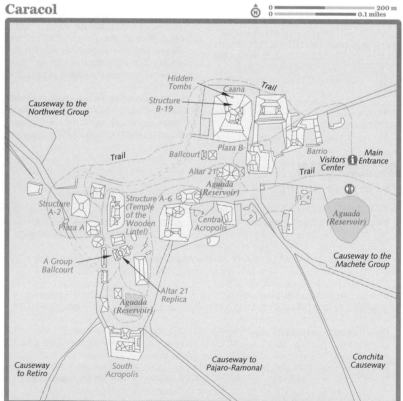

EXCAVATION HISTORY OF CARACOL

In 1937 a logger named Rosa Mai first stumbled upon the ruins. In 1938 commissioner of archaeology AH Anderson named the site Caracol (Spanish for snail), perhaps because of all the snail shells found in the soil. In 1950 Linton Satterthwaite from the University of Pennsylvania recorded the visible stone monuments, mapped the site core and excavated several tombs, buildings and monuments. Many stelae were removed and sent to Pennsylvania.

Since 1985 Drs Diane and Arlen Chase have led the **Caracol Archaeological Project** (www.caracol.org), with annual field seasons conducting surveys and excavations that have revealed Caracol's massive central core and complex urban development. From 2000 to 2004, the Tourism Development Project carried out an excavation and conservation program led by Belizean archaeologist Jaime Awe, which also improved road access to the site.

Tours

Most tour companies and lodges in and around San Ignacio run tours to the Mountain Pine Ridge and Caracol. On a typical day tour (usually BZ$140 to BZ$180 per person), you'll visit the Río On Pools, Río Frio Cave and one of the waterfalls. Caracol trips also stop at Río On Pools and Río Frio Cave on the way back.

Getting There & Away

Most people come on a guided tour but it's possible to drive here on your own. The road to Caracol, once the stuff of rugged travel legend, is now graded and no worse (and in many places better) than other unpaved roads in the area. All visitors – individuals and groups alike – travel to Caracol in a convoy that departs Douglas D'Silva (Augustine) ranger station at 9:30am every morning. On the return trip, the convoy departs at 2pm. Each car must sign in and out. The convoy is accompanied by two park ranger vehicles to ensure the safety of all passengers – this system was instituted after several reported incidents of tourist vehicles being stopped by armed robbers a decade ago. Since the convoy's institution, there have been no further reports of incidents on the long Caracol road.

The road to Caracol from the Western Hwy can be done in about two hours, give or take.

SAN IGNACIO

POP 19,200

Together with neighboring **Santa Elena**, on the east bank of the river, San Ignacio forms the chief population center of Cayo District. Staying here is generally the more economical option for travel in Cayo; furthermore, there is no shortage of tour operators who are willing to show you the attractions and activities in the surrounding area. It is a friendly, functional base for your explorations of the region.

But San Ignacio is not one of those towns that exist only for tourists. It has a very positive local vibe, with a bustling market and a steady influx of immigrants. Residents are Mestizos, Maya and Garifuna, as well as a bunch of free-spirited expatriates from Europe and North America. San Ignacio is on the west bank of the Macal River, a couple of miles upstream from its confluence with the Mopan River – a meeting of waters that gives birth to the Belize River. On the river's east bank is the town of Santa Elena. Two bridges cross the Macal.

Burns Ave, running north–south, is San Ignacio's main street, taking you past the football field and terminating at the traffic circle in the south, where you'll find the town hall and the police station. There is no bus terminal in San Ignacio, but nearly all buses stop in the market square, just east of Burns Ave.

Sights & Activities

Cahal Pech RUIN
(Map p158; 824-4236; admission BZ$10, 2hr tours BZ$20; 6am-6pm) High atop a hill on the southern outskirts of San Ignacio, Cahal Pech is the oldest known Maya site in the Belize River valley, having been first settled between 1500 and 1000 BC. Less impressive than Xunantunich and Caracol, it's still a fascinating example of Preclassic Maya architecture. It was a significant Maya settlement for 2000 years or more.

Cahal Pech (kah-*hahl* pech) is Mopan and Yucatec Mayan for 'Place of Ticks,' a nickname earned in the 1950s when the site was surrounded by pastures grazed by tick-infested cattle. Today it's a pleasantly shady site with plenty of trees and few tourists. Its core

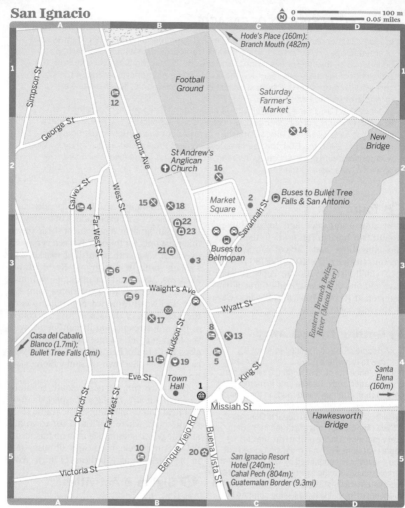

San Ignacio

area of seven interconnected plazas has been excavated and restored since the late 1980s.

The earliest monumental religious architecture in Belize was built here between 600 and 400 BC, though most of what we see today dates from AD 600 to 800, when Cahal Pech and its peripheral farming settlements had an estimated population of between 10,000 and 20,000. The place was abandoned around AD 850.

A small **visitors center** explains some of the history of Cahal Pech. Sometimes independent guides hang around here offering **tours**. Otherwise, walk about 150yd to the

area of excavated and restored plazas and temples. **Plaza B** is the largest and most impressive complex; **Structure A-1**, near plaza A, is the site's tallest temple. Two ballcourts lie at either end of the restored area.

Cahal Pech is 1 mile south of central San Ignacio. Head up Buena Vista St and turn left immediately before the Texaco gas station.

Branch Mouth   PARK
Branch Mouth is the meeting place of the Mopan River, coming from Guatemala, and the Macal River, flowing down from Mountain Pine Ridge. The confluence of these riv-

San Ignacio

ers forms the beginning of the Belize River, which flows northeast to the sea.

The surrounding parkland is home to an abundance of **birdlife** as well as an **iguana reserve**. The confluence of these rivers forms a sweet **swimming hole**, which is an enticing prospect on a hot day. To get there, cycle or walk 1.5 miles north on scenic Branch Mouth Rd to the Hammock Bridge.

Green Iguana Exhibit & Medicinal Jungle Trail GARDEN
(Map p158; ✆824-2034; www.sanignaciobelize.com; 18 Buena Vista St; adult/child BZ$12/$6; ⊗8am-noon & 1-4pm, tours every hr; 🐾) 🌿 On the lush Macal Valley grounds of the San Ignacio Resort Hotel, this program collects and hatches iguana eggs, raising the reptiles until they are past their most vulnerable age. The iguanas are then released into the wild, but not before giving guests a chance to get to know them. You'll get plenty of face time (and photo ops), as well as fun facts about iguanas. On the way back from the exhibit, learn about local herbs and plants on the **medicinal jungle trail** that winds through the forest.

San Ignacio & Santa Elena House of Culture MUSEUM
(✆824-0783; 7 King St; ⊗9am-noon & 1-6pm Mon & Wed-Fri, to noon Sat) FREE Opened in 2010, this small museum displays works by artists from Belize as well as arranging performances, classes and interactive happenings (occasionally extending past normal oper-ating hours). Museum curators are looking for a larger space, so by the time you read this, the museum may be elsewhere in San Ignacio, but for now it's right underneath the Town Council building.

🕝 Tours

Many of the most exciting sights and activities in Cayo District are most easily reached on a guided trip; some (such as Actun Tunichil Muknal and Barton Creek Cave) cannot be visited without a guide.

Typical day-trip prices per person are BZ$170 for Actun Tunichil Muknal (p157), BZ$60 to BZ$90 for a half-day trip to Barton Creek Cave (p161), BZ$140 to BZ$180 for Caracol (p167), BZ$130 for a cave-tubing trip to Nohoch Che'en (p150), BZ$60 to BZ$90 for Mountain Pine Ridge (p164) and BZ$200 to BZ$240 (plus border fees) for Tikal (p232) in Guatemala.

Leading tour companies or booking agencies based in or near San Ignacio include:

Pacz Tours GUIDED TOUR
(✆824-0536; www.pacztours.net; 30 Burns Ave) Offers reliably excellent service and knowledgeable guides to ATM and Tikal. Pacz rents good-quality mountain and road bicycles for BZ$70 a day, with long-term discounts available.

Belizean Sun CAVING
(✆665-2808; www.belizeansun.com) Based in San José Succotz, Belizean Sun provides

personalized caving experiences to some of Cayo's lesser-known caves, including Actun Chapat and Halal Cave. Whether your interests are flora, fauna, archaeology or cave geology, Belizean Sun guides will be sure to provide you with as much information and adventure as you desire.

Paradise Expeditions
BIRD-WATCHING
(✑ 610-5593, 820-4014; www.birdinginbelize.com; Crystal Paradise Resort, Cristo Rey village, Cristo Rey Rd) Run by the accomplished local bird guide Jeronie Tut, Paradise Expeditions does trips for both the casual and serious birder from its base at Crystal Paradise Resort.

Belize Nature Travel
TOUR
(✑ 824-3314; www.experiencebelize.com; Santa Elena) BNT specializes in cave tours such as ATM (BZ$190 per person, all inclusive) and does twice-weekly trips to Caracol (BZ$170 per person, minimum of two people, all inclusive). Check the website for other tour packages.

River Rat Expeditions
ADVENTURE TOUR
(✑ 824-2166, 605-4480; www.riverratbelize.com) Specialist in kayaking, river-tubing and cave trips. Enjoy a relaxing paddle down the Mopan River near Clarissa Falls, or take on some white water near Paslow Falls. Also books multiday kayaking and camping adventures, but arrangements must be made in advance.

David's Adventure Tour
ADVENTURE TOUR
(✑ 804-3674) Based just across the street from the Saturday market, David's offers ecofriendly tours to sites throughout the area. Among David's specialties are river canoe trips (BZ$40 to BZ$60 per person), overnight camping trips (BZ$75 per person) and full-on all-night jungle tours (BZ$150 per person).

Mayawalk Tours
ADVENTURE TOUR
(✑ 824-3070, 610-1129; www.mayawalk.com; 19 Burns Ave) Does trips to Caracol, ATM, Tikal (Guatemala) and many other adventure tours geared toward adventurers of all levels and interests.

🛏 Sleeping

San Ignacio accommodations are mostly in the budget bracket but there are also some excellent-value establishments here. More luxurious options can be found at lodges out of town.

Casa Blanca Guest House
HOTEL $
(✑ 824-2080; www.casablancaguesthouse.com; 10 Burns Ave; s/d/tr BZ$50/60/70, s/d with air-con BZ$80/100; ❉) Intimate and immaculate, the Casa Blanca gets rave reviews for its simplicity and hospitality. Decent-sized rooms have clean white walls and crisp fresh linens. Guests have a comfy sitting area, a clean kitchenette and a breezy rooftop terrace from which to watch the world go by.

Hotel Mallorca
HOTEL $
(✑ 824-2960; mallorcahotel@gmail.com; 12 Burns Ave; s/d BZ$45/55) Colorful quilts on firm beds in dark, spacious rooms with cable TV and hot showers are the main selling points of Hotel Mallorca. Super service is provided by managers Yolanda and Carlos, who live upstairs. All guests have access to the kitchen, a pleasant lounge area and a tiny balcony overlooking Burns Ave.

Western Guesthouse
GUESTHOUSE $
(✑ 824-2572; 54 Burns Ave; s/d with fan BZ$60/70, with air-con BZ$80/90, family ste BZ$140; P ❉ ⊗) The Urbina family's guesthouse on the quiet west side offers visitors a family atmosphere and access to a fully furnished kitchen. Fresh coffee is served in the morning, and guests have full kitchen privileges. Each of the family's six clean and comfortable guestrooms has two beds, its own TV and a hot shower, and there is also a large family suite with three double beds and full bathroom. Laundry services are available, and the Urbinas are a wealth of information about the area.

Rainforest Haven Inn
HOTEL $
(✑ 674 1984; www.rainforesthavens.com; 2 Victoria St; r BZ$90; ❉ @ ⊗) San Ignaciao's newest budget hotel is a real find; located on the east side of town right by Hawksworth bridge, the three-story hotel has lovely rooms with minifridges, cable TV, hot showers and comfortable beds. The best room in the house is on the 3rd floor. Featuring two queen-sized beds made from jungle wood and spectacular 360 degree views, this room is the same price as the others (so book in advance). There's a cool chill-out spot on the 2nd floor and a kitchen on the 3rd. The 1st floor features a separate internet cafe, popular with kids, and a hair salon owned by the Williams family who run the hotel.

Mana Kai Camp & Cabins
CAMPGROUND $
(Map p158; ✑ 824-2317, 624-6538; Branch Mouth Rd; s/d BZ$35/45, camping per person BZ$10; ⊗) Just north of the football grounds, Mana Kai

is a big swath of swampy land with colorfully painted cottages. There is plenty of space to spread out, with hammocks strung up around the grounds and an open-air wood stove for cooking. Inside, the cabins are basic and clean, with hot-water showers and private bathrooms. It's an excellent, affordable option if you are feeling stifled by the big city of San Ignacio.

Bella's Backpacker's HOSTEL $
(☎824-2248, 671-2248; bellabackpackers@yahoo.com; 4 Galvez St; dm BZ$15/20, r per person BZ$25; ☜❀) Located on a quiet street up the hill from the bus station, Bella's has two well-laid-out multistory dorm areas with new bunk beds and bathrooms with showers. Private rooms are fan cooled with big screened-in windows and a rock-motif bathroom. There's a 1st-floor communal kitchen and a breezy top-floor communal chill-out spot with hammocks and comfy couches.

Hi-Et Guest House GUESTHOUSE $
(☎824-2828; thehiet@btl.net; 12 West St; r with/without bathroom BZ$50/25) Friendly, funky Hi-Et occupies two connected houses, each with its own veranda overlooking the busy street below. Some rooms have shared bathrooms, but all are clean and comfy.

Elvira's Guesthouse GUESTHOUSE $
(☎804-0243, 620-5940; 6 Far West St; r with bathroom BZ$40-55, r without bathroom BZ$30; ❀) Simple and spacious rooms all have colorful paint jobs and warm woven blankets. Upstairs from Elvira's is a cool and cozy cafe, an excellent place for coffee, cakes, sandwiches and snacks.

Rosa's Hotel HOTEL $
(☎804-2265; Hudson St; d with fan/air-con BZ$50/75; ❀☜) Rooms are pretty bare, but they do have the basic necessities, including hot showers.

Cahal Pech Village Resort RESORT $$
(Map p158; ☎824-3740; www.cahalpech.com; Cahal Pech Hill; d/family ste BZ$158/198, dinner mains BZ$12-20; ▣❀@☜☒❀) Atop Cahal Pech hill, half a mile up from the town center, you can enjoy splendid views from this upscale resort. The hotel has 21 bright, tile-floored, air-con rooms and nine full-sized suites in the large main building. Built around the main building and offering the same exceptional views are 27 comfortable *cabañas* with thatched roofs. Wherever you stay, you'll enjoy a view of the Maya Moun-

tains or surrounding villages, either from your veranda or from the hotel's amazing two-level cascading pool. (Even if you aren't a guest you can still enjoy the pool for BZ$10). The onsite **restaurant** serves good international, Belizean and Maya food, so you don't need to trek into town for dinner. The hotel also has its own onsite tour service, booking trips to Caracol, Tikal, Xunantunich and any place else in Belize.

Martha's Guesthouse HOTEL $$
(☎804-3647; www.marthasbelize.com; 10 West St; r BZ$90-100, with air-con & breakfast BZ$110-120; ❀☜) This family-run guesthouse has bright, sparkling-clean rooms, each with a private balcony. Woven Maya tapestries accent the mahogany walls and furniture, while tile floors keep the rooms cool. Hotel amenities include a laundry and an excellent restaurant.

San Ignacio Resort Hotel HOTEL $$$
(Map p158; ☎824-2034; www.sanignaciobelize.com; 18 Buena Vista St; s/d with balcony BZ$342/376, regal r/family ste BZ$501/$376; ▣❀@☜☒) About 400yd uphill from the town center, this is San Ignacio's most upscale spot (indeed, the Queen stayed here in '94). The lobby is graced with a gorgeous mahogany staircase, marble floors and huge bouquets of orchids and bromeliads. Family-sized suites comfortably house six, while standard rooms are more cozy. Rooms with private balconies offer a great view, and garden rooms open up directly into the hotel's lush garden. All rooms are newly renovated, and the large stone-tiled showers in the bathrooms are downright sexy. Green Iguana Exhibit tours leave every hour on the hour from the lobby. Also onsite are a restaurant and bar, and next door is a casino for those in a gambling mood.

✖ Eating

Pop's Restaurant DINER $
(West St; breakfast BZ$8-10; ⊘breakfast, lunch & dinner) Friendly and clean six-booth old-school style hole-in-the-wall diner run by an older gentleman with a bushy white beard called – you guessed it – Pops. All-day breakfasts and bottomless cups of coffee. What more could you ask for?

Great Mayan Prince BELIZEAN $
(Map p158; ☎824-2588; 28 Benque Viejo Rd; breakfast & lunch BZ$8-10, Sun brunch buffet BZ$15; ⊘7am-9pm Mon-Thu, 7am-10pm Fri & Sat, 7am-3pm Sun; ☜❀) Off the main tourist

STREET FOOD & FARMERS MARKET

When it comes to street food, San Ignacio takes the prize for best street food, hands down (sorry, Orange Walk – you come in second). There's a plethora of stalls serving breakfast, burritos and other cheap eats on Burns Ave and more still down by the market on Savannah St.

To experience the true cultural tapestry of Belize firsthand, head down to the **Farmers Market** on Saturday, when San Ignacio's open-air market draws farmers and food producers from all ends of Belize (culturally and geographically) to buy and sell all manner of fruits, vegetables, jams and dairy products. Expect plenty of crafts and cooked foods as well.

drag, the Great Mayan Princess is worth the short hike up Benque Viejo Rd. Besides serving the best breakfast burrito in town, the restaurant also has a sweeping view of Cayo out to Guatemala. The Sunday brunch buffet is excellent as well.

Sweet T'ing   BAKERY $
(Map p158; ☑ 610-4174; 96 Benque Viejo Rd; cakes from BZ$3, coffee from BZ$2; ⊙ noon-9pm) A tiny bakery at the top of the hill with an exceptional variety of local chocolates (including made-in-Belize favorites Cotton Tree and Goss), Sweet T'ing is definitely worth the walk up. Also sells local and imported specialty items.

New French Bakery   BAKERY $
(baked goods from BZ$2; ⊙ 6:30am-6:30pm Mon-Sat) New location, same owners, this place serves excellent sticky buns, breads, coffee and even goat cheese.

★**Ko-Ox Han-nah**   MAYA $$
(☑ 824-3014; 5 Burns Ave; breakfast BZ$8-12, Belizean dishes BZ$10-12, Indian dishes BZ$15-20; ⊙ 6am-9pm) The name means 'let's go eat' in Mayan, and there's a reason why Han-nah's (as it's called) is the most popular spot in town any time of day. All food served comes from the owner's farm in nearby Calla Creek, including the lamb, pork and chicken (no factory farming here). Breakfasts are excellent and dinners unbeatable, with plenty of meatless options for vegetarians.

Serendib   SRI LANKAN $$
(Burns Ave; mains from BZ$15; ⊙ lunch & dinner) San Ignacio's only Sri Lankan restaurant serves excellent curries, spicy chicken tandoori and all manner of other delicacies from the Indian subcontinent. Friendly owners, sensational food and a peaceful courtyard dining area are bound to promote serendipity.

Cahal Pech Restaurant   INTERNATIONAL $$
(Cahal Pech Village Resort; mains BZ$9-20; ⊙ breakfast, lunch & dinner) If it's food with a view you're after, you won't get better than this unless you have your own chef and a zeppelin. International menu includes Belizean faves such as Mayan pork chops (BZ$22).

Martha's Kitchen   INTERNATIONAL $$
(10 West St; mains BZ$15-20; ⊙ breakfast, lunch & dinner) Highlights at Martha's Kitchen run the gamut from tasty pizza and delicious fish burritos to juicy steaks and vegetarian kebabs. Take a seat inside the wood-accented dining room or outside on the foliage-fronted terrace, but don't be surprised if you have to wait.

Hode's Place   BELIZEAN, AMERICAN $$
(Map p158; Branch Mouth Rd; mains BZ$12-20; ⊙ 10am-midnight) Locals love this rambling place north of the center. A large terrace restaurant opening onto a citrus orchard and kids' playground, it's a popular spot for families (a jukebox and games room also help). Friendly service and satisfying food – from burritos and fajitas to steaks, seafood and rice and beans – complete this place's recipe for success.

Mr. Greedy's   PIZZA, ITALIAN $$
(Burns Ave; burgers from BZ$7, pizzas from BZ$13; ⊙ breakfast, lunch & dinner) Great – though somewhat noisy – little pizzeria, bar and burger joint on the main drag that uses homemade ingredients, makes cocktails and milkshakes, and even sells slices.

Heat Wave   PIZZERIA $$
(Map p158; ☑ 824-4770; Benque Viejo Rd; slices BZ$3, pies from BZ$25; ⊙ 4-10pm) Good pizza pies and slices. Take-out only.

🍷 Drinking & Entertainment

Canta's Bar BAR
(8 Hudson St; ⊙10am-midnight) On the grounds of the former Cocopela, this bar has exchanged the pool table and foosball for a karaoke machine. The deck out back is a great place for a drink on a warm night.

Soul Project Space for the Creative Arts ART SPACE
(⊘653-1855; guanamon@yahoo.com; Buena Vista Rd, across from Police Station; ⊙11am-11pm; 🛜🍴) 🍴 Art space, restaurant, cafe and bar....Cayo's newest venue is difficult to categorize. Opened in December, 2012 by local artist, filmmaker and conservationist Daniel Velazquez, Soul Project is housed inside of a distinctly New Orleans–esque building on San Ignacio's less trammeled east side (just on the way to Cahal Pech). As well as being a cafe serving excellent and healthy Belizean and international cuisine (all foods locally sourced and, for the most part, organic), Soul Project is also a venue for local artists and musicians, featuring exhibits and performances by local and international artists. There's also a bar featuring beer, wine, smoothies and coffee. Furniture is eclectic, featuring swings, hammocks and tables made from recycled materials. Come in for the art, stay for a meal, nap on a hammock.

Stork Club BAR
(Map p158; ⊘824-2034; San Ignacio Resort Hotel, 18 Buena Vista St; ⊙bands & DJs 9:30pm-2am Fri & Sat) This hotel is a bit of a social hub, attracting tourists, expats and something of an older crowd. Call in advance to find out if there's live music.

🛍 Shopping

Belize Gifts ARTS & CRAFTS
(⊘824-4159; 21 Burns Ave, JNC Mall) This place has an excellent selection of high-quality souvenirs, including beautiful salad bowls, jewelry boxes and other wooden items. There is also a small selection of books and guidebooks about Belize, including the useful *Guide to the Maya Sites of Belize* by Jaime Awe.

New Hope Woodworking ARTS & CRAFTS
(Map p158; ⊘824-2188; Buena Vista St) South of the center, this carpentry workshop is a worthwhile stop if you are in the market for wooden furniture, cabinetry or smaller items made from mahogany or native woods. Be prepared to check it in with your luggage, because it is prohibitively expensive to ship.

Jungle Remedies HEALTH
(Map p158; ⊘663-0248; miracle@btl.net; Orange St) From gastric distress and asthma to high blood pressure, gall stones and gout, Dr Harry Guy claims his jungle remedies can cure nearly any ailment. Many locals swear by his potions, made from locally harvested roots, barks and leaves. Try his Noni Juice, made from a stinky fruit said to have curative properties.

Arts & Crafts of Central America ARTS & CRAFTS
(⊘824-2253; 24 Burns Ave) This little shop sells a wide variety of handmade jewelry, handbags and textiles, mostly from Guatemala. This is also the place to book your tours with Easy Rider.

Back to My Roots ARTS & CRAFTS
(⊘824-2740; 30 Burns Ave) Offers cool handmade jewelry, including silver, amber and other semiprecious stones. The name of the place refers to the drums and other Roots gear for sale.

Books & Stuff BOOKS
(21 Burns Ave) Formerly known as Amber Mystic Books, this wonderful shop inside the Burns Avenue Mall sells books, art and music, and welcomes trade-ins.

ℹ Information

Belize Bank (16 Burns Ave) and **Scotiabank** (cnr Burns Ave & King St) both have ATMs that accept international Visa, MasterCard, Plus and Cirrus cards.
La Loma Luz Hospital (⊘824-2087, 804-2985; http://lalomaluz.org; Western Hwy; ⊙emergency services 24hr) This Adventist hospital in Santa Elena is one of the best in the country.

ℹ WATCH WHERE YOU PARK

In January of 2011 three travelers had their car tires slashed while parked overnight on Burns Ave, the second such occurrence in six months. Parking in front of the **police station** (⊘824-2022; cnr Missiah & Buena Vista Sts) is advised. Otherwise, San Ignacio isn't a dangerous place. Still, travelers should always exercise caution, especially after dark.

❶ GETTING TO GUATEMALA

Direct buses from San Ignacio into Guatemala have ceased as of this writing but may be back by the time you read this. (There are buses coming from Flores to Belize City, but these are not technically permitted to stop anywhere but Belize City.)

Luckily, getting into Guatemala from San Ignacio isn't too challenging. *Colectivo* taxis (charging per person and leaving when they have a full car) head from a vacant lot on Savannah St to Benque Viejo del Carmen (BZ$4) and then directly to the Guatemalan border (BZ$6). Once you've crossed the border, you'll need to walk about a mile or hop on a taxi to get to the *colectivo* stand in Melchor de Mencos for Q10, from where you can catch a ride to Flores or El Remate.

Post office (✆824-2049; Hudson St)
Tradewinds (✆824-2396; 5 Hudson St, next to post office; per hr BZ$4; ⊗7am-10pm Mon-Sat, to 10pm Sun) A friendly internet spot with free coffee.

❶ Getting There & Around

BUS
For bus schedules, stop by the **Savannah Taxi Association** (✆824-2155) stand in the center of Market Sq. This is where buses stop en route to/from Belize City (BZ$6, two hours), Belmopan (BZ$4, one hour) and Benque Viejo del Carmen (BZ$3, 30 minutes). Buses run in both directions just about every half-hour from 7am to 9pm, with a less frequent service on Sunday. One bus a day goes to Dangriga (BZ$12, three hours), Friday to Monday only.

From a vacant lot on Savannah St, buses leave for Bullet Tree Falls (BZ$1, 15 minutes) at 10:30am, 11am, 11:30am, 12:30pm, 3:30pm, 4pm and 5pm, Monday to Saturday. From the same spot, buses go to San Antonio (BZ$3, 45 minutes) at 10:45am, 1:15pm, 3:15pm and 5:15pm, Monday to Saturday.

CAR
To really explore Cayo, you'll want a car. Don't even think about heading to Caracol without a 4WD. Rates include third-party insurance and unlimited mileage at the following agencies:
Cayo Auto Rentals (✆824-2222; www.cayo-autorentals.com; 81 Benque Viejo Rd) Daily rates start at BZ$164 for a Kia Sportage; rent six days and the seventh day is free.

Matus Car Rental (✆824-2005, 663-4702; www.matuscarrental.com; 18 Benque Viejo Rd) Rates start at BZ$125/700 per day/week for a Chevy Tracker and Four Runners.
Premium Auto (✆607-8945; premiumauto-belize@gmail.com; Western Hwy, Santa Elena; ⊗7am-5pm) Rents vehicles for BZ$130 per day; weekly and monthly rates available.
Safe Tours Belize (✆824-4262; 278 Western Hwy, Santa Elena; ⊗7am-9pm) Rents vehicles for BZ$164 per day; inquire at the office just north of Hannah's.

TAXI
Several taxi stands are around the town center. Sample fares: BZ$20 to the Guatemalan border (9 miles) or Crystal Paradise Resort (5 miles); BZ$60 round trip to Xunantunich; BZ$80 to BZ$100 one way to the Mountain Pine Ridge lodges. Taxis to Bullet Tree Falls (*colectivo*/private BZ$4/15) go from Wyatt St, just off Burns Ave.

NORTHWEST OF SAN IGNACIO

A paved road leads northwest out of San Ignacio, through green pastures and farmland to Bullet Tree Falls, a pretty little town straddling the Mopan River. Beyond Bullet Tree Falls a rough track covers the 8 miles to the remote Maya site of El Pilar on the Guatemalan border.

Bullet Tree Falls

Bullet Tree Falls is a quiet and quaint little village, home to a few laid-back lodges overlooking the Mopan River. Although it's on the edge of the jungle, it offers easy access to San Ignacio, even if you don't have your own vehicle. There is also a handful of outdoor adventure activities at your doorstep, including hiking in the nearby forests and river-tubing down the Mopan River.

As you come into the village you'll see the bus stop at the junction of a road to the right (which leads to Iguana Junction and Cohune Palms). Straight ahead, the main road continues 200yd to the bridge over the Mopan. The **Bullet Tree Internet Café** (per hour BZ$3; ⊗Mon-Thu 10am-9pm, Fri-Sun to 5pm) is north of the bridge, just across from the police station.

◉ Sights & Activities

El Pilar   RUIN
(Map p158; admission BZ$20; ⊗8am-4pm) The rough road to **El Pilar** heads off to the left,

400yd past the bridge in Bullet Tree Falls. Be prepared for a bumpy ride: 4WD is required for the 7-mile jungle trek.

El Pilar was occupied for at least 15 centuries, from the middle Preclassic period (around 500 BC) to the late Classic period (about AD 1000). Long before present-day political borders, El Pilar stretched to modern-day Pilar Poniente in Guatemala, and the two countries are now working as partners to preserve the area. The **El Pilar Archaeological Reserve for Maya Flora & Fauna** straddles the international boundary.

With 25 plazas and 70 major structures, El Pilar was more than three times the size of Xunantunich. Despite excavations since 1993, not much of El Pilar has been cleared; this has been to avoid the decay that often follows the clearing of ancient buildings. While appreciating El Pilar's greatness requires some imagination, this may help to give you the feeling that you're discovering the place rather than following a well-worn tourist trail.

Six archaeological and nature trails meander among the mounds. The most impressive area is **Plaza Copal**, which has four pyramids from 45ft to 60ft high. A partly visible Maya causeway runs 500yd west from here to Pilar Poniente. The site attracts archaeology enthusiasts as well as bird nerds. Toucans, orioles, toucanets, hummingbirds, woodpeckers and even the occasional scarlet macaw are sighted here.

If you have your own vehicle, it's an incredible, remote and rewarding place to wander on your own. Otherwise, you can hire a taxi (BZ$50 from Bullet Tree Falls) or take a tour. Bullet Tree local **Teddy Waight** (🖉664-9599; vlteddy@yahoo.com) brings small groups here for BZ$40 per person, including transportation.

Masewal Forest Garden GARDEN
(admission BZ$10) Up the road to the left, past the town of Bullet Tree Falls, you'll find the Masewal Forest Garden, an herbal and botanical garden created by renowned local healer Hilberto Cocom.

🛏 Sleeping & Eating

Bullet Tree Falls has about half a dozen small restaurants serving Belizean favorites on the cheap. **Gloria's Pizza and Fast Food** (Map p158; ☺breakfast, lunch & dinner), next to Chun's Supermarket, serves *garnaches* and

panades (both variations on the tortilla, beans and cheese theme) for a dollar each.

Parrot Nest Jungle Lodge CABINS $$
(Map p158; 🖉660-6336, 669-6068; www.parrotnest.com; treehouses or cabins without bathroom BZ$90, q cabins with hot showers & bathrooms BZ$105, breakfast BZ$8-12, dinner BZ$24; 🅿🐾📶♿) If you ever wanted to live like the monkeys, here is your chance to sleep in the branches of a massive guanacaste tree. Nine cabins – some on stilts, some in trees – all have sturdy wood construction, tin roofs and shared bathrooms; four larger cabins have private bathrooms and inviting verandas. Kids will love playing on the jungley grounds, a haven for wildlife-watching, river swimming and hammock swinging. Guests enjoy free use of kayaks, tubes and bicycles. The free morning shuttle to San Ignacio is still operating, but guests should take a *collectivo* home (BZ$2).

Cohune Palms CABINS $$
(Map p158; 🖉664-7508; www.cohunepalms.com; s/d/tr BZ$128/172/216, breakfast/lunch BZ$16/24; 🅿📶) Always laid-back but absolutely lovely, Cohune Palms is set on the riverbank, surrounded by its namesake tree. Four spacious *cabañas* – all topped with a thatched roof – have high ceilings, wood carvings, tile floors and woven tapestries. They share access to a shady deck, where meals are served. Spend the day swinging in a hammock or sign up for one of the many tours on offer. Cohune Palms also offers week-long yoga retreats several times a year.

Iguana Junction LODGE $$
(Map p158; 🖉824-2249; www.iguanajunction.com; d cabañas BZ$110) All four accommodations (two private rooms and two *cabañas*) are simple and clean with private bathrooms, fans and details such as locally made furniture and lamp shades. The central *palapa* is generously draped with hammocks, making it the ultimate hang-out place. The onsite restaurant is now open only for guests.

Hotel El Pilar HOTEL $$
(Map p158; 🖉824-3059; hotelpilar@live.com; s/d with fan BZ$60/95, with air-con BZ$95/125) A bright-yellow two-story building right in town offers clean tile-floor rooms with fans, air-con, cable TV and hot showers. Rooms are spacious and clean, and management is quite friendly.

★ **Mahogany Hall** BOUTIQUE HOTEL **$$$**
(Map p158; ☑844-4047; www.mahoganyhallbelize.com; d/ste BZ$350/660, colonial family r BZ$1200; ❋ 🎐 🕸 🛁) This beautiful three-story colonial mansion sits on the eastern bank of Mopan River, about a mile away from Bullet Tree Falls village. Rooms feature deep, dark mahogany floors and beds, classic French doors and bathrooms with exquisite brass fixtures. All rooms have air-con and LCD-screen TVs with cable; suites have Jacuzzis with French windows overlooking either the Mopan River or the rainforest. There's even a small, chic pool and a patio overlooking the rushing river. Onsite restaurant Rico's Restaurant and Bar offers three meals a day and cocktails with a traditional colonial West Indies feel.

Casa del Caballo Blanco CABINS **$$$**
(Map p158; ☑824-2098, in USA 707-760-4544; www.casacaballoblanco.com; Bullet Tree Rd; s/d/tr BZ$216/252/287, breakfast/lunch/dinner BZ$21/26/42; 🅿) ✦ About a mile out of San Ignacio on the way to Bullet Tree Falls, the 'House of the White Horse' is a concrete yellow ecolodge set on 23 acres of rolling hills and forest overlooking the Mopan River valley. Guests stay in spacious high-ceilinged thatched-roof *cabañas* that are sparingly decorated with hardwood furniture and Maya fabrics. Homegrown veggies and locally produced baked goods cover the tables at meal time. Aside from the sweeping views, the highlight of the White Horse is the bird sanctuary, an impressive facility that is used for the rehabilitation and release of native species. (Nonguests are welcome to the sanctuary, but are asked for a donation of BZ$10, which covers juice and snacks.)

ⓘ Getting There & Away

Seven daily buses (except Sunday) run from San Ignacio to Bullet Tree Falls (BZ$1, 15 minutes) and back. Alternatively, *colectivo* taxis pick up passengers at the bus stop at the junction.

SOUTHWEST OF SAN IGNACIO

Southwest from San Ignacio the Western Hwy runs across rolling countryside toward Benque Viejo del Carmen and the Guatemalan border. There is a variety of places to stay strung out along the highway. Buses between San Ignacio and Benque Viejo del Carmen will drop you anywhere along this stretch.

Between San Ignacio & San José Succotz

As the Western Hwy heads out of San Ignacio, it passes through the suburbs – basically a series of resorts scattered around the forested hills. The location is ideal, with the highway providing easy access into town, but the secluded atmosphere makes the place feel like it's tucked far away from anywhere.

🛏 Sleeping & Eating

Log Cab-Inn CABINS **$$**
(Map p158; ☑824-3367, 670-0711; www.logcabinnbelize.com; Mile 68 Western Hwy; s/d BZ$120/140, incl 3 meals BZ$181/267; 🅿 ❋ @ 🎐 🕸) Abraham Lincoln meets jungle resort on a citrus tree and palm-dotted hillside. Sixteen cabins are built from mahogany logs, with furniture crafted at the onsite carpentry workshop. All cabins have air-con, hot showers and cable TV – with the air-con mandatory in some, thanks to management's decision to seal the windows. Meals are served in an open-air restaurant and bar, and kids under 12 stay free with their parents.

★ **Ka'ana Resort & Spa** RESORT **$$$**
(Map p158; ☑824-3350; www.kaanabelize.com; Mile 69 Western Hwy; r from BZ$550, casitas from BZ$750, 1-/2-bedroom villas BZ$1600/2400, breakfast BZ$16-24, lunch & dinner BZ$40-60; 🅿 ❋ @ 🎐 🕸 🛁) ✦ If you are in the market for some indulgence, this unique boutique resort and spa is a good place to start. Meaning 'Heavenly Place' in Kekchi Mayan, Ka'ana offers luxurious rooms and *casitas* fully equipped with high-thread-count sheets, down comforters, LCD TVs and iPod docking stations. Decor is contemporary Maya, with artwork by local Belizean artists and changed between rooms every fourth night to ensure maximum appreciation by guests. Newly built private pool villas (yes, they have their own pools!) offer the height of both privacy and luxury. Private terraces overlook the lush grounds. The gourmet **restaurant** offers innovative, organic local cuisine – including herbs and vegetables from Ka'ana's 1-acre onsite garden – and a well-stocked wine cellar. Most tempting is the full menu of spa treatments at the **Caribbean Spa** (open 7:30am to 8:30pm), ranging from facials and pedicures to mud wraps and Ka'ana's special coffee massage (a massage which incorporates organic coffee beans). Nonguests are also welcome to enjoy all facilities, but reservations are recommended.

San José Succotz

Located 6.5 miles west of San Ignacio on the Western Hwy, San José Succotz sits at the doorstep of Xunantunich. A handful of restaurants are located in the town itself, and there are a few miniresorts catering to archaeology buffs and other adventurers strung out along the Western Hwy and the river. Though Xunantunich can be done as an outing from San Ignacio, you may prefer to use this slow-paced *barrio* as your base for exploring Cayo.

⊙ Sights & Activities

Xunantunich   RUIN
(admission BZ$10; ⊙7:30am-4pm) Set on a leveled hilltop, Xunantunich (pronounced shoo-nahn-too-neech), is one of Belize's most easily accessible and impressive Maya archaeological sites. To reach the ruins, take the free, hand-cranked ferry across the Mopan River. From the ferry, which comes and goes on demand, it's about 1 mile uphill to the parking lot and ticket office. It's a semi-strenuous walk with great opportunities for sighting birds and butterflies. At the end, your reward is a complex of temples and plazas that date back to the 7th century.

Xunantunich may have been occupied as early as 1000 BC but it was little more than a village. As mentioned, the large architecture that we see today began to be built in the 7th century AD. From AD 700 to 850, Xunantunich was possibly politically aligned with Naranjo, 9 miles west in Guatemala. Together they controlled the western part of the Belize River valley, although the population probably never exceeded 10,000. Xunantunich partially survived the initial Classic Maya collapse of about AD 850 (when nearby Cahal Pech was abandoned), but was deserted by about AD 1000. A good **visitors center**, located between the ticket office and the hilltop ruins, explains this history.

The site centers on **Plazas A-2** and **A-1**, separated by Structure A-1. Just north of Plaza A-2, Structure A-11 and **Plaza A-3** formed a residential 'palace' area for the ruling family. The dominant **El Castillo** (Structure A-6) rises 130ft high at the south end of Plaza A-1. El Castillo may have been the ruling family's ancestral shrine, where they were buried and/or represented in sculpted friezes. Structures A-1 and A-13, at either end of Plaza A-2, were not built until the 9th century and would have had the effect of separating the ruling family

from the rest of the population, possibly a response to the pressures that came with the decline of Classic Maya civilization at that time.

You can climb to the top of El Castillo to enjoy a spectacular 360-degree view. Its upper levels were constructed in two distinct phases. The first, built around 800, included an elaborate **plaster frieze** encircling the building; the second, built around 900, covered over most of the first and its frieze. The frieze on the east end of the building and part of the western one have been uncovered by archaeologists; these depict a series of Maya deities, with Chac, the rain god, probably the central figure at the east end. The friezes you see today are replicas, with originals underneath for safekeeping.

South of El Castillo is a partly overgrown area of lesser structures (Group C) that were abandoned as the city shrank after 900, leaving El Castillo (formerly at the center of the ancient city) on the southern edge of the occupied area.

Xunantunich

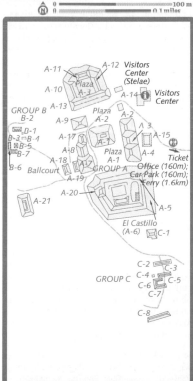

Tropical Wings Nature Center   GARDEN
(Map p158; 823-2265; www.thetrekstop.com; Mile 71 Western Hwy; adult/child BZ$6/3; 9am-5pm;) Perhaps you're looking for something to do on a rainy day or need a low-key afternoon activity after spending an exhausting morning at Xunantunich? You've found it. This interactive ecology exhibit is aimed at kids, but even adults will enjoy the butterfly house and medicinal gardens. If you crave some more active recreation, try your hand at **Frisbee golf** (per person BZ$6), a newfangled sport that requires floating the disk through the trees and into baskets. It's all on the grounds of the Trek Stop, whose guests enjoy free access to the nature center.

🛏 Sleeping & Eating

★ **Trek Stop**   BACKPACKER RESORT $
(Map p158; 823-2265; www.thetrekstop.com; Mile 71 Western Hwy; camping per person BZ$10, d/tr/q with bathroom BZ$83/109/131, s/d/tr/q without bathroom BZ$33/52/83/96, breakfast BZ$7-12, main dishes BZ$10-15; restaurant 7am-8pm;) The Trek Stop offers a unique combination of ecolodge and backpackers' outpost, perfectly located to provide a remote jungle setting and easy access to all the local sites. Hand-hewn cabins have simple wood furnishings and private verandas. Toilets are self-composting, but there is one new cabin with a flush toilet (BZ$120). There is plenty of hang-out space, including a shady hammock lounge, a self-catering kitchen and a highly recommended (and affordable) restaurant. The entrance to the Trek Stop is right on the Western Hwy (just before San José Succotz), but its 22 acres extend back into the wilds, where you can enjoy Frisbee golf, nature trails and other jungle activities.

Maya Vista   RESORT $$
(Map p158; 823-3020, in USA 609-828-1163; www.mayavistabelize.com; Mile 70 Western Hwy; cabañas from BZ$200;) This family-run resort is set on 68 acres of garden-filled jungle savanna with a killer view of the highest temple in Xunantunich. Eight comfortable cabins have tile floors, air-con, private bathrooms with hot showers and beautiful Maya carvings. Call first to make sure that someone is there to meet you when you arrive.

Benny's Kitchen   BELIZEAN $$
(Map p158; 823-2541; Mile 72 Western Hwy; meals BZ$10-20; 7am-10pm Sun-Thu, to midnight Fri & Sat;) Ah, Benny's! This local institution just gets better with every visit, serving local specialties like tangy *escabeche* (spicy chicken with lime and onions), fiery BBQ, cowfoot soup and more. Visit on the weekend for a chance to sample more exotic rotating specials like *gibnut* (small rodent similar to a guinea pig) stew and venison steak. A wide selection of beer and libations are available. Benny's also has a small store, children's playground and an air-conditioned internet cafe (open 10am to 9pm). Just a stone's throw from the Xunantunich ferry, Benny's is about 50m off the Western Hwy; turn off the road that heads south in Succotz.

Chial Road

Chial Rd, heading southeast off the Western Hwy, 5 miles from San Ignacio, gives access to three exquisite lodges on the west bank of the Macal River. In operation for as long as 30 years, these are some of the region's longest-established and best-loved lodges. Aside from the rather luxurious accommodations, they also offer an extensive range of activities, including some unique nature attractions that are open to nonguests.

Getting here is half the fun: Chial Rd is unpaved and very bumpy, traversing miles of agricultural fields, orange and lemon orchards and untamed wilderness. A 4WD may be required, especially outside the driest months. If you don't have your own vehicle, any of the lodges can provide airport transfers.

◉ Sights & Activities

Belize Botanic Gardens   GARDEN
(Map p158; 824-3101; www.belizebotanic.org; per person unguided/guided tour BZ$10/15, under 12 free, guided tour with transport BZ$50, includes entrance & round-trip ride from San Ignacio; 7am-3pm) The magnificent Belize Botanic Gardens houses samples of roughly one-quarter of the approximately 4000 species of plants in Belize. One of the region's highlights, the bountiful 45-acre zone boasts 2 miles of trails, many fruit trees and four different Belizean habitats: wetlands, rainforest, Mountain Pine Ridge (with a lookout tower) and medicinal plants of the Maya. Two ponds attract a variety of waterfowl; Hamilton Hide allows birders to bring their binoculars and spy on various species. The garden's native orchid house is the largest of its kind in Belize.

One worthwhile tour is called **Plants of the Maya** (per person BZ$100; ☺6am), which includes the entrance fee, a shuttle from San Ignacio, a traditional knowledge tour, with lunch and lessons in cooking or crafting with a local Maya guide. Or spend a **Day at the Gardens** (per person BZ$85), which includes transportation, guided tour and your choice of horseback riding or canoeing.

The gardens are situated adjacent to duPlooy's Jungle Lodge, whose guests enjoy free admission.

Chaa Creek NATURE RESERVE
Set along the banks of the Macal River, beautiful Chaa Creek is a 365-acre nature reserve offering extensive facilities to guests and nonguests alike.

Running through the jungle just above the river, the **Rainforest Medicine Trail** (Map p158; guided tours BZ$10; ☺tours hourly 8am-5pm) was established by Dr Rosita Arvigo. This is just one of a series of projects that aim to spread knowledge of traditional healing methods and preserve the rainforest habitats, from which many healing plants come. It identifies about 100 medicinal plants used in traditional Maya and/or modern medicine. A gift shop near the start of the trail sells a guide to the trail's plants and some of Dr Arvigo's books.

From here, hike up the tree-covered hillside to the **Chaa Creek Natural History Center & Butterfly Farm** (Map p158; guided tours BZ$10; ☺tours hourly 8am-4pm), a small nature center with displays on Belize's flora and fauna, as well as the early Maya. The highlight is the butterfly farm, which breeds the dazzlingly iridescent blue morpho *(Morpho peleides)* for export.

There's also **Spa at Chaa Creek** (Map p158; ☑824-2037; www.chaacreek.com; 1-day packages BZ$474) which offers a spectacular panorama of the Macal River valley. Enjoy the view while indulging in a massage, facial, aromatherapy, body wrap or some other sensual treat.

🛏 Sleeping & Eating

Macal River Camp at Chaa Creek CABINS $$
(Map p158; Macal River Camp; cabin per person incl dinner & breakfast BZ$130; 🐾) ✦ A half mile away from the Lodge at Chaa Creek, the Macal River Camp at Chaa Creek offers screened-in wooden cabins on stilts with comfy cots inside and a shady veranda outside. The place is not landscaped, but rather

inhabits the jungle without disturbing the environs. All cabins share clean bathrooms and excellent hot showers. A campfire is lit nightly, creating an atmosphere of camaraderie. Your hosts are Francelia and Docio Juarez, a local couple who tend the campsite and cabins, cook meals and lead tours.

To reach the Camp at Chaa Creek, you'll have to park in the designated area and hike in through the jungle for about half a mile. Room rates at both the lodge and the camp include canoeing, guided bird walks and visits to the onsite rainforest medicine trail, natural history center and butterfly farm.

★**Black Rock River Lodge** RESORT $$$
(Map p158; ☑834-4049, 834-4038; www.blackrocklodge.com; r BZ$210-420, extra person BZ$22, breakfast BZ$20, lunch items BZ$8-10, dinner BZ$80; Ⓟ) ✦ High up the Macal in beautiful Black Rock Canyon, this is a stunning setting for a jungle adventure. Slate-and-wood cabins, fully furnished, are fan cooled and have lovely verandas that look down on the rushing river and up toward the towering cliffs of the canyon and 13,000 acres of protected national park. From here you can hike a signed trail up the mountain behind the lodge, ride a horse to Vaca Falls up the Macal, or ride state-of-the-art specialized mountain bikes to the little-visited **Flour Camp Cave**, with its abundant ancient Maya pottery, stalactites and stalagmites. Black Rock's vast dining area and deck, covered by a *palapa*, is fantastic for birding (the grounds are home to a nesting pair of orange-breasted falcons, all three species of toucans, white hawks, and the distinctive blue crown and toady motmots). You may also spot howler monkeys, otters and iguanas. The same holds for a newly built hardwood floor *palapa* halfway to the river, used for retreats and yoga classes (Kelly, co-owner of Black Rock, is a yoga instructor). An onsite organic farm provides produce for some of the meals served in the restaurant, and all electricity is solar and hydro produced.

Black Rock River Lodge is at the end of a good, well-signposted, 6-mile unpaved road that leaves Chial Rd 0.8 miles off the Western Hwy.

duPlooy's Jungle Lodge RESORT $$$
(Map p158; ☑824-3101; www.duplooys.com; r/bungalow BZ$431/540, ste or casita incl breakfast BZ$695, 3 meals BZ$92; Ⓟ@🛜) Well-managed, family-run duPlooy's sits in large and lovely grounds above the Macal. Founded in 1989

it's one of the longest-running Cayo lodges. The duPlooys have bucked the thatched-roof trend, instead going with stone and wood tile-roofed cabins with full kitchens and living areas that sleep up to four people in two queen- or king-sized beds. Other suites and the *casitas* on the property can comfortably sleep as many as eight people (perfect for student groups). All lodging options have private verandas overlooking the jungle grounds.

Mother nature has been good to the area, and guests can enjoy swimming (and canoeing) in the river, hiking along the jungle trails, and coffee and bird observation from the bar in the morning, all for free. An elevated 30ft-high skywalk offers a unique vantage point of the surrounding jungle, and the onsite restaurant is both excellent and inexpensive. There are 11 horses residing on the property, and the lodge employs two guides who lead equestrian trips throughout the area.

To reach duPlooy's, turn right off Chial Rd after 2.5 miles and go on for 1.7 miles. Another perk is free access to the Belize Botanic Gardens, adjacent to duPlooy's.

Lodge at Chaa Creek　　ECOLODGE **$$$**
(Map p158; ☑824-2037, 824-4111; www.chaacreek. com; cottage s/d/tr BZ$470/660/750, ste BZ$760, lunch/dinner BZ$24/72; P@🛜🏊) ⌀ Consistently rated among the best lodges in Belize, Chaa Creek's tropical gardens and beautifully kept thatched cottages spread across a gentle slope above the Macal, 3 miles from the highway. Owned and operated by Lucy and Mick Fleming since 1977, Chaa Creek blossomed from an overgrown farm into Belize's original jungle lodge. The cottages, richly decorated with Maya textiles and local crafts, all have decks, fans and private bathrooms. Newly added accommodations for 2013 include the three-level treetop Jacuzzi suite (BZ$1071) overlooking the jungle, the amazing garden suite (BZ$833) and the spa villa (BZ$1370), which has three bedrooms and sleeps up to seven people.

An array of tours and activities is offered, and Chaa Creek is proud of its state-of-the-art spa on a hilltop overlooking the river. Chaa Creek is one of the original ecolodges, with its rainforest medicine trail and organic Maya farm. Breakfast is included.

Benque Viejo del Carmen

POP 6700
About a mile from the Guatemalan border and 7 miles from San Ignacio, Benque Viejo del Carmen is a small town with a surprisingly sophisticated cultural scene.

◉ Sights & Activities

Aside from the interesting attractions in the vicinity, Benque is home to the **Benque Viejo House of Culture** (☑823-2697; 64 St Joseph St; ⊙9am-4pm Mon-Fri), which hosts exhibits relevant to local art, history and culture. It's also home to **Stone Tree Records** (www.stonetreerecords.com), which produces some of Belize's best-known music.

The centerpiece of the town is **Our Lady of Mount Carmel Church**, visible from all corners. On Good Friday (the Friday before Easter) the church hosts a dramatic procession through town, culminating in a rendition of the Passion Play. In mid-July Benque breaks out of its tropical somnolence, when the **Benque Viejo del Carmen Fiesta** celebrates the town's patron saint with several days of music and fun.

Poustinia Land Art Park　　PARK
(Map p158; ☑822-3532; www.poustiniaonline.org; Mile 2½ Hydro Rd; admission BZ$20; ⊙by appointment only) Drive about 2.5 miles southeast of Benque Viejo along the unpaved, overgrown Hydro Rd and you will come to one of the hidden jewels of Western Belize. Created by Benque brothers Luis and David Ruiz, this highly unexpected avant-garde sculpture park set in 60 acres of rainforest displays some 30 works by Belizean and international artists. Poustinia was conceived as an environmental art project, in which, once in place, the exhibits – including a car, a greenhouse and a strip of parquet flooring – become subject to the action of nature, which may rot, corrode or otherwise transmute them.

One piece, *Stone Labyrinth,* is set on top of an unexcavated Maya mound with views to Xunantunich. Poustinia is best enjoyed if you have time to contemplate the art and the natural environment it's set in. Allow at least two hours, preferably more.

Make arrangements and buy your admission ticket at the Benque Viejo House of Culture, just off Campo Santo Memorial Park. The House of Culture can also arrange for a taxi cab to take you to Poustinia (BZ$20). Otherwise, turn south off George Price Blvd onto Hydro Rd, beside the Long Luck Super Store, and drive 2.5 miles to the park.

There's no restaurant in the park, but visitors are welcome to bring their own food as long as they don't leave any litter behind.

Camping is permitted for the small charge of BZ$10 per person.

Che Chem Ha   CAVE
(Map p158; Mile 8 Hydro Rd; tour per person BZ$40) William Morales' dog was busy chasing down a *gibnut* on his lush property one day in 1989, when the dog seemingly disappeared into a rock wall. Morales pressed into the 'wall' and found it was actually a cave mouth; inside he came upon probably the largest collection of Maya pottery ever discovered. This was Che Chem Ha, the 'Cave of Poisonwood Water.'

Morales' family has been farming this land since the 1940s and today they also conduct tours through the cave, offering lunches and simple lodgings to visitors. The cave, about 800ft long, was used by the Maya for many centuries for food storage and rituals.

Narrow passages wind past ceremonial pots, many of them intact, to a stela at the end of the tunnel. Short ladders enable you to climb up rock ledges. Bring strong shoes, water and a flashlight. The tour lasts about 90 minutes, following an uphill jungle walk of about 30 minutes to the cave mouth. After the cave, you can visit a lovely waterfall on the property and/or hike about 30 minutes down to Vaca Falls for a swim in the Macal River.

There is no current number for Che Chem Ha. You can make arrangements for transportation from San Ignacio or Benque Viejo del Carmen; continue south on Hydro Rd, about 5.5 miles beyond Poustinia.

🛏 Sleeping & Eating

Maxim's Palace   HOTEL $
(Map p158; ☎823-2360; cayobenque@yahoo.com; 41 Church Hill St; d with fan/air-con BZ$60/75; P ❄) If you are passing through en route to/from Guatemala, consider crashing chez Maxim. Spacious rooms, warm hospitality and affordable rates make it a decent place to use as a base as you explore the sights around the border.

Benque Resort & Spa   HOTEL $$
(Map p158; ☎666-3185; www.benquehouse.com; 22 Riverside; dm BZ$35, s/d BZ$75/120; ☎) Formerly known as Benque House, this charming three-story home on the south bank of the Mopan River offers unexpected B&B-type amenities, including beautiful woodwork (carved with scenes of Maya splendor), colorful tiled bathrooms with hot showers and very comfortable living quarters. There's a professional-quality onsite massage studio (BZ$60 for one hour), and an additional 3rd-floor skydeck with a gorgeous view, bar and three VIP rooms is currently being added. All rooms feature queen-sized beds, safes and full bathrooms. Larger rooms offer more space and a veranda with a river view.

Comida Mexicana   MEXICAN $$
(☎633-0748; lacasadeteresa@yahoo.com; cnr Independence St & Arenal Rd; meals BZ$10-25; ☺lunch & dinner Thu-Mon) The prettiest restaurant in Benque, Comida Mexicana sits on a hill with a commanding view of the town and surrounding jungle, and serves excellent Mexican fare in a colorful art and piñata-filled dining room. A full menu of tortillas, steaks and a few vegetarian options should keep all diners happy. Comida's smoky salsas and chips are particularly excellent, and included in the wide range of juices is a unique beverage called a Jamaican, a delicately flavored, slightly sweet, slightly tart drink made from flowers.

❶ Getting There & Away

Buses depart for San Ignacio (BZ$2, 30 minutes), Belmopan (BZ$6, 1½ hours) and Belize City (BZ$10, 2½ hours) about every half-hour from 7am to 5:30pm (and about every hour on Sundays).

Southern Belize

Best Places to Eat

➡ Rumfish, Placencia (p212)

➡ Maya Beach Bistro, Placencia (p211)

➡ Omar's Creole Grub, Placencia (p212)

Best Places to Stay

➡ Belcampo Belize, near Punta Gorda (p228)

➡ Thatch Caye Resort, Thatch Caye (p195)

➡ Singing Sands Inn, Placencia (p210)

Why Go?

Cultural, social and ecological diversity are the hallmarks of Southern Belize. It's here in the south that open savanna and citrus-filled farmland give way to forested hills dotted with Maya villages and ruins, while towns like Hopkins and Placencia offer sun, sand and a bit of local culture.

Adventurers will find no shortage of opportunities to get off the beaten path in Toledo's jungles, while trekkers who wish to splurge can choose from a number of five-star jungle lodges tucked away in remote corners. Those of more modest means will be able to have a great time on the cheap in the small villages and communities of the Deep South.

The south also has cayes all of its own boasting stunning coral reefs, where snorkeling, boating and diving enthusiasts can experience Belize's nautical wonders while avoiding the crowds (and the significantly higher price tags) of the Northern Cayes.

When to Go

The high season is from December to April, when heavy rainfall ends and the weather is at its mildest. If you go between May and July, you'll enjoy lower occupancy rates and prices (and you can eat lobster starting June 15). August and September are the dog days of summer, with hot weather, occasional showers and bargains galore.

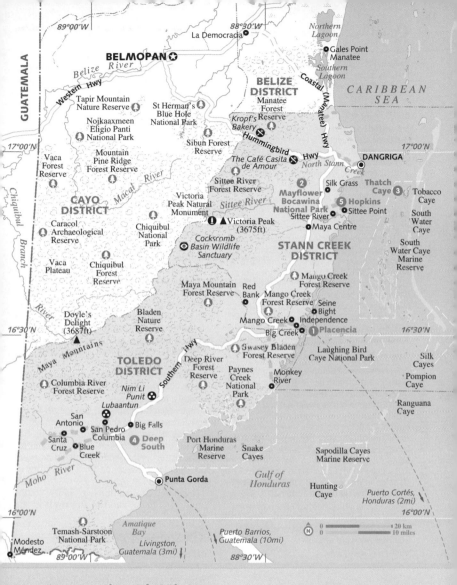

Southern Belize Highlights

❶ Eating, drinking and slacking out in **Placencia** (p204)

❷ Jungle hiking in **Mayflower Bocawina National Park** (p198)

❸ Living like a posh castaway on **Thatch Caye** (p195)

❹ Trekking through Maya Villages in the **Deep South** (p221)

❺ Garifuna drumming under the full moon in **Hopkins** (p195)

ⓘ Getting There & Around

AIR

Daily flights head from Belize City to Dangriga, then Placencia, then Punta Gorda (in other words, a flight from Belize City to PG is done in three hops).

BOAT

Scheduled boat services link Dangriga and Placencia with Puerto Cortés in Honduras, and Punta Gorda with Puerto Barrios and Lívingston in Guatemala. Boats cross to Tobacco Caye from Dangriga daily; boats to the other islands can be organized through tour operators, dive shops, accommodations or boat owners.

BUS

Buses from Belize City and Belmopan head down the Hummingbird Hwy to Dangriga then on to the Southern Hwy to Independence and Punta Gorda. Other services run from Dangriga to Hopkins and Placencia, and from Punta Gorda to the villages in the far south. As Belize no longer has a national bus service, buses are operated by smaller companies, which tend to go in and out of business. Schedules fluctuate, so adopt a Belizean attitude towards bus travel. (In other words: relax, you'll get there.)

CAR

Two roads connect Southern Belize to the Belize District and Northern Belize: the Hummingbird Hwy (which runs from Belmopan to the start of the Southern Hwy near Dangriga) and the Coastal (Manatee) Hwy, an unpaved road that stretches from the Belize District just south of the zoo to the Hummingbird Hwy west of Dangriga (along the way stretching the very definition of the term 'highway.') Though shorter in terms of miles, unless you're planning to visit Gales Point Manatee on your way down south, the Manatee isn't worth the chiropractic trauma.

The Southern Hwy meets the Hummingbird west of Dangriga then continues 100 miles south to Punta Gorda. Both the Hummingbird and Southern Hwys are well paved, but use caution when driving at night.

STANN CREEK DISTRICT

Bordering the Belize District to the north, Cayo to the west and Toledo to the south, the Stann Creek District is home to a number of spots popular with visitors, from the coastal villages of Hopkins and Placencia, to amazing inland parks and jungle sanctuaries and some of Belize's least visited cayes. Dangriga, Belize's second-largest town, is located on the district's northern coastal edge.

Dangriga

POP 11,500

Dangriga is the largest town in Southern Belize, and the spiritual capital of the country's Garifuna people. Stretching along the coast, Dangriga has a funky vibe about it – it's tumbledown and mildly untidy. Despite sharing a similar ramshackle exterior with Belize City, Dangriga exudes little of the larger city's menace, and is generally a safe place to explore. Dangriga is a proud, festive town, one that does its best to make the most of its vibrant Garifuna heritage. The cultural cache here entices visitors to spend an extra day.

The name Dangriga comes from a Garifuna word meaning 'sweet water' – the town's name having been changed from Stann Creek Town in the 1980s. Dangriga is the birthplace of punta rock (a fusion of acoustic Garifuna and electric instruments), and is home to a number of notable Garifuna artists, artisans and festivals, not to mention Belize's only Garifuna museum. With good access to both the central cayes and the Southern and Hummingbird Hwys, Dangriga is also an excellent place from which to launch nautical or jungle excursions.

Dangriga stretches about 2.5 miles along the coast and up to 1000yd inland. North Stann Creek empties into the Caribbean roughly in the middle of town. The main street, stretching most of the length of the town, runs through the names Havana St, St Vincent St and Commerce St. The main bus station is toward its south end (Havana St); most boats to the central and other cayes dock on South Riverside Dr, near the bridge over North Stann Creek.

Most accommodations are in the southern half of town, and the airstrip is at the north end.

⊙ Sights & Activities

Gulisi Garifuna Museum　　　　MUSEUM
(☑669-0639; www.ngcbelize.org; Stann Creek Valley Rd, Chuluhadiwa Park; admission BZ$10; ⊙10am-5pm Mon-Fri, 8am-noon Sat) This museum, operated by the National Garifuna Council (NGC), is a must for anyone interested in the vibrant Garifuna people. The museum is 2 miles out of town, on Stann Creek Valley Rd, but is easily reached by bicycle. It brings together artifacts, pictures and documents on Garifuna history and culture, including film of the original punta rockers, Pen Cayetano and the Turtle Shell Band, in Dangriga back in 1983. The mu-

seum is currently hosting an exhibit on the life and music of the late Garifuna musician Andy Palacio, who passed away in 2009.

Drums of
Our Father's Monument LANDMARK
This monument in the traffic circle south of Dangriga's main bus station underscores the importance of percussion in Garifuna (and Belizean) life, with its large bronze representations of ritual *dügü* drums and *sisira* (maracas). It was sculpted by Stephen Okeke, a Nigerian resident of Dangriga. Up at the other end of town, at the meeting of Commerce and Front Sts, stands a **statue of Thomas Vincent Ramos** (1887–1955), an early promoter of Garifuna culture, who also inaugurated Garifuna Settlement Day.

Pen Cayetano Studio Gallery GALLERY
(📞 628-6807; www.cayetano.de; 3 Aranda Cresent; admission BZ$5; ☺9am-noon & 2-5pm Mon-Fri, 9am-noon Sun) Renowned throughout Belize for his art and music, Pen Cayetano's workshop and gallery displays Garifuna artifacts and crafts. It also has works of art and music by Pen and the textile artwork of his wife, Ingrid, available for sale. Among the most unique items are drums made of turtle shells, which sell for around BZ$50. There are also occasional musical shows by Pen and drum workshops led by local drummers. The gallery is a bit tricky to find, located on a side-street west of the main drag. Give Pen or Ingrid a ring for directions.

Marie Sharp's Factory LANDMARK
(📞 532-2087; www.mariesharps-bz.com; ☺7am-4pm Mon-Fri) The super-hot bottled sauces that adorn tables all over Belize and beyond are made from habanero peppers (purchased from local farmers) here, at Marie Sharp's Factory, 8 miles northwest of town on Melinda Rd. Casual tours, often led by Marie herself, are offered during business hours, and the factory shop sells hot sauces and jams at outlet prices. If you can't make it to the factory but would still like to peruse the full line of sauces and jams, Marie Sharp's also has a **store** (📞 522-2370; 3 Pier Rd; ☺8am-noon & 1-5pm Mon-Fri) in Dangriga.

🎉 Festivals & Events

Día de los Reyes CULTURAL
(Three Kings' Day) On the nearest weekend to January 6, Dangrigans celebrate Día de los Reyes with the *wanaragua* or *jonkonu* (John Canoe) dance: male dancers wearing bright feather-and-paper headdresses, masks representing European men, and rattling bands of shells around their knees move from house to house dancing to Garifuna drums.

Garifuna Settlement Day CULTURAL
On November 19 Dangriga explodes with celebrations to mark the arrival of Garifuna in Dangriga in 1832. Dangrigans living elsewhere flock home for the celebrations, and drumming, dancing and drinking continue right through the night of the 18th to the 19th, while canoes reenact the beach landing in the morning.

🛏 Sleeping

D's Backpacker Hostel HOSTEL $
(📞 502-3324; valsbackpackerhostel.com; cnr Mahogany Rd & Sharp St; dm BZ$25; @🛜) Though the name has changed (it used to be known as Val's), management is still the same, and this, Dangriga's one and only hostel, is still a local institution. D's enjoys a large porch facing the park and a semi-finished rooftop chill out spot overlooking the park and a clean stretch of beach. The three dorm rooms are fan cooled with bunk beds and separate bathrooms with hot showers. Windows face the sea, so you can fall asleep to the sound of the ocean. There's a communal kitchen with movies, wi-fi and luggage lockers for guests. Dangriga native Dana (she's the D) is a great source of local information. D's also has bicycle rental (BZ$10 per day), a book exchange, freshly brewed coffee and more.

Ruthie's Cabanas GUESTHOUSE $
(📞 502-3184; 31 Southern Foreshore; s cabañas BZ$54, additional person BZ$10) Ruthie's comprises four pleasant, seaside, thatched-roof huts on the north side of Havana Creek. It offers hot and cold showers, plenty of coconut-tree shade and a chill and cheap place to stay in 'Griga. Ruthie also serves home-cooked meals for an additional charge.

Chaleanor Hotel HOTEL $
(📞 522-2587; www.toucantrail.com/chaleanor-hotel.html; 35 Magoon St; s/d/tr with bathroom BZ$76/121/150, without bathroom BZ$27/44/57, with air-con add BZ$30; P✳🛜) Rooms in this family-run hotel are clean and comfortable, with the ones upstairs having the best views. The cheaper units on the side of the hotel are fairly run-down and best suited to those placing budget above comfort. The owners will also be glad to help you arrange any trips or boat charters.

Dangriga

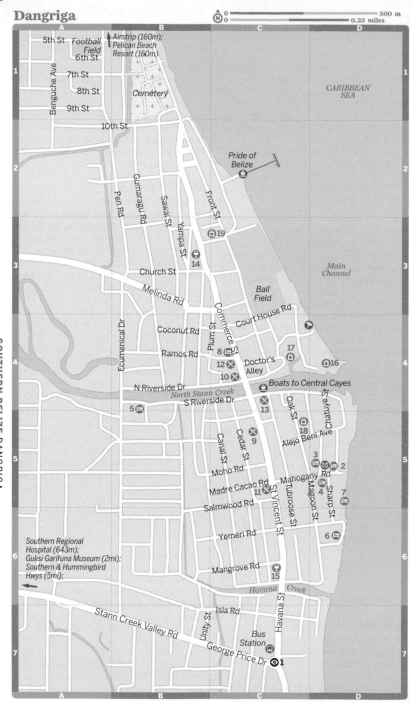

0 — 500 m
0 — 0.25 miles

CARIBBEAN SEA

5th St
Football Field
6th St
7th St
8th St
9th St
10th St

Benguche Ave
Pen Rd
Gumaragu Rd
Sawai St
Yampa St

Cemetery

Airstrip (160m);
Pelican Beach Resort (160m)

Front St

Pride of Belize

Main Channel

19

14

Church St

Melinda Rd

Ecumenical Dr

Coconut Rd

Ramos Rd

Plum St

Commerce St

Court House Rd

Ball Field

8

Doctor's Alley

17

12

10

16

N Riverside Dr

North Stann Creek

S Riverside Dr

5

13

Boats to Central Cayes

Oak St

Charves St

18

Canal St

Cedar St

9

Alejo Beni Ave

3

2

Moho Rd

Madre Cacao Rd

11

St Vincent St

Tubroose St

Mahogany Rd

Magoon St

Sharp St

4

7

Salmwood Rd

Yemeri Rd

6

Mangrove Rd

15

Havana Creek

Southern Regional Hospital (643m);
Gulisi Garifuna Museum (2mi);
Southern & Hummingbird Hwys (5mi);

Stann Creek Valley Rd

Unity St

Isla Rd

George Price Dr

Bus Station

1

Havana St

Dangriga

Wayohan   HOTEL $
([☎]522-2278; 105 Commerce St; s/d with fan BZ$50/65, with air-con BZ$70/90; [✳]) This hotel offers antiseptic rooms, hot showers, TVs and little in the way of charm. Not a bad choice for travelers on the cheap.

Jungle Huts Resort   RESORT $$
([☎]522-0185; junglehutsresort@gmail.com; 4 Ecumenical Dr; d BZ$116, cabañas BZ$160, ste BZ$180; [P][✳][@][🛜]) Philip Usher's riverside continually upgrading resort has nine rooms, three suites and three *cabañas*; all units have one double and one single bed, en-suite bathrooms and showers and air-con, but only the suites and *cabañas* have TV with cable. Jungle Huts' secluded feel belies its central location, and its facilities – on-site laundry, restaurant and plenty of hammocks for chilling out – make it a popular spot.

Pelican Beach Resort   RESORT $$
([☎]522-2044;   www.pelicanbeachbelize.com; 1st St; d with fan BZ$188, with air-con BZ$235; [P][✳][@][🛜]) If it's upmarket you're looking for, the Pelican is basically your only choice. The north-side hotel is close to the airport and has spacious, clean rooms with TVs, phones

and colorful local artwork. Most rooms have beach-facing porches with hammocks. The beachside restaurant has a good vibe, and while most of the dishes are a bit pricey for Dangriga, the Belize chicken plate (BZ$8) brings in locals and travelers alike.

Sea Breeze Restaurant & Inn   HOTEL $$
([☎]522-3766; Southern Foreshore; d with air-con BZ$90-130, with fan BZ$75, meals BZ$7-15; [✳][🛜][♿]) The newest entry to Dangriga's slim accommodation scene, the family-run Sea Breeze offers clean and cheery rooms with balconies and double beds, all with bathrooms and showers. More expensive rooms have air-con, while cheaper ones have standing fans. There's also a restaurant onsite offering a good variety of home-cooked Belizean, Creole and Mexican favorites, with rotating daily specials, as well as a fully stocked bar.

Bonefish Hotel   HOTEL $$
([☎]522-2243; www.bluemarlinlodge.com; 15 Mahogany Rd; r BZ$130-180; [✳][🛜]) Upper floors are not without charm, but the ones on the lower floor are darker and somewhat less cheery, though no less functional. All rooms have two double beds, fan, air-con and cable TV.

🍴 Eating

Food is good and generally inexpensive in Dangriga, though there tends to be less variety than you'll find in Placencia or Cayo. The best bet for budget travelers is to hit any one of a number of food-serving shacks in town. If you want fresh vegetables, hit the market (still open behind the old market building, currently being renovated). Dangriga also has several supermarkets for DIY diners.

Pomce   MEXICAN, BELIZEAN $
(Commerce St; dishes from BZ$1; ⊙ lunch & dinner) Serving excellent burritos, *salbutes*, *garnaches* and tacos on the cheap, a meal here will fill your belly with nary a dent on the wallet. There's no sign on this local favorite, so look for a pink and yellow shack with three picnic tables across from a grocery store called Best Buy.

Norman's Bakery   BAKERY $
(Madre Cacao Rd; burgers from BZ$3.50, sandwiches from BZ$7; ⊙8am-7pm Mon-Sat) This hole-in-the-wall bakery serves sandwiches, freshly made muffins, bread, rolls and pizza.

SOUTHERN BELIZE DANGRIGA

LOCAL KNOWLEDGE

MARIE SHARP, HOT SAUCE MAKER

Marie Sharp's eponymous hot sauces (p187) grace tables and tickle taste buds throughout Belize and around the world.

What is Belizean cuisine?
We're a multi-ethnic country, so Belize enjoys a multi-ethnic culinary tradition. Creole dishes like rice and beans, Mestizo dishes like *escabeche* and tacos, Garifuna dishes like hudut, even Chinese dishes...they're all Belizean!

Must-try Belizean dishes?
Rice and beans with stew chicken cooked on 'fire heart', or hudut served with baked fish and vegetables.

Best place for street food?
I like Dangriga (p186). Lots of great food vendors sell all sorts of local dishes on Dangriga's sidewalks.

Favorite restaurants?
In Hopkins I go to Chef Rob's (now Love on the Rocks) for a good meal, or I head to Hamanasi. In Dangriga I like the Pelican Beach Resort (p190) or the Phoenix Restaurant when I'm in the mood for Chinese.

Are Marie Sharp's sauces too hot for Marie Sharp?
'Fiery Hot' is my favorite, but I can't take it past that. 'Beware' and 'Belizean Heat' are just too hot for me!

Any dish you wouldn't put your own sauce on?
I use my hot sauce on most things I prepare, from rice, meat and soups to chips and crackers. I'd hold off putting it on *escabeche* since it already has enough jalapeño pepper.

King Burger BELIZEAN **$**
(Commerce St; dishes BZ$4-15; ⊙ breakfast, lunch & dinner Mon-Sat) Reliably fresh breakfasts of eggs, beans and fry-jacks for BZ$6.50, as well as hamburgers and plates of fried shrimp. Coffee is instant, but juices are fresh.

Family Restaurant CHINESE **$$**
(Commerce St; mains BZ$8-20; ⊙ 10am-11pm) A clean, fun (check out the swinging tables and chairs out back) and well-run Chinese restaurant that serves both Sino-Belizean fare and dishes to cater to the tastes of local Chinese who still remember what Chinese food is supposed to taste like. Best of the authentic Chinese menu items: *zhe jiang beef* (BZ$17.50), a spicy taste of Sichuan in the Caribbean.

Riverside Café SEAFOOD **$$**
(S Riverside Dr; mains BZ$10-25; ⊙ breakfast, lunch & dinner) Just east of the Stann Creek bridge, this cafe is the place to meet fishers and the folk who do boat tours to the outlying cayes. Food is good and the fish is always fresh. The Riverside is the place to go to arrange your boat to the cayes.

🍷 Drinking & Nightlife

Wadini Shed BAR
(St Vincent St; ⊙ 4pm-midnight) One thatched roof, no walls and a mainly local clientele make this a great spot to have a stout and get down with Dangriga culture. Though busier at night, you'll find a good crowd here during the day as well. During the week of Garifuna Settlement Day (November 19) the place practically explodes with music and dancing.

Roxy Club BAR
(Commerce St; ⊙ Tue-Sun) To quote a pair of Dangriga-based Peace Corps volunteers: 'The Roxy is a good place. Stumpy and Penny are very friendly, and Penny makes great *panadas* (small fish-filled fried tortillas), three for a dollar.' It's at the north end of the city, about three blocks north of the police station in Harlem Sq.

Pelican Beach Resort BAR
(www.pelicanbeachbelize.com; 1st St) The Friday happy hour at this beachfront resort bar, from 6pm to 8pm, usually pulls in a crowd.

🛍 Shopping

Dangriga Central Market MARKET
(On Beach behind Doctor's Alley; ⊙ 6am-4pm) The old Dangriga Central Market was under renovation at the time of research. The stalls and merchants are now doing their thing in a temporary building closer to the beach. You'll still find the microcosm of Dangriga society, including traders selling shoes,

clothing, crockery and Maya crafts operating alongside farmers and fishmongers (who still pause between deals to shoo away thieving pelicans). The market is busiest in the morning (where it's a great place to get a cheap breakfast), and most stalls stay open all day. Should the renovation be completed by the time you read this, you'll have slightly less far to walk.

Austin Rodriguez ARTS & CRAFTS
This master artisan carves Garifuna drums from mahogany, cedar and mayflower wood in his thatched-roof workshop by the water's edge (southeast of Dangriga Central Market). Though Austin's drums are sold all over Belize, you can cut out the middleman by going straight to the maker himself. Mr Rodriguez will be happy to answer any questions you might have on the drum-making process.

Garinagu Crafts ARTS & CRAFTS
(📞523-2596; grigaservices@yahoo.com; 46 Oak St) With the mission statement of 'keeping the black diaspora alive,' Dangriga native Francis M Swaso's shop is part crafts store, part museum. The shop sells a wide range of arts and handicrafts made by Garifuna artists, including drums, maracas, paintings and dolls, and displays a number of historical Garifuna artifacts as well.

Viola's Shells and Jewelry ARTS & CRAFTS
(St Vincent St) Jimmy sells handmade jewelry made from mother-of-pearl, conch and coconut as well as drums, shells and other souvenirs from his shop on the main drag. As long as you're here, check out the store just up the street from Jimmy's spot, which sells oils, candles, potions and other items used in Santeria rituals.

🛈 Information

Belize Bank (St Vincent St), **Scotia Bank** (St Vincent St) and **First Caribbean International Bank** (Commerce St) all have 24-hour ATMs that accept international Visa, MasterCard, Plus and Cirrus cards.

Immigration Office (📞522-3412; St Vincent St; ⊙8am-noon & 1-5pm Mon-Thu, 8am-noon & 1-4:30pm Fri) Offers 30-day visa extension stamps for BZ$50.

Police (📞522-2022, 911, 90; Commerce St) No longer handles visa extensions; for these, go to the Immigration Office.

Post Office (📞522-2035; Mahogany Rd)

Southern Regional Hospital (📞522-2078; Stann Creek Valley Rd) Good-standard public hospital.

D's Laundry (cnr Mahogany Rd & Sharp St; internet per hr BZ$4, laundry wash & dry per lb BZ$2; ⊙7:30am-7pm; 📶) Get your clothes cleaned and surf the web at D's (formerly Val's) Laundry/Backpacker Hostel.

🛈 Getting There & Away

AIR

From Dangriga airport (DGA), **Maya Island Air** (📞522-2659) and **Tropic Air** (📞226-2012) serve the city with flights also stopping at Placencia, Punta Gorda and Belize City.

BOAT

Dangriga is the jumping-off point for trips to Belize's central cayes, as well as for chartered trips up and down the coast and regularly scheduled trips to Honduras. The best spot to arrange sea transit is just outside the Riverside Café on South Riverside Dr. Stop by around 9am to 10am, or the afternoon before, to check when boats will be leaving. The more people you can get for one trip (within reason), the cheaper it works out per person.

Among the spots best reached from Dangriga are Thatch Caye, South Water Caye, Tobacco Caye and Glover's Reef; most of the lodges on these islands will organize your boat for you.

Companies doing the Dangriga–Central Cayes run include:

Topsy's Boat Service (📞623-9764) Day and longer trips to South Water Caye and Tobacco Caye can be arranged, as can excursions to Glover's Reef.

Riverside Water Taxi (📞627-7443; captain-doggy@gmail.com) Run by the colorful Captain Duggy, whose 25-foot boat travels between Dangriga, Hopkins and all of the cayes.

D-Bottom Line Water Taxi (📞633-0160; dalila56@yahoo.com) Does trips out to all the cayes as well as fishing and other privately chartered trips.

BUS

A major transit point for all bus companies servicing southern Belize, Dangriga's main bus station is across from the Drums of Our Father's Monument.

> 🛈 **DANGRIGA TO HONDURAS**
>
> Pride of Belize (p64) runs one weekly boat each Saturday between Belize City and Puerto Cortés (Honduras). The boat stops to pick up passengers and clear customs in Dangriga at 10:30am and arrives in Honduras at 2:30pm. The fare between Dangriga and Puerto Cortés is BZ$110.

Central Cayes

Less crowded (and often less costly) than those in the north, the cayes off Belize's central coast are smack in the middle of some of the country's most amazing diving, snorkeling and fishing sites. Slackers take note: there's no shortage of tropical breezes and palm-tree-slung hammocks.

Tobacco Caye

Sitting right on the barrier reef 12 miles from Dangriga, tiny Tobacco Caye is 200yd long, 100yd wide and mainly composed of sand, palm trees and guesthouses. Part of the South Water Caye Marine Reserve, the caye is a great place for **snorkeling**, **diving**, **fishing** or hanging out on a hammock. Tobacco Caye is sociable, friendly and popular with travelers on a limited budget looking for *a Gilligan's Island* experience.

🛏 Sleeping & Eating

Equipment rental and meal packages are available at most lodgings. Most also sell meals to guests staying in other lodges.

Fairweather Place   HOTEL $
(☑802-0030, 660-6870; hevf7@yahoo.com; s & d per person BZ$30) Over on the western edge of Tobacco Caye sit the islands, cheapest digs. Run by the friendly Upton Pandy, Fairweather has four rooms with one double bed each, electric fans and a small bookshelf filled with paperbacks. There's a shared bathroom with a cold-water shower, and out front is a sea-facing porch with a couple of chairs and hammocks. The Pandys don't provide meals, but their 1st-floor kitchen is open for use by guests wishing to prepare their freshly bought or caught fish, lobster and conch.

Tobacco Caye Paradise   CABINS $
(☑532-2101; r/cabañas per person BZ$25/80) The best deal on Tobacco, this place offers eight sizable rooms with shared bath plus six lovely *cabañas* (some over the water) with private baths and cold-water showers. Room prices are per person without meals, while prices per *cabaña* include three meals.

Gaviota   CABINS $
(☑509-5032, 621-1953; rezmanagerdean@yahoo.com; r per person from BZ$50, cabañas without/with bathroom per person BZ$60/70) On the eastern end of the island, Gaviota's offers *cabañas* in two flavors – with and without bathrooms – and comfortable and basic rooms in the beachside bunkhouse/hotel. Prices include three meals per day at the attached restaurant. Snorkeling-equipment rental is available for BZ$10 per day.

Lana's   HOTEL $
(☑520-5036; s & d per person incl meals BZ$70) On the west side of the island, Lana's has four rather cramped rooms, but offers good meals.

Tobacco Caye Lodge   RESORT $$
(☑532-2033; www.tclodgebelize.com; per person incl meals BZ$110, non-guest breakfast/lunch/dinner BZ$20/20/30) This place on the east side of the island has six simple but clean and fairly spacious rooms with private bathrooms, fans and beautiful verandas. Food is cooked by chefs Rhoda and Carl, renowned on the island for their culinary skills; non-guests are welcome with advance notice. Snorkel-gear rental is BZ$15 per day for guests, and canoes are free.

Reef's End Lodge   LODGE $$
(☑522-2419, 670-3919; www.reefsendlodge.com; r/cabañas per person BZ$130/150) At the south end of the island, Reef's End has eight sizable rooms plus a couple of ramshackle *cabañas*. There's also a nice restaurant over the water offering three meals a day. Inquire about off-season discounts.

South Water Caye

Three times as big as Tobacco but with half as many resorts, the 15-acre South Water Caye has excellent **sandy beaches** and an interesting combination of palm and pine trees. Like Tobacco Caye, it's part of the South Water Caye Marine Reserve. A seemingly bottomless 8-mile-long underwater cliff on the ocean side of the reef makes for excellent **wall-diving**, usually with good visibility. Snorkelers will find healthy coral reefs in the lagoon. Trips to Belize's offshore atolls are possible from here and there's excellent **fishing**, too.

South Water Caye's three resorts all offer a variety of multi-day packages including activities, meals and passage to the island from Dangriga.

🛏 Sleeping & Eating

⭐**Pelican's Pouch**   CABINS $$$
(☑522-2044; www.southwatercaye.com; s/d incl meals BZ$350/520, s/d cottages incl meals

---

ℹ️ THE CAYE THAT'S RIGHT FOR YOU...

Stann Creek has offshore cayes to suit every vacationer's need.
Choosing the right one is key...

Tobacco Caye

Pros Cheapest of the southern cayes to get to, with the best variety of budget accommodations. You'll never be lonely on Tobacco Caye.

Cons With half a dozen accommodations in a small space, Tobacco can feel a bit cramped. Alas, the coral around the island isn't as healthy as it once was.

South Water Caye

Pros Excellent diving and snorkeling opportunities and great space-to-resort ratio make this a good choice for visitors looking for a sublime island experience.

Cons Lack of cheap accommodations keeps South Water Caye off-limits to travelers on a budget.

Glover's Reef

Pros The best of both worlds, Glover's is surrounded by amazing coral, provides access to good dive sites, and the resorts along the atoll offer the full spectrum of budget accommodations.

Cons The boat ride out takes between an hour and a half and three hours. Glover's remoteness makes it a less-than-ideal choice for those looking to spend just a couple of days.

Thatch Caye

Pros Beautiful and ecofriendly, Thatch Caye is a good choice for honeymooners and families looking for luxury with a low carbon footprint.

Cons The campsite is the only budget option, and with only one resort on the island, Thatch might not be the best place for singles looking to mingle.

BZ$440/590; 🛜🏊) The solar-powered Pelican's eight comfortable wooden cottages at the south of the island are well spaced, giving a feeling of seclusion. Heron's Hideaway is probably the pick of the bunch, with a big porch and two hammocks overlooking the surf crashing onto the reef. The main building (once an island retreat for Belize's Sisters of Mercy) houses the dining room and five guest rooms opening on to long verandas. If you want to dive from here, book at least a week ahead. Kayaks are available free of charge.

Blue Marlin Lodge RESORT $$$
(📞520-5104, in USA 800-798-1558; www.blue-marlinlodge.com; r from BZ$400; @🛜) At the northern end of the island, Blue Marlin has its own full-service PADI dive center and a restaurant serving particularly good seafood. The resort has a series of *cabañas* and rather odd (but cool looking) igloo-shaped 'dome *cabañas*'. The complicated rate sheet published on their website gives the lowdown on the dozens of offered packages including longer stays, meals, transits and diving. The Dangriga office is inside the Bonefish Hotel (p189).

International Zoological Expeditions RESORT, CABINS $$$
(IZE; 📞520-5030, in USA 800-548-5843; www.ize2belize.com; packages per person per night from BZ$320; @🛜) Massachusetts-based IZE operates this site in the middle of the island with dorms for students and beautiful spacious wooden shoreline cottages for other guests. The main building incorporates a field station (with reference books and videos), an attractive wood-furnished dining room, internet access and a great bar. The basic package (minimum three nights) includes meals, transfers to/from Dangriga, snorkeling and sightseeing boat trips, and use of kayaks and sports equipment.

Glover's Reef

If you're serious about getting away from it all, Glover's Reef is the place to come. Named after the 18th-century English pirate John Glover (who attacked Spanish merchant ships from here), the 16-mile-long by 7-mile-wide atoll is pretty much as far from mainland Belize as you can get. Lying like a string of pearls in a blue sea, Glover's consists of half a dozen small cayes of white sand, palm trees, and a handful of low-key resorts, diving and kayaking bases.

The reef's unique position atop a submerged mountain ridge on the edge of the continental shelf makes it home to some of the world's finest **dive sites**. Divers here regularly see spotted eagle rays, southern stingrays, turtles, moray eels, dolphins, several shark species, large groupers, barracudas and many tropical reef fish. In the shallow central lagoon, 700 coral patches brim with marine life, brilliant for **snorkelers**. Turtles lay eggs on the beaches between June and August. Glover's Reef is included in the Belize Barrier Reef World Heritage listing, and it's also a marine reserve with a no-take zone covering most of the southern third of the atoll. As a protected marine reserve, guests at all resorts pay a park fee of BZ$30 per week.

🛏 Sleeping & Eating

Glover's Long Caye is home to camps and resorts for North American–based Slickrock Adventures (p37) and Island Expeditions (p36).

Glover's Atoll Resort   CABINS $
(☏520-5016; www.glovers.com.bz; per person per week camping BZ$198, dm & on-site tents BZ$298, cabins BZ$498-598 ; 🛜🍽) Occupying the atoll's northeast caye, this ramshackle backpackers' paradise is the perfect place to leave your troubles behind. The Lamont family's private 10-acre island has a total of 16 cabins (both over the water and on the beach, the former being more spacious and more costly), one basic dorm room, and eight private campgrounds from which to base your island adventure. Weekly prices include cooking facilities and boat transfers (leaving Sunday and returning Saturday) to/from the owners' mainland Glover's Guest House in the village of Sittee River, but you'll also need to think about the cost of water, food, equipment rentals and any excursions. Drinking water costs BZ$5 per gallon on the island, though water from the many coconuts is free.

There is an open-air thatched **restaurant** (breakfast/lunch/dinner BZ$24/24/36), or you can make your own meals – a few basic groceries plus fish, lobster and conch are available on the island, but the rest (including any alcohol) you must bring

over yourself. Snorkel gear rents for BZ$72 a week, kayaks from BZ$190 a week, and the resort has a PADI shop offering a range of courses and dives. (Serious divers may want to bring their own gear, as the shop's rental equipment has seen better days!) If a Sunday-to-Saturday stay doesn't suit you, there are nightly accommodations rates but the boat trips there and back will push costs up.

Isla Marisol Resort   RESORT $$$
(☏532-2399, 610-4204, in USA 866-990-9904; www.islamarisol.com; cabañas per day BZ$330-500, meals per person BZ$100, packages per week incl meals BZ$2200-3000; ❄🛜) The atoll's 18-acre southernmost island (called Usher Caye by some) is home to Glover's most upscale resort. Eleven sturdy and comfortably furnished wooden cabins with zinc roofs, hot showers, fans and air conditioners are laid out along the island, while two family-size reef houses provide accommodations for six closer to the water. There's also an excellent **restaurant** (try the lionfish *ceviche!*) and a bar on stilts over the water. Prices include boat transfers to and from Dangriga, with boats running on Wednesday and Saturday. Activities at Marisol include snorkeling, kayaking, sunbathing, fishing and, of course, diving. Isla Marisol also boasts an excellent PADI shop with two full time instructors. Individual dives go for BZ$100, with four-day and week-long packages available. Details available on the website.

Off the Wall   CABINS $$$
(☏532-2929; www.offthewallbelize.com; per person per week from BZ$2790; 🛜🍽) 🐟 Located on Long Caye, the solar- and wind-powered Off the Wall is a small and intimate PADI five-star island resort offering a variety of packages. Owners Jim and Kendra Schofield (both PADI-certified dive instructors, who met and married on the island itself) strive to provide a personalized island experience incorporating diving, kayaking, snorkeling, fishing, paddle-boarding, and just about any other nautical activities imaginable. All wooden *cabañas* come with queen-size posturepedic mattresses with Egyptian high-thread linens, and if you feel like sleeping outside, suspended swing beds allow you to doze beneath the stars. Other touches include yoga mats in every room and a scenic yoga deck to practice on,

and a candle-lit path for romantic walks. Centrally located bathrooms and showers (the former composting, the latter beautifully tiled) complete the ecofriendly picture. All packages include three gourmet meals a day, all nonalcoholic beverages, and travel to and from Dangriga.

Thatch Caye

★**Thatch Caye Resort**   RESORT $$$
(☑603-2414; www.thatchcaye.com; camping per person BZ$30, all-inclusive 4-day/3-night packages per person from BZ$1390; ☎) ◢ Sitting 8 miles off the coast, Thatch Caye is a privately owned island resort with environmental sustainability built into almost every aspect of its design. Eleven beautiful thatched-roof *cabaña* built from local hardwoods sit on stilts over the ocean, connected by paths winding through native mangroves. Electricity for both private and communal facilities is generated from both solar and wind sources, with a single diesel generator kept as backup.

Other nice touches include hand-carved Mahogany doors and furniture in every *cabañas*. Meals are served at Thatch's excellent **restaurant**, which employs local chefs and serves organic Garifuna, East Indian, Maya and North American dishes, and in the evenings guests can sip drinks beneath the stars while watching tropical fish swim below their feet at the newly built **Starfish Bar** (an over-the-water watering hole). Beachside campsites accommodate travelers on a budget.

Coco Plum Caye   CABINS $$$
(☑in USA 512-786-7309; www.cocoplumcay.com; 5-day packages from BZ$2600) More ramshackle than Thatch (but just a Frisbee-throw away – you can actually wade across during low tide and have a drink at the bar), Coco Plum's colorful Caribbean-style *cabañas* offer air conditioning and private bathrooms. All packages include three meals a day, full use of the island and transportation from Dangriga.

ℹ️ Getting There & Away

Most listed hotels and resorts will arrange your passage. The Central Cayes can be reached from Placencia, Hopkins and Dangriga, with the latter town being closest to all but Glover's Reef.

Hopkins
POP 1800

Located off the main Southern Hwy, the friendly coastal village of Hopkins attracts travelers looking to soak up sea breezes and Garifuna culture. Smaller than Dangriga and more rustic than Placencia, beachy Hopkins is an excellent place to meet other travelers and to base yourself for explorations of the cayes, reefs and islands to the east, and of the jungles, mountains and parks to the west.

Founded in 1942 by people from Newtown, a nearby Garifuna settlement that was destroyed by a hurricane, the village is named for Frederick Charles Hopkins, a Catholic priest who (in perhaps a cautionary tale to future travelers) drowned in the waters here in 1923.

Hopkins stretches about 1.5 miles along the coast. The road in from the Southern Hwy reaches the village at King Cassava bar, roughly the village's mid-point. There are plenty of guesthouses south of this intersection, either on the beach or on the town's single street (hence the lack of street addresses in our listings). The northern end of town is more densely populated, though there are fewer guesthouses and restaurants to be found.

🏃 Activities

Like Dangriga and Placencia, Hopkins is a fine place from which to access some of Belize's best **dive sites**. The barrier reef is less than a 40-minute boat ride away, and Glover's Reef is about 90 minutes away on a fast skiff. Diving can be arranged at Hamanasi Adventure & Dive Resort (p201). Hamanasi and Hopkins Inn offer reef-snorkeling trips, as does **Noel's Fishing & Snorkeling** (☑609-1991, 523-7219), which can be found outside the Watering Hole Restaurant. Noel charges two people BZ$250 for a day's outing. He also rents snorkel sets for BZ$10 a day.

Several accommodations have **kayaks** available for their guests, and Hopkins also has some good spots for **windsurfing**; Windschief (p197) offers lessons and gear rental.

Lebeha   DRUMMING
(☑665-9305; North Side) Set up by local drummer Jabbar Lambey and his wife Dorothy, Lebeha functions both as an educational and cultural center for local kids and as a general happening spot for travelers interested in Garifuna drumming. Lessons

Hopkins & Sittee Point

0 ———— 200 m
0 ———— 0.1 miles

Southern Hwy (4mi)

HOPKINS

CARIBBEAN SEA

SITTEE POINT

Diversity Tours and Treasures

Sittee River (1mi)

for individuals and groups are available for reasonable prices, and there's drumming almost every night beginning at around 7pm. Most definitely Hopkins' 'in' spot, Lebeha is a place that nobody with an interest in Garifuna music and culture will want to miss. Full-moon drumming parties are an especially great reason to visit.

👉 Tours

**Motorbike Rentals
& Alternate Adventures**   ADVENTURE
(📞665-6292; info@alternateadventures.com; South Side) MR & AA rents 200cc and 125cc street

bikes (lower and capable of carrying two) motorcycles. Prices are BZ$118 per day, helmets, cellphone and maps included. Emma, the owner, offers helpful suggestions for independent-minded travelers and is a wealth of local knowledge. MR&AA also has camping and snorkeling gear, underwater cameras and electric golf carts, as well as providing guide services to ruins and other sites of interest. The office is just north of the turn-off to the highway, about 20yd south of Thongs Cafe.

In addition to offering tours throughout the region, Alternate Adventures also offers what may be Belize's first food tour, hitting the country's culinary hotspots such as Marie Sharp's, local spice farms and other unique spots for fruit, food and gourmet culture.

Belize by Horace TOUR
(✔ 603-8358; www.belizebyhorace.com) Offers tours out to the cayes and through the lagoons and rivers around Sittee River on a 26-foot skiff, as well as land trips to Mayflower, Cockscomb and Red Bank.

Bullfrog Adventures DIVING, FISHING
(✔ 669-0046; issymcm@yahoo.com) Bullfrog does snorkeling, scuba diving, fishing and general island-hopping throughout the area on a 28-foot high bow skiff with a shade canopy, providing all the appropriate gear.

Charlton's Inland Tours TOUR
(✔ 661-8199; charltoncasstillo@yahoo.com) Birdwatching, Maya-ruin and hiking tours throughout Stann Creek, Cayo and beyond for between BZ$100 and BZ$220, with a four-person minimum group size.

Hopkins Underwater Adventures DIVING
(✔ 633-3401; www.hopkinsunderwateradventures. com) Located on the grounds of Parrot Cove, Hopkins Underwater Adventures is a PADI certified dive shop offering scuba instruction and trips to the Reef and beyond.

Lloyd Nunez FISHING
(✔ 662-0873, 603-2970) Lloyd is a professional fly-fisherman who leads expeditions into both the inner and outer cayes (BZ$500 to BZ$600 for two people, depending on the tour). His brother **Noel Nunez** (✔ 523-7219) also offers fishing and snorkeling tours at reasonable prices.

🛏 Sleeping

Lebeha CABINS **$**
(✔ 665-9305; North Side; dm BZ$20, s/d cabañas BZ$30/50, cabins from BZ$124; 🛜) On the north end of town, the Garifuna drumming school set up by local drummer Jabbar Lambey and his wife Dorothy also has a dorm room, two beachfront cabins and three *cabañas* for rent. The nicest of the *cabañas* is the honeymoon suite, which has a double bed, private bathroom and screened-in porch. Two smaller *cabañas* share a bathroom and cold-water showers. For those more inclined to fall asleep to the music of the sea, Lebeha also rents two beachfront houses with queen and single beds, hot-water showers and screened-in porches with hammocks. Freshly brewed coffee is available every morning, and Dorothy and Jabbar are warm, friendly people who'll go out of their way to make your stay in Hopkins memorable.

Funky Dodo HOSTEL **$**
(✔ 667-0558; www.thefunkydodo.com; South Side; dm BZ$15, d/tr/q BZ$38/51/68; 🛜) Hopkins' only hostel is becoming the byword for hostels in Belize, with locals using the phrase "Funky Dodo" and "hostel" interchangably. The centrally located Funky Dodo has 24 beds in a rough and rustic screened-in wooden bunkhouse, and four private rooms that sleep two to four each. Beds are comfortable, sheets clean, blankets colorful, and there's a communal kitchen as well. A short wooden boardwalk leads to shared bathrooms with cold-water showers, and a thatched-roof bamboo patio provides a fine spot to hang out and watch Hopkins go by. There's also a 2nd-story thatched-roof bar serving libations, guaranteeing a funky party vibe.

Whistling Seas CABINS **$**
(✔ 668-3665; Williams_Marcello@yahoo.com; South Side; s/d BZ$60/75) The five fan-cooled blue-and-white cement shacks here are comfortably furnished with wooden beds, colorful blankets, Maya art and even house plants. Private bathrooms and hot showers make Whistling Seas a good choice for the price range, and close proximity to Rainbow's Chinese restaurant on the south end of town means you won't have to travel far for chop suey.

Windschief Cabanas CABINS **$**
(✔ 523-7249; www.windschief.com; South Side; small/large cabañas BZ$60/90; 🅿 @ 🛜) Run by Oliver and Pamela Guthoff, the Windschief offers two basic *cabañas* with private bathrooms and hot showers. Windschief's bar is a very happening spot on weekends (and sometimes during the week). It is located on the beach at the south end of town.

DON'T MISS

MAYFLOWER BOCAWINA NATIONAL PARK

Looking to get off the beaten path? This beautiful 11-sq-mile **park** (admission BZ$10; ⏱8am-4pm) offers jungle, mountains, waterfalls, walking trails, swimming holes and small Maya sites, and on most days the only other person you'll encounter will be the park ranger who collects your entrance fee. You'll probably see lots of birds, though, and the park is rumored to be home to a few larger mammals as well. And the roaring? That'll likely be members of Mayflower's resident black howler monkey population.

A 4-mile unpaved access road, leaving the Southern Hwy 2 miles north of Silk Grass village, brings you to a small **visitors center** (⏱8am-4pm), where you pay a BZ$10 park fee, and the partly excavated **Mayflower Maya site**, with two pyramids and nine other structures, occupied in the late 9th and early 10th centuries. **Antelope Trail** leads down over Silk Grass Creek to the larger, unexcavated, partly tree-covered **Maintzunun temple mound**, 250yd away (built around AD 800). Continue on a further 1.7 miles – steep and strenuous in places – up to the beautiful 100ft-high **Antelope Falls**, and enjoy the great panoramas. The less-demanding **Bocawina Hill Trail** (1.4 miles) leads to the lower and upper **Bocawina Falls**: there's a cool swimming pool at the foot of the 50ft upper falls. Branch trails, for which a guide is recommended, lead to **Peck Falls** and **Big Drop Falls**.

Camping is permitted in the park. Campers are advised to bring their own food and water. Mayflower Bocawina National Park is home to the newly renovated **Mama Noots Eco Resort** (☑670-8019, in USA 928-300-1969; www.mamanootsbelize.com; Mayflower Bocawina National Park; Mayan r BZ$150, cabañas from BZ$300-370; P 🕸 🛜 🛗) 🍴 and **Bocawina Adventures & Eco Tours** (Zip Lines & Waterfall Rappelling; ☑ 670-2622, in USA 501-670-8019; Bocawina Park).

Day tours to the park from Hopkins or Maya Centre cost around BZ$90 per person. A taxi from Dangriga is about BZ$60.

Seagull's   CABINS $
(☑663-5976; South Side; s/d BZ$35/65) Just south of Dolly's bicycle rental on the southern end of town, Seagull's has comfortable *cabañas* at a budget price.

★**All Seasons Guest House**   GUESTHOUSE $$
(☑523-7209; www.allseasonsbelize.com; South Side; r BZ$86-150, family cabins BZ$196; P 🕸 🛜) All Seasons may just be the prettiest guesthouse in town, with its octagonal, thatch-covered upstairs porch and its four uniquely decorated rooms with big private bathrooms. Our favorite is the zebra-striped room, which is great for a couple (and also the cheapest). All rooms have air-con, coffee makers and hot showers. There's a great patio out front with a massive grill and picnic area. Ingrid (All Seasons' European owner) is a delightful person who also owns three beach apartments across the road with kitchenettes and two brand new cabins next to the guesthouse. All of the separate units are fully furnished and beautifully decked out, and can comfortably house four people. Weekly and monthly prices (BZ$1200/3000) are available. There's also a little shop in front of All Seasons that serves healthy breakfasts (BZ$14) and smoothies.

★**Coconut Row Guesthouse**   GUESTHOUSE $$
(☑670-3000, in USA 518-223-9775; www.coconutrowbelize.com; Beachside, South of King Cassava; d BZ$198, apartments BZ$250-290; P 🕸 🛜 🛗) Hopkins' newest hotel is the brightly painted Coconut Row. Run by Damian and Nisha Grieco, this colorful hotel offers five rooms, two of which are full two-bedroom apartments, two rooms with two double beds and one with two queen-sized beds. Rooms are absolutely beautiful (designed by the amazing Ingrid at All Seasons down the road). Beds have hand-carved headboards, ceramic sinks have bright mosaic patterns, and local art on the walls.

Apartments have state-of-the-art coffee makers and fridges, and all guests are treated to a welcome coconut. The more expensive apartment has a balcony with seafront view and cable TV with all premium channels. Discounts are available for stays of a week and longer.

Jungle Jeanie by the Sea   CABINS $$
(☑533-7047; http://junglebythesea.com; camping BZ$25, basic cabaña BZ$110, deluxe cabaña BZ$180-

240) A 10-minute walk south of Hopkins takes you to Jungle by the Sea, also known as Jungle Jeanie's. With accommodations available at all price ranges, Jungle J's offers beautiful hardwood single and duplex cabins on stilts, nestled in the trees with lovely sea views of the property's beautiful and seemingly endless beach. Each has a double bed, futon, bathroom, mosquito screens and veranda. One has a loft with a second double bed. At the north end of the property there are a few older, more basic wooden *cabañas* with similar amenities. Kayaks are available for guests for a small charge, and there's also a pontoon boat that rents for BZ$70 per person (minimum six people). Other activites include bocci ball, sunset dinner cruises and early morning bird-watching trips. Yoga classes (BZ$20) are at 3pm on Sunday, Tuesday and Thursday.

Tipple Tree Beya   HOTEL **$$**
(533-7006; www.tippletree.com; South Side; r BZ$70-110;) This sturdy wooden beach-side place rents three cozy, clean, fan-cooled rooms sharing a sociable veranda beneath the owner's quarters upstairs. Two rooms have private hot-water bathrooms, while the cheapest one has a cold-water shower. All have coffee makers and seafront views. There's also a larger private *cabaña* for BZ$110 that has the same amenities, hot shower and a microwave. The owner, Tricia, has a number of sustainable practices including composting, recycling and keeping the place as energy efficient as possible.

Hopkins Inn   HOTEL **$$**
(523-7013; www.hopkinsinn.com; South Side; cabaña incl breakfast BZ$99-199; P) Four cabins right by the beach are on offer at this well-run establishment where breakfast is brought to you. Each cabin has a coffee maker, veranda, mosquito screens and a nice, clean, white-tiled bathroom. A catamaran (per day BZ$40), bicycles (per day BZ$15) and free snorkeling gear are available, and owner Greg, a registered tour guide, takes snorkelers out in his boat.

Laru Beya Cabins   HOTEL **$$**
(604-7186, 523-7229; South Side; cabins BZ$100; P) These four log cabins right by the beach are done up in an Afro-Caribbean style. Located in the center of town, all cabins have dark-wood furniture, hot showers, coffee makers and soft beds.

✕ Eating

Iris's Place   BELIZEAN **$**
(South Side; mains BZ$8-15; breakfast, lunch & dinner) Iris serves good Belizean dishes like fried chicken, stewed beef, stir-fried shrimp and conch (in season). Decor is simple and prices are easier on the pocket than nearby Yugadah, but consider buying a couple of cookies from village kids to tide you over: Iris' service can be very slow.

★ Love on the Rocks   INTERNATIONAL **$$**
(South Side; meals BZ$22-45; lunch & dinner) Right at the southern end of town, Love on the Rocks is Belize's only (to our knowledge) hot-stone restaurant, serving meat grilled on – you guessed it – hot stones. The lobster (in season) is said to be the best in town and seafood is always a good bet. Formerly known as Chef Rob's; the owner has another restaurant in Sittee River.

Driftwood Beach Bar & Pizza Shack   PIZZERIA **$$**
(North Side; pizza from BZ$16; 11am-10pm Thu-Tue) Driftwood sits on the northern end of Hopkins, on the beach, and serves excellent pizza beneath a thatched roof. Ingredients are a mix of locally sourced and imported, and dough is made using a secret recipe. Something of a social hub, there are also weekly events like Saturday bloody Mary brunches and Sunday beach BBQs with ribs, chicken, fish, beer and volleyball.

Sandy Beach Women's Cooperative Restaurant   GARIFUNA **$$**
(sandybeachhopkins@gmail.com; South Side Beach front; meals BZ$10-15; 11am-9pm Mon-Sat, 10am-3pm Sun) The colorfully dressed ladies of the Sandy Beach Women's Cooperative serve up daily Garifuna specials like hudut (a creamy fish stew served with mashed plantain) with distinctive local flair. The newly opened restaurant also promises to soon have a full menu of local cuisine including plantain chips, sandwiches, quesadillas and burritos. It also offers a daily dessert. The beachfront space is available for events like weddings, retreats, student groups and conferences. Feel like camping on the beach? The ladies are cool with that.

Taste of India   INDIAN **$$**
(South Side; meals from BZ$16; lunch & dinner) Fish and chicken tikka masala, beef korma, papadum, lassis and many vegetable dishes from the Indian subcontinent provide

travelers with a break from Belizean food at this beachside restaurant. Service is a bit on the slow side, but the food is worth the wait. Look for the sign on the side of the road painted with the colors of the Indian flag.

Yugadah Café BELIZEAN **$$**
(South Side; mains BZ$8-25; ☺ breakfast, lunch & dinner) Long a local favorite, Yugadah Café serves delicious Belizean fare as well as burgers, burritos and sandwiches. Food is excellent, but travelers on a budget might find the menu (the cheapest item, humble chicken with stew beans, is a hefty BZ$18) a bit pricey. Lunches are cheaper (BZ$8 to BZ$12), and desserts are famously exquisite.

King Cassava BELIZEAN **$$**
(South Side; mains BZ$8-20; ☺ 11am-midnight) This Hopkins institution serves meat and seafood dishes as well as Belizean standards such as stew chicken, fry fish, and rice and beans. King Cassava is also Hopkins' leading cool spot at night.

Thongs Café CAFE **$$**
(South Side; mains BZ$8-23; ☺ 8am-2pm Wed-Sun, 6-9pm Fri & Sat; 🐾) This colorful cafe serves up an esoteric variety of moderately priced meals, not to mention hands-down the finest coffee drinks in town. Bonus: free wireless!

🍷 Drinking & Nightlife

Windschief BAR
(📋 523-7249; South Side) This local watering hole offers all kinds of cocktails, beer and stout, as well as light snacks like burgers and nachos from BZ$6. It's owned and operated by the same couple that run Hopkins Internet, so why not have a drink or six and then email your family to tell them how much fun you're having?

King Cassava BAR
(South Side; ☺ 11am-midnight) In the middle of town, this is a beer, pool and reggae hub for both locals and travelers.

Lebeha LIVE MUSIC
(📋 608-3143; North Side) This drumming center is one of the coolest spots in Hopkins to be on any given evening from about 7pm, when local Garifuna drummer Jabbar Lambey hosts drum-ins for friends, students and travelers alike. Lambey also teaches drumming in the day and his wife Dorothy runs the attached guesthouse.

🛍 Shopping

Hopkins is an especially good place to buy local crafts. Some restaurants and hotels carry items made by local craftspeople, but to get the real flavor, you'll want to go to the source.

Joy Jah's Arts ARTS & CRAFTS
(📋 669-1744; South Side) This place is run by George Estrada and his wife Andrea, the artists who painted the huge mural that greets visitors as they arrive in town. It sells lovely paintings, hand-carved wooden statues and other Belizean-flavored curios. You can't miss this shop: it's fluorescent green and has a plaster dolphin and turtle out the front.

David's Woodcarving ARTS & CRAFTS
(South Side) David makes exquisitely carved staffs, masks, canes, mortar-and-pestle sets and wooden jewelry in a workshop behind his shop by night, selling his creations at very reasonable prices during the day. When he gets the time to sleep is anybody's guess. The shop is inside a little green building with a thatched roof just south of Joy Jah's.

Kulcha Gift Shop ARTS & CRAFTS
(📋 523-7075; South Side) Kriol for 'culture,' Kulcha Gift Shop sells drums made by Belizean artists, as well as other arts and crafts. It's also the place to go for Cuban cigars (BZ$25).

ℹ Information

Cue the trumpets! Hopkins now has a genuine Belize Bank ATM (though not a branch) where you can get cash with nearly any ATM card. It's next to the grocery store just north of King Cassava. Wireless, once rare, is now everywhere, and if you're without a netbook you can check your email at Windschief's **Hopkins Internet** (📋 523-7249; per hr BZ$8; ☺ 1-9pm Fri-Wed).

ℹ Getting There & Around

Two buses a day leave Hopkins for Dangriga, at 6:30am and 12:30pm, except on Sunday. It's quite common to hitch to the Southern Hwy junction and pick up a bus there. A taxi to Hopkins from Dangriga costs about BZ$80.

You can rent single-speed bicycles at **Lebeha, Dolly's** and **Tina's** by the hour (BZ$5) and day (BZ$20). Dolly's and Tina's are both on the south side of town, and Lebeha is on the north.

With the motto 'Faster than a Sand Fly', Sittee Point–based **Smart Cart** (📋 651-3101; www.gosmartcart.com) rents four- and six-seater golf carts for exclusive use in Hopkins, Sittee River and Sittee Point for BZ$90 and BZ$140 respectively with a BZ$200 credit-card deposit. Discounts are available for rentals of three or more days.

Sittee Point

About 1.5 miles south of Hopkins sits Sittee Point. Where Hopkins ends and Sittee Point begins is the subject of mild debate, so we'll leave it to you to decide. The area itself (closer to Hopkins than to Sittee River, with which it should not be confused) mostly has high-end resorts and a few exceptionally pleasant midrange surprises. Too far to walk (for most), Sittee Point is about 20 minutes from Hopkins by bicycle.

🛌 Sleeping & Eating

⭐ **Beaches & Dreams** B&B $$
(☑523-7259; www.beachesanddreams.com; r incl continental breakfast BZ$190; P@🖳) If it's a personalized family atmosphere you're after, this might be the place for you. The family-owned Beaches & Dreams is run by Tony and Angela Marsico, two professional chefs who traded catering in Alaska for running a high-quality inn on the Belizean shore. Four rooms in two solid, octagonal wooden *cabañas*, with king-size beds, tiled bathrooms and futons for lounging are good for couples or small families, while the two-story treehouse (BZ$320) can comfortably fit five. Tony and Angela are renowned for their culinary skills, so even if you're not spending the night, stop in for a delicious 'Mediter-ibbean' (Caribbean ingredients, Mediterranean flair) meal (BZ$15 to BZ$50). Bikes and kayaks are available for guests, and discounts are available during the low season and for stays over three days. Rum-flavored impromptu jam sessions featuring local musicians often happen on weekend evenings.

Hamanasi Adventure & Dive Resort RESORT $$$
(☑533-7073, in USA 877-552-3483; www.hamanasi.com; r BZ$790-1380; P🖳@🖳🖳🖳) Easily the premier resort of the area, Hamanasi (Garifuna for 'almond tree') combines the amenities of a top-class dive resort with an array of inland tours and activities and a gorgeous 400ft beachfront. All of Hamanasi's 25 large, very comfortable rooms and suites face the sea, except for the popular wood-floored treehouses, which lie secluded among the foliage behind the beach. The best deals at this exclusively priced resort are available as packages including room, meals and tours. Hamanasi's professional PADI dive operation can carry divers out to all three

of Belize's atolls (Lighthouse, Turneffe and Glover's), as well as the barrier reef's best dive spots; it is also equipped with the latest in nitrox dive technology. Kayaks and bikes are available free for guests, and the on-site bar and restaurant are excellent.

Hamanasi also employs licensed local tour guides who are able to facilitate tours into the many jungle, waterfall and ruin sites of Southern Belize and Cayo.

Jaguar Reef Lodge RESORT $$$
(☑520-7040, in USA 800-289-5756; www.jaguarreef.com; cabañas BZ$400, beachfront d BZ$540; P🖳@🖳🖳) A luxury resort with a long, sandy beachfront and ample amenities and activities on land and water, Jaguar Reef is good for families or wary adventurers with deep pockets. The breezy and beautifully furnished cabañas here feature king-size beds, full bathrooms with tiled tubs, and end tables made from traditional Garifuna drums. As well as snorkeling, birding, diving, jungle hiking, fishing and river kayaking, guests can enjoy a wide variety of other activity packages available through the resort.

Parrot Cove Lodge RESORT $$$
(☑523-7225, in USA 877-207-7139; www.parrotcovelodge.com; d from BZ$300; P🖳@🖳🖳) This beachfront lodge has eight beautifully appointed rooms with air-con, full bathrooms with hot showers, TVs and coffee makers. There's also a beach-house next door with apartment suites sleeping up to six for BZ$750 to BZ$800. These suites are fully furnished and have DVD-equipped TVs. The lodge has its own dock, a courtyard pool with a small waterfall, and an excellent beachfront bar. It's also the home of Chef Rob's Restaurant.

ℹ Information

Diversity Tours and Treasures (☑661-7444; www.secondnaturedivers.com) offers information and arranges tours around the area. It also rents four- and six-seater golf carts (per day BZ$90/140).

Sittee River

The tranquil Creole village of Sittee River, with an increasing population of North American expats, stretches alongside the beautiful jungle-lined river of the same name, about 3 miles by unpaved road southwest of Hopkins. Sittee River is known for its spectacular river, its plethora of birds and other wildlife, and for its nigh-invisible and perpetually ravenous sand flies.

◎ Sights & Activities

Nearby **Boom Creek** (inhabited by otters, a few crocodiles and plenty of birds) and **Anderson's Lagoon** make for good canoeing. One good birding spot is the ruined (but under restoration) 19th-century **Serpon Sugar Mill**, 3 miles from the village toward the Southern Hwy.

🛏 Sleeping

Glover's Guest House   GUESTHOUSE $

(☎509-7099; www.glovers.com.bz; camping per person BZ$6, dm BZ$16, r with/without bathroom BZ$56/40; P) Though most visitors come to Glover's Guest House on Saturday night prior to catching the catamaran to Glover's Atoll Resort (p194), this riverside guesthouse is actually a pretty decent destination in its own right. One large bunkhouse and two comfortable cabins-on-stilts offer budget travelers a quiet cheap base from which to explore the area. Mind the sand flies, though!

River House Lodge   HOTEL $$

(☎603-0298; www.riverhouselodgebelize.com; r BZ$96-136; P❋@🛜🏊) With a lovely riverside setting, River House Lodge provides six comfortable, though somewhat generically decorated, air-con rooms with TV/DVD units and screened verandas in two-story wooden houses. There's also an excellent bar and a small indoor pool. Bikes and kayaks are available free of charge to guests, as are motorbikes with a BZ$500 deposit. Meals and tour information are available by request.

❶ Getting There & Away

Buses that serve Hopkins also go through Sittee River at about 1pm and 6pm heading out to the Southern Hwy and on to Placencia, and at around 6:30am (7:45am Sunday) heading to Hopkins and Dangriga.

Cockscomb Basin Wildlife Sanctuary

The **Cockscomb Basin Wildlife Sanctuary** (admission BZ$10) is Belize's most famous sanctuary; at 200 sq miles, it's also one of its biggest protected areas. On some maps the place appears simply as 'jaguar reserve,' but despite the moniker, your chances of seeing a jaguar here are slight at best. This great swath of tropical forest became the world's first jaguar sanctuary in 1984, thanks to the efforts of American zoologist Alan Rabinowitz. Today, this critical biological corridor is home to an estimated 40 to 50 jaguars and a vast array of other animal, bird and botanical life.

The sanctuary is part of the eastern Maya Mountain range. Most visits are restricted to a small eastern pocket of the sanctuary, which contains a visitors center, the sanctuary's accommodations and a network of excellent walking trails. The visitor sighting book does record instances of people spotting jaguars, so it is possible. What you can hope to spot are plenty of birds – egrets, toucans and hummingbirds are just a few that live in or pass through the park. You can also expect to see iguanas, local rodents such as *gibnuts*, and maybe, with a little luck, some jaguar paw prints.

Mornings are the best time for wildlife watching, as most animals seek shelter in the heat of the day. Though many visitors come as part of large (and inevitably noisy) tours arranged through nearby lodges or travel agencies, your best bet for viewing more elusive wildlife is to come alone or in as small and quiet a group as possible. Regardless, the trails are still magnificent.

Despite its size, the sanctuary itself isn't big enough to support a healthy breeding population of jaguars; however, its position adjacent to other reserves and swaths of jungle make it part of a biological corridor that, many believe, offers promise for the jaguar's future in Central America. Belize's four other wild cats, the puma, ocelot, margay and jaguarundi, also reside in and pass through the sanctuary, as do tapirs, anteaters, armadillos (the jaguar's favorite prey – crunchy on the outside but soft and chewy on the inside), brocket deer, coatimundis, kinkajous, otters, peccaries, tayras and other animals native to the area.

The sanctuary is also home to countless birds: over 290 feathered species have been spotted, including the keel-billed toucan, king vulture, great curassow and scarlet macaw. There's also a thriving community of black howler monkeys living close to the visitors center (these were reintroduced here from the Community Baboon Sanctuary (p67) in 1992). If you don't see them near the center, you'll definitely hear their eerie, cacophonous howling should you choose to spend the night. And herpetologists take note: large boa constrictors, small (and deadly poisonous) fer-de-lances and tiny coffee snakes are just some of the snakes that call the sanctuary home.

👉 Tours & Trails

Following the creation of the sanctuary, residents of the nearby Maya village were relocated, many of them to **Maya Center village**. Most of these villagers now make their living from the sanctuary, running tourist accommodations or tours, or working as park staff. It's an interesting situation, as the guides will show you not only the animals and the history of the park, but also where they lived just 20 years ago. A typical day tour to the sanctuary from Maya Centre costs around BZ$100 per person and includes transportation, a couple of guided walks (usually including a waterfall in the route), lunch and maybe river-tubing. An exciting option is a night tour (per person BZ$50), which offers increased chances of seeing nocturnal animals.

Though a guide is useful, the well-maintained 12-mile network of trails that fans out from the park office is pretty user friendly. Most of the walks are flat along the bottom of the basin, but the moderately strenuous **Ben's Bluff Trail** (1.25 miles and steep in parts) takes you up to a lookout point with fantastic views over the whole Cockscomb Basin and the Cockscomb Mountains.

An easy 1.4-mile **self-guided nature walk**, looping together the Currassow Trail, Rubber Tree Tail and River Path, can be followed with the trail map from the park office. The **River Path** (0.4 miles) and the **Wari Loop** (a 2.3-mile loop from the office) are good early-morning bets for seeing a variety of birds. Jaguar tracks are often spotted on the Wari Loop and the **Victoria Peak Path**. The **Antelope Loop** (a 3.4-mile loop from the office) rises and falls through a variety of terrain and vegetation, and offers walkers a good overview of the basin's geological features.

The office also rents tubes (BZ$5) for hour-long **river-tube floats** down South Stann Creek from the River Overlook on Wari Loop.

🛏 Sleeping & Eating

In the Sanctuary

Staying in the sanctuary gives you easy access to the trails, and enables you to experience the sounds of the jungle at night and be up at dawn when the wildlife is most active. You'll have to bring all of your own food and drinks.

Maya Centre has a couple of grocery stores selling basic supplies, so stock up before you come to the sanctuary (unless you want to live on chocolate bars and Pringles from the visitors center). The accommodations options range from camping under *palapas* (thatched-roof shelters; bring your own tent, per person BZ$10) to a 'rustic cabin' with two beds and kerosene lamps (per room BZ$40). There's also a lovely dorm with bunks and a flushing toilet (per person BZ$40), and four cabins that sleep up to eight people and go for BZ$96 to BZ$108 each. Use of a communal kitchen is included with all options except camping, for which grill pits are available. You can rent kitchen utensils for up to five people for BZ$10 per day.

In Maya Centre

Nu'uk Che'il Cottages   CABINS $
([📞]665-1313; www.mayacottages.com; camping per person BZ$7, dm BZ$20, d & tr with bathroom BZ$60; dishes BZ$8-16; ⊙restaurant 7am-8pm; [P][📶]) Spread around a verdant garden about 500yd along the sanctuary road, Nu'uk Che'il is owned by Aurora Saqui and her husband Ernesto, a former Quan Bank villager who was director of the Cockscomb Sanctuary from 1988 to 2004. Rooms are simple, though slightly buggy, and have hot-water bathrooms. There is a craft shop and a large fan-cooled *palapa* **restaurant** with Maya dishes available (if ordered ahead), as well as more standard Belizean fare and lovely fresh fruit juices.

Niece and apprentice of the legendary Maya healer Eligio Panti, Aurora performs consultations using locally harvested herbal medicines from an on-site herbal clinic, treating everything from the common cold to flu and gastric distress, as well as cupping, acupuncture and various other traditional treatments. She also maintains a medicinal plant trail (BZ$5 per person with a self-guiding leaflet, BZ$20 per group for 30-minute guided tours).

MAYA VILLAGE HOMESTAY

An excellent way to learn about the local Maya and their community is by living with a Maya family. The Maya Village Homestay program can be arranged through the Saquis at Nu'uk Che'il Cottages. The price for the homestay is BZ$45 per person per day, which includes accommodations and two meals.

Tutzil Nah Cottages
CABINS $

(📞 533-7045; www.mayacenter.com; s/d BZ$28/36, meals BZ$10-24; 🅿) On the Southern Hwy, 100yd north of the Maya Centre junction, the three Chun brothers provide four clean rooms in houses on stilts decked out in basic Maya style. Rooms have shared bathrooms, but there is a fifth with its own bathroom for BZ$44. The brothers also lead a series of hikes throughout the area.

Cockscomb Diner/Maya Museum
CAFE $

(📞 660-3903; mains BZ$8-12; ⏰ 6:30am-9pm) Mrs Heliadora and Julio Saqui operate this combination eatery-museum. The restaurant side serves Belizean and Maya dishes, burgers, sandwiches and fresh juices, but keeps sporadic hours. The adjoining thatched-roof Maya Museum has a series of local artifacts, as well as offering cooking demonstrations and Maya music and dancing performances.

Jaguar Mountain Café
CAFE $

(📞 666-1633; mains BZ$10; ⏰ 7:30am-5pm, extended hr for groups) Sitting directly on the Southern Hwy intersection, this cafe serves basic Belizean standards like rice and beans and baked chicken. It also prepares traditional Maya feasts with advance notice.

ℹ Information

The **sanctuary office** (⏰ 7:30am-4:30pm, night warden on duty after hours), where you pay the admission fee (BZ$10, BZ$2.50 for Belizeans), is at the end of a 6-mile road that begins at Maya Centre. The office has trail maps (BZ$5) plus a few gifts, soft drinks and chocolate bars for sale. You can also rent binoculars (per day BZ$5), hammocks (BZ$15) and tents (single tent BZ$5, three-person tent BZ$10).

ℹ Getting There & Away

Any bus along the Southern Hwy will drop you at Maya Centre, but there is no public transportation into the sanctuary. A taxi from Hopkins to Maya Centre or the sanctuary costs around BZ$80. Most of the Maya Centre tour guides offer taxi services to the sanctuary for around BZ$36/60 one-way/return. From there to the center it's a two-hour walk over flat terrain.

Placencia

POP 2000

Perched at the southern tip of a long, narrow, sandy peninsula, Placencia has long enjoyed a reputation as 'the caye you can drive to.' This is more true today than ever since the 27-mile road from the Southern Hwy is no longer spine-crushing, having now been fully paved.

How you wind up feeling about Placencia really depends on what you're looking for. If it's laid-back ambience, varied accommodations and some of the best restaurants in Southern Belize, this beachfront paradise may well prove to be your personal Margaritaville. If it's off-the-beaten-path adventure and cheaper living you're after, Placencia might serve better as a way-station. Come on down for a few days of sandy beaches, sunny skies and great seafood before heading off to less trodden paths.

The village of Placencia occupies the southernmost mile of the peninsula. On the eastern side is a sandy beach, and between the beach and the road (which ends at a fuel station and a handful of piers) is a narrow pedestrian-only footway.

Placencia's airport is about 1 mile north of the village; 6 miles beyond that is the Maya Beach. Between the village and the airport lie an increasing number of accommodations, including some of the swankiest in Belize and a growing number of luxury housing units.

High season in Placencia begins the week before Christmas and lasts until late April. During the full moons of May and June the town hops as whale sharks come to spawn in the nearby waters. Bargain hunters should be able to get discounted rates when the mercury rises.

🏄 Activities

Watersports

Placencia is close enough to a plethora of cayes, reefs and dive sites to make it a good base for **diving** and **snorkeling**. The more distant the area, the more expensive the trip. Most operators will charge around BZ$200 per person for a two-tank dive trip to a nearby dive spot. Longer outings to spots like Glover's Reef or the Sapodilla Cayes should be between BZ$250 and BZ$300. For some sites you may need to add admission fees of between BZ$8 and BZ$30. Advanced divers take note: March, April, May and June are especially good months to see whale sharks in the area. One of these trips should cost between BZ$300 and BZ$340. Most dive operators also run snorkeling trips. A snorkeling day trip to nearby cayes, often with a beach barbecue included, costs around BZ$70 to BZ$100 per person.

SEINE BIGHT

Most visitors to Placencia just breeze through Seine Bight, the Garifuna village in the center of this tourists' peninsula, which, with its shacks, shanties and cheap restaurants sticks out like a Rastafarian at a GOP fundraiser. But as the home of many of the folks who keep the surrounding resorts running, Seine Bight is worth a stop. In addition to offering some of the cheapest food on the peninsula (any of the roadside BBQ shacks are good bets, especially on a Saturday afternoon), Seine Bight is home to renowned artists. Painter and sculptor Lola Delgado, of the shop **Lola's Art** (☑601-1913, 523-3342; lolasart@btl.net), offers some of the same paintings, handcrafted jewelry, sculpture and assorted crafts you'll find adorning (and being sold at higher prices in) hotels and resorts around the area.

Opportunities for **fishing** are equally amazing, and in the waters off Placencia you can troll for barracuda, kingfish or tuna, spincast or fly-fish for tarpon, bonefish or snook, and bottom-fish for snapper or jack. **Sailing** is also popular in the waters around Placencia. In addition to Belize's cayes and other ports, Río Dulce in Guatemala and Honduras' Bay Islands are close enough to sail to.

As the whole town is geared toward tourism and aquatic fun, any hotel in Placencia can arrange your tour for you. Most beachside accommodations, particularly the mid-priced ones north of the village, have free **kayaks** or **canoes** for guests' use, and some will even provide fishing poles and bait to use on their private docks.

Inland Trips

Despite its peninsular nature, Placencia isn't too bad a spot to base yourself for inland exploration. A half-day tour of the **Placencia lagoon** shouldn't set you back more than BZ$80 per person. Expect to see plenty of birds and, if you're lucky, manatees or dolphins. Trips to **Monkey River** are around the same price, and include a sea cruise to Monkey River Town before a short trip brings visitors into howler monkey territory. Crocodile viewing and bird-watching are also on the agenda, as may be a couple of jungle walks and a swim or river-tube float, followed by a Creole lunch in the village. The forests here are still recovering from hurricane damage.

Several tour companies also offer full-day trips to the village of **Red Bank** for BZ$130 to see that area's beautiful scarlet macaws (best seen from January to March), as well as day trips to **Cockscomb Basin Wildlife Sanctuary** for around BZ$120. Both of these places can also be visited fairly easily on your own.

Bowling

Placencia is a slacker's paradise, so let out your inner Lebowski by bowling a few games at Cat and Dale Harshbarger's **Jaguar Lanes Bowling** (☑664-2583; Maya Beach, Peninsula; per person per game BZ$6, shoe rental BZ$2.50; ☺2-10pm Fri-Wed). It's a small alley by US standards, but the opportunity to do something cool and incongruous like bowling in the tropics is one fans of strange juxtaposition won't want to miss. Beer and snacks are available, but sorry, dude, it's BYOWR (Bring Your Own White Russian).

⛴ Tours

We've listed some reputable operators for land, sea and diving trips.

★ **Splash Dive Center**   DIVING
(☑523-3058; www.splashbelize.com) Operated by Patty Ramirez, Splash teaches PADI courses to divers of all levels, as well as offering diving and snorkeling tours to islands and reefs throughout the area. Patty is an extremely patient instructor, making her suitable for first time divers and experts alike. Patty and her husband Ralph also lead tours inland, including trips to ruins, jungles and other spots around the country.

Seakunga Adventure   ADVENTURE
(☑523-3644, in USA 800-781-2269; www.seakunga.com; Peninsula) On the peninsula, just south of Maya Beach, Seakunga does multi-day river and ocean kayaking tours and day adventure trips. In addition to renting hobiecat catamarans (per day BZ$4120) and windsurfing gear (per day BZ$80, lessons BZ$160), Seakunga is also the only place in Placencia that rents kite-surfing equipment (per day BZ$160).

Placencia

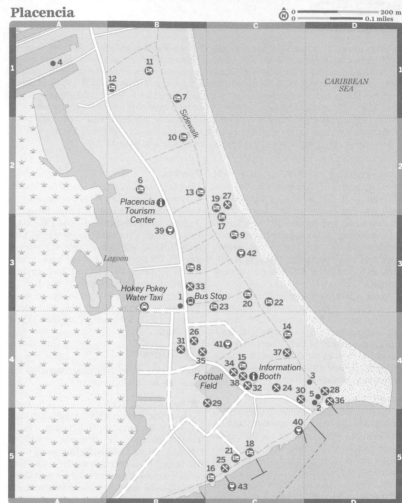

CARIBBEAN SEA

Sidewalk

Placencia Tourism Center

Lagoon

Hokey Pokey Water Taxi

Bus Stop

Football Field

Information Booth

Cayequest Tours TOUR

(☎633-6330, 664-8699; cayequest@hotmail.com)
Ever wanted to make your own chocolate
bar? Learn how to spear a fish with a Hawaiian
sling? Visit an organic chocolate farm
on the Caribbean coast? Or just experience
the nautical and jungle splendors of Belize?
Newly opened Cayequest tours can facilitate
all this, and more. Cayequest is an independent
and highly mobile guide service based
in Placencia offering tours from BZ$130 to
an all-inclusive overnight adventure package
that goes for BZ$700 per person. Call or
email Lyra and Mark for more details.

Avadon Divers DIVING

(☎503-3377, in USA 888-509-5617; www.avadon
diversbelize.com) Avadon Divers specializes
in nautical expeditions using a 46-foot boat
complete with all the mod-cons and fully
customized for a day out at sea. Three-
tank dive trips go for between BZ$300 and
BZ$400 depending on the dive sites. Avadon
also uses Nitrox and does certification
courses.

Joy Tours TOUR

(☎523-3325, in USA 917-446-6610; www.belize
withjoy.com) Offers a variety of fishing, snorkeling
and diving activities. Staff will also be

Placencia

glad to arrange hiking tours to Maya ruins around southern Belize.

Nite Wind Guide Service TOUR
(☑523-3487, 609-6845) Offers a variety of land and nautical tours.

Ocean Motion Guide Service TOUR
(☑523-3162, 512 3363) Does fishing and snorkeling trips.

Sailing Belize BOAT
(☑523-3138; http://sailingbelize.com) Day sails on a 50ft-monohull (BZ$240 per person).

★ Festivals & Events

Sidewalk Art Festival ARTS
(☉mid-Feb, nearest weekend to Valentine's Day) Features art, crafts and music, with scores of participants from all over Belize.

Lobsterfest CULINARY
(☉last weekend of Jun) Celebrates the opening of the lobster-fishing season with music, boat races, a fishing contest, a huge variety of lobster dishes to eat and a lot of fun.

🛏 Sleeping

Lodgings range from budget to midrange; most are small and family-run, and there are plenty of beachside *cabañas* (though your neighbor may be just a few feet away). Most places on the peninsula offer free airport pick-ups and a full range of tours and activities, usually at slightly higher prices than the agencies in town. During high season, beds can be hard to find; book ahead or your quest for accommodations may be lengthy. During low season some places close, and those that stay open may offer discounts of 10% to 25%, or more.

Manatee Inn HOTEL $
(☑523-4083; www.manateeinn.com; s/d/tr BZ$70/ 80/90; ℗🔊) Built by Slavek Machacka in 1999, this classical wooden hotel wins 'best in show' for the budget category. Set back a bit from the noisy center of town, the Manatee puts you close enough to the beach to feel a constant breeze. Amenities are as good (if not better) than some of Placencia's pricier hotels. Rooms are especially airy, with high ceilings, hardwood floors, refrigerators and private bathrooms with hot-water showers. In addition to the overall loveliness of the place, Manatee Inn is fairly unique in the area for having been operated by the same family for more than a decade.

Deb & Dave's Last Resort GUESTHOUSE $
(☑523-3207; debanddave@btl.net; r without bathroom BZ$50; 🔊) One of the cheaper options

---

LOCAL KNOWLEDGE

BERT SMITH: THE COCONUT MAN

Bert Smith, also known as 'Coconut Man', makes jewelry and other items from coconuts on Placencia Beach.

Where do you hail from? I came originally from the Cayo District, but once I found Placencia, I knew I'd found home.

Why Placencia? Because I'm an artist. I just love the vibe. Meeting different cultures, North American, European, Caribbean. Plus Placencia has the beach, one of the prettiest I've ever seen. I'm Belizean. I own the beach. But I'm willing to share it with the world!

Why coconuts? Coconuts are an amazing thing to work with. I make so many things with the shells – beautiful bowls, necklaces, bracelets, jewelry of all kinds. They're a great medium. They also have a lot of medicinal uses. The water inside has electrolytes that detoxify the system instantly, clean out the urinary tract and help rebuild tissue and blood cells. Coconut oil is good for all types of ailments…it is also an aphrodisiac!

Perfect day in Placencia? The sea is calm, the sky is bright and I can see the beautiful Cockscomb mountains, unmolested by clouds to the west. I head out on my canoe with my snorkel gear, and catch some lobster from underneath the rocks. I bring 'em home and cook 'em on the beach.

---

in town, D&D's offers comfortable, compact rooms with fans, surrounded by a leafy garden. A screened-in space offers a communal chill-out spot complete with a coffee maker.

Omar's Guesthouse GUESTHOUSE $
(☎634-4350; dm/s/d BZ$25/40/45, d with bathroom BZ$55) Small and unpretentious, Omar's is a perennial favorite with backpackers and others doing Belize on the cheap. Rooms are fan-cooled, bathrooms shared and showers cold. The eponymous Omar also runs Omar's Creole Grub (p212), which serves some of the best Creole food in town.

Lydia's Guesthouse GUESTHOUSE $
(☎523-3117; www.lydiasguesthouse.com; r BZ$45; ☎) Lydia's, with eight rooms and one studio apartment with a full kitchen (BZ$65), occupies a quiet stretch of sidewalk on the northern side of town. Look for the white house with yellow trim and the colorful hammocks hanging out front. Lydia's offers a communal kitchen with purified drinking water.

Yellow House GUESTHOUSE $
(☎523-3481; info@ctbelize.com; r BZ$50-70; ℗) This budget hotel in the center of Placencia has clean, basic rooms with double beds, kitchenettes, bathrooms and ceiling fans.

Casa Placencia SUITES $$
(☎630-7811; www.casaplacencia.com; r BZ$90-230; ℗❀☎) On the quiet northern end of town, Casa Placencia offers beautifully deco-

rated rooms with kitchenettes, cable TV and wi-fi. There's a great organic and pesticide-free garden with bananas, mangoes and papayas (all for the enjoyment of guests), and a chill-out spot with a beautiful tiled BBQ in the back. Guests are provided with free bicycles, and long-term rentals are available.

Sea Glass Inn HOTEL $$
(☎523-3098; www.seaglassinnbelize.com; s/d/tr BZ$158/158/188, per additional person BZ$20; ❀@☎) Formerly known as Dianni's Guest House, the newly renovated Sea Glass Inn offers unobstructed ocean views and endless sea breezes thanks to its position a stone's throw from Placencia's southern shore. Rooms are newly renovated, and all have coffee makers, microwaves and refrigerators. The wide, wood-floored veranda has chairs and hammocks for long-term lounging.

Colibri House APARTMENT $$
(☎605-0586; www.colibrihouseplacencia.com; weekly apt rental BZ$1040–1320; ❀☎☎) The octagonal Colibiri house is one of a kind; built from a mix of hardwoods (including bullet tree and sapodilla), the house is fully furnished with treasures from Tibet, Bali, Italy and India. The upper apartment features a downstairs bedroom and living room and a 2nd-floor loft space with a low bed; both floors feature large wraparound balconies. Discounts are available during the low season. Gregarious Stefano (the Italian-born manager of Colibri house) also manages a number of

other properties around Placencia. Call him for more information.

Captain Jak's
CABINS $$
(✉ 628-6447; www.captainjaks.com; cabañas from BZ$190; P 🛜) The Captain offers three *cabañas* and two larger cottages surrounding a quiet garden (weekly rates are available). All rooms are fan-cooled and come with kitchenettes, hot water and private bathrooms. There is also an immaculately furnished, very airy, two-story private villa that sleeps up to eight for BZ$630.

Captain Jak also rents funky egg-shaped electric carts for BZ$130 a day, kayaks for BZ$40 per three hours and bicycles for BZ$40 per day (BZ$26 per half day).

One World Rentals
HOTEL $$
(✉ 523-3103, 620-9975; studio apt BZ$98; P ✳ 🛜) These clean, fully equipped studios with well-stocked kitchenettes are on the south side of town behind the Rumfish. One World is run by a gregarious Swiss woman named Claudia who also runs a gift shop, information stand and laundromat at the front.

Julia's Guesthouse
GUESTHOUSE $$
(✉ 503-3478; r BZ$80-150; 🛜 🏠) A beachfront place on the tightest-packed part of the shore, Miss Julia has three cabins, four duplexes and one apartment. All are painted in Julia's signature tropical yellow and orange and offering TVs, hot showers, private bathrooms and sea views. The best deal for the money is the apartment, which has two bedrooms, a living and dining room, and a small kitchen. Laundry facilities are available, and guests are invited to use the BBQ and beachside hammocks and lounge chairs.

Paradise Vacation Hotel
BOUTIQUE HOTEL $$
(✉ 523-3179; r without/with sea view BZ$178/278; 🛜) This 12-room hotel lies across the peninsula's southern edge, offering rooms with sea and village views. Rooms are tastefully appointed in an island nautical theme, and come with flat-screen televisions, air conditioners and soft, comfy beds. Guests enjoy free use of kayaks and bicycles, and also have access to the hotels guest-only rental golf carts for BZ$130 per day.

Ranguana Lodge
CABINS $$
(✉ 523-3112, 610-2287; www.ranguanabelize.com; garden/seaview cabins BZ$176/188; ✳ 🛜) Ranguana offers five good-sized mahogany cabins on a small stretch of lovely beach. Two have kitchens; the others (smaller) have

sea views and air-con. All have two double beds, hot-water bathrooms, cable TV and microwaves, not to mention lovely verandas. Chefs take note: garden units have actual gas stoves. There's also an onsite grill.

Serenade Guesthouse
HOTEL $$
(✉ 601-4965, 523-3388; www.belizecayes.com; Sidewalk; r BZ$80-120; P ✳ 🛜) Rooms in this big wooden house just off the beach all have private bathrooms and cable TV. More expensive rooms have sea views, air-con and their own coffee makers. There's also a barber shop and full beauty salon on the 1st floor!

Westwind Hotel
HOTEL $$
(✉ 523-3255; www.westwindhotel.com; s/d/ste BZ$131/164/327; ✳ 🛜) Travelers speak highly of George and Lisa Westby's Westwind Hotel, a funky two-story wooden place with large, clean rooms and a definite family-run feel. Most rooms face the sea and all have a balcony, terrace or patio and hot-water bathrooms. The six-hammock *palapa* out front on the sand is a great place to eat, play board games and chill out in general.

Seaspray Hotel
HOTEL $$
(✉ 523-3148; www.seasprayhotel.com; r BZ$50-130; ✳ @) Owned and operated by the Leslies (one of Placencia's most established families), this lovely hotel has seven grades of room (all with private hot-water bathrooms) of varying degrees of luxury and proximity to the ocean.

Michelo Hotel
HOTEL $$
(✉ 523-3519; harbour21@gmail.com; d from BZ$130; P ✳ 🛜) This small hotel on the north end of town has four suites with queen-sized bed and futon, cable TV, wi-fi, and full kitchenettes with microwave and fridge. Air conditioning is available for an additional charge of BZ$30. The owners, Mr and Mrs Ardoulli, have built an absolutely beautiful temple and meditation space around the back that is open to guests and non guests alike.

Southwater Resort
CABINS $$
(✉ 523-3308; cabañas BZ$185, ste BZ$436; 🛜) Four beautiful sea-facing *cabañas* and three fully furnished suites that can sleep four to six people.

Miramar Properties
APARTMENT $$$
(✉ 523-3658; www.miramarbelize.com; studio BZ$250, ste BZ$370, 3-bed 2-bath r BZ$470; ✳ 🛜) These apartments, which can also be rented by the week or the month, come fully furnished; bath and beach towels are provided

AN OFFER YOU CAN'T REFUSE

This is it. **Turtle Inn** (📞523-3486, 523-3244, 824-4912, in USA 800-746-3743; www.turtleinn.com; s/d/tr cottages from BZ$862-966, villas from BZ$1208-1592 + tax and service charge; 🅿@🛜🏊) is the ultra-chic lodge owned by Mr Francis Ford Coppola, where the director himself maintains his own Belizean villa. It's the beachside complement to Coppola's hill-country Blancaneaux Lodge. There is, of course, little need for a lengthy review of this Balinese-themed, opulent-in-every-way resort; it is everything you'd expect from a place of both its price-tag range and Hollywood pedigree. (Its cinematic website – perhaps created with input from Coppola himself – paints an accurate picture.)

Yes, it is wonderful, combining luxury with a hint of the rustic, equipped with two beachfront pools, a fully equipped PADI dive shop and a spa complete with Thai masseurs. Would you expect anything less from the man who brought the world *Apocalypse Now*? Of course not. Instead, let's skip to the question you really want to ask: 'How much to live in Mr Coppola's personal villa...the actual one he lives in when he's in town?'

Renting the fabulous Pavilion House, a two-bedroom, two-bathroom villa with private entrance, pool, dining pavilion and personal attendant, costs a mere $2100 per night in the high season (that's in US currency, exclusive of tax or service charges). So, on to your second question: 'At that price, do I get full access to Mr Coppola's private DVD stash, including the *real* director's cut of the *Godfather* trilogy?'

No. While all accommodations at the Turtle come equipped with iHome units where you can plug in your iPod and enjoy your own music to your heart's content, neither the Pavilion House nor any of the villas have TV sets. This is, after all, where the director comes to get away from the movies. And at these prices, shouldn't you, too?

at no extra cost. Look for the flamingo-colored building with the white peace symbol on the northern end of the sidewalk.

Around Placencia

If laid-back Placencia town is too busy for you, there's always the peninsula. Most accommodations also boast restaurants, bars and various recreational facilities.

⭐ **Singing Sands Inn**　　BOUTIQUE HOTEL **$$**
(📞533-3022; www.singingsands.com; cabañas BZ$200-240; 🅿@🛜) Tucked away in a beautifully landscaped garden, the newly renovated Singing Sands offers an affordable ocean-side tropical oasis. Accommodations at Singing Sands Inn consist of thatched-roof *cabañas* and garden-view rooms with hardwood floors, custom-designed doors and furniture made by local craftspeople. The bathrooms, with imported hand-painted sinks and tiles, are especially nice. The Korean aesthetics of the owners are especially felt at the table of the on-site restaurant (the Bonefish Grille), which, in addition to serving continental and Belizean dishes, also makes Korean dumplings, noodles, and other dishes linking the Placencia and Korean peninsulas. Fans of the Paleo diet will want to try the lettuce wrap (BZ$14), sauteed ground steak

served on fresh lettuce wrap with sweet hoisin sauce – pure caveman delight! Energy-efficient LED lighting gives the Sands a warm nighttime glow. There's also a great swimming pool, beach, and free kayak use for guests.

Maya Beach Hotel　　　　HOTEL **$$$**
(📞533-8040; www.mayabeachhotel.com; Maya Beach; r BZ$178-318, rental houses BZ$318-1000; 🅿❄@🛜🏊🚲) The Maya Beach offers clean air-con rooms with custom-made wooden furniture on a beautiful beachfront location in the center of the Placencia peninsula. Rooms are fully furnished and adorned with eclectic art from both local and international artists. The hotel also manages five beautiful beachfront houses ranging from one to three bedrooms with full kitchens, living rooms and desks. There's an amazing pool (with a swim-up bar!) and free use of kayaks and bicycles.

Inn at Robert's Grove　　　RESORT **$$$**
(📞523-3565, in USA 800-565-9757; www.robertsgrove.com; r incl continental breakfast BZ$310-1190; 🅿❄@🛜🏊🚲) 🌊 From the Grecian fountain in the front driveway to the beautiful beachfront patio bar and restaurant, Robert's Grove is classy all the way. Least expensive on offer are Robert's Classic Vista room, a studio-style room with king-sized

bed, futon, mini-fridge and cable-equipped flat screen TV. Classic Vista Family rooms are slightly larger and have an additional bunk bed for the kids. The one-bedroom villas have kitchenettes, master bedroom and living room areas. The two and three bedroom villas sleep five and seven, respectively. All units are spacious, comfortable, terracotta-floored and brightly decorated with colorful art and fabrics. Guests at the Inn enjoy a wide variety of amenities, including three pools, a five-star PADI dive center employing three full-time instructors, complimentary bicycles, a full gym, windsurfers, kayaks, hobie cats and a spa full of exotic body treatments. There's also a small organic garden in the front. Check the website for full rates listings.

Robert's has three on-site restaurants, including the newly opened Sweet Mama's. Serving local Belizean breakfasts, lunches and dinners from BZ\$8 to BZ\$15, Sweet Mama's is quickly becoming a favorite with locals and travelers alike.

Green Parrot CABAÑAS **\$\$\$**
(☑ 523-2488, in USA 734-667-2537; d BZ\$300, per additional person BZ\$20; P ☎) Owned and operated by the Allardice family, Green Parrot offers six two-story beach houses and two *cabañas*, all within hopping distance of the sea. Beach houses feature all-wood interiors, high ceilings and huge screened-in windows for maximum breeze. *Cabañas* are slightly smaller, with thatched roofs and outdoor showers for a tropical feel. All units are beautifully furnished with wood and colorful hand-painted sinks, and guests enjoy complimentary use of bicycles, snorkeling equipment, kayaks and glass-bottom canoes. If you're considering staying a while, medium-term discounts are available.

✗ Eating

When it comes to good food, Placencia definitely takes the gold! If you're looking to stock up on supplies for an extended trip to the jungle or cayes, there are a number of good supermarkets.

Radi's Fine Food BELIZEAN **\$**
(lunch specials BZ\$10; ☺ lunch) What you see is what you get: a shack, a porch, a kitchen and three daily specials cooked by Creole chef Radiance, aka Radi. Shrimp dishes are a given, and the other two dishes can be anything from conch soup to meatloaf to lasagna. All are delicious, and portions are always more than ample. Check the board on the side of the road for the day's specials.

Dawn's Grill n Go BELIZEAN **\$**
(meals BZ\$6-35; ☺ breakfast, lunch & dinner) Good things come in small packages, and good food comes from a small kitchen at Dawn's Grill n Go. Chicken, fish ball snapper and other dishes are usually on order at Dawn's, where you'll also find excellent desserts (try the Baileys cheesecake or bread pudding with rum sauce, made from scratch right there). Dawn also makes her own amazing hot sauce from scratch.

Above Grounds CAFE **\$**
(coffee from BZ\$3, espresso drinks BZ\$5; ☺ 7am-4pm Mon-Sat, 8am-noon Sun; ☎) This coffee shop stilt-shack offers great coffee drinks, bagels, muffins and other freshly baked pastries on a raised wooden veranda deck overlooking a small patch of jungle. All coffee is organic, and the owner, Keith, buys his beans directly from the farmers themselves through the NGO As Green as It Gets (www.asgreenasitgets.org), which facilitates direct trade between merchants and producers. Wireless internet is free, music is way eclectic, and a good whack of the profits from every double-shot espresso drink sold sends money directly to the farmers themselves.

Friends CONTINENTAL **\$**
(Southern end of Sidewalk; meals from BZ\$8-12; ☺ breakfast & lunch; ☎) Formerly called the Boson's Chair, this bright yellow shack has friendly service. Specialties of the house include the lobster omelet (BZ\$14), cinnamon banana french toast (BZ\$10) and a variety of excellent sandwiches.

Tutti Frutti ICE-CREAM **\$**
(☺ 9am-9pm Thu-Tue) If you don't like the ice cream here, you won't like ice cream anywhere. It's that simple. Lactose intolerant? No problem. The gelato is even better.

Sweet Dreams BAKERY **\$**
(☺ 6am-6pm; ☎) Freshly baked personal pizzas, multigrain breads and baked goods of all sorts are served all day at this family-run European bakery. There's also good coffee, porch-front seating and, yes, free wireless.

★ Maya Beach Bistro INTERNATIONAL **\$\$**
(☑ 533-8040; www.mayabeachhotel.com; Maya Beach; meals BZ\$16-46; ☺ breakfast, lunch & dinner Tue-Sun) Maya Beach Hotel's popular bistro is a veritable Placencia landmark,

offering excellent (and creative) international dishes using top local ingredients. Try the spicy 'sassy shrimp pot,' with tequila-flambéd and caramelized pineapple tossed in coconut curry. This is the restaurant where folks who run the restaurants in town come to eat on their days off, so you know it has to be good!

★ Rumfish   FUSION $$
(☎523-3293; www.rumfishyvino.com; mains BZ$22-36; ⊙noon-midnight, kitchen closes at 10pm) 'A gastro-bar, Central American style' is how John and Pamela bill their 2nd-floor eatery, opened in 2008. Try the pan-seared snook (BZ$38), a fish dish made with banana coconut curry, served on a bed of sauteed vegetables with potato latkes. At BZ$7 a pop, travelers on a budget should try the Rumfish tacos: beer-battered fillets are served with shredded cabbage and *pico de gallo*. For dessert, try the chocolate habanero canoli (BZ$12), sweet on the front with a little kick on the back end. Teetotalers should try John's Virgin Mojito, a delightfully cooling mint-lime infusion. Imported wines, beers and cocktails and a breezy colonial veranda complete the picture.

Purple Space Monkey Bar & Grill   FUSION $$
(☎523-3169; ⊙11am-midnight; @ 🜚 ⚟) Under new management since our last visit, this Placencia landmark's latest incarnation has a decidedly more international flair than its predecessors, having hired American chef Rick Labonte (former head chef at The Placencia). Utilizing locally sourced ingredients, the menu offers dishes from around the world, including baked lobster tail (BZ$42), five-spice chicken breast (BZ$24) and honest-to-god *sushi rolls* for between BZ$12 and BZ$14. With a full bar, the Monkey occasionally hosts live music acts.

Omar's Creole Grub   SEAFOOD $$
(mains BZ$16-22; ⊙breakfast, lunch & dinner, closed Friday night and Sat lunch) How does Omar serve both the freshest and cheapest seafood in Placencia? By cutting out the middleman and catching it all himself. Crab, lobster, conch, shrimp and fish of all description, all trapped, speared or otherwise caught by Omar and grilled to perfection. The only way to get it fresher would be to catch it yourself (Omar can even facilitate this; inquire within). Since our last update, Omar's small shack has been enlarged (seat-ing 40), but the same small town Creole atmosphere still prevails. Even if you have to wait, a meal at Omar's is well worth it.

Galley   BELIZEAN $$
(☎523-3133; mains BZ$12-22; ⊙10am-2:30pm & 6-10pm) This unpretentious restaurant located on the far side of the sports field offers simple, good Belizean fare like shrimp, chicken, conch and lobster (in season). For dessert, try a slice of Galley's famous lemon pie, cheese cake or bread pudding.

Café Merlene   CARIBBEAN $$
(breakfast from BZ$10, meals from BZ$20; ⊙breakfast, lunch & dinner) On the peninsula's southern coast, this airy lime-green and peach restaurant caters to a combination of Belizean and North American tastes. Specialties of the house include locally caught seafood cooked in chef Merlene's homemade secret sauce. Breakfasts are served all day and are a good excuse to try Miss Merlene's excellent homemade jams.

Shak   CAFE $$
(dishes BZ$10-15; ⊙7am-6pm) Since moving to the southern ocean-facing end of town, this pretty restaurant has only gotten better. Sip a healthy shake while watching hummingbirds sip nectar from flowers growing up the sides of the building. All-day breakfasts, Indian curries, healthy Mexican dishes and excellent smoothies are served up along with the best view in town.

De-Tatch Café   CARIBBEAN $$
(breakfast & lunch dishes BZ$10-12, dinner mains BZ$12-26; ⊙7am-9:30pm Thu-Tue) Can too much delicious shrimp be a bad thing? Head to this popular, thatched-roof, open-air beachside place and order one of their shrimp dishes and decide for yourself. Caribbean, Belizean and North American food are De-Tatch signatures (not to mention the decent portions). Favorites include the coconut shrimp curry, charbroiled steaks and delightful chicken in mango-rum sauce.

Hidden Falls Gourmet Cafe   CAFE $$$
(☎667-4146; www.belizebamboo.net; Placencia Point, 2nd floor; Meals from BZ$22-50) Offers a unique farm-to-table experience featuring produce, herbs, teas, juices and spices all grown locally. Owner Sol is also a fisherman who catches his own fish, lobster and crab. Ask about the cafe's 'cook your catch of the day', a snorkeling/fishing trip in which visitors can cook their own catches.

PLACENCIA'S BEST KEPT SECRET

Difficult to categorize, this quiet spot in Placencia's busiest quarter is a semi-cooperative encompassing two businesses. The **Secret Garden Restaurant** (⊘breakfast, lunch & dinner) is a low-key bar and restaurant serving an eclectic variety of meals and drinks. Behind the restaurant and across a placid patch of sand sits the **Secret Garden Massage & Day Spa** (☑624-6096; per hour BZ$100; ⊘by appointment), where US-trained and licensed massage therapist Lee Nyhus offers a variety of bodywork treatments to soothe body and soul.

🍷 Drinking & Entertainment

Pickled Parrot　　　　　　　　　　BAR
(www.pickledparrotbelize.com; ⊘noon-midnight or later) Under new management, this thatched-roof Caribbean-style bar and restaurant a block from the ocean has been a popular spot for locals and tourists alike for over 15 years. Beer is cheap (BZ$4) and their food – including amazing wings, ham and cabbage plates and Philly cheese steaks - is excellent as well!

Barefoot Bar　　　　　　　　　　BAR
(⊘11am-midnight; ☎) Placencia's most happening spot for drinking and entertainment, the Barefoot Bar has live music five nights a week, fire dancing on Wednesdays, full-moon parties and more. Happy hours are from 5pm to 6pm, with bitters and cheap rum. Stiff drinks, tasty food and good times.

Tipsy Tuna Sports Bar　　　　　　BAR
(⊘7pm-midnight Sun-Wed, to 2am Thu-Sat) Occasional live bands spice up the program at Placencia's shiniest bar, featuring pool tables, a big-screen TV and a concrete apron spreading onto the sands. A fun-loving crowd gathers most nights, and happy hour runs from 5pm to 7pm, featuring local rum and beer for BZ$3, BZ$6 coladas and daiquiris and BZ$1 wings.

Yoli's　　　　　　　　　　　　　BAR
(regantrehewey@hotmail.com; ⊘noon-midnight or later) This covered bar over the water is especially popular on Sundays, when sea air, spirits and libations mix with the smells of ribs and chicken coming off Yoli's BBQ grill.

J-Byrds　　　　　　　　　　　　BAR
(⊘10am-midnight or later) This dockside bar can get pretty lively with locals and visitors, especially at the Friday dance party (9pm to 2am).

ℹ️ Information

There's no shortage of info on Placencia, both on the web and around Belize. Check out a copy of the monthly *Placencia Breeze* (also online at www.placenciabreeze.com) or **Placencia Online** (www.placencia.com) before you get here. The **Placencia Tourism Center** (☑523-4045; ⊘9-11:30am & 1-5pm Mon-Fri) has moved from its old spot in a shack by Rumfish and pending a permanent home, is now located temporarily just north of the police station on the main drag.

Belize Bank and **Scotiabank** (⊘8:30am-2:30pm Mon-Thu, to 4pm Fri) are both on the main drag and have 24/7 ATM access for all your money needs. There's an Atlantic Bank branch on the far north end of town as well.

Check your email at **Placencia Office Supply** (☑523-3205; internet per hr BZ$10; ⊘8:30am-7pm). Do your laundry as well at **Julia's Laundry** (☑503-3478; laundry by weight, internet per hr BZ$10; ⊘7am-7pm).

Need a visa extension? The nearest immigration office is just across the lagoon in **Mango Creek**, a Hokey Pokey Water Taxi and 2-mile taxi ride away.

ℹ️ Getting There & Away

AIR

Between them, from Placencia airport (PLJ), **Maya Island Air** (☑523-3475; www.mayaairways.com) and **Tropic Air** (☑523-3410; www.tropicair.com) fly around 16 times daily to Belize City (one-way/return BZ$190/328, 35 minutes), 12 times to Dangriga (BZ$90/180, 15 minutes), eight times to Punta Gorda (BZ$98/180, 20 minutes) and twice a day to Belmopan (BZ$99/180, 40 minutes). The airstrip is just north of town.

BOAT

The **Hokey Pokey Water Taxi** (☑665-7242) runs skiffs between the southern tip of Placencia and the town of Independence (one-way BZ$6, 12 minutes, every hour from 6:30am to 6pm); from Independence you can connect with any of the buses that traverse the Southern Hwy.

WORTH A TRIP

RED BANK'S SCARLET MACAWS

What brings people to the Maya village of **Red Bank**, just south of the Placencia turnoff on the Southern Highway? It's the rare and spectacularly plumaged scarlet macaws that gather in the trees surrounding the village for around three months of the year (January to March, though sometimes they will arrive as early as December) to feast on the fruits that grow in the area. Lush, verdant and almost entirely off the tourist trail, the surrounding jungles are filled with brooks, rivers and swimming holes. A group of villagers composed of 10 local families manage the area and arrange tours deep into the surrounding jungles to see not just the macaws, but other unique animals that inhabit the area, including tapirs, jaguars, *gibnuts* and agoutis.

The best times to see the birds are early mornings and late afternoons, so it makes sense to spend the night at the village guesthouse, a long house with a thatched roof and clean, basic accommodations for BZ$40 per person. A village restaurant prepares local Maya and Belizean dishes for around BZ$12 per meal.

It's a truly unique experience, and as both the guesthouse and local tours are locally owned and operated, all money spent stays in Red Bank village. For more info, contact Red Bank native **Florentino** (☑660-6320; scarletmacawb3d@gmail.com), who helps coordinate.

The 45-passenger **D Express** (☑Placencia Tourism Center 523-4045; 1st floor) sails from Placencia dock to Puerto Cortés, Honduras (BZ$120, 4½ hours, including immigration time) at 9:30am on Friday. Tickets are sold at the Placencia Tourism Center (p213), and the boat leaves from in front of J-Byrds Bar on the southern end of the penisula. The return trip leaves Puerto Cortés at 11am on Monday.

BUS

Ritchie (☑523-3806; www.ritchiesbusservice.com) bus line runs four daily buses to Dangriga, from where you can transfer to Belmopan and points beyond. Buses (BZ$10) leave at 6:15am, 7am, 1pm and 2:30pm. The ride to Dangriga is 90 minutes. To get to Hopkins ask to be let you off at the Hopkins junction. Passengers heading to Toledo can save time by taking the Hokey Pokey Water Taxi (p213) to Independence for a south-bound James bus.

CAR & MOTORCYCLE

Barefoot Services (☑629-9602, 523-3056; http://www.barefootservicesbelize.com) Rents cars, scooters, motorcycles and golf carts from their office across from Barefoot Bar in Placencia. Arranges pickup and drop off at the airstrip.

✪ Getting Around

Many accommodations north of the village offer free airport transfers and free use of bicycles for guests.

Taxis meet many flights. The ride to or from the village costs BZ$10. A taxi from the village costs around BZ$20 to Seine Bight or BZ$30 to Maya Beach.

Bicycles can be rented at Captain Jak's (p209) and Dawn's Grill n Go (p211) for BZ$20 per day. Golf carts can be rented from **Paradise Resort** (☑523-3179) and **Barefoot Rental** (☑523-3438; www.barefootrentalsbelize.com).

TOLEDO DISTRICT

Bordering Guatemala to the south and west and the Stann Creek and Cayo Districts to the north, the 1669-sq-mile Toledo District encompasses an area most Belizeans refer to lovingly as 'The Deep South.' Around 27,000 people live in this huge area, and about half the district is under protection as national parks, wildlife sanctuaries, forest reserves or nature reserves.

Toledo's attractions – jungle trails, lagoons, wetlands, rivers, caves, waterfalls, countless birds – and its archaeological heritage are much less trumpeted than those of Belize's other districts, which makes them all the more magnetic to those looking to get off the beaten path. Toledo's capital, Punta Gorda, is also its only major town.

Punta Gorda

POP 5100

Most casual travelers in years past didn't make it as far as Punta Gorda (or PG as it's called throughout Belize); if they did, they only used this low-key seaside town as a jumping-off point into Guatemala. Recently though, the worm seems to be turning (at a typically slow Belizean pace, naturally), with the number of visitors coming to chill out in this unpretentious southern town increasing. Some base themselves here for longer-term trips out to the southern cayes or for lengthy explorations of Belize's deep Maya south.

Though it lacks the beaches of Placencia, there are plenty of docks from which to take a dip in the Gulf of Honduras' blue waters. A pretty town, a good part of PG's charm lies in its unassuming character. PG also boasts a good variety of mid-priced guesthouses, hotels and B&Bs, as well as a number of backpacker budget accommodations.

The town of Punta Gorda spreads along the Gulf of Honduras, its downtown area stretching lazily for several blocks just in from the coast. The town center is a triangular park with a distinctive blue-and-white clock tower; the airstrip is northwest, on the inland edge of town. Wednesday, Saturday and, to a lesser extent, Monday and Friday, are market mornings, when villagers from the mostly Maya settlements of southern Toledo come to town to buy, sell and barbecue around the central park and Front St.

🏃 Activities

Punta Gorda is a cool place to chill out for a few days, but outside of eating, lounging around the park and swimming off various docks, it isn't exactly activity central.

In the town's immediate environs, however, it's a different story: you can kayak on **Joe Taylor Creek**, which enters the sea at the eastern end of town, **hike** in the jungle around Hickatee Cottages or take **kayak trips** on other rivers in the area, where you may see monkeys, crocodiles and even manatees or dolphins (a typical trip like this costs around BZ$350 for up to four people).

Offshore, some of the islands of the **Port Honduras Marine Reserve**, northeast of Punta Gorda, present good snorkeling and diving, especially the **Snake Cayes** (named for their resident boa constrictors!), 16 miles out, with white-sand beaches. The beautiful **Sapodilla Cayes** on the barrier reef, some 38 miles east of Punta Gorda, are even better, with healthy coral reefs, abundant marine life and sandy beaches. A day trip for four costs around BZ$500 to the Port Honduras Marine Reserve or BZ$650 to Sapodilla Cayes.

Fishing for bonefish, tarpon, permit, snook, barracuda, kingfish, jacks and snapper is superb in the offshore waters and some coastal lagoons and inland rivers: fly- and spin-fishing and trolling can be practiced year-round. Any of the tour operators listed can help you arrange fishing and sailing trips, as well as other activities.

Drum Lessons

Local Drummer Ronald Raymond (Ray) McDonald teaches Garifuna beats at his **Warasa Garifuna Drum School** (☎ 632-7701; New Rd) on New Rd (about 15 minutes walk out of town). There are one-on-one classes, group lessons, options for kids and adults, and for all skill levels. McDonald also performs and lectures about Garifuna culture at Hickatee Cottages.

If it's Creole beats you're interested in, check out the Maroon Creole Drum School, where Creole drum-master Emmeth Young teaches drumming and drum-making on his jungle farm just outside of Punta Gorda.

Maroon Creole Drum School MUSIC (☎ 668-7733, 632-7841; methos_drums@hotmail.com; Joe Taylor Creek, Punta Gorda;) Students have a bit further to trek to study beats and drum-making at Emmeth's new location on the outskirts of Punta Gorda, but those looking to study with a master will find the trip well worth it. When he's not touring the country performing, Young (easily one of Belize's most respected Creole drummers) hosts drum-making workshops and group presentations. His new place is off Joe Taylor Creek, ¼ mile out of PG, so look for sign on the highway. Prices vary, but for around BZ$250 students can spend a few days learning both drumming and drum making, leaving with their own hand-crafted drum. Camping at the school is available for

---

WORTH A TRIP

FAJINA CRAFTS CENTER

Operated cooperatively by a women's association with members from 13 villages around southern Toledo, the **Fajina Crafts Center** (Front St; ⏰ 8am-noon, sometimes later, Mon-Sat) sells handmade necklaces, belts, bracelets, baskets, clothing, bags, earrings, wood carvings and many other items made by Toledo's indigenous peoples. All items sold here are guaranteed to be locally produced, and proceeds earned at the shop go directly back to the craftspeople themselves.

Punta Gorda

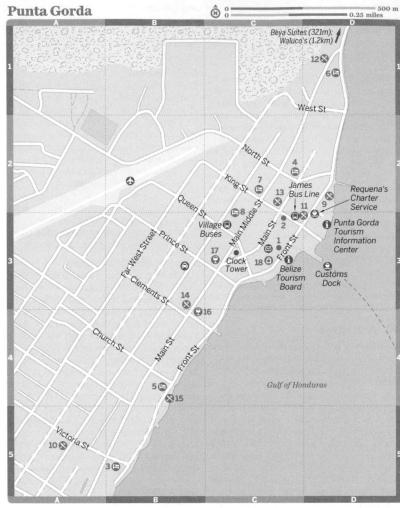

BZ$10, and other courses – including wine-making, medicinal-plant identification, and even cooking classes – are also possible.

👉 Tours

Ideally located for exploring Belize's Deep South, Punta Gorda has a number of certified tour guides who lead day trips and longer, both terrestrial and nautical, as well as renting out canoes, kayaks and other gear. The **Punta Gorda Tourism Information Center** (📞722-2531; btiatoledo@btl.net), a bright green and yellow circular building on Front St just down from immigration,

can also direct you to recommended guides, guesthouses or anything else.

Tide Tours   TOUR
(📞722-2129; www.tidetours.org) ✏ Always eco-friendly, Tide does tours in the Toledo area, including inland adventures to caves, waterfalls, birding trips and cultural tourism to local Maya villages, chocolate-making trips and more. It also does boating adventures out to the Southern Cayes including snorkeling, sport fishing, diving tours and more. Inland trips go for around BZ$100 per person, while marine trips start at BZ$150. Stop

Punta Gorda

at the Front St office to use the internet or to get free information.

Wild Encounters   TOUR
(📞 722-2300; www.seafrontinn.com; 14 Front St) Operated out of the colorful Sea Front Inn, Wild Encounters is one of the original PG tour companies.

**Toledo Cave and
Adventure Tours**   TOUR
(📞 604-2124; www.suncreeklodge.com) Operated by the owner of Sun Creek Lodge, if it's adventure you want, Bruno will help you find it.

Wild Thing   ADVENTURE
(📞 663-4559; Snack Shack) Offers custom tours around the Toledo District, including snorkeling trips, temple expeditions, kayaking, fishing and more. Head to the Snack Shack and ask for Roberto.

🎆 Festivals & Events

Two days of fishing, beer drinking, punta dancing, kayaking and volleyball contests, plus music, drumming and plenty to eat and drink add up to a big weekend at the **Toledo Fish Fest**, held close to Garifuna Settlement Day (November 19). The **Toledo Cacao Festival**, organized by local organic cacao businesses, happens at the end of May and beginning of June.

🛏 Sleeping

Whether you're traveling on a tight budget or living off a trust fund, you'll have little problem finding suitable accommodations in Punta Gorda.

Tate's Guest House   GUESTHOUSE $
(📞 722-0147; tatesguesthouse@yahoo.com; 34 Jose Maria Nunez St; s/d BZ$38/76, additional person BZ$11; ❄ @ 🛜) Since retiring from his job as Punta Gorda's postmaster, Mr Tate has channeled his energies into his guesthouse – and the latest refurbishment includes a beautiful garden out front and an all-over purple exterior. Rooms in this quiet guesthouse are still as clean and safe as they come (nobody messes with the guests of the postmaster, retired or not), and all are equipped with cable TV and hot showers. The costlier rooms have air-con and kitchenettes, the cheaper ones are fan-cooled. Long-term rental discounts are available.

Charlton's Inn   HOTEL $
(📞 722-2197; wagnerdm@btl.net; 9 Main St; s/d/ tr BZ$66/77/98; ❄ @) With 25 clean rooms with air-con and cable TV, not to mention a good location at the north end of town, Charlton's is a good choice for those looking for a place in the upper level of the budget category. Triples are more like suites, with two stand-alone bedrooms. Some rooms have their own bathtubs, a rarity in this area.

Nature's Way Guest House   GUESTHOUSE $
(📞 702-2119; natureswayguesthouse@hotmail.com; 82 Front St; s/d/tr/q BZ$28/38/48/58) Clean, safe and affordable, with a terrific breakfast, freshly brewed coffee and ocean breezes to die for, this family guesthouse is a longstanding favorite of backpackers and students (group rates are available). Simple, screened-in, ocean-breeze-cooled wooden rooms are upstairs, and a large airy communal area with TV, music and internet is below. There's also one big communal sleeping area where a bunk with mosquito netting goes for BZ$18, and two new private rooms with private bathrooms. Nature's Way also offers kayaks for BZ$15 per day.

Nature's Way Guesthouse is the head office of the Toledo Ecotourism Association (p227).

St Charles Inn
HOTEL **$**

(☎722-2149; 23 King St; s/d/tr BZ$40/50/65; ❋) Lilac-colored walls, verandas with hammocks, and budget rooms are the main draws of this aging guesthouse in the center of Punta Gorda (just down from Grace's Restaurant). All rooms come with private bathrooms, coffee makers and cable TV.

★ Hickatee Cottages
RESORT **$$**

(☎662-4475; www.hickatee.com; cottages BZ$130-190, d den BZ$150, Wilby Suite d/tr/q BZ$220/240/260; P@❷❋) ✈ In a world where an increasing number of businesses are flying a green flag to appeal to the ecoconscious crowd, Ian and Kate Morton's does more than just talk the green talk. The couple have gone out of their way to create a beautiful and unique solar-powered resort that leaves as light an ecological footprint as possible. Hickatee now sports six cottages, fully furnished with beautifully crafted items made of locally harvested wood. The newest are the Hickatee Den (a small detached unit that sleeps two and overlooks the plunge pool) and the family sized Wilby Suite with a queen bed, double futon and lounge area. The property itself, a mixture of intentional garden and wild jungle space, has a 3-mile trail network (including one very cool jungle maze) and is home to a wide variety of bird and butterfly species. Ian and Kate encourage visitors to explore Toledo on their well-maintained bicycles (free for guests). Activities at Hickatee include nature walks, tarantula spotting and bird-watching. Kate and Ian also run free visits to the Fallen Stones butterfly farm over in San Pedro Columbia each Friday. Finally, there are weekly drumming performances and lessons by Ronald Raymond McDonald every Wednesday.

Hickatee's restaurant serves breakfast and dinner to non-guests by reservation.

Blue Belize Guest House
B&B **$$**

(☎722-2678; www.bluebelize.com; 139 Front St; ste BZ$150, honeymoon ste BZ$190, 2-bed ste BZ$270; @❷❋) ✈ The beautiful Blue Belize leaves a light environmental footprint with its high ceilings (which, combined with the ocean-front location, nicely eliminate the need for air-con) and rainwater-fed plumbing system. BB's six breezy and beautifully decorated suites are more like serviced apartments than hotel rooms, offering well-furnished living rooms and kitchenettes, in addition to a comfortable master bedroom. Suites in the newly built north wing include flat-screen TVs for watching DVDs (Blue Belize has an extensive book and film library for guests); the north wing also has an amazing veranda for stargazing.

Coral House Inn
BOUTIQUE HOTEL **$$**

(☎722-2878; www.coralhouseinn.net; 151 Main St; d incl continental breakfast BZ$165-200; ❋❷❋) This excellent seaside inn at the southern end of town boasts a lovely garden and an oddly narrow, in-ground swimming pool (perfect for laps or one-on-one water volleyball matches). All rooms in this renovated house are clearly decorated by someone with an eye for style, giving the place a classic (but not at all pretentious) colonial feel. A spacious veranda overlooks the sea on one side and a quaintly picturesque old cemetery on the other. Chilling at the quiet poolside bar and exploring the area by bicycle (provided free) are just some of the options available to guests.

Sea Front Inn
HOTEL **$$**

(☎722-2300; www.seafrontinn.com; 4 Front St; s/d BZ$130/160; P❋❷) A strong contender for the quirkiest-looking hotel in Belize, this four-story gabled stone, wood and concrete construction was partly inspired by owner Larry Smith's travels in Europe. It's a comfortable and hospitable place, where each of the good-sized, air-con rooms (some

---

RANGER FOR A DAY

The unique 'Ranger for a Day' program enables travelers to experience the life and work of jungle rangers as they go about their daily activities in the **Golden Stream Corridor Preserve**, protecting the area from illegal activity and monitoring biodiversity. To the untrained eye, it's a pile of poop, but to a ranger, the scat tells many-a-tale. Participants in the program have a unique chance to learn various skills such as species recognition, identifying edible and medicinal plants and jungle-survival in general while exploring a 15,000-acre wildlife reserve with local park rangers. For more information, contact **Ya'axché Conservation Trust** (☎722-0108; www.yaaxche.org).

IXCHEL WOMEN'S GROUP

Toledo travelers looking to bring home souvenirs and put their dollars to good use should know about the Ixchel Women's Group (☑709-2006; Indian Creek Village, Toledo; ☺7am-5:30pm). Run from a small hut just about a mile past the turnoff for Nim Li Punit (on the west side of the road), the group is run collectively by 10 Kekchi Maya women who produce traditional handicrafts and sell them throughout the area. Among the items you'll find here are bracelets, bags, necklaces and *kalaba* shakers (a local instrument). Income generated at the shop goes directly back to the people of the Indian Creek community, skipping the middlema...er, the middlewoman.

boasting their own balconies) has a different theme (jaguar, blue morpho, manatee) - try for the emperor angelfish with its exotic sculptures! The top-floor restaurant serves excellent breakfasts of locally grown tropical fruits. The rear building – no less unusual looking – houses three apartments for medium and long-term visitors.

Beya Suites HOTEL **$$**
(☑722-2188; www.beyaste.com; 6 Hopeville; s/d/tr BZ$120/150/180; ❋🛜) Brightly colored (it's the pink building on the edge of town) and breezy, this seaside hotel about half a mile north of PG is a good find for those looking to balance comfort and economy. The rooms are well appointed and comfortable, with wireless internet, air-con, hot-water bathrooms and private verandas. Beya's on-site restaurant serves breakfasts for around BZ$15.

A Piece of Ground HOTEL **$$**
(☑665-2695, 702-0044; www.apieceofground. com; 1050 Pelican St; d BZ$100; ❋🛜) Nicely appointed spot on the southern end of town, the chief features of APOG are its communal areas. On the 3rd floor is a beautiful large open-air rooftop deck with a view out to the cayes in the east and the mountains in the west, and a large pool table. The 4th floor also has a deck perfect for lounging. All four rooms have a single double bed, wooden cabinets, bathrooms with hot and cold showers and cable TV.

✖ Eating

★Cotton Tree Chocolate CHOCOLATE **$**
(2 Front St; ☺8am-noon & 1:30-5pm Mon-Fri, to noon Sat) 🍃 The chocolate center of the universe? A big claim you might say, but come on down and try some of Cotton Tree's chocolate and you may leave convinced. Owner and chief chocolatier Julie Puryear buys her beans from Toledo Cacao Growers Association, a local co-op of about 900 small

growers, promoting both fair trade and local production. In addition to offering tours of her small factory (a fiendishly clever plan, if we do say so ourselves), Julie also has a small gift shop selling only locally made (and some chocolate-themed) handicrafts, including soaps, cacao-bean jewelry and other items.

Marian's Bayview Restaurant CARIBBEAN **$**
(76 Front St; mains BZ$8-14; ☺lunch & dinner) A 3rd-floor outdoor eatery with an amazing view over the Gulf of Honduras, this place is worth visiting for the ambience alone. But add to the mix excellent East Indian cuisine dished up by Marian and her husband Hubert, and some of the wickedest homemade hot sauce south of the Rio Grande (you can bring a bottle home for BZ$5; watch out, it's a slow burn!), and you've got one of the best little restaurants in Punta Gorda. Lunch and dinner are served buffet style, and the always-good variety keeps locals and visitors (and Peace Corps recruits) coming back.

Driftwood Cafe ECLECTIC **$**
(☑632-7841; 9 Front St; meals from BZ$8; ☺7am-4pm; 🍃) Run by the lovely Jill Burgess (wife of the famed Belizean drummer Emmeth Young), the Driftwood serves a unique variety of dishes drawing on local ingredients and inspiration from North American culinary traditions. Specialties of the house include the 100%-vegan chocolate chili, the green fruit freeze (orange juice and callaloo, a local green amaranth), milkshakes made with local cacao, coffee drinks made with local Belizean coffee and tamales and quesadillas.

The restaurant is festooned with local art and Mr Young's drums, giving it a local gallery feel. Come for the food, stick around for the culture. Jill and Emmeth also teach cooking classes at the cafe.

ℹ THE LONELIEST CAFE

Driving the Southern Hwy? Few and far between are roadside eateries between Independence and Punta Gorda. One of the very few is **Coleman's Café** (☑ 630 4432; Big Falls; ⊘ 11am-3pm & 6-9pm) 18 miles north of PG, near the rice mill. On the menu are solid Belizean and North American favorites like fry fish, fry chicken, burgers and fries, as well as more esoteric stuff like garlic shrimp and cream potato. Coleman's also serves beer, liquor and other beverages, including freshly squeezed juices.

Gomiers   VEGETARIAN $
(5 Alejandro Vernon St; meals BZ$6-16; ⊘ 11am-2pm & 5:30-10pm; ✍) Already becoming a PG institution, this small restaurant serves excellent vegetarian cuisine, fresh juices and a variety of tofu-based creations (including ice cream). Gomier also opens his shop to classes, teaching the craft of soy-making to students. Call for schedule or come by.

Snack Shack   CAFE $
(Main St; mains BZ$10-20; ⊘ 7am-3pm Mon-Sat) This popular outdoor eatery with a wooden porch serves Belizean breakfasts and generally healthy lunch items like shrimp salads and sandwiches all day. For something really unique, try a soursop slushie (BZ$3.50).

Fajina Maya Food   MAYA $
(mains BZ$5; ⊘ 6am-9pm Mon-Sat) Located on the 2nd floor above the Fajina Crafts Center, this small restaurant serves interesting Maya soups and stews with vegetables and poultry from farms in the outlying communities. The specialty of the house is *caldo*, a chicken soup colored red with annatto, a local vegetable. Lack of ambiance is more than made up for by the sea breeze and ocean view.

Di BoneVille   CAFE $
(Jose Marie Nunez St; meals from BZ$4, snacks from BZ$2.50, coffee drinks from BZ$4; ⊘ 10am-9pm Mon-Fri, closed Wed; 🛜✍) This church-run cafe is in the south end of town across from the university. Offering a variety of American-style eats (burgers, fries and milk-shakes) at prices so low as to be nearly saintly, it also serves up biblically named coffee drinks, baked goods and burritos in a pleasant youth-center environment. Weighing about a pound, the BZ$6 'Goliath' burrito is the best deal in town. Smaller appetites will want to stick to the 'David' (BZ$4).

Grace's Restaurant   BELIZEAN $
(16 Main St; breakfast BZ$5-10, mains BZ$7-12; ⊘ 6am-10pm) A longtime favorite of locals and travelers alike, Grace's offers a wide range of dishes, from Belizean specialties such as stew chicken, fry fish and rice and beans, to more exotic fare.

Hang Cheong Restaurant   CHINESE $
(cnr Main & Clements Sts; dishes BZ$6-18; ⊘ 10:30am-2:30pm & 5pm-midnight) An increasing number of Chinese restaurants dot the PG foodscape. If lunchtime crowds are anything to go by, Hang Cheong seems to enjoy the best reputation.

Mangrove Restaurant   SEAFOOD $$
(Milestone One, Cattle Landing; mains BZ$16-20; ⊘ noon-3pm & 5-10pm) Located in a screened-in area below the **Casa Bonita** (s/d BZ$50/60), a small guesthouse with two simply furnished but comfortable rooms, this is the first restaurant on the stretch of road leading in to PG. Chef Iconie is well known for her fusion Belizean meals, incorporating locally caught seafood, curries and pasta dishes.

🍷 Drinking & Nightlife

PG has a fair number of bars, from small waterfront pubs located on Front St to larger places over on Main. The town is also home to some top performers, such as *paranda* (serenading music) maestro Paul Nabor, *brukdown* (19th-century Creole music) queen Leela Vernon, and local punta rock favorites, the Coolie Rebels. Don't miss a chance to hear them on their home turf at one of the bars in town.

Olympic Bar and Grill   BAR, GRILL
(cnr Main & Clements Sts; ⊘ 7am-11pm) The latest hotspot with the PG expat crowd serves ice-cold beers, spicy-hot wings, homemade ice cream, and snacks galore. Alvan and Yvette Vernon also do catering for group functions, including snacks, pastries and local delicacies.

Waluco's   BAR
(Front St) If you're wondering where everybody is on Saturday or Sunday afternoon, they're probably out at this big, breezy *palapa* a mile northeast of town, swimming off the pier, enjoying the BBQ and knocking back a few Belikins. It's normally open Tues-

day to Saturday evenings, too, and Garifuna drummers often play here.

PG Sports Bar BAR
(cnr Main & Prince Sts; ⊙8pm-midnight Tue-Thu, to 2am Fri & Sat) A good-sized, fairly standard bar, incongruously enhanced by a staggering collection of US sports photos and posters. There's usually a DJ or live music on Friday and Saturday.

ℹ Information

Belize Bank (30 Main St) and **Scotia Bank** (1 Main St) both cash traveler's checks and have 24-hour ATMs accepting most international cards.

Belize Tourism Board (☑227-2420; Front St; ⊙8am-noon & 1-5pm Mon-Fri, to noon Sat) Among the services provided here are timetables for buses going out to the villages, current bus schedules to points north, and information and advice on guesthouses and attractions around Toledo.

Customs & Immigration (☑722-2022; Front St; ⊙9am-5pm Mon-Fri) This is your first port of call when coming to Punta Gorda by boat from Guatemala or Honduras; it should also be your last stopping place when leaving by sea (there's a departure tax of BZ$7.50). Head here for visa extensions too – it's next to the dock.

Punta Gorda Hospital (☑722-2026; Main St)

Punta Gorda Laundry Service (wash & dry per lb BZ$1.75; ⊙8:30am-5pm Mon-Sat)

V-Comp Technologies (29 Main St; per hr BZ$8; ⊙8am-8pm Mon-Sat) Check your email here.

ℹ Getting There & Away

AIR

Tropic Air (☑722-2008; www.tropicair. com) has flights five times daily to Placencia (one-way/return BZ$98/184, 20 minutes), Dangriga (BZ$156/299, 40 minutes), Belize City (BZ$209/406, one hour) and Belize City International (BZ$250/487, one hour). **Maya Island Air** (☑722-2856; www.mayaairways.com) does the same trips three times daily. Specials are often available, and ticket offices are at the airstrip (airport code PND).

BOAT

Requena's Charter Service (☑722-2070; 12 Front St) Operates the *Mariestela*, departing Punta Gorda at 9am daily for Puerto Barrios, Guatemala (BZ$50, one hour), returning at 2pm. Tickets are sold at the office and the customs dock down the street.

Memo's Boat Service (☑630-5889, in Guatemala 00502-4896-9215; memosboatserviceandtours@yahoo.com; Front St) Departs Punta Gorda daily at 12:45pm for Livingston and Puerto Barrios, Guatemala (BZ$50/60,

30/45 minutes). Returning, Memo's boat leaves Livingston at 2pm and Puerto Barrios at 3pm, with identical prices. The office is across from Customs & Immigration.

BUS

James Bus Line (☑722-2625, 702-2049; King St) Hourly buses run from Punta Gorda to Belize City (BZ$22, seven hours) from 4am to 4pm. Buses stop at Independence (BZ$9, two hours), Dangriga (BZ$14, 3½ hours) and Belmopan (BZ$20, 5½ hours). All buses leave from the main bus station on King St and cruise around PG a bit before heading north.

ℹ Getting Around

Tide Tours (☑722-2129; Prince St) and **Benjiman's Bike Rental** (☑629-4266; Far West St) both rent bikes for BZ$3/12/20 per hour/half day/day.

Aliram Auto Rental (☑722-2753; aliram@btl. net; Far West St) rents cars for use in the Toledo area. Serious adventurers should check out **Sun Creek Lodge** (☑604-2124; belizegate@gmail. com) which rents more jungle-ready vehicles like diesel pickups, Land Rovers and even school buses with daily, weekly and monthly rates.

Galvez's Taxi (☑722-2402; 61 Jose Maria Nunez St) A dependable option. Other taxis congregate around Central Park.

THE DEEP SOUTH

Beautiful, remote and largely untrodden by travelers, Belize's Deep South is a hotbed of culture, history, nature and environmentalism. The region is also home to some of the country's swankiest ecolodges.

Visitors to Belize's Deep South have a unique opportunity to simultaneously experience both ancient and contemporary Maya culture. Over 60% of the population of Toledo District is Maya and these people, with more than 30 villages, have done a great deal to keep their culture alive and intact. The Maya of Southern Belize who survived European diseases were mostly driven into Guatemala by the British in the 18th and 19th centuries. But two groups crossed back from Guatemala to Southern Belize in the late 19th and early 20th centuries, fleeing taxes, forced labor and land grabs by German coffee growers. The Mopan Maya settled in the uplands of Southern Belize, while the Kekchi Maya, from the Alta Verapaz area of Guatemala, settled in the lowlands. The Mopan and Kekchi speak distinct Mayan languages, as well as English and sometimes Spanish.

The Deep South

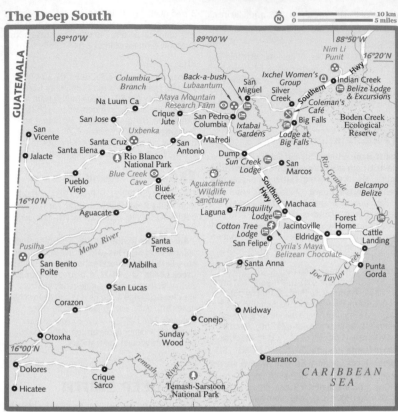

While Maya men generally adopt Western styles of dress, most women still wear plain, full-length dresses with bright trimmings, or calf-length skirts teamed with embroidered blouses. Rituals and folklore continue to play an important role in Maya life, with masked dances such as the Cortés Dance and Deer Dance performed in some villages at festivals, including All Saints' and All Souls' Days (November 1 and 2) and Easter week. If your village visit coincides with one of these, it will be all the more memorable.

Villages & Ruins

San Pedro Columbia

Around 20 miles northwest of Punta Gorda is the village of San Pedro Columbia, the largest Kekchi Maya community outside Guatemala. Columbia (as locals call it) was established by Kekchi families who left Pueblo Viejo to look for new farmland around 1905. The village has seen boom and bust, with mahogany and cedar felling, chicle collection and, in the 1970s and 1980s, marijuana cultivation. There are currently around 1500 residents. The village has one restaurant, Maggie's, by the crossroads, which serves uninspired fare and cold beer, and there are several shops where handicrafts and food can be bought.

Two miles up the river is the source of the Columbia branch of the Rio Grande, where water bubbles out from beneath the rocks. Local guides can take you to see the source; it's a 45-minute walk from the center of town (try floating down on a river-tube!). Behind the village, up in the hills, is the **Columbia Forest Reserve**, which has thousands of acres of forest, sinkholes, caves and ruins hidden in the valleys.

There are also local guides who can take you there. Maya Mountain Research Farm (p301) is just a few miles upriver from the village. Columbia is also walking distance to Lubaantun and 20 minutes by bus from Nim Li Punit, making the village an ideal place from which to explore two of the area's most complex and amazing ruins.

San Miguel

Just down the road from San Pedro Columbia, this Kekchi village of 400 people is on the road close to the Lubaantun ruins and the Southern Hwy. You can walk to Lubaantun or make a little expedition to **Tiger Cave**, 1½ hours' walk away, returning by canoe along the Rio Grande. For sleeping and eating, San Miguel offers the budget options of Back-a-bush (p227) and, down the road toward San Pedro Columbia (it's walkable), **Ixtabai Gardens** (✆632-7841; www.columbiarivercooperative.com; San Pedro Columbia; dm BZ$20; ☎⛱). Both also make good bases for exploring Lubaantun and rural Toledo.

◉ Sights

Lubaantun   RUINS
(admission BZ$20; ☺8am-5pm) The Maya ruins at Lubaantun, 1.3 miles northwest of San Pedro Columbia, are built on a natural hilltop and display a construction method unusual in the ancient Maya world of mortar-less neatly cut black slate (rather than the more typical limestone) blocks. In 1924, Belize's then-chief medical officer Thomas Gann, an amateur archaeologist, bestowed the name Lubaantun (Place of Fallen Stones) on these ruins. Perhaps the name has to do with the mortar-free composition of the structures. Or maybe Gann's naming of the site was inspired by his own practice of dynamiting temple tops to remove earth and rocks. History doesn't tell. More professional work has taken place since 1970 and much of the site is now cleared and restored.

Archaeologists postulate that Lubaantun, which flourished between AD 730 and 860, may have been an administrative center regulating trade, while nearby Nim Li Punit was the local religious and ceremonial center. The Maya site comprises a collection of seven **plazas**, three **ballcourts** and surrounding structures. Lubaantun is known for the numerous mold-made **ceramic figurines** found here, many of which represent ancient ball players.

Lubaantun

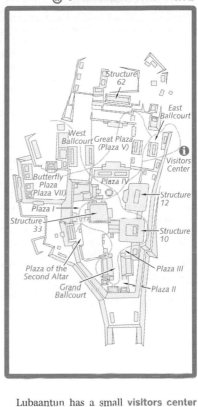

Lubaantun has a small **visitors center** displaying pottery, ceramic figurines, maps and other items pertaining to the place. When not giving tours, the caretakers of the site can be found here, and are generally glad to answer any questions you might have.

If making your own way to Lubaantun from Punta Gorda, follow the Southern Hwy for 15 miles until 2 miles past Dump Junction, where you'll see a sign reading 'Lubaantun'. The dirt road takes you through the village of San Miguel before a second dirt road heads half a mile to the site itself.

Laguna

About 13 miles northwest of Punta Gorda, Laguna is just 2 miles off the Southern Hwy and quick and easy to get to. About 300 Kekchi Maya villagers live here. The lagoon the village is named for, about a two-hour walk away, is at the heart of the 8.6-sq-mile **Aguacaliente Wildlife Sanctuary**, an extensive

WORTH A TRIP

THE CAYES OF THE DEEP SOUTH

Glover's Reef and the other islands of Central Belize a bit too crowded for your tastes? Then head seriously off the beaten path to the seldom-visited cayes of the Deep South.

About a two-hour boat ride from Punta Gorda (and right on the barrier reef!) is the **Sapodilla Cayes Marine Reserve**. A protected reserve (visitors pay a daily BZ$20 conservation fee), the Sapodillas offer superlative opportunities for swimming, snorkeling and diving. **Lime Caye**, most popular of the Sapodillas, has wonderful white-sand beaches, basic *Gilligan's Island* hut accommodations (s/d BZ$60/80), beach camping (BZ$30) and meals for BZ$20. A round-trip fare to Lime Caye is around BZ$600 per boat (maximum of 6 passengers). Trips to other cayes in the chain are also available.

Sapodilla's a bit too far? Close enough to PG to be seen from the terrace of Marian's Bayview is the **Port Honduras Marine Reserve**, which contains 130-plus mangrove cayes. The marine reserve is managed by the Toledo Institute for Development and Environment, AKA TIDE (☑722-2274; www.tidebelize.org; One Mile San Antonio Rd, Punta Gorda), and there's a daily charge of BZ$10 for visiting.

Trips to the Port Honduras reserve begin at **Abalone Caye**, where a short presentation is given by the rangers in charge. Visitors will then be brought to different cayes in the reserve, including **West Snake Caye** (known for its white-sand beaches), **East Snake Caye** (excellent snorkeling) and **Frenchman Caye** (a prime spot for Manatee watching). Depending on the trip, you may also get to see **Wild Cane Caye**, an ancient Maya center of obsidian trade and production.

To arrange trips to either Sapodilla or Port Honduras, contact **Garbutt's Marine/ Fishing Lodge** (☑722-0072; garbuttsmarine@yahoo.com; Joe Taylor Creek, Punta Gorda; ◷8am-5pm). In addition to managing a property on Lime Caye, Garbutt's also arranges a variety of marine tours around the area, including fishing, scuba and snorkeling trips, with price dependent on distance.

---

wetland area. The area provides great birdwatching and is home to flocks of ibis and woodstork, many raptors including ospreys, plenty of kingfishers and herons and the odd jabiru stork. There's a **visitors center** on the trail from the village. The hike can be wet and muddy and is sometimes impossible at the height of the rains.

San Antonio

The largest Mopan Maya community in Belize (population about 2500), San Antonio was founded in the mid-19th century by farmers from San Luis Rey in El Petén, Guatemala. A wooden idol (of San Luis) was taken from the church in San Luis Rey by settlers who returned to Guatemala to retrieve their saint. The idol remains in the beautiful **stone church** in San Antonio, which has wonderful stained-glass windows with Italian and Irish names on them (because the glass was donated by parishioners from St Louis, Missouri). The **Feast of San Luis**, a harvest festival where the famous Deer Dance is performed, is celebrated in town from about August 15 to 25. There is a TEA (Toledo Ecotourism Association)

guesthouse in the village, and **Bol's Hilltop Hotel** (r without bathroom BZ$15) has very basic rooms, if you can get Mr Bol to come to the door (he's a bit hard of hearing). San Antonio has a large concentration of cacao farmers growing cacao for export and use in Belizean-made chocolate products.

⊙ Sights

Uxbenka   RUIN

FREE Smaller in size and far less developed than Lubaantun and Nim Li Punit, the Maya ruins of Uxbenka are located close to the village of Santa Cruz on the road from San Antonio. The site is mostly undeveloped and the visible part is merely the center of a larger, yet-to-be-excavated city. Archaeologists believe Uxbenka dates back to the Classic period, with stelae erected in the 4th century. There is evidence that it had a close relationship with Tikal to the north. The open site has a large plaza with some excavated tombs and sweeping views to the sea. On a clear day it is possible to see the mountains of Honduras and Guatemala. At the time of writing, there were no entry fees for Uxbenka; a local guide can take you, or you can make your own way there.

Nim Li Punit   RUIN
(admission BZ$20; ⊙8am-5pm) The Maya ruins of Nim Li Punit stand atop a natural hill half a mile north of the Southern Hwy, 26 miles from Punta Gorda. Buses along the highway will drop you off or pick you up at the turnoff. Only discovered in 1976 by oil prospectors, Nim Li Punit was inhabited from some point in the middle Classic Period (AD 250–1000) until sometime between AD 800 and 1000. It was probably a town of 5000 to 7000 people at its peak, a political and religious community of some importance in the region.

The site is notable for the 26 stelae found in its southern **Plaza of the Stelae**. Four of the finest are housed in the stela house beside the visitors center. **Stela 14**, at 33ft, is the second-longest stela found anywhere in the Maya world (after Stela E from Quirigua, Guatemala). It shows the ruler of Nim Li Punit in an offering or incense-scattering ritual, wearing an enormous headdress which is responsible for the name Nim Li Punit ('Big Hat' in Kekchi Maya).

The most interesting part of the site is the south end, comprising the Plaza of the Stelae and the Plaza of Royal Tombs. The Plaza of the Stelae is thought to have acted as a calendrical observatory: seen from its western mound, three of the small stones in front of the long eastern mound align with

sunrise on the equinoxes and solstices. The **Plaza of Royal Tombs**, with three open, excavated tombs, was a residential area for the ruling family. Archaeologists uncovered four members of this family in Tomb 1, along with several jadeite items and 37 ceramic vessels.

Like Lubaantun, Nim Li Punit has a good **visitors center** where you can view various items preserved from earlier excavations, as well as hire tour guides or get general information.

Río Blanco National Park   PARK
(admission BZ$10) Halfway between Santa Cruz and Santa Elena sits the 105-acre Río Blanco National Park. The protected wildlife area is home to a variety of flora and fauna, but the highlight is definitely **Río Blanco Falls**, a beautiful 20-foot-high waterfall leading into a clear blue swimming hole (considered one of the best swimming holes in the country). After paying your entrance fee at the ranger station, the falls are a five minute hike. Other activities in the park include bird-watching, nature-trail hiking, and kayaking (you can rent a kayak for BZ$5 per hour at the ranger station). Guests who want to stay the night can do so in a very basic bunkhouse attached to the ranger station (BZ$20), which has a small stove for cooking, or they can camp in the park itself (BZ$10). Guesthouse stays in **Santa Elena** (a small Mopan village of 300 souls about 6 miles west of San Antonio) can also be arranged through the ranger station.

Pueblo Viejo

Sitting 3 miles beyond Santa Elena, the name of Pueblo Viejo (Old Town) is appropriate for this village, the first Mopan village settled in Belize. Today it is home to about 550 people. It's still an isolated place, without electricity. There are beautiful **waterfalls** close by and you can take **jungle hikes** or go **horseback riding**.

San Jose

Also known as Hawaii (a Mopan word, pronounced ha-wee-ah), this Mopan village of 700, known for practicing organic farming, is located in the foothills of the Maya Mountains. The rainforest surrounding it is among the most pristine in Toledo. From here you can take jungle hikes to **Gibnut Cave** and a 200ft **sinkhole**. The village honors

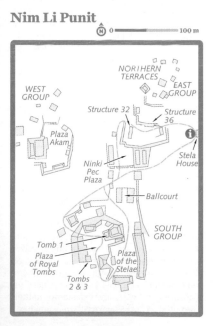

Nim Li Punit
Ⓝ 0 ▬▬▬▬▬ 100 m

NORTHERN TERRACES
WEST GROUP
EAST GROUP
Structure 32
Structure 36
Plaza Akam
ℹ
Stela House
Ninki Pec Plaza
Ballcourt
SOUTH GROUP
Tomb 1
Plaza of Royal Tombs
Plaza of the Stelae
Tombs 2 & 3

SOUTHERN BELIZE VILLAGES & RUINS

MAYA MOUNTAIN RESEARCH FARM

Those interested in learning about permaculture, Maya farming techniques and sustainable living should consider an internship at Maya Mountain Research Farm (p301). Located in a beautiful jungle valley 2 miles upriver from San Pedro Columbia, the 70-acre organic farm and registered NGO is run by permaculture teacher Christopher Nesbitt. With the philosophy of promoting fully sustainable food production, the farm offers internships for those interested in learning about organic farming, biodiversity and alternative energy. Accommodations are simple and beautiful: students can choose from a series of rustic *cabañas* and thatched-roof *palapas,* all of which come equipped with beds and blankets. Interns pay BZ$350 for the week, or BZ$1200 for the month, which includes everything.

All aspects of life at MMRF are geared toward environmental sustainability. Interns take part in every stage of meal preparation, from harvesting fruits, vegetables, nuts and herbs to cooking over a wood-burning stove inside the farm's outdoor kitchen (hand-built with stones from the river that marks the border between MMRF and the surrounding farms). Even the toilet – an outhouse with fantastic views of the valley – is set up to recycle nutrients back into the soil.

Rustic, beautiful in the extreme and completely off the grid (phone service, no; satellite internet, yes!), the farm is located in one of the least-touristy sections of Belize. MMRF also offers short-term courses lasting between one and three weeks in both permaculture design and solar electricity management.

its patron saint with three days of eating and dancing to marimba and harp music around March 19.

Blue Creek

This village of some 250 people, part Kekchi and part Mopan, does indeed have a pretty, blue-tinted river running through its center. Howler monkeys inhabit the surrounding hilly jungles, otters live along the creek and green iguanas are plentiful. Blue Creek is a tourist stop for the **Blue Creek Cave** (Hokeb Ha Cave; admission BZ$2), a walk of about 0.75 miles along a marked jungle path from the bridge in the middle of the village. The cave has a 'wet side,' where you swim and wade up to an underground **waterfall** (about one hour in the cave), and a 'dry side,' where you can try a more difficult venture involving climbing, and emerge at a different entrance. Guides are obligatory inside the cave. Another good hike here is up the hill known as **Jungle Height** (about 1½ hours to the top), which affords great views.

Near Blue Creek is the **Tumul'kin School of Learning**, a Maya boarding school that hosts students from throughout Toledo and other parts of Belize, providing a learning venue that inculcates pride in being Maya and gives students an education that values traditional knowledge.

San Benito Poite

One of the most rural villages in Toledo, San Benito Poite sits on the border of Guatemala and is close to a small Maya site called **Pusilha**. Barely excavated, the site contains one of the only remaining ancient Maya bridges. Pusilha's main temple offers views into the jungles of Guatemala. San Benito Poite is home to the independently and locally operated **Kehilha Jungle Lodge** (http://kehilha.com; 🛜) 🍃. This completely solar-powered lodge offers visitors a variety of activites, including jungle-medicine lessons, rainforest hikes, river fishing, horseback riding, caving and more. Though the town lacks phone service, the lodge is connected to the world via an internet cafe, also solar-powered!

Jalacte

Few visitors make it to this small village, known mostly for being the end of the line on the road leading from the Southern Hwy into the Maya villages of western Toledo. The hilly village sits right on the border of Guatemala, and while it isn't officially a land border crossing (not yet), unofficial crossings occur just west of the village (not a good idea for travelers, as the one thing Belize and Guatemala both agree on is the need for visitors to have entry and exit stamps in their passports!). There's heavier-than-average soldier presence in Jalacte as a result, so if you drive here, don't be surprised if your vehicle is searched for contraband. The village itself is very pretty, with some traditional hillside housing overlooking a lovely river (and a dangerous-looking suspension bridge). If you get stuck here, the town's only guesthouse is right across from the bus stop. It's BZ$15 a night, and basic doesn't begin to describe it.

Barranco

Barranco is an anomaly indeed, a Garifuna community surrounded by Maya villages. It is both the oldest settlement in Toledo and, despite its distance from major Garifuna population centers such as Dangriga and Hopkins, is a major spiritual homeland of the Garifuna. Though the area was once heavily farmed, nowadays the village supports itself primarily through fishing, as its population has dwindled to about 150 (men of working age head for the cities and better economic opportunities). Still, many are working to revitalize Barranco, both because of its spiritual importance to the Garifuna and its proximity to **Temash-Sarstoon National Park**, an amazing and remote 64-sq-mile protected reserve of rainforest, wetlands, estuaries and rivers lined by towering mangroves and stretching all the way to Guatemala.

The park harbors a huge variety of wildlife, from jaguars, tapirs and ocelots on land to ospreys in the air, large snook and tarpon in the rivers and manatees in the estuaries. Two Barranco natives deeply involved in both local tourism and park conservation are **Egbert Valencio** (☑ 626-7684; egbertvalencio@yahoo.com) and **Alvin Loredo** (☑ 604-8564; alvinloredo@yahoo.com); both lead land and river tours into the nearby park, and will both be glad to help arrange tours for groups and individuals, as long as they're given a few days' notice.

Other activities available at Barranco include **drumming** and **dory building** (a dory is a traditional Belizean canoe).

Sleeping & Eating

Back-a-bush   HOSTEL $
(☑ 631-1731; www.back-a-bush.com; dm BZ$25, d per person BZ$30, meals BZ$12-15) In the village of San Miguel just a few miles from Lubaantun sits this simple chilled-out jungle guesthouse and farm, owned and operated by Naud and Elsbeth Brouwer, two transplanted Dutch farmers. Accommodations are rustic but peaceful, and guests can enjoy meals made with cacao, coffee and vegetables grown on the farm itself.

TRAVEL WITH TEA

A unique opportunity to be welcomed into local villages and experience village life firsthand is provided by the **Toledo Ecotourism Association** (☑ 722-2531; btiatoledo@btl.net). TEA is a community organization that manages guesthouses in several picturesque Maya villages, offering travelers the chance to really get to know the families and faces that make up the area. Through TEA, travelers can arrange to explore these villages, living in local guesthouses, taking meals with Maya families and participating in a variety of local activities. The villages are gorgeous – simple, neat, clean, surrounded by lovely scenery and usually with a river or stream at their heart – and the villagers friendly without being overly so. Around the villages are waterfalls, caves and ancient Maya ruins that are best experienced with a local guide. Currently, villages with TEA guesthouses include San Jose, Santa Elena, San Antonio, Laguna, San Miguel and Medina Bank.

Rates for all guesthouse stays are BZ$22 per person per day. In addition to housing, meals prepared in local families' homes are available for around BZ$8 each. Main meals usually consist of tortillas and *caldo*, a stew made from root vegetables and meat, usually chicken. If you're vegetarian, be sure to specify this clearly and in advance.

Most of the funds collected through the programs go directly to the villages themselves. Activity options range from guided hikes, caving, canoeing and bird-watching to classes in textiles, basket weaving or cooking, or village tours and after-dinner storytelling. Most of these cost around BZ$8 per person per hour. Performances of traditional dance and music (using the harp in Kekchi villages, marimba among the Mopan) can also be arranged.

To get specific contact information for key people in individual villages, stop by Nature's Way Guest House (p217), who can arrange stays and provide information on ways to get to the villages themselves, all of which have regular (but not always daily) buses.

Check out www.teabelize.org for more information about the TEA program.

Sun Creek Lodge RESORT $$
(☏604-2124; www.suncreeklodge.com; cabañas from BZ$80, villas from BZ$160) Situated close to the village of San Marcos, this tropical garden lodge consists of four individual thatched-roof *cabañas* and one beautifully appointed one-bedroom villa. Accommodations are a comfortable blend of modern and rustic, with more expensive *cabañas* having bathrooms with hot showers. All of Sun Creek's dwellings are made of (and furnished with) dark tropical hardwoods; splashes of color coming from Maya-print curtains and bed linens are a lovely touch. Sun Creek owner Bruno Kuppinger also runs Toledo Cave and Adventure Tours (p217), which does a variety of treks and tours throughout the area.

★ **Belcampo Belize** LODGE $$$
(☏722-0050; www.belcampobz.com; ste BZ$660-1050 incl breakfast; ✳🏠🛜♨️🛗) ✎ Formerly Machaca Hill Lodge, the fabulous Belcampo Belize enjoys a superb hilltop setting overlooking miles of protected jungle stretching to the Gulf of Honduras. This lodge offers luxurious accommodations (while leaving only a light ecological footprint). The 12 beautiful rooms boast solid wood furniture, ceramic-lined bathrooms (fed with rain-water catchment systems), two queen-size beds and verandas overlooking jungle and sea. Further enhancing the lodge's eco-friendly bona fides, a good proportion of the food served in the dining room comes from its own organic farm, which produces fruits and vegetables, chicken, eggs, cacao, vanilla and jungle spices.

ℹ️ RURAL TRAVEL ON THE FLY

While tourism in rural Toledo is picking up, aside from the TEA program (p227) and a few independent hotels and fancy eco-lodges, there aren't many hotels in the Deep South. This doesn't mean you'll wind up sleeping in the jungle (although that can be arranged), it just means that outside swanky jungle lodges you'll have to look a bit harder to find a bed. If you end up in one of the villages without making prior arrangements, your best bet is to ask at the village candy store. Someone will generally find you a place to bunk. Nearly every village has at least one bar and restaurant (sometimes called 'cool spots'). These don't always have signs, so you may need to ask.

Activities include hiking, mountain-biking on Belcampo's fleet of high-quality fat-tire fliers, bird-watching, kayaking, fishing and more. Organized events include Garifuna drumming and Maya musical performances. Different vacation packages are available, all of which include room, airport transfer and breakfast, and a variety of add-on activities available. The lodge is 2.4 miles off the Southern Hwy, from a turnoff 3 miles out of PG.

Belcampo also offers a culinary course utilizing fruits, vegetables and meats from the resort's own organic farm and pasture. Its fantastic restaurant, serving farm-fresh meals, is open to the public, though reservations are requested. Dinner menu changes nightly, breakfast and lunch are set.

Lodge at Big Falls RESORT $$$
(☏610-0126, 732-4444; www.thelodgeatbigfalls.com; s/d/tr incl full breakfast BZ$320/460/530; 🅿️@🛜♨️🛗) At the village of Big Falls, on a loop of the jungle-clad Rio Grande, 18 miles from Punta Gorda, sits Lodge at Big Falls, where tiled-floor, palm-thatched cabins are spread about beautifully tended gardens. Popular with bird-watchers (and rightly so, as over 300 species have been spotted here) and butterfly enthusiasts, the lodge is also a fine place from which to enjoy a host of activities, from snorkeling in the southern cayes to caving, kayaking and river-tubing. It's a good base for excursions into the wilds of southern Belize, too. Activities at the lodge include kayaking, river tubing, disc throwing on one of Belize's finest frisbee lawns, and badminton. Meticulously maintained by owners Rob and Marta Hirons, the Lodge at Big Falls is an island of Anglo-American calm in the jungles of southern Belize. The lodge also has a fine restaurant serving meals from between BZ$22 and BZ$70. Transfers to or from PG are BZ$100 for up to four people.

Cotton Tree Lodge RESORT $$$
(☏670-0557, in USA 866-480-4534; www.cottontreelodge.com; luxury cabins incl meals & tours from BZ$400, student group discounts available; 🅿️✳@🛜♨️) ✎ Luxury, environmentalism and intense beauty meet a few miles north of the village of San Felipe and 10 miles from PG at Cotton Tree Lodge. The 100-acre property offers amazing views of the nearby Maya Mountain Range on the western horizon. All of Cotton Tree's 11 thatched-roof cabins are luxuriously furnished in a superb jungle/hardwood motif, and all (including

the remote 'jungle cabin,' nearly 0.25 miles away) are connected to the main restaurant-bar area via a network of elevated wooden boardwalks that spans the entire property. The resort's power is partially provided by 15 solar panels, and plans are in the works to commit even further to alternative energy. Most of the food served in the lodge's excellent restaurant is bought locally, with some of the vegetables coming from the on-site organic garden. Activities include hiking, horseback riding, kayaking, canoeing, caving and bird-watching.

Tranquility Lodge RESORT $$$
(📞 665-9070, 677-9921, in USA 800-819-9088; www.tranquility-lodge.com; cabañas BZ$230, r incl breakfast BZ$270; P❄🛜🍴) The Tranquility Lodge is 8 miles from PG just off the road to Barranco and offers three thatched-roof *cabañas* and four lodge rooms set amid pretty gardens and jungle. Rooms are equipped with air-con and flat screen televisions. The *cabañas* are big, breezy, fan-cooled and TV-free. All have hot showers and iPod docking stations. Prices are based on double occupancy, with an extra charge of BZ$40 for additional guests (children under 12 are free), and come with breakfast. There's a regulation pool table and a shuffleboard deck in the lodge, not to mention an excellent swimming hole on the property. Transfers from PG are available for BZ$40.

👉 Tours

Cyrila's Maya Belizean Chocolate TOUR
(http://www.cyrilaschocolate.org; San Felipe Village; ⊙ 9am-5pm; 🍴) 🌿 Love chocolate? Visit Juan and Abelina's beautiful cacao farm and chocolate factory in the Maya village of San Felipe, where the gregarious Juan will walk you through the traditional chocolate making process – from harvest and fermentation to drying and roasting, to deshalling and grinding. Visitors do not merely experience the process, they get to taste it at every step along the way. Tours are held daily, and the couple will also cook traditional Mayan lunches of corn tortilla, vegetable rice, chocolate chicken, salads made from organic vegetables for the farm and, yes, hot chocolate. Day tours are BZ$60, and include lunch, tours, chocolate making and more. Drop-in visitors are welcome, and can experience just the chocolate making for BZ$20, with lunches available for a separate charge of BZ$10.

The family who runs Cyrila's also has a small homestay bunkhouse next to the fac-

tory with two double rooms and two sets of single bunk beds; student groups often live here, but travelers are also welcome to stay for a nominal charge of BZ$40, which includes breakfast and dinner. Students who are volunteering on the farm can stay for BZ$40, including all meals and chocolate-making activities.

ℹ Getting There & Around

Any northern-bound bus leaving PG will drop you off at the Dump or Lubaantun intersections, from where people often hitchhike to many of the villages listed.

One daily bus leaves Punta Gorda at 6am, stopping at the villages of Eldridge, Dump, Mafredi, San Antonio, Santa Cruz, Santa Elena and Pueblo Viejo before reaching Jalacte. On Monday, Wednesday, Friday and Saturday there is a second Jalacte bus leaving at 11:30am. The return bus leaves Jalacte at 3am, getting to PG at 5:30am.

The Barranco bus leaves at noon on Monday, Wednesday, Friday and Saturday, returning from Barranco at 6am the next day. Another goes to San Jose at 11:30am and again at noon, leaving San Jose at 4pm and 5pm.

To get to Lubaantun, take the 11am bus to Columbia or the 11:30am bus to Silver Creek. Return buses pass through Silver Creek at 4pm.

Schedules fluctuate; stop by the BTB office in Punta Gorda for the latest (they can also help arrange meals and housing). Village buses cost between BZ$2 and BZ$6 (depending on distance). All village buses leave from Jose Maria Nunez St, in Punta Gorda (just north of Tate's Guest House).

THE ROAD AHEAD

Southern Belize may soon have a legal border crossing with Guatemala; as this book goes to print, the eight-million dollar road connecting the two countries through the still-remote towns of Southern Toledo was underway, with asphalt being laid as far out as San Antonio. When completed, the 23-mile road should link the Southern Highway with the once remote villages of Mafredi, San Antonio, Santa Cruz, Santa Elena, Pueblo Viejo and Jalacte.

While impossible to say what changes the road will bring to these communities, one thing is certain: the Deep South's days as a quiet, dead-end backwater are numbered.

Tikal & Flores, Guatemala

Includes ➡

Best Places to Eat

➡ Sugar Sap (p241), El Remate

➡ Las Orquideas (p242), El Remate

Best Places to Stay

➡ Tikal Inn (p236), Tikal

➡ Gucumatz (p242), Lago de Petén Itzá

➡ Gran Hotel de la Isla (p246), Flores

Why Go?

The glory and splendors of the ancient Maya world await you, just over the border in the lush rainforests of Eastern Guatemala. The region is especially important to the Maya people, being home to many temples, pyramids and ruins with significance to the alignment of 12/21/2012, which recently completed a major cycle of the Maya calendar and began another.

The most fabled (and easiest to reach) of Guatemala's slice of La Ruta Maya is Tikal. Larger and more completely restored than any of the Maya sites in Belize, Tikal offers visitors the unique opportunity to spend the night at the ruins, waking up in the middle of the jungle, thanks to its in-park campground and lodges. Alternatively, the nearby lakeside villages of Flores and El Remate are peaceful, picturesque places to recover from some intensive archaeological exploration.

When to Go

From January to March, few bugs and little rain make for optimum jungle travel conditions. The Unificación Maya Festival takes place at Maya sites throughout the area in December.

ⓘ Getting There & Around

AIR

Belizean Carrier **Tropic Air** (☑ Belize 226-2012, in USA 800-422-3435; www.tropicair.com; one-way/return BZ$230/450) has two daily flights between Belize City International and Flores, Guatemala. The flight takes close to 60 minutes, but leave time for customs and immigration proceedings on both sides.

BUS

Independent adventurers can take a direct express bus to Flores from Belize City or San Ignacio. Alternatively, local buses go from these cities to Benque Viejo del Carmen, in Belize, where you can get a taxi for the 2 miles to the border.

Melchor de Mencos is the village on the Guatemalan side of the border. From here, you can catch a *colectivo* (a shared minibus) to Santa Elena; from there you can hop in a taxi or walk to Flores. The road is now fully paved. If you choose to go to El Remate first, the driver will let you off at the Puente Ixlú (also called El Cruce) junction, from which it's a half-mile walk into town. From El Remate, you can catch a taxi or *colectivo* 22 miles further to Tikal.

Linea Dorada (☑ Belize City 223-2225, Guatemala 7924-8535; www.lineadorada.com.gt) runs daily buses between Flores and Belize City.

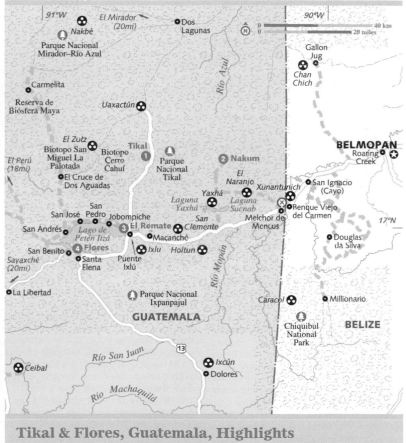

Tikal & Flores, Guatemala, Highlights

❶ Climbing Temple IV for a 360-degree view of the jungle-shrouded ruins in **Tikal** (p232)

❷ Camping at night in the ancient, seldom-visited city of **Nakum** (p237)

❸ Watching the sun set over Lago de Petén Itzá in **El Remate** (p238)

❹ Wandering the cobblestone streets of **Flores** (p243)

❶ TRANSITIONING: BELIZE TO GUATEMALA

Language

Spanish is the main language in Guatemala. Most Tikal tour guides speak English, as do the staff of some upscale hotels. But most hotel and restaurant employees, bus drivers, taxi drivers and other people on the street are unlikely to speak English, so brush up on your Spanish before arriving. For all your language needs in Guatemala, pick up a copy of Lonely Planet's Latin American Spanish phrasebook.

Money

The unit of currency in Guatemala is the quetzal (Q). Moneychangers hang around the border, but there are no ATMs or banks on either side. The nearest ATMs are in Santa Elena and Flores. US dollars are widely accepted.

Visas & Fees

First, the good news: citizens of the USA, Canada, EU countries, Norway, Switzerland, Australia, New Zealand, Israel, Iceland, South Africa and Japan are among those who do not currently need visas to visit Guatemala. (Regulations can change, so check with your travel agent or a Guatemalan embassy or consulate before your trip.)

Now, the bad: there's a BZ$37.50 departure tax when you leave Belize, and even if you're only going to Tikal for the day, you'll have to pay it. Belizean and US dollars are both accepted. And on the way back, Guatemala will expect their cut; there's a Q250 departure tax if you're flying and a mere Q20 if leaving by land.

Tikal

Towering pyramids pierce the jungle's green canopy and catch the sun. Howler monkeys swing noisily through the trees, as brightly colored birds dart from perch to perch amid a cacophony of squawks. The region's most significant Maya site – both historically and spatially – is contained within the jungles of **Tikal National Park** (☑ 2367-2837; www.tikalpark.com; admission Q150; ☉ 6am-6pm), a Unesco World Heritage site. While the park's 222 sq miles contain thousands of structures, it's estimated that only 7% of the original buildings have been excavated. As for the remaining 93% of this city (which once rivaled Rome in size and population), well...it still lies beneath a millennium's worth of soil, vines and trees. Six majestic temples – some reaching heights over 200ft – have been partially restored. Hundreds of other structures lie in various states of deterioration, giving visitors an impression of the grand civilization that existed here over a thousand years ago.

Although Tikal National Park is spread over a vast area, the part that has been excavated occupies only about 10 sq miles. This central area is located about 12 miles north of the park entrance.

Your bus will bring you all the way to the parking lot near the central excavated site, which is where you pay the entrance fee. If you want to visit outside normal opening hours, you can get a sunrise or sunset ticket for Q100. Multilingual guides are available at the nearby visitors center (per half day for up to five people Q390). There is also a museum in the visitors center.

For more complete information on the monuments at Tikal, pick up a copy of *Tikal – A Handbook of the Ancient Maya Ruins,* by William R Coe, available at Tikal and in Flores.

❍ Sights & Activities

Gran Plaza   HISTORIC SITE
The path leading to the plaza goes around **Templo I**, the Templo del Gran Jaguar (Temple of the Great Jaguar), built to honor – and bury – Lord Chocolate, or King Moon Double Comb. The king's rich burial goods included 16lb of jewelry, 180 jade objects and 90 bits of bone carved with hieroglyphs. Archaeologists also found stingray spines, which were used for ritual bloodletting.

At the top of the 144ft temple is a small enclosure of three rooms that is covered by a corbeled arch. The lofty roof comb (ornamental structure) that crowned the temple was originally adorned with reliefs and bright paint, and may have symbolized the 13 realms of the Maya heaven.

Since at least two people tumbled to their deaths, the stairs up Templo I have been closed. But the views from Templo II just across the way are nearly as awe-inspiring. Templo II was once almost as high as Templo I, but now measures 124ft without its roof comb.

The **Acrópolis del Norte** (North Acropolis), while not as impressive as the two temples, is of great significance. Archaeologists have uncovered about 100 structures, with evidence of occupation as far back as 400 BC. The Maya rebuilt on top of older structures, and the many layers, combined with the elaborate burials, added sanctity and power to their temples. Look for the two huge, powerful wall masks. The final version of the acropolis, as it stood around AD 800, had more than 12 temples atop a vast platform.

Acrópolis Central   HISTORIC SITE
On the southeast side of the Gran Plaza, this maze of courtyards, little rooms and small temples is thought by some to have been a residential palace for Tikal's nobility. Others believe the tiny rooms may have been used for sacred rites.

Plaza Oeste   HISTORIC SITE
North of Templo II is Plaza Oeste (West Plaza). To its north is a late Classic temple. To the south, across the Calzada Tozzer (Tozzer Causeway), is **Templo III**, which is 181ft high and yet to be uncovered. Calzada Tozzer, the causeway leading to Templo IV, was one of several sacred ways built among the complexes for astronomical and aesthetic reasons.

Acrópolis del Sur & Templo V   HISTORIC SITE
Excavation is ongoing at Acrópolis del Sur (South Acropolis), a 5-acre mass of masonry south of the Gran Plaza. The palaces on top are from late Classic times, but earlier constructions probably go back a thousand years.

East of the Acrópolis del Sur, Templo V is 190ft high and was built around AD 700. Unlike the other great temples, it has rounded corners and one tiny room at the top, less than 3ft deep, but with walls up to 14ft thick. Restoration of this temple took from 1996 to 2003. The temple is currently in a state of partial excavation, with one half remaining little more than an earthen hill, offering an excellent illustration of what may lie beneath Tikal's yet-unexcavated 93%.

A wooden stairway (not for the fainthearted) leads to the top, offering excellent views.

Plaza de los Siete Templos   HISTORIC SITE
Located on the other side of the Acrópolis del Sur is the Plaza de los Siete Templos (Plaza of the Seven Temples). The little temples, which are clustered together, were built in late Classic times. Note the skull and crossbones on the central temple. On the plaza's northern side is an unusual triple ballcourt; another, larger version in the same design stands just south of Templo I.

El Mundo Perdido   HISTORIC SITE
About a quarter-mile southwest of the Gran Plaza is El Mundo Perdido (The Lost World), a complex of 38 structures surrounding a huge pyramid. Unlike the rest of Tikal, where late Classic construction overlays earlier work, El Mundo Perdido holds buildings of many different periods. The **large pyramid** is thought to be Preclassic, with some later repairs and renovations, the **Templo del Talud-Tablero** (Temple of the Three Rooms) is an early Classic structure, and the **Templo de las Calaveras** (Temple of the Skulls) is late Classic.

The pyramid, 105ft high and 262ft along its base, had huge masks that flanked each stairway but no temple structure at the top. Each side of the pyramid displays a slightly different architectural style. Tunnels dug by archaeologists reveal four similar pyramids beneath the outer face; the earliest (Structure 5C-54 Sub 2B) dates from around 700 BC, making the pyramid the oldest Maya structure in Tikal.

Templo IV & Complejo N   HISTORIC SITE
Standing at 210ft, Templo IV is the highest building at Tikal. It was completed by about 741, in the reign of King Moon Double Comb's son. From the base it looks like a precipitous little hill. A series of steep wooden steps and ladders takes you to the top for a panoramic view across the jungle canopy. If you stay up here for the sunset, climb down immediately, as it gets dark quickly.

Complejo N (Complex N), near Templo IV, is an example of the 'twin-temple' complexes popular in the late Classic Period. These complexes are thought to have commemorated the completion of a *katun* (20-year cycle) in the Maya calendar. This one was built in 711 by King Moon Double Comb to mark the 14th *katun* of Baktun 9. (A *baktun* – 144,000 days, about 394 years – consisted of 20 *katun*.) The king is portrayed on Stela 16, one of Tikal's finest stelae (stone shafts).

Templo de las Inscripciones (Templo VI)   TEMPLE
Compared to Copán or Quiriguá, there are relatively few inscriptions on buildings at

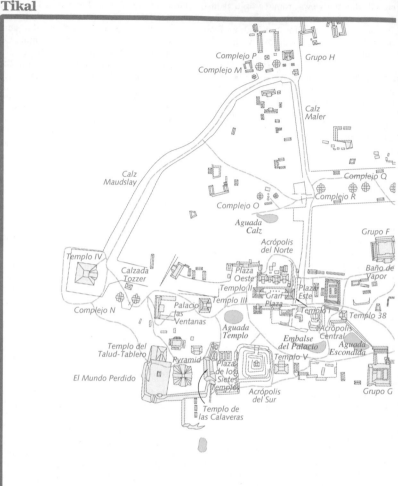

Tikal. The exception is this temple, 1.2km southeast of the Gran Plaza. On the rear of the 12m-high roofcomb is a long inscription; the sides and cornice of the roofcomb bear glyphs as well. The inscriptions give us the date AD 766. Stele 21 and Altar 9, standing before the temple, date from 736. The stele had been badly damaged (part of it was converted into a *metate*, a stone for grinding corn!) but has now been repaired.

Museo Lítico
MUSEUM

(Stone Museum; admission, also valid for Museo Tikal, Q10; ☺9am-noon & 1-4:30pm) The larger of Tikal's two musuems is in the visitor center. It houses a number of stelae and carved stones from the ruins. Outside is a large model showing how Tikal would have looked around AD 800. The photographs taken by Alfred P Maudslay and Teobert Maler of the jungle-covered temples in various stages of discovery, in the late 19th century, are particularly striking.

Museo Tikal
MUSEUM

(free with ticket from Museo Lítico; ☺9am-5pm Mon-Fri, 9am-4pm Sat & Sun) This museum offers some fascinating exhibits, including artifacts from the tomb of Lord Chocolate.

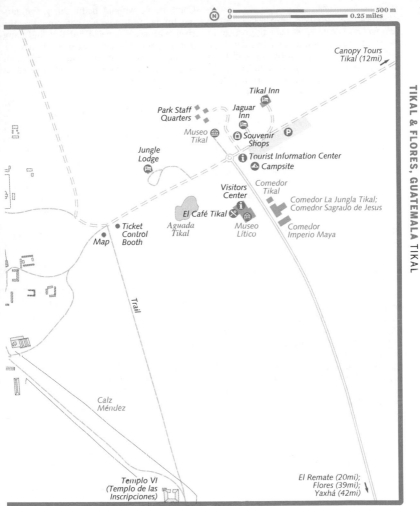

☞ Tours

One-day tours to Tikal from Flores cost between Q300 and Q500. As a general rule of thumb, the more expensive the tour, the smaller the group will be. Taking an overnight tour is one of the easiest ways to get a reservation at a hotel in the park. Recommended tour operators include:

Roxy Ortiz   TOURS
(☎ 5197-5173; tikalroxy.blogspot.com) If it's a personalized, knowledgeable guide you're after, look no further. Archaeologist Roxy Ortiz has 35 years experience trekking throughout the Maya world and does early-morning tours around Tikal. She also does personalized treks to Uaxactún, Yaxhá and other less-visited sites with her 15-seat military vehicle.

Martsam Travel   TRAVEL AGENCY
(Map p244; ☎ 7867-5377; www.martsam.com; Calle 30 de Junio, Flores) Works with Comités Comunitarios de Ecoturismo (Community Ecotourism Committees), which employ local guides from jungle communities, in the villages of El Cruce de Dos Aguadas and Carmelita.

Turismo Aventura RUIN
(Map p249; 7926-0398; www.toursguatemala.com; 6a Ave) Located just over the bridge in Santa Elena. Offers one- and two-day trips to Tikal, as well as a boat trip around Lago de Petén Itzá. Single-day tours start at Q350. Prices for overnight trips range from Q2100 to Q2800 including hotel and transfer.

Canopy Tours Tikal ADVENTURE
(5819-7766; www.canopytikal.com; admission Q235; 8am-5pm) By the national park entrance, this outfit offers a one-hour tour through the forest canopy, with the chance to ride a harness along a series of cables linking trees up to 300m apart and several hanging bridges. The fee includes transport from Tikal or El Remate.

🛌 Sleeping & Eating

The three hotels at Tikal are often booked in advance by groups, but staying here allows you to savor the dawn and dusk, when the jungle fauna is most active. Book ahead, especially in summer and between Christmas and Easter. All three hotels have their own restaurants. The hotels and campsites all depend on generators for electricity and hot water, which are available at set hours.

By the entrance road, an official **camp-site** (tent space per person Q15, tents for rent Q60) is set in a large, open lawn with some shady trees. You can hang your hammock under a *palapa* (thatched-roof shelter) here, too.

As you arrive at Tikal, you'll see the little **comedores** (meals Q40-60; breakfast, lunch & dinner) on the right-hand side of the road. These places offer rustic and agreeable surroundings and huge plates of tasty food, including burgers, pasta and hot chicken and meat dishes.

★**Tikal Inn** HOTEL $$
(7861-2444; www.tikalinn.com; s/d Q395/470, bungalow Q470/590;) Built in the late '60s, this resort-style lodging offers rooms in the main building and thatched bungalows alongside the pool and rear lawn, with little porches out front. All are simple, spacious and quite comfortable. The most secluded accommodations are the least expensive, in a handful of cabins at the end of a sawdust trail through the forest.

Jaguar Inn HOTEL $$$
(Map p249; 7926-0002; www.jaguartikal.com; camping own/rented tent Q25/80, s/d bungalows Q395/590; restaurant mains Q60-80;)

Comfortable without being fancy, the Jaguar Inn is inside a secure compound by the river, with wood-paneled, faded rooms along a leafy patio. It's a decent deal, though its out-of-the-way location, 150m off the main road near the airport, may only appeal to travelers with vehicles.

Jungle Lodge HOTEL $$$
(2477-0570; www.junglelodgetikal.com; s/d Q622/772, without bathroom Q298/338;) The largest and loveliest of the hotels was originally built to house archaeologists working at Tikal. Self-contained bungalows are well spaced throughout rambling, jungly grounds where ocellated turkeys and agoutis roam. The restaurant-bar is the classiest around these parts, serving veggie pastas, crepes, pepper steak and other international dishes in a tropical ambience (main dishes Q80 to Q100).

Restaurante El Café Tikal RESTAURANT $
(visitors center; mains Q60-80) Enjoy table service amid the hum of the generator. Picnic tables beneath shelters are located just off Tikal's Gran Plaza, with soft drink and water peddlers standing by.

ℹ Information

Near the visitors center are Tikal's hotels, a camping area, a **tourist information center** (8am-4pm), a few small *comedores* (eateries) and another museum. From the visitors center, a network of trails leads around the ruins, past the massive ceiba tree, the national tree of Guatemala. It's about a 1-mile walk southwest to the Gran Plaza. To visit all the major building complexes, you must walk at least 6 miles, so wear comfortable shoes with good rubber treads, as the ruins can be very slick. Bring plenty of water, sunblock and insect repellent.

ℹ Getting There & Away

Plenty of travelers do Tikal as a day trip from Belize, though if you're going to do this it's best to join one of the tour groups advertising such trips in Cayo. Shuttles to Belize advertised at Tikal may detour to Flores to pick up passengers. The **Jaguar Inn** (7926-0002; www.jaguartikal.com; campsite per person Q25, with tent Q80, s/d Q395/590;) has a colectivo bus going to the Belize border at 7am daily (Q275).

Microbuses by Agencia Exploradores de la Cultura Maya depart from Flores (Q50, 1¼ hours, 62km) at 5am,7am, 9am and 1pm, returning at noon, 1:30pm, 3pm and 6pm. You could also take the Uaxactún-bound bus (Q35) at 2pm, which goes a bit slower. **Autobuses del Norte**

(☑ 7924-8131; www.adnautobusesdelnorte. com) provides Pullman service at 6am and 8am (Q80). A taxi from Flores airport to Tikal costs about Q400.

Yaxhá

High upon a hill, overlooking the twin lakes of Laguna Yaxhá and Laguna Sacnab, this late Classic Maya site (admission Q80; ⊘ 7am-5pm) is the third-largest in Guatemala. Yaxhá translates as 'green water', likely in reference to its lakeside location. (By the way, don't be tempted to swim in the lakes – the crocs will get you!) During its heyday in the 8th century, Yaxhá was home to a population of 20,000. Its 400-plus structures included five acropolises, two astronomical observatories and three ballcourts.

These days, excavations are ongoing. It still takes at least a couple of hours to look around the main groups of ruins. The high point (literally), towering above all else, is Templo 216 in the Acrópolis Este (Eastern Acrópolis), which affords magnificent views in every direction.

On an island near the south shore of La guna Yaxhá is a separate, Postclassic archaeological site, Topoxté. The dense covering of ruined temples and dwellings may date back to the Itzá, the pre-Columbian civilization that occupied Flores island.

About 17 miles north of Yaxhá, Nakum is an old river port on the Holmul River. You'll need a 4WD to get there, but once you make it, you can observe the ongoing archaeological excavation. Nakum is a spectacular place to spend the night, though you'll want to make arrangements in advance and bring your own camping gear. The admission price to Yaxhá includes all three sites.

If you have a hankering to stay near the lesser explored, more mysterious site at Yaxhá, book a room at El Sombrero Eco Lodge (☑ 4147-6380; s/d with shared bathroom Q165/370, s/d with private bathroom Q330/430; ℗). On the southern shore of the pristine Laguna Yaxhá, the lodge has thatched-roof bungalows with breezy views from the shaded porches. The on-site restaurant is excellent – important information if you are coming on a day trip. El Sombrero offers boat tours to Topoxté and horseback-riding trips to Nakum.

❶ Getting There & Away

Halfway between Puente Ixlú and Melchor de Mencos, Yaxhá is 7 miles north of the main road. The access road can get rough in the rainy season. A taxi from Flores will be about Q500, and about Q400 from El Remate. Check with tour companies in Flores or El Remate to find out about organized tours.

Uaxactún

Uaxactún (wah-shahk-toon), 14 miles north of Tikal along an unpaved road through the jungle, was Tikal's political and military rival in late Preclassic times. It was conquered by Tikal's Chak Toh Ich'ak I (King Great Jaguar Paw) in the 4th century, and was subservient to its great sister to the south for centuries thereafter. Uaxactún village lies either side of an unused airstrip, which now serves as pasture and a football field.

The pyramids at Uaxactún were uncovered and stabilized so that no further deterioration would result, but they were not restored. White mortar is the mark of the repair crews, who patched cracks in the stone to prevent water and roots from entering. Head south from the airstrip to reach Grupo E, a 10- to 15-minute walk. Perhaps the most significant temple here is E-VII-Sub, among the earliest intact temples excavated, with

---

TIKAL SUNRISE, TIKAL SUNSET

Though they still draw a fair number of travelers, not everyone who goes on the Tikal 'sunrise tour' (which leaves Flores around 4am in order to arrive in time to watch the sunrise from Temple IV) finds it worth the early wake-up. The jungle is indeed most alive (and the park least crowded) at dawn, but on most mornings the jungle mists don't lift until well after dawn, making for a bit of a muted sunrise. Still, if you'd like to come yourself, joining a tour isn't necessary; public transportation starts at 5am and the park opens at 6am.

More to the liking of many (especially those who prefer sleeping in) is the Tikal sunset experience. Visitors can watch the sun go down from the top of Temple IV (a spectacular sight almost any day) before retiring to one of the park's hotels or campgrounds.

Tickets for sunrise or sunset cost Q100 and are in addition to the park entrance fee.

foundations going back perhaps to 2000 BC. On its flat top are holes, or sockets, for the poles that would have supported a wood-and-thatch temple. The pyramid is part of a group with astronomical significance: seen from the pyramid, the sun rises behind Templo E-I on the longest day of the year and behind Templo E-III on the shortest day. Also, look for the somewhat deteriorated jaguar and serpent masks on this pyramid's sides.

About a 20-minute walk to the northwest of the runway are **Grupo B** and **Grupo A**. Some unfortunate early excavation work at Grupo A destroyed many of the temples, which are now in the process of being reconstructed.

If you are visiting Uaxactún from Tikal, there is no fee. But if you are going to Uaxactún without stopping to visit Tikal, you still have to pass through the Parque Nacional Tikal and will have to pay a Q10 fee at the park entrance. Tours to Uaxactún can be arranged in Flores or at the hotels in Tikal.

You can spend the night near Uaxactún at **Aldana's Lodge** (campsite per person Q20, r per person Q25) or **Campamento, Hotel & Restaurante El Chiclero** (7926-1095; campamentochiclero@gmail.com; campsites per person Q25, r per person Q50), both of which are very simple.

❶ Getting There & Away

A bus leaves Santa Elena for Uaxactún (Q25) at 1pm daily, passing through Tikal about 3pm to 3:30pm, and starting back for Santa Elena from Uaxactún at 6am the following day. Its schedule is rubbery though and it can arrive in Tikal any time up to about 5pm and in Uaxactún up to about 6:30pm. During the rainy season (from May to October, sometimes extending into November), the road from Tikal to Uaxactún can become pretty muddy: locals say it is always passable but a 4WD vehicle might be needed.

El Remate

POP 2000

Quaint and beautiful, the village of El Remate wraps lazily around the northeastern corner of Lago de Petén Itzá. Eighteen miles south of Tikal, the village is ideally located for those looking to explore Guatemala's most famous Maya site. It's also close enough to other ruin sites to make it a viable base for exploration of the area's wealth of treasures, both natural and historic. Even if you've come to the region for reasons other than exploration of the ancient Maya world,

you'll still find plenty of things about El Remate to love. For starters, the town itself is quite pretty, and the sight of the sun setting over the lake while horses graze the banks will leave lasting impressions. The lake itself is also an ideal location for bicycling, canoeing and kayaking, the gear for all of which is easily rented in town.

El Remate begins about half a mile beyond Puente Ixlú (also called El Cruce), which is the village where the road to the Belize border diverges from the Tikal road. The town is strung along the Tikal road, also known as Main Rd, for a half mile to another junction, where an unpaved road branches west along the north shore of Lago de Petén Itzá to the Biotopo Cerro Cahuí and beyond. Called the Jobompiche (*Ho mom biche*) road as well, this road continues all the way to the villages of San José and San Andrés near the west end of the lake, making it possible to go all the way around the lake by road. The road is rough (even by local standards) but worth exploring. Several more places to stay and eat can be found dotted along the way.

🏃 Activities

Hiking & Nature Walks

Biotopo Cerro Cahuí NATURE RESERVE
(admission Q40; 7am-4pm) The entrance to this 6.5-sq-km subtropical forest reserve is 1.75km west along the north-shore road from El Remate. The vegetation here ranges from *guamil* (regenerating slash-and-burn land) to rainforest. Trees include mahogany, cedar, ramón, broom, sapodilla (the extremely hard wood used in Maya temple door lintels) and cohune palm, along with many types of bromeliads, ferns and orchids.

More than 20 species of mammal roam the reserve, including spider and howler monkeys, ocelots, white-tailed deer, raccoons and armadillos. Bird life, as well, is rich and varied. Depending on the season and migration patterns, you might see kingfishers, ducks, herons, hawks, parrots, toucans, woodpeckers and the famous ocellated (or Petén) turkey, a big bird resembling a peacock.

A network of loop trails starts at the road and goes up the hill, affording a view of the whole lake and of Laguna Salpetén to the east. The trail called Los Escobos (4km long – it takes about 2¼ hours), through secondary growth forest, is good for spotting monkeys. The guards at the entrance can give you directions.

DON'T MISS

DEEPER STILL INTO THE MAYA WORLD

Though the most visited, Tikal and Yaxhá are far from El Petén's only Maya sites. Indeed, the entire area is so rich with history that any hill you see could well be a temple, pyramid or other ancient structure awaiting discovery. Some of the area's sites sit behind (in some cases, beneath) present-day villages close to major roads. Others are beyond the reach of anyone without a military-caliber vehicle, helicopter or several days to trek. If you've got the time and the passion for serious exploration, consider checking out these off-the-beaten-track ruins.

➡ **Sayaxché** On the south bank of the Río de la Pasión, 38 miles southwest of Flores, this is the closest town to nine or 10 scattered Maya archaeological sites, including Ceibal, Aguateca, Dos Pilas, Tamarindito and Altar de Sacrificios.

➡ **El Perú** In the Parque Nacional Laguna del Tigre, 39 miles northwest of Flores. These trips are termed La Ruta Guacamaya (the Scarlet Macaw Trail) as the chances of seeing these magnificent birds are high, chiefly during their February-to-June nesting season.

➡ **El Mirador** (www.miradorbasin.com) Archaeologists believe that the Preclassical-era city of El Mirador flourished from about the 6th through the 1st centuries BC, making it a far older city than Tikal; it was as large as Tikal though. At 230ft from forest floor to top, El Mirador's La Danta temple is among the largest pyramids in the world. The city's extremely remote location (without a helicopter the full return trek takes around six days) makes it almost unknown to tourists.

➡ **San Clemente** Less than an hour out of El Remate and relatively close to the Melchor/Flores road, this small site has three excavated pyramids and an excavated central courtyard. There's no admission fee, but a guide may be necessary to help you find the site.

Three guides who specialize in trips to these out-of-the-way ruins are:

➡ **Roxy Ortiz** (p235) In addition to leading tours around Tikal, Roxy also does longer personalized treks to Uaxactún, Yaxhá and other less-visited sites with her 15-seat military vehicle, as well as helicopter trips to Mirador. An archaeologist with 35 years of experience, she can also provide information on just about any Maya site in the area.

➡ **Ramon Puga** (☑ 3110-0730; ramonremate@yahoo.com) When not helping to run Sugar Sap cafe in El Remate, archaeologist Ramon Puga assists interested and motivated visitors to explore the ancient Maya world.

➡ **Mayan Adventure** (Map p244; ☑ 5830-2060; www.the-mayan-adventure.com; Calle 15 de Septiembre, Flores) Coordinated by a German Mayanologist, it offers 'scientific' tours to sites currently under excavation, with commentary by archaeologists working at the sites.

The admission fee includes the right to camp or sling your hammock under small thatch shelters inside the entrance. There are toilets and showers.

The dock opposite the entrance is the best place to swim along the generally muddy shore of the lake.

Horseback Riding

Horses have always been an important part of life in rural Guatemala, and equestrians will find the sight of dozens of horses wandering and grazing along the shores of Lago de Petén Itzá and around El Remate particularly inspiring. We'd advise against hopping on random horses, however, as some of El Remate's horses (or so we're told) are feral (literally, as in, unbroken and unowned). But there are

opportunities to ride. Schnoken Jungle Tours (p242) can arrange trail rides and horse rentals with locals. Hotel Palomio Ranch (p240) offers free rides on their property for guests and also does longer guided trail rides.

🛏 Sleeping

Accommodations are either on the main road (that is, the road to Tikal) or on unpaved Jobompiche Rd, which winds along the lake's northern edge.

Hotel Sun Breeze HOTEL $
(☑ 7928-8044; sunbreezehotel@sunbreeze.net; Main Rd; s/d Q80/120) Down the lane toward the lake, nearly at the junction, is this excellent-value homey guesthouse. Rear units are

best, with lake views through well screened windows. It's a short stroll to El Remate's public beach.

Casa de Ernesto
BUNGALOW **$**

(☑ 4915-8309; hotelcasadernesto@gmail.com; Jobompiche Rd; s/d Q100/150, without bathroom Q40/80; ✸) Ernesto and his clan offer cool and comfortable adobe huts in the woods with thatched roofs, tile floors, and good rustic-style beds. Add Q50 for air-con. Canoe rentals, horseback riding to Laguna Salpetén and expeditions for the great white fish are among the activities offered.

Sak Luk Tikal
HOSTEL **$**

(☑ 5048-3982; http://www.tikalsakluk.com; Main Rd; dm Q30, r shared/private bath Q40/60; @) Look for the massive, multicolored Maya mask at the side of the road for these affable and ultra-affordable accommodations in El Remate. Climb the steep stone stairs to find a place to pitch your tent, hang your hammock or take your choice of beds. The most inviting options are the loft-like, open-air dorm rooms, which offer inspiring views of the sunset over the lake. There's also a communal cooking area, a DVD player with English- and Spanish-language movies, and other activities for social people.

Las Gardenias
HOTEL **$**

(☑ 7928-8377; www.hotelasgardenias.com; Main Rd; r from Q 85/125; ✸ @ ☎) Right at the junction with the north shore road, this cordial hotel/restaurant/shuttle operator has two sections: the wood-paneled rooms at the front are bigger, those in the rear are appealingly removed from the road. All feature comfortable beds with woven spreads, attractively tiled showers and porches with hammocks. The restaurant across the courtyard serves dishes from Q30 and makes a pretty good milkshake.

Gringo Perdido Ecological Inn
RESORT **$$**

(☑ 5804-8639; www.hotelgringoperdido.com; Jobompiche Rd; camping Q50, s/d Q150/300, with breakfast & dinner Q360/720; P) ✈ Waking up here is like waking up in paradise, with no sound but the lake lapping at the shore a few steps from your door. Eight rooms have one double and one single bed or bunk bed, mosquito nets and full-wall canvas roll-up blinds to give you the sensation of sleeping in the open air. A few lakeside bungalows offer a bit more seclusion. There's also a grassy campground with thatched-roof shelters for slinging hammocks and a Maya sauna. The Gringo Perdido is 3km along the north-shore road from the main Tikal road.

Hotel Mon Ami
HOTEL **$$**

(☑ 7928-8413; www.hotelmonami.com; Jobompiche Rd; dm/s/d Q50/150/200; ☎) A 15-minute walk from the Tikal road and a stone's throw from the Biotopo Cerro Cahui, this maintains a good balance between jungle wildness and Euro sophistication. Quirkily furnished cabins and dorms with hammocks are reached along candlelit paths through gardens bursting with local plant life, though the bathhouse needs a feng-shui overhaul. Fans of French cuisine will appreciate the open-air restaurant.

Hotel Palomio Ranch
HOTEL **$$**

(☑ 7298-8419, 4044-4473; El Remate; s/d Q150/300; P ✸ ✈) A genuine slice of the old west in Guatemala, this lovely hotel is furnished with replica antiques. Air-conditioned rooms are furnished in an old-west motif (the antique desks offer an interesting juxtaposition with the televisions), with private bathrooms with hot showers. There's a lovely swimming pool, and the surrounding grounds are filled with horses (guests are allowed to ride around the grounds for free from 7am to 4pm, and trail rides can be arranged as well). The on-site restaurant serves food and beverages all day long.

La Casa de Don David
HOTEL **$$**

(☑ 5306-2190; www.lacasadedondavid.com; Jobompiche Rd; s/d incl breakfast from Q235/360; ☉ restaurant 6:30am-9pm; ✸ @ ☎) Just west of the junction, this full-service outfit has spotless, modern rooms with Maya textiles for decor. All feature verandas and hammocks facing the broad lakefront lawn, dotted with wacky topiary. Owner David Kuhn – the original Gringo Perdido – is a botanist from Florida, who'd love to show you his garden, including a young ceiba tree and the night-blooming *pitaya petenera*.

Hotel La Mansión
del Pájaro Serpiente
HOTEL **$$**

(☑ 5702-9434; Main Rd; s/d/ste from Q264/352/528; ✸ ✈) Dotted along a steep hillside, these cottage-like cabins all make the most of their perch, with wraparound windows and front lounges overlooking the lake. Peacocks strut around the landscaped grounds, which feature a pool with hammocks under

RAMON PUGA, ARCHAEOLOGIST

Why is El Remate such a good base for explorers? Obviously it's close to Tikal, but there's so much more within striking distance of El Remate, so many smaller Maya sites worth visiting. San Clemente, for example, has three pyramids and a couple of palaces, completely in their natural state. Almost nobody even knows about it. In fact, though it's just east of El Remate and not far from the main road, you still need a local just to help you find it.

Most sacred spot? Nakum is a very special place. Each time I go there my sense that this city must have been quite sacred to the Maya people grows. It must have been a very important center of spirituality in its time. Nakum is small but very elaborate. It is my opinion that Nakum is more beautiful than Tikal.

Good multi-day trip? You would want to spend two days exploring the three cities of Yaxhá (☑5204-1851; admission Q80; ☺6am-5pm), Nakum and El Naranjo. You can camp in Nakum before heading to El Naranjo the next day. Outside of Yaxhá, chances are good that the only people you would run into would be archaeologists working at the other two sites.

Site still on your to-see list? I've yet to visit El Mirador (p239). A friend has invited me to take a month-long trek through the area, but obligations to my family have thus far kept me from being able to devote the time. One day, perhaps.

nearby *palapa* shelters, and a reasonably priced restaurant-bar.

El Muelle
HOTEL $$
(☑5501-8087, 5514-9785; elmuelle_reservaciones@hotmail.com; Main Rd; r without/with view Q300/400; P❊☎☒) El Muelle is the preferred hotel of Guatemalan families who appreciate practicalities such as the huge on-site restaurant and the well-stocked gift shop. The rooms are pretty plain, but there is no need for decoration if you opt for one with a lovely lake view.

Hostal Hermano Pedro
HOSTEL $$
(☑4326-6253; www.hhpedro.com; dm/s/d Q96/152/208; ☎) Set in a two-story wood-and-stone house, 20m off to the right from the main road, the spacious rooms are refreshingly simple and comfortable, with a few frills like lacy curtains, big fans and balcony porches. Guests can use the kitchen or grab a hammock in the common room.

Pirámide Paraiso
HOTEL $$$
(www.hotelgringoperdido.com; Jobompiche Road; r Q1600; ☎) Built in time for the dawn of the new *baktún* is this glitzy addition to the Gringo Perdido Ecological Inn, a smooth white structure that rises surreally from the forest like a Maya temple. Each of the eight huge, luxuriously decorated suites features its own exterior Jacuzzi.

✗ Eating

★ Sugar Sap
CAFE & INN $
(☑3110-0730; coffee drinks Q15-25, sandwiches Q25; ☺8am-8pm) ✎ The Sugar Sap is run by April Puga and her husband, archaeologist Ramon Puga, who occasionally leads tours throughout the area. Offering something of a southwestern feel (thanks in no small part to the building itself, a pseudo-adobe made of recycled materials designed to stay cool on the hottest of days), this beautiful lakeside spot on the road to Jobompiche offers hands-down the best coffee in El Remate. As if this wasn't enough, Sugar Sap serves sandwiches made with homemade bread and organic vegetables from the owner's own garden, as well as other traditional Guatemalan snacks. Sugar Sap's two rooms – each done with the same beautiful design as the restaurant – are an excellent choice for those looking to stay with this amazing family; both have two double beds and full mod-cons. The larger room rents for Q350, and the smaller for Q250.

Restaurante Cahui
GUATEMALAN $$
(Main Rd; meals Q60-90) At any time of day or night, the big wooden deck overlooking the lake at this local eatery is a great place to be. The food is simple and filling, the views

superb and the healthy selection of beers on the menu won't go astray either. Just before the north shore turnoff, this is also a good stop for information and souvenirs from the gift shop out front.

Las Orquideas ITALIAN $$
(☎5819-7232; Jobompiche Rd; pastas Q55-80; ☺noon-9pm Tue-Sun) Las Orquideas has a genial Italian owner-chef cooking up genuine Mediterranean fare, with tempting desserts too.

Nakun's PIZZERIA $$
(pizza Q35; ☺9am-8pm) Out on the main drag, this cheery shack features a lakeside balcony. Pizzas are the main attraction, made with real mozzarella cheese.

❶ Information

Schnoken Jungle Tours (Main Rd; ☺10am-9pm) This shop sits across from the lake just before the northern turnoff. In addition to selling handicrafts, the shop also rents out bicycles (Q65 per day), motorbikes (Q250 per day) and kayaks (Q35 per hour). Fluent in English, French, Spanish and German, the shop's owner is also a good source of information about the area.

❶ Getting There & Away

Any bus or minibus going north from Santa Elena to Tikal can drop you at El Remate.

To get to the Belize border, catch a lift to Puente Ixlú, from where you can flag a bus en route from Flores. A taxi to/from Puente Ixlú is about Q2. Alternatively, you can hail any passing bus or minibus on the Flores–Tikal road, but traffic is light after midmorning. Taxis from Flores to El Remate cost around Q170.

North Shore, Lago de Petén Itzá

The road running west of El Remate along the northern shore of Lago de Petén Itzá gets mighty rough past Biotopo Cerro Cahuí, resembling less a road and more a monster truck off-road course until somewhere around San José. For about 15 miles, this beautiful but treacherous bit of track runs along the lakeshore, passing by beautiful swimming spots and through small villages with plenty of off-the-beaten-track exploration potential.

Among the villages you'll pass through on your journey around the lake are **Jobompiche** and **San José** before reaching the town of **San Andrés**. A pretty town of a few thousand, San Andrés has a few hotels and restaurants, as well as a waterfront park (with a water-slide). The region as a whole doesn't see many tourists but it's home to a number of good private-run Spanish-language immersion programs and organizations offering a variety of volunteer opportunities.

⚲ Courses

Eco-Escuela de Español LANGUAGE COURSE
(☎3099-4846; San Andrés) This community-owned school emphasizes ecological and cultural issues and organizes environmental trips and volunteer opportunities; Q1180 a week includes room and board with a local family.

🛏 Sleeping & Eating

⭐**Gucumatz** B&B $$
(☎5729-2183; www.gucumatz.com; San Pedro; s/d incl breakfast Q200/400; @) Pronounced 'gookoomatz', this charming bed-and-breakfast run by the Stenton family is about 12 miles west of El Remate on Lago de Petén's northern shore. Sitting on a tree-filled hillside (complete with howler monkeys!) overlooking the lake, it would be hard to imagine a more idyllic setting. Clean and well-furnished rooms have private bathrooms with hot-water showers and are surprisingly luxurious for the price, and the Stenton family will arrange pickup from either El Remate or Flores with advance notice. Mountain bikes, kayaks, pedal boats and rowboats are on the premises and free for guest use, and the family can arrange horseback trips as well.

La Lancha RESORT $$$
(☎7928-8331; www.blancaneaux.com; Aldea Jobompiche; s/d/tr casitas with lake views Q1562/2422/2828, with rainforest views Q1094/1562/1960; P☀) Featuring his signature blend of exclusivity and adventure, Francis Ford Coppola has created a lodge of rustic luxury about 8 miles west of El Remate. Secluded *casitas* have exquisite furniture from native woods and wide verandas with amazing views of the surrounding rainforest or the blue-green waters. The grounds are alive with howling monkeys and squawking birds. All room prices here include breakfast, use of mountain bikes and hiking trails, as well as a 10% service charge.

Ni'tun Ecolodge RESORT $$$
(☑5201-0759; www.nitun.com; s/d incl breakfast from Q1100/1770 ; P @) A few kilometers west of San Andrés is this beautiful property, set on 35 hectares of grounds where six species of hummingbird nest year-round. Bernie and Lore, who built and operate the lodge, are adventurers and conservationists. There are four spacious huts, with accommodation in the rustic vein. Room rates include airport transfers and breakfast. They also offer adventure trips with transport in Land Cruisers to such destinations as Ceibal, Yaxhá and Tikal, with prices ranging from Q1000 to Q1200 per person per day.

❶ Getting There & Away

If you're coming from El Remate, your only option is hiking, bicycling or renting a motorcycle. From Santa Elena, you can take a bus from the market to San José or San Andrés for Q10. You might also be able to negotiate for a boat to take you across from Flores.

Flores & Santa Elena

Perched on an island in the middle of lovely Lago de Petén Itzá, Flores (population 3000) is a tranquil town of red-roofed houses and cool lake breezes. It's really a traveler's town: pastel-painted hotels line the lakeshore, providing easy access to the water and sunset views, and travel agencies, internet cafes and souvenir stands are in no short supply. But it's free of hassle and hustle, which makes it easy to stick around longer than anticipated.

Across the causeway is its sister city, Santa Elena (population 25,000), a rumpled place of dusty streets and honking horns, with a hot, chaotic market. The main street is strung with bus depots, which is the main reason travelers make their way here (there is no bus station in Flores). Arriving long-distance buses drop passengers on or just off Santa Elena's main drag, 4a Calle. The airport is located 1.2 miles east of the causeway in Santa Elena.

◉ Sights & Activities

Most visitors use Flores as a base to explore (or to recuperate from) the region's Maya ruins. But there are a number of spots in and around the cobblestone-paved town worth checking out (besides the town itself!).

Boats at the *embarcaderos* (docks) beside Hotel Santana in Flores and Hotel Petén Espléndido in Santa Elena can be hired for **lake tours**. Prices are very negotiable. Expect to pay about Q200 for about an hour on board.

Centro de Información Sobre la Naturaleza, Cultura y Artesanía de Petén MUSEUM
(Cincap, Petén Nature, Culture & Handicrafts Information Center; ☑7926-0718; Parque Central, Flores; ⊘9am-noon & 2-9pm) This center has some interesting displays on archaeological sites, conservation areas and the local way of life in El Petén. It also sells handicrafts from the region and has an information desk, where you can ask about visits to some of the region's more remote natural and archaeological sites.

Museo Santa Bárbara MUSEUM
(Isle of Santa Bárbara; admission Q15; ⊘8am-noon & 2 5pm) On an island to the west of Flores, this museum holds a grab bag of Maya artifacts from nearby archaeological sites, yellowing articles from National Geographic, and radio broadcasting equipment, all crammed into a small room. There are over 9000 pieces, according to the caretaker who has a story about every one of them. The old radios and phonographs were contributed by his father, who was an announcer for 40 years at Radio Petén, which still broadcasts from an adjacent building. After browsing the museum, enjoy chilled coconuts at the cafe by the dock. It's a stone's throw from San Benito dock: phone or whistle for the boatman, who'll take you across for Q10.

San Miguel OUTDOOR ACTIVITY, RUIN
You can also explore the slow-moving lakeside village of San Miguel, which sits on a peninsula that juts into Lago de Petén Itzá just north of Flores. Catch a *lancha* (small boat) from the northeast side. There is a pleasant 1-mile walk up to a treehouse lookout called **El Mirador**, with fine views of Flores and around Lago de Petén Itzá. The path traverses part of the **Tayazal archaeological site**, which is a set of chiefly Classic-era mounds scattered around this western end of the peninsula. (Confusingly, this is not the same as Tayasal – the original name for Flores – as these overgrown ruins predate the Itzáes' arrival in the area and the founding of Flores.) The walk is best done in the morning, to avoid afternoon heat and the danger of being overtaken by dusk.

Flores

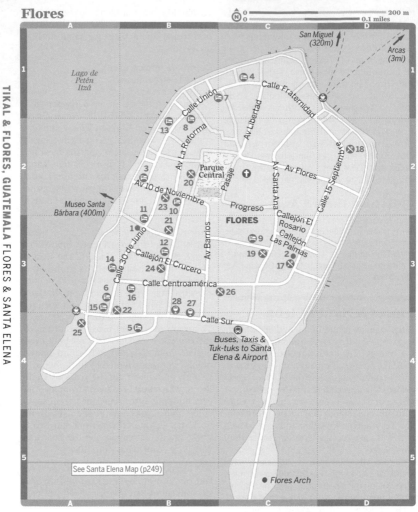

🛏 Sleeping

Most visitors choose to stay in Flores, which has plenty of choices in all price ranges and a better selection of restaurants and services catering to travelers. Santa Elena, closer to the bus station, offers cheaper eating options and feels a bit grittier.

Flores

Hospedaje Doña Goya   HOSTEL **$**
(Map p244; ☎7867-5513; Calle Unión, Flores; dm Q35, s/d Q80/120, without bathroom Q70/90; ☎) This family-run guesthouse is one of the best budget choices in town and, therefore, often full. The beds are comfortable, the water's hot and there's a roof terrace with a palm-thatched shelter and hammocks for enjoying lake views. The dorms are spacious and spotless. Breakfast is served with a smile in the cafe downstairs.

Hospedaje Doña Goya the 2nd   HOTEL **$**
(Map p244; ☎7867-5516; hospedajedonagoya@ yahoo.com; Calle Unión, Flores; s/d Q80/120, r with balcony Q160; ☀@☎) Doña Goya's second effort is even spiffier than her first – this one's got a jungle theme, with banisters made to look like climbing vines. Rooms are plain,

Flores

airy and well scrubbed, with screened windows, and most give some kind of view. And like its predecessor, DG2 features a hammock-slung terrace.

Hotel La Unión   HOTEL $
(Map p244; ☑ 7867-5531; gulzam75@hotmail.com; Calle Unión, Flores; s/d Q90/130; ☞) Considering the location beside the waterfront promenade, this well-maintained property is quite a deal, with relatively stylish decor in fan-cooled rooms. Check email at the downstairs cybercafe or enjoy cocktails on the lakeside terrace.

Hostel Los Amigos   HOSTEL $
(Map p244; ☑ 7867-5075; www.amigoshostel.com; Calle Central, Flores; dm/r Q55/120; ☺) Flores' one true hostel, with a 10-bed dorm, hammocks and even a tree house, has grown organically in its nine years of existence. All the global traveler's perks are here in abundance: nightly bonfires, happy hours, heaping helpings of organic food, yoga and cut-rate jungle tours. A new annex around the corner is quieter, with seven originally designed rooms.

Green World Hotel   HOTEL $
(Map p244; ☑ 7867-5662; greenworldhotel@gmail. com; Calle 30 de Junio, Flores; s/d Q110/160, with air-con Q190/260; ☀☺) This low-key shoreline property features an interior patio and an upstairs terrace overlooking the lake. Compact, low-lit rooms have safes, enormous ceiling fans and good hot showers – No 8, with its rear balcony, is by far the nicest.

Posada de la Jungla   HOTEL $
(Map p244; ☑ 7867-5185; www.posadadelajungla.com; Calle Centroamérica 30, Flores; s/d/tr Q100/150/200) Also worth considering is this slender, three-story building with front balconies. Though a bit cramped, rooms are comfortably arranged, with quality beds.

Hotel Isla de Flores   HOTEL $$
(Map p244; ☑ 7867-5173, 2476-8775; www.hotelisladeflores.com; Av La Reforma; s/d Q305/367; ☀) This upscale option calls itself 'an island in the jungle,' much like Flores itself, but there is nothing savage about the white wicker furniture and potted plants that provide the ambience here. All rooms are comfortable and fully equipped with cable TV and hot-water showers (some rooms even have tubs); the ones on the upper floors have balconies where you can catch a glimpse of the lake over the red rooftops.

Casazul   BOUTIQUE HOTEL $$
(Map p244; ☑ 7867-5451; www.hotelesdepeten. com; Calle Unión, Flores; s/d/tr Q325/390/480; ☀☞) They're not kidding when they call this the blue house – there's shades of it everywhere, from the plantation-style balconies to the nine individually decorated, spacious and comfortable rooms. A couple have their own balconies and everyone can enjoy the 3rd-floor terrace.

Casa Amelia   BOUTIQUE HOTEL $$
(Map p244; ☑ 7867-5430; www.hotelcasamelia.com; Calle Unión, Flores; s/d Q220/340; ☀◉☞) Amelia has an eye for aesthetics, and her artistic touches are evident throughout the 12 guest

rooms and lobby of this inviting inn. The walls are hung with interesting exotic art; rooms are furnished in rosewood and mahogany. (Rooms 301 and 302 are best, opening on the superb roof terrace.) The restaurant is definitely one of the perks of this place.

Hotel La Mesa de los Mayas   HOTEL $$
(Map p244; ☑ 7867-5268; mesamayas@hotmail. com; Av La Reforma, Flores; s/d Q125/150, with air-con Q150/200; ❋ 🛜) Alongside a narrow alley, the Mesa's one of the stalwarts on the Flores hotel scene. Rooms are very neat and decked out with pretty, checkered bedspreads and reading lamps; some feature plant-laden balconies.

Hotel Petén   HOTEL $$
(Map p244; ☑ 7867-5203; www.hotelesdepeten. com; Calle 30 de Junio, Flores; s/d/tr incl breakfast Q376/464/600; ❋ @ 🛜 ≋) Rooms are cheerily decorated here with a dash of chintz. Definitely choose the lake balcony units as they cost no more than interior ones. A good-sized indoor/outdoor swimming pool is inside the courtyard, and a restaurant/bar opens on a lakeside terrace.

Hotel La Casona de la Isla   HOTEL $$
(Map p244; ☑ 7867-5203; www.hotelesdepeten. com; Calle 30 de Junio, Flores; s/d/tr Q410/475/560; ❋ @ ≋) Popular with groups, this has a definite Caribbean flavor, augmented by cheery blue-and-yellow paint. Decorated with restraint, the smallish rooms line a long veranda facing a pool with a rock garden and an adjacent lake-view deck. The most appealing units, 31, 303 and 304, have windows facing the lake and gorgeous sunsets.

Hotel Santana   HOTEL $$
(Map p244; ☑ 7926-0262; www.santanapeten.com; Calle 30 de Junio, Flores; s/d/tr Q370/440; ❋ @ ≋) 'Eclectic' best describes the melange of concrete, wood, thatch and wickerwork here, but it all hangs together somehow. Rooms are generously sized with ceiling fans and aquamarine walls, and if you get one out the back, you'll have a little balcony looking over the lake onto Isla Santa Bárbara.

Gran Hotel de La Isla   HOTEL $$$
(Map p244; ☑ 7867-5549; www.granhoteldeflorespeten.com; Calle Sur, Flores; s/d Q560/640; P ❋ @ 🛜 ≋) This glossy business-class lodging holds a commanding presence at the west end of the Playa Sur. Along arched corridors with images of Maya royalty, the 46 rooms are luxuriously appointed, though the

lake-view balconies are skimpier than you might expect. Leisure moments can be spent soaking in the outdoor and indoor pools or downing daiquiris in the Fisherman's Bar.

Santa Elena

Mayaland Plaza Hotel   HOTEL $$
(Map p249; ☑ 7926-4976; mayalandplaza@yahoo. com; 4a Calle; s/d/tr Q225/285/375; P ❋ @ ≋) The spacious comfortable rooms are set colonial-style around a peaceful courtyard. All services are on hand, including a recommended restaurant and travel agent.

Hotel Maya Internacional   HOTEL $$$
(Map p249; ☑ 7926-2083; www.villasdeguatemala.com; 1a Calle, Santa Elena; s/d Q585/829; P ❋ @ 🛜 ≋) One of the best reasons to stay in Santa Elena is this tropical-chic resort spreading over a landscaped marsh by the waterfront. The thatched big-top dining room is the center of activity; an adjacent wooden deck with a small infinity pool is great for sunset daiquiris. A boardwalk snakes through tropical gardens to reach the 26 rooms, thatch-and-teak affairs combining a jungly ambience with modern comforts. Rooms 49 to 54 give the best lake views.

La Casona del Lago   HOTEL $$$
(Map p249; ☑ 7952-8700; www.hotelesdepeten. com; 1a Calle; s/d/tr Q616/760/904; P ❋ @ 🛜 ≋) The horseshoe shape here allows all the rooms to enjoy the vista of Lago de Petén Itzá and Isla de Flores. At the center of the horseshoe is the lovely terrace, complete with swimming pool and hot tub. Rooms are equally appealing, with sparkling white tiles and ocher-colored walls.

Hotel Petén Espléndido   HOTEL $$$
(Map p249; ☑ 7774-0700, 7926-0880; www. petenesplendido.com; 1a Calle 5-01; s/d/tr/q Q784/880/976/1096; P ❋ 🛜 ≋) Standing alongside the causeway with its own marina, the most formal hotel in the region pulls out all the stops, featuring room safes, bathroom telephones, great balcony views and possibly the only elevator in all of El Petén. Rooms could be bigger, but they're definitely comfortable and a couple of good restaurants and a poolside bar can keep you happy. If you're flying in, hook up a free shuttle from the airport.

Hotel del Patio   HOTEL $$$
(Map p249; ☑ 7926-0104; www.caminoreal.com.gt; cnr 8a Av & 2a Calle; r Q780; P ❋ @ 🛜 ≋) Shady corridors lined with terra-cotta floors wind

around a stunning courtyard, centered on a gurgling fountain. Rooms are tasteful and comfortable, though not quite as luxurious as the courtyard.

✗ Eating

Most restaurants keep long hours and prepare international foods. A few may even have some dishes featuring local game animals like *tepescuintle* (agouti), *venado* (venison), armadillo and *pavo silvestre* (wild turkey). The specialty of the area is *pescado blanco* (white fish). For atmospheric dining, grab a table at one of the shady shacks built over the water north of Calle 10 de Noviembre, in Flores. By night, these candlelit, waterside spots are the most romantic in town. If it's eating on the cheap you're in the market for, the plaza west of Parque Central has a number of inexpensive **food stands**.

✗ Flores

Cool Beans CAFE $
(Map p244; Calle 15 de Septiembre, Flores; coffee & snacks Q8-25; ⊗7am-10pm Mon-Sat; 🖥) Also known as Café Chilero, this laid-back place is more clubhouse with snacks than proper restaurant, featuring salons for chatting, watching videos or laptop browsing. The lush garden with glimpses of the lake makes a *tranquilo* spot for breakfast or veggie burgers. Be warned – the kitchen closes at 9:01pm sharp.

UK@'s CAFE $
(Map p244; Calle Centroamérica; coffee from Q10; ⊗7:30am-3pm; 🖥) This pretty cafe serves strong Guatemalan coffee and light breakfasts. Green wrought-iron chairs and decorative candles make up the decor, and friendly management offers free internet with your order.

★ Il Terrazo ITALIAN $$
(Map p244; Calle Unión, Flores; pasta Q65-75; ⊗8am-10pm Mon-Sat) Inspired by a chef from Bologna, this Italian gourmet restaurant covers a romantic rooftop terrace. The fettuccine, tortellini and gnocchi are all produced inhouse, the panini are amply stuffed, and the fruit smoothies are simply unbelievable. All this, and the service is the most attentive in town.

Raíces STEAKHOUSE $$
(Map p244; Calle Sur, Flores; mains Q80-110; ⊗4-10pm Sun-Thu, 4pm-1am Fri & Sat) A broad deck and a flaming grill are the main ingredients at this stylish lakefront restaurant/bar. Chargrilled meats and seafood are the specialty, and you can choose your grills by the pound or half-pound.

Capitán Tortuga INTERNATIONAL $$
(Map p244; Calle 30 de Junio, Flores; pizzas Q45-100; ⊗8am-10:30pm) A barnlike venue with a pair of lakeside terraces, this Carlos & Charlie's clone serves heaped helpings of comfort food – especially pizzas – at medium prices.

Café Arqueológico Yax-ha CAFE $$
(Map p244; www.cafeyaxha.com; Calle 15 de Septiembre, Flores; mains Q35-65; ⊗6:30am-10pm) Wallpapered with photos and articles relating to Maya sites, this cafe-restaurant is home base for an archaeological tour outfit. Apart from the usual egg-and-bean breakfasts, what's special here is the pre-Hispanic and Itzá items – pancakes with ramón seeds, yucca scrambled with mora herbs, chicken in chaya sauce.

La Guacamaya RESTAURANT $$
(Map p244; Av la Reforma; mains Q40-60; ⊗lunch & dinner) Local artworks adorn the walls, while bright colors and wooden furniture enhance the atmosphere. This Maya-themed place verges on gourmet: if you're feeling fancy, try the baked haddock or filet mignon. Otherwise, burgers and burritos will sate your hunger without breaking the bank.

La Luna MEDITERRANEAN $$
(Map p244; cnr Calle 30 de Junio & Av 10 de Noviembre, Flores; mains Q60-120; ⊗noon-11pm Mon-Sat; 🖉) This deservedly popular restaurant cultivates a tropical ambience with low-lit patio dining. Aside from the usual steak and pasta dishes, Spanish cuisine is its strong suit (the owner hails from the *madre tierra*): go for the gazpacho.

La Hacienda del Rey RESTAURANT $$
(Map p244; Calle 30 de Junio; mains Q60-80; ⊗4pm-9pm) This open-air affair at the west end of Playa Sur has an inviting tropical feel, where you can catch an evening breeze and quaff a cold Gallo before tearing into a juicy steak. A 'Pyrex,' consisting of a pound and a half of Argentine cuts, feeds two or three (Q165). If it's just a snack you're after, order a couple of tacos de *arrachera* (skirt steak, Q15).

Fonda Ixobel CAFE $$
(Map p244; cnr Calle Central & Av Santa Ana; breakfast Q15-25, mains Q60-80; ⊗8am-late Mon-Sat) An airy, atmospheric salon where overhead fans whir and sweet-natured Q'eqchi' women

TIKAL & FLORES, GUATEMALA FLORES & SANTA ELENA

work the bar, Las Puertas prepares an eclectic choice of dishes highlighted by pasta variations and abundant salads. There's live jazz or reggae most nights.

El Pescador
SEAFOOD **$$$**

(Map p244; www.petenesplendido.com; Calle Surs; dishes from Q65-150; ☺breakfast, lunch & dinner) The restaurant on the first floor of the Gran Hotel de la Isla specializes in seafood, especially the famed *pescado blanco* and various kinds of *ceviche*. Families will appreciate more kid-friendly items like hamburgers and spaghetti.

La Mesa de los Mayas
MAYA **$$$**

(Map p244; Av La Reforma; dishes from Q50-125; ☺breakfast, lunch & dinner) This is the place in Flores to sate your craving for exotic dishes, from armadillo to wild boar to the hard-to-find *tepescuintle* (it's a large rodent and tastier than it sounds). There's plenty on the menu for less adventurous palates.

🍴 Santa Elena

Restaurante Mijaro
RESTAURANT **$**

(Map p249; 6a Av; meals Q15-40; ☺breakfast, lunch & dinner) You'll find good home cooking at both branches of Restaurante Mijaro, a friendly, locally popular *comedor,* one on the main street and the other round the corner on 6a Av. The latter features a thatch-roofed garden area. Besides the grub, it does good long *limonadas* (lime-juice drink).

Restaurante El Puerto
SEAFOOD **$$**

(Map p249; 1a Calle 2-15, Santa Elena; mains Q100; ☺11am-11pm) Seafood is the star attraction at this breezy, open-air hall by the lakefront in Santa Elena, with a well-stocked bar at the front. Restaurante El Puerto is an ideal setting to enjoy shellfish stews, *ceviches* or the famous *pescado blanco* – white fish from the lake.

🍷 Drinking & Nightlife

Flores is a chilled-out town, where sunset drinks on the lakefront followed by quiet conversation over a few Cuba Libres at one of the many hotels and restaurants that have terraces constitutes a typical evening out. If you're looking for something more lively, head over the causeway to Santa Elena.

El Trópico
BAR

(Map p244; Calle Sur, Flores; ☺4:30pm-1am Mon-Sat) The candlelit terrace here is a nice spot to start the night, as the lights of Santa Elena reflect pleasingly off the lake.

Casa de Palmas
BAR

(Map p244; Calle Sur, Flores) Aside from drinking and conversing at the terrace tables, there's non-stop dancing on the crowded dance floor. It's a mostly middle-class Guatemalan scene.

Mi Disco
DISCO

(Map p249; cnr Calle Central & Av Santa Ana, Santa Elena; ☺Mon-Sat) The combination of eardrum-exploding music and bouncers armed with pump action shotguns should leave no uncertainty in your mind that you're in for a fun night, Guatemalan style. In addition to well-armed security guards, Mi Disco also boasts an excellent dance floor and cheap drinks. If you'd rather croon than dance, Monday to Wednesday evenings are reserved for karaoke.

ℹ️ Information

Flores now has a number of ATMs in stores and alcoves; just look for signs reading ATM. One reliable **ATM** (Calle 30 de Junio, Flores) is next to Hotel Petén.

In Santa Elena, two reliable banks with ATMs are **Banco G&T Continental** (4a Calle, Santa Elena; ☺9am-7pm Mon-Fri, to 1pm Sat) and **Banco Industrial** (4a Calle, Santa Elena; ☺9am-4pm Mon-Fri, 10am-2pm Sat).

The main hub in Flores for internet cafes and travel agents is Calle Centroamérica. One such internet stop is **Tikal Net** (Calle Centroamérica, Flores; per hr Q10; ☺8am-9pm), which also has an office in **Santa Elena** (4a Calle, Santa Elena; per hr Q10; ☺8am-8pm Mon-Sat, 9am-5pm Sun). You can make domestic and international phone calls from either branch.

Other tourist and travel-related information can be obtained here:

Inguat Tourist Office (☎7926-0533; Santa Elena Airport; ☺7am-noon & 3-5pm) The only official tourist information around is at this office out at the airport, which is on the eastern outskirts of Santa Elena, 2km out on the causeway connecting Santa Elena and Flores.

Aventuras Turísticas (☎4034-9291; www.aventurasturisticas.com; Av Barrios, Flores) Tours to Tikal.

ℹ️ Getting There & Away

AIR

The international departure tax at Flores airport (FRS) is Q240.

Santa Elena

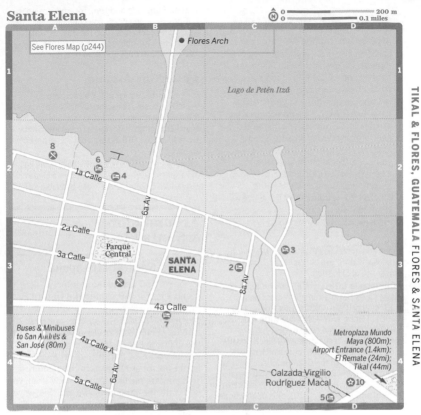

Belizean carrier **Tropic Air** (📞 7926-0348; www.tropicair.com) currently operates two flights daily between Flores and Belize City, charging Q1015 each way for the one-hour trip.

Grupo Taca (www.taca.com) has flights to/from Guatemala City (Q1255, two daily).

BUS

Long-distance buses use the Terminal Nuevo de Autobuses in Santa Elena, located 1km south of the causeway along 6a Av. It is also used by a slew of microbuses, with frequent services to numerous destinations. Second-class buses and some micros make an additional stop at 5a Calle, in the market area (the 'old' terminal) before heading out. You can reduce your trip time by 15 minutes by going straight to the market, though the vehicle may be full by then.

Departures include the following (as always, schedules are highly changeable and should be confirmed before heading out):

➡ **Belize City** (four to five hours, 137 miles) Línea Dorada & Mundo Maya (Q60, 7am). This bus connects with boats to Caye Caulker and Ambergris

Santa Elena

☺ Activities, Courses & Tours
1 Turismo Aventura B3

🛏 Sleeping
2 Hotel del Patio C3
3 Hotel Maya Internacional C3
4 Hotel Petén Espléndido B2
5 Jaguar Inn D4
6 La Casona del Lago A2
7 Mayaland Plaza Hotel B4

☻ Eating
8 Restaurante El Puerto A2
9 Restaurante Mijaro B3

☻ Entertainment
10 Mi Disco D4

Caye. It's cheaper but slower to take local buses from Flores to the border and go on from there.

➡ **El Remate** (Q20, 40 minutes, 15 miles) Microbuses leave every half hour from 5am to 6pm.

❶ STOCKING UP@THE MALL

Metroplaza Mundo Maya (Airport Rd, Santa Elena) is the closest thing to a modern mall greater Santa Elena has to offer, and as such, is a good place to stock up on a variety of items in one fell swoop. The mall has a supermarket, a bank, two ATMs, a video arcade, a store selling mobile phones and computer gear, another selling lingerie, several clothing stores, and half a dozen shoe stores. As far as food goes, there's a bakery, a Pizza Hut, and a rather fancy looking restaurant called **Beijing** (☑ 7884-3454; mains from Q50; ⊙ 11am-11pm) that serves some of the region's most excellent Chinese food.

Buses and minibuses to and from Melchor de Mencos will drop you at Puente Ixlú junction, 2km south of El Remate.

➡ **Guatemala City** (eight to nine hours, 258 miles) Línea Dorada runs first-class buses at 10am and 10pm (Q150), plus a deluxe bus (Q190) at 9pm. Autobuses del Norte has 1st-class (Q150) and deluxe (Q200) buses at 9pm and 11pm, respectively. All Línea Dorada and Autobuses del Norte buses pick up passengers in front of the Gran Hotel de la Isla an hour prior to the Santa Elena terminal departure. Fuente del Norte runs 16 buses between 3:30am and 10:30pm (Q110), plus deluxe buses at 10am, 2pm, 9pm and 10pm (Q160), although security problems have been reported by passengers using this line.

➡ **Melchor de Mencos/Belizean border** (two hours, 62 miles) Microbuses (Q25) go about every hour, 5:45am to 6pm. Línea Dorada Pullmans en route to Belize City depart at 7am (Q35).

➡ **Tikal** (Q50, 1¼ hours, 62km) Microbuses by Agencia Exploradores de la Cultura Maya depart at 5am, 7am, 9am and 1pm, returning at noon, 1:30pm, 3pm and 6pm. You could also take the Uaxactún-bound bus (Q35) at 2pm, which goes a bit slower. Autobuses del Norte provides Pullman service at 6am and 8am (Q80).

❶ Getting Around

Flores, Santa Elena and the airport are connected by buses, taxis and *tuk-tuks* (open-air, three-wheeler vans). *Tuk-tuks* will take you anywhere within or between Flores and Santa Elena for about Q10. A taxi from the airport costs about Q25.

Rental-car companies are in the arrivals hall at the airport. Fill your fuel tank in Santa Elena or just before El Remate; no fuel is available at Tikal.

Around Flores & Santa Elena

Parque Natural Ixpanpajul

If you're wild about the rainforest, plan to spend a day at the **Ixpanpajul Nature Park** (☑ 7863-1317, 5619-0513; www.ixpanpajul.com; adult/child Q200/120), a nature preserve and activity center on Km468 on the road from Río Dulce to Flores. It's not a huge place, but it packs a lot of fun into its 1112 acres, and it takes place at all levels of the rainforest.

If you are partial to the canopy level, you will enjoy the Tarzan Tour, or **zip-line**, or you can saunter at your own pace along the **Skywalk**, a network of hanging bridges at the same level. You can explore the understory on **horseback** or by **mountain bike**, and arrange **birding tours** and **night safaris**. Simple *cabañas* and campsites are also available. Ixpanpajul is about 6 miles from Santa Elena on the road to Río Dulce; call ahead for a **shuttle bus service** (☑ 5897-6766; Q40) from Flores.

Understand
Belize

Belize Today

According to the most basic benchmarks, Belize is flourishing, with compulsory primary education, a relatively stable democracy, a thriving tourism industry and an economy that is plugging along. Unfortunately, many people in Belize have not seen the benefits of these positive developments.

Best on Film
Mosquito Coast (1986) Harrison Ford and River Phoenix star as members of an American family in search of a simpler life in Central America.
Apocalypto (2006) Mel Gibson's visually arresting – if not historically accurate – Mayan thriller.
Curse of the Ixtabai (2012) Belizeans are quite proud of this feature-length horror film, the first to be 100% filmed and produced in Belize using local scenery, cast and crew.

Best in Print
Beka Lamb (Zee Edgell) A heart-wrenching novel about a girl's coming-of-age amid political upheaval.
The Last Flight of the Scarlet Macaw (Bruce Barcott) An unflinchingly honest account of Sharon Matola's fight against the construction of the Chalillo Dam on the Macal River.
Jaguar (Alan Rabinowitz) A first-person account of two years living among the Maya and the jaguars.

Greeting People
Don't be shy about making eye contact and greeting strangers on the street. Belizeans are friendly! The most common greeting is the catch-all 'Aarait?' (Alright?), to which you might respond 'Aarait, aarait?'

Tourism

Tourism is the country's top source of employment and investment. The challenge moving forward seems to be one of balancing the needs of the tourism industry with Belizeans' desire – expressed time and again – to protect the environment.

While the benefits of tourism for the country as a whole are acknowledged by Belizeans at nearly every level of society, Belize does not yet have the infrastructure to support the massive numbers of tourists that arrive each year. The most contentious tourism-related issue today concerns cruise-ship passengers. Belize is among the most popular stops on the Caribbean cruise-ship circuit, but many Belizeans believe these day visitors do not contribute enough to the local economy to justify their impact on environment and infrastructure. The past few years have seen increasing opposition to opening new areas to cruise-ship passengers, especially in Placencia, which is being opened to cruise tourism despite widespread local objection.

It's never easy to maintain the delicate balance between preserving natural resources and cashing in on economic opportunity. Most Belizeans are proud of their natural heritage and recognize that the goals of environmental conservation and economic prosperity are not mutually exclusive. How to pursue those goals is the subject of much debate.

Persistence of Poverty

Economic prosperity remains elusive for most people. A few entrepreneurs have made big money, and a small middle class survives on business, tourism and other professions. But many more Belizeans live on subsistence incomes in rudimentary circumstances. In 2010 an estimated 43% of the population lived below the poverty line.

Unemployment has reached 13% in recent years. And labor – whether washing hotel sheets, cutting sugarcane or packing bananas – is poorly paid when compared with the high cost of living. Although Belize has the second-highest per capita income in Central America, this does not reflect the huge disparity that exists between rich and poor.

Crime & Corruption

Crime is a fact of life in Belize, especially in Belize City whose murder rate slightly exceeds the average for Central America. Most violent crime is related to gang warfare and drug transactions, and incidents of violent crime against tourists are relatively infrequent. Still, petty crime (such as pickpocketing and break-ins) is common in tourist areas such as San Pedro and Placencia.

Belize's small Chinese minority has reported feeling especially targeted by criminals, and over the last few years has petitioned the government publicly for stronger law enforcement.

Perceived corruption in the government is also an issue. At election time both political parties come up with strategies to combat the corruption they claim the other party is perpetrating. Journalist and former police officer Wellington Ramos has written about the culture of corruption among civil servants, including in the police force. In an article published in *Caribbean News Now!* he speculates that some illegal activity – including drug running – is allowed to continue because of a few well-placed financial donations to political campaigns.

Belizeans tend to lean towards the side of optimism in general, but on issues concerning crime and corruption most express a deep sense of cynicism about the judicial process.

POPULATION: **333,200**

AREA: **8867 SQ MILES**

PROTECTED AREA: **4062 SQ MILES**

ANNUAL VISITORS: **1,040,000**

LITERACY RATE: **77%**

UNEMPLOYMENT RATE: **13%**

if Belize were 100 people

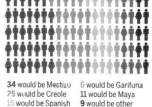

34 would be Mestizo
25 would be Creole
15 would be Spanish
6 would be Garifuna
11 would be Maya
9 would be other

languages

(% of population)

| Kriol | Spanish | English |
| 33 | 46 | 4 |

| Garifuna | Maya Kekchi | Other |
| 6 | 5 | 6 |

population per sq mile

BELIZE   USA   UK

♦ ≈ 36 people

History

Don't be fooled into believing that Central America's youngest independent nation is short on history. Though independence came only in 1981 (peacefully, we might add), many Belizean families trace their connection to the land back many generations. Most Belizeans have at least a tale or two to tell about the role played by their relatives in the creation of the nation they now proudly call home.

Joyce Kelly's *An Archaeological Guide to Northern Central America* offers the best descriptions of the Maya sites of Belize, along with those in Guatemala and Mexico.

Historians normally divide Maya chronology into three periods: Preclassic (around 2000 BC to AD 250), Classic (about AD 250 to 1000) and Postclassic (around AD 1000 to the arrival of the Spanish). It was in the Classic period that the Maya attained the intellectual, architectural and artistic achievements that set them apart. Maya civilization in Belize reached its peak between the 6th and 9th centuries AD, after which the Maya reverted to a more primitive cultural level, with a much-reduced population living away from their once great cities.

The first Spanish ships may have visited Belize's coast in 1508, possibly already bringing diseases that would later decimate the Maya population. Spanish expeditions – mostly from Mexico – succeeded in conquering Maya settlements as far south as Tipu. The Spanish set up Christian missions, but the Maya rebelled frequently and the Spanish did not stay.

All around the Caribbean, the 17th century was the golden age of piracy, as fortune-seekers looted slave and silver from trade ships. Another attractive prize from Spanish ships was logwood, a timber used by the wool industry in Europe. Some pirates decided that cutting this wood themselves might be as profitable as stealing it. The British pirate-wood-cutters ended up congregating in the area of present-day Belize, where Spain exercised no effective control.

British settlements expanded around the mouth of the Belize River, eventually gaining the moniker British Honduras. Treaties in the late 18th century allowed the loggers to extract not only logwood, but also mahogany. In return, Britain agreed to abandon the Mosquito Coast of Nicaragua, bringing to the Crown Colony thousands of new settlers, most of whom were slaves of African origin.

TIMELINE	2400 BC	2000 BC –AD 250	AD 250 –1000
	The earliest known settlement in Belize is at Cuello in Orange Walk. It predates even the Preclassic period, and some archaeologists attribute the settlement to Mayan predecessors.	The earliest sedentary Maya communities are formed during the Preclassic period. Among the earliest Maya settlements are Cahal Pech in Cayo and Lamanai in Orange Walk.	The Classic period of the Maya civilization is characterized by the construction of cities and temples and other artistic and intellectual achievements. The population reaches around 400,000.

Mexico and Spain's Central American colonies won their independence in the 1820s, but this didn't improve the lot of the Maya in the Yucatán and Guatemala. They finally rose up in bloody rebellion, however unsuccessfully. Large numbers of refugees from both sides of the conflict fled into British Honduras, founding the towns of Orange Walk and Corozal.

Organized political action against colonialism did not begin in British Honduras until after the Great Depression in the 1930s. The newborn nationalist movement started out protesting against unemployment and injustice in colonial society. The 1950s saw the formation of new political parties, national strikes and – eventually – the implementation of universal adult suffrage. In successive decades, British Honduras became an internally self-governing colony and changed its name to Belize, before finally gaining independence in 1981.

From Lordly Realm to Lost World: Ancient Maya

Belize hosted one of the great Mesoamerican civilizations of ancient times, the Maya. The Maya created vibrant commercial centers, monumental religious temples and exquisite artworks. They possessed sophisticated knowledge about their earthly and cosmological environments, much of which they wrote down. The Maya thrived from roughly 2000 BC to AD 1500, before succumbing to domestic decline and alien assault. The stone foundations of their lordly realm became a lost world submerged beneath dense jungle.

The Maya ranged across Central America, from the Yucatán to Honduras, from the Pacific to the Caribbean. They were not ethnically homogeneous but only loosely related, divided by kinship, region and dialect. The different communities sometimes cooperated and often competed with one another, building alliances for trade and warfare.

Archaeological findings indicate that Maya settlements in Belize were among the oldest. In the west, Cahal Pech, an important commercial center between the coast and interior, was dated to around 1200 BC. In the north, majestic Lamanai, a major religious site for more than 2000 years, was founded as early as 1500 BC. In Belize today, three distinct Maya tribes still exist: the indigenous Mopan in the north; the Yucatec, who migrated from Mexico, also in the north; and the Kekchi, who migrated from Guatemala, in the west and south.

The Maya were organized into kingdoms, in which social and economic life was an extension of a rigid political hierarchy. At the top were the king – or high lord – and his royal family, followed by an elite stratum of priests, warriors and scribes; next came economically valued artisans and traders; and finally, holding it all up were subsistence farmers and servant workers. The system rested on a cultural belief that the high lord

History Books

Thirteen Chapters of a History of Belize, Assad Shoman

Belize: A Concise History, PAB Thomson

The Caste War of the Yucatán, Nelson Reed

900–1000	1000–1600	1540s	1638
The great Maya civilization declines, possibly as a result of drought, disease or environmental disaster. Large urban centers come under stress and their populations disperse throughout the region.	During the Postclassic Period, the Maya civilization continues to develop, although populations are not as concentrated. Political and cultural centers migrate to northern Belize and the Yucatán.	Spanish conquistadors sweep through northern and western Belize, attempting to establish strongholds in Chetumal near Corozal, Lamanai in Orange Walk, and Tipu in Cayo.	British Baymen 'settle' Belize when former pirate Peter Wallace lays the foundations for a new port at the mouth of the Belize River, on the site of today's Belize City.

had some influence with the powerful and dark gods of the underworld, who sometimes took the form of a jaguar when intervening in human affairs. This view was reinforced through the ruling elite's elaborately staged power displays, a temple theater of awe.

Even before the germ-ridden Europeans arrived, the cultural underpinnings of Maya society were already coming undone. A prolonged drought had caused severe economic hardship, leaving the impression that the kings and priests had somehow lost their supernatural touch. It was left to the Spanish, however, to officially cancel the show.

Possibly the most impressive of the Maya kingdoms in Belize was at Caracol, in the western Mountain Pine Ridge. At its height, in the 6th and 7th centuries, Caracol was a major urban metropolis, with more than 100,000 residents. It boasted first-rate jewelers and skilled artisans, an intricately terraced agriculture system, a prosperous trading market, and 40 miles of paved roads (considerably more than it has today). According to the story carved by Maya artists into commemorative stone, the king of Caracol, Water Lord, defeated his chief rival, Double Bird, king of Tikal, in a decisive battle in AD 562, ushering in a long period of Caracol supremacy in the central highlands. The pictographic stone inscriptions also suggest that Water Lord personally sacrificed Double Bird to further emphasize the Caracol triumph. Perhaps this had something to do with the still-simmering feud between Belize and Guatemala.

In the 1500s, the jaguar kings were forced to take cover in the rainforest when the sword-wielding Spanish arrived in Belize with the aim of plundering Maya gold and spreading the word of God. The Maya population of Belize at this time numbered about a quarter of a million, but their ranks were quickly decimated by as much as 90%, from the lethal combination of the disease and greed of the Spanish. In the 1540s, a conquistador force based in the Yucatán set out on an expedition through much of present-day Belize, down the coast and across to the central highlands. Disappointed by the lack of riches uncovered, they left a bloody trail of slaughtered victims and abandoned villages in their wake. Religious sites, such as Lamanai, were forcibly converted to Catholicism.

In the early 1600s, the Maya finally staged a counteroffensive that successfully drove out the few Spanish settlers and missionaries that had decided to stay. Weakened and fearful, the Maya did not return to the now desolate old cities, choosing instead to stay huddled in the remote interior.

Emory King's *The Great Story of Belize* is a fun read, and quite detailed, even though it has come under criticism for glamorizing the swashbuckling ways of the early British settlers.

Baymen of the Caribbean: British Settlement

When Columbus accidentally bumped into the continental landmass soon to be known as the Americas, his Spanish royal patrons Ferdinand and Isabella had it made. Soon, Aztec gold and Incan silver overflowed in

1638–40

Maya rebellion finally drives out the Spanish for good, although they never relinquish their claim to the territory. The Maya population drops dramatically due to war, drought and disease.

1667

Britain and Spain sign a treaty which grants freedom of trade, as long as Britain agrees to control piracy. The result is an increase in logging and the acceleration of settlement of Belize.

DANITA DELIMONT / GETTY IMAGES ©

➜ The Maya site of Xunantunich (p179)

the king's coffers, making Spain a transatlantic superpower. In 1494, the Treaty of Tordesillas established an exclusive Iberian claim on the region, declaring New World riches off-limits to old-world rivals. But the temptations were too great, and the hiding places too many. Spain's spoils were set upon by British buccaneers, French corsairs and Dutch freebooters. In times of war, they were put into the service of their Crown as privateers; at other times, they were simply pirates.

Belize emerged as one of several Caribbean outposts for Britain's maritime marauders. In the early 17th century, English sea dogs first began using the Bay of Honduras as a staging point for raids on Spanish commerce; henceforth the Brits in the region came to be known as Baymen.

The Belizean coast had several strategic advantages from a pirate's perspective. The land was both bountiful and uninhabited, as the Spanish had already driven the Maya out but never bothered to settle in themselves. It was just a short sail away from the heavily trafficked Yucatán Straits, where – if luck be with ye – the Treasure Fleet might be gathering in Havana or the Silver Train passing through on its way from Panama. And the shoreline, concealed behind thick mangroves and littoral islands, offered protective cover, while the long barrier reef was a treacherous underwater trap that kept Spanish war galleons at a distance.

For the sake of historical record, the year 1638 was made the official founding date of a British settlement at the mouth of the Belize River. It was around then that a Scottish pirate captain, Peter Wallace, decided to organize the building of a new port town. Legend has it that he laid the first foundations of what became Belize City with woodchips and rum bottles, presumably empty.

Meanwhile, the Baymen found yet another activity to annoy the Spanish crown – poaching its rainforest. The settlement became a rich source of hardwoods, especially mahogany, much valued by carpenters, furniture-makers and shipbuilders back in Britain. In addition, the lowland forest was abundant in logwood trees, which provided a valuable dye extract used to make woolen textiles.

By the 18th century, Britain's monarch finally had a navy and merchant fleet to match Spain's. Privateers were no longer needed, and pirates were a nuisance. In 1765 Jamaican-based British naval commander Admiral Burnaby paid a visit to the rough-hewn Baymen and delivered a code of laws on proper imperial etiquette: thieving, smuggling and cursing were out; paying taxes and obeying the sovereign were in.

As the British settlement became more profitable, the Spanish monarch became more irritable. Spain's armed forces made several unsuccessful attempts to dislodge the well-ensconced and feisty squatters. With the Treaty of Paris, in 1763, Spain instead tried diplomacy, negotiating a deal in which the Brits could stay and harvest wood as long as they

The virtually un-explored Glover's Atoll is named for the pirate John Glover, who hung out there in the 1750s; there are supposed to be pirate graves on Northeast Caye.

1724	1717–63	1786	1798
The first African slaves are recorded in Belize. Slaves are put to work cutting logwood and mahogany, as well as doing domestic work and farming.	Spanish attacks attempt to end British extraction of hardwoods. Finally, the Treaty of Paris gives Britain the right to cut and export logwood, but the Spanish still claim the land.	The Convention of London gives loggers the right to fell the forest, but not to establish any agriculture or government. However, an informal group of magistrates governs and agriculture exists.	During the seven-day Battle of St George's Caye, British Baymen and Creole slaves defend their settlement from Spanish invasion, finally ending Spanish claims on the territory.

THE FIRST MESTIZO

In 1511, the Spanish ship *Valdivia* was wrecked at sea when a reef ripped through its hull. About 15 survivors drifted for several days before making it to shore in northern Belize, where they were promptly apprehended by anxious Maya. Just to be on the safe side, the locals sent 10 to the gods and kept five for themselves.

One of the captives was conquistador Gonzalo Guerrero, a skilled warrior and apparently not a bad diplomat either. Guerrero managed to win his freedom and a position of status with the Maya chief at Chetumal. He became a tribal consultant on military matters and married the chief's daughter; their three children are considered the first Mestizos (mixed-race Spanish and indigenous people) in the New World.

Eight years later, Hernán Cortés arrived in the Yucatán and summoned Guerrero to serve him in his campaign of conquest. But Guerrero had gone native, with facial tattoos and body piercings. He turned down the offer, saying instead that he was a captain of the Maya. Cortés moved on in his search for gold and glory. Guerrero, meanwhile, organized Maya defenses in the wars that followed. It would take the Spanish more than 20 years to finally defeat the Maya of Yucatán and Belize.

paid rent to the Spanish Crown and promised not to expand the settlement. The Baymen did neither.

Spain finally got the better of the Baymen in 1779, burning down Belize City in a surprise attack and consigning the prisoners to slavery in Cuba. The conflict reached a decisive conclusion in 1798 at the Battle of St George's Caye when a squadron of 30 Spanish warships was met and turned back by the alerted Baymen operating in smaller but faster craft. From this point, Spain gave up trying to boot the Brits from Belize. And the battle made such a good story that it eventually inspired a national holiday (Battle of St George's Caye Day).

In 1872 the Crown Lands Ordinance established Carib Reserves and Maya Reserves, which stripped the Garifuna and Maya of their property rights.

In Living Color: British Honduras

In the 19th century, modern Belize began to take form, largely shaped by its economic role and political status in the British Empire, where it was officially dubbed British Honduras. At first it was administered from Jamaica, but later was made a Crown Colony with its own appointed royal governor. Belizean society was an overlapping patchwork of British, African, Maya and Spanish influences. It was a haven for refugees and a labor camp for slaves, a multicultural but hierarchical Crown Colony in living color.

At the top of the colonial social order were the descendants of the Baymen. In earlier times, their outlaw ancestors comprised an ethnically mixed and relatively democratic community. But as the colony grew

1832	1838	1847	1854
A group of Garifuna from Honduras settle in present-day Dangriga. This ethnic enclave was previously deported from the British-ruled island of St Vincent, after being defeated in the Carib Wars.	According to the Abolition Act, slavery is outlawed throughout the British Empire, including Belize. Former slaves are unable to own property and are dependent on their ex-master's for work.	Spanish, Mestizo and Maya peoples engage in the War of the Castes in the neighboring Yucatán Peninsula. The violence sends streams of refugees into Belize.	A new constitution establishes a Legislative Assembly of 18 elected, property-holding members, thus consolidating British political control of the territory.

larger and ties with the empire stronger, an oligarchy of leading families emerged. They may have descended from anti-establishment renegades, but now they were all about aristocratic manners. They touted their white, cultured British lineage, and used the Crown's authority to reinforce their status. By order of His Majesty's Superintendent for British Honduras, they alone were given political rights in colonial affairs and private entitlement to the forest and land. This elite colonial cohort managed to hold sway until the early 20th century.

As the economy was centered on timber exports, strong bodies were needed to perform the arduous labor of harvesting hardwoods from the dense rainforest. As elsewhere in the Americas, African slaves provided the muscle, along with much sweat and pain. By 1800 the settlement numbered about 4000 in total: 3000 black slaves, 900 mixed-race coloreds and free blacks, and 100 white colonists. Slave masters could count, and acted shrewdly to stay on top. Male slaves were kept divided into small work teams based on tribal origins. They were forced to do long tours of duty in remote jungle camps, separated from other teams and from their families. Slave women performed domestic chores and farm work. Interacial separation, however, did not mean interracial segregation, as mixed-race Creoles (descendants of African slaves) would eventually make up nearly 75% of the population.

In 1838 slavery was abolished in the British Empire. The plight of Afro-Belizeans, however, did not much improve. They were forbidden from owning land, which would have enabled them to be self-sufficient, and thus remained dependent on the white-controlled export economy. Instead of slaves, they were called 'apprentices' and worked for subsistence wages.

When the timber market declined in the 1860s, landowners diversified their holdings by introducing fruit and sugarcane. One persistent historical narrative has it that slave life in Belizean logging camps was more benign than the harsh conditions that existed on Caribbean sugar plantations. While this may be so, the facts remain that Belize experienced four major slave revolts between 1760 and 1820, and recorded a high annual incidence of runaways, suggesting instead that repressive inhumanity may come in different packages.

Toward the mid-19th century, British colonists finally came into contact – and conflict – with the indigenous Maya. As loggers penetrated deeper into the interior, they encountered the elusive natives, who responded with hit-and-run assaults on the encroaching axmen.

At this time in the neighboring Yucatán Peninsula, an armed conflict broke out among the lowly Maya, second-class Mestizos and privileged Spanish-descended landlords. The bloody War of the Castes raged for over

Colonial Sights

Government House, Belize City

Museum of Belize, Belize City

St John's Cathedral, Belize City

HISTORY IN LIVING COLOR: BRITISH HONDURAS

1862	1865	1871	1927
The settlement in Belize is declared a Crown Colony and named British Honduras. Initially it is administered from Jamaica, but a separate royal governor is appointed soon after.	The Serpon sugar mill – the country's first steam-powered mill – is built on the Sittee River, ushering in an era of economic development.	A new constitution establishes a nine-member Legislative Council, which governs the colony alongside the lieutenant governor.	Successful international trading ties give rise to a prosperous Creole elite, which gains formal means of power when several representatives are appointed to the Legislative Council.

BELIZEAN STARS & BARS

At the end of the US Civil War, several thousand Confederate soldiers chose not to return to their defeated and occupied homeland. The rebels instead accepted an invitation to resettle under the British flag in Belize.

The white colonial elite of Belize sympathized with the Southern cause during the conflict. During the war, they supplied the Confederacy with raw materials and guns. After the war, colonial officials enticed the war veterans with promises of land grants and other economic incentives. It was hoped that these expatriate Americans could help rejuvenate the Belizean economy, which suffered from a decline in timber exports, by sharing their expertise of the plantation system.

As many as 7000 American Southerners made it to Belize in the 1860s, mostly arriving from Mississippi and Louisiana, with the dream of re-creating the Old South in tropical climes. Their initial attempts to cultivate cotton, however, were dashed by the inhospitable steamy jungle climate. They had better luck with sugarcane. The Confederate contribution to the colonial economy was notable, as Belizean sugar exports between 1862 and 1868 increased four-fold, from 400,000lb to 1,700,000lb.

But the move did not go smoothly. The American newcomers had run-ins with the local white landowners, who resented their presence and privileges, and with the local black workforce, who refused to submit and serve. All but a couple of hundred of the Confederate contingent eventually cashed out and returned home.

a decade and forced families to flee. Caste War refugees more than doubled the Belize population, from less than 10,000 in 1845 to 25,000 in 1861.

The movement of peoples redefined the ethnic character of northern Belize. Mestizo refugees, of mixed Spanish-Indian stock, brought their Hispanic tongue, corn tortillas and Catholic churches to scattered small-town settlements. Yucatecan Maya refugees, meanwhile, moved into the northwestern Belizean forest, where they quickly clashed with the logging industry. In 1872 the desperate Maya launched a quixotic attack on British colonists at Orange Walk, in what was a fierce but futile last stand. Diminished and dispirited, the remaining Maya survived on the territorial and social fringes of the colony.

Patience & Resistance: Belizean Independence

Belize remained a British colony until 1981, rather late for the West Indies. Spain and France lost most Caribbean possessions in the early 19th century, while Her Majesty's island colonies were liberated in the 1960s. With its ethnic divisions, a unifying national identity formed slowly, and the Belizean independence movement displayed more patience than resistance.

1931	1950	1961	1971
The deadliest hurricane in Belizean history hits on September 10, when the country is celebrating the national holiday. Belize City is destroyed, as is most of the northern coast; 2500 people die.	A severe economic crisis sparks anti-British protests, and the pro-independence movement is launched under the leadership of George Price and the People's United Party (PUP).	Hurricane Hattie devastates Belize, killing hundreds of people and destroying Belize City. British naval troops arrive to control widespread violence and looting.	In response to the devastation wrought by Hurricane Hattie, a new inland capital is established at Belmopan. The new National Assembly building is designed to resemble a Maya temple.

As the 19th century closed, the orderly ways of colonial life in British Honduras showed signs of breakdown. The old elite was becoming more isolated and less feared. Its cozy connections to the mother country were unraveling. By 1900 the US surpassed Britain as the main destination of the mahogany harvest; by 1930 the US was taking in 80% of all Belizean exports.

The colonial elite's economic position was further undercut by the rise of a London-based conglomerate, the British Estate and Produce Company, which bought out local landowners and took over the commodity trade. Declining timber fortunes caused colonial capitalists to impose a 50% wage cut on mahogany workers in Belize City, which provoked riotous protests and the first stirrings of social movement.

During the first half of the 20th century, Belizean nationalism developed in explosive fits and starts. During WWI, a regiment of local Creoles was recruited for the Allied cause. The experience proved both disheartening and enlightening. Ill-treated because of their dark skin, they were not even allowed to go to the front line and fight alongside white troops. They may have enlisted as patriotic Brits, but they were discharged as resentful Belizeans. Upon their return, in 1919, they coaxed several thousand into the streets of Belize City in an angry demonstration against the existing order.

It was not until the 1930s that a more sustained anticolonial movement arose. It began as the motley 'Unemployed Brigade,' staging weekend rallies in Battlefield Park in Belize City. The movement fed on the daily discontents of impoverished black workers, and spewed its wrath at prosperous white merchants. It soon was organizing boycotts and strikes, and shortly thereafter its leaders were thrown into jail.

Finally, in the early 1950s, a national independence party, the People's United Party (PUP), became politically active. When WWII caused the sudden closing of export markets, the colony experienced a severe economic crisis that lasted until well after the war's end. Anti-British demonstrations spread all across Belize, becoming more militant and occasionally violent. Colonial authorities declared a state of emergency, forbidding public meetings and intimidating independence advocates.

In response, the PUP organized a successful general strike that finally forced Britain to make political concessions. Universal suffrage was extended to all adults and limited home rule was permitted in the colony. The imperial foundations of the old ruling elite crumbled, as the colony's ethnically divided peoples now danced to a common Belizean drum beat.

Full independence for Belize was put off until a nagging security matter was resolved. Spain never formally renounced its territorial claim to Belize, which was later appropriated by Mexico and Guatemala. In the

In 1988 the Duke of Edinburgh and World Wildlife Fund head, Prince Philip, was on hand to celebrate the creation of the Cockscomb Basin Wildlife Sanctuary, the world's first wildlife sanctuary for the jaguar. By 1998, the protected realm of the Belizean jungle's king eventually reached more than half a million acres.

HISTORY PATIENCE & RESISTANCE: BELIZEAN INDEPENDENCE

1972

Jacques Cousteau takes his research ship *Calypso* to the Blue Hole, bringing unprecedented publicity and kicking off its popularity as a destination for divers and snorkelers.

1975

Young activist attorneys Said Musa and Assad Shoman begin an intensive campaign to obtain international support for an independent Belize.

1981

After years of anticolonial and pro-independence political movements, Belize receives formal international recognition of its independence. George Price (PUP) is the first prime minister.

BURNETT & PALMER / GETTY IMAGES ©

→ Diving at Blue Hole (p120)

MAYAN CODE

19th century, Britain signed agreements with both claimants to recognize the existing colonial borders, but the one with Guatemala did not stick.

Guatemala's caudillo (Spanish/Latin American military dictator) rulers remained very preoccupied with the perceived wealth of British Honduras. The 1945 Guatemalan constitution explicitly included Belize as part of its territorial reach. Britain, in turn, stationed a large number of troops in the west. Guatemala barked, but did not bite. By the 1960s, the border threat was stabilized and the demand for independence was renewed.

Belizeans waited patiently. In 1964 the colony became fully self-governing, installing a Westminster-style parliamentary system. In 1971 the capital was relocated to Belmopan, a geographic center symbolically uniting all regions and peoples. In 1973 the name was officially changed from the colonial sounding British Honduras to the more popular Belize. And in September 1981 Belize was at last declared an independent nation-state within the British Commonwealth. Even Guatemala recognized Belize as a sovereign nation in 1991, although to this day it maintains its territorial claim.

Return of the Jaguar King: Contemporary Belize

Independence did not turn out to be a cure-all. The angry nationalists that led Belize to independence turned into accommodating capitalists. The country had a small economy whose fortunes were determined beyond its control in global commodity markets. Belizeans eventually discovered that rather than remain vulnerable to exports, they had something valuable to import: tourists. The rise of ecotourism and revival of Maya culture has reshaped contemporary Belize, and cleared the jungle overgrowth for a return of the jaguar king.

Belizean politics were long dominated by the founder of the nationalist People's United Party (PUP), George Price. His party won nearly every parliamentary election, consolidating political independence and promoting a new middle class. In 1996, at the age of 75, Price finally stepped down with his national hero status intact; the PUP, however, looked vulnerable.

The party was tainted by corruption scandals: missing pension funds, selling off of public lands and bribery. Supporters argue that other parties' politicians are guilty of similar crimes.

The frail economy inherited at the time of independence was slow to recover. Many Creoles began to look for work outside the country, forming sizeable diaspora communities in New York and London. As much as one-third of the Belizean people now live abroad. Meanwhile, civil war and rural poverty in neighboring Guatemala and Honduras sent more refugees into Belize, whose demographic profile changed accordingly, with Spanish-speaking Mestizos becoming the majority ethnic group.

In 1984, 18-year-old David Stuart became the youngest person to receive a McArthur Genius Award for his work in cracking the Mayan hieroglyphic code, which he had been working on since the age of 10.

1991	1994	1998	2002
Guatemala finally recognizes Belize as a sovereign, independent state. Tensions continue, however, as the neighbor to the west refuses to relinquish its territorial claim over parts of Belize.	The United Kingdom withdraws military forces, with the exception of the British Army Training & Support Unit, which is established to assist the new Belize Defence Force.	Promising to 'Set Belize Free,' the People's United Party (PUP) takes the national elections, winning 26 of 31 seats in the House of Representatives. Party leader Said Musa becomes prime minister.	The purpose-built Tourism Village opens in Belize City to welcome cruise-ship passengers to Belize. The following year, the tiny country hosts more than half a million cruise-ship tourists.

From the time of independence, the Belize nation has doubled in size, from 150,000 in 1981 to 333,200 in 2010.

Belize was an ideal candidate for a green revolution. Wide swaths of lowland rainforest were unspoiled by loggers, while sections of the interior highland had never even been explored by Europeans. The jungle hosted a rich stock of exotic flora and fauna, feathered and furry, while just offshore was the magnificent coral reef and mysterious Blue Hole, which Jacques Cousteau had already made famous.

A Tourist Ministry was created in 1984, but it was not until the 1990s that the government began to recognize ecotourism as a viable revenue source and invested in its promotion and development. Infrastructure associated with various sites improved, small business loans became available, training programs were organized for guides, and a bachelor's degree in tourism was created at Belize University.

Over the next decade, more than 20 sites from the western mountains to the eastern cayes were designated as national parks, wildlife sanctuaries, forest reserves and marine preserves. More than 40% of Belizean territory received some form of protective status, including 80% of its pristine rainforest. The number of visitors rose steadily, from 140,000 in 1988 to more than a million in 2010. By the end of the 1990s, tourism was Belize's fastest-growing economic sector, surpassing commodity exports.

The ecocraze coincided with archaeological advances to spur a revival of Maya culture. In the 1980s, significant progress was made in cracking the Mayan hieroglyphic code, enabling researchers to gain deeper insights into this once-shrouded world, while NASA satellite technology revealed over 600 previously unknown sites and hidden temples beneath the Belizean rainforest. In 2000 the government allocated nearly $30 million to support excavation projects. A lost culture became a live commodity. Maya descendants re-engaged with traditional ceremonies, craftmaking, food preparation and healing techniques, often in response to touristy curiosity. However, the commercial aspects of cultural revival can be controversial, and one doesn't have to look far for examples where tourism and sanctity clash. One example concerns Cayo's Actun Tunichil Muknal cave, which is at once a sacred spot to the Maya and a top tourist attraction. After one visitor dropped a camera, fracturing an ancient human skull, cameras were banned from the cave. This example, among others, begs the question of how to promote cultural tourism while avoiding a carnival atmosphere.

In contemporary Belize, the new understanding of the Maya past fostered a changed attitude in the Maya present. The Maya culture is no longer disparaged at the fringe of society, but now is a source of pride and a defining feature of Belizean identity.

HISTORY RETURN OF THE JAGUARKING: CONTEMPORARY BELIZE

In 2008, the Belize and Guatemala governments signed an historic agreement to refer their territorial conflict to the International Court of Justice, pending approval from their electorates. The referenda – which must be held in both countries simultaneously – have not been scheduled due to the volatile political climate in Guatemala.

2006
Black gold. After more than four years of exploration around the country, oil is discovered in commercially viable quantities in the Mennonite village of Spanish Lookout.

2008
Led by Dean Barrow, the United Democratic Party (UDP) overwhelmingly defeats the PUP in countrywide elections, capturing 25 out of 31 seats in the House of Representatives.

2011
Under pressure from local residents and hotel owners, the Belize Tourism Board decides against the development of a new cruiseship port on Placencia peninsula.

2012
While the United Democratic Party (UDP) loses several seats in the general election, it holds onto its majority with 17 seats to the PUP's 14.

Ancient Maya

Though the Maya population of Belize is small (around 10% of the nation's population), imagining contemporary Belize without the Maya would be difficult. From the Cayo District's Caracol (which covers more area than Belize City and still boasts Belize's tallest structure) and Xunantunich to smaller archeological sites stretching from the nation's far north into its deep south, remnants of ancient Maya glory abound.

Dr Allen J Christenson has an MA and a PhD in Pre-Columbian Maya Art and Literature, and works as a professor in the Humanities, Classics and Comparative Literature department of Brigham Young University in Provo, Utah. His works include *Popol Vuh: The Sacred Book of the Maya* (2003), a critical translation of the Popol Vuh from the original Maya text.

Nearly all aspects of Maya faith begin with their view of the creation, when the gods and divine forebears established the world at the beginning of time. From their hieroglyphic texts and art carved on stone monuments and buildings, or painted on pottery, we can now piece together much of the Maya view of the creation. We can even read the precise date when the creation took place.

In AD 775 a Maya lord with the high-sounding name of K'ak' Tiliw Chan Yoat (Fire Burning Sky Lightning God) set up an immense stone monument in the center of his city, Quirigua, in Guatemala. The unimaginative archaeologists who discovered the stone called it Stela C. This monument bears the longest single hieroglyphic description of the creation, noting that it took place on the day 13.0.0.0.0, 4 Ahaw, 8 Kumk'u, a date corresponding to August 13, 3114 BC on our calendar. This date appears over and over in other inscriptions throughout the Maya world. On that day the creator gods set three stones or mountains in the dark waters that once covered the primordial world. These three stones formed a cosmic hearth at the center of the universe. The gods then struck divine new fire by means of lightning, which charged the world with new life.

This account of the creation is echoed in the first chapters of the *Popol Vuh*, a book compiled by members of the Maya nobility soon after the Spanish conquest in 1524, many centuries after the erection of Quirigua Stela C. Although this book was written in their native Maya language, its authors used European letters rather than the more terse hieroglyphic script. Thus the book gives a fuller account of how they conceived the first creation:

This is the account of when all is still, silent and placid. All is silent and calm. Hushed and empty is the womb of the sky. These then are the first words, the first speech. There is not yet one person, one animal, bird, fish, crab, tree, rock, hollow, canyon, meadow or forest. All alone the sky exists. The face of the earth has not yet appeared. Alone lies the expanse of the sea, along with the womb of all the sky. There is not yet anything gathered together. All is at rest. Nothing stirs. All is languid, at rest in the sky. Only the expanse of the water, only the tranquil sea lies alone. All lies placid and silent in the darkness, in the night.

All alone are the Framer and the Shaper, Sovereign and Quetzal Serpent, They Who Have Borne Children and They Who Have Begotten Sons. Luminous they are in the water, wrapped in feathers...They are great sages, great possessors of knowledge...Then they called forth the mountains from the water. Straightaway the great mountains

Books on Maya Art & Architecture

Maya Art & Architecture by Mary Ellen Miller

The Ancient Maya by Robert J Sharer

came to be. It was merely their spirit essence, their miraculous power, that brought about the conception of the mountains.

The Maya saw this pattern all around them. In the night sky, the three brightest stars in the constellation of Orion's Belt were conceived as the cosmic hearth at the center of the universe. On a clear night in the crisp mountain air of the Maya highlands, one can even see what looks like a wisp of smoke within these stars, although it is really only a far-distant string of stars within the M4 Nebula.

Popol Vuh: The Sacred Book of the Maya

Maya Cities as the Center of Creation

Perhaps because the ancient Maya of northern Belize didn't have real mountains as symbols of the creation, they built them instead in the form of plaza-temple complexes. In hieroglyphic inscriptions, the large openair plazas at the center of Maya cities are often called *nab'* (sea) or *lakam ja'* (great water). Rising above these plastered stone spaces are massive pyramid temples, often oriented in groups of three, representing the first mountains to emerge out of the 'waters' of the plaza. The tiny elevated sanctuaries of these temples served as portals into the abodes of gods that lived within. Offerings were burned on altars in the plazas, as if the flames were struck in the midst of immense three-stone hearths. Only a few elite persons were allowed to enter the small interior spaces atop the temples, while the majority of the populace observed their actions from the plaza below. The architecture of ancient Maya centers thus replicated sacred geography to form an elaborate stage on which rituals that charged their world with regenerative power could be carried out.

Many of the earliest-known Maya cities were built in Belize. The earliest temples at these sites are often constructed in this three-temple arrangement, grouped together on a single platform, as an echo of the first three mountains of creation. The ancient name for the site known today as Caracol was Oxwitza' (Three Hills Place), symbolically linking this community with the three mountains of creation and thus the center of life. The Caana (Sky-Place) is the largest structure at Caracol and consists of a massive pyramid-shaped platform topped by three temples that represent these three sacred mountains.

The Belizean site of Lamanai is one of the oldest and largest Maya cities known. It is also one of the few Maya sites that still bears its ancient name (which means Submerged Crocodile). While other sites were abandoned well before the Spanish Conquest in the 16th century, Lamanai continued to be occupied by the Maya centuries afterward. For the ancient Maya the crocodile symbolized the rough surface of the earth, newly emerged from the primordial sea that once covered the world.

Preclassic Maya Sites

Cuello (p127), Orange Walk

Lamanai (p130), Orange Walk

Cerro Maya (p143), Corozal

Caracol (p167), Cayo

Altun Ha (p69), Belize District

ANCIENT MAYA MAYA CITIES AS THE CENTER OF CREATION

For a lively discussion of Maya religion and the creation, pick up a copy of *Maya Cosmos* by David Freidel, Linda Schele and Joy Parker.

THE HERO TWINS

According to the *Popol Vuh,* the Lords of Xibalba (the underworld) invited Hun Hunahpu and his brother to a game in the ballcourt. Upon losing the game, the brothers were sacrificed and the skull of one of them was suspended from a calabash tree as a show of triumph.

Along came an unsuspecting daughter of Xibalba. As she reached out to take fruit from the tree, the skull of Hun Hunahpu spat in her hand, thus impregnating her. From this strange conception would be born the Hero Twins, Hunahpu and Xbalanque.

The Hero Twins would go on to have many adventures, including vanquishing their evil half-brothers. Their final triumph was overcoming Xibalba and avenging the death of their father – first by fooling the Lords, and then by sacrificing them. After this, the twins ascended into the sky, being transformed into the sun and moon.

Mara Vorhees

POPOL VUH

The name of the city reveals that its inhabitants saw themselves as living at the center of creation, rising from the waters of creation. Its massive pyramid temples include Structure N10-43, which is the second-largest pyramid known from the Maya Preclassic period and represents the first mountain and dwelling place of the gods.

The Maya Creation of Mankind

According to the *Popol Vuh,* the purpose of the creation was to give form and shape to beings who would 'remember' the gods through ritual. The Maya take their role in life very seriously. They believe that people exist as mediators between this world and that of the gods. If they fail to carry out the proper prayers and ceremonies at just the right time and place, the universe will come to an abrupt end.

The gods created the first people out of maize (corn) dough, literally from the flesh of the Maize God, the principal deity of creation. Because of their divine origin, they were able to see with miraculous vision:

> Perfect was their sight, and perfect was their knowledge of everything beneath the sky. If they gazed about them, looking intently, they beheld that which was in the sky and that which was upon the earth. Instantly they were able to behold everything...Thus their knowledge became full. Their vision passed beyond the trees and the rocks, beyond the lakes and the seas, beyond the mountains and the valleys. Truly they were very esteemed people.
>
> *Popol Vuh: The Sacred Book of the Maya*

The oldest known copy of the *Popol Vuh* was made around 1701–03 by a Roman Catholic priest named Francisco Ximénez, in Guatemala. The location of the original Popol Vuh from which Ximénez made his copy, if it still survives, is unknown.

In nearly all of their languages, the Maya refer to themselves as 'true people' and consider that they are literally of a different flesh than those who do not eat maize. They are maize people, and foreigners who eat bread are wheat people. This mythic connection between maize and human flesh influenced birth rituals in the Maya world for centuries.

Maya Kingship

The creation wasn't a one-time event. The Maya constantly repeated these primordial events in their ceremonies, timed to the sacred calendar. They saw the universe as a living thing. And just like any living thing, it grows old, weakens and ultimately passes away. Everything, including the gods, needed to be periodically recharged with life-bearing power or the world would slip back into the darkness and chaos that existed before the world began. Maya kings were seen as mediators. In countless wall carvings and paintings, monumental stone stelae and altars, painted pottery and other sacred objects, the Maya depicted their kings dressed as gods, repeating the actions of deities at the time of creation.

A common theme was the king dressed as the Maize God himself, bearing a huge pack on his back containing the sacred bits and pieces that make up the world, while dancing them into existence. A beautiful

AMAZING MAIZE

No self-respecting Maya, raised in the traditional way, would consider eating a meal that didn't include maize. They treat it with the utmost respect. Women do not let grains of maize fall on the ground or into an open fire. If it happens accidentally, the woman picks it up gently and apologizes to it. The Maya love to talk and laugh, but are generally silent during meals. Most don't know why; it's just the way things have always been done. As one elder explained, 'For us, tortillas are like the Catholic sacramental bread: it is the flesh of god. You don't laugh or speak when taking the flesh of god into your body. The young people are beginning to forget this. They will someday regret it.'

GUIDE TO THE GODS

The Maya worshiped a host of heavenly beings. It's practically impossible to remember them all (especially since some of them have multiple names), but here's a primer for the most powerful Maya gods.

Ah Puch God of Death

Chaac God of Rain and Thunder

Itzamma God of Priestly Knowledge and Writing

Hun Hunahpu Father of the Hero Twins, sometimes considered the Maize God

Hunahpu & Xbalanque The Hero Twins

Ixchel Goddess of Fertility and Birth

Mara Vorhees

example of this may be seen on the painted *Buena Vista Vase,* one of the true masterpieces of Maya art. Discovered at Buenavista el Cayo, a small site in the Cayo District of Belize, right on the river (north side) close to the border with Guatemala, it is now one of the gems of the Maya collection housed in the Department of Archaeology, Belize City. These rituals were done at very specific times of the year, timed to match calendric dates when the gods first performed them. For the Maya, these ceremonies were not merely symbolic of the rebirth of the cosmos, but a genuine creative act in which time folded in on itself to reveal the actions of the divine creators in the primordial world.

In Maya theology, the Maize God is the most sacred of the creator deities because he gives his very flesh in order for human beings to live. But this sacrifice must be repaid. The Maya, as 'true people,' felt an obligation to the cosmos to compensate for the loss of divine life, not because the gods were cruel, but because gods cannot rebirth themselves and need the intercession of human beings. Maya kings stood as the sacred link between their subjects and the gods. The king was thus required to periodically give that which was most precious - his own blood, which was believed to contain the essence of godhood itself. Generally, this meant that members of the royal family bled themselves with stingray spines or stone lancets. Males did their bloodletting from the genital area, literally birthing gods from the penis. Women most often drew blood from their tongues. This royal blood was collected on sheets of bark paper and then burned to release its divine essence, opening a portal to the other world and allowing the gods to emerge to a new life. At times of crisis, such as the end of a calendar cycle, or upon the death of a king and the succession of another, the sacrifice had to be greater to compensate for the loss of divine life. This generally involved obtaining noble or royal captives through warfare against a neighboring Maya state in order to sacrifice them.

Altar 23 from Caracol shows two captive lords from the Maya cities of B'ital and Ucanal, on the Guatemala–Belize border, with their arms bound behind their backs in preparation for sacrifice, perhaps on that very altar. If this were not done, they believed that life itself would cease to exist.

The beauty of Maya religion is that these great visions of creation mirror everyday events in the lives of the people. When a Maya woman rises early in the morning, before dawn, to grind maize for the family meal, she replicates the actions of the creators at the beginning of time. The darkness that surrounds her is reminiscent of the gloom of the primordial world. When she lights the three-stone hearth on the floor of her home, she is once again striking the new fire that generates life. The

Like ancient Greece, there was no unified Maya empire. Each city had its own royal family and its own patron gods. Warfare was often conducted not for conquest, but to obtain captives who bore within their veins royal blood to be sacrificed.

grains of maize that she cooks and then forms into tortillas are literally the flesh of the Maize God, who nourishes and rebuilds the bodies of her family members. This divine symmetry is comforting in a world that often proves intolerant and cruel.

Maya Hieroglyphic Writing

More than 1500 years prior to the Spanish Conquest, the Maya developed a sophisticated hieroglyphic script capable of recording complex literary compositions, both on folded screen codices made of bark paper or deer skin, as well as texts incised on more durable stone or wood. The importance of preserving written records was a hallmark of Maya culture, as witnessed by the thousands of known hieroglyphic inscriptions, many more of which are still being discovered in the jungles of Belize and other Maya regions. The sophisticated Maya hieroglyphic script is partly phonetic (glyphs representing sounds tied to the spoken language) and partly logographic (glyphs representing entire words), making it capable of recording any idea that could be thought or spoken.

The Maya hieroglyphic writing system is one of only five major phonetic scripts ever invented – the others being cuneiform (used in ancient Mesopotamia), Egyptian, Harappan and Chinese.

Ancient Maya scribes were among the most honored members of their society. They were often important representatives of the royal family and, as such, were believed to carry the seeds of divinity within their blood. Among the titles given to artists and scribes in Maya inscriptions of the Classic period were *itz'aat* (sage) and *miyaatz* (wise one).

Counting System

Maya arithmetic was elegantly simple: dots were used to count from one to four, a horizontal bar signified five, a bar with one dot above it was six, a bar with two dots was seven etc. Two bars signified 10, three bars 15. Nineteen, the highest common number, was three bars stacked up and topped by four dots.

HOW THE MAYA CALENDAR WORKED

The ancient Maya used three calendars. The first was a period of 260 days, known as the Tzolkin, likely based on the nine months it takes for a human fetus to develop prior to birth. The second Maya calendar system was a solar year of 365 days, called the Haab. Both the Tzolkin and Haab were measured in endlessly repeating cycles. When meshed together, a total of 18,980 day-name permutations are possible (a period of 52 solar years), called the Calendar Round.

Though fascinating in its complexity, the Calendar Round has its limitations, the greatest being that it only goes for 52 years. After that, it starts again and so provides no way for Maya ceremony planners to distinguish a day in this 52-year Calendar Round cycle from the identically named day in the next cycle. Thus the Maya developed a third calendar system that we call the Long Count, which pinpoints a date based on the number of days after the day of creation on August 13, 3114 BC it takes place.

Let's use the date of Friday April 1, 2011 as an example. The Maya Long Count date corresponding to this day is 12.19.18.4.10, 3 Uayeb 11 Oc.

The first number, '12,' of this Long Count date represents how many *baktuns* (400 x 360 days: 144,000 days) have passed since the day of creation (thus 12 x 144,000 = 1,728,000 days). The second number, '19,' represents the number of *katuns* (20 x 360: 7200 days) that have passed, thus adding another 19 x 7200 = 136,800 days. The third number, '18,' is the number of *tuns* (360 days), ie 6480 days. The fourth number, '4,' is the number of *uinals* (20 days), ie 80 days. Finally the fifth number, '10,' is the number of whole days. Adding each of these numbers gives us the sum of 1,728,000 + 136,800 + 6480 + 80 + 10 = 1,871,370 days since the day of creation.

The Maya then added the Calendar Round date: the Haab date (3 Uayeb) and the Tzolkin date (11 Oc).

The Mayan Calendar System

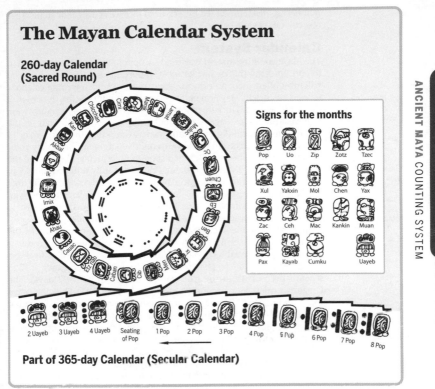

260-day Calendar (Sacred Round)

Signs for the months

Pop · Uo · Zip · Zotz · Tzec

Xul · Yakkin · Mol · Chen · Yax

Zac · Ceh · Mac · Kankin · Muan

Pax · Kayab · Cumku · Uayeb

2 Uayeb · 3 Uayeb · 4 Uayeb · Seating of Pop · 1 Pop · 2 Pop · 3 Pop · 4 Pop · 5 Pop · 6 Pop · 7 Pop · 8 Pop

Part of 365-day Calendar (Secular Calendar)

The Maya didn't use a decimal system (which is based on the number 10), but rather a vigesimal system (that is, a system that has a base of 20). The late Mayanist Linda Schele used to suggest that this was because they wore sandals and thus counted not only their fingers but their toes as well. This is a likely explanation, since the number 20 in nearly all Mayan languages means 'person.'

To signify larger sums the Maya used positional numbers – a fairly sophisticated system similar to the one we use today and much more advanced than the crude additive numbers used in the Roman Empire. In positional numbers, the position of a sign and the sign's value determine the number. For example, in our decimal system the number 23 is made up of two signs: a 2 in the 'tens' position and a 3 in the 'ones' position; two tens plus three ones equals 23.

In the Maya system, positions of increasing value went not right to left (as ours do) but from bottom to top. So the bottom position showed values from one to 19 (remember that this is a base-20 system so three bars and four dots in this lowest position would equal 19); the next position up showed multiples of 20 (for example four dots at this position would equal 80); the next position represents multiples of 400; the next, multiples of 8000 etc. By adding more positions one could count as high as needed.

Such positional numbers depend upon the use of zero – a concept that the Romans never developed but the Maya did. The zero in Maya

> The Maya likely used their counting system from day to day by writing on the ground, the tip of the finger creating a dot. By using the edge of the hand they could make a bar, representing the entire hand of five fingers.

numbering was represented by a stylized picture of a shell or some other object – but never a bar or a dot.

Calendar System

The Maya counting system was used by merchants and others who had to add up many things, but its most important use – and the one you will most often encounter during your travels – was in writing calendar dates. The ancient Maya calendar was a way of interpreting the order of the universe itself. The sun, moon and stars were not simply handy ways of measuring the passage of time, but living beings that influenced the world in fundamentally important ways. Even today, the Maya refer to days as 'he.' The days and years were conceived as being carried by gods, each with definite personalities and spheres of influence that colored the experience of those who lived them. Priests carefully watched the sky to look for the appearance of celestial bodies that would determine the time to plant and harvest crops, celebrate certain ceremonies, or go to war. The regular rotation of the heavens served as a comforting contrast to the chaos that characterizes our imperfect human world.

In some ways, the ancient Maya calendar – still used in parts of the region – is more accurate than the Gregorian calendar we use today. Without sophisticated technology, Maya astronomers were able to ascertain the length of the solar year as 365.2420 days (a discrepancy of 17.28 seconds per year from the true average length of 365.2422 days). The Gregorian calendar year works out to be 365.2425 days. Thus the Maya year count is 1/10,000 closer to the truth than our own modern calendar.

Maya astronomers were able to pinpoint eclipses with uncanny accuracy, a skill that was unknown among the brightest scholars in contemporary medieval Europe. The Maya lunar cycle was a mere seven minutes off today's sophisticated technological calculations. They calculated the Venus cycle at 583.92 days. By dropping four days each 61 Venus years and eight days at the end of 300 Venus years, the Maya lost less than a day in accuracy in 1000 years!

The ancient Maya believed that the Great Cycle of the present age would last for 13 *baktun* cycles in all (each *baktun* lasting 144,000 days), which according to our calendar ended on December 23, AD 2012, beginning a new cycle. The Maya saw the end of large cycles of time as a kind of death, and they were thus fraught with peril. But both death and life must dance together on the cosmic stage for the succession of days to come. Thus the Maya conducted ceremonies to periodically 'rebirth' the world and keep the endless march of time going.

The Maya never expected the end of this Great Cycle to be the last word for the cosmos, since the world regularly undergoes death and rebirth. Koba Stela 1 (the first stela from the site of Koba) records a period of time equivalent to approximately 41,341,050,000,000,000,000,000,000,000 of our years! (In comparison, the Big Bang that is said to have formed our universe is estimated to have occurred a mere 15,000,000,000 years ago.)

When the Spaniards arrived, Christian missionaries zealously burned all the Maya hieroglyphic books they could find. Only four are known to have survived and are held in Dresden, Madrid, Paris and Mexico City.

If you are curious about how scholars unlocked the secrets of Maya hieroglyphics, read Michael Coe's *Breaking the Maya Code*. It reads like a detective novel.

The People of Belize

Belize is a tiny country (population around 333,200), but it enjoys a diversity of ethnicities that is undeniably stimulating and improbably serene. Four main ethnic groups – Mestizo, Creole, Maya and Garifuna – comprise 76% of the population. The remaining 24% includes East Indians (people of Indian subcontinent origins), Chinese, Spanish, Arabs (generally Lebanese), the small but influential group of Mennonites, and North Americans and Europeans who have settled here in the last couple of decades.

Mestizo
Mestizos are people of mixed Spanish and indigenous descent. Over the last couple of decades, Mestizos have become Belize's largest ethnic group, now making up about 34% of the population. The first Mestizos arrived in the mid-19th century, when refugees from the Yucatán flooded into northern and western Belize during the War of the Castes. Their modern successors are the thousands of political refugees from troubled neighboring Central American countries. While English remains Belize's official language, Spanish is spoken by over half of the population; this has caused some resentment among Creoles, who are fiercely proud of their country's Anglo roots.

Creoles
Belizean Creoles are descendants of African slaves and British baymen, loggers and colonists. In the 1780s, after much conflict, the Spanish and the British finally reached an agreement allowing Brits to cut logwood from the area between the Rio Hondo and the Belize River (essentially the northern half of Belize). Three years later, according to the Convention of London, the area was extended south.

The convention also permitted the British to cut mahogany, a hardwood that was highly valued in Europe for making furniture. In return, Britain agreed to abandon the Mosquito Coast of Nicaragua, prompting 2214 new settlers to come to Belize and quadrupling its non-Maya population. Three-quarters of the newcomers were slaves of African origin.

This influx of slave labor was convenient for the loggers. Mahogany is a much larger tree than logwood, and

WHO ARRIVED WHEN

2000 BC–AD 250
The oldest Maya sites in Belize – including Cahal Pech and Lamanai – date to the Preclassic period of this indigenous civilization.

16th century
By now dispersed and depopulated, the Maya nonetheless resist the Spanish attempts to convert and conquer them. Early Spanish explorers do not stay.

17th century
Belize becomes a popular hideaway for British Baymen, who eventually establish settlements along the coast and move inland.

1786
Britain cedes the coast of Nicaragua, bringing to Belize an influx of African slaves – the beginning of today's Creole population.

1832
After being deported from St Vincent and migrating from Honduras, a group of Garifuna settles in present-day Dangriga.

1847
Spanish, Mestizo and Maya peoples engage in the War of the Castes in the neighboring Yucatán Peninsula, sending streams of refugees to settle in Belize.

1958
After being driven out of Mexico, the first group of Mennonites settles in Belize.

it is more scattered in the forest, meaning that its extraction required more labor. Thus it was that mahogany played a key role in the creation of the Afro-Belizean population. After several generations of mixing with the loggers and other colonists, the so-called Creoles became the most populous ethnic group in Belize.

Belizean Creoles now form only about 25% of Belize's population, but theirs remains a sort of paradigm culture. Racially mixed and proud of it, Creoles speak a fascinating and unique version of English: it sounds familiar at first, but it is not easily intelligible to a speaker of standard English. Most of the people you'll encounter in Belize City and the center of the country will be Creole.

Experts estimate that the number of Belizeans living overseas is roughly equal to the number of Belizeans living at home.

Maya

The Maya of Belize make up almost 11% of the population and are divided into three linguistic groups. The Yucatec Maya live mainly in the north, the Mopan Maya in the southern Toledo District and the Kekchi Maya in western Belize, and also in the Toledo District. Use of both Spanish and English is becoming more widespread among the Maya. Traditional Maya culture is strongest among the Maya of the south.

Garifuna

In the 17th century, shipwrecked African slaves washed ashore on the Caribbean island of St Vincent. They hooked up with the indigenous population of Caribs and Arawaks and formed a whole new ethnicity, now known as the Garifuna (plural Garinagu, also called Black Caribs).

France claimed possession of St Vincent in the early 18th century, but eventually ceded it to Britain according to the Treaty of Paris. After prolonged resistance, the Garifuna finally surrendered in 1796, and Britain decided to deport them. Over the course of several years, the Garifuna were shuffled around various spots in the Caribbean, with many dying of malnutrition or disease. Finally, 1465 of the original 4000-plus deportees arrived at the Honduran coastal town of Trujillo. From here, these people of mixed Native American and African heritage began to spread along the Caribbean coast of Central America.

Garifuna History, Language & Culture of Belize, Central America & the Caribbean, by Sebastian Cayetano, gives an easily understood overview of the Garifuna people and their culture.

BILEEZ KRIOL

Although English is the official language of Belize, when speaking among themselves most locals use Kriol (Creole). According to one local journalist, Kriol is 'di stiki stiki paat,' or 'the glue that holds Belize together.' While this patois sounds like English, most anglophones will have a hard time understanding it. It is a language that 'teases but just escapes the comprehension of a native English speaker,' as one frustrated American traveler so aptly stated.

Kriol derives mainly from English, with influences from Mayan and West African languages, as well as Spanish. Linguists claim that it has its own grammatical rules and a small body of literature, as well as speaking populations in different countries – criteria that determine the difference between a dialect and a language.

In 1995 the National Kriol Council was established to promote Kriol language in Belize. The council believes that the use and recognition of the language can solidify national identity and promote interaction and cooperation among different ethnic groups. Kriol is used by more than 70% of the population; not only by Creoles, but also many Garifuna, Mestizos and Maya who speak Kriol as their second language. The council believes that a better understanding of Kriol will actually improve local English. As people recognize that Kriol is a different language – and not just improper English – both children and adults will make the effort to learn the differences in grammatical construction.

> ## WHAT THEY BELIEVE IN BELIZE
>
> Ethnicity is a big determinant of religion in Belize, with most Mestizos, Maya and Garifuna espousing Catholicism as a result of their ethnic origins in Spanish- or French-ruled countries or colonies. Catholicism among Creoles increased with the work of North American missionaries in the late 19th and early 20th centuries. Approximately a quarter of Belizeans are Protestants, chiefly Anglicans and Methodists. Today, the number of Pentecostalists and Adventists is growing due to the strength of their evangelical movements. Mennonites also constitute a small minority.
>
> Among the Garifuna, and to a lesser extent the Maya and Creoles, Christianity coexists with other beliefs. Maya Catholicism has long been syncretized with traditional beliefs and rites that go back to pre-Hispanic times, while some Creoles (especially older people) have a belief in *obeah*, a form of witchcraft.
>
> Belize's tradition of tolerance also encompasses Hindus, Muslims, Baha'i, Jehovah's Witnesses and a small (but eye-catching) number of Rastafarians.

The first Garifuna arrived in Belize around the turn of the 19th century. But the biggest migration took place in 1832, when, on November 19, some 200 Garifuna reached Belize in dugout canoes from Honduras. The anniversary of the arrival is celebrated as Garifuna Settlement Day, a national holiday.

Today the Belize Garifuna number around 20,000, about 6% of Belize's population, most of whom still live in the south of the country, from Dangriga to Punta Gorda. The Garifuna language is a combination of Arawak and African languages with bits of English and French thrown in.

The Garifuna maintain a unique culture with a strong sense of community and ritual, in which drumming and dancing play important roles. The *dügü* ('feasting of the ancestors' ceremony) involves several nights and days of dancing, drumming and singing by an extended family. Its immediate purpose is to heal a sick individual, but it also serves to reaffirm community solidarity. Some participants may become 'possessed' by the spirits of dead ancestors. Other noted Garifuna ceremonials include the *beluria* (ninth-night festivity), for the departure of a dead person's soul, attended by entire communities with copious drumming, dancing and drinking; and the *wanaragua* or *jonkonu* dance, performed in some places during the Christmas-to-early-January festive season.

Garifuna culture has been enjoying a revival since the 1980s, due in no small part to the punta rock phenomenon. In 2001 Unesco declared Garifuna language, dance and music to be a 'Masterpiece of the Oral and Intangible Heritage of Humanity' – one of the initial selections for what has become the cultural equivalent of the World Heritage list.

The Mennonites

It almost seems like an aberration, an odd sight inspired by too much sun: women in bonnets and drape-like frocks; blond-haired, blue-eyed men in denim overalls and straw hats; the whole family packed onto a horse-drawn carriage, plodding along the side of the highway. In fact, it is not something your imagination has conjured up; you're looking at Belizean Mennonites.

The Mennonites originate from an enigmatic Anabaptist group that dates back to 16th-century Netherlands. Like the Amish of Pennsylvania, the Mennonites have strict religion-based values that keep them isolated in agricultural communities. Speaking mostly Low German, they run their own schools, banks and churches. Traditional groups reject any form of mechanization or technology (which explains the horse-drawn buggies).

Conservative Mennonite Groups

Shipyard, Orange Walk

Little Belize, Corozal

Progressive Mennonite Groups

....

Blue Creek, Orange Walk

....

Spanish Lookout, Cayo

Mennonites are devout pacifists and reject most of the political ideologies that societies have thrust upon them (including paying taxes). So they have a long history of moving about the world trying to find a place to live in peace. They left the Netherlands for Prussia and Russia in the late 17th century. In the 1870s, when Russia insisted on military conscription, the Mennonites upped and moved to isolated parts of Canada. After WWI, the Canadian government demanded that English be taught in Mennonites' schools and their exemption from conscription was reconsidered. Again, the most devout Mennonites moved, this time to Mexico. By the 1950s Mexico wanted the Mennonites to join its social security program, so once again the Mennonites packed up.

The first wave of about 3500 Mennonites settled in Belize (then called British Honduras) in 1958. Belize was happy to have their industriousness and farming expertise, and the settlements expanded.

Today, Belize has many different Mennonite communities. The progressives – many of whom came from Canada – speak English and have no qualms about using tractors or pickup trucks; other groups are strongly conservative and shun modern technologies.

Belize has been good to the Mennonites and in turn the Mennonites have been good to Belize. Mennonite farms now supply most of the country's dairy products, eggs and poultry. Furniture-making is another Mennonite specialty and you'll often see them selling their goods at markets.

Rhythms of a Nation

Belize knows how to get its groove on. You'll hear a variety of pan-Caribbean musical styles, including calypso (of which Belize has its own star in Gerald 'Lord' Rhaburn), soca (an up-tempo fusion of calypso with Indian rhythms) and, of course, reggae. But what's special about the music is that the styles are uniquely Belizean.

Punta & Punta Rock

Musicians and linguists speculate that 'punta' comes from the word *bunda*, which means 'buttocks' in many West African languages. The word derivation is not certain, but it is appropriate. Heard at any sort of celebration or occasion, this traditional drumming style inspires Garifuna peoples across Central America to get up and shake their *bunda*.

The crowd circles around one couple, who gyrate their hips while keeping the upper body still. Traditionally, it is associated with death and ancestor worship, which explains why the dance is often performed at funerals and wakes.

Punta rock was born in the 1970s, when punta musician Pen Cayetano, a native of Dangriga, traveled around Central America and came to the realization that Garifuna traditions were in danger of withering away. He wanted to inspire young Garifuna people to embrace their own culture instead of listening to and copying music from other countries – and so he invented a style that is cool, contemporary but uniquely Belizean. He added the electric guitar to traditional punta rhythms and so was born punta rock.

Punta rock can be frenetic or it can be mellow, but at its base are always fast rhythms designed to get the hips swiveling. Like traditional punta, the dance is strongly sexually suggestive, with men and women gyrating their pelvises in close proximity to each other. The lyrics are almost always in Garifuna or Kriol, which differs from traditional punta.

Andy Palacio was a leading ambassador of punta rock until his untimely death in 2008. Palacio was known for mixing the Garifuna sound with all sorts of foreign elements, including pop, salsa and calypso beats. He deserves the credit for widening the audience for punta rock and turning it into the (unofficial) national music of Belize.

Another recent sensation is Supa G, who provides a fusion of punta rock, techno and even a spot of Mexican balladeering. Cayetano's Turtle Shell Band spread the word, and the rhythm, to neighboring Guatemala, Honduras (both with their own Garifuna populations), Mexico and even the USA (where there are sizable Belizean and Garifuna communities), and Ideal, Mohobub and Myme Martinez are all members of the Turtle Shell Band who are enjoying success in their solo careers.

Originally from Hopkins, Aziatic has blended punta with R&B, jazz and pop, earning him an international audience, particularly in the US, where he now lives. The Coolie Rebels are a popular East Indian punta rock group from Punta Gorda.

Pen Cayetano is a polymathic figure who started the punta rock musical phenomenon, but he also does oil paintings portraying the Garifuna culture.

After musician Andy Palacio's untimely death, an estimated 2500 people descended on his home village of Barranco, where he was laid to rest following a Catholic Mass, a Garifuna ceremony and an official state funeral.

PARANDA

Paranda

Shortly after the Garifuna arrived in Central America, they started melding African percussion and chanting with Spanish-style acoustic guitar and Latin rhythms. The resulting mix is known as *paranda*, named after a traditional African rhythm that is often at the root of the music. Unlike punta rock, paranda music is totally unplugged, played on wooden Garifuna drums, acoustic guitars and primitive percussion instruments such as shakers and turtle shells. It combines fast rhythms and lyrical melodies.

Although musicians have been playing *paranda* since the 19th century, it was not recorded and therefore rarely heard outside Garifuna communities. It is another genre of folk music that is in danger of dying out, as very few young musicians are making new *paranda* music. In the mid-1990s, producers from Stonetree Records recognized the importance of making a recording before the great *paranderos* passed. The so-called Paranda Project resulted in an album that featured eight of the most esteemed *paranda* musicians from Belize and Honduras.

The Belizean master of *paranda* is Paul Nabor from Punta Gorda, born in the 1920s, while the rising star is Aurelio Martínez, considered the future of the musical genre. The title of Martínez' album *Garifuna Soul* gives a good idea of what *paranda* is all about.

In the liner notes of the album *Paranda*, Aurelio Martínez writes 'I feel very proud to be in the same album with such great paranderos. And in a symbolic way I feel like they are passing me the torch to carry on the tradition. To me this is more than a Grammy.'

Brukdown

In the 18th and 19th centuries, most of the hard labor of logging – the intensive cutting and heavy lifting of the massive mahogany trees – was carried out by African slaves and their descendents. Here, in the logging camps of the Belize River valley, workers soothed their weary bodies and souls by drinking, dancing and making their own unique music, known as *brukdown*.

Belize's most prominent Creole music, *brukdown* is deeply rooted in Africa, with layered rhythms and call-and-response vocals. Back in the camps, it was normally played by an ensemble of accordion, banjo, harmonica and a percussion instrument – usually the jawbone of a pig, its teeth rattled with a stick. Nowadays, modern musicians might add a drum or an electric guitar.

Like the Garifuna music, *brukdown* is predominantly a rural folk tradition that is rarely recorded. The exception is the so-called King of Brukdown, Wilfred Peters, and his band Mr Peters' Boom & Chime. Mr Peters made music for more than 60 years before his death in 2010, and became a national icon and the country's best-loved Creole musician. In 1997 Queen Elizabeth II awarded him an MBE for his cultural contributions.

GARI-FUSION

In contemporary Belize there has been a resurgence of Garifuna music, popularized by musicians such as Andy Palacio, Mohobub Flores and Adrian Martinez. These musicians have taken many aspects of traditional Garifuna music and fused them with more modern sounds. Andy Palacio's last album, *Watina,* was a collaboration with other musicians, known as the Garifuna Collective. Each track on the album is based on a traditional Garifuna rhythm, and all of the songs are in the Garifuna language, which is a novelty itself. Rooted in musical and folkloric tradition, the album exhibits remembrance of the past and hope for the future of the Garifuna people.

Umalali, which means 'voice' in the Garifuna language, is the name of an album created by the Garifuna Women's Project. In 2002, Garifuna women from all around Central America met in the village of Hopkins to record their most beloved songs and musical stories. Their voices were then layered on top of the rhythms and instrumentation of the Garifuna Collective, fusing many elements of the rich but endangered culture.

> ### THREE KINGS OF BELIZE
> Three men. Three different geographic regions, three different cultures, three different musical traditions. What these men have in common – besides their native land – is their passion for an art that is fading, even as they fade.
>
> *Three Kings of Belize* is a documentary by Katia Paradis (2007) that follows three pre-eminent musicians, each considered the 'king' of his genre. Paul Nabor is a legendary Garifuna *parandero* from Punta Gorda, Wilfred Peters was a Creole *brukdown* accordionist from Belize City, and Florencio Mess is a traditional Maya harpist living in the farming village of San Pedro Columbia. The film captures the artists in their homes, interacting with their families, recalling stories from their lives and, of course, making music.
>
> The recurring theme – expressed by all three gentlemen – is a frustration, and perhaps a fear, that young people no longer make this music. There is a sense that when these old guys die, their music might die too. But *Three Kings* is not just about frustration or fear. It is wistful, perhaps, but ultimately accepts that nothing is eternal.
>
> In June 2010, Wilfred Peters died at the age of 79. Hundreds of people attended his funeral, including the prime minister and the leader of the opposition – proof that music is greater than politics. The local newspaper noted that the funeral service was 'far from a solemn occasion,' with plenty of *brukdown* beats to accompany the hymns. 'The service concluded with a rising rendition of *brukdown* music with the cathedral's bells tolling in the background,' it said.

If Mr Peters was the King of Brukdown, the Queen of Brukdown is undoubtedly Leela Vernon. A resident of Punta Gorda, Leela Vernon is a high-energy singer and dancer. In addition to making four albums, she has also started a dance group to preserve traditional Creole dance.

Kungo Muzik
'This muzik is one of the heart beats felt out of Afrika coming by way of Belize.' So says Brother David Obi, better known in Belize as Bredda David. And he should know, as he created the fast-paced fusion of Creole, Caribbean and African styles known as *kungo muzik*.

Maya
The Maya have been making music for thousands of years. In contemporary Maya music, bones and rattles are used for percussion, while other instruments include whistles, flutes and horns made from conch shells. The ocarina is an ancient wind instrument that is something like a flute with a wider body and 10 to 12 finger holes. The same types of instruments have been found as artifacts at archaeological sites all around Central America.

Originally from Guatemala, Pablo Collado is a Maya flautist who now resides in Benque del Carmen. His new-age-style music is light and relaxing, often incorporating sounds that mimic nature, such as the gurgling of water or the calls of birds or insects.

Also popular among the Maya is the marimba, a percussion instrument that resembles a xylophone, except it is made of wood and so produces a mellower sound. Marimba music is used during Maya religious ceremonies.

Stringed instruments like the guitar, violin and harp are used in Maya ceremonial and recreational music. Crafted from native woods like mahogany or cedar, harps were traditionally carved with animal symbols, representing the Maya gods. Florencio Mess not only plays the Maya harp, but also makes these instruments from hand in the traditional style. His music – based on age-old melodies and rhythms – has been called 'a living connection to ancient Maya culture.'

Top Albums

Best of Punta Rock, Pen Cayetano & Mohobub Flores

Bumari, Lugua Centeno

Garifuna Soul, Aurelio Martínez

Brukdown Reloaded, Mr Peters' Boom & Chime

Beyond Rice & Beans

A staple of Belizean cuisine, rice and beans comes in two varieties: 'rice and beans,' where the two are cooked together; and 'beans and rice,' where beans in a soupy stew are served separately in a bowl. Both variations are prepared with coconut milk and red beans, which distinguishes them from other countries' rice and beans. You're bound to eat a lot of rice and beans (or beans and rice) while you are in Belize, but Belizean cuisine has more depth than would first appear.

Rice and Beans (www.riceand beansindc. blogspot.com) is a blog about mindful eating, written by a Belizean ('I love me some spicy food') with organic roots ('I want my food straight from the dirt').

Seafood

When it comes to seafood in Belize, lobster plays the starring role. Distinguished from the American and European lobster by their lack of claws, the Caribbean crustaceans are no less divine, especially when grilled. Lobster is widely available in coastal towns, except from mid-February to mid-June, when the lobster season is closed.

Conch (pronounced 'konk') is the large snail-like sea creature that inhabits conch shells. Much like calamari, it has a chewy consistency that is not universally appreciated. During conch season, from October to June, it is often prepared as *ceviche* (seafood marinated in lemon or lime juice, garlic and seasonings) or conch fritters (and it's considerably cheaper than lobster).

Aside from the shellfish, the local waters are home to snapper, grouper, barracuda, jacks and tuna, all of which make a tasty filet or steak.

Belizeans really know how to prepare their seafood, be it barbecued, grilled, marinated, steamed or stewed. A common preparation is 'Creole-style,' where seafood, peppers, onions and tomatoes are stewed together.

Meat & Poultry

Seafood is popular on the coast (and especially in tourist towns), but most often the main course in Belize comes from a chicken. Poultry serves as an accompaniment for rice and beans, a stuffing for burritos and *salbutes* (a variation on the tortilla), and a base for many soups and stews.

Belizeans do not eat a lot of beef, but they do love cow-foot soup. This is a glutinous concoction of pasta, vegetables, spices – and an actual cow's foot. Cow-foot soup is supposed to be 'good for the back'; in other words, an aphrodisiac.

Cookbooks

Mmm... A Taste of Belizean Cooking, Tracy Brown da Langan

Foods of the Maya, Nancy & Jeffrey Gerlach

Pastries

Almost every town in Belize has at least one shop where the shelves are lined with sweet and savory pastries to make you drool. If you're looking for a quick, tasty and cheap snack, you can't go wrong at the local bakery. Grab a tray and a pair of tongs and make your selection from the delectable treats on display.

While these pastries are pretty to look at and delicious to eat, they are not the best in Belizean baked goods. That title belongs to fresh-baked johnnycakes, or biscuits, smothered in butter, beans or melted cheese.

Johnnycakes are the quintessential breakfast in Belize, but they are also served throughout the day as a snack or side dish.

Every cuisine in the world includes some version of fried dough, usually topped with fruit or sugar. In Belize, it's called fry jacks. Again, it can be served sweet or savory, usually for breakfast but also throughout the day.

Maya Specialties

Maya meals are sometimes on offer in the villages of southern Belize and in Petén, Guatemala. *Caldo* is a hearty, spicy stew, usually made with chicken (or sometimes beef or pork), corn and root vegetables, and served with tortillas. Ixpa'cha is steamed fish or shrimp, cooked inside a big leaf. The Maya also make Mexican soups-cum-stews such as *chirmole* (chicken with a chili-chocolate sauce) and *escabeche* (chicken with lime and onions).

Garifuna Specialties

Garifuna culinary traditions come from St Vincent. When the Garifuna people came to Belize, they brought their own traditions, recipes and even ingredients, meaning that cuisine is one more way that Garifuna culture is unique.

One of the most important staples, cassava, is a starch, like a sweet potato, used to make cassava bread. A *varusa* is like a tamale, but it's made from a fruit that is a cross between a banana and a plantain, picked while it's still hard and cooked until it's soft.

A 'boil-up' is a stew of root vegetables and beef or chicken. This is the dish that is most common on restaurant menus, although it is traditionally prepared for Garifuna Settlement Day.

Other Garifuna specialties feature fresh fish, bananas or plantains, and coconut milk. *Alubundiga* is a dish of grated, green bananas, coconut cream, spices, boiled potato and peppers, served with fried fish fillet (often snapper) and rice. *Sere* is fish cooked with coconut milk, spices and maybe some root vegetables. Possibly the most beloved Garifuna dish, hudut is made from plantain, cooked until tender, mashed with a big mortar and pestle, then cooked with local fish like snapper and coconut milk.

Food Festivals

Lobster Festivals in Placencia, Caye Caulker and San Pedro

Fish Fest, Punta Gorda

Cashew Festival, Crooked Tree

Cacao Festival, Toledo District

BEYOND RICE & BEANS MAYA SPECIALTIES

JOHNNYCAKES

There is no more satisfying Belizean breakfast than a fresh-baked johnnycake with a pat of butter and a slice of cheese. These savory biscuits – straight from the oven – steal the show when served with eggs or beans.

Ingredients

2lb flour
6 teaspoons baking powder
½ cup shortening
½ cup margarine
1 teaspoon salt
2 cups coconut milk or evaporated milk

Method

Sift dry ingredients. Heat oven to 400°F. Use fingertips or knife to cut margarine and shortening into flour. Gradually stir in milk with a wooden spoon. Mix well to form a manageable ball of dough. Roll out dough into a long strip and cut into 1½in to 2in pieces. Shape into round balls and place on greased baking sheets. Flatten lightly and prick with a fork. Bake in hot oven for 10 minutes or until golden brown.

Mestizo Specialties

Just like their Caribbean and Central American neighbors, Belizeans like to cook with habaneros, jalapeños and other peppers. Most restaurants have a bottle of hot chili sauce on the table next to the salt and pepper so guests can make their meals as spicy as they like.

In small towns, the best breakfast is usually found at the local taco vendor's cart, where tortillas stuffed with meat and lettuce are sold. Other Mexican snacks are also ubiquitous, including *salbutes, garnaches, enchalades* and *panades* – all variations on the tortilla, beans and cheese theme (*salbutes* usually add chicken, *panades* generally have fish). You'll also come across burritos and tamales (wads of corn dough with a filling of meat, beans or chilies).

Restaurants for Foodies

Sandro, Caye Caulker

Ko-Ox Han-nah, San Ignacio

Hidden Treasures, San Pedro

Capricorn Restaurant, San Pedro

Rumfish, Placencia

Cerros Beach Resort, Cerros

Drinks

If you want to know what tropical paradise tastes like, sample the fresh fruit juices that are blended and sold at street carts and kiosks around the country. Usually available in whatever flavor is seasonal (lime, orange, watermelon, grapefruit, papaya and mango), they're delicious and refreshing – and healthy!

In recent years, Belize has started catering to coffee drinkers with its own homegrown beans, even though Belize lacks the high altitudes that benefit other Central American coffee-growing countries. On a *finca* (farm) in Orange Walk, a local company called Gallon Jug is producing shade-grown beans for commercial distribution. Caye Coffee in San Pedro gets its beans from Guatemala, but roasts them in its facility right in San Pedro, producing such popular blends as Belizean Roast and Maya Blend.

SHARP ON THE TONGUE

Belizean meals are not usually very spicy, but your table and your meal are always enlivened by the inimitable presence of Marie Sharp's fiery sauces, accurately labeled 'Proud Products of Belize.'

Marie Sharp got into the hot-sauce business in 1981. One season she and her husband found themselves with a surplus of habanero chili peppers at their family farm near Dangriga. Hating to see them wasted, Marie experimented with sauce recipes in her own kitchen. She felt that other bottled hot sauces were often watery and sometimes too hot to be flavorful. She wanted one that would complement Belizean cuisine and would not have artificial ingredients. She tried out some of her blends on her friends and family, and by far the favorite was one that used carrots as a thickener and blended the peppers with onions and garlic.

Once she had her formula, Sharp embarked on a guerrilla marketing campaign, carrying samples of the sauce, along with corn chips and refried beans, door-to-door to shopkeepers all over Belize. When proprietors liked what they tasted, Marie asked them to put the sauce on their shelves and agreed to take back the bottles that didn't sell. The sauce, initially bottled under the name Melinda, caught on and was soon not only in stores but also on restaurant tables all over the country.

Marie bottled the sauces from her kitchen for three years, finally bringing in a couple of workers to help her mix the zealously guarded formula. She eventually hybridized her own red habanero pepper – a mix of Scotch bonnet and Jamaican varieties – which contributes to the distinctive color of her sauces. She opened her own factory in 1986 with two three-burner stoves and six women to look after her pots, and moved to her current factory outside Dangriga (p187) in 1998.

Today, Sharp's hot red-habanero sauces come in six heat levels: 'Mild,' 'Hot,' 'Fiery Hot,' 'No-Wimps-Allowed,' 'Belizean Heat' and 'Comatose.' Sharp also produces a range of mixed sauces (habaneros with prickly pears or citrus fruit), pepper jellies and tropical-fruit jams.

Belikin is the native beer of Belize. You'll be hard-pressed to find any other beer available, as there are severe import duties levied on foreign brews. Fear not, however, as Belikin is always cold and refreshing. Belikin Regular is a tasty lager, but Belikin also brews a lower-calorie, lower-alcohol beer, called Lighthouse Lager, as well as Belikin Stout and Belikin Premium.

In a Caribbean country that produces so much sugarcane, it's not surprising that Belize's number one liquor is rum. The country has four distilleries; the Travellers distillery in Belize City has won several international awards with its thick, spicy One Barrel rum.

Cuba libre (lime, rum and coke) and piña colada are the most popular ways of diluting your fermented sugarcane juice. But according to Belize bartenders, the national drink is in fact the 'panty-ripper' or 'brief-ripper', depending on your gender. This concoction is a straightforward mix of coconut rum and pineapple juice, served on the rocks.

'Belikin' is Mayan for 'road to the east' and the main temple of Altun Ha is pictured on the label of Belikin beer.

BEYOND RICE & BEANS DRINKS

Wild Things

Belize's sparse human population and its history of relatively low-key human impact have yielded a vast diversity of animal and plant species. The country has an admirable conservation agenda, pursued by governments and nongovernmental organizations (NGOs) since Belizean independence in 1981. This has led to the nation becoming a top destination for anyone interested in the marine life of the coral reefs, the vegetation and animal life of the forests, or the hundreds of bird species that soar, flutter and swoop through the skies.

Jaguar: One Man's Struggle to Establish the World's First Jaguar Preserve is the story of American zoologist Alan Rabinowitz' efforts to set up what has become the Cockscomb Basin Wildlife Sanctuary.

Animals

Land Mammals

Felines

Everyone dreams of seeing a jaguar in the wild. Jaguars are found across the country, and live in large expanses of thick forest. The largest populations and most frequently reported sightings are near Chan Chich Lodge and at the Río Bravo Conservation & Management Area in Orange Walk. You might also see their tracks or the remains of their meals in Cockscomb Basin Wildlife Sanctuary, which was established in Stann Creek as a jaguar reserve in the 1980s. But although Belize has healthy numbers of the biggest feline in the western hemisphere (which measures up to 6ft long and 250lb in weight), your best chance of seeing one is still at the Belize Zoo.

Belize has four smaller wildcats, all elusive like the jaguar: the puma (aka mountain lion or cougar), almost as big as the jaguar but a uniform gray or brown color (occasionally black); the ocelot, spotted similarly to the jaguar but a lot smaller; the margay, smaller again and also spotted; and the small, brown or gray jaguarundi.

Monkeys

The endangered black howler monkey exists only in Belize, northern Guatemala and southern Mexico. Its population has made a comeback in several areas, especially in the Community Baboon Sanctuary in Belize District, established in the 1980s to protect this noisy animal. The sanctuary is now home to some 3000 individual monkeys. Other places to see and hear howlers include: Lamanai in Orange Walk; Cockscomb Basin Wildlife Sanctuary in Stann Creek; Chan Chich and Río Bravo in Orange Walk; and Tikal National Park in Guatemala. The howler's eerie dawn and evening cries – more roars than howls – can carry 2 miles across the treetops.

Less common are the smaller, long-tailed spider monkeys, though you may still spot some in similar areas.

Other Land Mammals

Visitors and residents alike are often surprised to learn that the national animal of Belize is Baird's tapir (sometimes called the mountain cow). The tapir is related to the horse, but it has shorter legs and tail, a stouter build and small eyes, ears and intellect. Baird's tapir is a herbivore and –

MIND THE MANATEES

Belonging to a unique group of sea mammals comprising only four species worldwide, manatees are thought to be distantly related to elephants. However, with at least 55 million years separating the two, their kinship is only apparent in a few fairly obscure anatomical similarities and a broadly similar diet. Like elephants, manatees are herbivores and require huge amounts of vegetation each day. Grazing on a wide variety of aquatic plants, a large adult can process as much as 110lb every 24 hours, producing a prodigious amount of waste in the process – fresh floating droppings (similar to a horse's) and almost continuous, bubbling streams of flatulence are useful ways to find them. (Not too appetizing, but it does make them easier to spot.) The best places for a chance to observe manatees are around 'blowing holes' or *sopladeros* (deep hollows where manatees congregate to wait for the high tide).

Manatees are reputed to have excellent hearing, but they're most sensitive to fairly high frequency sounds, such as their squeaking vocalizations. Apparently, the engine of a motorboat is not a high-frequency sound, which means that quiet approaches are often rewarded with good viewing, although sadly it also makes them vulnerable to collisions with these boats.

interestingly – a daily bather. It tends to be shy, so it's infrequently spotted and likely to run like mad when approached.

You have better chances of catching sight of a peccary, a wild pig that weighs 50lb or more. There are two types, whose names - white-lipped peccary and collared peccary – define their differences. Both types of peccaries are active by day and they travel in groups, making them relatively easy to check off your wildlife list. Be aware that these meanies can run fast. If you get in the way of a pack of wild peccaries, experts advise you to climb a tree (they can't catch you up there).

Resembling a large spotted guinea pig, the *gibnut* (or *paca*) is a nocturnal rodent, growing up to 2ft long and weighing up to 22lb, that often lives in pairs. You might see a *gibnut* in the wild, and you are also likely to see one on the menu at your local Belizean restaurant. The agouti is similar but diurnal and more closely resembles a rabbit, with strong back legs. The tayra (or tree otter) is a member of the weasel family and has a dark-brown body, yellowish neck and 1ft-long tail. The coatimundi (or quash) is a cute, rusty-brown, raccoon-like creature with a long nose and ringed tail that it often holds upright when walking. It's not uncommon to see coatimundi in daylight on the sides of roads or trails. Also in the raccoon family is the nocturnal kinkajou (or nightwalker), mainly a tree-dweller.

Marine Life

West Indian manatees inhabit the waters around river mouths, in coastal lagoons and around the cayes. The sure-fire places to spot these gentle, slow-moving creatures are Southern Lagoon, near Gales Point Manatee village, and Swallow Caye, off Belize City. Manatees are the only vegetarian sea mammals in existence. Typically 10ft long and weighing 1000lb, adults eat 100lb to 150lb of vegetation each day (especially sea grass). Only a few hundred manatees survive in Belizean waters.

Belizean waters are home to the world's largest fish. Whale sharks grow up to a whopping 60ft (although the average length is 25ft) and weigh up to 15 tons. They hang out at Gladden Spit, near Placencia. Between March and June – usually during the 10 days after a full moon – these filter-feeding behemoths come in close to the reef to dine on spawn. Fun fact: whale sharks can live up to 150 years.

Wildlife-Watching

Community Baboon Sanctuary

Río Bravo Conservation & Management Area

Shipstern Nature Reserve

Gales Point Manatee or Swallow Caye

Cockscomb Basin Wildlife Sanctuary

Belize Zoo

WILD THINGS ANIMALS

Other sharks – nurse, reef, lemontip and hammerhead – and a variety of rays often make appearances around the reefs and islands. Sharing the water with the larger animals is a kaleidoscope of reef fish, ranging from steely-eyed barracuda and groupers to colorful parrotfish, angelfish and butterfly fish. The fish frolic amid a huge variety of coral formations, from hard elkhorn and staghorn coral (named because they branch like antlers) to gorgonian fans and other soft formations. Belizean waters host more than 500 species of fish and 110 species of coral, plus an amazing variety of sponges.

The best all-in-one wildlife guide is *Belize & Northern Guatemala: The Ecotravellers' Wildlife Guide,* by Les Beletsky, offering helpful descriptions along with full-color drawings and photographs.

Reptiles

The protected green iguana is a dragon-like vegetarian lizard that can grow to 6ft in length and is often spotted in trees along riverbanks. You can also see it in iguana houses at Monkey Bay Wildlife Sanctuary in Belize District and at the San Ignacio Resort Hotel.

Belize is home to two species of crocodile: the American crocodile and Morelet's crocodile, both of which are on the endangered species list. The American usually grows to 13ft and can live in both saltwater and freshwater. The smaller Morelet's crocodile, which grows to 8ft, lives only in fresh water. Belizean crocs tend to stick to prey that's smaller than the average adult human. Still, it's best to keep your distance.

Hawksbill, loggerhead, leatherback and green sea turtles can be seen in the waters of Belize. They live at sea and the females come ashore only to lay their eggs. Sea turtles are victims of poaching and egg hunting, as their eggs are believed by some to be an aphrodisiac. However, while all sea turtles are endangered, the hawksbill, which was hunted for its shell, is the only one currently protected in Belize. Turtle-viewing outings are organized in the May to October laying season from Gales Point Manatee village.

Up to 60 species of snake inhabit the forests and waters of Belize, but only a handful are dangerous. The nasties include the poisonous fer-de-lance (commonly known as the yellow-jaw tommygoff), which is earth toned and a particular threat to farmers when they're clearing areas of vegetation; the coral snake, banded with bright red, yellow and black stripes; the tropical rattlesnake; and the boa constrictor, which kills by constriction but can also give you a mean (but venomless) bite.

Bird-Watching

Crooked Tree, Belize

Half Moon Caye, Lighthouse Reef

New River, Orange Walk

La Milpa, Orange Walk

Red Bank, Stann Creek

Birds

Ornithologists have identified 570 bird species in Belize, 20% of them winter migrants from North America. You're likely to see interesting birds almost anywhere at any time, although February to May are particularly good months. Wetlands, lagoons, forested riverbanks and forest areas with clearings (the setting of many jungle lodges and Maya ruins) are good for observing a variety of birds.

Sea Birds

Magnificent frigate birds constantly soar over the coastline on pointed, prehistoric-looking wings which have a span of up to 6ft. They have difficulty taking off from the ground, so their method of hunting is to plummet and catch fish as they jump from the sea. They often hang out around fisherfolk and other birds so that they can swoop in on discarded or dropped catches. Males have red throats that are displayed during courtship.

Swooping and soaring with the frigate birds are neotropic cormorants, brown pelicans, nine species of heron, eight species of tern and six species of gull. The rare red-footed booby bird lives at Half Moon Caye.

BIRDS OF BELIZE

Raptors & Vultures

Raptors are predators that usually hunt rodents and small birds. The most common species in Belize include the osprey (look for their huge nests atop houses and telephone posts), peregrine falcon, roadside hawk and American kestrel. Most of these birds of prey are territorial and solitary. The majestic harpy eagle is rarely seen in the wild, but is a resident at the Belize Zoo, as is the ornate hawk eagle, which is a beautiful large raptor with a black crest, striped tail and mottled breast.

Inland along the sides of the road and flying overhead you'll see large turkey, black and king vultures. Their job is to feast on dead animals. The turkey vulture has a red head, the king has a black-and-white color scheme with a red beak, and the black vulture appears in black and shades of gray.

Other Well-Known Birds

The national bird of Belize is the keel-billed toucan. This is the species of Toucan Sam, the hungry bird who knows to 'follow your nose' to find the fruit loops. A black bird with a yellow face and neck, it has a huge multicolored bill. The 'keel bill' is actually very light and almost hollow, enabling the bird to fly with surprising agility and to reach berries at the end of branches. Toucans like to stay at treetop level and nest in holes in trees. They are surprisingly aggressive and are known to raid other birds' nests for breakfast.

The beautiful scarlet macaw, a member of the parrot family, is highly endangered. Belize's small population of the bird – possibly under 200 – lives most of the year in remote jungles near the Guatemalan border, but from January to March they can be seen at the southern village of Red Bank, where they come to eat fruit.

The jabiru stork is the largest flying bird in the Americas, standing up to 5ft tall and with wingspans of up to 12ft. Many of the 100 or so remaining Belizean jabirus gather in Crooked Tree Wildlife Sanctuary in April and May.

You'll also have the chance to see (among others) many colorful hummingbirds, kingfishers, motmots, parrots, woodpeckers, tinamous, tanagers and trogons.

In 2004 Belize finally got its own birding guide with the publication of the comprehensive *Birds of Belize*, by H Lee Jones, which is well illustrated by Dana Gardner.

BELIZE'S WORLD HERITAGE SITE

In 1996 Unesco designated the Belize Barrier Reef Reserve System a World Heritage Site. The World Heritage listing covers seven separate reef, island and atoll areas, not all of which include bits of the barrier reef. The seven sites were recognized for demonstrating a unique array of reef types (fringing, barrier and atoll) and a classic example of reef evolution; for their exceptional natural beauty and pristine nature; and for being an important habitat for internationally threatened species, including marine turtles, the West Indian manatee and the American crocodile. The sites are:

➡ Bacalar Chico National Park & Marine Reserve, Ambergris Caye

➡ Blue Hole Natural Monument, Lighthouse Reef

➡ Half Moon Caye Natural Monument, Lighthouse Reef

➡ Glover's Reef Marine Reserve, Central Cayes

➡ South Water Caye Marine Reserve, Central Cayes

➡ Laughing Bird Caye National Park, Central Cayes

➡ Sapodilla Cayes Marine Reserve, Punta Gorda

Plants

Belize is home to more than 4000 species of flowering plant, including some 700 trees (similar to the total of the USA and Canada combined) and 304 orchids. Nonspecialists can usefully distinguish three chief varieties of forest in the country: coastal forests (19%), moist, tropical broadleaf forests (68%), and pine and savanna (13%).

'One perceives a forest of jagged, gnarled trees protruding from the surface of the sea, roots anchored in deep, black, foul-smelling mud, verdant crowns arching toward a blazing sun...Here is where land and sea intertwine, where the line dividing ocean and continent blurs.' – Klause Rutzler and Ilka Feller, *Scientific American*, March 1996

Coastal Forests

Coastal forests comprise both the mangrove stands that grow along much of the shoreline and the littoral forests slightly further inland. Mangroves serve many useful purposes as fish nurseries, hurricane barriers and shoreline stabilizers, and they are credited with creating the cayes: when coral grows close enough to the water surface, mangrove spores carried by the wind take root on it. Mangrove debris eventually creates solid ground cover, inviting other plants to take root and eventually attracting animal life. There are four common species of mangrove: red, buttonwood, white and black.

Trees of the littoral forests typically have tough, moisture-retaining leaves. They include the coconut palm, the Norfolk Island pine, the sea grape and the poisonwood, the sap of which causes blistering, swelling and itching of the skin, as well as (happily) the gumbo-limbo, with its flaky, shredding bark that acts as an antidote to poisonwood rashes. The sandy bays off the coast are covered in sea grass, including turtle grass, manatee sea grass and duckweed sea grass.

Tropical Broadleaf Forest

Tropical broadleaf grows on thin clay soils where the principal nutrients come not from the soil but from the biomass of the forest – that is, debris from plants and animals. Buttressed trunks are a common phenomenon here. These forests support a huge diversity not only of plants but also of animal life.

MAYA MEDICINE

The Maya have not only long-depended on the forest for food and shelter, but also for hygiene and healing. These days in Belize, tour guides are quick to recommend a herbal remedy for everything from stomach ills to sexual failures. But there are only a few remaining healers who are skilled and knowledgeable in Maya medicine. If you are curious about this holistic and natural approach to medicine, consult a professional (eg at the Chaa Creek Rainforest Medicine Trail in Cayo). Here is a sampler of what might be prescribed:

➔ **Bay cedar** *(Guazuma ulmifolia)* The bark is boiled and used to calm the stomach and to treat dysentery.

➔ **Cockspur** *(Acacia cornigera)* The tea from cockspur thorns is used to treat acne, while the bark can be used to treat some snake bites.

➔ **Cohune palm** *(Orbignya cohune)* The oil is used for cooking and as a skin moisturizer. The shell can be used for fuel, as charcoal.

➔ **Guava** *(Psidium guajava)* Boil the bark of a guava and drink the tea as an antidote for dysentery or diarrhea.

➔ **Gumbo-limbo tree** *(Bursera simaruba)* The gumbo-limbo tree always grows near poisonwood, which causes an itchy rash similar to poison ivy. The sticky inner bark of the gumbo-limbo is effective treatment for the poisonwood rash.

➔ **Skunk root** *(Petiveria alliacea)* The skunk root – boiled into a tea – is an effective way to treat stomach ulcers.

Source: Rainforest Remedies: One Hundred Healing Herbs of Belize, by Rosita Arvigo & Michael Balick

One of the fascinating elements of these forests is their natural layering. Most have at least three layers: ground cover (a ground or herb layer); a canopy layer formed from the crowns of the forest's tallest trees; and, in between, shorter subcanopy or understory trees. Throughout the layers grow hanging vines and epiphytes, or 'air plants,' which are moss and ferns that live on other trees but aren't parasites. This is also the habitat for more than 300 species of orchids, including the national flower, the black orchid.

The national tree in Belize is the majestic mahogany, known for its handsome hardwood. Also important is the ceiba (the sacred tree of the Maya), with its tall gray trunk and fluffy kapok down around its seeds. The broad-canopied guanacaste (or tubroos) is another tree that can grow more than 100ft high, with a wide, straight trunk and light wood used for dugout canoes (its broad seed pods coil up into what look like giant, shriveled ears). The strangler fig has tendrils and branches that surround a host tree until the unfortunate host dies. The flowering calophyllum, sometimes called the Santa Maria tree, is used for shipbuilding, while its resin has medicinal uses.

Pine & Savanna

The drier lowland areas inland from Belize City and the sandy areas of the north are designated as lowland savanna and pine forest. Growth here is mostly savanna grasses and Honduran and Caribbean pine, as well as Paurotis palm, giant stands of bamboo, and some oak and calabash.

The Mountain Pine Ridge is a fascinating phenomenon. As you ascend these uplands, the forest changes abruptly from tropical broadleaf to submontane pine, due to a transition to drier, sandier soils. Predominant species include Mexican white pine, Pino amarillo (or Mexican yellow pine) and Hartweg's pine.

The tropical broadleaf is often called rainforest, although technically only far southwestern Belize receives enough rain to officially support rainforest.

RAINFOREST

WILD THINGS PLANTS

Land & Environment

Happily, the Belize government and the populace have recognized that their country's forests and reefs are natural treasures that need to be preserved – not only for their intrinsic ecological value, but also for attracting tourism. Early on, the government developed a large network of national parks and reserve areas; however, these areas are only as inviolable as the degree to which the community is able to protect them.

Forest cover in 1980: 75.9%

Forest cover in 2010: 62.7%

National Parks & Protected Areas

About 44% of Belizean territory, a little over 4062 sq miles, is under official protection of one kind or another. Belize's protected areas fall into six main categories:

Forest reserve Protects forests, controls timber extraction and conserves soil, water and wildlife resources.

Marine reserve Protects and controls extraction of marine and freshwater species; also focuses on research, recreation and education.

National park Preserves nationally significant nature and scenery for the benefit of the public.

Natural monument Protects special natural features for education, research and public appreciation.

Nature reserve Maintains natural environments and processes in an undisturbed state for scientific study, monitoring, education and maintenance of genetic resources; not usually open to the general public.

Wildlife sanctuary Protects nationally significant species, groups of species, biotic communities or physical features.

Environmental NGOs

Belize Audubon Society (www.belizeaudubon.org)

Oceanic Society (www.oceanic-society.org)

Programme for Belize (www.pfbelize.org)

Toledo Institute for Development & Environment (www.tidebelize.org)

Wildlife Conservation Society (www.wcs.org)

Ecotourism

Belize practically invented the concept of ecotourism. Its ecolodges allow guests to live in luxury but also in harmony with the creatures and plants in their midst, while its educational tours and activities allow travelers to learn about the forest and the reef without harming the fragile ecosystems. Conscientious enterprises minimize their environmental impact by employing alternative and renewable energy sources; avoiding destruction of surrounding habitats; effectively managing waste and employing recycling programs; and using locally grown produce whenever possible. Dedicated entrepreneurs also give back to the community by employing local people and investing in local causes, thus sharing the wealth.

Ecotourism depends on a precarious balance: welcoming tourists, but not too many of them; allowing access to natural sights, but not too much access; maintaining an infrastructure to support the visitors, but not having too much infrastructure. Belize is constantly struggling to maintain this balance, with varying degrees of success.

There is no doubt about the economical boon of tourist dollars flowing from visiting cruise liners; however, the recent increase in cruise-ship traffic in Belizean waters has worried many conservationists and citizens, who view the huge numbers of tourists as disturbing wildlife and overwhelming the infrastructure.

Development along the coast caters to the growing demands of tourists. A recent study suggests that as much as 80% of coastal property is foreign-owned, with construction planned or underway. Construction of buildings and pavement of the roads on Ambergris Caye has dramatically changed the aesthetics and the atmosphere of that island, once a sleepy outpost and now a destination for package-tourists and partiers. In a recent struggle, San Pedro developers petitioned to eliminate the protected status of the southern portion of Bacalar Chico National Park & Marine Reserve. To the relief of many, the petition was rejected.

Of course, there is no hard and fast rule about how many tourists are too many or how much development is too much. Many Belizeans compare their country to Cozumel or Cancun and they are proud of the way that ecotourism is preserving their paradise. On Ambergris, few locals would stop the construction of condos and resorts that is taking place up and down the coast. It's predominantly the expats – who came to Belize to 'escape civilization' – who complain about the rampant level of development. Locals, by contrast, appreciate the influx of cash into the economy – the jobs, the roads, the restaurants – not to mention the constant flow of tourists who keep bringing money to spend.

Deforestation

Despite the impressive amount of protected territory, deforestation in Belize has been slow and steady since independence. Agriculture and aquaculture, development and illegal harvesting all contribute to the felling of the forests, which is taking place at a rate of 0.6% per year.

This contradiction is a result of poor management and monitoring. Protection requires money and even at the best of times Belizean governments are short of cash. Underfunding means understaffing, which impedes the fight against poaching and illegal extraction.

There is a perception in Belize that illegal Guatemalan immigrants are responsible for many of these incursions into protected areas. The ongoing territorial dispute between Guatemala and Belize exacerbates the situation, as many Guatemalan peasants believe they have a right to hunt and harvest there.

Energy Management

The problem of power is certainly not unique to Belize. Like many other countries, Belize consumes more than it can produce, and its consumption is increasing by 10 to 15% per year. Historically, Belize has imported much of its electricity from Mexico, although the country is implementing a multiprong strategy to reduce this dependency.

Hydro

Two plants harness the power of the Macal River in Cayo to produce hydroelectric power. Built in 1995, the Mollejon Dam is limited by the storage capacity of its reservoir, but since 2006, the huge Chalillo Dam has fed both plants. The dam has the advantage that it can generate power in the evening (peak consumption hours), when the imported electricity is more expensive. The construction of the Chalillo Dam sparked massive controversy, as critics voiced concerns about the damage inflicted on wildlife habitats in the river valley, as well as the financial viability of the project.

LAND & ENVIRONMENT DEFORESTATION

Ecolodges

Calypso Beach Retreat, Long Caye

Cerros Beach Resort, Corozal

Chan Chich Lodge, Orange Walk District

Black Rock River Lodge, Cayo District

Thatch Caye Resort, Central Cayes

Cotton Tree Lodge, Deep South

Estimated number of cruise ship tourists in 2011: 788,494

Estimated number of overnight tourists in 2011: 250,000

Bruce Barcott investigates the construction of the Chalillo Dam and the efforts of Sharon Matola (founder of the Belize Zoo) to stop it, in his fascinating book The Last Flight of the Scarlet Macaw.

BELIZE'S PROTECTED AREAS AT A GLANCE

PROTECTED AREA	FEATURES
Actun Tunichil Muknal	spectacular cave with ancient Maya sacrificial remains
Bacalar Chico National Park & Marine Reserve	northern Ambergris Caye barrier reef and surrounding waters
Blue Hole Natural Monument	400ft-deep ocean-filled sinkhole home to sharks
Caracol Archaeological Reserve	Belize's biggest and greatest ancient Maya city
Caye Caulker Marine Reserve	barrier reef reserve with plentiful marine life
Cockscomb Basin Wildlife Sanctuary	large rainforest reserve for jaguars, with huge range of wildlife
Community Baboon Sanctuary	forest sanctuary for black howler monkeys
Crooked Tree Wildlife Sanctuary	wetland area with huge bird population
Gales Point Wildlife Sanctuary	inland lagoons with Belize's largest colony of manatees
Gladden Spit & Silk Cayes Marine Reserve	barrier reef and island reserve visited by whale sharks
Glover's Reef Marine Reserve	beautiful atoll with coral-filled lagoon and seas swarming with marine life
Guanacaste National Park	small forest park centered on huge guanacaste tree
Half Moon Caye Natural Monument	lush bird-sanctuary atoll island with spectacular underwater walls offshore
Hol Chan Marine Reserve	waters off Ambergris Caye with the famous Shark Ray Alley Protected Area
Laughing Bird Caye National Park	island on unusual faro reef in waters full of marine life
Mayflower Bocawina National Park	rainforest park with hills, waterfalls, howler monkeys and hundreds of bird species
Monkey Bay Wildlife Sanctuary	small private sanctuary on savannah and tropical forest
Mountain Pine Ridge Forest Reserve	upland area with rare pine forests and many waterfalls
Nohoch Che'en Caves Branch Archaeological Reserve	stretch of Caves Branch River running through caverns
Port Honduras Marine Reserve	inshore islands and coastal waters important for marine life
Río Bravo Conservation & Management Area	large rainforest reserve with great wildlife diversity
St Herman's Blue Hole National Park	small rainforest park with cave and swimming hole
Sapodilla Cayes Marine Reserve	beautiful barrier reef islets with healthy coral and abundant marine life
Shipstern Nature Reserve	wetlands and rare semideciduous hardwood forests with diverse wildlife, including wood-stork colony
South Water Caye Marine Reserve	large reserve encompassing parts of barrier reef and inshore islands
Swallow Caye Wildlife Sanctuary	small island with permanent manatee population
Temash-Sarstoon National Park	rainforests, wetlands and rivers with huge variety of wildlife

ACTIVITIES	BEST TIME TO VISIT	PAGE
caving	year-round	p157
diving, snorkeling, bird-watching and wildlife-watching	year-round	p83
diving, snorkeling	Dec-Aug	p120
exploring ruins, bird-watching	year-round	p167
diving, snorkeling	year-round	p105
hiking, wildlife and plant observation, river-tubing	Dec-May	p202
wildlife-watching, bird-watching, horseback riding	year-round	p67
birding, walking, canoeing, horseback riding	Feb-May	p71
manatee and turtle observation, bird-watching, fishing, sailing	year-round	p77
diving, snorkeling, kayaking	Mar-Jun	p31
diving, snorkeling, swimming, fishing, sailing, kayaking	Dec-Aug	p193
bird-watching, swimming, plant identification	year-round	p150
diving, snorkeling, bird-watching, kayaking	Dec-Aug	p121
diving, snorkeling	year-round	p82
diving, snorkeling	Dec-Aug	p31
hiking, bird-watching, swimming	year-round	p198
bird-watching, wildlife-watching, canoeing, caving	year-round	p76
walking, swimming, bird-watching, horseback riding	year-round	p164
river-tubing	year-round	p150
diving, snorkeling	Dec-May	p215
bird-watching, wildlife-watching, trail hikes, canoeing	year-round	p133
swimming, caving, hiking, bird-watching	year-round	p155
diving, fishing, kayaking, snorkeling, swimming	Dec-May	p215
wildlife observation	year-round	p144
diving, snorkeling, bird-watching, kayaking	Dec-May	p192
manatee observation	year-round	p108
wildlife observation, walking, boat trips	Dec-May	p227

BLACK GOLD

Early in the millennium, the possibility of sweet crude oil in Belize caused dollar signs to start flashing inside the minds of Belizean officials and international prospectors. Eighteen oil companies obtained licenses for exploration all around the country, sometimes without conducting an environmental impact survey or campaigning for community involvement.

After several years, the Irish-owned Belize Natural Energy (BNE) found what they were looking for in Spanish Lookout: oil fields with commercially viable quantities. In 2010, BNE discovered another oil field near Belmopan.

Conservationists fear the environmental degradation that may result from further oil exploration and extraction. There is also significant overlap between the petroleum map and the protected-areas map, threatening the sanctity of these spots. In the wake of the 2010 oil spill in the Gulf of Mexico, an umbrella group of NGOs called for a ban on all offshore drilling, especially in the Belize Barrier Reef, which has been designated as a World Heritage site.

Under pressure from local communities and conservationists, in 2007 the government of Belize instituted a 40% tax on oil production profits, declaring that the 'petroleum fund' would be used to improve education, fight poverty and strengthen the Belizean dollar. Several years down the line, however, there are concerns about the success of this fund, with the local press asserting the revenues – estimated to be in the hundreds of millions of dollars – have been 'absorbed by the government for its day-to-day operating expenses.'

The highest peak in the Maya Mountains is Doyle's Delight (3687ft), named after Arthur Conan Doyle, author of *The Lost World*. He wrote 'there must be something wild and wonderful in a country such as this, and we're the men to find it out!'

Cogeneration

A byproduct of the processing of sugarcane, *bagasse* is also a fuel. In 2009, the sugar industry opened a cogeneration facility that would supply 13.5 megawatts to the national grid, in addition to powering the sugar mill and other industry facilities.

Solar

Solar power is becoming more viable on a small scale, but it does not yet offer a feasible solution for the energy needs of the country. Solar power is still relatively expensive and – significantly – it can't produce power at night. That said, it has become a popular alternative for some ecolodges and even some villages that are off the grid. In 2011, the government of Belize signed an agreement with the University of Belize to construct photovoltaic panels, which generate solar electricity. Proponents of alternative energy are hopeful that the so-called Photovoltaic Project might lead to a long-term, large-scale commitment to solar energy.

Survival
Guide

Directory A–Z

Accommodations

Budget Categories

Budget Within this range the best value is usually provided by small, often family-run guesthouses. Only the cheapest budget options have shared bathrooms or cold showers; a few places provide dorm accommodations.

Midrange Midrange embraces many hotels, more-comfortable guesthouses and most of the small-scale lodges and resorts. Many places in this range have their own restaurants and bars, and offer arrangements for activities, tours and other services. The range of accommodations and service is wide within this category.

Top End Top-end accommodations can be seriously sumptuous. These are resorts, lodges and classy hotels with large, well-appointed rooms and plenty of other facilities, from restaurants and bars to private beaches, spas, pools, horse stables, dive shops and walking trails. Many of these places have

their own unique style and atmosphere created with the help of architecture, decor, location and layout.

Seasons

Most establishments have high- and low-season prices, often with extra-high prices for the peak weeks.

Low season May to November

High season December to May

Peak season December 15 to January 15, plus Easter week

Taxes & Service Charges

Prices listed by Lonely Planet do not include the 9% hotel room tax or the (sometimes obligatory) service charges which might be added at some top-end places. There is some talk of this tax being raised to 12.5% sometime in the future.

Types of Accommodations

Cabañas & Cabins
These two terms are pretty well interchangeable and can refer to any kind of free-standing, individual accom-

---

GREEN ACCOMMODATIONS

Ecotourism means big business in Belize, and sometimes it seems like every hotel, hostel, lodge, resort and guesthouse is a friend and protector of Mother Earth. But attaching 'eco' to the front of a name does not necessarily make it so. This prefix may mean that the enterprise is taking serious steps to reduce its environmental impact, whether by practicing recycling, implementing alternative energy, participating in conservation programs or educating its guests. On the other hand, it may mean nothing more than a remote location or rustic accommodations. Most likely, the truth is somewhere in between.

Many lodges, resorts, hostels and guesthouses *are* implementing 'ecopolicies' (with varying degrees of effectiveness). Look for the 🍂 icon in the listings.

BOOK YOUR STAY ONLINE

For more reviews by Lonely Planet authors, check out http://hotels.lonelyplanet.com. You'll find independent reviews, as well as recommendations on the best places to stay. Best of all, you can book online.

modations structure. You'll find cabins in every class of accommodations: they can be made of wood, concrete or brick, and be roofed with palm thatch, tin or tiles. They may be small, bare and cheap, or super-luxurious and stylish, with Balinese screens, Japanese bathrooms and Maya wall hangings. Locales vary from beachside, riverside or jungle to on the grounds of a hotel alongside other types of accommodations.

Camping

Belize does not have many dedicated campsites, but there are some (mainly budget) accommodations that provide camping space on their grounds, and just a few of those have gear for rent.

Guesthouses

Guesthouses are affordable, affable places to stay, with just a few rooms and usually plenty of personal attention from your hosts. Most are simply decorated but clean and comfortable. Rooms usually have a private bathroom with hot water. You'll find guesthouses in towns or on the coast or cayes. Some guesthouses (also called B&Bs) provide breakfast.

Located in the southern Toledo District, the Toledo Ecotourism Association (p227) runs an excellent village guesthouse program that enables travelers to stay in the area's Maya villages.

Hotels

A hotel is, more or less, any accommodations that generally doesn't give itself another name (although some smaller hotels call themselves inns). You'll find hotels in villages and towns of all sizes. Some offer lovely rooms and extra amenities like a restaurant or a pool, while others have fewer creature comforts. Hotels generally don't offer a vast range of tours and activities to their guests, but there will be exceptions to this.

Lodges

In Belize the term 'lodge' usually means a comfortable hotel in a remote location, be it in the Cayo jungles or the offshore cayes. Most lodges focus on activities such as diving, fishing, horseback riding or jungle or river adventures, aiming to provide comfortable accommodations and good meals to sustain their guests between outings. Many lodges have gorgeous island, beach or forest settings, and they tend to be on the expensive side, due mainly to their high standards, wide range of amenities and sometimes remote locations.

Rental Accommodations

In main tourist destinations such as San Pedro, Caye Caulker and Placencia, there are houses and apartments for rent for short stays or by the week or month. If you plan a long stay you'll certainly cut costs by renting your own place. Plan ahead: these places can get booked up.

Resorts

Resorts have a great deal in common with lodges – again they tend to be among the more expensive options and can be found both inland and by the sea. If there is any real distinction, it's that the emphasis in resorts tends to be marginally less on activities and slightly more on relaxation.

Customs Regulations

Duty-free allowances on entering Belize:

➡ 1L of wine or spirits.

➡ 200 cigarettes, 250g of tobacco or 50 cigars. It is illegal to leave the country with ancient Maya artifacts, turtle shells, unprocessed coral and fish (unless you have obtained a free export permit from the Fisheries Department). It is also illegal to take firearms or ammunition into or out of Belize.

Climate

Belize City

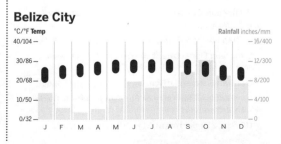

Electricity

110V/60Hz

Embassies & Consulates

A few countries have embassies in Belize. Many others handle relations with Belize from their embassies in countries such as Mexico or Guatemala, but may have an honorary consul in Belize to whom travelers can turn as a first point of contact.

Australian Embassy (☎+52-55-1101-2200; www.mexico.embassy.gov.au) The Australian embassy in Mexico handles relations with Belize.

Canadian Honorary Consul (☎223-1060; cdncon.bze@btl.net; 80 Princess Margaret Dr, Belize City; ⊙9am-2pm Mon-Fri)

French Honorary Consul (☎223-0399; malas@btl.net; 109 New Rd, Belize City)

German Honorary Consul (☎222-4369; seni@cisco.com.bz; Western Hwy, Mile 3½, Belize City)

Guatemalan Embassy (☎223-3150; embbelice@minex.gob.gt; 8 A St, Belize City; ⊙8:30am-12:30pm Mon-Fri)

Honduran Embassy (☎224-5889; embahonbe@yahoo.com; 6199 Buttonwood Bay, Belize City; ⊙9am-noon & 1-4pm Mon-Fri)

Mexican Embassy (☎822-0406; www.sre.gob.mx/belice; Embassy Sq, Belmopan; ⊙8am-5pm Mon-Fri)

Netherlands Honorary Consul (☎223-2953; mchulseca@btl.net; cnr Baymen Av & Calle Al Mar, Belize City)

UK High Commission (☎822-2146; http://ukinbelize.fco.gov.uk; Embassy Sq, Belmopan; ⊙8am-noon & 1-4pm Mon-Thu, 8am-2pm Fri)

US Embassy (☎822-4011; http://belize.usembassy.gov; Floral Park Rd, Belmopan; ⊙8am-noon & 1-5pm Mon-Fri)

Food

More more details on Belize's culinary delights, see the Beyond Rice & Beans chapter (p278).

Gay & Lesbian Travelers

GLBT travelers should be advised that male homosexuality is illegal in Belize, although female homosexuality is legal. Tourists have not been prosecuted for homosexuality, but local people have been arrested and jailed. Generally speaking, Belize is a tolerant society with a 'live and let live' attitude. But underlying Central American machismo and traditional religious belief, as well as legal prohibitions, mean that same-sex couples should be discreet. Some useful resources:

Gay Travel Belize (www.gaytravelbelize.com) Includes country-wide information and accommodations, although it's primarily focused on San Pedro.

International Gay & Lesbian Travel Association (http://www.iglta.org) General information on gay and lesbian travel in Latin America.

Purple Roofs (www.purpleroofs.com) Includes some listings in San Pedro and Cayo District.

Undersea Expeditions (www.underseax.com) Gay and lesbian scuba-diving company.

Health

Travelers to Central America need to be concerned about food- and mosquito-borne infections. While most infections are not life-threatening, they can certainly ruin your

---

GOVERNMENT TRAVEL ADVICE

Official information can make Belize sound more dangerous than it actually is, but for a range of useful travel advice (including information on healthy traveling) you should consult the travel advisories provided by your home country's foreign-affairs department.

➡ **Australian Department of Foreign Affairs** (www.smarttraveller.gov.au)

➡ **British Foreign Office** (http://www.fco.gov.uk/en/)

➡ **Canadian Department of Foreign Affairs** (www.voyage.gc.ca)

➡ **German Foreign Office** (www.auswaertiges-amt.de)

➡ **New Zealand Ministry of Foreign Affairs & Trade** (www.safetravel.govt.nz)

➡ **US State Department** (www.travel.state.gov)

DIRECTORY A–Z HEALTH

trip. Besides getting the proper vaccinations, it's important that you pack a good insect repellent and exercise great care in what you eat and drink.

Medical Checklist

It is a very good idea to carry a medical and first-aid kit with you, in case of minor illness or injury:

➡ antibiotics

➡ antidiarrheal drugs (eg loperamide)

➡ acetaminophen/paracetamol (Tylenol) or aspirin

➡ anti-inflammatory drugs (eg ibuprofen)

➡ antihistamines (for hay fever and allergic reactions)

➡ antibacterial ointment (eg Bactroban) for cuts and abrasions

➡ steroid cream or cortisone (for poison ivy and other allergic rashes)

➡ bandages, gauze, gauze rolls

➡ adhesive or paper tape

➡ scissors, safety pins and tweezers

➡ thermometer

➡ pocketknife

➡ insect repellent containing DEET for the skin

➡ insect spray containing permethrin for clothing, tents and bed nets

➡ sunblock

➡ oral rehydration salts

➡ iodine tablets (for water purification)

➡ syringes and sterile needles

Bring medications in their original containers, clearly labeled. A signed, dated letter from your physician describing all medical conditions and medications, including generic names, is also a good idea. If carrying syringes or needles, be sure to have a physician's letter documenting their medical necessity.

Potential Hazards
Mosquitoes & Ticks

To avoid mosquito and tick bites, wear long sleeves, long pants, hats and shoes or boots (rather than sandals). Use insect repellent that contains DEET, which should be applied to exposed skin and clothing, but not to eyes, mouth, cuts, wounds or irritated skin. In general, adults and children over 12 should use preparations containing 25% to 35% DEET, which

RECOMMENDED VACCINES

VACCINE	RECOMMENDED FOR	DOSAGE	SIDE EFFECTS
Hepatitis A	all travelers	one dose before trip with booster six to 12 months later	soreness at injection site; headaches; body aches
Hepatitis B	long-term travelers in close contact with the local population	three doses over a six-month period	soreness at injection site; low-grade fever
Chickenpox	travelers who've never had chickenpox	two doses one month apart	fever; mild case of chickenpox
Measles	travelers born after 1956 who've had only one measles vaccination	one dose	fever; rash; joint pain; allergic reaction
Tetanus-diphtheria	all travelers who haven't had a booster within 10 years	one dose lasts 10 years	soreness at injection site
Typhoid	all travelers	four capsules by mouth, one taken every other day	abdominal pain; nausea; rash
Yellow fever	required for travelers arriving from yellow-fever-infected areas in Africa or South America	one dose lasts 10 years	headaches; body aches; severe reactions are rare

last about six hours. Children between two and 12 years of age should use preparations containing no more than 10% DEET, which will usually last about three hours. Products containing lower concentrations of DEET are as effective, but for shorter periods of time.

For additional protection, you can apply permethrin to clothing, shoes, tents and bed nets. Permethrin treatments are safe and remain effective for at least two weeks, even when items are laundered. Permethrin should not be applied directly to skin.

Traveler's Diarrhea

To prevent diarrhea, avoid tap water unless it's been boiled, filtered or chemically disinfected (with iodine tablets); only eat fresh fruit or vegetables if cooked or peeled; be wary of dairy products that might contain unpasteurized milk; and be highly selective when eating food from street vendors.

If you develop diarrhea, be sure to drink plenty of fluids, preferably an oral rehydration solution containing salt and sugar. A few loose stools don't require treatment, but if you start having more than four or five stools a day, you should start taking an antibiotic (usually a quinolone drug) and an antidiarrheal agent (such as loperamide). If diarrhea is bloody, persists for more than 72 hours or is accompanied by fever, shaking chills or severe abdominal pain, you should seek medical attention.

Recommended Vaccinations

Since most vaccines don't produce immunity until at least two weeks after they're given, visit a physician four to eight weeks before departure. Note that some of the recommended vaccines are not approved for use by children and pregnant women; check with your physician.

Insurance

Travelers should take out a travel insurance policy to cover theft, loss and medical problems. Some policies specifically exclude 'dangerous activities,' which can include scuba diving, motorcycling and even trekking. Check that the policy you are considering covers ambulances as well as emergency flights home.

You may prefer a policy that pays doctors or hospitals directly rather than requiring you to pay on the spot and claim later. If you have to claim later, make sure you keep all documentation.

Internet Access

Belize has plenty of internet cafes, with typical rates ranging from BZ$4 to BZ$8 per hour. Many hotels and lodges also provide computers where their guests can access the internet, as indicated by the @ icon in the listings. Skype is blocked by Belize Telecom, but some internet cafes offer Skype service through satellite or virtual private networks.

For those traveling with a laptop, most accommodations also have wireless access in the rooms or in common areas, as indicated by the 🛜 icon. This access is fairly reliable, but is easily overburdened if there are several people working simultaneously. For more information on traveling with a portable computer, see www.teleadapt.com.

Legal Matters

Drug possession and use is officially illegal and, if caught in possession of larger amounts of marijuana or possession or use of any other illicit drugs, offenders will generally be arrested and prosecuted.

Persons found having sex with a minor will be prosecuted; the age of consent for both sexes is 16. Travelers should note that they can be prosecuted under the law of their home country regarding age of consent, even when abroad.

You are not required to carry ID in Belize but it's advisable to do so. If arrested you have the right to make a phone call. The police force does not have a reputation for corruption as in many countries in Central America, and it is highly unlikely that you will be asked for a bribe. A special **tourist police force** (☎227-6082) patrols tourist areas, including central Belize City, San Pedro, Caye Caulker and Placencia. The tourist police wear a special badge on their left shoulder.

For detailed information on the Belize legal code, check out the **Belize Legal Information Network** (www.belizelaw.org).

Maps

Lonely Planet maps will enable you to find your way to many of the listed destinations, but if you'd like a larger-scale, more detailed travel map, you cannot beat the 1:350,000 *Belize* map, published by International Travel Maps of Vancouver. It is widely sold in Belize.

You can buy high-class 1:50,000 topographic sheets for BZ$40 each at the **Ministry of Natural Resources & Environment** (☎822-2226; www.mnrei.gov.bz; ⏰8am-noon & 1-4:30pm Mon-Fri) in Belmopan. These maps cover the country, including the cayes, in 70 different sheets; however, most of them were last updated in the 1990s.

Drivers will find *Emory King's Driver's Guide to Beautiful Belize* useful. Sold in bookstores and gift shops in

PRACTICALITIES

Currency
The Belizean dollar (BZ$) is pegged to the US dollar at two to one (BZ$1 = US$0.50). Nearly every business in Belize accepts US dollars and prices are sometimes quoted in US dollars at upscale resorts and hotels.

Newspapers
Amandala (www.amandala.com.bz) The twice-weekly, left-wing newspaper has the largest circulation.
Belize Times (www.belizetimes.bz) Represents the People's United Party (PUP) perspective, Sunday only.
Guardian (www.guardian.bz) The voice of the United Democratic Party (UDP), Sunday only.
Reporter (www.reporter.bz) Presents the most independent coverage, Sunday only.

Radio
Love FM (www.lovefm.com) The most widely broadcast radio station in Belize, with spots at 95.1MHz and 98.1MHz.
KREM FM (www.krembz.com) Plays a modern selection of music at 91.1 MHz and 96.5MHz.

Taxes
Hotel room tax is currently 9%, though there is talk of raising it to 12.5% in the future. Restaurant meals are subject to an 8% sales tax. Some hotel owners quote prices with taxes already figured in.

Television
Channel 5 (www.channel5belize.com) Tagline 'Great Belize TV.'
Channel 7 (www.7newsbelize.com) Tagline 'Where News Comes First.'

Tipping
Tipping is not obligatory but is always appreciated if guides, drivers or servers have provided you with genuinely good service. Rounding up the check by somewhere between 5% and 10% is usually a suitable tip. Some hotels and restaurants add an obligatory service charge to your check (usually 10%), in which case you definitely don't need to tip.

Weights & Measurements
➡ Belize measures distance in miles.
➡ Gasoline is sold by the (US) gallon.
➡ Laundry is usually weighed and paid for by the pound.

Belize City, it's a compilation of route diagrams and user-friendly tips about turnoffs you might miss and speed bumps you might hit. A new edition is published annually.

Opening Hours
Standard business hours are as follows, unless otherwise noted in the text:
Banks 8am to 2pm or 3pm Monday to Thursday and 8am to 4pm or 4:30pm Friday.
Pubs and bars Noon to midnight.
Restaurants and cafes 7am to 9:30am (breakfast), 11:30am to 2pm (lunch) and 6pm to 8pm (dinner).
Shops 9am to 5pm Monday to Saturday.

Public Holidays
Many of Belize's public holidays are moved to the Monday nearest the given date in order to make a long weekend. You'll find banks and most shops and businesses shut on these days. Belizeans travel most around Christmas, New Year and Easter, and it's worth booking ahead for transportation and accommodations at these times.
New Year's Day January 1
Baron Bliss Day March 9
Good Friday March or April
Holy Saturday March or April
Easter Monday March or April
Labor Day May 1
Sovereign's Day May 24
National Day September 10
Independence Day September 21

Day of the Americas
October 12

Garifuna Settlement Day
November 19

Christmas Day December 25

Boxing Day December 26

Telephone

Belize has no regional, area or city codes. Every number has seven digits, all of which you dial from anywhere in the country. When calling Belize from other countries, follow the country code with the full seven-digit local number.

Cell Phones

You can rent cell phones from Belize Telecommunications Ltd (BTL) at the Philip Goldson International Airport in Belize City. They require prepaid DigiCell phone cards, which you can buy where you see green signs announcing 'BTL's PrePaid Cards Sold Here.' If you're staying for more than a week or two, a cheap phone with a pre-paid SIM card can be had for less than BZ\$120.

International cell phones can be used in Belize if they are GSM 1900 and unlocked. You can buy a SIM pack for US\$25 from DigiCell distributors around the country.

International roaming is provided by T Mobil, Cingular and MexTel, but coverage is patchy – check with your service provider back home about coverage in Belize.

Phone Cards

Public phones are plentiful, with about 500 around the country. Buy phone cards wherever you see the green signs announcing 'BTL's PrePaid Cards Sold Here.' You scratch the back of the card to reveal its PIN number, then to make a call you dial the access number given on the back of the card. Automated messages will direct you through the call.

Time

Belize uses North American Central Standard Time (GMT/UTC minus six hours), as in Guatemala and southern Mexico. Belize and Guatemala do not observe daylight saving, so there is never any time difference between them, but Mexico does observe daylight saving from the first Sunday in April to the last Sunday in October, so Belize is one hour behind Mexico during that period.

When it's noon in Belize, it's 1pm in New York, 6pm in London, 10am in San Francisco and 4am the next day in Sydney (add one hour to those times during daylight saving periods in those cities).

Tourist Information

Belize Tourism Board (www.travelbelize.org) The official tourist agency has information offices in Belize City and Punta Gorda, and there are good local tourist information offices in San Pedro and Placencia.

Belize Tourism Industry Association (BTIA; ☎227-1144; www.btia.org; 10 N Park St, Belize City; ☉8am-noon & 1-5pm Mon-Fri) An independent association of tourism businesses, actively defending 'sustainable ecocultural tourism'. The office provides leaflets about the country's regions, copies of its *Destination Belize* annual magazine (free), and information on its members, which include many of Belize's best hotels, restaurants and other tourism businesses. The website has a plethora of information.

Travelers with Disabilities

Belize lacks accessibility regulations and many buildings are on stilts or have uneven wooden steps. You won't see many ramps for wheelchair access. More difficulties for wheelchair users come from the lack of footpaths, as well as plentiful rough and sandy ground. With assistance, bus travel is feasible, but small planes and water taxis might be a problem.

Visitors with limited mobility do come to Belize. Accommodations suitable for wheelchair users include the Radisson Fort George Hotel (p57) in Belize City; Corona del Mar (p93) on Ambergris Caye; Mara's Place (p112) and Blue Wave (p113) on Caye Caulker; Orchid Palm Inn (p128) in Orange Walk; Hok'ol K'in Guest House (p139) in Corozal; El-Rey Inn (p153) and the Bull Frog Inn (p154) in Belmopan; Jungle Huts Resort (p189) in Dangriga; and Turtle Inn (p210) in Placencia.

There are a number of useful organizations and websites for travelers with disabilities, though there's little information that is specific to Belize.

Access-Able Travel Source (www.access-able.com) Has good general information.

Global Access Disabled Travel Network (www.globalaccessnews.com) Good website with interesting general travel information.

Mobility International (www.miusa.org) US-based website that advises travelers with disabilities or mobility issues; you can organize a mentor and someone to help you plan your travels.

Royal Association for Disability and Rehabilitation (Radar; www.radar.org.uk) A network of disability organizations and people with disabilities that lobbies for policy changes.

Visas

Information on visa requirements is available from Belizean embassies and consulates, and the **Belize Tourism Board** (www.travel-belize.org). At the time of writing, visas were not required for citizens of EU or Caricom (Caribbean Community) countries, nor Australia, Canada, Hong Kong, Mexico, New Zealand, Norway, the USA or Venezuela. A visitor's permit, valid for 30 days, will be stamped in your passport when you enter the country. This can be extended by further periods of one month (up to a maximum of six months) by applying at an immigration office (there's at least one in each of Belize's six districts). For further information you can contact the **Immigration & Nationality Department** (☎822-2423; fax 822-2662) in Belmopan.

PREVENTING CHILD SEX TOURISM IN BELIZE

Tragically, the exploitation of local children by tourists is becoming more prevalent throughout Latin America, including Belize. Various socioeconomic factors make children susceptible to sexual exploitation, and some tourists choose to take advantage of their vulnerable position. Sexual exploitation has serious, lifelong effects on children. It is a crime and a violation of human rights.

Belize has laws against sexual exploitation of children. Many countries have enacted extraterritorial legislation that allows travelers to be charged as though the exploitation happened in their home country.

Responsible travelers can help stop child sex tourism and exploitation by reporting it to websites such as the **CyberTipline** (www.cybertipline.com). You can also report the incident to local authorities and, if you know the nationality of the perpetrator, to their embassy.

Travelers interested in learning more about how to fight sexual exploitation of children can find more information through **End Child Prostitution & Trafficking** (ECPAT; www.ecpat.org).

Volunteering

There are a lot of opportunities for volunteer work in Belize, especially on environmental projects. In some cases, you may have to pay to participate (costs vary).

Belize Audubon Society (BAS; www.belizeaudubon.org) BAS invites volunteers with experience in developing countries, community development, teaching, tourism development, art, small business development, conservation or park management, and who are available to work for at least three months, to assist in the main office or in education and field programs. Divers can volunteer for marine research projects for a month at a time. Volunteer bird-watchers are always required for the Christmas bird count. Payment and housing are not provided.

Belize Wildlife and Referral Clinic (http://www.belizewildlifeclinic.org) Offers short term internships in wildlife medicine ranging from two to six weeks for veterinary and non-veterinary students. Various scholarships and work exchanges are available for students with sincere interests and skills, and the clinic is flexible and always interested in speaking with potential interns and long-term volunteers.

Cornerstone Foundation (www.cornerstonefoundationbelize.org) This NGO, based in San Ignacio, hosts volunteers to help with AIDS education, community development and other programs. Most programs require a two-week commitment, plus a reasonable fee to cover food and housing.

Earthwatch (www.earthwatch.org) Paying volunteers are teamed with professional scientific researchers to work on reef restoration and shark conservation. Most projects are 10 to 14 days.

Eco-Escuela de Español (☎3099-4846; San Andrés) A Spanish-language school in El Petén, Guatemala, that also organizes educational programs and environmentally related volunteer opportunities.

Gapforce Worldwide (www.gapforce.org) Catering to gap-year travelers, Gapforce organizes one- to five-month programs that combine work such as trail-cutting, visitor-center building in protected areas, rural teaching or archaeological work, with optional jungle treks, diving and Spanish courses.

Global Vision International (www.gvi.co.uk) Volunteer programs of over one month or more. Projects include conservation of national parks and Maya ruins; trail maintenance and boundary clearance; contributing to crocodile surveys; assessing jaguar populations; and running environmental field courses. Placements available at Belize Audubon and the Belize Institute of Archaeology.

Help for Progress (www.helpforprogress.interconnection.org) A Belizean NGO that works with local community development organizations in fields such as education, gender issues, citizen participation and environment.

Maya Mountain Research Farm (www.mmrfbz.org) The 70-acre organic farm and registered NGO in Toledo offers internships for those interested in learning about organic farming, biodiversity and alternative energy.

Monkey Bay Wildlife Sanctuary (☎822-8032; www.belizestudyabroad. net; Mile 31½ Western Hwy; canoeing per person BZ$70) ☞ Monkey Bay's programs provide opportunities in conservation and community service. It also has many links to other conservation organizations in Belize.

Oceanic Society (☎in USA 800-326-7491; www.oceanic-society.org; Blackbird Caye; 5-day research programs from BZ$3750, family-education programs per week adult/child BZ$3900/3580; 🖩) ☞ Paying participants in the society's expeditions assist scientists in marine research projects at the society's field station on Blackbird Caye and elsewhere.

Plenty International (www. plenty.org) Opportunities for working with grassroots organizations (such as handicraft cooperatives) and schools, mostly in Toledo District.

ProWorld Service Corps (www.proworldvolunteers.org) Like a privately run Peace Corps, ProWorld organizes small-scale, sustainable projects in fields such as healthcare, education, conservation, technology and construction.

Volunteer Abroad (www. volunteerabroad.com) A sort of clearing house for volunteer opportunities around the world. The database includes a few dozen organizations that work in Belize.

Volunteer Petén (☎5711-0040; www.volunteerpeten. org) Focuses on educational projects and management of a public reserve in Petén, Guatemala. Cost includes homestay, meals and activities; Spanish lessons are also available.

WWOOF Belize (www.wwoof-belize.org) WWOOF stands for 'World Wide Opportunities on Organic Farms,' some of which are in Belize. One of them is at **Spanish Creek Rainforest Reserve** (☎668-3290, 670-0620; www. belizebamboo.com; Rancho Delores), but there are many other opportunities to get your hands dirty.

Women Travelers

Women can have a great time in Belize, whether traveling solo or with others. Of course, you do need to keep your wits about you and be vigilant, as does any solo traveler. Keep a clear head, and keep in mind that excessive alcohol will make you vulnerable.

If you don't want attention, try to wear long skirts or trousers and modest tops when you're using public transportation and when on solo explorations. Some men can be quite forward with their advances or even aggressive with their comments. Such advances are rarely dangerous: be direct, say no and ignore; they're likely to go away. A bicycle can be an asset in this scenario: you can just scoot.

Avoid situations in which you might find yourself alone with unknown men at remote archaeological sites, on empty city streets, or on secluded stretches of beach. For support and company, sign up for group excursions or head for places where you're likely to meet people, such as guesthouses that serve breakfast, backpacker lodgings or popular mid-range or top-end hotels.

Transportation

GETTING THERE & AWAY

Travelers can get to Belize by land, sea or air. Overland, travelers might enter Belize from Guatemala or Mexico. Boats also bring travelers from Honduras and Guatemala. Air carriers service Belize from the United States and El Salvador. Flights, tours and rail tickets can be booked online at lonelyplanet.com/bookings.

Entering the Country

Entering Belize is a simple, straightforward process. You must present a passport that will be valid for at least three months from the date of entry. Officially, visitors are also required to be in possession of an onward or return ticket from Belize and funds worth BZ$120 per day for the duration of their stay

in the country, but it's rare for tourists to be required to show these.

Tourists are generally given a 30-day stay, extendable once you're in Belize.

Air

Airports & Airlines

Philip Goldson International Airport (BZE; www.pgiabelize.com), at Ladyville, 11 miles northwest of Belize City center, handles all international flights. With Belize's short internal flying distances it's often possible to make a same-day connection at Belize City to or from other airports in the country.

Airlines Flying To & From Belize

American Airlines (www.aa.com) Direct flights to/from Miami and Dallas/Fort Worth.

Continental Airlines (www.continental.com) Direct flights to/from Houston.

Delta Air Lines (www.delta.com) Direct flights to/from Atlanta.

Grupo TACA (www.taca.com) Direct flights to/from Houston and San Salvador (El Salvador).

Maya Island Air (www.mayaairways.com) Flights to Cancun, Guatemala City and San Pedro Sula in Honduras.

Transportes Aeros Guatemaltecos (www.tag.com.gt) Regular flights between Belize and Guatemala City and Flores, Guatemala, only.

Tropic Air (www.tropicair.com) Daily flights to Flores, Guatemala and charter flights to Roatan, Honduras. They may have flights to Cancun by the time you read this.

US Airways (www.usairways.com) Direct flights to Charlotte, North Carolina.

CLIMATE CHANGE & TRAVEL
....

Every form of transport that relies on carbon-based fuel generates CO_2, the main cause of human-induced climate change. Modern travel is dependent on aeroplanes, which might use less fuel per person than most cars but travel much greater distances. The altitude at which aircraft emit gases (including CO_2) and particles also contributes to their climate change impact. Many websites offer 'carbon calculators' that allow people to estimate the carbon emissions generated by their journey and, for those who wish to do so, to offset the impact of the greenhouse gases emitted with contributions to portfolios of climate-friendly initiatives throughout the world. Lonely Planet offsets the carbon footprint of all staff and author travel.

Land

Mexico

There are two official crossing points on the Mexico–Belize border. The more frequently used is at Subteniente López–Santa Elena, 9 miles from Corozal Town in Belize and 7 miles from Chetumal in Mexico. The all-paved Northern Hwy runs from the border to Belize City.

The other crossing is at La Unión–Blue Creek, 34 miles southwest of Orange Walk Town. If you happened to be driving in from Mexico straight to La Milpa Field Station or Chan Chich Lodge, you might consider using this crossing, as the road is paved all the way from the border on the Mexican side; otherwise you face 28 unpaved miles on the road to Orange Walk from Blue Creek.

Bus

The Guatemalan company San Juan Travel runs one daily express bus from the Ado bus terminal in Chetumal, which arrives at the Caye Caulker Water Taxi terminal in Belize City (BZ$20, three hours). San Juan makes no other stops in Belize (though it does continue on to Flores, Guatemala). At the time of research, the foreign-owned bus companies were prohibited from picking up passengers in Belize City and taking them to Chetumal on the way back.

Many regular Belizean buses ply the Northern Hwy between Belize City and Chetumal. In Chetumal, bus-es bound for Corozal Town (BZ$2 to BZ$4, one hour), Orange Walk Town (BZ$6 to BZ$8, two hours) and Belize City (BZ$10 to BZ$14, four hours) leave the north side of Nuevo Mercado, about 0.75 miles north of the city center, once or twice an hour from about 4:30am to 6pm.

Car & Motorcycle

To bring a vehicle into Belize, you need to obtain a one-month importation permit at the border. This obliges you to take the vehicle out of Belize again within the validity of the permit. To get the permit you must present proof of ownership (vehicle registration) and purchase Belizean motor insurance (available for a few US dollars per day from agents at the borders). Permit extensions can be obtained by applying to the **Customs Department** (☑227-7092) in Belize City. In the unlikely event that a Mexican or Guatemalan car-rental agency permits you to take one of their vehicles into Belize, you will also have to show the rental documents at the border.

It's not unusual to see US license plates on cars in Belize, as driving from the USA through Mexico is pretty straightforward and car rental in Belize is expensive. The shortest route through Mexico to the crossing point between Chetumal and Corozal is from the US–Mexico border points at Brownsville–Matamoros or McAllen–Reynosa, a solid three days' driving.

You are required to obtain a temporary import permit for your vehicle at the border when you enter Mexico; as well as the vehicle registration document you'll need to show your driver's license and pay a fee of around BZ$50 with a Visa, MasterCard or American Express credit card. You'll also have to buy Mexican motor insurance, also available at the border.

Guatemala

The only land crossing between Belize and Guatemala is a mile west of the Belizean town of Benque Viejo del Carmen at the end of the all-paved Western Hwy from Belize City. The town of Melchor de Mencos is on the Guatemalan side of the crossing. The border is 44 miles from the Puente Ixlú junction (also called El Cruce) in Guatemala, where roads head north for Tikal (22 miles) and southwest to Flores (18 miles). The road is now fully paved.

Bus

Two companies run express buses to/from Guatemala. From the Caye Caulker Water Taxi terminal in Belize City, you can go to Flores (BZ$50, five hours) or Tikal (BZ$60, 5½ hours), or connect all the way to Guatemala City (BZ$110, 13 hours).

You can also take any of the frequent westbound Belizean buses to Benque Viejo del Carmen and then use the local service to the border. There are plenty of buses and minibuses that link Flores with Guatemala City and other destinations in Guatemala.

Sea

It's now possible to arrive in Belize by boat from all three of its neighboring countries. See the boxed text, p306.

GETTING AROUND

Air

Belize's two domestic airlines, **Maya Island Air** (www.mayaairways.com) and **Tropic Air** (☎226-2012; www.tropicair.

SEA DEPARTURE TAX

The only fee you have to pay when leaving Belize by sea is the BZ$7.50 (US$3.75) PACT (Protected Areas Conservation Trust) fee. It's payable in cash (Belizean or US dollars).

com), provide an efficient and reasonably priced service in small planes on several domestic routes, with plenty of daily flights by both airlines on the main routes:

➤ Belize City–Dangriga–Placencia–Punta Gorda

➤ Belize City–Caye Caulker–San Pedro

➤ Belize City–San Pedro–Sarteneja–Corozal

➤ Belize City–Belmopan (Tropic Air only)

➤ Belmopan–Placencia (Tropic Air only)

➤ Belize City–Cayo

Belize City flights use both the Philip Goldson International Airport and the Municipal Airstrip, about 12 miles from the international airport; flights using the Municipal Airstrip are usually BZ$20 to BZ$40 cheaper than those using the international airport.

Bicycle

Most of Belize, including all three of the main highways, is pretty flat, which makes for pleasant cycling, but traffic on the main highways does tend to travel fairly fast; make sure you're visible if riding along these roads. Belizeans use bicycles – often beach cruiser-type bikes on which you brake by pedaling backward – for getting around locally, but you don't see them

doing much long-distance cycling unless they're into racing.

Bikes are available to rent in many of the main tourist destinations for around BZ$20 per day. You don't usually have to give a deposit. It may be possible to purchase a used bike from one of these rental companies for longer-term use.

Boat

There are several boat services operating between the mainland and the islands (mainly Caye Caulker and Ambergris Caye). Lodges and resorts on the smaller islands usually arrange transportation for their guests.

Otherwise, getting to and around Belize's islands and reefs is a matter of taking tours or dive-and-snorkel trips, using boats organized by island accommodations or chartering a launch. As a rough rule of thumb, launch charters cost around BZ$200 per 10 miles. They're easy to arrange almost anywhere on the coast and on the main islands.

The regular services include:

Belize City–Caye Caulker–San Pedro At the time of research, three different companies handled this route four or five times a day, so there are plenty of options. The stalwart is the Caye Caulker Water Taxi Association, but the others offer similar price and level of service.

Corozal–Sarteneja–San Pedro The Thunderbolt has a monopoly on this route, taking passengers in each direction once a day during high season, and several times a week (based on demand) during low season.

Dangriga–Central Cayes Not exactly offering a regularly scheduled service, but there is a handful of water taxis that make the run frequently. It's easy to arrange and cheaper to share.

Placencia–Independence
The Hokey Pokey Water Taxi travels between Placencia and Independence, saving travelers a long road detour between Placencia and Punta Gorda.

Bus

To the untrained eye, the Belize bus system still seems to be in chaos. However, all you need to know is that there are still regular buses plying the regular routes, and that they charge – more or less – the same prices.

There are three main bus routes, all of which originate in Belize City:

Northern Hwy From Belize City to Orange Walk and Corozal (and on to Chetumal, Mexico). At last count there were six companies servicing this route, and between 25 and 30 buses a day going in each direction.

Western Hwy From Belize City to Belmopan, San Ignacio and Benque Viejo del Carmen. Several companies service this route, resulting in a regular service that runs in both directions every half-hour throughout the day.

Hummingbird and Southern Hwys Buses from Belize City and Belmopan head down the Hummingbird Hwy every hour or so, stopping in Dangriga then continuing on to the Southern Hwy to Independence and Punta Gorda. Other regular services run from Dangriga to Hopkins and Placencia.

Most Belizean buses are old US school buses. Regular-service buses stop anywhere to drop and pick up passengers. Express buses, sometimes air-conditioned, have limited stops and as a result are quicker and usually less crowded. They cost a bit more but they save a lot of time, especially on longer trips, so it's worth the extra few dollars.

A variety of smaller bus companies serve villages around the country. They often run to local work and school schedules, with buses going into a larger town in the morning and returning in the afternoon.

Occasional breakdowns and accidents happen with Belizean buses but their track record is at least as good as those in other Central American countries. Luggage pilfering has been a problem on some buses in the past. Carry valuables with you on the bus and give your stored baggage to the bus driver or conductor only, and watch as it is stored. Be there when the bus is unloaded to retrieve your luggage.

Car & Motorcycle

Having a vehicle in Belize gives you maximum flexibility and enables you to reach off-the-main-road destinations and attractions (of which there are many) without having to depend on tours and expensive transfers. Though car rental is costly in Belize, it doesn't look so exorbitant when you consider the alternatives, especially if there are three or four people to share the expenses.

Belize has four asphalt-paved two-lane roads: the Northern Hwy between Belize City and the Mexican border north of Corozal; the Western Hwy between Belize City and the Guatemalan border near Benque Viejo del Carmen; the Hummingbird Hwy from Belmopan to Dangriga; and the Southern Hwy, which branches off the Hummingbird Hwy a few miles from Dangriga and heads south to Punta Gorda. Connecting the Western Hwy just south of Belize City with the Southern Hwy just west of Dangriga, the unpaved Manatee Hwy will save you a few miles but isn't recommended for cars without 4WD.

Most other roads are one- or two-lane unpaved roads. The most oft-used roads are kept in fairly good condition, but heavy rains can make things challenging. Off the main roads you don't always need a 4WD vehicle but you do need one with high clearance, such as a Chevy Geo Tracker.

Driver's License
If you plan to drive in Belize, you'll need to bring a valid driver's license from your home country.

Fuel & Spare Parts
There are plenty of fuel stations in the larger towns and along the major roads. At last report, regular gasoline was going for around BZ$12 per US gallon, with prices on the rise. Premium (unleaded)

ENTERING BELIZE BY SEA

FROM	TO	FREQUENCY	DURATION	PRICE	FOR MORE INFO'
Dangriga	Puerto Cortés, Honduras	weekly	3-4hr	BZ$110	p191
Placencia	Puerto Cortés, Honduras	weekly	3-4hr	BZ$110	p214
Punta Gorda	Livingston, Guatemala	daily	30min	BZ$50	p221
Punta Gorda	Puerto Barrios, Guatemala	twice daily	45min	BZ$50-60	p221
San Pedro	Chetumal, Mexico	twice daily	2hr	BZ$60-70	p122

MAIN DRIVING ROUTES

Northern Hwy Belize City to Orange Walk Town (1½ hours, 57 miles), Corozal Town (2¼ hours, 86 miles) and Santa Elena (Mexican border; 95 miles, 2½ hours)

Western Hwy Belize City to Belmopan (1¼ hours, 52 miles), San Ignacio (1¾ hours, 72 miles) and Benque Viejo del Carmen (Guatemalan border; 80 miles, two hours)

Hummingbird and Southern Hwys Belmopan to Dangriga (1½ hours, 55 miles), Hopkins (two hours, 63 miles), Placencia (3½ hours, 98 miles) and Punta Gorda (4½ hours, 148 miles)

is a few cents more. Spare parts and mechanics are most easily available in Belize City, although San Ignacio, Belmopan and Orange Walk Town also have parts suppliers. Check the Belize **Yellow Pages** (www.yellowpages.bz).

Rental

Generally, renters must be at least 25 years old, have a valid driver's license and pay by credit card.

Most car-rental companies have offices at Philip Goldson International Airport as well as in Belize City; they will often also deliver or take return of cars at Belize City's Municipal Airstrip or in downtown Belize City. Rental possibilities are few outside Belize City, but it is possible to rent cars in San Ignacio and Placencia.

Rental rates, including taxes, insurance and unlimited mileage, generally start at BZ$160 a day for an economy vehicle with 4WD and air-con. If you keep the car for six days you'll often get the seventh day free.

Most rental agencies will not allow you to take a vehicle out of the country. One agency that allows cars to be taken into Guatemala is **Crystal Auto Rental** (223-1600; www.crystal-belize.com; Mile 5 Northern Hwy) in Belize City.

Insurance

Liability insurance is required in Belize. There are occasional police checkpoints on the main highways, where you may be required to produce proof of it – you face possible arrest if you can't. You won't be able to bring your own vehicle into Belize without buying Belizean insurance at the border, but rental companies always organize the necessary insurance for you.

Road Conditions & Hazards

Outside Belize City, traffic is wonderfully light throughout the country, but there are some potential hazards to be aware of:

➡ On the main roads, watch out for erratic and dangerously fast driving by others. Drive defensively.

➡ Watch for speed bumps (also known as sleeping policemen): these are sometimes well signed, but sometimes not signed at all.

➡ Off the major highways, most roads are unpaved: be careful of potholes.

➡ After a lot of rain, some roads may become impassable; make inquiries before you set out, and if you're in doubt about whether you'll get through a stretch, don't risk it.

➡ Always have water and a spare tire, and always fill your tank before you head off into the back country (and turn back before you've used half of it!).

Road Rules

➡ Driving in Belize is on the right-hand side of the road.

➡ Speed limits are 55mph on the open highway, and either 40mph or 25mph in villages and towns.

➡ Seat belts are compulsory for drivers and front-seat passengers.

➡ Mileposts and highway signs record distances in miles and speed limits in miles per hour, although many vehicles have odometers and speedometers that are calibrated in kilometers.

Golf Carts

If you're spending some time at the beach and you can't fathom being dependent on your own leg-power, you might consider renting a golf cart. It's relatively inexpensive (compared to a car) but it still gets you to the beach and back without causing you to break a sweat. The golf cart is a popular form of transportation in Placencia, San Pedro and – to a lesser degree – Caye Caulker. Both gas-powered and battery-powered golf carts are available: gas goes further and faster, but battery is better for the planet. Expect to pay about BZ$130 per day for a four-seater.

Hitchhiking

Hitchhiking is never entirely safe in any country and in Belize, like anywhere, it's imperative that you listen to your instincts and travel smart. Travelers who decide to hitchhike should understand that they are taking a small but potentially serious risk. You're far better off traveling with another person, and never hitchhike at night. Also keep in mind that buses in Belize are cheap and fairly efficient; you might decide that a bus is a safer and more comfortable bet.

HITCHHIKING IN BELIZE

Guidebook writers dread the day they get an email – perhaps months or years after the publication of a book – telling the ghastly story of a reader who's been hurt (or worse) doing something that the writer had ostensibly suggested was 'safe.' For that reason, Lonely Planet gives a boilerplate warning against hitchhiking. That said, it would be remiss of us not to mention the fact that hitchhiking is a common mode of transportation in Belize, especially down south, where buses between villages and towns are few and far between.

During my first research trip in Belize, I was lucky to have both pickup truck and driver (the amazing Christopher Nesbitt, who, behind the wheel of the green Maya Mountain Research Farm Toyota 4WD, proved nigh-unstoppable on even the worst roads), and giving lifts to hitchhikers was a regular part of our trip. During that journey – which ranged from the furthest southern villages and back roads of Toledo to the Mexican border with Corozal – the pan of the truck served as ad-hoc public transit for more people than I can recall. We gave rides to dozens of teenagers, university-aged students, Maya farmers, tourists, Mennonites, young mothers with babes-in-arms, and one rather gruff police constable (him we let ride up front; the baby-toting mother, too). Only once (a group of three teenagers with an air of trouble about them) did we fail to pick up anyone who needed a lift.

During my second Belize research trip I found myself without a vehicle and on the opposite side of the hitchhiking equation. This time I was the one humbly thumbing down rides throughout rural Belize, riding in the pan along with fellow travelers from all walks of Belize society. In many weeks of hitching, only once did I experience any trouble: on the road from Independence to the Southern Hwy a fellow hitcher misinterpreted a blue bandanna I'd unwisely chosen to wear as protection against the sun as a sign of membership in a gang. He seemed to feel great antipathy toward the gang in question, which resulted in his making several menacing comments as we both stood on the side of the road.

Ever the diplomat, I assured the gentleman that I was in no way affiliated with any gang, removing the offending bandanna as a gesture of goodwill. He responded by not murdering me, and soon we were both riding peacefully together in the back of a farmer's pickup truck.

Although this trip ended well, the incident serves as a reminder that hitchhiking is never 100% risk free. But the fact remains that hitchhiking is a common way that Belizeans get around themselves. If you do hitchhike in Belize, the best ways to minimize the risks are to travel in pairs if possible, ride in the backs of pickup trucks where possible, and never hitch at night. As for headgear, Mennonite straw hats work best. If you must wear a bandanna, blue or red are best avoided.

Joshua Samuel Brown

Hitchhiking is a fairly common way for Belizeans to get around. In a country where vehicle owners are a minority and public transportation is infrequent to places off the main roads, it's common to see people trying to catch a lift at bus stops or at speed bumps, where traffic slows down. If you too are trying to get some place where there's no bus for the next three hours, it's likely that you'll soon get a ride if you hold out your hand and look friendly. Offering to pay a share of the fuel costs at the end of your ride never goes amiss. But always be aware of the potential risks.

Local Transportation

All of Belize's towns, including the parts of Belize City that most visitors frequent, are small enough to cover on foot, although for safety reasons you should take taxis for some trips within Belize City. Taxis are plentiful in all mainland towns and are also an option for getting to places out of town. Rates vary depending on where you are: the 7-mile ride from Corozal to Consejo costs BZ$20, but the 6-mile trip from Maya Centre to Cockscomb Basin Wildlife Sanctuary is BZ$36.

Bicycling is an enjoyable way of getting around local areas and bikes can be rented at around BZ$20 per day in many tourist haunts (and are free for guests at some accommodations). On the cayes, of course, you get around by boat if you're going anywhere offshore.

Behind the Scenes

SEND US YOUR FEEDBACK

We love to hear from travelers – your comments keep us on our toes and help make our books better. Our well-traveled team reads every word on what you loved or loathed about this book. Although we cannot reply individually to postal submissions, we always guarantee that your feedback goes straight to the appropriate authors, in time for the next edition. Each person who sends us information is thanked in the next edition – the most useful submissions are rewarded with a selection of digital PDF chapters.

Visit **lonelyplanet.com/contact** to submit your updates and suggestions or to ask for help. Our award-winning website also features inspirational travel stories, news and discussions.

Note: We may edit, reproduce and incorporate your comments in Lonely Planet products such as guidebooks, websites and digital products, so let us know if you don't want your comments reproduced or your name acknowledged. For a copy of our privacy policy visit lonelyplanet.com/privacy.

OUR READERS

Many thanks to the travelers who used the last edition and wrote to us with helpful hints, useful advice and interesting anecdotes:
Alice Maria Donati, Brock Houston, Rae Knutson, Kainie Manuel, Anne Miller, Julija Otto, Arislea Parissi, James 'Chip' Petersen, Mike Poirier, Katherine Shea, Alexa Talbot, Edwin Van Unen, Janice Vettese, Daniëlle Wolbers

As for individuals who have made this trip particularly worthwhile, in no particular order: my mad henchman of the road, Dave Narby; in Toledo, Christopher and Celini; in Belize City, Demian and Nicole; in Dangriga, David and Nikki; in Placencia, Jacki, Nick, John and Pam; in Cayo, Matthew, Yosiah and Linda; and in Corozal, Gwyn.

Special thanks to Misty for the last one and Bill K & Aimee for being a small part of yet another long, strange trip.

AUTHOR THANKS

Mara Vorhees
Now that I am a parent myself, I feel like I can never express enough gratitude to my own parents, for everything they encouraged and endured over the years. But this is hardly the place for it anyway, so I'll just try to express my gratitude to them for being such awesome grandparents. I never could have taken on this project if we didn't have the best kind of built-in babysitters accompanying us in Belize. Thanks for sharing in the family adventure.

Joshua Samuel Brown
At the tail end of the fourth month of my fourth journey through Belize, I'd like to thank first and foremost the entire nation and everyone who calls it home, from the northern edge of Corozal to the remotest jungles of Toledo.

ACKNOWLEDGMENTS

Climate Map Data Climate map data adapted from Peel MC, Finlayson BL & McMahon TA (2007) 'Updated World Map of the Köppen-Geiger Climate Classification', Hydrology and Earth System Sciences, 11, 1633–44.

Maya Medicine (p286) Reproduced with permission from Rainforest Remedies: One Hundred Healing Herbs of Belize, by Rosita Arvigo and Michael Balick, Lotus Press, a division of Lotus Brands, Inc., PO Box 3205, Twin Lakes, WI 53181, USA, www.lotuspress.com © 1998 All Rights Reserved.

Cover photograph Trumpetfish in corals, Belize, Tim Rock/Getty Images.

THIS BOOK

This 5th edition of Lonely Planet's *Belize* guidebook was researched and written by Mara Vorhees and Joshua Samuel Brown. The previous two editions were also written by Mara Vorhees and Joshua Samuel Brown.

It was commissioned in Lonely Planet's Oakland office, and produced by the following:

Commissioning Editor Catherine Craddock-Carrillo

Coordinating Editor Nigel Chin

Assisting Editors Janice Bird, Justin Flynn, Carly Hall, Alan Murphy

Senior Cartographer Alison Lyall

Assisting Cartographers Jeff Cameron, Rachel Imeson, Robert Townsend

Coordinating Layout Designer Adrian Blackburn

Managing Editors Barbara Delissen, Annelies Mertens, Martine Power

Managing Cartographer Anita Banh

Managing Layout Designer Jane Hart

Cover Research Naomi Parker

Internal Image Research Kylie McLaughlin

Thanks to Shahara Ahmed, Bruce Evans, Ryan Evans, Larissa Frost, Mark Griffiths, Genesys India, Jouve India, Trent Paton, Kerrianne Southway, Branislava Vladisavljevic, Gerard Walker, Tony Wheeler

Index

NOTES

Map Legend

Sights

- Beach
- Bird Sanctuary
- Buddhist
- Castle/Palace
- Christian
- Confucian
- Hindu
- Islamic
- Jain
- Jewish
- Monument
- Museum/Gallery/Historic Building
- Ruin
- Sento Hot Baths/Onsen
- Shinto
- Sikh
- Taoist
- Winery/Vineyard
- Zoo/Wildlife Sanctuary
- Other Sight

Activities, Courses & Tours

- Bodysurfing
- Diving/Snorkelling
- Canoeing/Kayaking
- Course/Tour
- Skiing
- Snorkelling
- Surfing
- Swimming/Pool
- Walking
- Windsurfing
- Other Activity

Sleeping

- Sleeping
- Camping

Eating

- Eating

Drinking & Nightlife

- Drinking & Nightlife
- Cafe

Entertainment

- Entertainment

Shopping

- Shopping

Information

- Bank
- Embassy/Consulate
- Hospital/Medical
- Internet
- Police
- Post Office
- Telephone
- Toilet
- Tourist Information
- Other Information

Geographic

- Beach
- Hut/Shelter
- Lighthouse
- Lookout
- Mountain/Volcano
- Oasis
- Park
- Pass
- Picnic Area
- Waterfall

Population

- Capital (National)
- Capital (State/Province)
- City/Large Town
- Town/Village

Transport

- Airport
- Border crossing
- Bus
- Cable car/Funicular
- Cycling
- Ferry
- Metro station
- Monorail
- Parking
- Petrol station
- Subway/Subte station
- Taxi
- Train station/Railway
- Tram
- Underground station
- Other Transport

Note: Not all symbols displayed above appear on the maps in this book

Routes

- Tollway
- Freeway
- Primary
- Secondary
- Tertiary
- Lane
- Unsealed road
- Road under construction
- Plaza/Mall
- Steps
- Tunnel
- Pedestrian overpass
- Walking Tour
- Walking Tour detour
- Path/Walking Trail

Boundaries

- International
- State/Province
- Disputed
- Regional/Suburb
- Marine Park
- Cliff
- Wall

Hydrography

- River, Creek
- Intermittent River
- Canal
- Water
- Dry/Salt/Intermittent Lake
- Reef

Areas

- Airport/Runway
- Beach/Desert
- Cemetery (Christian)
- Cemetery (Other)
- Glacier
- Mudflat
- Park/Forest
- Sight (Building)
- Sportsground
- Swamp/Mangrove

OUR STORY

A beat-up old car, a few dollars in the pocket and a sense of adventure. In 1972 that's all Tony and Maureen Wheeler needed for the trip of a lifetime – across Europe and Asia overland to Australia. It took several months, and at the end – broke but inspired – they sat at their kitchen table writing and stapling together their first travel guide, *Across Asia on the Cheap*. Within a week they'd sold 1500 copies. Lonely Planet was born.

Today, Lonely Planet has offices in Melbourne, London and Oakland, with more than 600 staff and writers. We share Tony's belief that 'a great guidebook should do three things: inform, educate and amuse'.

OUR WRITERS

Mara Vorhees

Coordinating Author, Belize District, Northern Cayes, Northern Belize Mara first visited Belize as a student of international development, when she traveled the country on a backpacker's budget, researching the outcomes of US-sponsored foreign aid projects. She fell in love with the reef, the rasta guys, and the rice and beans (although she was not so enamored of US development policy). The pen-wielding traveler has since taken to seeing and saving the world by other means. Besides this book, she has worked on *Costa Rica*, and a slew of other titles for Lonely Planet. Her articles and photographs of Central America have appeared in the *Boston Globe* and the *Miami Herald*, among other national newspapers. Follow Mara's latest adventures at www.maravorhees.com

Joshua Samuel Brown

Cayo District, Southern Belize, Tikal & Flores (Guatemala) Born and raised in New York City, Joshua Samuel Brown has lived in Taiwan, Hong Kong, China, Singapore, Canada, Belize and America. He is the author of *Vignettes of Taiwan* (2005) and co-author of ten travel guides for Lonely Planet. His work has appeared in numerous publications, including the *South China Morning Post*, *The Standard* (Hong Kong), *Beijing Scene*, the *Asia Literary Review*, *Destination Belize* and *Cat Fancy*. He has also contributed four stories to Lonely Planet's *The World's Best Street Food* guide (2012), is a regular contributor to the Lonely Planet website and has maintained the high-traffic travel blog Snarky Tofu (www.josambro.blogspot.com) since 2006. When not on the road for Lonely Planet, Joshua writes comedy sketches, short stories and screenplays.

Published by Lonely Planet Publications Pty Ltd
ABN 36 005 607 983
5th edition – Sep 2013
ISBN 978 1 74220 444 4
© Lonely Planet 2013   Photographs © as indicated 2013
10 9 8 7 6 5 4 3
Printed in China